WOMEN'S STUDIES ON ITS OWN

NEXT WAVE

New Directions in Women's Studies

A series edited by Inderpal Grewal,

Caren Kaplan, and Robyn Wiegman

WOMEN'S STUDIES ON ITS OWN

A Next Wave Reader in Institutional Change

Edited by Robyn Wiegman

Duke University   Durham and London 2002

© Duke University Press
All rights reserved
Printed in the United States of America on acid-free paper ∞
Typeset in Scala by Keystone Typesetting, Inc.
Library of Congress Cataloging-in-Publication Data appear
on the last printed page of this book.
Robyn Wiegman's essay, "The Progress of Gender: Whither
'Women'?" first appeared in a slightly different form in the vol. 26,
no. 2 issue of *Signs* under the title "Object Lessons: Men,
Masculinity, and the Sign *Women*."

III : IN THE SHADOW OF CAPITAL

IV : CRITICAL CLASSROOMS

Introduction: On Location

The idea for this collection of essays began over dinner in Berkeley in 1998 when a small group of faculty in Women's Studies gathered to discuss our situations in programs and departments in the United States and Canada. We were drawn to this conversation because of a mutual recognition: It was rare to have the opportunity to talk to not one or two but five faculty members with full-time appointments in Women's Studies. After our indulgence in the familiar litany of frustration—about the absence of adequate funding, the way intellectual disagreement was often recoded as generational strife, and the daily difficulty of inter-disciplinary teaching and research—we turned in necessity to a consideration of why Women's Studies as an institutional location had hailed all of us. What was it about the contemporary opportunity of Women's Studies that drew us not only to take up full-time appointments, but also to become on our own campuses its most vociferous supporter, if not department chair or program director? If being in Women's Studies was often difficult, why did we nevertheless find it not simply necessary but intellectually and politically indispensable?

My own answers to these questions go back much further than our conversation that evening. In 1977, at age 19, I found myself in a Women's Studies course at Indiana University. To this day, I don't remember how I ended up turning to the proper page of the course catalogue, so nonexistent was my formal knowledge about feminism, but I have always valued the way that incoherence—and the haphazard—is a central feature of my own institutional origin story. I did learn in time what it was about Women's Studies that I wanted to pursue. Initially, it had to do with the open discussion of what other courses seemed so resistant to broach: the majority of Shakespeare's sonnets, the politics of women's bodies, the implications of being white and in the First World. I liked the political nature (I use that word purposely) of Women's Studies and the way it made what one thought to be nature so irreversibly political.

My attachments to the field and to its animating politic—feminism— have changed over the years. At first I needed Women's Studies to be trained critically on everything about me; today, I want its knowledge formation to resist the narcissistic encounter in order to make claims on those domains that twentieth-century feminism has not taught me to think about well: scientific method, for instance, or issues of institutional power, or even something as common-sensical as the past before feminism became a term by which to define and study it. But more than this, I want the question of Women's Studies, along with the difficulties that are discussed at conference dinners, to be valued as crucial aspects of this thing that we are in the midst of: a historic project, to be sure, but one whose political intervention into knowledge practices necessitates a challenge to every impulse of celebratory self-narration. It is the tension here between respect for the visionary labor of the past and academic commitment to critique that seems today to animate Women's Studies as a political project. Although this tension generates certain divisions (between founders and their successors, the academic "inside" and a "real" world, the past and the future), feminism has taught many of us to value the enduring sense of being in struggle, which makes the struggle today within Women's Studies a project of possibility in a strangely utopian sense. My contemporary attachment to the field collates around just this struggle, where those of us trained by the founding generation have the opportunity to carry something forward, and to do so from within the positions of power that feminism in the academy has made possible for us.

In raising the issue of feminism's contemporary academic power as a positive political inheritance, I want to foreground a situation that some scholars have interpreted as a debilitating one: that the inaugurating critique of institutional power that founded feminism's academic intervention now exists in contradiction with the contemporary production of both academic feminists and their proliferating objects of study. This perspective has generated a number of familiar questions, each regularly cast at conferences or in print as the source of academic feminism's self-produced harm. Has academic feminism betrayed its radical political roots, substituting abstraction for action, legitimacy for risk? Have the emergent generations of professionally trained feminists abandoned their foremothers' tradition by making of feminism an academic career? Has our success, in short, engendered failure, transforming grassroots social movement and anti-institutional ethics into prototypically liberal and hence reformist, not revolutionary, ideals? To answer these questions affirmatively is to cast contemporary academic feminism in general, and Women's Studies in particular, as monstrous creations, undone in present time by their own inability to remain on progressive historical time. To answer them negatively is to commit ourselves to a constant demonstration of continuity with academic feminism's inaugurating ideals, which may not offer us adequate understanding of the present contexts of academics, public culture, capital formation, and feminist subjectivities within which we must negotiate the field's future.

My tactic in assembling this collection has been to ask Women's Studies practitioners to think about the field *otherwise*. Instead of finding the present at fault for its lack of coherence with the past, I wanted scholars to trace the difference that resides in the present and to judge that difference in relation to the institutional project of academic feminism. The force of this limitation—of directed study of the institutional project—allows us to turn from the issue of women's social subjectivity (which has been, arguably, the central focus of feminist theory) to the question of feminist intellectual formation and, with it, the problematic of identity as the institutionalized object of study for Women's Studies as a field. These issues are not unconnected, of course, as so much of the critique of the unity of women as a sign for social collectivity has animated the theoretical interests of Women's Studies, even inaugurating a kind of object crisis for the field. Such object crises, while read as detrimental to social movements based on collective identifications, are crucial to academic formations in part because they sustain the interrogation of the object (whether "society," "being," "culture," "nation," "text," or "woman"). For academic feminism, of course, the present object crisis that generates the disciplinary and interdisciplinary project of Women's Studies raises the kind of generational anxieties I noted earlier, indicating to some observers that the academy has brought feminism's project of illuminating women to a sudden and terrifying halt. By imposing the limit of thinking about the academy as the specific material site for feminist knowledge, this volume paradoxically escapes the generational enclosure by authorizing, even legitimating, the interrogation of institutionalization and the academy as such. *Women's Studies on Its Own* thus works to trace, in a positive political grammar, the difference that the present makes for thinking about Women's Studies as a knowledge formation, academic institution, agency of the state, and pedagogical insurgency.

The volume is organized into four sections, each designed to foreground a different register of critical analysis and concern. The first section, "Histories of the Present," explores the various contexts that inform our theoretical understanding of Women's Studies as a field. We open with Sneja Gunew's thoughtful consideration of the current dystopic impulse in Women's Studies' own self-narration, the "malaise that appears to have descended on the area at least in some parts of the world." In particular, Gunew is interested in thinking about the issues—interdisciplinarity, activism, identity politics, and difference—that seem to render Women's Studies difficult, if not, using Wendy Brown's term, "impossible" as an intellectual and institutional site. But rather than assenting to the powerful affect of exhaustion that she diagnoses, Gunew models the strategy adopted by contributors to this collection as a whole: She finds in the very problems that are identified as central to Women's Studies' contemporary "impossibility" an important critical project, one whose future lies in the deliberate curricular and pedagogical confrontation with the seeming impasses that we face. She hopes, in short, to find a "useful way for feminist theory to 'make strange' the current paralysis in Women's Studies in relation to identity, difference, and critique." In this, "Feminist Cultural Literacy: Translating Differences; Cannibal Options" offers critical acumen and hesitant optimism about a field that has changed profoundly since its inauguration and is perhaps now in the midst of its most challenging epistemic transformation as it marshals the energy to reconsider nearly everything it had assumed it knew. What, precisely, is the interdisciplinarity that we have heralded as our critical difference from the disciplines? Where have our interdisciplinary initiatives proved unable to go? How have the histories of U.S. nationalism and racialization performed themselves within Women's Studies curricula and research? How does the theoretical formulation of identity as it has emerged in the First World affect the current call to internationalize Women's Studies as a field? What are the intellectual consequences of our current ways of thinking about activism—and about Women's Studies as the academic unit that produces activist subjectivities? And finally, what does "the political" mean in a field formation overwritten by its own claims to politicization?

"Feminist Cultural Literacy" considers these questions by beginning in a startling place: a feminist conference on pleasure and power at the Central European University in Budapest in late May 1999, when the war in Kosovo was escalating. From this location, Gunew ponders the difficulty not simply of forging commonalities among feminists worldwide, but also of "the salience of translation" as a fundamental problem of the university and its organization of knowledge. Taking interdisciplinarity at one point as a key example of translation as a fundamental practice, she explores the possibilities and limits of producing new knowledge for feminism from the disciplines. Her essay is an important reexamination of the effect that disciplinary translations have on the Women's Studies curriculum, where, as she notes, we tend to rely on a "smorgasbord" approach: Students enroll in a variety of cross-listed courses; their instructors hail from the disciplines; and interdisciplinarity becomes an effect of disciplinary accumulation, not a strategy of instruction at either the undergraduate or doctoral level. At the same time, Gunew is interested in the emergent forms of disciplinarity that structure Women's Studies from within. When she considers, for instance, why it is that "theoretical and intellectual work [is] so often perceived as non- or a-political," she draws us into a broader consideration of the way that Women's Studies' own self-defined justification as the academic arm of the women's movement can function as a territorial one, foreclosing in the present the interdisciplinary extension of feminist knowledge into domains that will have no obvious connection to the field's self-narration (such as the sciences). Too often, she writes, "Activism remains more comfortable with . . . the here and now," which means that the temporality of social change defined by an overtly activist agenda will by necessity view some forms of knowledge production as extraneous to, if not wasteful of, academic feminism's critical definition. The issue then is about the disciplining of Women's Studies by its own activist self-narration, not as others might argue by the institutional apparatus of the broader academy.[1]

Gunew is not, however, dismissive of the activist sensibilities that have defined Women's Studies; far from it. Rather, she is concerned, as are other contributors to this volume, with the way in which we understand the scope and shape of activism, and with activism's critical positioning within Women's Studies as a field. Why, for instance, does the emphasis on activism rarely move outside the United States? If "difference" is not only a multicultural project within the nation-state but part of the possibility of translation as a critical enterprise, then what happens to the categories of both activism and feminist academics when the history of U.S. social struggle is placed within Cold War politics, institutionalized nationalisms, and modernity? These are the questions that motivate Caren Kaplan and Inderpal Grewal, whose chapter, "Transnational Practices and Interdisciplinary Feminist Scholarship: Refiguring Women and Gender Studies," seeks nothing less than an entire rethinking of the history and context of "women's" epistemic emergence as the foundation of Women's Studies as a field. In particular, Kaplan and Grewal are concerned with what they identify as the problems of comparativist international models for thinking about the Women's Studies project outside its prototypically national U.S. framework—models that urge the U.S.-based scholar and student to produce a global feminist politics that is still tied to a history of knowledge production in the Cold War apparatus of the U.S. state. To bring that history into critical view, Kaplan and Grewal look at the way in which area studies and American Studies were formulated in relation not only to each other but to race, class, and nation formation. They also point out how the call to "internationalize" Women's Studies can itself reproduce the binary division between American Studies and area studies that emerged in the 1950s as a strategy to contain both the challenges of ethnic struggle to the U.S. state and that of decolonization in Western colonial sites throughout the world. To the extent that the "U.S. woman of color" and the "Third World woman" have emerged in Women's Studies as iconic figures for these geopolitical divisions, Women's Studies, they argue, reconstitutes the Cold War production of knowledge that relies methodologically on comparing world regions to the U.S. Their project hopes instead to begin to establish transnational linkages to understand exploitation, subject production, and the uneven effects of modernity, colonization, nation formation, and racialization worldwide. Such linkages disrupt the comparison model by refusing the boundary logic that area studies and American Studies have epistemologically established.

Kaplan and Grewal ground their discussion by providing a long overdue critique of the way the typical Women's Studies introductory course remains tied to a U.S. national rubric that implicitly, if not explicitly, enforces a notion of feminist politics as an originary struggle within a nationalist domain. Such a focus not only underestimates the way that differences among women in the United States are effects of geopolitical processes that have always exceeded the nationalist narrative of U.S. belonging; it also dismisses the opportunity to craft a transnational critical consciousness that can unsettle the faulty and damaging divides within contemporary feminist theory around First World and Third World, theory and practice, and activism and academy. Although Kaplan and Grewal recognize that introductory courses have functioned, strategically, to situate the analysis of gender within the activist dimensions of the field's origins in the United States, they believe that we have not adequately prepared our students to understand, much less critique, nation-state formations as part of a broader history of capitalism, imperialism, and colonization. Without such a critique, Women's Studies will remain bound to an organization of knowledge that forwards a critical analysis of the United States as part of fulfilling the nation's idealized self-narration as democracy. In this, a liberal feminism that cannot account for capitalism or the effects of histories of colonization and racialization will be secured as the legitimate discourse of gender studies in the contemporary academy, thereby further entrenching Women's Studies within the university as a form of neoliberal "diversity."

This does not mean, as Kaplan and Grewal go to lengths to explain, that their model of a transnational feminism is "an improved or better or cleaned-up kind of international or global feminism. Transnational feminism . . . is not to be celebrated as free of these oppressive conditions. In fact, there is no such thing as a feminism free of asymmetrical power relations. Rather, transnational feminist *practices*, as we call them, involve forms of alliance, subversion, and complicity within which asymmetries and inequalities can be critiqued." Kaplan and Grewal thus seek a way of thinking about feminism—and of practicing feminist knowledge production—that makes no claim that feminism exists outside of or opposed to power. Their "transnational" is a term that is "useful only when it signals attention to uneven and dissimilar circuits of culture and capital," which means that feminism's own self-narration as an agent of liberating women must itself come into critical view. In doing so, the linkages among various forms of patriarchy, colonialism, racialization, and feminism can be examined. This examination positions feminism as itself historical (and not, as our own celebratory narratives often have it, as a revolutionary agency of history's making), with all its complicit and resistant ties to modernity, capitalism, and various forms of patriarchy exposed. Such a call for making Women's Studies the institutional domain for critiquing the convergences as well as the differences between historically constituted feminist discourses and "women" has critical effects that reverberate beyond the introductory course. Certainly it calls into question the field's own imperative to produce positivist knowledge accounts of the life experiences of diverse women, because it raises *as a question* the equation of humanism's construction of the self-authorizing subject as feminism's political destination. It also asks us to rethink the imposition of the subjective as the critical domain within which feminist scholars can know their objects of study, "women."

Rachel Lee takes up the problematic of the subjective and of the scholar's relationship to "women" in her careful explication of the categorical function of "women of color" in Women's Studies curricula today. She begins her consideration by talking about the now ubiquitous undergraduate curricular requirement: the "Women of Color" course. This course functions to foreground one of academic feminism's own exclusions, but in such a way, Lee claims, as to guarantee for the field a progressive, democratic self-narration. In its potential to signal a better critical future for academic feminism, "women of color" as a category of knowledge is made secondary to its figural function as the ghostly presence that both haunts and promises to repair a faulty history. Lee is concerned with this positioning of "women of color" for four primary reasons:

1. It produces a curricular demand, made most difficult for the women of color assigned to teach the class, that the course function structurally to resolve the crisis of race in Women's Studies;
2. Its prominence as a course devised by and found solely in Women's Studies curricula—and found there as a corrective—casts it as the exceptional and always marginal nomination that cannot *not* speak to a racializing center;
3. In this fetishistic mode of marginality, it nurtures an idealist notion that "women of color" as both a social category and an intellectual practice exist outside and against power; and hence

4. It forecloses the possibility of producing "women of color" as a category of knowledge that could begin to explore the incommensurabilities between and among the many social groups, theoretical perspectives, and geopolitical divisions that are often undifferentiatedly collected under its rubric. Instead, "women of color" occupies a temporal no-place—simultaneously, the corrective to the past (the "not that") *and* the mythic embodiment of a future (the "not yet").

In its temporal position between the "was" and the "will be," "women of color" functions as a kind of mobile screen, absorbing projections from white women and scholars of color alike. Lee's essay explores several kinds of projections. In two recent narratives written by white women, she finds "women of color" configured as the site of overinvestment and affect, a kind of centered marginality that seems to risk undoing academic feminism (in Susan Gubar's formulation) or Women's Studies (in Wendy Brown's) by deploying guilt or anger instead of intellect. In both these cases, "women of color" come to interrupt the utopian position as the projected future by failing to bring resolution to the categorical crises that the term has historically and curricularly named. For Gubar, this has to do with the acrimony of the critique of white feminism by feminists of color; for Brown, it is tied to the structural implications of founding a curricular project on an identitarian social movement collated around a singular axis (gender). Lee's point is not to fault Gubar or Brown but to identify how a certain exhaustion with race is part of "a deepening uncertainty over feminism's and Women's Studies' own future. . . . 'Will the breast-beating over race never end?' shades into the question of 'Why can't we get to an end? Have an end? Guarantee an end?'" This desire for completion is itself an important aspect of the way in which academic feminism in general, and Women's Studies in particular, produce, through their own regulatory discourses, racialized subjects. In her reading, Lee finds the contemporary production of a white feminist subject overwhelmed by the failure of the future, a failure she hopes to relocate in the field's structural inability to define "women of color" as a category of knowledge.

If white feminist subjectivity seems now overcome by a political imaginary that sees race as immobilizing, scholarship by feminists of color, Lee observes, repeatedly figures mobility as the defining characteristic of "women of color" as a political subjectivity. Through a careful reading of Chela Sandoval's "U.S. Third World Feminism: The Theory and Method of Oppositional Consciousness in the Postmodern World," Lee diagnoses how the blind spot of white feminism—which was produced by a failure to read the mobility of women of color across multiple axes of difference as anything other than "a blank"—has been turned into the theoretical basis for celebrating a kind of nomadism as characteristic of women of colors' political consciousness itself. Lee is skeptical of this tactic not because it figures mobility as a vehicle for resisting modes of domination, but because it devises that tactic in the hope of averting "becoming dominant and thereby 'repeat[ing] the oppressive authoritarianism from which [they attempt] to free [themselves].'"

For Lee, the extraterritorial roving position locks "women of color" into what she calls "the prisonhouse of reactiveness," in which a fantasy of unity among women of color posits them against the dominating center of white feminism. Lee argues instead for a women-of-color criticism that risks articulating its own desire for territory and hence for power by acknowledging its "distinctive terrain" and turning to the ways in which its own codification as a body of knowledge has been imperfectly produced. This would entail, for instance, examining the reliance on civil-rights discourse that has been central to women-of-color writing, thereby critiquing how "modes of political redress attendant on a concept of justice inhering in rights and in possessive, capitalist individualism and subjectivity" have often been forwarded as the liberationist rhetoric of women-of-color scholarship as a field. For Lee, then, as for other contributors to this volume, "the challenge for Women's Studies in developing a slate of classes on 'women of color' will be to collaborate, paradoxically, on points of disagreement and catalysts of disidentification . . . conceptualizing and narrating 'women of color' as also a site of difference and struggle—as itself a discourse in need of critique and deconstruction."

The first three essays in "Histories of the Present" thus pose questions about the possibilities of decolonizing Women's Studies, with the colonial understood alternately in the historical, discursive, geopolitical, and curricular registers. In so doing, each essay offers a critical meditation on the problematic that *women* presents to Women's Studies as a field. My contribution, "The Progress of Gender: Whither 'Women'?" extends this critical interest by exploring how the crisis of women's categorical insularity has been countered in some institutional contexts by a change of name from Women's Studies to Gender Studies (or Women and Gender

Studies). By tracking the way that race- and sexuality-inspired critiques of the singularity of academic feminism's woman opened masculinity studies for Women's Studies, my essay deliberates on a conceptual shift: where "gender" in the earliest years of academic feminism was used interchangeably with "women," it was reconfigured in the 1990s to signal women's narrowness—if not, at times, its exclusiveness. Thus, when scholars talk today about "gender studies," they often do so to announce a more expansive domain, a territorial extension of critical investigation beyond women to a host of identity designations—not only men but gays, lesbians, the transgendered, the transsexual, and the intersexed. Although I find it absolutely critical for Women's Studies as a field to refuse to discipline itself into a singular object of study, my essay raises questions about the desire for representation that has motivated many of the debates about women and forwarded the notion that the political work of identity-based studies is representation via the nomination of the object itself. My chapter thus works to interrupt as a strategy of theoretical elaboration any move that seeks commensurability between field name and object domain in order to consider what identity-based institutional sites might now, intellectually speaking, do. For the move from women to gender does not overcome the elisions of the former so much as reproduce women's own originating ideal to guarantee a relationship of justice between scholars and the objects they have come to both represent and study. That this ideal has failed is surely beyond dispute.

"The Progress of Gender" reflects, in many ways, my critical concern with how we understand the institutionalization of identity—that is, what happens as an identity rubric becomes refracted through the lens of academic critique, especially when identity has had such enormous utility in organizing social transformation in various parts of the world in the twentieth century. To the extent that identity seems to come undone by critical elaboration, to the extent that it ceases to signify solely along representational (indeed, referential) lines, it begins to achieve, seemingly at the cost of its political utility, the status necessary for disciplinarity. The conflict here—between the structure of a discipline that guarantees its academic reproduction by perpetuating its object as something *to be known* (an infinite deferral) and the political mobility of identity as a form of identification and self-nomination for social movement (a forceful *now*)—speaks to the enduring problem of defining and creating feminist politics across intersecting but incommensurate social domains. Certainly, it marks the differing temporalities that govern identity's deployment in academic institutions and public cultures, temporalities that pose the long haul of institutionalization against the emergency of the present demanded by the now of social change.

The kind of conflict that I am describing points to the necessity of thinking critically about temporality as difference, and enables a general intellectual investigation into the problematic of time not simply for thinking about politics but also for organizing an intellectual field. It is this that Jane Newman offers in "The Present and Our Past: Simone de Beauvoir, Descartes, and Presentism in the Historiography of Feminism," which challenges practitioners in Women's Studies to cast a critical gaze on our own infatuation with feminism as a heroic, modernist progress narrative. Newman thus gives theoretical delineation to the irony of "progress" in the title that advances my discussion of gender's failure to resolve the problematic of a representational deployment of *women*. Her essay begins with a clever reading of Gary Ross's back-to-the-future cinematic odyssey *Pleasantville*, which provides an analogy for thinking through academic feminism's method of keeping time—a method that repeatedly, even obsessively, narrates the past only through the lens of the present and finds the future as the only credible temporal locus for imagining feminist politics. By raising "alterity as an issue of change over time as well as of geographical distance, ethnic difference, and sexual choice," Newman uses a Renaissance scholar's particular understanding of both feminism and intellectual genealogy to question the way the field understands—indeed, produces—its own history of knowledge. Why, for instance, does Simone de Beauvoir so often stand as the beginning of feminism's theoretical tradition and not as a major thinker at its current "end"? How does the specter of the Enlightenment function to reiterate a First World presentism that undercuts the ability of Women's Studies to render in historically diverse ways the various objects of its study: women, gender, and sexuality? To what extent is this inability an effect of difficulties born of Women's Studies' negotiation of the contradictory discourses of disciplines? Newman's hope in answering these questions is less to define an agenda for transcending the Enlightenment than diagnosing the field's need to ground itself in a coherent temporality.

Above all, Newman is concerned with academic feminists' own investments in the progress narrative and its quick, often simplistic writing of the past as the error against which the heroism of the present can be constructed: "The overall inclination of many programs and courses in interdisciplinary Women's Studies [is] to assume that the key issues of feminism about which students need to know began to emerge only in the 1960s and '70s, if not in the 1990s, and have moved only forward ever since. Accompanying this assumption is the implicit claim that reaching back before these years can represent nothing other than antiquarian—and potentially politically incorrect—knowledge projects." For Newman, this construction of the past is a defensive maneuver for an academic feminism now confronting its own incorporation into the "traditional mechanisms of mass instruction, administrative bureaucracy, and, in particular, the trap of a kind of quick and competitive knowledge production that can be measured only in the currency of the late postmodern academic realm—namely, publication."

In Women's Studies' own complicity with the speedup of knowledge as information and relay, it contributes to the devaluing of whole arenas of knowledge production: dead and dying languages, classics, comparative religious studies—all those realms in which the modern is not simply held at bay but temporally out of sync for critical understanding. Although Newman is not unaware of the entertainment quality that a cultural-studies–based presentism brings to the Women's Studies classroom (after all, she, too, begins her essay by reading a film), she questions our willingness to sacrifice feminism as an academic entity to the consumptive logic of popular present time. In addition, she reads such willingness as part of a disciplinary anxiety, a complex form of compensation that attempts to generate disciplinary security "by identifying all that is . . . representative of humanism, the Enlightenment, 'the canon,' and the past . . . as different from and even antithetical to 'our concerns.' " The fantasy encoded in the presentism that Newman delineates works to produce Women's Studies as a field distinct from the disciplines, but in this distinction we undermine, to the point of paralysis, our own claims to interdisciplinarity by refusing to posit feminist knowledge as an intellectual project outside the daily emplottment of revolutionary (which is always future) time.

The presentism that Newman describes can be found throughout the Women's Studies curriculum and is reiterated in both the rhetoric and the critical methods through which academic feminism often produces itself: in the self-conscious articulation of political consciousness as the goal of feminist instruction; in the delineation of difference as a matter of representation, visibility, and voice; in the figure of the live, suffering woman for whom academic feminism bears its guilty obligation of justice; in the rhetorical gesture toward the priority of discerning the materiality of the everyday; in the live encounter between researcher and researched. In these and other formulations, a tacit presentism inhabits, as the defining political force, Women's Studies as a field. Although Newman does not take up these considerations in detail, it is nevertheless important to assert how crucial her discussion of presentism—and by implication the political—is to any long-term consideration of the research agenda of Women's Studies. As the pressure to articulate that agenda grows more intense in coming years, in part because of the emergent emphasis on the doctoral degree as signifier of the progress of our march through the university, it will be important to think both critically and well about how Women's Studies can build alliances among academic domains, not in the name of a transcendent future, but to comprehend temporality as one of the most crucial blind spots in our approach to the organization of knowledge.

The essays offered to delineate "The History of the Present" are not, of course, comprehensive enough, even collectively, to define all the theoretical debates and challenges that today constitute the intellectual imaginary, much less the critical history, of Women's Studies as a field. But they do articulate a number of nodal concerns about how Women's Studies might achieve a self-definition for its intellectual production that can continue what is, for all of us, the messy implication of identity as a critical object of inquiry. In the context of the postcolonial inflections that inaugurate the collection, such messiness arises under a political imperative to give our students knowledge that can intervene in the very transformations in capital that are now reconfiguring subject formation in the U.S. academy. At the same time, we resist the call to understand the political labor of Women's Studies solely along the lines of subject formation, as it is that understanding that has often rendered various fields either superfluous to Women's Studies or significant only in their relation to a certain articulation of the political urgency of the present.

All of the issues raised in the first section remark in some way on the processes of institutionalizing identity as an object of study, and in this they establish identity as the problematic that animates as well as limits

Women's Studies as a field. In the second section, "Institutional Pedagogies," we turn to the question of the institution in a more direct way, as contributors take up a series of conflicting positions about the practices that constitute the project of institutionalization: interdisciplinarity, governance, administration, faculty review, professionalism, corporatism, fiscal autonomy, and fiscal constraint. Each contributor to this section was asked to keep her comments brief and pointed—in essence, to produce a position statement about a particular aspect of institutionalization that she found to be most in need of critical articulation. Kathleen Blee begins with a chapter titled "Contending with Disciplinarity," which entails a discussion of how the disciplinary organization of knowledge and its structures of judgment, review, and promotion affect the interdisciplinary designs—in curriculum, teaching, and faculty relations—of Women's Studies. Taking the feminist theory course as a case study for the difficulty of transmitting the interdisciplinarity that has long served as a chief characteristic of Women's Studies' difference in the academy, Blee explores the contradictions that ensue in the clash between feminist intervention in specific disciplines and the desire to produce a distinct academic tradition of our own. Her essay does not provide solutions as much as set the stage for thinking about how the materiality of knowledge production in the disciplines produces dis-identification, ambivalence, and at times deep contention within Women's Studies.

Bonnie Zimmerman extends Blee's opening consideration of the category of theory by tracing its place in the founding texts of Women's Studies as a field, with particular attention to the way in which the current conception of Women's Studies as an academic entity is articulated in tension, if not contradiction, with the activist. Wanting both to appreciate the political insurrection that accompanied the move of Women's Studies from social movement to academic institutionalization, Zimmerman seeks to adjust our understanding of the present as one defined by very different social formations and political challenges. She rightly points out how certain attempts to maintain the ethos of second wave feminism within Women's Studies programs—service learning, for instance—is contradictory in the context of the disestablishment of the welfare state, as it now proffers a liberal solution to what once signified as a distinctly socialist practice. In articulating the academic as a critical politics, Zimmerman offers readers a deliberation on the central issue that motivated the creation of this volume: how both to understand and to negotiate effectively in our present and future the certain consequence of feminism's twentieth-century path in the academy—that is, the institutionalization of feminist knowledge via Women's Studies programs and departments.

These issues are taken up as well by Judith Kegan Gardiner and Jean Robinson, both of whom consider the impact of Women's Studies' own institutionalization—as degree-granting entity, tenure home, and professional culture—on the politics of programs and departments. Gardiner offers a history of governance transformation at her institution, weighing the changing dynamic between inclusiveness and community to the more enclosed structure predicated on tenure review and faculty mentorship. Whereas Gardiner remains hopeful that Women's Studies can find an appropriate balance for its egalitarian goals, Robinson counters in a more doubtful tone, focusing in detailed ways on the various costs of institutional incorporation. For Robinson, the drive to protect Women's Studies' own curriculum, to hire and tenure its own faculty, and to preserve its own judgments about the content of feminist scholarship has had the negative effect of closing the doors of the Women's Studies academic community and endorsing aspects of professionalization that feminist scholars have long critiqued. Still, she does not fault the generation that has come to occupy those positions as much as provide a compelling and generous account of the different kinds of feminist subjects that have been created in and by the academic institution. From both of these discussions, we can understand generational difference not simply as a matter of age, but also in terms of the structural production of feminist subjectivity as an effect of our own practices and processes of institutional transformation.

Devoney Looser highlights the question of generation by thinking about it through the lens of Women's Studies administration. Specifically, she is concerned with the way in which, thirty years into our institutional history, many Women's Studies programs are still forced to rely on junior faculty administrators, often in contexts in which the senior faculty are experiencing massive burnout from the struggles of the inaugurating years. In using her own experience as a chronologically young and institutionally junior administrator, Looser is interested in how "generation" plays out across academic hierarchies and how narratives of past struggles (and the history of institutional affiliations that accompanied those struggles) significantly limit the possibilities of moving programs toward something other than a continued institutional existence of marginality. One very important issue emerges here that is often kept under wraps in Women's Studies program cultures: the desire for—indeed, the dedication to—marginality that over time becomes a false emblem of a program's security and success. Looser resists the idea that continuity in Women's Studies must be registered by the perpetuation of marginality. Her chapter struggles both to respect the labor that has gone into the building of Women's Studies and her own desire for a utopian future that less ambivalently embraces the possibility that institutionalization is itself a form of feminist power.

The final three chapters in "Institutional Pedagogies" move forward the conversation begun by Looser about administrative issues in Women's Studies. In "Taking Account of Women's Studies," Diane Elam interrogates the relationship between disciplinarity and departmentalization—and the fiscal and intellectual stakes that accompany Women's Studies' historical resistance to claim for itself either disciplinary or departmental status. Drawing on findings from her 1997 national review of Women's Studies in Switzerland, Elam provides important critical linkages between feminist knowledge and the state, demonstrating the ways in which any claim within Women's Studies to marginality as a guarantee of political difference works to reinforce the secondary status of feminist knowledge and places the critical possibilities of interdisciplinarity in a stranglehold. For Elam, Women's Studies must have a departmental location in the institution from which to perform and extend its understanding of the intellectual project of interdisciplinarity. The resulting contradiction—that Women's Studies organizes itself more like a discipline to provide an institutional basis for interdisciplinarity—does not, in her view, deprive Women's Studies of a radical institutional politics. Rather, such a politics is made possible by harnessing funds and tenure lines to an interdisciplinary project formed in the name of feminist knowledge.

Robyn Warhol takes a different tack on the question of institutional autonomy by thinking about the project of Women's Studies in colleges and universities that will not provide the funding necessary to secure tenure lines or departmental status. Her chapter, "Nice Work, If You Can Get It—And If You Can't? Building Women's Studies Without Tenure Lines," offers a sobering intervention into the national conversation that sets as a standard for defining the field's success in terms of departmental status, tenure-track faculty, and the development of autonomous undergraduate and graduate degrees. For Warhol, these conversations often rely on a faulty characterization of the disciplines as "traditional" thought police who are fundamentally opposed to feminist scholarship. She offers instead a more dynamic way of thinking about the relationship between interdisciplinary and disciplinary sites in order to consider how transformations of each are ongoing and productive—and how the incursion of interdisciplinarity in general, and of feminist knowledges in particular, has visibly changed what count as legitimate methods and objects of inquiry throughout the humanities and social sciences. "The long-term radical transformation of 'traditional departments' is as worthy a goal," she argues, "as the more obviously exciting project of developing Women's Studies tenure lines in those institutions where it is possible to do so." By paying attention to the unevenness of the institutional security achieved by Women's Studies in diverse academic settings, Warhol reminds us that strategies of intervention always have local inflections, which is one way of saying that the "institution" cannot be paradigmatically invoked in its materiality without sacrificing some of the critical possibilities of Women's Studies, as a diverse institutional project, in its present tense.

In the chapter that closes the "Institutional Pedagogies" section, "The Politics of 'Excellence,' " Jeanette McVicker moves the conversation from the local to the global by examining how economic and ideological transformations in the university are finding their impact on and within Women's Studies. Using Bill Readings's critique of the emergence of the discourse of "excellence" as the founding feature of administrative justification for the university's work at the end of the twentieth century, McVicker tracks the characteristics of what she calls "the university-becoming-transnational corporation." For McVicker, the bureaucratic forms of administration that Women's Studies, like other academic units, is increasingly asked to use—in languages of assessment, accountability, outcome, efficiency, and productivity—point to the new conditions within which tensions, felt at all levels of the social formation, between nation-state forms of governance and transnational corporatism are being negotiated. Rather than seeing the nation as fully superceded by the corporate model, as some have argued, McVicker finds nation and corporation oddly entwined in the territorial fight within universities and colleges over general education curricula and the student-subjects such curricula inevitably produce. Thus, the "idea of America," so crucial to the Cold War institution and its legacy of educational nationalism, is recast but not displaced when the transnational corporatist model offers the United States as the referent for and agency of economic globalism. For McVicker, transdisciplinary sites such as Women's Studies are threatening to both forms of subject production in the university, which is why, she argues, the very legitimacy of the field came under scrutiny in the recent curricular battles in the State University of New York system. How Women's Studies understands its own political project within this transforming institutional context will be crucial, she predicts, to its ability to think broadly and with critical impact on education as an instrument of capital and the state. Certainly, the issues she raises have crucial implications for a Women's Studies project that now seeks to "internationalize" its curriculum and to produce various kinds of workers (including activists) for an increasing array of global organizations.

McVicker's contribution thus returns us, from a different analytic angle, to the questions of difference and of the relationship between a seemingly domestic interior and a global exterior that troubled various critics who, at the outset, questioned the geopolitical dimensions of Women's Studies as a field formation. At the same time, "The Politics of 'Excellence' " acts as a bridge to the third section of this volume, "In the Shadow of Capital." In this section, issues of capital, labor, and the managed university take center stage, providing an unprecedented and urgent critical analysis not simply of the material conditions under which feminist knowledge is created, but also of the institutional shape and everyday labor of Women's Studies practitioners. In addition, scholars explore the institution's demand for a rationalized outcome to Women's Studies education by studying statements of expectations and career paths of our graduates at the baccalaureate level. Such a consideration faces the conundrum of Women's Studies' own relationship to the managed university by talking about the complexity of training students who increasingly view themselves as consumers—indeed, as consumers of Women's Studies. The volume thus moves from position statements about the kinds of institutional practices that challenge and enable Women's Studies to negotiate its own process of institutionalization to a set of concerns about the labor of our endeavors as part of—and, indeed, as vital to—the managed university itself. In this collision between our ideals about academic political struggle and the institution as a site of profession/professionalization, capital shadows our every move. For contributors to this collection, such an observation enables us to grapple more fully with the location of academic feminism.

"In the Shadow of Capital" opens with Dale Bauer's deliberation on the sexual division of labor that has shaped the development of Women's Studies programs, where a great deal of the labor that accompanies the political struggle to institutionalize the field remains imperceptible except as part of that increasing arena of generally uncompensated labor called "service." For Bauer, this situation is only one aspect of the broader problem of labor facing Women's Studies, whose own academic culture often reinforces the very practices of exploitation attending feminism's "Academic Housework." Too often, as Bauer notes, the university positions Women's Studies as labor to be performed "after hours"—after the work of the home department or discipline has been completed. This after-hours approach, which dovetails ideologically with Women's Studies' own ambivalence about its institutional legitimacy, means that feminists—especially those in joint appointments—do the second shift in the academy, performing various kinds of unwaged labor that replicates (are we surprised?) women's housework in dual-career heterosexual families.

"The "real work" of the academy goes on, business as usual in traditional departments, and most female faculty working within those departments must then do two sorts of labor. The first is that for which they are hired, promoted and rewarded; the second—they are told—is that which they do out of their commitment or interest. And so they perform the domestic work of academe, the nurturing, sustaining, fostering of students, a labor made "natural" because of their interest in furthering a Women's Studies agenda.

Bauer's concern is not only to diagnose the labor structure that makes visible in concrete ways the patriarchal organization of the university, but also to offer alternatives that will enable Women's Studies to challenge its own domestication as a feminized work site. This begins, she argues, by recognizing how the ambivalence that is the inescapable consequence of the feminist academic's double shift (or "double shaft") position "may also be the site of new resistance." Resistance is possible through a new agenda of internal assessment and documentation that, first, makes their own unwaged labor visible to Women's Studies faculty as precisely a problem of labor (and not as a matter of choice borne of politics), and second, makes the issue of service a labor concern in Women's Studies' own processes of governance and review. As Bauer writes, students "come to us for personal as well as academic guidance on abortion, sexual assault and harassment, and . . . career counseling. . . . This generally unrecognized and usually unremunerated part of our labor must be logged, made explicit, and counted as part of merit and promotion advancements. . . . This may be Women's Studies' next great educational step: to broadcast the demands on female faculty and on Women's Studies as a program."

Bauer calls for the creation of a "Feminist Dossier" that will become part of the review process to document and thereby politicize for the institution the various ways in which women faculty are positioned as caretakers by students and administrators, and within the ideology of feminist pedagogy itself. "Such a dossier," she writes, "might include: (1) the scope of extra-pedagogical topics we need to address for our students; (2) the interdisciplinary range of our syllabi; (3) our most effective non-traditional assignments, along with a description of the range of our students, many of whom are nontraditional students; (4) our emphasis on ability-based curricula, and especially reports of peer and administrator visits to our classes, to attest to the kinds of teaching methods and successes in feminist classrooms; and (5) the administrative burdens of running interdisciplinary programs." By using accountability to its own ends, Women's Studies can challenge both the university's sexual division of labor and its tacit acceptance of the second shift as the inevitable, if exhausting, cost of feminist change.

Crucially, "Academic Housework" demonstrates how important it is for Women's Studies to confront its own entrenchment in a service mentality that has often been justified, if not celebrated, as evidence of shared political commitments to feminist change. Certainly, such commitments have functioned as a kind of culture-making glue for the community-building aspects of underfunded programs in which the shared lack of compensation for institutionalizing the field has productively allied scholars and students in a collective endeavor. But the costs of this mechanism of community building have been unevenly distributed, for all bodies in the labor market of the academy are not, we know, the same. Scholars of color, in fact, may be re-racialized in the structure of service production cast in Women's Studies as an emblem of belonging, and in this, belonging to Women's Studies becomes a material burden overwritten by the economic hierarchies at work in capitalist delineations of "race." This is even more the case when programs and departments establish service requirements as part of their governance structure, thereby institutionalizing for scholars with political commitments to other identity-based and routinely underfunded sites the dilemma of difference (race or gender; double or triple shift) described in our scholarship. To the extent that Women's Studies functions as a site that extracts ever greater amounts of surplus labor as a condition of inclusion, even if the rhetoric of such extraction is about political change, it participates in a form of diversity management that requires those who labor under the sign of "minority" identities to fulfill the university's obligation to difference quite literally on their own backs. The political costs of service-driven cultures of belonging in Women's Studies is one of the most important issues we face today in discussions about labor and shared governance.

The program cultures that are created in our own negotiation of the sexual and racialized divisions of labor that operate in the university extend, of course, beyond the professoriat and are variously entwined in the way adjuncts, teaching assistants, and research assistants are situated in our units. Sivagami Subbaraman's contribution to this volume, "(In)Different Spaces: Feminist Journeys from the Academy to the Mall," sets forth some of the most salient issues for thinking about part-time labor in the contemporary university, challenging feminists across the disciplines to be more diligent in analyzing the complexity of feminization on wages and labor conditions. She begins by looking at recent studies from the Modern Language Association (MLA), the U.S. national organization for the study of literature, that examine the increasing use of part-time labor in English departments nationwide. These studies, she notes, rely on an interpretative strategy that seeks to disavow the forms of exploitation that accompany the use of part-time labor to staff introductory writing and literary studies courses. In particular, she analyzes how the heterosexual family form is assumed as a wage unit for part-time instructors, which has the effect of rendering women's employment in this sector as a secondary, non-necessary contribution to a phantasmatic stable family wage. By looking especially at how the MLA's rhetoric comes to pit the "love" of teaching against the financial rewards offered, Subbaraman demonstrates how discourses of family, romance, and female subordination intertwine to render the feminization of academic labor invisible as prototypical unwaged labor. Her chapter is especially important in the context of thinking about Women's Studies programs, whose own economic marginality in the institution (and, at times, economic dependence on the disciplines) generates a pipeline of exploitation, with the very functioning of feminist curricula contingent on the feminization of academic labor.

Although Subbaraman's chapter is primarily concerned with part-time labor and with the different female bodies that have been given access to the university as a "home" for their academic production, her discussion also opens a conversation for thinking about the current situation of teaching assistants, who, throughout the 1990s, worked to bring issues of their status as expendable labor into critical view in university settings throughout the United States. In the struggle to unionize, teaching assistants have found themselves at times pitted against the very culture of surplus labor as political service in Women's Studies that I discussed earlier. The shock for many Women's Studies professors of thinking about and approaching teaching assistants as workers—much like the shock of recognizing what we call our political struggle as itself a form of surplus labor—demonstrates the need for complex delineations of the way in which the university has come quite brilliantly to manage Women's Studies' own project of political change. At the same time, it can often be the case that unionization efforts will function as vehicles of overexposure for such institutional sites as Women's Studies, which can never shake off the constraining perception that they are primarily advocacy units and hence political in the narrowest self-interested and (to some administrations) anti-intellectual sense. It is not uncommon for Women's Studies programs to surface as targets of administrative surveillance during student campaigns for unionization in ways that the traditional disciplines do not. These complexities, where marginalization and exploitation are structurally institutionalized both in Women's Studies' general position in the university and in the fiscal order that has underwritten the field's emergence as a degree-granting entity, is surely part of the complexity of thinking labor and capital as key elements of institutionalization itself.

But it is simply not enough to raise the issue of Women's Studies as marginalized vis-à-vis the university in the context of these discussions of labor as if such a statement can adequately negotiate the problems we face in accounting for the many ways in which our programs, as well as our faculty, bear and deploy institutional power. The teaching assistant who makes $4,890 for teaching an introductory course with 240 students while a full professor makes $25,000 for the same course surely has no faith in our analytic abilities if we ask her to remember, in the context of unionizing struggles, that Women's Studies is marginalized. Nor should any amount of shared governance or collaborative teaching with students serve to defend Women's Studies programs from apprehending and grappling with the actual hierarchies that inhabit our institutional sites.

This problem—of having power to wield—is one of the greatest challenges many Women's Studies practitioners face. Certainly, it is the case that continued efforts to build programs into departments, to hold and tenure faculty, and to create autonomous doctoral programs will increase the ways in which the everyday life of Women's Studies in the institution is defined by divisions of labor—divisions that emerge through economic arrangements and through the processes of credentialing, judgment, and review that accompany our growth. In this regard, the expansionist mentality that often underlies our ways of marking program success does not counter the institution's discourse as much as it employs feminism as a desiring agent of accumulation within its purview.

The issue of complicity is at the heart of Miranda Joseph's contribution to this volume, which importantly links issues of academic labor to the managerial work that identity-based studies are currently performing for the university. "Analogy and Complicity: Women's Studies, Lesbian/Gay Studies, and Capitalism" begins by situating questions of labor within the larger political economy of the university as a subject-producing entity for capital and the state. For Joseph, although the work of institutionalizing discrete identity-based academic sites opens "a space for interventionist and emancipatory scholarship and activism," it is nevertheless "implicated in and determined by transformations in the global formation of capitalism in ways that undermine their emancipatory potential." This is the case in part because of feminism's own political genealogy within liberal capitalism, which links feminism's emphasis on liberal humanist notions of autonomy to the consumer subject wrought by modernization and globalization. But it is also the case because of the structure of analogy that adheres to identity production: where notions of the internal coherence of gender, race, sexuality, and class produce subjects (of scholarship as well as citizens) that register their difference as the value of equivalences. Such value, Joseph argues, arises from the logic of capital itself, where equivalence functions ideologically to mask the disparity in value that accompanies the wage-labor system. By thinking about how singular identity forms have emerged as categories of value within consumer capital, Joseph contemplates the value for capital of identity-based studies, with special attention to the increasingly tense relationship between Women's Studies and lesbian/gay/bisexual Studies.

The story that Joseph tells about these entities begins in her own university setting, where she was hired as the "sexuality studies person" in a Women's Studies program that had been under both institutional and programmatic pressure to resolve the tension between gender and sexuality as analytic modes and objects of study in its curriculum. This resolution, according to Joseph, was impossible not only because of the culture that had come to function within Women's Studies, where the program's founding around "women" served as the glue for its functioning as a scholarly community, but also because the idea that gender and sexuality can be made internally coherent and hence externally different from each other can be neither intellectually nor socially sustained. Gender and sexuality cannot, in short, be rendered equivalent to each other (or to race, class, or nation). The political project of identity thus cannot be forced on analogies among categories of identification. Rather, she argues, affiliations can be made because of the political and intellectual potential of the negative recognition of non-equivalence; indeed, for Joseph, much of the possibility of Women's Studies (to invert the trajectory of the title of Wendy Brown's essay) arises from the prospect that it might function as one (though not the only) institutional site for exploring identity's problematic history both in modernity and as the taxonomy for human categorization in various social formations. To the extent that Women's Studies refuses this possibility, setting its sights instead on the political resolution of identity claims, it will function to bolster and extend capital's disciplining of identity into valued equivalence.

Joseph's use of her own institutional experience and candid discussion of issues that affect the everyday shape and culture of her working life is a risky kind of critical maneuver for a number of reasons, not the least of which is her willingness to expose and question her own political investments in both identity and the academic institution. Remaining skeptical of the role as sexual informant that she was hired to play, but finding herself politically mobilized by the lack of a curriculum in Women's Studies that could make sexuality at least provisionally a primary object of study, Joseph's narrative gives us insight into the consequences of hiring practices that use identity categories as the intellectual basis for defining positions and fields of competence. In ways that crisscross with conversations staged in this volume by Rachel Lee and Minoo Moallem concerning the "Women of Color" course and the bodies assumed to staff it, the demand that "difference" operate representationally one for critics and their objects of study—that, in fact, you are what you teach—carries a high intellectual and social cost for Women's Studies programs. It carries forward the assumption that the academic labor of decolonizing the curriculum comes from a reorganization of fields of study, establishing "expertise"—almost always understood as experientially based—in specific identities for whom the program's obligation to difference can be met because one representative is most assuredly enough (at least, given the long fight for even one faculty position, it is all that a program or department can afford). Often it is the new generation of Women's Studies faculty who are asked to play the role of identity representatives, with the senior faculty composed of those who represent the disciplines, not social bodies, as such. This division, which asks junior faculty to bear the burden of an expertise written on their bodies, produces a strange kind of mind-body split within Women's Studies program cultures, exacerbating the alienation that comes from the duty of "being" while setting disciplinary knowledge against the categories of difference articulated as politically urgent in the present (race, sexuality, postcoloniality).

I am not arguing that fields of study and identities need to be made distinct; rather, it is the assumption of an equivalence between the two, along with the political desire that such an equivalence will settle identity's incoherencies by representing greater specificity in the curriculum, that must be critically challenged. Crucially, Joseph offers us a narrative that articulates the difficulty of negotiating identity logics in the contemporary university. But more than this, her contribution to the volume demonstrates that there are theoretical discourses that need to be brought to bear on identity and that in this, students and scholars alike can demand pedagogical practices that make the legibility of identity's incoherence their political and critical goal. This is at least one way of reading her essay's opening delineation of the political economy of identity, which offers a critical apparatus for helping us understand both that identity is part of a modern interpretative framework and that it is a concept in need of explanation. To the extent that Women's Studies programs have used identity as a referential discourse to explain our political desire for difference, we have short-circuited the very challenge that identity as an object of study critically opens; in the process, we have also forged a gap between theoretical commitments to the non-unity of identity categories and the operation of institutional domains. When Joseph points out how the discrete production of identity sites in the university demonstrates our own forgetting of our scholarship, it is this that she means: that we have wagered a territorial understanding of women that continues the practices of disciplining bodies and knowledges into managed units of difference for the university.

The disciplining that Joseph describes is not, in her narrative or my interpretation of it, lodged solely in Women's Studies. Indeed, part of the power that adheres to identity's particularist formulation comes from the way that sexual identity has long threatened the legitimacy of any feminist deployment of the category of woman. Thus, Joseph talks about how her program had been sexually policed by administrative bodies that were concerned with the number of lesbians hired into it (though not hired under the proliferation of identities as object domains). This surveillance, performed also by the legislature as the state agency overseeing all curricular reform, makes visible the institutionalized hierarchies of power (from program to college, university, system, and the state) that must be negotiated by Women's Studies at state universities.

Marcia Westkott's "Institutional Success and Political Vulnerability: The Importance of Allies" develops this trajectory of discussion further by providing readers with a thoughtful narrative about how her Women's Studies program negotiated its relationship to governmental power by successfully establishing a Women's Studies major in a public institution governed by a conservative, and indeed homophobic, state legislature. Using interviews with key administrative and faculty personnel who supported the major, Westkott examines the social psychology of institutional change, demonstrating the strategic usefulness and possibilities of constructing allies in tense political encounters. Most important perhaps, her essay foregrounds not only how practices of institutionalization can perform profound activist functions, but also how facile are notions of the academy as a site distanced from the political in its most overt sense. Westkott's example serves as an important index of the force of coalitional struggle, as the instillation of the major required a deft negotiation of the legislature's perception of Women's Studies as a "lesbian" entity and of subsequent right-wing efforts to deny all funding to the university as long as its officials supported Women's Studies. By foregrounding the difficulties of creating a stable site for the production of feminist knowledge in a public institution, Westkott provides readers with a way to understand institutional transformation as both social and psychic transformation for Women's Studies faculty and their allies.

Westkott's essay is especially important because of its ability to describe the complexities of a political situation that Women's Studies faculty have long faced: The program could not prevail without strong advocacy from outside forces, especially in the administration. But how to mobilize the administration to take up pedagogically the banner of Women's Studies as a necessary and legitimate intellectual site? At Westkott's university, Women's Studies had garnered institutional prestige through a number of avenues, from the publication records of its faculty to the historical growth of its curriculum to the enormous diversity of its faculty vis-à-vis the whiteness of the institution as a whole. It had also raised money for the renovation of its building and had a healthy history of collaboration with the local community. These strengths were the effects of a concerted strategy to build the program's reputation on its academic standing and thus to redefine how the university administered both identity studies and diversity in its faculty. In addition, the program benefited from the larger history of Women's Studies in the university, as some of its administrative supporters had been trained within—or, at least, in critical conversation with—Women's Studies as a field. In this regard, the struggle for the major at Colorado was embedded in the successes of the institutionalization of Women's Studies at other Research-I public universities, and informed administrators could field questions about the political context of Women's Studies without becoming defensive—without, in fact, defending Women's Studies on anything other than intellectual grounds. The struggle for the major was thus a pedagogical lesson in institution building. It "awakened us afresh not only to our political vulnerability, but also to the political importance of our task," Westkott writes. "Thus, we find ourselves toeing the narrow line between the twin goals of survival and change, a political-institutional dance that is, indeed, an art form."

Students made up a second, though no less significant group, of allies, teaching the faculty a thing or two about the political utility of consumer subjectivity. By pointedly adopting the discourse of education as consumption and of the student as the consumer of the marketplace of ideas, Women's Studies students were able to garner both administrators' and legislators' attention in their coalitional efforts to secure the new major. Given that Women's Studies faculty have long resisted the bureaucratic call to define the value of Women's Studies in market-based terms, the students' savvy ability to do so is an important index of the ways in which "the political" as a set of strategies and "subjectivity" as a political effect are being transformed in the very processes of our academic institutionalization. Whereas Women's Studies faculty once might have assumed that a student who mobilized the discourse of consumption and posited education in market terms needed a Women's Studies curriculum as a political counter, new evidence from students indicates their willingness (indeed, their ability) to exist in the contradictions among capital, the state, and a politicized education in Women's Studies in ways we may not have anticipated. This is at least one of the conclusions of the study of career trajectories of Women's Studies graduates offered by Maryanne Dever, Denise Cuthbert, and Lindsey Pollak in this section's final essay. "Life After Women's Studies: Graduates and the Labor Market" addresses the "vocational" as it shapes both life decisions of our students and, with increasing force, our fiscal and rhetorical administrative practices.

The authors begin with a useful consideration of how the question of the vocational has been dismissed or repressed in Women's Studies conversations as well as in our program statements for outcome-driven administrations of the precise kinds of training we are providing to students. Chiefly, the authors note that the very consideration of students' relationship to the labor market has often indicated to Women's Studies faculty their programs' capitulation to the ethos of commodity education now dominating many public institutions. Hence, the feminist imperative to think about education as a response to the constraining choices offered by patriarchal institutions (the family, the church, the state, the military) has inculcated a critical distaste for thinking about the convertibility of feminist knowledge to a capitalist wage-labor system. But the authors of this essay are convincing in their assertion that it is not possible today to ignore the challenge of crafting a feminist politics through which the question, "What do you do with a Women's Studies major?"

can be refracted. This is the case not only because of shrinking resources for education, but also because of our students' own expectations that Women's Studies will both teach them about alternatives and prepare them materially to achieve agency over their life directions. "We would suggest," the authors write, "that consideration of our students' post-graduation experiences in general, and their vocational aspirations in particular, is essential if we are to maintain some meaningful fit between our professed teaching and learning objectives; our students' needs, desires, and aspirations; and the wider context in which important educational and vocational decisions are negotiated."

After surveying the limited research that currently exists on students' expectations and career outcomes of a Women's Studies education, "Life After Women's Studies" presents important new findings produced by the authors' pilot survey of first-year Women's Studies students. The survey sought to understand the relationship between students' decision to enroll in a Women's Studies class and their anticipated career paths, "replacing the question, 'What do you do with Women's Studies?' with "What do you think you can do with Women's Studies?' or 'What do you want to do with Women's Studies?'" The survey's findings were both predictable and surprising. Most predictable was that 61 percent of the respondents choose either personal interest or interest in the subject matter as the primary reason for enrolling in Women's Studies, whereas only 3 percent said that anticipated career trajectories governed their decision. And yet, when students were asked directly to note their anticipated career paths, 25 percent were not satisfied with the list provided by the survey's authors, thereby "producing a radically different profile from the one we anticipated." Although the authors expected the category of public service and administration to draw the most responses, only 4 percent of the students chose it. "Likewise, 'women's organizations' was selected by only 8 percent of respondents," they write. "Of the fields of employment we nominated in the questionnaire, only the education and social work-welfare areas rated significantly, both registering 32 percent." The students who chose "other" provided a wide range of possible careers, "in order of popularity: health, including psychology and nursing; drama and theater; media, including journalism, film, television, and advertising; the environmental movement; sports and leisure industries; and the armed forces." These choices indicated to the authors of the survey how constrained their own sense of the vocational outcome for Women's Studies education had been, leading them to consider the extent to which their own pedagogical practices might actually mistake the diversity of students' expectations and aspirations for a Women's Studies degree.

By arguing that feminist research on the post-graduation labor-market aspirations and experiences of Women's Studies students can play a critical role in challenging prevailing models of economic rationalism, Dever, Cuthbert, and Pollak encourage new research on vocational expectations as a crucial part of intervening in the discourses of the institution. In particular, they cite three primary areas for continued study:

1. Comparative international studies that will allow Women's Studies practitioners to track both the differing career paths taken by Women's Studies graduates and the impact of our work across a variety of national domains;
2. The broader community, including graduate recruiters, personnel officers, careers counselors, and human-resources managers, which will allow us to discover popular understandings of Women's Studies as an academic program and the range of attitudes that our students will confront as they seek post-graduate education and employment; and
3. Women's Studies faculty, in order to understand better how the aspirations of practitioners in the field influence students.

Through research in these areas, Dever, Cuthbert, and Pollak believe, we can better craft an understanding of the complexities of "what our students hope to be able to do with their Women's Studies education . . . what the labor market expects of graduates and how the skills and attributes of Women's Studies graduates mesh with these expectations; and whether and in what ways Women's Studies programs and their staff address the post-graduation aspirations of their students and the world of work beyond the walls of the university."

"Life After Women's Studies" is in many ways an inaugurating analysis, by which I mean that it is more interested in defining both the scope of preliminary research into post-graduate career paths and future research directions than it is invested in analyzing the discourse of assessment and outcomes used by the university. It begins by accepting the critiques of the university's relationship to capitalism that have been articulated in this volume (and elsewhere) but responds by offering research as the political strategy that will aid us in challenging the managerial rationalism of the university as marketplace while maintaining our obligation to students who seek through education to control their economic fates. Our complicity in the reproduction of the class system of which higher education is a primary apparatus cannot, as all of the "In the Shadow of Capital" chapters concede, be resolved. And yet the hope, provisional and small though it may be, is that we are learning something significant about the psychic and material terrain of feminism's institutionalization.

The first three sections of this collection take us through a number of pressing questions related to the present of Women's Studies as an institutional site. The final section focuses on what, for many of us, is the most palpable political space of our academic lives: the classroom. Each of the chapters in "Critical Classrooms" thinks about the pedagogical implications of the various divisions of knowledge—racial, sexual, disciplinary, geopolitical, economic—that have been discussed by previous contributors. Sabina Sawhney's "Strangers in the Classroom" begins by offering a studied meditation on introductory Women's Studies courses that rely on team-teaching to achieve the desired interdisciplinarity of the field. Drawing on her experiences as the "humanist" scholar paired with a social scientist to teach "Introduction to Women's Studies," she defines the various forms of inequality that emerge among knowledges in a classroom setting quite explicitly devoted to disciplinary equality. When the course material is drawn from the humanities, and hence when the epistemological force of investigation is linked to language and subjectivity, she writes, the social sciences are constructed as "raw data" in need of the sophistication that the interpretative languages of the humanities will bring. In the obverse situation—when the course focuses on issues derived from the social sciences—the humanities tend to function as the ephemeral stepchild to social science's methodological coherency. In each of these scenarios, the particular histories of these large disciplinary rubrics, along with the complexities of the interpretative and methodological modes of the disciplines organized within them, are lost to practices of appropriation and, at times, a kind of chauvinistic intellectual neglect. By analyzing the way interdisciplinarity is assembled in such a classroom, Sawhney considers the pedagogical impact on students as well as implications for Women's Studies as a field.

Sawhney's consideration of the introductory course is part of a larger deliberation on the structures of belonging that produce both the social and the intellectual modes of production in Women's Studies program cultures. Her chapter works to situate the course she has team-taught within the specificities of her own institution while also mapping it onto some of the larger assumptions about modes of belonging that organize the field imaginary of Women's Studies. In particular, Sawhney is concerned with how belonging to the category of women served initially as the vehicle for constituting Women's Studies as an intellectual site, which left intact certain aspects of disciplinary identity: One was, for instance, a feminist literary critic or a feminist sociologist. This meant "subscribing to the structure of . . . disciplines" even as feminist scholars remained "firmly opposed to their contents." In such a context, Women's Studies served as the institutional location for resolving the abjection wrought by the disciplines, a resolution contingent on a shared collaboration between feminist scholars and their gendered object of study (women). Making women the glue for a solidarity born of abjection is of course one of the most mobilizing aspects of identity politics. But the institutionalization of this relationship for Women's Studies has led, in Sawhney's analysis, to a number of damaging effects. Not only does it gloss over the contentiousness around which women can be apprehended as a coherent object of study; it also wagers the project of interdisciplinarity against the reified identity structures of disciplinary knowledge. In this, the feminist scholar working in Women's Studies can participate in what Sawhney calls a "fantasy" of interdisciplinarity by assuming that the composite accumulation of disciplinary difference is adequate to the pedagogical project of Women's Studies as a field. Hence, as she puts it, "the very organizations of identity and discipline, which were the premier objects of attack [for the inauguration of Women's Studies], become incorporated in precisely those courses that [are] introduced to rectify the problem."

What, then, should the introductory Women's Studies course do? For Sawhney, this question seems impossible to answer with any satisfaction at the pedagogical level because it raises the problem of what precisely Women's Studies is. That problem that has grown more, not less, urgent for Women's Studies practitioners in the course of the field's thirty-year sojourn. "Strangers in the Classroom" does not, however, seek a definitive response to this problem as much as it constructs Women's Studies as a site of intellectual opportunity for the ongoing deliberation of the dilemmas that frustrate the field. By viewing Women's Studies "at a slant, as it were, to the mainstream disciplinary formations," Sawhney calls for a strategy of "anti-disciplinarity": courses that "include discussions of the histories and the current structures of various disciplines, their rationales and philosophies. . . . [For what] is common to all the disciplines are the aporias, the gaps in their structures, the organizing principles that have been forgotten or ignored in the name of professionalism. Women's studies, along with other similarly oriented knowledge projects such as African American studies, postcolonial studies, and gay and lesbian studies, would initiate a displacement in the conception and organization of knowledge in contemporary academia." This is, of course, a difficult task in itself, as it places a great deal of emphasis on both faculty and curricular development, neither of which can happen without adequate institutional support. In the long run, then, Sawhney's deliberation on the introductory course points out the fiscal fantasy that interdisciplinarity has come to represent in the humanities and social sciences—a kind of dream formulation where new knowledges can be made with perfect economic efficiency. On the surface, they cost no one. Sawhney's chapter, however, demonstrates the intellectual cost to the university and to Women's Studies of program cultures that reproduce the hegemony of the disciplines in their construction of feminist knowledge as the consequence of the study of women (itself understood as the nomination for a social identity).

Sawhney's chapter implicitly approaches the construction of curricula and syllabi as theoretical activities. In this, she reads the classroom and its intellectual agenda, as well as its pedagogical practices, as one of the places in which institutional possibilities and limits are made most productively legible. Minoo Moallem's " 'Women of Color in the United States': Pedagogical Reflections on the Politics of 'the Name' " takes a similar tack, using the classroom as a site and teaching as an activity as the basis for critical investigation. The study of the classroom, she writes, "is important not only for an examination of institutional regimes of power and knowledge, but also for tracing the covert operations of governmentality within the academy." Moallem is especially interested in thinking about governmentality in a number of registers—not only the ways in which the university polices the production of subjects for the state and capital, but also how the implicit assumption about the relationship between bodies and knowledge performs a strategic function in articulating and ordering cultural identities. Her example is the "Women of Color in the United States" course, which she has taught in different university settings in the United States and Canada and to vastly different student audiences. This course, as Rachel Lee discussed in the volume's first section, has emerged as a standard in Women's Studies curricula through a particular history of knowledge formation, serving as the corrective to the tacit whiteness of the field's institutionalized object of study. For this reason, as Moallem writes, the course has often been the only site "where issues of race are legitimately addressed." From this space of both responsibility to the critical project of race and the burden of its non-appearance elsewhere, Moallem analyzes both the history of, and her discomfort with, the specificities named in the course's title: women, color, the United States.

First the history. Here, Moallem begins with the story about Women's Studies as a field that has become a regular part of our own critical self-narration. She describes the ways in which Women's Studies was pressured from both within and without to respond to racism. Throughout the 1980s, new textbooks appeared, faculty of color were hired, and a seemingly standard course became required for certification in the major. In the 1990s, however, a second, related transformation occurred, one wrought by the "internationalization of the women's studies curriculum and the expansion of the category of 'women of color' to include a speaking position for women from Third World countries." In this context, which refracted changes in the hegemonic position of the United States in the global economy, tensions around the deployment of race in Women's Studies and its categorical signification emerged. Although a political and theoretical project was crafted, by Chandra Mohanty and others, that sought to link the two most significant categories delineating a racialized subject—women of color in the United States and Third World women—Moallem notes that no amount of "coalition-building vis-à-vis White feminist movements in the West" could obviate the contradictions for Women's Studies of this new "inclusion of diasporic Third World women." This is the case in part because "the projection of U.S. racial politics onto the global situation disguises cultural imperialism as a major component of postcolonial societies. In this sense, cultural politics in the context of academia cannot be separated from the importance of making social, cultural, political, and economic issues the primary categories for understanding the curriculum."

Hence the discomfort. As a Third World feminist scholar in the U.S.

academy, Moallem expresses concern about the nominations set forth in the course that she has repeatedly been asked to teach, a concern that is born of the entanglement of the various histories of identity formation, cultural appropriation, and violence that simultaneously mark her as a woman of color and delegitimate her as an authority on or for the United States. "While the connection of the category 'woman of color' to 'Third World' facilitates a 'speaking' position for me," she says, "the framing of the course 'in the United States' raises a whole series of questions in terms of what should or should not be discussed, and who may or may not legitimately teach it." More than once she has encountered student resistance to her authority to teach the course based on her "foreignness." In this reiteration of the nationalist contours of the Women's Studies curriculum, the students of color in the classroom demonstrate that they understand all too well the territorial ideologies through which "women of color" has been offered as their now politicized, but no less "proper," place. In this proper place, where they are valued precisely as the object of study, students are unsettled when the processes whereby race is normalized are revealed. For Moallem, such processes are the content of a course on "women of color in the United States," which means that, rather than consecrate new racialized subjects under the sign of Women's Studies, she hopes to interrupt "the universalization of the category of women of color and its epistemological distancing from its genealogy." This will entail articulating as a critical problem both the utopian gesture around race consciousness encoded in the "Women of Color" course and the political failure that accompanies the course as it seeks a relationship of justice between Women's Studies as an institutionalized entity and racialized women.

Moallem's chapter is especially important because of its deft negotiation of the contradictory impulses and possibilities of the "Women of Color" course and its ability to use that course to contemplate how students are produced as specific kinds of intellectual and political subjects by a curricular structure. Her concern arises in part from the set of assumptions that have accompanied the institutionalization of race as a pedagogical focus in Women's Studies. But while she, like other contributors to this volume, is critical of some of the effects generated by the field's method of producing politicized subjects, this does not mean that Moallem or other contributors are dismissive of the attempt to counter consumptive subjectivities with critical agency. The point is, rather, that the political intentions that accompany curricular development cannot finally be guaranteed; nor can the classroom serve without contradiction as the scene for a faculty's own version of feminist self-fashioning.

For Moallem, as for others in this volume, the ethics of the classroom require instead a certain deliberation on the very limits of feminism's own historical critical agency, which is one way to relinquish feminism as the identity to be achieved and repositioning it as that which the field engages in its historical, epistemological, and anti-disciplinary specificities. Such an engagement will by necessity proceed in different ways across the course of an undergraduate curriculum. Although the introductory level must offer the rudiments of an analysis of gender and other forms of identity-based discriminations, subsequent courses need to historicize categories of identity, subjectivity, governmentality, and representation so that students have a critical relationship to that which feminism has purported to know. The final three chapters in this volume collaboratively contribute to an examination of the pedagogical issues at stake in the temporalizing modality of a Women's Studies curriculum. Nancy Naples, for instance, addresses the complexity of defining a concrete project for the introductory course that can teach students how to approach community action in their everyday lives. Susan Stanford Friedman focuses on what is often called the "capstone course," the senior seminar, in order to think about how a Women's Studies major might most productively come to a close. And Laura Donaldson and her colleagues Jael Silliman and Anne Donaday offer a theoretical consideration of the Women's Studies Ph.D.

Naples's "Negotiating the Politics of Experiential Learning in Women's Studies" returns to a founding category in Women's Studies curricular transformation in order to provide a close examination of the political and pedagogical history, theoretical formulations, and current critiques of experience as a basis of feminist pedagogical practice. For Naples, the current dismissal in many Women's Studies programs and departments of experiential pedagogy belies its utility to teach students, through an activist-oriented pedagogy, about concrete agencies for social change. By differentiating between personalized deployments of experience as autobiographical and emotional and critical deployments of experience as the basis of collective social action, Naples calls for a reassessment of the contribution that experiential learning can make to Women's Studies— especially at the introductory level, where students do not have critical tools for thinking about institutionalized forms of inequality and the historical processes through which social change has been, and can be, effected. Her chapter uses the Community Action Project, a pedagogical exercise she developed for an introductory Women's Studies course on institutional power, as an example of how experiential learning can work to transform students' agency and critical consciousness. In doing so, Naples demonstrates the ways in which critics of experience have too often read it as a further expressive function for the bourgeois subject and not as a mechanism for motivating beginning students toward thinking about politics as coalitional and collective.

Naples's return to experience is presented explicitly as a critical response to the way in which the institutionalization of Women's Studies has generated distance from the modalities of subject construction wrought by feminist work in the public sphere. Her take on institutionalization thus repeats what some of the essays collected here have tended to critique: the characterization that posits the failure of academic success in an increasing distance between the university and the political life of the community. Yet her chapter shows how the pedagogical work of translating students' political consciousness into a form of community action found its greatest effect in various kinds of interventions in the culture of the university—meaning that, for many students in her introductory course, the force of the Community Action Project lay in its ability to direct their attention to the organization of politics, knowledge, and labor in the everyday institutional life of their campus. In this, students were given a critical apparatus that compelled their realization that the work, learning, and living space of the university was not disconnected from those issues about organization and equality and inequality they studied as central to law, the family, the state, or church. Instead, the university was itself a key institution for their understanding of social formation. In addition to this way of making legible the everyday operation of institutions, the Community Action Project gave students an important opportunity to learn about activism less as an animating ideal than as a set of carefully wrought practices. In trying to help students understand the possibilities and the limits of such practices, the Community Action Project could turn the inevitable failures that arise in collectivity (around shared leadership, equal distribution of labor, or clarity of intended goal) into a powerful pedagogy, deepening their sense of social transformation as struggle in multiple ways.

One of the most important aspects of Naples's contribution to the collection is its closing meditation on the relationship between the use of the Community Action Project in the introductory course and the larger Women's Studies curriculum. Here, she rightly recognizes that the emphasis on praxis must be followed by more extensive instruction in the meaning and scope of social change—instruction that offers students both critical vocabularies and historical contexts for understanding forms of social action ranging from female club movements, volunteerism, and '60s style activism to NGOs and other emergent political organizations in a global world. Her suggestion that Women's Studies undergraduate majors take a required course on activism seeks to address the ways in which the curriculum has functioned under a fairly idealist and often nostalgic image of its own knowledge practices as a form of activism in and of itself. Such an understanding of the curriculum not only leads to the kind of presentism that Jane Newman has already diagnosed; it also has the damaging effect of casting activism as both everywhere and nowhere at once—as the most celebrated raison d'etre of the field and its least interrogated categorical assumption.

Naples's concern for a more studied approach to the pedagogical place of activism in the Women's Studies curriculum is not disconnected from one of the most crucial and difficult questions that now animates curricular discussions in the field: What is "core knowledge" for the undergraduate major? Because of the many imperatives that have become central to Women's Studies in its academic development—including intersectional and international analytic frameworks, action-oriented pedagogy, historical nuance, and a rigorous interdisciplinarity that refuses to keep the disciplines in place—problems abound in deciding, no less than institutionalizing, a set of course requirements that are coherent in their diversity. In "What Should Every Women's Studies Major Know? Reflections on the Capstone Seminar," Susan Stanford Friedman confronts this issue head on as she contemplates the various strategies she has adopted in designing and teaching the final course in the Women's Studies undergraduate major. For Friedman, the complexities of this course arise in part from divisions among the faculty over how Women's Studies as an academic entity is understood. "For some," she writes, "Women's Studies is an interdisciplinary field in which feminist questions and knowledge from a variety of disciplines are brought to bear on work in one of the traditional disciplines. For others, Women's Studies is a new discipline, with its own body of knowledge and methodology, the basis for newly proliferating Ph.D. degrees."

These differing understandings are often connected to the resources available in Women's Studies programs and tend to reflect, in material terms, the particular configuration of courses (autonomous or cross-listed) and faculty (lent by departments or housed in Women's Studies) that structure the unit at the time of any individual faculty's affiliation. This situation—the unevenness of the modes of intellectual belonging for Women's Studies faculty—is mirrored in the undergraduates in our courses, many of whom come to Women's Studies, even as majors, late in their undergraduate careers and most often as an addition to disciplinary course work. From their perspective, too, Women's Studies can appear as a collaborative correction to the blind spots of the disciplines or as an academic field of its own. Contributors to this volume have documented many of the struggles around which Women's Studies programs have negotiated their institutional existences, with the material implications of the field's growth and development in any specific place leading to the need for institutional contextualization at almost every step. The radical disparity between the field imaginary (what is projected in print and at conferences about its political and intellectual foundations) and the daily life of institutions, with their specific administrative structures and histories of undergraduate education, makes the determination of core knowledge in Women's Studies even more difficult. And yet, the very burden of a Women's Studies major as a degree conferred by hundreds of institutions in the United States necessitates deft negotiation of these issues.

Friedman's chapter seeks to accomplish this by situating the capstone seminar in the particular history of the Women's Studies unit in which she teaches it—and in the context of her own academic formation as a literary scholar. In addition, she provides a brief survey of the various functions that the capstone seminar has been asked to play in Women's Studies curricula across the United States, where it has typically taken one of four forms:

1. A research-oriented course for student-designed projects;
2. An introduction to feminist theory;
3. A topics course based on a faculty member's area of expertise; or
4. A seminar focusing on interdisciplinarity itself.

Friedman's course, taught since 1992, takes none of these directions in part because she has found the limitations of all of them. "After one unfortunate experience," she says, "I discovered that most students were very unhappy with a seminar aimed at deepening their knowledge of feminist theory. . . . Having watched a colleague face wholesale revolt against her attempt to teach an aspect of her research specialization, I didn't even attempt to focus the capstone on a narrow topic that I happened to know a great deal about. . . . For related reasons, I hesitated as well to attempt a seminar in which the goal was to get each student to design a research topic. . . . How could I—with thirty-some students ranging over the humanities, social sciences, and sciences—effectively direct all those projects, particularly when a large number of them would inevitably require knowledge of scholarly literatures and methodologies with which I was not familiar?" Now her course seeks to be "ambitiously interdisciplinary," even as it remains "rooted in fields and methods I can handle; extensively theoretical without being directly devoted to feminist theory; and analytically rather than research-oriented." It functions by thematizing and theorizing the temporal place it occupies in student development by looking backward and looking forward. The course thus has three organizing rubrics:

1. The History and Theory of Women's Studies;
2. Feminist Epistemologies: Theory and Practice in Reading and Writing Women's Lives; and
3. The Third Wave: The New Generation of Feminists and Your Future.

Friedman's purpose in describing her course and its developmental history is not to assert a new or standardized paradigm for the Women's Studies capstone seminar as a whole. Rather, she hopes to inaugurate a conversation about the various pressures that faculty face in designing the "final course in a cumulative Women's Studies curriculum in different academic settings and with different kinds of students." Because capstone courses "come at a very special moment in the lives of undergraduates," they are especially useful for broader considerations of the difficulties of curricular cohesion in a field that has a decidedly uneven institutional history. "What Should Every Women's Studies Major Know?" is thus a question, Friedman suggests, that we not only should not, but will not be able to, answer definitively—at least not now, when the institutional apparatus supporting the field and producing the intellectual subjects who come to teach in our programs and departments varies so greatly from one site to another. In this, the question that motivates her chapter is a provocation as well a deferral: It defines an anxiety about the lack of cohesion that her essay says we cannot escape while mobilizing an obligation toward students to engage critically the institutional dilemmas of the present in course development and curricular structure. In this tactic of ascertaining the material conditions of feminist knowledge production alongside the long-term goals of institutionalizing a self-justifying undergraduate degree, Friedman seeks to negotiate what-is-not-yet with the ideals of what-will-be to give us a cogent way to think about the profound challenges of this "stage," if you will, of curricular development and transformation.

In Friedman's estimation, a certain amount of the present urgency of the question of core knowledge for Women's Studies arises from the emergence in the 1990s of a new set of expectations around graduate study in the field. Although she is on record elsewhere as hesitant about the move toward doctoral training at a time of heavy economic retrenchment for higher education as a whole, the issues she raises about the capstone seminar will resonate for scholars involved in the development of graduate curricula: What constitutes interdisciplinary training? How do we negotiate the multiple and contradictory methodologies that feminist scholars utilize? Does Women's Studies have its own method? Is it, in fact, a discipline? The final essay in this section takes up a number of these questions, as the authors draw on their experience founding a Women's Studies Ph.D. at the University of Iowa. But rather than settling their focus on justifying (or not) the turn toward doctoral training, Laura E. Donaldson, Anne Donadey, and Jael Silliman consider what is for them the danger of institutionalizing our history of curricular formation at the graduate level. Their "Subversive Couplings: On Antiracism and Postcolonialism in Graduate Women's Studies" explores the risk in defining courses, methods of evaluation, and admission policies that do not sufficiently grapple with the history of race and nationalism within the field's imaginary and its operational cultures. Their contribution thus focuses on "the often sharp divide between faculty who privilege gender, or gender and sexuality, as analytical frameworks and those who also incorporate race, colonialism, and class; the pedagogical strategies that will foster multiaxial analysis in the next generation of feminist scholars; and the curricular content that will facilitate this kind of learning."

In particular, "Subversive Couplings" works to demonstrate the co-implications of ethnic studies and postcolonial knowledge formations, with the overall goal of undermining the strict divides that have arisen around "national" and "area" knowledges. Echoing chapters by other contributors, Donaldson, Donadey, and Silliman argue for a rethinking of the ways in which the categories of Third World women and women of color function to dis-articulate the necessary connections that enable both historical and critical understanding of the legacies of imperialism, white supremacy, and the formation of the nation-state on divisions of both labor and knowledge in an international theoretical context. "Post-colonial critiques are essential for understanding both gender issues within the United States and the neocolonialist relationships of the United States to the rest of the world," they write, "while experiences of race and class are profoundly inflected by the colonial forces that produce and maintain them." Crucially, the authors enfold their critique of Women's Studies in a detailed discussion of the strategies they used in the design and implementation of Iowa's Ph.D. to make foundational the interconnections between race and postcolonial studies. Readers will appreciate their attention to various details of program and departmental practices. Take, for instance, their discussion of course-evaluation forms. Their institution had used an evaluation at the undergraduate level that asked students to rate courses on their level of "feminist perspective." Donaldson, Donadey, and Silliman had evidence that students often used this particular question to police materials on race, sexuality, and post-coloniality by casting them as external to feminism (thus, professors who focused their courses in this way suffered from low ratings for a feminist perspective). Any adoption of this evaluative criteria at the graduate level threatened to reproduce an effect that the graduate curriculum was designed to negotiate. In this and other ways, "Subversive Couplings" makes tangible how the organization of knowledge within Women's Studies curricula bears intimate connections with the micro practices of institutionalization.

In asking how the most definitive sign of institutionalization—doctoral programs—can focus our collective attention on the question of the intellectual future of Women's Studies as a political entity in the academy, the critical conversation launched by Donaldson, Donadey, and Silliman returns readers to some of the central concerns motivating contributors to this volume: What constitutes the knowledge questions that currently condition the political horizons of Women's Studies programs and departments? And how do we think about Women's Studies as a political entity within radically reconfiguring university cultures? Indeed, how do we understand the ways in which institutionalization transforms our objects of study, self-narration, interdisciplinary potentials, and relationship to the governmental and administrative aspects of our labors in higher education? These questions are not new to Women's Studies, as Gloria Bowles reminds us in her afterword, "Continuity and Change in Women's Studies." But the local and geopolitical conditions—not to mention the theoretical conditions—in which we ask them today demonstrate how non-identical are our motivating factors and how newly legible are the contexts and problems that generate this important rethinking of the interventionary project of the field. After all, never before has Women's Studies faced the question of its self-identity as a political entity in the context of so much concern over its institutional success; nor has it felt the burden, in quite the same way, of ascertaining a set of intellectual goals that perform an institutional politics by bringing various feminist knowledges to bear on the daily conditions, pedagogical practices, and research agendas that define its self-production. This is not to say that the issues foregrounded in *Women's Studies on Its Own* represent a comprehensive mapping of the current dilemmas of the field. But they do signal our collective hope that the issues we have raised refract the question of the politics of institutionalization in productive ways.

Notes

1   The point here is not, however, to dismiss activism altogether. It is to put pressure on the way in which we currently understand the term as our singular reference for social change. As the chapters in this volume will demonstrate, there are various temporalities to the projects of social change. The institutionalization of feminist studies is one of them.

Feminist Cultural Literacy: Translating Differences, Cannibal Options

In trying to write this chapter over several months, I've been mystified by my internal resistance to the project. After all, feminism and Women's Studies have been part of my life for more than two decades. As part of the process of deferral, as though waiting for a sign, I was musing about this paper while in Budapest at the end of May 1999 when the war in Kosovo, in the former Yugoslavia, seemed to escalate daily. The occasion was a feminist conference being held at the Central European University (an institution set up by the Soros Foundation as part of its grand plan to facilitate the creation of "open societies"). The conference's title was "Pleasure and Power," and the ironies were manifold—not least of which the knowledge that we were engaging in an "open society" project on the threshold of war. How could we come to terms with the disaster on our doorstep—war as the most extreme fracturing of the social, the ultimate symbol of a closed society? What could feminism offer here?

The participants were drawn in the main from other parts of Eastern and Central Europe, although to my knowledge no Albanians were present. At the conference, the dominant theoretical paradigm was that of psychoanalysis in the particular versions in which it is applied to cultural analyses. I pondered this. Discussions concerning race and ethnicity or references to multiculturalism were conspicuous by their absence, particularly for those of us from the so-called First World who are used to such interrogations in the conferences we attend. Psychoanalysis can after all be used as a way to analyze individual relationships without ever having to embed them in a sociopolitical context, despite the fact that it is precisely in Eastern Europe that theorists such as Slavoj Žižek and Renata Salecl have brilliantly attempted to change this.[1] We conference delegates represented our nations in a broad sense, but we were not segmented into any further subgroups. Indeed, it was difficult to raise the issue of subgroups or ethnicity or of processes of racialization or multiculturalism. The proximity of Kosovo was palpable and ultimately unspeakable both in its own right and in the ways in which it made certain conversations impossible, particularly public ones. Yet in spite of our many differences and the ensuing silences I've tried to indicate, a tenuous sense of a shared project prevailed, and that project continues to be named as feminist. That feeling of commonality riven by differences was to me an enigmatic and fragile, but nonetheless palpable, image of continuity, and I was able to place it alongside the frustrations that have marked my teaching in Women's Studies over the past few years.

But what also struck me about this experience was the salience of translation in its most profound and structuring form. The assumption that the common project of feminism implied a common language or even common "cultural literacy" was certainly not reinforced by this event. Rather, we were plunged, in both productive and unproductive ways, into those incommensurabilities that are at the heart of the translation element present in all communication and that in postcolonial studies is perceived to be inherent in all articulations of cultural difference (Bhabha 1994). But just as translations proceed in spite of the conceptual impossibilities of the task, so might Women's Studies prevail in spite its own impossibilities, as flagged, for example, by Wendy Brown's controversial essay (Brown 1997). Was it possible to conceive of trying to translate the cultural differences permeating global feminisms or to find a kind of common cultural literacy for a Women's Studies prepared to engage with international feminisms and its own incommensurabilities?

I have taught Women's Studies in Australia and Canada and have been involved in it since the late 1970s—those heady early days that we later came to characterize rather more severely (and interrogatively) as the institutionalization and professionalization of Women's Studies. I find myself both reluctant and impelled to analyze the malaise that appears to have descended on the area, at least in some parts of the world (Clark et al. 1996; Stanley 1997). It is difficult at times to disentangle what is particular to Women's Studies and to what extent we are dealing with the implications of university corporatization (Evans 1997; Threadgold 1998), which has had a profound impact on the humanities and social sciences in general (Nussbaum 1997). The appearance of special issues of relevant journals (*differences, Atlantis*, etc.) and of anthologies such as *Knowing Feminisms* (Stanley 1997), *Anti-Feminism in the Academy* (Clark et al. 1996), and *Generations* (Looser and Kaplan 1997) help us focus on the problems specific to Women's Studies.

Restructuring: Marginality as Institutional Advantage

There is no doubt that we are in the midst of a huge restructuring of knowledge that questions the monopoly universities have traditionally enjoyed as privileged purveyors of knowledge. Within this, Women's Studies has things both to offer and to learn. What it has to offer is, to my mind, particularly related to interdisciplinarity—a way of reorganizing knowledge that is being acclaimed (sometimes for wrong, cost-cutting reasons) by university administrators everywhere. Women's Studies has the kind of track record in interdisciplinarity (in all its permutations) that can offer cautions as well as insights. Paradoxically, the precarious institutional history of much Women's Studies (see, e.g., Threadgold 1998) could turn out to be its strength. Being marginal means that one can respond more quickly and have less to lose by risking greater pedagogical experimentation. I think it is true that, for a while now, Women's Studies has represented in various ways a continuing experiment in interdisciplinarity, as the interdisciplinary model, for good and bad reasons, is increasingly being explored by universities. Women's Studies is able to offer a tradition of experimentation in interdisciplinarity in areas ranging from curriculum design to pedagogical principles, team-teaching, and, at least, course articulation. This does not always mean that Women's Studies has been able to pursue these experiments systematically or to theorize them clearly, but as in cultural studies, for example, one can point to its grappling with interdisciplinarity in ways that traditional disciplines have found more difficult to pursue. In some ways I feel, at least from the programs with which I have been associated, that we in Women's Studies need to learn more about integrated interdisciplinarity—that is, we have ourselves been guilty at times of taking it for granted merely because we assumed we had the common focus of women. Much of what I've experienced has been a putting of disciplines side by side in a multidisciplinary way rather than working for an integrated model. Indeed, one can support a nonintegrated model as long as the mix of courses and methods is overtly addressed rather than simply allowed to exist in haphazard fashion, with no guidance for students. And, as I elaborate later, both models involve us in the task of translating among the disciplines. Having taken part in many interdisciplinary projects, I learned very quickly that concepts as well as terminology do not mean the same things across the disciplines. For example, what counts as evidence in sociology as distinct from literary studies? What is meant by politics? What is assumed about identity as distinct from a more dispersed poststructuralist subjectivity?

Initially, for the first two decades, one could describe Women's Studies relatively unproblematically as a field that functioned as a critique of masculinist knowledge structures.[2] This is where it gained its impetus and gradually a kind of idiosyncratic legitimacy. However, now, as many have pointed out, when we are faced with declining numbers in both students and faculty, we are also confronted with the need to rethink the curriculum. For me, this was clearly delineated as a problem when I transposed a feminist theory in the humanities course that I had been teaching for several years in Women's Studies to my cross-appointed field of English. The modifications I needed to make, and the assumptions about what I expected my students to know, in each case clarified some dilemmas for me. The experience reminded me that feminist work is vigorously being generated within the disciplines but that this work does not always have a self-evident relationship with programs in Women's Studies.

The feminist work within disciplinary areas is intrinsically embedded in a larger framework of accreditation and professionalization associated with specific disciplinary training. And it is not as though this ceases to function, albeit in a semi-conscious manner, within Women's Studies courses themselves. Because many programs use cross-appointed or cross-listed faculty and courses—in part as a matter of principle and otherwise for economic efficiency—few programs are staffed entirely by those trained only in Women's Studies. In other words, the skills that faculty bring to the programs are thoroughly informed by their own disciplinary training. This can be at odds with the rhetoric that Women's Studies offers genuine interdisciplinarity. Often, the reality is a smorgasbord that is structured along the disciplinary lines familiar to the faculty teaching in the program. In practice, this can, for example, lead to a split between humanities and social sciences and certainly to a further distancing from the sciences, medicine, and so on. That is, because of the institutional history of Women's Studies as primarily occurring in faculties of humanities and the social sciences, as well as its being subjected to a legacy of underfunding and marginalization, there has often not been either the time or the resources to articulate fully an interdisciplinarity that has been thought through and translated in terms of finding a common language of pedagogy.

In relation to Women's Studies, the question therefore arises as to what exactly we are trying to achieve in such programs. Echoing Brown (1997), what do we want our students to know? It is clear that we cannot simply or exclusively remain with the concept of Women's Studies as the place from which to critique the rest. Although this may be a continuing element and a legacy of Women's Studies in its first stage, it cannot remain its primary identification. This dilemma was addressed by the graduate student Renea Henry when she stated: "There is the question of which kind of training a student receives. What are you prepared to teach? What have you learned? If you turn these programs into a sort of center to critique power, what is it that you are prepared to address substantively and how?" (Cook et al. 1997: 142). What kind of "disciplining" are we providing, and what therefore authorizes us—what legitimizes our pedagogy? One assumption is that we are training agents for social change, but if this stays at an inchoate level, it invites the kind of charge that leads long-time opponents to accuse Women's Studies of being staffed simply by ideologues who contaminate the objectivity of university-generated knowledge. Among ourselves, the rhetoric that surrounds the idea that we are engendering a kind of activism often is not thought through in terms of what has been described as the uneasy history of the relationship between politics and theory or, more simply, intellectual knowledge.

Capitalizing on my good fortune in having taught in several different contexts, I will introduce some Canadian reflections at this point. A special issue of the Canadian Women's Studies journal *Atlantis* published about a decade ago, in 1990, dealt with the findings of a very interesting project called the Canadian Women's Studies Project. As described by one of the coordinators, Margaret Eichler, the project consisted of widespread interviews with women teaching in Women's Studies across the country and charted how and by whom such programs were instituted. Eichler herself has examined the relationship between Women's Studies and feminism, calling the first a subject area and the second an approach. She argues that we cannot take the relationship between the two for granted, just as, increasingly, we cannot make the two synonymous. It is therefore important that we label our work "feminist" in order to signal its distinction from Women's Studies courses that do not have a feminist approach (Eichler 1990).[3] In the same issue, Rhonda Lenton looks at the relationship between academic Women's Studies and the wider women's community and concludes that the incorporation of Women's Studies within the academy has rendered it more conservative, particularly among younger scholars. She concludes: "If feminist scholars are to retain a critical position toward the discipline and if they are to provide leadership within the feminist movement, they will need to maintain ties with political activists outside of academia" (Lenton 1990: 67). Although statements such as this one allow us to point to Women's Studies as a model to offer the restructuring agents in the university at large who are looking for ways to bring the community and university together (for reasons of sheer survival), we also need to consider carefully our own ties with community groups and to think about this in relation to the academic project in general. Does entry into the academy automatically uncouple Women's Studies from a supposedly self-evident feminist politics? Why is theoretical and intellectual work so often perceived as non- or a-political?

The urgency is compounded by another institutional "success story" for Women's Studies that relates to the growth of practicum programs. Part of the call for accountability that has been linked with the increasing intervention of local political concerns into the funding and business of universities has resulted in greater attempts to bring the community and university into proximity with each other. Women's Studies has had a long record, once again, in doing this through its ties to the women's movement. Although academic feminism has often been accused of severing this link (as exemplified by Lenton's statement quoted earlier), it is certainly the case that Women's Studies programs have generally preserved a much closer liaison with varieties of community women's groups than have other disciplines in the university. This has now been consolidated into practicum programs.[4] In Australia, it has also taken the form of policy work, and there is a long tradition there of universities providing consultancy bases for policy work for government agencies

(Yeatman 1990, 1998). But once again, the relationship is an uneasy one and needs to be carefully monitored so that it does not, among other implications, help support the growing perception that university knowledge and training are only of value insofar as they prove their immediate and instrumentalist "relevance" to contemporary community issues or that the practicum is a guarantee of activism that otherwise does not exist within the university boundaries.

To complicate this tendency, it would be very helpful to pool our knowledge about the university itself as a site for feminist politics. My first four years in Canada were acutely marked by two separate and extremely painful cases of charges of sexual and racial harassment, occurring, oddly enough, in politics departments at the two universities where I was teaching (Chilly Collective 1995; Emberley 1996; Fekete 1994; Marchak 1996). I learned a great deal from both examples about the litigious nature of North American society and about the limits of tolerance for gender and race concerns within universities. But one thing both these experiences accomplished—as do the recent writings of Jane Gallop—was to politicize staff and students and show without doubt that the university itself was a charged political space (Gallop 1995, 1997, 1999; Gallop and Francis 1997).

A further problem, one that has been tackled in the theorization of Women's Studies for decades, concerns the differences within and among feminists, which many have described as a fragmentation into feminists of difference (those who query the definitions of women and certainly of the commonality initially attributed to women's experience) and feminists who feel that we cannot (politically) afford such interrogations. For example, if we look at the "third wave" in North America, its prime concern with race and sexuality involves, among other things, an interrogation of orthodoxies that are also perceived to reside within mainstream feminism. In the United States, Devoney Looser speaks as a third-wave feminist, which she describes as "the new feminisms and feminists emerging in the late 1980s and 1990s, many of whom purport to interrogate race, nation, and sexuality more thoroughly than did the second wave, and many of whom are skeptical about the unity of the category 'women'" (Looser 1997: 38). She also contends that in the writing of second wave feminists her generation are often perceived as the mangy strays betraying the ideals of the "purebreds" (Looser 1997: 37). This characterization also seems to haunt the exchange between Susan

Gubar and Robyn Wiegman in *Critical Inquiry* (Gubar 1998; Wiegman 1999). It might also be useful to bear in mind Canadian feminist Jill Vickers' caution that "there are currently two major barriers impeding our progress toward the goal of effective women-centered knowledge in the social sciences: first, our difficulty in dealing with difference as a theoretical and research problem and second, the constant lure of subjectivism and radical individualism which comes from feminism's privileging of individual experience and our tendency to reject authority (even feminist authority) as the basis for knowledge" (Vickers 1996: 222). One of the most pernicious directions taken by this subjectivism is that of identity politics, a development that has paralyzed many women's projects (Elam 1997). How might one locate or construct intellectual and pedagogical interventions that avoid the general reductionism of identity politics?

The debates about identity politics have a particular resonance within global feminism, although their detailed meanings are often dependent on local contexts. The phenomenon might be traced to the "consciousness-raising" tactics that are historically associated with second-wave feminism and led from the articulation of women's collective differences to the delineation of other group differences. But increasingly, these differences have congealed into imprisoning essentialisms that are often perceived as obscuring more than they illuminate, of occluding intragroup differences and "intersectional identities" (Crenshaw 1995: 333). Martha Minow has argued that identity politics "may freeze people in pain and also fuel their dependence on their own victim status as a source of meaning" (Minow 1997: 54). She goes on to state that "identity politics tends to locate the problem in the identity group rather than the social relations that produce identity groupings" (Minow 1997: 56). Jodi Dean contends that "the articulation of particular identities has led to the rigidification of these very identities. At the legislative level, this rigidification appears as the reinforcement of minority status with its negative connotations of inferiority" (Dean 1996: 5). In the context of the struggle by "women of color" to assert their own politics of difference, Analouise Keating cautions "not to abandon all references to personal experiences but rather to take experientially based knowledge claims even further by redefining identity" (Keating 1998: 36). Keating draws on Chela Sandoval's concept of "differential consciousness" (quoted in Keating 1991: 34) and on Homi Bhabha's notion of "ambivalent identification" (Bhabha

1994) as a way to move to such new definitions of identity. At its worst, identity politics are invoked as part of individualized experience and prevent the kind of theoretical analysis that is at the very heart of the academic enterprise. Such anti-intellectualism has led feminists such as Wendy Brown to identify a serious split between academic feminism functioning within the disciplines and a version of Women's Studies that "consolidates itself in the remains, impoverished by the lack of challenges from within" (Brown 1997: 84).

Without in any way wishing to invoke the specter of identity politics in any essentialist manner, what is not always identified to the same extent in these inquiries is the changing nature of Women's Studies students themselves. I experienced some disturbing manifestations in translating, as mentioned earlier, a curriculum from Women's Studies to English. While some of my Women's Studies students were reluctant to do the historical and theoretical work that underpinned our exploration of representation in a range of texts, some of the English honors students were comparably uncomfortable talking about the political implications of these representations and their embeddedness within social relations. One explanation resides in the general assumption that, if Women's Studies is a training ground for activism, then there is not much patience among students either for historical inquiry or for epistemological questioning. Activism remains more comfortable, with categorical certainties preferably confined to the here and now. Nor is there necessarily much curiosity about activism elsewhere on the globe. At its worst, this manifests itself in the profoundly chauvinist manner of the kind alluded to by Shirley Yee in her statement that "foregrounding any understanding of 'women' from a U.S.-based trajectory is inherently problematic when attempting to internationalize 'Women's Studies'" (Yee 1997: 57–58).

This dilemma is complicated by the fact that differences are also becoming more obvious in the changing nature of the student body in many of the countries that have been offering Women's Studies. The diversification in terms of ethnicity, class, and sexuality has not necessarily been fully addressed by either the curriculum or pedagogy in more general terms. My own interests relate particularly to postcolonial issues—that is, to ethnicity and cultural differences. I taught for several decades in a university system in Australia where multiculturalism (particularly in relation to cultural issues) was minimally recognized as a field of research or as worthy of archival work; thus, it was hardly surprising that the various ethnic affiliations of our increasingly multicultural student body were not being adequately addressed (Gunew 1994). While teaching in Canada for the past six years, I have found a far greater commitment to acknowledging the cultural diversity of the national culture, but this has not necessarily flowed into the local specificities of curriculum (Bannerji 1996; Miki 1998; Philip 1992, 1995). Universities have traditionally been concerned with the eternal verities and with the continuities of knowledge construction. The implications of a changing student body at best were perceived as ephemera that required the compensatory stability of pedagogical uniformity. The fact that a large percentage of the student body where I now teach have affiliations (over several generations) to a range of Asian cultures is only very gradually being recognized in the curriculum in general. Given this situation, the complexities of devising a common cultural literacy for feminism and Women's Studies is profoundly challenging.

Translation: Globalization Translated into Internationalization

In oversimplified terms, "globalization" in this chapter refers to the dissemination of communication technology and the attendant economic rationalization; by contrast, "internationalization" conveys the ways in which global issues are interpreted at a local level. Outside North America (and even within it if we are taking a Canadian perspective) globalization often translates into U.S.-centrism—that is, the charge that U.S. culture is colonizing the world. What is left out of this glib binarism are the multiple differences within the United States, where there are indeed local interpretations of and oppositions to globalism not unlike those that proliferate outside the United States. To take up these tactics in more detail, recent statements in the various collections I mentioned earlier as registering the malaise within Women's Studies and feminist projects are rife with warnings that key terms do not mean the same thing globally that they mean locally. Global feminism as currently practiced in North America, for example, tends to naturalize rather than deconstruct terms such as "Third World" and "First World" (Narain 1997; Yee 1997: 59). If we were to imagine that the intersection of two versions of feminism were comparable to what happens when texts in two languages intersect, then Anna Loewenhaupt Tsing's concept of "faithless translation" is an enabling possibility (Tsing 1997). Drawing on contemporary translation theory, she suggests that all translations are inherently faithless in that something new is created in the slippage between languages and texts. It is this slippage that needs to be explored when varieties of feminism and Women's Studies meet. But what does this mean in concrete terms? Tsing gives three examples informed by her postcolonial perspective:

> First, instead of tracing a Western history of social thought, we can trace the moves in which lists of Western thinkers appear to be History. Second, instead of following Western originals across non-Western cultural transformations, we can follow the narrative contests through which foci of cultural difference are identified. Third, instead of debating the truth of Western-defined universals, we can debate the politics of their strategic and rhetorical use across the globe. (Tsing 1997: 254)

What I note here is a somewhat easy invocation of the "West" and "Europe" in much postcolonial theorizing, and that this, too, is a category that needs to be deconstructed. This unease is also registered, for example, by Rosi Braidotti in an essay in the same volume when she calls for the need to "problematize and to historicize the question of what, if anything, constitutes European" (Braidotti 1997: 356). Echoing the groundbreaking work of Donna Haraway, among others, Braidotti offers a timely reminder of the need to consider all knowledge, including feminist knowledge, as "situated practices" (Braidotti 1997: 357). In very practical terms, Braidotti's essay goes on to delineate Women's Studies in the European Union, where she gives information concerning the Erasmus project of exchanging students and faculty across Europe. These kinds of intra- and inter-institutional collaborations have been part of the history of Women's Studies programs in many places. The new direction we are seeing now is to forge joint programs with Women's Studies teams in Asia and Southeast Asia of the kind that Braidotti identifies within Europe. These moves are facilitated by new technology that enables teams to collaborate across the globe to produce course materials—a clear example of a homogenizing global tool being transformed by local forces to create a truly diversified internationalism. Such collaborations will help dispel the prevailing notion that North American feminism is a homogeneous colonizing force and will help disseminate the recognition that there are many differing versions and differing politics within these supposedly unified metropolitan centers. It has become very clear to me in my own work not only that we are enmeshed in the phenomenon of traveling theory, where theories metamorphose in response to the local circumstances in which they are embedded, but also that terms we think of as global or universal have very particular local and national meanings. In the wake of the breakup of the Second World, and the development of what has been termed "globalization" or the "restructuring of the Third World," we have very different interactions among various versions of what counts as feminist and how that informs Women's Studies curricula and pedagogical practices. This is something I glimpsed at the Budapest conference.

But let us now move to concrete examples of the kinds of imbrications and "faithless translations" that some of us have attempted in recent pedagogical enterprises as a way to bring feminism and Women's Studies into challenging proximity. One such project with graduate students and colleagues involved examining a number of texts, written and cinematic, that dealt with the intersections of women, food, and ethnicity. Because digestion of food is the underlying metaphor for social assimilation, it is singularly appropriate to focus on the domain of food to bring to the fore the unassimilated incommensurabilities that abound in the relations between women and food. For example, there is the Canadian writer Hiromi Goto's *A Chorus of Mushrooms* (1994), in which three generations of women in a Japanese Canadian family direct their struggles with identity through language and food. To those of us familiar with Julia Kristeva's work, it was clear that whenever these two elements come together, cannibalism—symbolically, at least—lurks in the shadows. Drawing on the work of Kristeva (1982) and Maud Ellmann (1993) concerning the war between language and food within the subject, we also speculated about the ways this might have implications for the practices of citation and quotation in academic texts and, in particular, for textual relations in translation.

The examples that follow constitute some attempts to make more tangible what I have rather abstractly been trying to posit as the productive possibilities that may occur in an encounter between general theories relating to cultural difference when they meet very specific texts that are at a tangent to global feminism when it is conceived in a hegemonic, universalistic manner. These speculations are organized around the trope of cannibalism, chosen because its charged implications capture both the fascination and repulsion involved in registering the contact processes of two individuals or groups. I am not the first to consider the tactic of using this most shocking model of human interaction as a way of "fighting back" against imperialism, colonialism or, other hegemonic forces, as the example of the Brazilian modernists cited later makes clear. I am merely "translating" these tactics into ones that might provide a useful way for feminist theory to "make strange" the current paralysis in Women's Studies in relation to identity, difference, and critique.

Anthropophagy: Toward a Theory of Translation

In the variegated global domain of multicultural studies, one of the few consistently benign ways to refer to diversity is via ethnic cuisines, particularly within the anxious space of the nation. But what really is being consumed when multicultural food is celebrated? I would suggest that what may be at play here is assimilating the multicultural other, particularly as this is exemplified in texts (written and cinematic) by minority women. Recent anthologies such as *Hungry for You: From Cannibalism to Seduction: A Book on Food* (Smith 1996) or Slavenka Drakulic's *The Taste of a Man* (1996) exemplify the ways in which cannibalism is used to figure the pleasures of love, consuming the other as the ultimate expression of sexual (and other) consummations. At the same time, the rise in texts dealing with the experience of anorexia and bulimia also deal with self-consumption (the ultimate form of narcissism). A plethora of texts dealing with women's manipulation of food as metaphor for their roles in the family, the community, and the nation have been appearing over the past decade.

In a recent collection enticingly titled *Post-colonial Translation* (Bassnett and Trivedi 1999), the editors are particularly impressed with the trope of cannibalism developed by one of the authors as an apt encapsulation of the power differentials inherent in all translation events. Traditionally, the "original" text is given mystic powers, but what really is the original? This has long been a point of contention in postmodernist debates in particular.[5] The critic Else Viera explores the work of the Brazilian translator Haroldo de Campos in the context of the notorious Brazilian modernist manifesto, which structured itself according to anthropophagy. Drawing on the original Tupa Indians' supposed penchant for cannibalism, it intersects with the Jesuit mission of conversion, structured in turn by the symbolic cannibalism of the Christian Mass (Vieira 1999: 98). Both traditions, the colonized and the colonizer, are thus brought together in the trope of cannibalism, which elevates the former to the same symbolic and ethical level as the latter—or, at the very least, shows that they are structurally connected.

The Cannibal Looks and Answers Back.

In her recent book, *The Third Eye* (1996), Fatimah Tobing Rony explores (as does her film *On Cannibalism* [1996]) the nature of ethnographic cinema and what she calls the "third eye," a variant on W.E.B. Du Bois's double consciousness or Edward Said's "contrapuntal" perspective. In other words, it is a way for those who are objectified by, in this case, the European ethnographic gaze to look back, to resist being turned into objects "without history, without writing, without civilization, without technology, without archives" (Rony 1996: 7). Rony sets up the three stages of ethnography, from 1) Félix-Louis Regnault's ethnographic studies of time and motion in order to uncover a taxonomy of race through gesture; to 2) Robert Flaherty's restaging of Inuit culture in *Nanook of the North* set within the framework of the teleological certainty that indigenous races would die out; to 3) *King Kong,* which she sees as an ironic moment in ethnographic film. In Rony's *On Cannibalism,* the narrator identifies with the "bride of King Kong," which is used as a position from which to explore the "other's" or "cannibal's" knowing look back. In her exploration of what she calls "fascinating cannibalism," she draws attention to the voyeuristic consumers of ethnography, of the bodies of the "Savage" (Rony 1996: 10).

As the film illustrates, there is a long history of cannibalism within "European" culture, and as the postcolonial critic Peter Hulme points out, "Cannibalism is—as practice or accusation—quite simply the mark of greatest imaginable cultural difference and therefore the greatest challenge to our categories of understanding" (Hulme 1998: 20). Approaching these issues from a rather different perspective, Marina Warner's study of Western folklore, *No Go the Bogeyman* (1998b), is also replete with cannibalistic motifs and suggests that what postcolonialists designate as cultural difference extends to, or perhaps begins with, sexual difference, a point of particular interest to feminist researchers. In European folklore, cannibalism is mostly attached to relations between male figures and children, and according to Warner, women in Greek myth, for example, may kill their children, but they don't eat them (Warner 1998b: 56). However, there is also the witch or bad-mother figure who stalks more general folklore and who does indeed eat children (though not usually her own). Warner associates the devouring male figure, in turn, as representative of *couvade*, men's envy of women's ability to give birth:

> This cannibal motif conveys a threefold incorporation: sexual union by which a form of reciprocal devouring takes place, pregnancy, by which the womb encloses the growing child, and paternity, which takes over the infant after birth in one way or another. The metaphors are enchained, one to another—sex, obliteration, food—as language strains to convey the tension between union and separation, individuality and connection, autonomy and possession. Ogres, be they gods or fairy story giants, threaten the weak with an enduring metaphor of annihilation and loss of self—being eaten alive. The boundaries of the body are breached as that body is gnashed and ground and digested. (Warner 1998a: 165)

Warner considers the image of the bogeyman/ogre as an archetypal figure for male legitimacy and authority. In the eyes of the material historians, the prevalence of the cannibal motif supposedly derives quite rationally from the many famines in European history, but if one looks to psychoanalysis or the structuralism that ordered an earlier version of anthropology—the "deep structures" in various ways—one may encounter another kind of logic at play.

In relation to Warner's work on folklore, Hulme states: "Cannibalism here operates as family romance, its stories engaging with the fundamental enigmas of kinship: what is the relation between identity and origin?; how can doubleness of origin (from mother and father) be expressed?; how does biological origin convert into social relation?" (Hulme 1998: 33). But as in the case of the Brazilian translator referred to earlier, we, too, might speculate about the nature of origins, originals, progenitors. Drakulic's powerful (and in some ways comic) novel *The Taste of a Man* enables us to pursue some of these implications. Ostensibly, this text celebrates a familiar cannibalistic motif in relation to incorporation as sexual union—the kind in which the two beings are so caught up in each other that they form a whole, a closed circuit that is profoundly antisocial and that can end only in suicide or madness. (One thinks here as well of Oshima's famous film *In the Realm of the Senses*.)

The book begins with a scenario of Kristevan abjection, with the narrator pondering the difficulties of cleaning up after a murder. She recalls her mother, with her legacy of obsessive cleanliness and the maintenance of boundaries. In contrast, we are quickly presented with a rationale for the events recounted in flashback. The female narrator refers to her desire to merge with her lover, to erase all boundaries—the only solution to the fact that he must eventually return to his family. Because they come from two different cultures, they cannot communicate through language: "Had I been able to reach him through words . . . our relationship probably would have ended differently" (Drakulic 1996: 41). Thus, because they cannot converse in more prosaic manner, they connect primarily through their bodies—through sex and food. In her brilliant study of self-starvation, Ellmann, taking her departure from Freud, considers the contest between food and words—"words and food are locked in eternal rivalry" (Ellmann 1993: 46)—in that both attempt to occupy or colonize the same corporeal space, the mouth. We encounter Drakulic's narrator after she has killed her partner. She already feels that he animates her from inside her body (Drakulic 1996: 7). She recalls their first meal together after they had had sex for the first time. By then, the food had already become synonymous with their bodies: "We pounced voraciously on the food and then our hunger for food mixed with our hunger for each other. . . . I know now that I should have recognized that first shared meal as the true desire to feed ourselves to each other and thus become one. Food was part of our intimacy, our union, as important as touching itself " (Drakulic 1996: 35–36). At one stage, the narrator makes the kind of soup that signals commensality, the bringing of people together into family and community by women in particular (Drakulic 1996: 40). But this is a rare moment that ultimately functions to accentuate the couple's inability to be part of the social world around them.

Meanwhile, the surrounding world begins to send the narrator hermetic signs of their inescapable destiny. A poem by George Herbert signals for her an association of love with eating the beloved (Drakulic 1996: 84). José, the lover, dreams of eating his own sister (Drakulic 1996: 166–67). Later, after the narrator has fed him a drink laced with sleeping pills and he lies dying, she is overcome by an immense hunger that drives her out into the street in search of sustenance. She returns, and after killing her lover, she begins to eat him. The initial spiritual dimension of the ritual is overtaken by a physically voracious and bestial hunger: "I glanced in the mirror above the sink. My mouth was bloody like an open wound, or like the snout of a beast poking into a carcass" (Drakulic 1996: 186). At various points, the narrator compares her hunger to pregnancy; the notion of having to "eat for two" (Drakulic 1996: 176), a common euphemism for pregnancy, takes on a demonic meaning. She tells the reader that a normal pregnancy would have produced a new being that was only partly José (Drakulic 1996: 180); it is precisely the establishment of the social that she rejects. So on the face of it, this text deals with cannibalistic incorporation in terms of sexual union.

However, a further dimension of the text places it in the context of the postcolonial cannibal looking back and identifying the primacy of European cannibalism, as in Rony's work.[6] The lover, José, turns out to be an academic studying cannibalism, and the text is littered with knowing references to the literature. Moreover, José is Brazilian, and the shadow of his Indian ancestors lurks, in feminized manner, within his persona.

> Sometimes, when I looked at him for a long time, I would see another colour burning under his skin. His light complexion would seem a mere illusion then; his full lips, the black glint in his eyes, the small nose and wide nostrils, the slanting forehead would give him away. From beneath the pale skin would emerge the well-defined shadow of an Indian woman, his otherness which so fascinated me. Not only was he a separate being, which was painful enough, but he was doubly other—because of language, and because of the world he came from, a world about which I knew nothing. (Drakulic 1996: 44, see also 69)

There is also quite possibly a knowing wink to the Brazilian manifesto on modernism, which, as mentioned earlier, was symbolically structured around "anthropophagy." According to Sérgio Bellei, this involved the following tropes: "The stomach without ideas, ready to devour everything, already points to anthropophagy as a metaphor for the cosmopolitan enterprise of absorbing both foreign and native cultures as the means to construct a hybrid and unique Brazilian cultural identity . . . legitimating anthropophagy by transforming the taboo of the primeval father's parricide (the father being in this case the European colonizer) into the acceptable eating (by the colonized) of the totemized animal that symbolically replaced the primeval father" (Bellei 1998: 91–93). Before she returns to Poland, Darkulic's narrator visits a church, from which she emerges reborn (Drakulic 1996: 206). Like many European colonizers before her, she is able to purge her guilt through the rituals of the Christian church. José is better off within her. His surviving relic, the head that maintained his individuality after his body had been dismembered and disposed of, has decayed into an inhuman mess.[7] The narrator returns to Europe, sheathing the essential José within her own body, another demonic inversion of pregnancy, while bearing a Braun food mixer that she had exchanged for the electric saw that had enabled her to dismember his body. In sum, it is a brilliant satire on the cannibalistic motif that also casts a sly eye on certain feminist orthodoxies, particularly those connected with the privileging of essentialist identity politics. The "faithless translation" inherent in the trope of cannibalism may well help Women's Studies develop a common literacy that moves us beyond the recent paralyzing battles about identity politics.[8]

To speak about Drakulic's text in the "First World" might be interpreted as drawing parallels between Western European colonialism toward both South America and, later, Eastern Europe. To speak about colonialism in Eastern Europe is to invite a reading that has Eastern Europe speaking back both to its Western cousin and to the U.S. globalism discussed earlier. It also involves the wry restaging of a familiar erotic scenario in which the victim is male and the aggressor female. A reversal of gender-based orthodoxies takes place that may provide useful tools for estrangement when teaching these categories in Women's Studies. Using the symbolic framework of anthropophagy and this text as a case study suggests that these kinds of reversals and shock tactics might be required to stop the implosion within forms of Women's Studies in which members of the community turn on and silence one another, in ever-narrowing circles, about whose authority should be counted and whose voice should be heard and in designating victims and systems of oppression. In such instances, the traditional categories of analysis—class, gender, and race—function in increasingly universalized and unnuanced ways to prevent the very notion of porous cross-cultural, internationally sensitive collaborations that, for many of us, are the exciting future of Women's Studies. To maintain that model, a feminist theory that is ready at all times to question its own terminology and methodology—its own basis for authority—remains a given.

In Budapest, there was a great deal of questioning, but there were also many silences and many stereotypical notions of how our various feminist enterprises move in the world. The image of a cannibal, that most abject of humans (indeed, to designate someone a cannibal is to mark her or him as abject, beyond the pale) looking and speaking back to the taxonomists, the legislators or those in the know, could well function as a galvanizing icon or mascot for our future projects and our potential attainment of common cultural literacies.

Notes

1 See Salecl 1994. Žižek is so prolific that it is difficult to choose just a few texts, but see Žižek 1989, 1994.
2 This was exemplified in the two anthologies of feminist theory I edited for Routledge. See Gunew 1990, 1991.
3 Her comments have some resonance with Brown's comments (Brown 1997) almost a decade later.
4 See the section "Women's Studies in Focus: Field-Based Learning in the Practicum Course," *Atlantis* 22, no. 1 (fall-winter 1997): 109–34.
5 Jorge Luis Borges's story "Pierre Menard, Author of the *Quixote*" (1971) is often invoked as a paradigmatic text in these debates.
6 A particularly succinct favorite of mine is Witi Ihimaera's poem "Dinner with the Cannibal," *SPAN*, vol. 36, no. 1 (1993), 154–55.
7 It is difficult not to read this as an allusion to the ending of Stendhal's *Le Rouge et le Noire*, another famous example of *amour folle*.
8 Many feminists have written on these battles, but see Elam (1997) and Gunew (2000).

Transnational Practices and Interdisciplinary Feminist Scholarship: Refiguring Women's and Gender Studies

At the present time, any discussion of women and gender studies as an interdisciplinary field must be contextualized within the institutional politics of higher education. As Women's Studies faculty at San Francisco Bay area universities, we see the promise and the possibilities of working within this interdisciplinary field; in fact, our writing, our teaching, and our scholarship have been tremendously energized by joining departments of Women's Studies. In many ways, this is one of the best times to be working in this field. Programs are growing, interest is high and the scholarship is burgeoning. More and more, the emerging field of gender studies is being incorporated into the Women's Studies curriculum. All around the world, departments and centers of women's and gender studies have been created. Yet in our own institutions, we are constantly frustrated by a serious backlash that comes not only from administrators concerned about bottom lines and shrinking revenues but also from feminist scholars and academics as well as activists who view Women's Studies as the paramount problem or obstacle to their feminist projects.

Is interdisciplinarity the reason for this backlash? Based on our teaching and research, interdisciplinarity can mean many things and is practiced in different ways in different places. Nor is it a new phenomenon. We are arguing for an interdisciplinarity that destabilizes, critiques, and challenges rigid methodological practices—because the divide between disciplinary and interdisciplinary is often mystified. The rise of interdisciplinary programs and methods has to be understood in relation to the history of knowledge production and institutional politics in modern times. Transnational feminist cultural studies located within Women and Gender Studies as an interdisciplinary site can provide a space for critique and the production of new kinds of knowledges. We do not want to claim that Women's Studies has always been and will always be a vanguard in and of itself as some kind of unified field. But given the context of U.S. academia, Women's Studies, especially when combined with gender studies, can serve as a space for innovation and rigorous analysis.

Yet, in our institutions and in many others, Women's Studies is embattled, ridiculed, dismissed, and marginalized. Although this may always have been true, there are distinct characteristics to the current situation. How are we experiencing this new backlash against Women's Studies in our institutional sites? There are at least five versions of the backlash narrative offered as "critiques," feminist and non-feminist, of Women's Studies programs and departments.

—First, we are told by people in other disciplines and in our administrations that Women's Studies as an institutional site is redundant, moribund, and so on, because feminists are now able to work within the disciplines without being marginalized or penalized in any professional way.
—Second, we are told that the interdisciplinary framework of Women's Studies is irrelevant because now, of course, even people located within disciplines are doing feminist interdisciplinary work. Ergo, Women's Studies has been so successful it is no longer needed.
—Third, it is said that Women's Studies has always been less rigorous, too political, too ideological, unlike the other disciplines, which are supposed to be free of ideology, politics, and investment. Thus, Women's Studies not only is superseded by the more rigorous feminist versions emerging from disciplinary sites, but it also must be superseded because it only produces identities rather than knowledges.
—Fourth, Women's Studies is never sufficient in and of itself as a site, so it always needs to be supplemented by the disciplines. It can never produce adequate knowledges; it can only reflect local, invested politics. Thus, because you can never justify crowded full-time equivalent lines in Women's Studies, junior scholars are not able to establish their

careers in women's and gender studies at an early stage, doctoral programs are few and far between, and affiliation remains a matter of
volunteerism, with either risk or marginalization attached.
—Fifth, for some feminists, the deconstruction of the category "woman"
means that this subject ceases to exist and thus should not be reproduced and reified in an institutional site. In our view, woman as
subject exists in so many shapes and forms that we need to study how it
has been reproduced and scattered across popular, corporate, political,
and academic cultures in relation to other social categories such as
sexuality, nationality, class, religion, race, and so on. The perfect site for
such studies remains women's and gender studies.

There is, finally, a more glib consumption-oriented dismissal of Wom-
en's Studies as a 1960s-style product that no longer signifies novelty or
relevance, and thus no longer "sells." It must therefore be superseded by
whatever seems newer or trendier. Although this superficial critique says
volumes about the corporatization of higher education, it is not unrelated
to the other backlash examples we have mentioned thus far. This kind of
market-driven and funding-driven approach to higher education is pernicious, certainly, but not something we will discuss in much detail here.

These attacks are not haphazard or incoherent. They can be understood fully as generated by specific political and ideological needs and
practices—needs and practices that reflect dominant conventions of Cold
War and late capitalist knowledge production. It is our argument that
these conventions are themselves powerful machines that generate mystified, invisible, generic identities and knowledge frameworks that are
destructive to genuine political change and struggle.

Interdisciplinary practices, like disciplinary ones, are not natural. They
have histories, and they are produced in particular places and in specific
times to support hegemonic projects. What knowledges are needed, and
for what ends? Universities exist to produce and supply expertise and
knowledge. These are not neutral practices. Disciplines have created
dominant consensus through the creation of boundaries between different kinds of subjects and bodies of knowledge so that the boundaries
themselves become reified and legitimated. They have produced their
own subjects and reproduced their own practices. But simply to charge
the disciplines with inadequacy elides questions of the relationship between knowledge production and institutional histories, because almost

as soon as they establish credibility through discourses of coherence and rigor, disciplines tend to fall into crisis. Against the assertion of distinctive purity, it is possible to see disciplines as always already hybrid. Similarly, the emergence of interdisciplinary projects has sought disciplinary-like status in the process of institutionalization and thus have fallen into similar dynamics.

Creating a binary division between disciplinary and interdisciplinary practices cannot help us understand the puzzling devaluation of Women's Studies at the same time that other interdisciplinary programs, such as American studies, seem to be thriving and expanding. Solving the question of academic programmatic destinies requires understanding and analyzing local agendas; political expediencies; and the politics of gender, race, and sexuality, among other elements. Rather than reify the divide between disciplinary and interdisciplinary programs and practices, we need to focus on the histories of particular institutions and knowledges. One aspect of this history that has been ignored is the role of national boundaries in the creation of interdisciplinary programs in the United States.

Women's Studies Internationalism: Maintaining Divisions
Between Area Studies and American Studies

As Tani Barlow has argued, area studies was implicated in the production of Cold War cultural and political knowledges about other cultures and nations (Barlow 1993). American studies comes from a '30s Marxist, popular-front effort to critique and oppose capitalism. During the conservative backlash of the Cold War, it was co-opted and became articulated as American exceptionalism. At that point, the whiteness of "American" studies became distinguishable from what later emerged as "ethnic studies." The emergence of ethnic studies has to be understood as a response to this conservative retrenching of an otherwise limited but more radical initial vision. So both area studies and American studies as we know them today are Cold War productions generated to manage and negotiate the tensions that arose after World War II and during decolonization worldwide—that is, in distinction to the emergence of other nationalisms. Thus, the racialized nationalism of U.S. American studies comes to stand for the democratic genericism of the Western superpowers.

One consequence of these divisions has been that comparative work in area studies and in American studies remains bound by the nation-state. Although an analytic position of the comparison-studies mode has given us some useful insights, it naturalizes and reproduces the nationalist basis of modernist scholarship. By questioning the distinctness of "areas" presupposed by the comparative framework, and by respecting the specificities of historical and cultural conjectures, we might enable new and different insights into the workings of gender and patriarchy across various borders rather than simply within the parameters of the state or the nation. The changing nature of migrations and global flows of media and capital demand a different notion of transdisciplinary scholarship. Are we able to conduct this kind of scholarship today? And what sites will encourage, support, and generate these knowledges?

If American and area studies can be seen as products of the Cold War, reinforcing the boundaries of nation and state, the question remains: Why did U.S. Women's Studies arise in similar ways, using similar discourses and producing nationalist knowledges? Just as ethnic studies raised the question of the "Third World" within the "First World," and questioned the racial paradigms of American studies, U.S. Women's Studies added gender to the demand for equity and civil rights. By the 1970s and '80s, both popular and academic feminism concerned itself with cultural, racial, and sexual difference. However, most Women's Studies departments retained a U.S. framework even in area and development studies. This trajectory is no accident. The Cold War roots of Women's Studies have not been fully examined. The forms of knowledge production generated throughout the 1950s and '60s in North American universities cannot be ignored when we try to understand these issues. The nationalist biases that permeate U.S. Women's Studies are most obvious in the "Women in Development" paradigm, of course, but they can be seen just as powerfully in the "women of color" paradigm, among others.

The Women in Development paradigm is the most obvious example of international content in Women's Studies. The concept of development as a form of modernization of the so-called Third World has been widespread and influential, disseminated by the policies and practices of many international bodies, including the United Nations, the World Bank, and the International Monetary Fund. It has also been supported by a long-standing tradition of missionary discourses in circulation in the

West since the nineteenth century, discourses and practices in which Western women have played key roles. In the past fifteen years, this missionary model has been critiqued by many feminists from many regions and across many fields (Enloe 1990; Spivak 1987a; Ware 1992)— so much so that the United Nations and the World Bank are now aware of these critiques. It remains to be seen what they will do with them. The sustainable-development model that is now being widely embraced is a way to create a kinder and gentler version of these missionary development models (Gupta 1998). Without critiquing global finance capital and its practices, the sustainable-development model attempts to address globalized inequities. Within this context, we have witnessed the rise of a global feminist movement whose modernist politics are hotly debated and require more sustained research than we have at present. There is a great deal of evidence of these movements and activities on the Internet and in print. The NGO-ization of feminism is an important area of research for those of us who are interested in the future of Women's Studies (especially in relation to the privatization of public education in the United States as an ongoing trend) (Lang 1997). None of this work critiques the U.S.-bound frameworks of Women's Studies, even in its newer incarnation as women's and gender studies. For the most part, despite a rise in the stated discourse in "international" and "global" Women's Studies, U.S. agendas of nation and imperialism still pervade the curriculum and research.

The development- and global-feminism models give rise to a highly mystified figure and object of study: the "Third World woman." This figure has been critiqued and unpacked by many feminists, but it persists in yet another form, which needs to be examined (Alarcón 1990; Mohanty 1991). We want to make a link between the "Third World woman" as an object of study and the rise of the concept of "woman of color" in U.S. ethnic studies and Women's Studies. Both "Third World women" and "women of color" as political projects have had great salience in struggles for civil rights, decolonization, anti-racism, and progressive coalition politics in many contexts (hooks 1984a; Hurtado 1996; Sandoval 1991; Wong 1991). However, at a certain point, both of these concepts have come to represent the homogenized figure of racialized and sexualized difference. Thus, the term "global" has come to mean a "common difference," and despite racial and national differences, woman remains a reified category. This position argues that all patriarchies are essentially alike; that female bodies are transhistorical and cross-cultural; and that resistance has to be mounted against this common patriarchy (Daly 1978; Morgan 1984; Rich 1979). In gender studies, which does not include patriarchy as a primary analytical category, the reified "woman" reemerges in the argument that gender categories and sexual identities are universal (Morris 1994).

Reifying the subject of feminism as "woman" leads to new forms of globalization and cosmopolitanism. For example, the globalization of "domestic violence" activism leads to assertions that all kinds of violence within the family can be understood as "domestic violence," regardless of economic, political, or social context. In India, struggles against "wife-beating," as it is phrased, include in some instances opposition to the licensing of liquor stores by the state. These activists link local patriarchies to the state rather than simply identify family pathologies. In the United States, by contrast, domestic-violence activism has come to see the state as an ally: The Clinton approach to domestic violence was to fund more policing rather than welfare and education programs (Grewal 1999). Thus, some domestic-violence activists, especially those in poor and ethnic communities, may oppose police funding because their communities are disproportionately represented in the prison population, but mainstream domestic-violence activists see the police as allies rather than adversaries. None of these approaches, however, questions how North American nationalism frames its projects and constructs its subjects.

The recent emergence of human rights as a tool against domestic violence and violence against women continues the practice of eliding nationalist agendas under the rubric of the "international." Human rights is increasingly being used in other venues, as well (Grewal 1999; Koshy 1999; S. Joseph [forthcoming]). We see paradigms of gay and lesbian human rights, women's rights as human rights, children's rights, elders' rights, rights of the disabled, indigenous people's rights, consumer's rights, and so on. All of these movements represent struggles that have led to the formation of NGOs, both national and transnational, that produce subjects, practices, and policies. As feminist scholars, we need to study the forms of nationalism and internationalism that underlie these movements and groups rather than simply celebrate their humanist dimensions. In proposing such critiques and research agendas, we are not denying that violence and injury occur. Rather, we are saying that the ways we interpret, analyze, and address such phenomena must be linked to the legacies and histories of modernist knowledge production in late capitalism. The end of the Cold War has not meant liberation from the burden of nationalist bilateralism. Far from it. In fact, these structures have new and pernicious formations that generate and undergird our disciplinary and interdisciplinary practices.

From International to Transnational: Reconfiguring Women's Studies

At this point, we need to turn to a set of critical practices that help us recast and think through the legacy of development and modernization in academic knowledge production. In our collaborative work we have decided to use the term "transnational" instead of "international" in order to trace circuits that are produced by problematic political, economic, and social phenomena. Thus, if we speak of transnational circuits of information, capital, and labor, we refuse to valorize a system founded on inequality and exploitation. It would be impossible for us to advocate a transnational feminism as an improved or better or cleaned-up kind of international or global feminism. Transnational feminism, for example, is not to be celebrated as free of these oppressive conditions. In fact, there is no such thing as a feminism free of asymmetrical power relations. Rather, transnational feminist *practices,* as we call them, involve forms of alliance, subversion, and complicity within which asymmetries and inequalities can be critiqued.

"Transnational" as a term is useful only when it signals attention to uneven and dissimilar circuits of culture and capital. Through such critical recognition, the links among patriarchies, colonialisms, racisms, and feminisms become more apparent and available for critique or appropriation. The history of the term "international," by contrast, is quite different. Internationalism as a concept is based on existing configurations of nation-states as discrete and sovereign entities. The socialist model of internationalism posited a workers' alliance across the boundaries of nation and state to oppose capitalism; the liberal and conservative versions of internationalism arose after World War I in an effort to adjudicate and resolve conflicts among nations. The paramount example of this doctrine and mode of representation is the League of Nations and its offshoot, the United Nations. Liisa Malkki, for instance, sees the international as a pluralism of nations that is unevenly experienced by different parties (Malkki 1994). Malkki argues that old, nineteenth-century ethnological notions of culture remain embedded in these discourses of nations and internationalism, creating discrete cultures as nationally specific identities. Along with Malkki, we believe that internationalism relies on humanist notions of diversity, creating and incorporating local specificities. It is globalizing, hegemonic, and deeply unequal in its effects.

A critique of universalized internationalism has emerged in the concept of critical internationalism. For example, Benjamin Lee's essay of the same name critiques the separation between domestic and international studies in U.S. universities and calls for a renewed focus on difference as well as on what he calls the "global interarticulation" of cultural practices in different societies (Lee 1995). Because Lee envisions this new critical internationalism as a neutral space, his relativist argument reinforces a comparativist model of what he calls the "contextualization of value traditions." Another critical articulation of internationalism can be found in Chen Kuan-Hsing's work on "new internationalist localism" (Chen 1994). Across several essays, Chen has argued for "strategic maneuvering" in cultural studies to avoid the depoliticization that a relativist internationalism inevitably engenders. Chen calls for a notion of the local that is permeated by international, political, and economic power. He argues that the local struggle has to be conscious of the international and that there is no pure, authentic source of particularity. Calling for new international alliances, Chen's concern is for social relations to "escape capture and conditioning by the state" (1992: 482). It is not clear to us, however, how local subjects can escape capture and conditioning by the state, as even new international bodies such as NGOs have very dynamic, close, and mystified relations to the state and nation.

Both internationalism and critical internationalism display a stubborn reliance on state and nation that ignores the scattered hegemonic effects that evade governmentality. There is a vexed relationship among state, nation, and cultural nationalism even in U.S. multiculturalism. The legacy of cultural nationalism can be discerned within U.S. multiculturalism as it creates a diversity of cultures that are ethnically and racially distinct. U.S. multiculturalism has generated discourses of diversity that create notions of the local within its theorizing of difference. Critiques of this kind of multiculturalism argue that it reifies culture, replacing one set of stereotypes with another (Gordon and Newfield 1996; Grewal and Kaplan 1999; Shohat 1998). This representation of culture is often accomplished within yet another hegemonic framework, or the legacies of the dominant framework are incompletely critiqued and thus resurrected. A second critique of U.S. multiculturalism points to its co-optation by multinational business to market and develop new products as well as new consumers and producers. A new variant called "critical multiculturalism" argues for a continued critique of Eurocentric narratives of universalism and essentialism and for the value of opposition generated by counter-hegemonic cultural production. Although this critique of Eurocentrism and its anticolonial and antiracist agendas is extremely important, critical multiculturalism often relies on celebrations of hybridity in which cultures and nations remain discrete forms articulated as cultural rather than as also governmental or economic.

A related version of diversity discourse, cosmopolitanism, relies on humanist narratives of universality and individualism for the creation of subjects such as the world citizen, the nomad, the traveler, the diasporic subject, and all other romanticized figures of mobility (Cheah and Robbins 1998; Clifford 1988; Kaplan 1996). These subjects signify a hegemonic internationalism generated by metropolitan and elite groups who have material and ideological investments in international affiliations among states. Nationalism remains alive in such cosmopolitan discourses, which flatten and universalize the extremely uneven forms of displacement that affect people's lives. Such discourses also erase the specificities of various experiences of localism and transnationalism—again these scattered hegemonic effects cannot be accounted for by Enlightenment paradigms.

All of these terms and critical practices reinforce governmentality over and against cultural effects or reinforce cultural effects over and against governmentality and economic considerations. In this regard, the term "transnational" can mark critical practices that bring the economic and governmental into cultural criticism. Thus, using the term "transnational" rather than "international" does not avoid the conundrums of globalizing capitalism. Although practices of subversion always arise, they are always implicated in current conditions or dominant discourses. Transnational conditions signal dissimilar circuits of culture and capital, and it is these circuits that link patriarchies, colonialisms, cosmopolitanisms, racisms, and feminisms.

Transnational feminist practices of knowledge production thus must be distinguished from the humanist notion of comparative study. Because the regions, nations, locales, and cultures that come to be "compared" have been generated by a colonial episteme, it is necessary to question such a framework (Bernheimer 1995; Grewal 1996). In the past decade or so, new frameworks of knowledge production have emerged to destabilize the binary structure of comparative methodology by continually emphasizing the highly political nature of identity formation in modernity. Feminist scholarship along these lines examines the extent of collaboration and complicity across reified or naturalized institutional borders. Drawing on a notion of linkage rather than comparison helps us critique a reductionist and mystified world-systems model of center and periphery, a model that deploys notions such as "authenticity" and "tradition" along with other constructions of modernity. Even more sophisticated notions of center-periphery that stress hybridity can reproduce or recuperate the binary model by fixing or essentializing the terms of difference.

Ella Shohat has reformulated this notion of linkage in terms of what she calls a "relational approach," one that "operates at once within, between, and beyond the nation-state framework" (Shohat 1992–93). Thus, linkage theory is important not only to understand the connections among nations, patriarchies, colonialisms, racisms, and feminisms but also to destabilize the forms of hegemony that underwrite the production of knowledge in the modern period. The nationalisms and regionalism of area studies, the exceptionalism of American studies, the cultural nationalism of ethnic studies, and the domestic focus of mainstream Women's Studies are reworked by transnational feminist cultural practices of research and teaching.

Reconfiguring Women's Studies Pedagogy:
Teaching Introduction to Women's Studies

One of the most important dimensions of practice for us as professors in primarily undergraduate-oriented departments of Women's Studies is teaching the introductory gateway course. Introducing fields of study, disciplinary or interdisciplinary, must always be posed as a question. That is, designing any introductory course always raises questions of content and method, and can include considerations of the production of knowledge of the field or fields themselves. The introductory course is always a partial gesture—incomplete, sometimes inherently unsatisfactory, and always challenging.

The history of the "Introduction to Women's Studies" course is connected to a much larger discussion of the rise of academic Women's Studies over the past twenty-five years. What we have asserted so far is that the legacy of the Cold War and its geopolitics remains mostly unexamined in relation to the field of Women's Studies. Thus, the emphasis in U.S. Women's Studies first on sexual difference, then on racial difference and gender difference, has remained enmeshed in the disciplinary and interdisciplinary paradigms we have already discussed. Methodologically, Women's Studies needs to move away from these approaches.

In brief, "Introduction to Women's Studies" has developed along four trajectories that we believe demand critique:

—As cultural feminism supplanted socialist and radical feminism throughout the 1970s and '80s, a notion of unmediated experience established what is now referred to as "essentialist" identities at the foundation of Women's Studies. Thus, the socialist standpoint epistemology merged with cultural identity politics in a unique and quite interesting way that continues to plague the Women's Studies curriculum. The woman's standpoint, whether multicultural or intersectional or queer or racial or global, can never escape this history of ideas. Recourse to a transparent experience in the early "Introduction to Women's Studies" courses led to emphases on oppression—the socialization of individuals into oppression via identity and roles in the family and the workplace (Cochran et al. 1991; Freeman 1995). There is no mention of nation in these earlier versions, except in the mid-'80s with the emergence of the politics of location and "U.S. Third World Women of Color" approaches. The cultural feminist syllabus has been organized around sexual-difference topics, such as the origins of patriarchy, language acquisition, biological and psychological bases for gender differentiation, violence against women in the home and the workplace, women's rights, and women's culture.

—Obviously, this culturalist approach could incorporate race through multiculturalism only as "intersectionality": the intersection of standpoints of race, sex, and class, and so on (Crenshaw 1995). The focus on a unified identity, whether it takes a feminist or multicultural standpoint, means that links and complicities, as well as inequalities, often get erased in order to create positivist knowledge. In our classrooms, the effect of this practice creates hierarchies of students who can know only what they "are," and even of teachers who can teach only what they "are." The legacy of U.S. cultural feminism can be seen in the ideas that research counts for nothing before unmediated experience, and that the politics of reified identities replaces historical analysis.

—The U.S. focus of cultural feminism as it has been practiced in most Women's Studies departments has led to narrow articulations of universalized subjects such as "woman," "mothering," "family," and "feminist." This domestic focus universalizes particularities even as it exceptionalizes U.S. formations. For example, a concern we hear from administrators who learn that we are trying to "internationalize" our curricula is that all U.S.-specific content will be lost. The absurdity of this anxiety is remarkable given the deep-seated, foundational assumptions of Women's Studies in general. We dare say that it would be *impossible* to get the United States out of our curricula. But what underlies this fear that we might lose the United States? It must be that, at the root of this discourse, we find that the United States and the international are perceived to be opposed and separate rather than linked and contiguous. We also hear from some of our colleagues that any strong curricular effort to work toward the international will undermine U.S. women of color and the gains they have made in Women's Studies curricula. The arena of contest between the "United States" and the "international" in curriculum revision signals existing disciplinary divides in academic institutions—for instance, the division between area and American studies and the emerging divide between diaspora and ethnic studies. Historically, these divides have erased the racial in the international and the international in the racial. For instance, it is only now that discussions of Cold War military technology can be linked to the prison-industrial complex in the United States—that is, how global capital creates class and race in the United States.

—If this clearly demarcated "international" arena enters the Women's Studies curriculum at all, it does so under the auspices of "development" or "global" feminism. This configuration is directly linked not only to nineteenth-century colonial discourses but also to more modernized Cold War discourses and institutional practices. Can we afford to inculcate new generations of Women's Studies students with these geopolitics and these kinds of limited critiques? We believe that we have other alternatives in our research and in other curricula.

To move to this kind of practice, we need a notion of transnationality to help us differentiate our practices from the international—not that we can avoid or escape the implications of these foundational discourses, but we can mark an effort to subvert and displace them and to reflect the very different historical juncture of the present moment. Transnational feminist practices refer us to the interdisciplinary study of the relationships among women in diverse parts of the world. These relationships are uneven, often unequal, and complex. They emerge from women's diverse needs and agendas in many cultures and societies. Given a very heterogeneous and multifaceted world, how do we understand and teach about the condition of women? When we ask this question, relations among women become just as complicated as those among societies or among nations. Rather than simply use the model of information retrieval about a plurality of women around the world, a project that is both endless and arbitrary, we need to teach students how to think about gender in a world whose boundaries have changed. Because recent scholarship has shown that gender, class, religion, and sexuality produce different kinds of women in relation to different kinds of patriarchies, we must design classes that present a more complex view of how women become "women" (or other kinds of gendered subjects) around the world. In addition, we need to teach about the impact of global forces such as colonialism, modernization, and development on specific and historicized gendering practices that create inequalities and asymmetries.

In developing critical approaches that avoid information retrieval, we have focused on the following three points:

—Critiquing boundaries. In breaking down the divide between the national and international and utilizing the notion of linkage instead of comparison, our goal is to analyze the production of identities through demarcations among genders and nations. Given that people are subject to many institutionalized discourses, the emergence of specific identities can be linked to the ways in which boundaries are produced by hegemonic practices.
—Focusing on complicity and conflict as well as alliance and commonality. In our study of global feminism we have found that essentialized similarities tend to ground these practices. For instance, it is possible to view the 1995 United Nations Conference on Women in Beijing in a number of different ways. For example, although some feminists see

that conference as a triumph of internationalism and the unity of gendered interests across national and cultural divides, others have argued that the Platform for Action it generated shows just as many signs of conflict and difference as it does unity. Many of the debates that occurred in the meeting at large were left out of the final document. The question of unity and hegemonic interests, as opposed to the messy, uneven, and conflicted discourses, needs to be placed at the center of Women's Studies and gender studies.

—Critiquing the "natural" and "common sense." We have found that students are attached to notions of common sense, pragmatism, and individual choice. Our curricula need to address how these notions are products of various dominant knowledge frameworks. For instance, the demarcation between science and superstition emerged in the context of colonialism, as racial and civilizational divides were created between North and South.

—Deconstructing the divide between "high" and "low" culture. Under conditions of late capitalism, knowledge is produced primarily through new media and in visual modes. The curriculum must address how gender is implicated in these shifts and new modes of representation.

In the current version of the "Introduction to Women's Studies" course that we have researched and designed together, we are trying to incorporate these new frameworks. For instance, we do not discuss eating disorders or foot-binding or female genital surgeries as universalized patriarchal atrocities. We do discuss epistemic violence vis-à-vis cultural specificity, but we also discuss it through processes of globalization and modernization. Thus, female genital surgeries cannot be considered only via female genital mutilation discourse, the discourse generated by the World Health Organization and some feminist NGOs. It also must be considered within the history of the rise of gynecology as biomedicine *in the West*. In a transnational context, female genital surgeries across regions and time periods are both linked and unlinked in such a way that the constructions of empire can be seen to recast gendering practices (Abusharaf 1998; Grewal and Kaplan 1999; Gunning 1992; Kirby 1987; Lionnet 1995). Thus, practices such as sex assignment of intersex infants and the rise of transsexual surgeries throughout this century can be linked not only to the rise of medical technology but the transnational study of colonial patriarchies. In addition, the obsessive gaze of colonial and neocolonial medical and scientific authorities toward the "Third World woman's" reproductive and sexual organs cannot be understood apart from the racist policies of eugenics and the rise of Malthusian population-control initiatives. How these formations are recast by various nationalists who oppose colonial and neocolonial authorities must be included in a transnational study of this phenomenon. This is just one of many examples of the kind of recasting of the conventions of mainstream Women's Studies that we are advocating.

The question we return to over and over in this introductory course is how a variety of genders are reduced to a binary of sexual difference in Western and colonial modernity. Such a course must help students understand that a transnational world does not simply imply a plurality of nations, states, and cultures. Rather, the transnational world is structured unevenly by new technology, reconfigurations of national and governmental power, corporate restructuring, and the practices of flexible accumulation that create new citizens, consumers, and producers in late capitalism. Are existing disciplinary and interdisciplinary practices up to this challenge? We would argue that, in all of these sites, feminist work is necessary and is also emerging in newly viable ways. However, there are two final points to be made: No matter how necessary these emergent practices might be, without the institutional structure of Women's Studies and gender studies, there is no guarantee that these practices will be recognized or not marginalized. However, mainstream Women's Studies and gender studies must radically reconfigure themselves to participate in and support these scholarly and pedagogical initiatives.

Notes from the (Non)Field: Teaching and Theorizing Women of Color

We were not born women of color, but became women of color here.
—Jacqui Alexander and Chandra Mohanty (1997)

In their introduction to *Feminist Genealogies, Colonial Legacies, Democratic Futures,* Jacqui Alexander and Chandra Mohanty (1997: xiv) call attention to their formation as "women of color" in a particular location—the United States. Although they chart how their postcolonial feminist consciousness emerged with respect to anticolonial struggles in other parts of the world (Trinidad, Tobago, and India), it wasn't until they learned "the peculiar brand of U.S. North American racism" that they were confronted with this identity and discourse of "U.S. women of color" to which their own experiences were being domesticated (Alexander and Mohanty 1997: xiv). Although my own feminist formation has occurred primarily within educational institutions in the United States, I would nevertheless echo Alexander and Mohanty's words in saying that I was not born a "woman of color" but made so, here—meaning, even more specifically, at my home institution, the University of California at Los Angeles (UCLA). Specifically, I became a "woman of color," as opposed to an Asian American woman, an interpreter of literature, or even a professor of Women's Studies, when I was hired to teach the "women of color" core course, WS130, at UCLA.

Though it would be convenient to explain Women's Studies' curricular commitment to courses such as WS130 as a function of undergraduate demand, I would suggest that more complex and troublesome investments on the part of Women's Studies' faculty sustain this course and also incapacitate it deeply. WS130 and some, but not all, courses of a similar genealogy fulfill a diversifying, metacritical, and symbolic function for their sponsoring programs. Under this aspect, ws130 becomes freighted with the weight of a racial alibi, and the bodies of knowledge produced by and about women of color become less important than the hailing of "women of color" as a synecdoche for Women's Studies' own blind spots. When Angela Davis comments that "the term 'woman of color' is often used in a nominalistic way, without substantive meaning," she calls our attention precisely to those allusions to women of color that occur on the level of a theoretical gesture where they mark the ultimate space of invisibility and compounded exclusion (Davis and Martinez 1994: 45). Women of color have been protesting this nominalistic figuration of themselves,[1] calling for more tangible institutional commitments to building cross-racial coalitions. Thus, Davis contrasts this nominalistic approach to the work done in the Women of Color Research Cluster at the University of California, Santa Cruz, which has developed a slate of courses on the topic of women of color.[2] At the same time, this same program figures negatively in Wendy Brown's criticism of her local Women's Studies program and of the institutional formation of Women's Studies, more generally (see Brown 1997).

As this cursory review suggests, the politics surrounding "women of color" classes have much to tell us not only about the current relation of women of color to Women's Studies but also about how that relationship is entangled with Women's Studies' own negotiations of its intellectual, educational, and political roles in the institution. My exploration of these relations begins with the ws130 requirement at UCLA, the underscrutinized investments in colored bodies rather than in bodies of knowledge that motivate this class, and the peculiar resolution of this course's fulfillment through a kind of off-shore manufacturing precisely because the colored bodies desired to teach this class are situated for the most part outside of Women's Studies. The paradoxical incorporation into the program's core of "women of color" as a knowledge generated outside of that same space helps extend the metacritical and symbolic function of this course to Women's Studies' narrative of its "progress." Because ws130 serves notice of Women's Studies' diversification and awareness of its own faults, Women's Studies programs require this class to be both within the institution of Women's Studies and simultaneously outside or marginal to it.[3] More distressing, and as my reading of two recent essays will reveal, when "women of color" are perceived as too much "inside" the field, determining a new hegemony for Women's Studies, this state of affairs causes as much of a crisis for the field (it becomes the catalyst or symbolic nexus through which Women's Studies can voice anxiety over its institutional stature and its uncertain academic ends) as when "women of color" are felt to be wholly left out. Finally, I suggest some ways in which the scholarship of "women of color" can begin articulating its own historical formation as a function of its own blind spots rather than persist (merely) as a ghostly presence haunting Women's Studies. Thus, the "women of color" class crystallizes a number of seemingly disparate but connected events: the over-eagerness of Women's Studies to sustain this course; the attack on "women of color" scholarship and pedagogy in feminist journals; and the fetishization on all sides of marginality and non-territoriality.

Off-Shore Bodies

The ws130 "women of color" requirement at UCLA evinces a desire to represent women of color at the "core" of Women's Studies and yet replicates a structure at odds with how professors of color have already been conceiving of and teaching courses on the histories of feminist consciousness and culture within their own communities. As one of three core courses (the other two being ws10 "Introduction to Women's Studies" and ws110 "Feminist Theory"), ws130 is a required class that, though upper division, often functions as a feeder course, introducing students of color into the Women's Studies major. A number of women of color faculty, after teaching the course with mixed results, decided that their students were better served when they reconceived their classes under the auspices of their respective ethnic studies programs—for example, as "Chicana feminism" or "Asian American women." Attempting to resolve this disjunction between how faculty wanted to construct their courses and how the institution of Women's Studies itself wanted to act as a centripetal force bringing together various women of color under one umbrella topic, UCLA's program adopted a policy of offering one ws130 class—and hiring a faculty member (me) to teach the course. At the same time, the "core" requirement was redesigned so that either ws130 or a class in any one women of color subject (such as Native American women or African American women's literature) fulfills this distribution.[4]

The emphasis on ws130 as a feeder to the major hints that "women of color" does not name a body of knowledge analogous to feminist theory (though both occur at the 100 level). Rather, the class remains crucial to the program's institutional demography on the levels of both student enrollment and faculty representation. By counting on the conflation of course content with the body of the instructor, well-intentioned chairs and advisory boards commit to a curricular structure in which Women's Studies cannot fulfill its pedagogical mission without the participation of a woman of color in the ranks. This conflation leads to a curious overinvestment in ws130 as a course that must be part of the core course series, taught every year by a woman of color. At the same time, there is a peculiar dis-investment in the body of scholarship by and about "women of color" in which all core faculty must remain expert enough to teach. This body of knowledge remains decidedly plural, best apprehended through a slate of courses (such as that generated at Santa Cruz) rather than a single, stopgap measure.[5]

The challenge for Women's Studies programs with respect to women of color will be how to carve out a space unique among other institutional sites at the university to foster collaborative scholarship and pedagogy among individual African American, black Caribbean, Chicana, Latina, Native American, Middle Eastern, Asian and Pacific Islander, and Anglo-European professors. Otherwise, Women's Studies, failing to take seriously the bodies of knowledge produced at the intersection of race and gender, desiring only the bodies to diversify its program rosters, will only continue to see its own marginalization of women of color fulfilled, despite the expressed eagerness for (and even job offers extended to) individual black and brown women.

The policy of dispersing the "women of color" core course—or, rather, looking to its fulfillment through classes outside Women's Studies— reflect the broader educational philosophy of UCLA's Women's Studies program. Under significant budget constraints, this interdisciplinary unit works by staffing its courses and fulfilling its overall educational mission with a heavy reliance on cross-listing, an effect not unrelated to material inadequacies and its marginalization within the institution.[6] On the one hand, we can see this outsourcing of the Women's Studies "core" as an admirable practice: Women's Studies refuses to be territorial about its curricular program and ensures that its majors enjoy more traditional training in several disciplines. On the other hand (or perhaps on the same hand), we might imagine that, through this scattering of the Women's Studies curriculum throughout the university, an approach attuned to gender and sexual hierarchies will have become so thoroughly incorporated into traditionally defined departments that there will no longer be a need for a separate field of "Women's Studies." Drawn in this fashion, Women's Studies appears to be a "war of position" rather than a "war of maneuver" (cf. Hall 1986).[7] Yet cleaving to this style of guerrilla infiltration of Women's Studies precepts into traditional academic disciplines has been driven not by choice but by necessity. Although we try to reconfigure our weaknesses as our strengths, we also need to recognize how tiring guerrilla tactics can be and how alienating (of our labor) this commitment to dissipating the field—diffusing it into an everyplace that feels, too often, like no place—can be for those working in the trenches.[8]

Ironically, the theory and method of women of color as oppositional consciousness seems to endorse this very dwelling in multiple sites about which I am skeptical. In her landmark essay on U.S. Third World feminism, Chela Sandoval persuasively articulates women of color as superceding any singular political agenda, as no place and everyplace precisely because "U.S. Third World feminists" embody a type of "differential consciousness" that engages other oppositional ideologies selectively and weaves "between and among them" (Sandoval 1991: 14). Women of color's expansive consciousness is at once derivative of their material locations: They are characterized as situated at or between physical, often national, borders—in no one territory. In this scenario, women of color fade into a "no-place" of political nonrecognition precisely because of the inability of both the state and progressive countermovements to see "the intersection" (Crenshaw 1989), "the borderlands" (Anzaldúa 1987), or "the interstices" (Kim 1998) as, indeed, types of places.

Depicting this misrecognition more concretely, Sandoval recalls the charges lobbied against U.S. feminists of color for being only sporadically present in the "1970s white women's liberation movement." She writes: " 'When they were there, they were rarely there for long' went the usual complaint, or 'they seemed to shift from one type of women's group to another' " (Sandoval 1991: 13). Sandoval makes clear, however, that U.S. feminists of color were pre-eminently "mobile . . . members of this particular liberation movement. It [was] precisely the significance of this mobility which most inventories of oppositional ideology [could not] register" (Sandoval 1991: 14). The perception of women of color's absence did not, in fact, bespeak their absence. Rather, it signaled a problem in feminist codes of reading that could comprehend mobility only as a blank. Paraphrasing Aida Hurtado and Cherrie Moraga, Sandoval described " 'women of color [as] more like urban guerrillas trained through everyday battle with the state apparatus' " whose insurgent "fighting capabilities ha[d] 'not been codified' nor understood precisely because they were mobile and flexible (Sandoval 1991: 14–15).

After establishing that feminist codes of reading "opposition" must be enlarged to include women of color's mobile practices, the essay posits this mobility as a possible mode outside of domination, precisely because women of color do not strive for their own fixed, singular Truth but flexibly engage multiple ideologies. Sandoval draws on the force of a vehicular metaphor, "the clutch of an automobile," to describe the flexible practices that permit women of color to "select, engage, and disengage gears [or different programs of action, different oppositional ideologies] in a system for the transmission of power" (Sandoval 1991: 14). Notably, Sandoval does not argue for a separate gear for U.S. Third World feminists. Instead, "U.S. third world feminism represents a central locus of possibility, an insurgent movement which shatters the construction of any one of the collective ideologies [or gears] as the single most correct site where truth can be represented. Without making this move, any liberation movement is destined to repeat the oppressive authoritarianism from which it is attempting to free itself and *become trapped inside a drive for truth which can only end in producing its own brand of dominations*" (Sandoval 1991: 14; emphasis added). The insistence that Third World feminism not "[produce] its own brand of dominations" speaks to the essence behind Third World feminism's guerrilla tactics. This mode of "consciousness"—also defined as an activity of border- or threshold-crossing—does not aim to fortify a ground, territory, or place to stand. Within its logic, "there are no ultimate answers, no terminal utopia. . . . [Its practice must] not . . . become static" (Sandoval 1991: 23, n. 58).[9]

But how is this mobile practice, born of the desire not to repeat oppressive dominations, particularly attached to women of color? Why name this mobile activity "Third World feminism" if indeed this practice might be better apprehended as "flexible resistance" or "multiplicitous travel" or "guerrilla ideological tactics"? The desire to remain outside the mechanisms of institutional power ends up superceding the project of bringing into visibility, naming and fixing, even if temporarily, "a specific U.S. third world feminism"—in short, the project of staking out a territory. Instead, the focus of "oppositional consciousness" is retrained on dominant determinations, even as its own commitment to marginality would seem to suggest otherwise. Clearly, the desire to locate Third World feminism in a strictly tactical, mobile, non-territorial mode of consciousness proceeds in part from the very anxiety that Women's Studies as an institution, and Third World women as part of that institution, feel about becoming dominant and thereby "repeat[ing] the oppressive authoritarianism from which [they attempt] to free [themselves]." But as seductive as the exemption from producing dominations is, this extraterritorial roving position falters as a model for a program's effective operation in the university or for the developing and initiating of a comparative analysis of the resistant practices of various Third World women and women of color.

Not merely women of color, but Women's Studies as a whole, remains enthralled with this characterization of women of color as an extraterritorial roving position, especially as that critical mobility might be tapped into on behalf of the field's account of itself as an "outsider" knowledge, as the embodiment (the incorporation) of that which has been excluded, and even that which it has itself excluded.[10] In the contradictory logic of fetishized marginality, the narration of Women's Studies' critical progress inheres in the field's ability both to incorporate the "outside" and to substitute itself for the "outside." Thus, Women's Studies imagines itself as having, in the past, omitted a race-full perspective in its initial primary focus on gender, and, in the present, working toward a more inclusive analysis of simultaneous subjectivizing discourses of race, gender, class, sexuality, nationality, and so forth. Characterized as that which had been left out of Women's Studies' and ethnic studies' historical and current practices (the subject of multiple exclusions and the testament to Women's Studies' "exclusionary" practices), women of color symbolize the potentiality of feminist studies' critical future—the superordinate capacity to switch between and among different "gears" (or different ideologies and explanatory systems), which is also the capacity to occupy the space outside of itself (outside of its own explanatory systems). Thus, in their aspect as "oppositional consciousness"—as the residual subject never fully spoken for in any program of action or knowledge formation—women of color remain eminently useful to the progress narrative Women's Studies wishes to create for itself, where the fullness of women of color's arrival within Women's Studies is always "about to be."

Precisely this notion of "women of color"—as either a racial exclusion to be resolved or a non-territorial space of critical surplus—seduces both women of color and white women by holding out the promise of a victorious ending. "Women of color" are hailed as the final frontier—as our temporal and global end, the place where we end our seminars rather than begin them.[11] Moreover, this fantasy of "women of color" as a refinement, as the ultimate, non-exclusionary position, becomes the ghost that haunts ws130 classes. Though understandable, it is nevertheless a regrettable failure of an entire Women's Studies program (and curricular structure) that the resolution of race acts as the not-so-secret desire of students throughout this particular course's run.[12]

In my own "women of color" classes, my students have taught me not to take for granted any belief on their part that feminism ought to be concerned also about race, about the Third World, or about capitalist and (neo)colonial development.[13] That is, if feminism's agenda is to be as capacious as any political concern of any woman, the question haunting this dream of absolute inclusiveness is: What makes this agenda particularly feminist? As one student put it, "Should feminism also be concerned with saving the whales?" I think this question can be resolved only by helping students to recognize the split between our temporal domains of definition (for example, past and future) and resolving ourselves to the different capacities and potentials of these domains. Feminism may be unique only to the extent of its historicity—its narration as an evolving set of movements and methodologies—rather than in terms of its vision of the future and its vision of justice, which is, in most present-day assessments, not merely a gendered justice but also a more complete economic, racial, sexual, religious, and ecological justice. Feminism's definition is more narrowly identifiable as a narration of its past, whereas feminism's definition as a future agenda is always already an incomplete definition. Thus, feminism is defined by both the specifics of the past and the indeterminacy, struggle, and open-endedness of its future. What becomes the most interesting work for the classroom, then, is puzzling over what constitutes feminism's present, that space residing between historical specificity and indeterminate future.

In centering women of color in the classroom—in such debates over what constitutes feminism's present—we should be cautious, then, of elevating women of color to the future and to the promise of what we have yet to incorporate in our activism and scholarship. Just as vigilantly, however, we should be suspicious of attempts preemptively to relegate women of color to the past so that we can move on to greener, less troublesome pastures. Thus, in addition to focusing on how women of color speak to one another, our classrooms might also be considered workshops to explore in a critical fashion how women of color figure in the present teleological crises of Women's Studies.

At least two widely circulating essays on the topic of the current viability of Women's Studies (and its future directions) give a prominent place to the way in which feminism has been derailed because it has been colonized by a "women of color" pedagogical style and scholarly lexicon. In "The Impossibility of Women's Studies" (1997), Wendy Brown calls into question the wisdom of solidifying the victories of Women's Studies in degree-granting programs, suggesting that critical studies of gender and sexuality might be better pursued in the mainstream disciplines. Her urging of this new (and old) feminist project stems from her frustration with the inability of her own Women's Studies program to reach a consensus over curriculum reform, as well as from the lone curricular requirement on which her colleagues can agree: the "women of color" class. As she describes it, white and colored students in this class at Santa Cruz engage in an "intensely emotional . . . relentless, compensatory cycle of guilt and blame about race" that intellectually habituates these students to making narrow demands of "excessive specificity" (Brown 1997: 93–94). Brown rebuts the pluralist logic of such demands and, having characterized Women's Studies as cycling repeatedly around this issue (as opposed to moving forward), she implicitly calls for an end to this loop of "guilt and blame" by advocating the pursuit of the study of women outside of Women's Studies. Thus, if Women's Studies were to occur wholly within the traditional disciplines, it could focus not on women per se but on the modalities of subjection that produce gender as an effect, sexuality as an effect, or race as an effect, rather than what Women's Studies continually confronts in its own house: Its elisions of other categories of difference (race being the exemplary instance).

In declaring the "impossibility" of Women's Studies, Brown proclaims an end to what she portrays as a two-pronged hegemony within Women's Studies programs: 1) its focus on "one dimension of power . . . as primary and structuring" (Brown 1997: 93), echoing the broad critique of mainstream feminist theory by "women of color"; and 2) its cleaving to a pre-Foucauldian analysis of power as hierarchical ranking rather than as subjectifying modalities that produce even as they regulate subjects. Though never explicitly argued, Brown's citational practice indicates that this pre-Foucauldian construction of power has been a favored heuristic in "women of color" scholarship (Brown 1997: 86), and that this (to her mind) mistaken articulation of power along the lines of privilege (Hurtado 1989) and intersectional oppression (Crenshaw 1989) has obscured for Women's Studies the potential of Foucauldian analyses not only to make more complex our understandings of agency, subjectivity, and discourse, but also to resolve the cycle of guilt and blame enshrined in the "women of color" classroom.[14] Because this essay renders the passionate volleys of that classroom the sign of Women's Studies' breakdown, Brown obscures "guilt and blame" as possible effects of a particular cognitive leap made by students that Women's Studies is itself a site of regulation. Critiques by women of color not only expose Women's Studies' primary focus on "woman" as too narrow but also suggest that this primary focus bespeaks white and colored women's uneven relationship to the mode in which they are produced in Women's Studies—an unevenness that we can understand as a function not merely of "differences" (their production through different modalities) but also of *differences that are ranked*. We may all be different, but this does not mean that we are all equal. It is this simple—perhaps even simplistic—insight of which a pre-Foucauldian apprehension of power forcefully reminds us, and which scholarship by women of color finds unexpendable.[15]

Although it is true that we can never make Women's Studies a completely interrogatory rather than also a regulatory project, this does not mean that its dissolution is the only answer, though it is Brown's provisional one. Her essay suggests escaping the compensatory cycle of race enshrined in the Women's Studies curriculum by simply abandoning it—traveling elsewhere. This proposal of a mobile, non-territorial Women's Studies project, however, only partially proceeds from Brown's frustration over the inability of her own Women's Studies program to set a curriculum (to know its curricular beginnings and ends). In the detailed account of the particular pedagogical frustration in the "women of color" classroom, which is also the only curricular certainty that Brown's Women's Studies program has evolved, this article indicates that the more nettlesome point is the endless struggle, rather than resolutions achieved, in this course. "The Impossibility of Women's Studies" thus sheds light on how courses such as ws130—and the imputed failure of such classes to resolve critiques by women of color—have become central to a debate over the Women's Studies project on the whole.

Notably, in urging a new feminist project no longer under the aegis of Women's Studies programs but roving among the traditional disciplines, Brown proposes a vision uncannily similar to the oppositional Third World feminist consciousness proposed by Sandoval. Her suggestion to render Women's Studies a completely transitive project is a way to re-inhabit on behalf of Women's Studies the position of the lost object that travels in a ghostly fashion, haunting other disciplines rather than being haunted by cycles of guilt and blame around its own exclusionary prac-tices. Rather than being hailed as the future of Women's Studies, women of color are being taken to task for having degraded Women's Studies and feminism, not via their deconstruction of the myth of global sisterhood (a more familiar critique) but through their colonizing of the realm of the excluded, degraded, or lost object (that is, the haunting presence) for women of color specifically and not for women in general. Brown sug-gests that feminism is most critically useful when it shadows the main-stream disciplines, when it challenges "the seamless histories, theories, literatures, and sciences featuring and reproducing a Humanism star-ring only Man" (Brown 1997: 95), in essence revealing gender as an originary absence in humanistic study and, by doing so, injecting that loss into the mainstream disciplines. Through recolonizing the position of the "lost object," feminist studies tries to triumph over its own melan-cholia, or its repetitive, cyclical, guilt-ridden staging of its own exclusions.

While Brown's essay quite subtly handles its construction of women of color as crisis object, Susan Gubar's "What Ails Feminist Criticism" unapologetically dwells on the "censorious" tone of black and Third World women's scholarship that has won for them a "critical election" on the backs of white women's "critical abjection" (their deferring to women of color's words or their utter silence when faced with women of color's "condemnatory vocabulary") (Gubar 1998: 888–93).[16] Unlike Brown, Gubar does not engage the conceptual apparatus of Women's Studies—its narrow focus on "woman" and its pre-Foucauldian articulations of power—that have contributed to an impasse over race. Focusing on style as content, Gubar portrays the crisis in feminist criticism in terms of a general atmosphere of "crank[iness]," her solution appealing to that same register: "I find myself echoing the words of Braidotti . . . who exclaims, 'I wish feminism would shed its saddening, dogmatic mode to rediscover the merrymaking of a movement that aims to change life.' . . . I would like to think I'm supplying food for thought about how to find more mirthful scholarly lexicons" (Gubar 1998: 902). However, the foil to these mirthful tones is set in her essay by black and Third World women, and although ostensibly Gubar pleads for an end to the general "debilitating rhetorics of critical election, abjection, and obscurantism," the specific examples in her essay clarify that the particular end being asserted is the cessation of race critics' critical election, made possible by white women's deferring (making "obeisance") to these women of color and their mode of inquiry. Notably, Gubar does not dwell, in turn, on how asserting and demanding a superior, more decorous (literate, literary) style is also a well-worn mode of not only critical, but also material and historical, election that has often dovetailed with the maintenance of racial ranking and colonial domination (see Gates 1986). This is not to suggest that anger and accusation are better means of addressing racial privilege or examining race as a historical formation. Rather, the point to be registered is that the unseemly speech at which Gubar's essay takes aim has a racial particularity, even as the essay ostensibly impugns the state of feminist criticism more generally. As Robyn Wiegman cogently argues, Gubar's essay cannot conceive of scholarship by women of color as offering self-reflexive contributions to the Women's Studies project. Rather, it reduces that scholarship to its emotional effects on white women. The essay continually shifts focus from "the intentions of women of color to speak for themselves to the effects of their discourse on white women—demonstrat[ing], in symptomatic fashion, the inability of 'What Ails Feminist Criticism?' to analyze race in a critical vocabulary divorced from white women's emotional centrality" (Wiegman 1999: 378). As an alternative, Wiegman proposes that, although Gubar's essay gives legitimate testimony to "a certain feeling of feminism's fragility" (which is clearly linked to its lack of institutional support), it ultimately "misdiagnoses as illness academic feminism's difficult negotiation of these conditions" (Wiegman 1999: 379).

My point is not to fault Gubar's or Brown's positions in particular but to highlight the way in which their essays similarly suggest that the overwhelming success of women of color in inhabiting the center of feminist scholarship is what we must grapple with in our assessments of Women's Studies today. Both these essays exemplify a new mode of estrangement (misalliance, and sometimes outright hostility) in mainstream feminist scholarship vis-à-vis women of color. The estrangement is best expressed by an almost exhausted sentiment that the challenge made by women of color to Women's Studies is well worn and that as we narrate and proceed into the future of feminism, the only thing for sure is that Women's Studies ought not be invested in those angry charges made by women of color that they were excluded, because now they are included—even dominant—in Women's Studies. This sentiment of exhaustion contrasts with a previous and not always straightforward assessment of race and women of color as regretfully neglected components of Women's Studies, whose continued omission would impoverish feminism's analytical paradigms. Most interesting about this shift to a current mode of estrangement is that the exhaustion with race is a function not so much of what is ostensibly said—that we have achieved racial parity (the end has been achieved)—but of a deepening uncertainty over feminism's and Women's Studies' own future: its guarantee of a better mode of inquiry, a better scholarly challenge unassayed in the traditional disciplines. In a work of both denial and displacement, a pre-emptive proclamation that women of color are at the center of feminist criticism helps posit an achievement, any achievement, where other certainties and ends are less assured.

To put it another way, the teleological guarantee that feminism does not provide (or, at least, the variant of feminism that insists on its partiality, its self-admitted inability to see everything or to present a totality of knowledge and a totality of justice) becomes metonymically supplied by the teleological guarantee of getting over racial exclusion. If feminism cannot guarantee total justice, it can at least posit one sure thing about to be: that feminism will be adequate to racial challenges because feminism has made, or is on the verge of making, women of color central. Thus, we have a very odd contemporary moment in which we see the frustrations of Women's Studies—a manifest frustration at the insufficiently guaranteed end of racial guilt and anger—narrating obliquely and on some deeper level a frustration with the inability of feminism to guarantee its own challenges to the disciplines. "Will the breast-beating over race never end?" shades into the question, "Why can't we get to an end? Have an end? Guarantee an end?"

Women of color are thus peculiarly positioned in our contemporary moment, at once hailed as a phantasmic "pure space" outside domination but within Women's Studies, in which they have the dubious distinction of being celebrated for not speaking and not occupying—for the capacious space of the "not yet realized." They are simultaneously expected to act as a palliative agent, assuaging Women's Studies' anxieties over its uncertain ends and objects precisely by reassuring Women's Studies that the (inter)discipline has achieved something definite, because women of color, according to this viewpoint, are, indeed, central. Women of color thus serve Women's Studies in multiple fashions: as the idea of a triumphal end point and as a resented (envied) lost object that has wrested from Women's Studies its own phantom mobility.

Clearly, then, the seduction of non-territoriality, which I have examined as a persuasive force within women of color scholarship, is also a seduction to Women's Studies scholars more generally. This turn (seemingly back) toward a position of holding no territory, to my mind, parallels a kind of uncertainty principle that has rebounded on Women's Studies over whether it can have an end (whether Women's Studies can build a better mode of apprehension), especially when the end of which it had been somewhat certain—the end of racist analysis within feminism itself—is still questionable. What I suggest is that even though this status as lost object or as roving principle is immensely tempting to both women of color and feminist studies more generally, neither can afford to rest solely within that everywhere and nowhere space of critique.

More significantly, do we really want to stay mired in a struggle over who really "owns" (or is most radically dis-owned by) this critically useful, mobile oppositional consciousness? As Mohanty said nearly a decade ago, "Histories of feminism also document histories of domination and oppression. No noncontradictory or 'pure' feminism is possible" (Mohanty 1991b: 20). Yet, ironically, what is being seized in such yearnings for that status of pure, dislocated object is not a territory but a non-territoriality. The danger lies in both "women of color's" and (white) Women's Studies equal enthrallment with this threshold position.

Instead of jockeying over this mobile oppositional consciousness, I suggest that "women of color" scholarship look to the unchallenged assumptions underlying its own critical terrain as a way to challenge its predominant image as a reactive entity to the institution of Women's Studies. "Women of color" scholarship might understand its historical formation to be contingent on the narration of its own myopia, in the same way that the positive contours of mainstream feminist theory are indebted to critiques by women of color—that is, somewhat paradoxically, canonical feminist theory became something other than a supplement to men's knowledge when it went beyond the singular aim of analyzing and establishing the gendering of all knowledge to explore the racialized presumptions of its own growing body of representative texts. When feminist studies took a look at itself as a positive, palpable corpus that had its own blind spots—at angles skewed to or not commensurate with its (reactive) gender critique—feminism attained a level of legitimacy. It became "a field" (following Rey Chow's formulation) with positive territorial contours.[17] The silver lining in Women's Studies' recognition of its own complicity in hegemonic structures was a backhanded affirmation of its own dominance. In similar fashion, "women of color" criticism might exit the prisonhouse of reactiveness—negative definition—through the articulation of its own blind spots, which is simultaneously an acknowledgement of its distinctive terrain.

Our classrooms and our curriculum, to return to my point of departure, can crucially figure as sites in which to develop such an apprehension of women of color as a body of knowledge, codified in ways that are expedient and imperfect but nevertheless generative of identifiable contours that can therefore be scrutinized. One of the most enlightening moments in my classes occurs when we turn our attention to the privileges women of color unknowingly preserve that are at angles askew from the privileges they sought to critique in white feminism (e.g., racial privilege and middle-class normativity). One such skewed angle might be the U.S.-centrism of "women of color" writings and the reliance on civil-rights discourse in proposals for remedy. For instance, the lack of inclusion in U.S. legislative and judiciary processes is implicitly where Kimberlé Crenshaw aims her critique in her oft-cited essay "Demarginalizing the Intersection of Race and Sex" (1989). Yet, dispossessed indigenous groups colonized by the Anglo-European U.S. state might argue for land rights and territorial separation rather than for inclusion in the "civil rights" guaranteed by U.S. laws (see Guerrero 1997; Trask 1993). One key blind spot in much "women of color" scholarship, then, is its own imbrication in civil rights discourse and modes of political redress attendant on a concept of justice inhering in rights and in possessive, capitalist individualism and subjectivity.

At the same time, it is precisely because Crenshaw's essay does not shy away from seizing territory, so to speak, arguing for a palpable material

remedy, that can we tackle its narrowness, its embeddedness in a particular location. Forgoing the critical surplus of oppositional mobility, Crenshaw constructs a remedial agenda for black women that seeks redress
vis-à-vis the U.S. political economy in the late twentieth century rather
than celebrating "women of color's" marginality to the state. In this
respect, Crenshaw's essay spurs a critical reassessment of Sandoval's
"oppositional" mobility. While Sandoval highlights multiplicitous mobility as graceful, Crenshaw in contrast emphasizes the collision of several
routes as traumatic rather than as enlarging:

> If an accident happens in an intersection, it can be caused by cars
> traveling from any number of directions and, sometimes, from all
> of them. Similarly, if a Black woman is harmed because she is in the
> intersection, her injury could result from sex discrimination or race
> discrimination. . . . Providing legal relief only when Black women
> show that their claims are based on race or on sex is analogous to
> calling an ambulance for the victim only after the driver responsible
> for the injuries is identified. But it is not always easy to reconstruct
> an accident: Sometimes the skid marks and the injuries simply
> indicate that they occurred simultaneously. . . . In these cases . . . no
> driver is held responsible. (Crenshaw 1989: 149)

Where Sandoval heralds the guerrilla ability of a woman of color to
"transform [her] identity according to [one's] readings of power's formation" (Sandoval 1991: 15), Crenshaw characterizes shape-shifting (or
fitting one's shape into those forms already recognized by power formations, such as the court or current antidiscrimination statutes) as a deficit, because too often women of color—black women, in particular—
cannot fit their shape into the one size that is offered. Her enunciation of
the trauma rather than of the open-ended possibilities of "women of
color's" flexible identities might mark the emergence of a woman-of-
color *transformative* political subjectivity. I mean transformative precisely in the sense of seeing what we possess (guerrilla abilities, flexibility
and grace, a mobile disposition) not merely as heroic, though such
qualities certainly are, but also as something we can change. Portraying
black women as underserved by national protections—as "countryless
women," to use Ana Castillo's phrase (Castillo 1994: 24)—Crenshaw
characterizes justice as a more complete coverture of black women by the
interventionist state.

In claiming a terrain on which black women would be not merely the oppositional mode but the centered subject, Crenshaw stakes a claim that, in emphasis of the earlier point, has its own limited vision. For the Hawai'ian activist Haunani-Kay Trask, such appeals to the U.S. courts would be a misguided appropriation of territory already seized from indigenous peoples. Defining her feminist project in terms of indigenous land rights and woman's *"mana"* (power, authority), Trask refuses to romanticize her exquisite dispossession and argues for a political terrain, a sovereignty, and a transformative political subjectivity, albeit aimed at a different territorial object from that defined by Crenshaw. Can these two programs for action coalesce? The answer is, probably not. However, the contradictions internal to the different domains to which various women of color speak constitute the challenge represented by the bodies of knowledge produced by women of color in distinction to the ease of noting women of color's convergence in opposition to the center. Thus, the challenge for Women's Studies in developing a slate of classes on "women of color" will be to collaborate, paradoxically, on points of disagreement and catalysts of disidentification, controverting over-investments in "women of color" as a "new model for unity" (Zinn and Dill 1994: xv).[18] Although it is certainly admirable, this emphasis on "unity" tends to obscure the legitimacy of other modes of conceptualizing and narrating "women of color" as also a site of difference and struggle—as itself a discourse in need of critique and deconstruction.

In short, the struggle for women of color is not—as perhaps implicitly envisioned—to be answered in (white) feminism's self-ameliorating actions on race, not in some other agent's ability to read or see women of color's mobile practices, and not in our inhabiting the space of promised teleological guarantee on behalf of feminism, but in our scrutiny of our own articulations of women of color as community, methodological consistency, temporary coalition, or that which is secured by a teleological guarantee. (For instance, Sandoval seems not to want such a guarantee, whereas Crenshaw and Trask do.) Essentially, I suggest that women of color and Third World feminism seek out the places that are haunted by ghostly presences not yet articulated.[19]

The Yearning to Travel

To envision "women of color," and Women's Studies on the whole, as somehow a better mode of consciousness, as materially disposed to crossing borders and working beyond territorial, national, and institutional boundaries, is immensely tempting. The luster of (and lust for) this purely interrogative travel constitutes our most steadfast yearning. In fact, because of the old mind-body split, the lack of territory can appear as a prerequisite for an acute perceptual brilliance. In the case of women of color, because they seem not to reside in any single territory or ideological apparatus (a seeming deficit in the quest for political enunciation or for syllabi construction, one might argue), they are attributed with an especially expansive ability to embrace multiple causes: Their "no place" becomes "every place"—or, at least, a perch from which to see how other territories, communal formations, and emancipatory discourses are delimited. This idea of women of color as a standpoint (Collins 1990), as a lens through which one perceives better (Haraway 1988), or as a roving activist practice or stance (Sandoval 1991), rather than women of color as object of specular scrutiny, is decidedly seductive precisely because it attributes to the "women of color" viewing perch an optimum panorama from which one can see at the same time that one refuses to be seen. This characterization of women of color as all eye and no body seems counterintuitive, because one of the complaints around "women of color" is that they have an excess of visibility, that they are superabundantly constrained by their bodies or, more precisely, by social constructs about their bodies as hypersexual and exploitable.[20] Hence, to attribute to these hypervisible bodies an acuteness of perceptual power is a revolutionary act, yet one that has limitations, as well. The major limitations that I will underscore here with making "women of color" more or less synonymous with an exceptional perspective are that 1) women of color are precisely valued for that angle of vision onto feminism and minority manhood and are not given the opportunity to engage one another as subjects struggling together collaboratively and in conflict; 2) women of color, in being a ghostly angle of vision, can be deeply unsatisfying figures for undergraduate students, who would like to see women of color as authors, artists, and creators rather than strictly as a mode of inquiry; and 3) in a world that operates through fields, guerrilla action (or the espying of weakness in someone else's bunker), although a necessary maneuver, cannot be an end point unto itself. Guerrilla action must begin to seize territory or dissolve.

It is tempting, in short, to envision our exploitation, dispossession, and unsafe spaces as our strengths. But though we may be rich in our "psychic terrain"—in our ability to grasp dualities simultaneously precisely because we are not allowed a space in any singularity—we remain materially and practically impoverished, without stable ground on which to stand. Similarly, diminishing funding and territory for "women of color" within Women's Studies—relegating women of color to no place and every place—does not, I think, build a corpus of classes on women of color; solidify cultural, service-oriented, and political collaborations among women of color; or ultimately deepen students' understanding of "women of color" as anything other than a marginal perspective. Perhaps the time is ripe to begin enunciating "women of color" with respect to privilege and—dare I say?—within and through privilege.

Notes

A version of this essay was presented at the Annual Meeting of the Modern Language Association, San Francisco, Calif., December, 1998.

1 In the preface to their sociohistorical compendium *Women of Color in U.S. Society* (1994), Maxine Baca Zinn and Bonnie Thornton Dill address their audience's potential unease with this invented social grouping, saying: "Some readers may find the term 'women of color' itself troublesome because it reflects less the actual experiences of Native American women, African-American women, Latinas, and Asian-American women than it does the type of intellectual and political coalition that joins these groups. The term 'women of color' aims to foster unity and unwillingly flattens diversity" (Zinn and Dill 1994: xiv–xv). Zinn and Dill ultimately hold on to the term for its potential as an emergent identification that would go beyond the very experiences of women of color in order to help "construct new political and intellectual communities" and "new models of unity" (Zinn and Dill 1994: xv). However, this investment in women of color as a "new model for unity" is also problematic. (I develop this more fully in the body of this chapter.) On the vexaciousness of the "women-of-color" label, see also Alarcón 1990: 356–69; Mohanty 1991a: 1–47; and Alexander and Mohanty's (1997) subtle distinction between "women of color" feminism and Third World feminism.

2 Two different seminars on "Women of Color: Genders and Sexualities" and one course on "Women of Color and Visual Culture" are among the courses that have been fostered by Santa Cruz's Curriculum Development Project. Each of these classes is co- or team-taught. The Women of Color Research Cluster also lists several "related" classes, such as "Indigenous Women in the U.S. and Canada" and "Queer Politics."

3 The liminal siting of UCLA's "women of color" requirement both under and outside the auspices of Women's Studies literalizes at an institutional level the "outsider within" consciousness that Patricia Hill Collins (1990) attributes to black women and the mobile oppositional consciousness that Sandoval (1991) claims for Third World women. Evoking these metaphors of inside and outside—of territory, occupation, and

mobility—I mean to call attention not just to who is or isn't at home in Women's Studies (Martin 1986), but how dislocatedness and absence once figured as deficit has been reconstrued as a critical surplus—one that the institution of Women's Studies seems eager to reclaim for itself.

4 Within the pluralist logic that motivates WS130, this amendment to the core is an excellent system, because it preserves the fiction of "women of color" for Women's Studies' liberal self-portrait and yet partially concedes the point that Chicanas and African American, Native American, and Asian women are deciding for themselves the much narrower confines of their course proposals. However, it does not wholly concede that "women of color" represents a body of knowledge best pursued in racially specific classes, for Women's Studies needs to maintain its own WS130 in its core because of the metacritical purchase it gets from this maintenance. Hence, the "both-and" solution actually exacerbates the understaffing of the "women of color" class, which is still conceived as the province of only dark-skinned women, and does little to encourage pedagogical collaboration among Chicanas and African American, Native American, and Asian women.

5 I would argue that Women's Studies needs to spearhead a more vigorous growth of its own core course series, each one emphasizing race, rather than continue to imply that race can be set aside for coverage in WS130 or some other approved course. By growing the core, I do not mean merely the lengthening on paper of the courses offered by other departments that would count toward the major; rather, I mean the funding of collaborative pedagogies and the offering of material support for a group of faculty, and possibly graduate students, to create ensemble new knowledges through a comparative approach to feminist histories, theories, and cultural productions. In essence, I am arguing for less dispersing of the "women of color" core course—less looking to its fulfillment through classes outside Women's Studies—insofar as that policy reflects Women's Studies' undercutting both its own claims on the university and its own responsibilities to inaugurate scholarship on women of color.

6 As argued by Patrice McDermott, the institutionalized marginalization of Women's Studies in terms of budget allocation renders "the few institutional devices over which feminist scholars exert considerable control" all the more important. One of those devices is core curriculum, which may account for the heightened struggles now being staged around it. See her excellent summation of the ways in which Women's Studies, "when it comes to new curricular proposals, unlike traditional disciplines, is continually forced to defend its intellectual merit" (McDermott 1998: 92).

7 According to Stuart Hall, Gramsci drew a distinction "between two types of struggle— the 'war of manoeuvre,' where everything is condensed into one front [e.g., the single Women's Studies department] and there is a single, strategic breach in the 'enemy's defenses' [allowing for] a definitive (strategic) victory. Second, there is the 'war of position,' which has to be conducted in a protracted way, across many different and varying fronts of struggle." What really counts in a war of position is "the whole structure of society" and, to extend the metaphor, the whole structure of the university (Hall 1986: 17). See note 17 for an elaboration of Chow's analysis of Gramsci with respect to de Certeau.

8 Dale Bauer argues in this volume that such demands on Women's Studies scholars to

occupy multiple departmental homes often compounds the institutional denial of their second-shift of labor ("the nurturing, sustaining, fostering" of Women's Studies students), for which they are unrewarded and which the language of "care" and "feminist duty" often obscures. "The very language ascribed to Women's Studies is a language of academic 'service,'" she writes. Norma Alarcón characterizes the institution's expectations of ethnic studies scholars in a similar fashion: "[Ethnic studies] has been treated as a perpetual service department, pitting it, along with Women's Studies, and other interdisciplinary programs, against the 'major' or 'mainstream departments' and, in the process, treating them like 'maids, ranch hands, janitors, etc.,' who pick up or service the damages perpetrated upon minoritized students. Not only are we then obliged to pick up the damaged pieces, but it is simultaneously asked [of us that we] be 'intellectually vibrant in a highly competitive' elite institution" (Alarcón to ethnic studies faculty, letter, April 16, 1999, posted in the Internet news release, "Response to Last Week's Student Protests and Arrests: A Public Statement of Ethnic Studies Faculty at UC Berkeley," April 19, 1999, from L. Ling-chi Wang [http://www.aspenlinx.com/twlf/facultystatement.htm]). These accounts of multiple labors expected and unrewarded (insignificant in terms of tenure and promotion) attest to one of the material complications and further alienations that are exacerbated by a non-territorial institutional stature.

9   This enunciation of a Third World feminist consciousness as a celebratory mobile, flexible strategy contrasts strikingly with contemporary denunciations of mobility and flexibility as postindustrial capital's mode of choice (cf. Rouse 1995; Tadiar 1995). Although space constraints do not permit me to work through these affinities and contrasts here, the possibility that Sandoval's articulation of a differential consciousness might subtend or bespeak capitalist logic poses fertile ground for exploration. That is, Sandoval does not consider how mobility and multiplicity also can produce domination; how, if not the drive for truth, then the drive for surplus works preeminently through flexibility and extraterritoriality. In other words, mobile nonprivilege seeks a surplus not of territory and disciplinary power but of critical intervention, of surplus negativity or "elusive negativity" (Hayles 1991: 83).

10 Sandoval's depiction of women of color as mobile members of various liberation movements correlates to the (dis)location of UCLA's "women of color" course requirement in various sites outside Women's Studies, yet also ostensibly within Women's Studies. Echoing the point made in the introduction, by defining the "women of color" class as one of its three core or required courses for the major and simultaneously allowing the pursuit of this "core" requirement outside the confines of the program's sponsorship, Women's Studies extends the diversifying and metacritical importance of the "women of color" requirement with respect to the institution of Women's Studies. The metacritical function (the work of self-critique) is realized only when Women's Studies incorporates (moves to the inside) that which it has excluded—namely, the outside. Thus, the half-inside, half-outside location of the "women of color" requirement allows the operation of this metacritical exercise.

11 Countless critics have made exactly the point that women of color are continually posited, in syllabus construction and curriculum structure, as an omission that will

be rectified, rather than as a generative center for invigorating feminist analysis. Mohanty referred to this as "pivoting the center" (Mohanty 1991a: 2). Feminist analysis might be usefully engaged as first and foremost a response to First World anthropological scrutiny, to the collusion of patriarchies and colonial rules in the Third World, rather than first and foremost as an outgrowth of Enlightenment rights discourse or the civil-rights struggle in the 1960s.

12 At UCLA, the course series (WS10 "Introduction to Women's Studies"; WS110 "Feminist Theory"; WS130 "Women of Color"), through its very serial coding, plots out the postponement of women of color as a later (often upper-division) answer to the unwitting omissions of earlier introductory courses.

13 WS130 ("Women of Color in the U.S.") represents a particular crisis point for students who have come to the table learning that gender represents a centrally useful analytical paradigm. So why focus on race, too? Why take seriously the central critique made by women of color that feminism too strenuously privileges gender difference as the source of oppression (see Mohanty 1991b)? Or, as Alarcón puts it, "to acknowledge that 'one becomes a woman' [is a] much more complex [process] than . . . a simple opposition to men. . . . one may also 'become a woman' in opposition to other women" (1990: 360).

14 Foucauldian analyses of power, in Brown's articulation, might resolve the cycle of guilt and blame simply by sidestepping it. No longer will students be caught up in determinations of how one student has power over another or how certain social groups are ranked higher than others, as they will refocus their attention on power as multiple, unanalogous, simultaneously operating modalities that regulate and produce subjects. Susan Bordo characterizes this kind of articulation of Foucault as a misreading. In Foucault's reconstruction of power as "a dynamic of noncentralized forces, its dominant historical forms [attain] their hegemony, not from magisterial design or decree, but through multiple 'processes, of different origin and scattered location,' regulating and normalizing the most intimate and minute elements of the construction of time, space, desire, embodiment" (Bordo 1993: 260). Nevertheless, Bordo stresses that "this conception of power does not entail that there are no dominant positions, social structures, or ideologies emerging from the play of forces; the fact that power is not held by any one does not mean that it is equally held by all. It is in fact not 'held' at all; rather, people and groups are positioned differentially within it" (Bordo 1993: 261–62). See also Nancy Fraser's analysis of Foucault's ambivalent articulation of power as non-normative (refraining from setting up a moral anchor) yet also critical of liberal notions of power (Fraser 1989).

15 Although Brown's essay is still extremely valuable for its deconstruction of Women's Studies as itself an instantiation of an alternative but also a rescriptive regulatory modality, it is hampered by its covert romanticization of scholarship as mostly interrogative, or critically oppositional, and not as heavily regulatory (dogmatic, territorial) at the same time it "inquires."

16 The second essay by Susan Gubar has already been deconstructed and defended in several articles published in *Critical Inquiry* in 1998–99. See Gilbert 1999; Gubar 1998, 1999; Heilbrun 1999; and Wiegman 1999.

17 Chow draws from both Gramsci and de Certeau in her articulation of tactics versus strategies and the establishment of fields (Chow 1993: 15–17). Chow writes, "The notion of a 'field' is analogous to the notion of 'hegemony.' In Gramsci's sense, revolution is a struggle for hegemony between opposing classes. [Yet] I remain skeptical of the validity of hegemony over time" (Chow 1993: 16). Alluding to de Certeau, she advocates an alternative practice of working in the mode of "para-sites" (quasi-sites) rather than field maneuvers, a mode that refrains from "[taking] over a field in its entirety but [instead erodes] it slowly and tactically" (Chow 1993: 16). Although I find Chow's critical idioms useful to my argument—especially her distinction between "strategy [as belonging] to 'an economy of the proper place' and to those who are committed to the building, growth, and fortification of a 'field,'" versus a "tactic [which is] 'a calculated action determined by the absence of a proper locus'"—my specific position with regard to Women's Studies' current romance with institutional marginality differs somewhat from Chow's. She diagnoses correctly that "what academic intellectuals must confront is thus not their 'victimization' by society at large, but the power, wealth, and privilege that ironically accumulate from their 'oppositional' viewpoint" (Chow 1993: 17). However, following this analysis of marginality as a legitimizing mode (which I have referred to as the "seduction of non-territoriality"), Chow succumbs to this very desire to secure a non-territory or roving oppositional stance for intellectual inquiry: "How do we resist the turning-into-propriety of oppositional discourses, when the intention of such discourses has been that of displacing and disowning the proper? How do we prevent what begin as tactics—that which is 'without any base where it could stockpile its winnings'—from turning into a solidly fenced—off field, in the military no less than in the academic sense?" (Chow 1993: 17). I am less interested in how intellectuals can maintain their non-territoriality (and therefore their surplus of critical interventions) than with how the continuing investment in being without or outside a "field" leads both to Women's Studies' fetishization of "women of color" and to the overall neglect of "women of color" as itself a discourse in need of critique and deconstruction.

18 As my earlier characterization of Zinn and Dill's project indicates, these authors voice a healthy skepticism of the "women of color" label and do not expressly advocate an over-investment in "unity" as the mode of "women of color's" formation and narration. Rather, I want to underscore how Zinn and Dill's very language reveals their seduction by this potential "unity" as the justification for their collaboration. How radical would it be to form a collective that spoke primarily of distinctions and points of conflict? The seduction toward articulating "women of color" as unity is not Zinn and Dill's alone.

19 The generation of "women of color" scholarship and classes should be considered the project not of an individual but of a collective. However, institutionally, Women's Studies is approaching this as an individual problem and solution—some one woman of color will be the magic pill who cures the problems. As many others have pointed out, "women of color" is not a communal identity that has a singular native informant; rather, it is an invented coalition among women in disparate communities who might be unified in a shared context of struggle—even if that struggle is the invention

in the classroom of a body of works and enunciations named "women of color." There are pitfalls to resolving the institutional void of women of color through one course, or even a conglomeration of courses, focused on a single ethnically or racially defined women's community. If the spirit of coalition is for several people from different communities and different ideologies to converge on a single issue, then women of color as the coalition we are interested in disseminating might be better established through a series of courses that are issue-based and that draw participation from women of various minority and colonized communities. This sort of work is uncomfortable; it is not nurturing, as Bernice Reagon (1983) suggests.

A better way to generate "women of color" classes would be to solicit a number of courses on women of color—and fund the development of such a new course series—and encourage collaboration in the drawing up of these course syllabi, lesson plans, and research agendas. And importantly, not all of those instructors need be or ought to be women of color themselves. The safe space or barred room—protected by the fetishization of colored bodies—might finally give way to a coalition united in the seriousness of its consideration of "women of color" scholarship and imparting that seriousness to its students. If, indeed, women of color is a coalitional ideal to which we are still aspiring, then it follows that one site of generating such coalitions might be in our Women's Studies departments.

20 Bordo discerns a disavowal of the female body specifically in the long history of Western philosophy's refining cognitive modes through an increasing detachment from the body, figured as "impediment to objectivity" and a "heavy drag on self-realization" (Bordo 1993: 1–5).

The Progress of Gender: Whither "Women"?

In "Women's Studies on the Edge," a special issue of *differences,* Leora Auslander (1997) opens the volume by thinking about the composite intellectual projects that today coalesce under the framework of gender. Her essay, "Do Women's + Feminist + Men's + Lesbian and Gay + Queer Studies = Gender Studies?" offers an affirmative answer to the central question its title poses, finding in the move from Women's Studies to gender studies an intellectual expansion and revisioning of feminist objects of study "in which the study of masculinity, feminist gender studies, and gay, lesbian, and queer studies each have an equal voice" (Auslander 1997: 25). Positioned as the volume's optimistic answer to the dystopic diagnosis in one of its concluding essays, Wendy Brown's controversial "The Impossibility of Women's Studies," Auslander's keynote provides a kind of assurance that the edge can become an intellectually cutting one when gender rescues the field from a faulty *women.*

I am interested in the rhetorical gesture of inclusion, of "equal voice" that inaugurates and accompanies the move to gender studies, especially in those institutional domains that are contemplating or have recently changed their name from Women's Studies.[1] While Auslander's Center for Gender Studies at the University of Chicago never supplanted a Women's Studies program (because one never existed), more often than not the question of *gender*'s categorical function emerges in the context of heated debate about Women's Studies and its proper objects of study. At my former institution, the University of California-Irvine, which is the only Anglo-minority campus in a nine-campus system, however, *gender* was never able to withhold critique long enough to become the figure to undo *women*'s problematic heritage, in part because the significatory chain it enacts might be said to begin in a tacit subordination of race, class, and nation. *Gender* in this view signaled its own version of *women*'s categorical failure—a failure that becomes most legible when the analytic frame is widened to challenge the ideal that *women* so powerfully created: that field formations and their objects of study are one.

This chapter poses a number of questions about the expectations and ideals that seem to govern contemporary feminism's desire to settle the problematic of identity on which its institutional knowledge formation is founded. Most broadly, I ask: What generates our search for a consistent, non-contradictory sign to organize the many intellectual genealogies about bodies, identities, sex, gender, and both racial and economic difference that have come to exist uncomfortably and without identitarian coherency within the institutional domain first named Women's Studies? My exploration of this question is motivated less by the desire to retrieve or lament the potential loss of the category of *women* than to consider why feminism would want, in this era of the disestablishment of affirmative action, to concede the ground of *women* as analytically singular, if not altogether insular—and further, why we would willingly produce it as the site of a past "error" that can be righted by *gender,* as if *gender* will be immune to the kinds of exclusions and omissions we have found attached to *women.* It seems to me, in fact, that the move from *women* to *gender* does not displace the problematic of identity that *women* is said to represent. Rather, it mimics that problematic, which is to say that while *gender* may appear to be more intellectually capacious than *women,* it will ultimately fail to fulfill the demand for representational comprehensiveness as well. This is the case in part because of the way that identity objects of study disassemble in their transposition from political gestures and representations of social bodies to critical targets of an intellectual domain. My critique is aimed, then, at interrupting the demand for referential coherence in order to define the impossibility of coherence as the central problematic and most important animating feature of feminism as a knowledge formation in the contemporary academy.

To arrive at these issues, I trace the theoretical conversations that have functioned to give *gender* its critical mobility, paying attention to the emergence of men and masculinity as objects of study in three trajectories of feminist analysis. The first identifies how questions of differences among women, especially racial differences, compelled a rearticulation of feminism's hegemonic understanding of gender, making legible how difficult are such overarching concepts as "women's oppression" and "patriarchy" as precise terms for social worlds that operate along multiple axes of power and difference.[2] By focusing on the transition from identity as the favored ground for feminist critical vocabularies to difference, I demonstrate how critical interest in inequalities among men has advanced feminist theoretical understanding of the structure and ideological function of "male bonding" on one hand and the production of alternative masculinities on the other. The second trajectory takes up the poststructuralist challenge to the category of women in order to define how the broad critique of identity as a coherent referent for feminism has worked to reconfigure normative assumptions about the relationship between sex and gender. This reconfiguration has profoundly challenged ideals of corporeality as gender's natural domain of truth, making possible considerations of gender's performativity apart from the normative mapping of bodies, identities, and desire. In the third trajectory, the poststructuralist critique is taken to its critical extreme as masculinity and men are severed altogether in order to generate attention to female masculinity, transsexuality, and the politically activist theorizing on intersexuality. These critical domains not only raise issues about the structure and performance of gender identifications irreducible to the body as determinant sex; they also install a series of new identities as crucial sites of study for feminist scholars.

In tracking the theoretical elaboration of men and masculinity as objects of study, this essay demonstrates how feminism's critical interrogations of gender have productively disassembled the normative cultural discourse that weds masculinity to men and thinks about women only in the register of the feminine. Such "unmaking" of the category of men importantly remakes masculinity as pertinent to, if not constitutive of, female subjectivity, thereby rendering complex feminism's ability to negotiate the distinctions and interconnections among sex, sexuality, and gender. Given such critical possibility, why would anyone hesitate to redefine feminism's institutional domain under the sign of *gender*? My answer to this question takes shape in the essay's final section, where I return to the problem of representational coherence to consider how feminism as a knowledge project can never fulfill the demand to do justice to identity, its animating object of study.

Feminism's Mal(e)contents

Although Auslander cites *gender* as a term that suspends "the problems with the category of 'woman,' " she also points to the way in which it productively registers "the fact that men qua men . . . [are] legitimate and important subject[s] of research for feminist scholars" (Auslander 1997: 7).[3] The transformation characterized here is an importantly new one, and it is not an overstatement to suggest that one of the most proliferate areas of feminist inquiry in the 1990s has been the study of men and masculinity. Such proliferation does not mean, however, that men and masculinity have never elicited critical or cultural commentary. But compared with the endless speculation that has accompanied the seemingly enigmatic feminine, masculinity has most often existed as though its construction and social function were transparent—indeed, quite simple and commonplace. What we understand today about the history of masculinity's critical and cultural commentary arises more as an effect of the way knowledge has been produced than as a consequence of its articulation as a necessary object of investigation. The English literary canon, traditional history: These arenas have taught us a great deal about the relationship of men to masculinity, but only as evidence of the male body's abstraction into the normative domain of the universal where, shielded by humanism, both specificity and diversity are lost in the generic function of "man." To remove the generic fallacy, to unveil masculinity as a particularized ontology linked to a normative rendering of the male body, has been the task that feminism since the mid-1980s has been pursuing as a necessary political intervention.

Such an undertaking has not been without anxiety, as those familiar with contemporary critical discussions about men and masculinity well know. The turn toward examining masculinity has brought pressure to bear on a variety of earlier feminist assumptions. In the first, heady decade of the contemporary women's movement, for instance, men and masculinity tended to be melded together in a normative reiteration of the sex-gender equation and functioned as the foundational identity form for understanding such concepts as "patriarchy" and "women's oppression." By collapsing men and masculinity into a generalized category of "man" and wedding that generalization to the organizational practices and privileges of patriarchy, much feminist critical analysis relied on what seemed to many scholars and activists an unproblematic linkage among maleness, masculinity, and the social order of masculine supremacy. Although this linkage is legible today as the site of a certain kind of critical incomprehension concerning the complexity of power, it enabled feminist discourse to posit a political subjectivity for women that seemingly disrupted the sexual arena of women's primary social bonding: the heterosexual. By bringing into question women's allegiances to men as products of heterosexuality's compulsory production, feminism made imperative political solidarity among women. Thus, sisterhood became powerful, and the personal, in its multiple aspects of the everyday, took on a decidedly political signification.

As we all know, however, this utopian narrative of identitarian collectivity is itself a site of contestation as both concrete political struggle and the recognition of women's differences in power and privilege have combined throughout the "second wave" of feminist movement to undermine the saliency of *women* as a coherent identity project. For this reason, our narrative of second-wave origins might more accurately say that, although identity served at times productively to isolate woman's difference from man and to generate a collective identification in the face of that difference, the imperative toward differences among women—the race, class, national, and sexual dynamics of women's engendering—has from the outset unsettled any easy collapse of *women* into a monolithic or unified construction.[4] For some feminist thinkers, the concept of men as the common enemy was never an adequate explanatory framework, as it obviated the way in which women's political solidarities quite often transgressed the identitarian logics of gender. As feminists of color have routinely discussed, a monolithic understanding of man avoids the violent and discriminatory implications of white racial supremacy, displacing both white women's complicity with men of their own racial group and antiracist bonding across gender among the disfranchised.[5] Because all men do not share equal masculine rights and privileges—because some men are, in fact, oppressed by women of the prevailing race and class—assumptions about power as uniformly based on sexual difference (men as oppressor, women as oppressed) have long been under pressure to give way.

One of the most important expressions in the 1970s of how an examination of the social position of women of color rearticulates the status of men within a feminist theoretical framework was the Combahee River Collective's "A Black Feminist Statement." Founded in 1974, the collective wrote its statement in 1977 in order to establish "as our particular task the development of integrated analysis and practice based upon the fact that the major systems of oppression are interlocking" (Combahee River Collective 1982: 13). Dedicated then to what we would later call "intersectional" analysis, the collective explicitly explained the political relationship between black women and men: "Although we are feminists and lesbians, we feel solidarity with progressive Black men and do not advocate the fractionalization that white women who are separatists demand. Our situation as Black people necessitates that we have solidarity around the fact of race. We struggle together with Black men against racism, while we also struggle with Black men about sexism" (Combahee River Collective 1982: 16). What remains striking today about this passage is the "although" that opens it, which demonstrates how overwritten were the categories of feminist and lesbian by the force of a foundational and oppositional sexual difference, one that seemed to preempt the work of affiliation and collectivity across lines other than those of gender.[6] By drawing out the implications of an analysis of women's differences from one another in the context of socialist feminism's attention to race and class, the collective identified how the category of men could not be monolithically rendered. As other black feminists—bell hooks, Michele Wallace, Audre Lorde, and Angela Davis—added their critical analysis of the complexity of social-power arrangements to the feminist theoretical archive, the study of men and masculinity was disarticulated from its status as patriarchal business-as-usual.

My training in graduate school in the 1980s was drawn quite heavily toward the theoretical and political project of understanding differences among women, which led me (to my own surprise) to write a dissertation about men. As a feminist project, the dissertation was not fully legible to everyone on my committee, and indeed I felt a great deal of anxiety about the political consequences of its focus. What was a feminist project that didn't take women as its object of study? How could feminist theory find some kind of critical future in the study of men? These questions were made all the more urgent by the end of the decade, when conference presentations and articles began appearing that quite forcefully critiqued feminist interest in studying masculinity because of the way it seemed to reproduce the centrality of "man" against which Women's Studies as a broad, interdisciplinary field had long defined itself. Although various scholars were concerned both before and after 1991 about the implications of masculinity studies (and many remain so today), it was Tania Modleski's *Feminism Without Women: Culture and Criticism in a "Post-feminist" Age* (1991) that brought such anxieties to center stage. For Modleski, the turn toward masculinity studies in general, and the inclusion of men as critics of and speakers for feminism in particular, evinced a triumph "of a male feminist perspective that excludes women" (Modleski 1991: 14), thus returning critical practice to a "pre-feminist world" (Modleski 1991: 3) where women could be politically recontained within the masculine universalism that constituted every tradition of knowledge production in the humanities. As her title charged, any feminism that articulated itself without women as both subject and object—as knower and the category to be known—had acquiesced to the conservative political project of the 1980s, which succeeded, thanks to the nationalist masculinity of both Ronald Reagan and George Bush, in rendering "feminism" a very dirty word. The "post-feminism" that Modleski hoped both to diagnose and combat needed, in politically strategic and ideologically pointed terms, *women*.

Although *Feminism Without Women* took its urgency from the transformations in the popular public sphere that had indeed changed, radically, the conditions under which feminism (like other leftist discourses that proliferated in the 1960s) operated, Modleski identified the academic recuperation of feminism via masculinity studies as a consequence of theoretical shifts, as well—namely, poststructuralism's anti-humanist approaches to identity, experience, and subjectivity. The post-feminist formation that she critiqued in the study of masculinity was not, then, a consequence of the genealogy of analysis put into play by black feminism; it was instead the effect of feminist "intercourse" with French intellectual culture. From Judith Butler to Donna Haraway to Denise Riley, Modleski cited the critique of the subject and its attendant interrogation of the category of woman as a massive rejection by feminists of feminism's political imperative.[7] Lamenting that "every use of the term 'woman,' however 'provisionally' it is adopted, is [now] disallowed" (Modleski 1991: 14), Modleski argued for a non-essentialist, though identity-grounded, epistemology, a category of "women's experience" that could serve as locus for both political organization and "a sense of solidarity, commonality, and community" (Modleski 1991: 17). Without this epistemological assurance, Modleski wrote, "it is easy to see how a "man" can be a 'woman'" (Modleski 1991: 15), which is to say that it was easy to see how an anti-essentialist deconstructive move could banish the material implications of living in a body defined as *woman,* and hence how women within feminism could entirely disappear.[8] Thus indicting both male and female scholars for abandoning feminism's political project of doing justice to and for women, Modleski cast the study of men and masculinity as a theoretically driven appropriation, if not displacement, of feminist political struggle.[9]

If a decade of scholarship unsettles Modleski's argument by defining masculinity studies within and not against feminism as an intellectual and political project, it should not be assumed that Modleski's anxieties have disappeared from the critical scene or, further, that we have nothing to learn either from such anxieties or from her book. From the vantage point of nearly a decade later, we might interpret Modleski's work as an attempt to slow the commodification of feminist knowledge that accelerated at the end of the 1980s and defined whole field imaginaries as critical arenas of the past tense. She wanted, it seems to me, to stay put for a while longer with the problematic of differences among women, in part because the various critical moves that had transformed feminism's theoretical imperative from identity to difference had assumed that identity and difference were so antithetical that no subjective affiliation or critical transportation could occur between them. It is this, finally, that a great deal of critique about masculinity studies a decade ago seems symptomatically to speak: a desire to forge identification and political solidarity not to the exclusion of women's differences, but from within them—and hence from within those very contradictions that had animated *women* as the referent, no matter how troubled, for feminism. How this desire works itself out in the context of the institutional domain of Women's Studies will be part of my closing comments, but for now it is important to stress that Modleski was not alone in assuming that a critical intimacy between women and feminism provided the immunity necessary to resist patriarchal appropriations and recuperations. For her as for others, *women* as an object of critical analysis was what differentiated feminism from its foe and thereby guaranteed feminism's political effectiveness.

While Modleski sounded a powerful warning about the dangers she saw in the burgeoning rise of masculinity studies and of a male feminism that "banishes women," she tried in her introduction "to make it clear that I do not consider [the dangers] to comprise the whole picture" (Modleski 1991: 12, 11).[10] She thus turned, as have many feminist critics, to the work of Eve Kosofsky Sedgwick, whose 1985 *Between Men: English Literature and Male Homosocial Desire* not only extended feminist analysis by partaking in an important deconstructive move that gave both legibility and critical complexity to the dominant term of gender's powerful binary, but did so in the context of linking feminism to anti-homophobic critique. Modleski praised *Between Men* for "making feminists sensitive to issues of homophobia and making gay men aware of how constructions of homosexuality intersect with misogynist constructions of femininity," even as she felt obliged to criticize Sedgwick's inattention to the lesbian as a lurking postfeminist danger (Modleski 1991: 12).[11] In her acknowledgment of Sedgwick, Modleski recognized gay studies (and what would later be called, via Sedgwick, queer theory) as one of the most important analytic trajectories of masculinity studies to be developed in the 1980s.

Between Men worked in tandem with Gayle Rubin's controversial essay "Thinking Sex: Notes for a Radical Theory of the Politics of Sexuality" (1984) to forge a series of important deliberations on terms that had rather loose interchangeability in feminist studies: gender, sex, and sexuality. Interestingly, it was Rubin who had written in 1975 the foundational essay, "The Traffic in Women: Notes on the 'Political Economy' of Sex," that had cogently articulated the relation between sex and gender as a systemic one. As Sedgwick would later describe it, Rubin defined "the system by which chromosomal sex is turned into, and processed as, cultural gender," a strategy that yielded "analytic and critical leverage on the female-disadvantaging social arrangements that prevail[ed] at a given time in a given society, by throwing into question their legitimating ideological grounding in biologically based narratives of the 'natural' " (Sedgwick 1992: 274) Rubin's critical intervention was a de-essentializing one, giving anthropological weight to the analysis of cultural practices and providing feminist theory with a distinct and powerful way to ward off simple biological determinism.[12] Rubin's social analysis superceded the "nature-nurture" framework of analysis that held biology and culture in a dynamic tension by yielding primary analytic power to the "nurture" side of the equation. By wrenching the authority of sexual difference from the supposed natural domain of the body to the realm of the socio-cultural, Rubin's sex-gender distinction has profoundly affected nearly two decades of critical analysis by providing a theoretical perspective for a host of interconnections between the power arrangements of sexuality and gender.

In *Between Men*, which Naomi Schor has called the inaugural text in the "rise of gender studies" (Schor 1992: 276), Sedgwick used Rubin to interrogate thoroughly, to brilliant effect, the power dynamics of the erotic triangle of two men and one woman found throughout British literature (from Shakespeare to the English readers of Walt Whitman). As Sedgwick described it, Rubin's early essay revealed how "patriarchal heterosexuality can best be discussed in terms of one or another form of the traffic in women: it is the use of women as exchangeable, perhaps symbolic, property for the primary purpose of cementing the bonds of men with men" (Sedgwick 1985: 26). By linking the traffic in women to the homophobic injunction against male-to-male sex, Sedgwick's text transformed the kinds of questions feminist theory thought to ask not only about patriarchy as a historical organization of masculine supremacy, but about male sexuality in both its hetero and homosexual dimensions. In particular, *Between Men* returned issues of genital sexuality among men to the critical understanding of patriarchy as a structure of masculine bonds, challenging the important, but in Sedgwick's words "expensive leap of register" (1985: 26) that accompanied Luce Irigaray's formulation: "The exchanges upon which patriarchal societies are based take place exclusively among men. . . . This means that the *very possibility of a sociocultural order requires homosexuality* as its organizing principle. Heterosexuality is nothing but the assignment of economic roles" (Irigaray 1985a: 12). For Sedgwick, "the quicksilver of sex itself" was critical to thinking historically about the male "homosocial continuum" that structured patriarchal organization (1985: 26). Although for the ancients this continuum functioned without injunction to articulate sex between men as a part of the pedagogical instruction of class based gender privilege— activities that consolidated male bonds and normative masculinity—the violent homophobia of contemporary Western culture was quite clearly another story. And it was that story, as one deeply entangled with feminist aspirations to understand interconnected discriminatory structures, that interested Sedgwick. "The importance of women . . . in the etiology and the continuing experience of male homosexuality seems to be historically volatile (across time, across class). . . . Its changes are inextricable from the changing shapes of the institutions by which gender and class inequality are structured" (Sedgwick 1985: 26–27).

Sedgwick's historicist approach to the issue of male bonds revealed some of the ways in which both patriarchy and masculinity had been discussed and analyzed throughout humanistic-based feminist inquiry in a metaphoric register that collapsed both cultural and temporal distinctions. Where Irigaray and others read the realm of the masculine as an "economy of the same" and posited women as outside the symbolic orbit of male relations, Sedgwick simultaneously facilitated and came to represent a turn toward the ruptures, contradictions, and inconsistencies that had to be repressed, negotiated, or violently eradicated in the continual process of constituting and extending patriarchal power. More dissertations than mine were written under the auspices of this attention to differences among men, and it is striking that, although *Between Men* took class and sexuality as the main determinants for understanding the historical function and structure of gender, the author recognized in her introduction how powerful her analysis would be for interrogations into race and masculinity in U.S. culture. Turning briefly to Margaret Mitchell's *Gone With the Wind,* Sedgwick compared the two "rape" scenes in the novel—one by the black man seeking money he was told was hidden in Scarlet's bosom; the other the blissful marital moment of Scarlett and Rhett's union—in order to argue against the categorical deployment of rape in U.S. feminism as a crime against women and tool of patriarchal domination.[13] "To assume that sex signifies power in a flat, unvarying relation of metaphor or synecdoche will always entail a blindness," she wrote, "not to the rhetorical and pyrotechnic, but to such historical categories as class and race" (Sedgwick 1985: 10–11). Calling then for "more different, more complicated, more diachronically apt, more off-centered . . . applications of our present understanding of what it may mean for one thing to signify another," Sedgwick challenged the dominant imaginary of feminism not simply to think its own historicity, but to rethink most seriously a great deal of what it assumed it already knew (Sedgwick 1985: 11).

Susan Jeffords extended Sedgwick's intervention into feminist understanding of patriarchal social formation in general, and male bonds in particular, in 1989 by considering the prolific figure of the Vietnam veteran that had dominated U.S. popular culture throughout the 1980s. Taking film, television, cultural history, and contemporary fiction as its objects of analysis, *The Remasculinization of America: Gender and the Vietnam War* (1989) studied how these texts stressed, in a compulsive fashion, the significance of masculine bonds as the ideological counter to the feminizing influences of both a corrupt, betraying government (the United States) and an enemy (the Vietcong) who refused to fight, in Western parlance, "like a man." For Jeffords, these representational formulations established differences between men and women as the necessary precondition for defining and celebrating a commonality of gender among men. "The masculine bond," she wrote, "insists on a denial of difference—whether black or white, wealthy or poor, high school or college-educated, from north or south, men are the 'same'—at the same time that the bond itself depends for its existence on an affirmation of difference—men are not women" (Jeffords 1989: 59–60). Jeffords understood the postwar reassertion of a mythic masculine bond not only as a strategy for reinvigorating the national imaginary in the aftermath of the loss of the war, but also as a response to the feminist, civil-rights, and gay-rights struggles that forcefully criticized the exclusionary practices on which traditional structures of power had long depended.[14] Her interest in the male bond was thus in its function as a scene for the negotiation—indeed, celebration—of masculine sameness in the face of a variety of potentially disrupting differences (race, sexuality, and class, as well as gender).

In linking her project to *Between Men,* Jeffords reiterated in the context of a different century and in texts widely disparate from the canonical British tradition, the theoretical paradigm Sedgwick had witnessed in *The Country Wife:* "Men's heterosexual relationships . . . have as their raison d'etre an ultimate bonding between men . . . [which] if successfully achieved, is not detrimental to 'masculinity' but definitive of it" (1985: 50). Because the so-called theater of war functions in modern technological cultures as the primary scene of masculinity's hegemonic performance, Jeffords's investigation simultaneously situated the homosocial prominently within the national imaginary and detailed the ways in which popular culture by the end of the twentieth century functioned as the symptomatic domain for the production of masculinity as spectacle. In the proliferation of this spectacle—that is, in its incessant visuality—

Jeffords culled a vocabulary for thinking not only about crucial distinctions between patriarchy and masculinity, but also about the historically specific structural relationships between gendered discourses and social differences among men. As she remarks in the closing pages of her study,

> It is methodologically important to maintain a distinction between patriarchy and masculinity. Masculinity is the primary mechanism for the articulation, institutionalization, and maintenance of the gendered system on which patriarchy is based. The structural expression of patriarchal interests takes place through . . . the masculine point of view, distinct from masculinity in that it marks specific males as expendable in order to maintain the larger frame of masculine narration. . . . Although masculinity is by far the category of privilege within patriarchy . . . [it is] manipulated by other interests [race, sexuality, class] than those defined by gender. For this reason, an examination of masculinity, not as a direct oppressor of women, but as a category of definition itself is important to any feminist understanding of the operations of patriarchy. (Jeffords 1989: 181)

For Jeffords, then, as for Sedgwick, a feminist "analysis of the patriarchal system [limited solely] to relations between men and women . . . overlook[ed] much of its force" (Jeffords 1989: xii).

In hoping to pry apart masculinity and patriarchy as conceptual terms in the context of Vietnam War narration, Jeffords encountered a certain resistance in her objects of analysis that seemed to propel the analytic gaze away from those differences repressed by the homosocial bond and toward the mechanisms of their recuperation and hegemonic recontainment, as her study's signal term "remasculinization" would suggest. Other scholarship in the late 1980s and early 1990s would move, analytically, in the opposite direction, finding in the figure of a multiple object of study—masculinities—a way to fracture productively the consolidation of male bonds that underwrote patriarchal investments in sexual difference. Important studies of masculinities thus focused on the sexuality, race, and class differences that unsettled the ideological destination of homosocial bonding, hailing men not into a monolithic vision of essential sexual difference but toward contrary intellectual and political claims.[15] In *Slow Motion: Changing Masculinities, Changing Men* (1990), for instance, Lynne Segal sought to plumb the disparity between being male and being normatively masculine by focusing on what she called "competing masculinities." As she explained, "by looking not at 'masculinity' as such, but at certain specific '*masculinities*', it is . . . *differences* between men which [become] central to the struggle for change" (Segal 1990: x).

Taken together, the critical projects by Sedgwick, Jeffords, and Segal are important indices of the ways in which the study of men and masculinity has developed from Rubin's early intervention into the normative naturalization of sex as gender. As the forgoing discussion should suggest, the focus on the male bond has deepened feminist critical understanding of the way in which patriarchal investments are reproduced not only in the management of erotic and intimate life but also in the spheres of popular culture and national politics. In reading the dynamics of power in these realms, scholars draw our attention to the constructedness of masculinity and its complex dependence on discourses of sexual difference (sometimes with and sometimes without the figure of woman), thereby making visible and theoretically credible the analysis of the constitutional performativity of a variety of masculinities, from dominant heterosexual formations to more subversive gay, black, or antisexist articulations. The seeming naturalness of adult masculinity—heterosexuality, fatherhood, family governance, soldiery, and citizenry—can thus be viewed as a set of prescriptive norms that contain potential contradictions within and between men. These norms repress the male subject's constitution along multiple lines of the social: race, class, and sexuality in addition to gender. In unleashing masculinity from its assumed normativity and reading its function and structure as the product of a contested and contradictory field of power, a great deal of feminist work in masculinity studies has been motivated by the desire to intervene in the practices of patriarchal domination while locating the possibilities for men to challenge their constitution as men. That much of this challenge begins in a rethinking of the patriarchal structure of homosocial relations—what by shorthand we now call the male bond—is hardly a surprise, given the profound impact of feminist theoretical concern with the patriarchal "traffic in women" and its own utopic imagining of women's political bonding with one another.

Masculinity Without Men

Careful readers will note that my discussion of the fracturing of the monolithic understanding of the category of men and of the male bond in the previous section mentioned without adequate commentary Rubin's important essay "Thinking Sex" (1984). Although we might think of it as a piece historically akin to Sedgwick's *Between Men*, published a year later, its significance in this discussion of masculinity inaugurates what I consider a different line of critical investigation, one that disarticulates the feminist imperative to link gender and sexuality that had been a consistent call in lesbian feminist discourses since the early 1960s. For Rubin, the dominant discourse in feminism by the end of the 1970s concerning sexuality—by which she meant sex acts and activities—was so heavily prohibitive as to make feminism resemble a sexual temperance movement. In its anti-pornography and anti-lesbian s/m discourses, feminism was courting the state, quite literally, in order to resolve forms of discrimination and violence that sexuality as a realm not of pleasure but of coercion had come to represent. Rubin's essay, still one of the most controversial statements against sexual prohibition in the feminist archive, challenged the movement's conceptions not of sexual difference per se but of sex itself, forcing a reconsideration of feminism's understanding of the political struggles of various sexual minorities: homosexuals, prostitutes, sadomasochists, transvestites, pederasts, and onanists. Revising her theoretical stance in "The Traffic in Women," Rubin now argued "that it is essential to separate gender and sexuality analytically," to see them "as two distinct arenas of social practice" (1984: 33). Most crucially, she asserted that "feminist thought simply lacks angles of vision which can fully encompass the social organization of sexuality" (Rubin 1984: 34).

Rubin's position, as she would explain it to Judith Butler in a 1994 interview, was not a rejection of feminism per se; nor was it a claim that gender and sexuality should have no analytic traffic. Rather, it was a studied response to the increasing moralism and desexualization of critical analysis within the dominant imaginary of feminism in the 1970s, where even sexual relationships between women had been cast outside a sexual register as "woman identification," and every act of non-normative sexual behavior was interpreted as part of the system maintaining women's subordination. "I looked at sex 'deviants,'" she explained, "and frankly they didn't strike me as the apotheosis of patriarchy" (Rubin 1994: 78).[16] Rubin's desire to make sex, in analytical terms, a domain of practices and to think about how specific practices have been historically cast in juridical terms as deviant identities (as in the cases of homosexuality, prostitution, transsexualism, fetishism, and sadomasochism) opened a productive wedge between acts and identities that would enable greater critical commentary about not only feminism's own "abjected" categories but the definitional relationship between what bodies do and what bodies are. By interrupting the normative emplotment of the relationship among bodies, acts, and identities, a whole range of scholarly investigation has emerged to rethink desires, identifications, and psychic formations that, although not articulated directly under the banner of masculinity studies, have nevertheless made possible the trajectory of inquiry described by this section's title: masculinity without men. This domain is epitomized by queer theory's poststructuralist critique of identity's coherence, intersex activism and criticism, transsexual theory and political criticism, and deliberations on butch-femme, drag kings, and "female masculinity," to use Judith Halberstam's (1998) term.

Each of these arenas is critically inaugurated by a certain refusal to accede to the domain of the biological as the prior condition for gender's construction, as the "natural" material on which gender dimorphically depends. No text is more famous for making this point than Butler's *Gender Trouble: Feminism and the Subversion of Identity* (1990), which argued that while the idea of a male or female body functions as gender's seemingly neutral sexed referent, it can do so as only a consequence of the ideological structure of sexual difference. Hence, gender—as the name we give to the social apparatus that produces and maintains various kinds of sexual divisions—provides the conceptual framework for rendering the body biologically determinant. "Sex itself is a gendered category," Butler wrote, thereby defining "sex" not as gender's necessary precondition, but as one of gender's most powerful effects (1990: 7). In this, she reconfigured Rubin's argument in "The Traffic in Women" while challenging feminist scholarship that used a corporeal logic to define woman's difference from man.

Although so much critical memory of *Gender Trouble* has involved Butler's use of gay male drag as an example of what she defined as the constitutive performativity of gender, she actually devoted more pages to a figure far more important to her argument: the hermaphrodite in *Herculine Barbin, Being the Recently Discovered Memoirs of a Nineteenth Century Hermaphrodite* (Foucault 1980). Butler's discussion of Barbin, which focused on the seeming referential realness of what Sandy Stone has called "genetic" gender (1991: 294), was crucial to *Gender Trouble*'s analysis of the heterosexual regulatory strategies that normatively align sex, gender, and sexuality.[17] The intersexuality of Barbin's genitals and her/his passage in the course of a truncated lifetime through the categorical designations of both male and female challenged any definitive account of the trajectory of sexual desire—was she/he homosexual or heterosexual, seemingly "normal" or sexually "deviant"? The failure of gender identity to be mapped back onto the body, and for the body to function as gender's founding alibi, gave Butler one way, among many explored in *Gender Trouble*, to conclude that "gender ought not to be construed as a stable identity or locus of agency from which various acts follow; rather, gender is an identity tenuously constituted in time, instituted in an exterior space through a *stylized repetition of acts*. . . . This formulation moves the conception of gender off the ground of a substantial model of identity to one that requires a conception of gender as a constituted social temporality" (Butler 1990: 140–41).

In turning to Barbin, Butler was staging an argument with Foucault, whose editorial introduction to Barbin's autobiography strove to figure the hermaphrodite as outside the law precisely because of the body's failure to conform to the law's regulatory schema of dimorphic sex. More recent work on intersexuality returns, sometimes only implicitly, to Foucault's earlier work on the establishment of the clinic and prison, where he traced the production and productivity of medical-juridical discourses as disciplinary regimes that normalized and made bodies docile. In "Hermaphrodites with Attitude: Mapping the Emergence of Intersex Political Activism," Cheryl Chase (1998) documents the development in the twentieth century of intensive medical intervention into intersex births, detailing how a culture of experts has emerged to manage what is deemed a "medical crisis." This crisis necessitates swift action, often days after birth, in order to prevent the intersexed individual from knowing about her/his bodily history. Chase, who has been assigned at different times to both categories of dimorphic sex, questions not only the cultural invisibility of intersexed people but also the profound structure of medically sanctioned silence and secrecy that functions to eradicate the very possibility of intersex subjectivity. "We as a culture have relinquished to medicine the authority to police the boundaries of male and female, leaving intersexuals to recover as best they can, alone and silent, from violent normalization" (Chase 1998: 193). As a counter to this disciplinary tactic, Chase's essay also provides an important theoretical account of the recent emergence of "intersex people [who] have begun to politicize intersex identities, thus transforming intensely personal experiences of violation into collective opposition to the medical regulation of bodies that queer the foundations of heteronormative identifications and desires" (Chase 1998: 189). Intersex theory and activism thus draws its critical edge from a refusal to assent to the invasive maneuvers of medical science where the consolidation of the ideology of gender functions to inscribe dimorphic sex onto bodies and subjectivities in the violently ironic hope of returning such bodies to "nature."

This refusal, which seeks not only to instantiate ambiguity in the relationship between sex and gender, but also to establish as a political project the intersexed subject's own authority in the decision to be "remade" (or not) in the image of categorical completeness, has important parallels with Stone's foundational work in transsexual theory, "The *Empire* Strikes Back: A Posttranssexual Manifesto" (1991). As Stone's title begins to demonstrates, the "posting" of the transsexual reveals a political imperative to refuse the transposition of one unambiguous sex for another. By arguing against the social injunction for transsexuals to "pass," to render their interruption into the naturalized regulations of bodies and identities invisible, Stone calls for "a political action begun by reappropriating difference and reclaiming the power of the refigured and reinscribed body" (Stone 1991: 298–99). Here, as Stone puts it, "on the gender borders at the close of the twentieth century, with the faltering of phallocratic hegemony and the bumptious appearance of heteroglossic origin accounts," the possibility of speaking "beyond the constructed oppositional nodes which have been predefined as the only positions from which discourse is possible" begins (Stone 1991: 294–95).[18] In the theoretical archive of intersexuality and transsexuality, with their differing political and historical genealogies on one hand and their complex relationship to medical practices and knowledges on the other, we encounter a powerful rearticulation of the meaning of the sexed body and those regulatory discourses, including feminism, that have utilized genetic normativity to stabilize not only identity based social struggle but theoretical understandings of sex and gender.

This is not to say that the move to destabilize sex, whether medically managed or not, is always disruptive of the cultural imperative to return the body to a discourse of nature (even, perhaps especially, if the truth of nature is "made" by science). Nor am I suggesting that feminism as a critical discourse and set of cultural and political practices is the "other" against which a rigorous constructionist analysis of the body must always proceed. Certainly, Stone's work emerges from within the feminist theoretical archive. As much as it critiques some feminist critics' tendency to read the male-to-female transsexual (MTF) as an inauthentic woman, it also sets forth an important understanding, found elsewhere in feminist thought, that gives priority to the complexity of identification and offers productive thinking toward constructing a more nuanced feminist understanding of how affiliations toward and against "genetic" bodies shapes a wide variety of transgender identities.[19] This is the point, it seems to me, of Rubin's examination of the diversity of gender within lesbian identity formation. In "Of Catamites and Kings: Reflections on Butch, Gender, and Boundaries" (1992), she traces the way in which lesbian feminism had invested in the figure of a masculine butch while simultaneously denigrating the female-to-male transsexual (FTM) as a disloyal woman. While citing significant differences between FTMs and butches, Rubin argued that the boundaries between these transgender identities were in fact quite permeable. "Many of the passing women and diesel butches so venerated as lesbian ancestors are also claimed in the historical lineages of female-to-male transsexuals," wrote Rubin (1992: 473). And yet, in lesbian communities, "female-to-male transsexuals [are often treated] as treasonous deserters. . . . A woman who has been respected, admired, and loved as a butch may suddenly be despised, rejected, and hounded when she starts a sex change" (Rubin 1992: 474–75).[20] Thus defining U.S. lesbian culture's historical investment in celebrating a variety of transgender identifications, Rubin revealed how tense and contradictory was the value placed on masculinity as a lesbian attribute. In the context of the material she analyzed in this essay, the diversity of lesbian gender identity was itself made possible by an anxious relationship to genetic bodies and gender performances and the ideological distinction that in the 1970s had been erected between the two.

Although Rubin's essay was notable as a lesbian feminist criticism for its desire to refuse genetic sex as the precondition for licensing either gender's performative display or feminism's political project, her text was constrained by the linguistic divide that governs the lesbian butch, on one hand, and the FTM on the other—the transformation in self and social identification that "she" and "he," as the structural language of personhood in English, profoundly signify. By seeking to define butch as a category of persons in its own right (as not precisely "women"), Rubin put pressure on the linguistic domain of sexed subjectivity, trying to construct a continuum that could conceptualize masculinity across a range of bodies, identities, and practices. Yet her definition began in sexual difference: "Within the group of women labeled butch, there are many individuals who are gender dysphoric to varying degrees. Many butches have partially male gender identities. Others border on being, and some are, female-to-male transsexuals" (Rubin 1992: 468). The move from the beginning of this definition to the end becomes in its linguistic formulation an illogical one, for certainly if butch is a group of women, it is not possible for that term coherently to contain the FTM. Rubin, of course, was trying to find a way to define the difference between butch and FTM while rendering that difference more permeable than an absolutist understanding of dimorphic sex would allow. But the continuum that she hoped to construct was haunted from the outset by personhood's linguistic status as dimorphically sexed—this, even as her analysis repeatedly refused sex as a political identification by exploring butch as a domain of complex and diverse identificatory practices that confounded the normative routes of dimorphic sex, gender, and desire. The problem registered here—where the political project of forging a (masculine) identificatory relationship between butch and FTM and the difficulty of sex's representational hold on bodies and identities—marks one of the most profound challenges for feminist theory today: not simply addressing the persistence of the divide between genetic bodies and discursive gender, but offering a political analysis of the socially constructed affiliations between the two.

If it seems that this discussion has strayed far from a consideration of men and masculinity, that is, of course, precisely the point. For Rubin, the diversity of lesbian gender in general, and butch gender in particular, posed theoretical questions for thinking about masculinity as a structure of identification in ways that could be wholly disconnected from genetic male bodies (if not fully from female ones). The analytic focus on "masculinity without men," as Halberstam (1998) theorized, not only functioned to valorize those butch gender styles that mainstream feminism had often been embarrassed about, if not scared of; it also, more to the point, allowed for a deeper consideration of the relationship between gender variance and homosexuality.[21] Although for much of the twentieth century gender variance was located in both medical and political discourse as internal to homosexuality, indeed one of its most legible signs, in "the last part of this century," Halberstam wrote, "the invention of transsexuality as a medical category has partly drained gender variance out of the category of homosexuality" (1998: 142–43). Halberstam was interested in pursuing the theoretical implications of this shift, especially as it made possible interrogation of a range of female masculinities (of women who do not identify according to the logics and bodily tropes of femininity) without assuming that same-sex object choice defined either the horizon or parameter of such masculinities. By offering a kind of taxonomy of female masculinities from the androgyne, tribade, and invert to the stone butch and drag king—and differentiating from within and not simply across each "type"—Halberstam studied the cultural repression of gender variance in women. Although she was clearly committed to the project as a revalorization and diversification of the lesbian butch, it would be incorrect to limit her analysis of female masculinity to the province of lesbians. Indeed, at its broadest and most crucial critical intervention, *Female Masculinity* turned the tables on normative gender imaginaries by refusing to concede that most sacred terrain, masculinity, to men, seeking instead to figure *women* as a category of profound gender difference itself.

The theoretical distinctions among sex, gender, and sexuality that Halberstam both inherited and refined have had an enormous impact on masculinity studies, producing the three different and overlapping trajectories of critical investigation I have now defined. The first identified how differences among women mobilized an inquiry into the ways in which patriarchal power was consolidated by examining both the structure of the male bond and the various forms of masculinity and social hierarchy that the bond functions to deny. Through a social-construction rubric that disarticulates the normative wedding of sex and gender, alternative masculinities could be both politically imagined and critically analyzed. Using poststructuralism, the second trajectory builds radically on the sex-gender distinction to rethink the very idea of genetic sex, turning to considerations of gender's performativity apart from the normative mapping of bodies, identities, and desire. The third trajectory relocates the question of masculinity from genetic corporeality to the realm of identification, thereby defining a new "species" of masculinities that cannot be assimilated into the framework of patriarchal constructions of men. In these various conversations, the political stakes for feminism are high—so high, in fact, that we must now pause over one of the central questions that gave rise to the study of masculinity: What do men have to do with feminism? By deemphasizing the normative relationship between men and masculinity and seeking not simply alternative masculinities for men but also a broad rearticulation of masculinity as a production of gender distinct from, if not in contradiction with, so-called male bodies, feminist work in the 1990s has radically transformed the content, scope, and political project of masculinity as a domain of critical inquiry.[22] If the decade began with critical concern that feminism was abandoning women, it ended with the counterintuitive suggestion that even masculinity was no longer the proper domain of men. In other words, the knowledge objects once unquestioned as the definitive property of feminism—and those accepted as fully outside feminism's critical scope—had lost the logic of their critical place. Gender trouble indeed.

What's In a Name?

From the dire predictions of *Feminism Without Women* to the seemingly outrageous postulation of masculinity without men, then, feminist critical analysis has covered a great deal of theoretical ground in the past decade in its attempt to understand the complex relationships between and among bodies, identities, sexualities, and genders.[23] Whereas Modleski feared the loss of women, Halberstam celebrated woman's normative undoing, making sex and gender mobile across bodies and identities, and feminism mobile across sexed bodies and gender identities. For some critical observers, these differences are evidence that feminist theory is, at the beginning of the twenty-first century, decidedly torn between a modernist and postmodernist political interpretation—that is, between a desire for a materialist articulation of bodies versus their liberation in indeterminate or multiple resignifications. This rendering of the contradictions and contestations within feminist theory perpetuates the clichéd taxonomy that has occluded our present understanding of the paradox—the unresolvable constitutive constant—that feminism is not the scene of a seamless identification between so-called women and *women* but is crisscrossed and overwritten by a whole range of disidentifications, incongruities, and remappings of the material (bodies and identities) that it has taken as its primary knowledge objects. One does not need poststructuralism to detect the various ways in which feminism has sought both to diagnose and to heal through its own production of a counter-cultural imaginary the profound and unsettling social and psychic cost of living under the organizational sign of *woman*.[24] To the extent that it has done so by relying on identitarian sameness as its primary insurgent mechanism, it has repeatedly—at local, national, and international levels, in theory and in practice—confronted the unevenness of women's inhabitation in the psychic and social economies of gender. To say that the study of men and masculinity has been another route for confirming this insight is not to return a solidified woman to the center of feminist analysis. Rather, it is to demonstrate what the theoretical archive seems implicitly to assert: that feminism as an intellectual and political project is not finally bound to any prescribed domain of gender's complex universe.

Given this recognized and recognizable history, it is perhaps of little surprise that scholars in recent years have hoped to transform feminism's institutional domain from Women's Studies to gender studies (or the compromise figure women's and gender studies) in order to reflect more accurately the scope of knowledge projects undertaken by the field. Foregrounding the necessary critique of women as a coherent sign, such a transformation simultaneously identifies men and masculinity as potential objects of study (if not also practitioners in the field) and makes legible objects of analysis—lesbian and gay studies, intersexuality, cultures of sexual minorities, and emergent transgender identities and communities—that cannot be organized by the category *women*. It further works to identify, by allowing *gender* as a category to include women but signify beyond them, how potentially conservative *women* can be as the horizon of feminist knowledge, on one hand, and as its object of study, on the other. Most crucially, the transformation from Women's Studies to gender studies enables new subjects to locate an identitarian referent within feminism's institutional domain—subjects whose social formation may in fact be consolidated through such intense dis-identifications with the normative productions of woman that any organization of inquiry under that banner would provoke psychic as well as political disequilibrium, if not despair or disdain.

These are some of the most compelling intellectual arguments that I have encountered—at the National Women's Studies Association (NWSA) sessions on gender studies or by colleagues in my own program and elsewhere—that demonstrate the critical importance of a name change.[25]

There are (at least) four crucial issues embedded in these arguments that warrant attention, and I raise them here not to dismiss the important intellectual or pragmatic reasons that have motivated members of any program or department to engage the often productive, often fractious conversations that inaugurated a change of name. Nor am I interested in reconstituting a nostalgic or sentimental reclamation of women as the epistemological perspective and identitarian structure for understanding feminist knowledge formation. Rather, I want to suggest that the very issue of knowledge formation has yet to be rigorously and consistently thought in the field domain of Women's Studies or gender studies, and that this failure of consideration will not enable *gender* to escape the problematic of exclusion, contradiction, and incommensurability that now accompanies *women*. The following issues, which I provide in list format for the reader's ease, summarize the arguments that stage not simply a retention of Women's Studies as the appellation for a field domain, but also its resignification as a critical and political problematic.

1. *Field formations and identity objects of study.* When Women's Studies first emerged as a way to claim knowledge in the contemporary U.S. university, its practitioners described the project in the language of identity, as the study of women by women and, politically speaking, for women. This identitarian rubric has failed, it is now safe to say, because of the way in which the articulation of women as an object of study has proved different from, while nevertheless the referent for, its deployment as a political category.[26] Although we might define the theory-practice split in academic feminism as an effect of the differentiation of subject (knower) from object (the known) that knowledge formations generate, it is in fact just such deliberation that has transformed the field's imaginary, giving *gender* priority as the organizing trope for interrogations into a new set of bodies, identities, political acts, and critical practices.[27] Functioning now as the critical content of the category of *gender*, these new objects of study (alternative masculinities, transgender identities and identifications, transsexuality, intersexuality) and the subjects that might be said to mirror them (gay men, straight men, transsexuals, the transgendered) are by definition referents for *women*'s faulty universalism—that is, they function implicitly to claim identities as women's other. As a collective of new identity claims, their incorporation into feminism's field imaginary

displaces onto *gender* the optimistic hope that a relationship of compatibility, if not consistency, between field formation and its object of study can (finally) be won.

Although *gender* might interrogate the limit of *women*'s categorical content, then, it does not undo the political investment in identitarian logics that has defined feminism's formation of knowledge. "Gender studies" or "Women and Gender Studies" thus maintain a deep commitment—indeed, a persistent insistence—that an accurately expansive appellation for the institutional domain can overcome the problematic that accompanies the institutionalization of feminism: the incommensurability, that is, between the political development and transformations of utopian horizons and critical desires expressed as and through identity rubrics and the limitation imposed by and on an identity object of study. Rather than pursuing the investment in a realist referentiality, practitioners of academic feminism might train their attention on the failure of identity to function comprehensively as a measure or register for the many political projects that animate the field.

2. *Categorical coherence and mobility.* But why read gender as a surrogate for identity? Does it not function to indicate a set of practices and identifications that are irreducible to identity formations? In theoretical terms, after all, it has been the shift from identity to identification that has enabled a new critical lexicon—performativity—to define a highly mobile way of thinking social and psychic subjectivity, and much of the work that has gathered under the appellation of gender owes its critical genealogy to the performativity trajectory inaugurated by the critically queer. That *queer* has sought by definition to indicate non-identitarian and unpredictable mobilities of bodies, desires, and practices has placed it in critical proximity to identification as the other to identity, but the very practice of this differentiation has the effect of consolidating anti-identitarian identities on new identity grounds. This has certainly been the case with *queer,* which is now regularly appended as an identity extension to gay and lesbian (as in Lesbian, Gay, Bisexual, Transgender, and Queer Studies), and it is the functioning logic of *gender,* whose deployment within the institutional domain of Women's Studies carries with it most prominently gay men and anti-heteronormative queers. As a Women's Studies director at a recent professional meeting said: "In trying to develop a coali-

tional politics with gay, lesbian, and queer studies, we are thinking about changing our name to Gender Studies." The sudden shift from sexuality to gender that marks the transition between Women's Studies and gender studies demonstrates the end of gender's critical mobility to signify outside and beyond the domain of specific identities, becoming instead the collaborative term for new identities that need to be given representational visibility. It is at just such a moment that *women* takes on a most patriarchal signification, becoming the referent for the particular in a dynamic that reduces it to the normatively literal domain of sexual difference. Why feminism would want to author such a reduction of women is perhaps not immediately clear, although Biddy Martin (1996) has incisively diagnosed the utopian impulse that animates queer mobility against the static constant of distinctively female bodies. Writes Martin: "I am worried about the occasions when anti-foundationalist celebrations of queerness rely on their own projections of fixity, constraint, or subjection onto a fixed ground, often onto feminism or the female body" (1996: 71–72).

The notion, then, that *gender* is more critically mobile than *women* and that it will withstand what *women* could not—the interrogation into its historical, cultural, and contextual deployments—begins by "fixing" women as the price of its own utopian gesture. But more crucial than this is the implicit priority that *gender* gives to thinking about sexuality, masculinity, and men over and against other axes of analysis—namely race, class, and nationality. Given the now lengthy conversation in academic feminism concerning its theoretical and political imperative toward intersectional analysis—toward gender's imbrication with race, class, sexuality, and nationality—it is not clear how gender's isolation as a utopian horizon can adequately address the profound need to account for modalities of hierarchy and oppression that bear little in the way of utopian generation: white supremacy, imperialism, colonialism and postcolonialism, and global capitalism. In this context, it is worth contemplating again the impossibility of sustaining an institutional rubric that does not fail representational (or what I have been calling "referential") coherency. The point is not that race or class needs to be added to the appellation for the field, but that our way of thinking about identity is so deeply confounded by the need to develop ways to track something more than interpretative dyads (gender and sexuality; race and gender; class and nationality) that all gestures toward coherency will at this point reiterate the exclusivist conditions by which identity is itself theoretically, if not politically, configured. I would even argue that *women*'s theoretical inadequacy is, in fact, an important critical achievement: Rather than rushing to do away with it, in a replacement fantasy of categorical completeness, we might consider the intellectual uses to which its inadequacy can be put.[28]

3. *Historical-political time.* The third issue embedded in the conversation about the turn from Women's Studies to gender studies (or women's and gender studies) concerns the present social project of disestablishing affirmative action, which has succeeded in California and elsewhere to render *women* a term of partiality and exclusion. What does it mean to reconvene that very logic within the field, especially as *gender*'s capaciousness is often defined by its ability to include men? On one hand, we might say that *gender* represents a canny institutional move, a way to ward off the possible costs to identity-based institutional sites borne under the ethos, if not in the era, of affirmative action's own establishment. It can, in short, be a form of protectionism. On the other hand, the institutional renaming can work to confirm that those intellectual projects articulated around identity have themselves become the repositories of exclusionist practices, thereby undermining the meaning of democracy by giving preference to difference. Every director knows the political discomfort of being asked by a dean how many men are seated in Women's Studies courses, precisely because one's answer can so quickly slide into an administrative justification for further inadequate levels of funding.[29] The persistent priority given to men as normative subjects of the university and the increased fear in the 1990s that the academy is being feminized, not simply in the humanities but across the boards due to the greater ratio of female-to-male undergraduates nationwide, are critical contextual issues. After all, it is the sphere of education that has served throughout the twentieth century as a decisive battleground over the meaning of democracy and civil rights. Any consideration of transposing *gender* for *women* needs rigorously to consider the national anti-affirmative action agenda that hopes to render all counterinsurgent identities insular and exclusivist as part of the process of dismantling the juridical apparatus established by identity's public claim.

4. *Institutional time.* Finally, I want to think about timing in a broader

sense, in terms of the temporality of the human sciences and their historical commitment to an organization of knowledge under the epistemological framework of the generic, if not always genetic, man. We might say that the challenge that woman/women have posed to that epistemological framework is now, institutionally, thirty years old. Although feminist knowledge is often a requirement in doctoral preparation in fields as diverse as literary study and sociology, whole arenas of knowledge production, especially in the sciences, have yet to be significantly affected by the revolution in analysis wrought by feminism. From this perspective, *gender*'s analytic effectiveness is attached, like that of women and feminism, more to the humanistic and "soft" social sciences than to those realms most identified as methodological domains of masculine objectivism. How we understand what I call the sexual division of knowledge, and how we produce an institutional site that intervenes in the present and future of the university's organization of knowledge, is a necessary political project—one that will require the mobility of *women* to achieve a foothold in those areas that have failed to recognize how profoundly this category of persons has been excluded from those knowledge domains. We need, then, to think about the uneven development of feminist knowledge in the university and to explore the categorical constraints of identity's deployment in those realms that have been most distanced from the political history and theoretical form of academic feminism.

These issues are complex, of course, and although I have rendered them in outline form through practical necessity, I hope to have demonstrated—at least, provisionally—that there may be reasons to continue to produce *women* as signifier of feminism's institutional domain. Not the least of these is that domain's function as an important resource for understanding the problematic of identity that institutionalization simultaneously generates and demands. But my comments here are not meant as an injunction against name changes. Instead, I want to intervene in a critical moment—a moment of critical analysis—that seems to me to have come too early, in part because we are not late enough in our thinking about how to avoid dyadic rubrics and build critical vocabularies that make possible the intersectional imperative that we believe we believe in. Rather than forfeiting *women* to its most literal and dyadic meaning, and rather than circumscribing it as both insular and particular, we might better redeploy it as the critical framework under which the problematic of thinking about the relationship between identity and difference has been most productively made.

Notes

1 At a session on gender studies at the 1999 National Women's Studies Association (NWSA) meeting, Kay Trimberger distributed a compilation of programs and departments that have initiated a change in the name of their major, which often reflects a change in the institutional name of the unit. *Women's and gender studies:* American University, Amherst College, Eckerd College, Kenyon College, Louisiana State University, Macalester College, North Carolina State University, Sonoma State University, Sweet Briar College, and Yale University; *gender and women's studies:* Connecticut College, Grinnell College; *gender studies:* Bennington College, University of Chicago, Indiana University, Lawrence University, Lewis and Clark University, and New College of California. Bryn Mawr College calls its major "feminist and gender studies," and Pitzer's is titled "gender and feminist studies."

2 It is perhaps worth noting here how much the language of multiplicity and difference had seemed to turn into cliché by the end of the 1990s, becoming imprecise, even reductive, in relation to the political aspiration to speak without reiterating homogeneous formulations and fantasies of unity. Some of this is due, as others have cogently written, to the corporatization of multiculturalism that has refunctioned issues of diversity into management strategies and consumer niches. (See especially Gordon and Newfield 1996.) But it is also due to certain features of professional academic culture where whole domains of inquiry—and the political optimism that their investigation might be said to seek—quickly become truncated through the intellectual methodology of "critique." Although my ruminations at the end of this essay on the naming of institutional domains will in a certain sense challenge the way in which we participate in a "critical killing" of the memory trace of the intellectual genealogies that inhabit us, I will remark here on the necessity of further analysis of the incessant "presentism" of feminist theory, by which I mean the desire to write the present as the future's political—indeed, transcendent—guarantee.

3 To bring about the resignification of gender as more capacious than women, Auslander simultaneously articulates men and masculinity as objects of feminist inquiry while critiquing the operations of woman as producing an indifference, if not a critical inattention, to sexuality. It is this second move that seems most disingenuous, functioning as a kind of cover story to obscure the ways in which lesbian studies may chaff against the category of women but is not altogether outside it. Nor indeed has Women's Studies historically been an institutional domain devoid of lesbian scholarship.

4 My narrative of the identity-difference axis of twentieth-century feminist thought is devoted to countering the now normative assumption that early second-wave feminism was indifferent to race, class, sexuality, or nationality, an assumption that disturbingly casts both women of color and lesbians as belated arrivals to feminist critical

practice and movement. Actual examination of documents from the 1960s and 1970s demonstrates that issues of race and sexuality, especially, were given more than incidental discussion, and many of us trained as the first undergraduate generation of Women's Studies students were schooled in the lengthy discussions by Barbara Smith, Audre Lorde, and others about the content and politics of black women's studies. This is not a defense against the charges that feminism or Women's Studies were racist in their second-wave articulation; rather, it is an argument against writing out of the history of contemporary feminist thought the early and vibrant discussion of race and sexuality. Instead of producing a narrative of progress concerning feminism's ability to grapple with its own exclusionary thinking, we need to examine feminism's ties to a Western modernity that privileges liberal frameworks for thinking about social change, with our own narratives of democratic progress at the center of our critique.

5 See Davis 1983 (1981); hooks 1984b; and Lorde 1987.

6 Marilyn Frye reads gay male culture as "congruent with and a logical extension of straight male-supremacist culture" (1978: 144), a position that privileged the differential of gender over that of sexuality in the competing regimes of patriarchy and compulsory heterosexuality. Although her essay was intended as a call to gay men to abandon the "unconscious" of male privilege, it nevertheless performs the fundamental move of a great deal of lesbian feminist theorizing and organizing that the Combahee River Collective (1982) critiques. A decade after the publication of Frye's essay, of course, the political situation within lesbian and gay communities had radically shifted, because of the AIDS crisis, to such an extent that the kinds of affiliate discourses produced by women of color in relation to men of color became more normative within lesbian and gay—or, more properly, "queer"—critical endeavors: see Stein 1997; Stoller 1995.

7 In particular, Modleski critiques Butler 1990; Haraway 1990; and Riley 1988.

8 Modleski cites Boone and Cadden's *Engendering Men: The Question of Male Feminist Criticism* (1990), which, she says, "banishes women from its list of contributors," as an example of the dangers of male feminism (Modleski 1991: 12). As a project by men about men in feminism, *Engendering Men* ends, in Modleski's words, with a "complaint about the way heterosexual men have become invisible within feminism!" (Modleski 1991: 12). For Modleski, any male feminist project that wants to claim to be feminist will need to do something more than perform a kind of male-bonding scene around feminism as a political object or project.

9 Modleski in a sense found feminist traffic with poststructuralism a vehicle for enabling men to regain, through feminism, their historical authority as critics and commentators about women. Her essay thus echoed concerns that have persisted throughout feminism's late-twentieth-century proliferation concerning the relationship between a feminism committed to women-only spaces (both intellectual and political) and a sex-blind feminism. The 1999 controversy over Mary Daly's refusal to seat male students at Boston College is a case in point. Because the media coverage of this incident was so analytically poor, I direct readers to the conversational archive on the Women's Studies list service at listserv@umdd.umd.edu.

10 "But a little credit where credit is due," Modleski writes. "A body of male criticism supportive of the feminist project *is* beginning to develop, and the criticism that I have personally found most useful in thinking through my own subject is the kind that analyzes male power, male hegemony, with a concern for the effects of this power *on the female subject* and with an awareness of how frequently male subjectivity works to appropriate 'femininity' while oppressing women" (Modleski 1991: 6–7). Modleski cites Edelman 1990; Levernz 1986; and Newfield 1989 as examples of this body of work.

11 In citing the absence of the lesbian from the analysis, Modleski launched what has been one of the most persistent criticisms of *Between Men*. Yet in her introduction, Sedgwick establishes her analysis within the context of feminist theory and identifies the ways in which the asymmetries of gender arrangements and of sexual practices within homosocial networks will not yield comprehensive analytic purchase. For a discussion of how Modleski mobilizes the figure of the lesbian, see Jagose 1997.

12 Critics have since noted that Rubin does not challenge the biological notion of sexual difference so much as rearticulate the power of gender hierarchies to the realm of the cultural. See, for instance, Nicholson 1994.

13 In her use of the example of rape, Sedgwick was drawing from a lengthy conversation in African American scholarship on how white supremacy used rape in the nineteenth and twentieth centuries as a provocation for racial violence. Rape was thus not simply a crime against all women; it was also a vehicle for criminalizing black men, for whom, as Richard Wright put it in *Native Son*, "rape was the death before death came" (New York: Harper and Row, [1940] 1966: 228). In the figure of the black male rapist, which proliferated as a popular icon after the Civil War, the contestation between patriarchal and white-supremacist social formations is simultaneously made legible and managed: see Davis 1983 (1981): 172–201; Hall 1983; Harris 1984; V. Smith 1990; Wallace 1990 (1979); Wells 1970; and Wiegman 1995.

   In not citing this archive, Sedgwick remained within the field formation of "difference" that will be the object of my discussion at the end of the chapter, in which the trajectory of interrogation around sexuality, and to a lesser extent class, and that of race has more often been parallel, not intersecting. This has led to some of the contestation over the way in which "gender" has been raised to replace "women" in the institutional domain of Women's Studies, because the intersectional imperative for the study of gender's relation to race, class, sexuality, and nationality is thereby articulated into distinct lines of interrogation.

14 In reaffirming men's difference from women, dominant discourses in the contemporary period offer to men a narrative of power, privilege, and exclusivity based on the singular and seemingly irrefutable fact of maleness. This narrative not only demands and guarantees the excision of the feminine (and its representative, woman); it also represses those hierarchical differences among men that might expose the race, class, and heterosexist elitism that organizes social power arrangements. From this perspective, the continued hostility toward women's integration into the military seems hardly coincidental, as such hostility actually aids the process of assimilating racial, class, and religious differences among men, while constructing and emphasizing

physical and emotional disparities between men and women. As the most contested site of gender's rearticulation in U.S. culture, the struggle over women's participation in warfare, according to Jeffords (1989), brings into crisis the historical functioning of war as the exclusive scene of masculinity's performance. As she suggests, allowing women into the theater of war threatens to disrupt this masculine arena at a variety of levels—it threatens, in short, to steal its central and most dramatic scene.

15 For the historical archive on black masculinity, see Hine and Jenkins 1999; and Lowe 1996: 11–12.

16 In calling for an end to feminism's internal compulsion to police the proper domain of sexed, gendered, and sexual expression, Rubin later specified an arena of discussion—transsexuality—that had been an important impulse for writing "Thinking Sex," although one that did not appear as central in the essay's final form. As she explained in her interview with Butler,

> "Thinking Sex" wasn't conceived in a direct line or as a direct departure from the concerns of "Traffic." I was trying to get at something different. . . . I started to get more and more dissatisfied with what were then the stock feminist explanations for certain kinds of sexual behaviors. . . . A number of different debates . . . forced me to starting questioning the wisdom, if not the relevance, of feminism as the privileged political movement or political theory for certain issues of sexuality and sexual difference. One was the debate on transsexuality. Even before that debate hit print toward the late 1970s, the discussion really flipped me about because it was so biologically deterministic. When it finally erupted into print over the hiring of Sandy Stone, a male to female transsexual, by Olivia Records, there were a number of articles in the lesbian press about how women were born and not made which I found rather distressing. (1994: 67, 72)

17 "Genetic gender" does not seek to describe a biological truth about sexed embodiment; rather, it is a term that refers to the coherence between medically assigned sex and gender identification and performance: see Stone 1991: 294.

18 Jay Prosser challenges the *post*-transsexuality of Stone's political imperative. He writes,

> Fundamental to posttranssexuality is the belief that political subjectivity for transsexuals requires not simply a revision but a refusal of sexual difference—of what has been transsexuality's very purpose: passing, belonging, attaining realness in one's gender identity. In Stone's posttranssexuality there is no space for transsexuality as a progressive narrative—for continuing to value belonging, for an ongoing desire for a sexed realness and coherent embodiment: precisely the desire for a sexed place that galvanized transsexuality's narrative in the first place. . . . In pushing past a transsexual narrative ("post"), in ceding our claims to sexed location, we relinquish what we do not yet have: the recognition of our sexed realness; acceptance as men and women; fundamentally, the right to gender homes. (Prosser 1998: 203–204)

The political project of Prosser's *Second Skins* is thus a reconfiguration of the desire and demand for gender belonging, a belonging couched in the language of embodied coherence. Prosser is eloquent in his readings of the autobiographical narratives of transsexuals where this desire is most profoundly expressed—and in the claim that transsexuality itself must be thought of as and through narrative. But in thinking about Stone's work (or Butler's, for that matter), Prosser relies on a crucial contextual erasure: that of feminism. Instead, he locates queer theory as the generative discourse for transsexuality as a theoretical issue, without linking queer theory to feminism and its grappling with sex and gender.

This is not to say that any text dealing with transsexuality needs to have feminism as its object of study or its political commitment, especially given the historical difficulty that feminism has had in relinquishing its own disciplinary hold on a normative idea of *woman*. But the decontextualization of Stone's "Manifesto" from its place within feminist political analysis and organization is a costly critical omission. In the late 1970s, after all, it was literally around Stone's body that a major political eruption occurred when Olivia Records, a company owned and run by a woman, hired her. For a time, Stone, as an MTF, was the single individual around whom lesbian feminism's passionate commitment to "women born women" was expressed. "Manifesto" takes its political intervention in feminism as its primary domain, not queer studies, and it is precisely its lament that feminism has reproduced a discourse of regulation, shame, and critical abjection that motivates the imperative toward what Stone describes in the essay's closing words, "the next transformation" (1991: 299); this is a transformation not of the individual but of the social, "although *individual* change is the foundation of all things, it is not the end of all things" (1991: 299), she wrote.

For an account of the critical archive within feminist and lesbian theory concerning transsexuality, see Chapman and Du Plessis 1997.

19 Prosser (1998) has noted this inconsistency in which the notion of "transgender" does the vanguard work of delinking gender from sex by constituting identifications, desires, and pleasures in ways unmapped by normative regulatory schemas, but without displacing the status of originary sex embodiment. The term "transgender," he writes, was derived from "transgenderist," a term "coined in the late 1980s to describe a male subject with a commitment to living as a woman more substantial than that denoted by 'transvestite' or 'cross-dresser'" (Prosser 1998: 176). Although "transgender" tends now to function as an umbrella term for transsexuals, transvestites, intersexuals, butches, drag queens and kings, cross-dressers, and the gender dysphoric of all kinds, it was forged precisely to differentiate among acts, identifications, and performances that do or do not remake the body (or hope to) at the level of sex. For an articulation of the political utility of transgender as an umbrella term, see Stryker 1998.

20 Rubin concluded her essay by predicting that "the next debate over inclusion and exclusion will focus on the female-to-male transsexual" (1992: 475). In "Transgender Butch: Butch/FTM Border Wars and the Masculine Continuum" (in Halberstam 1998), Judith Halberstam traced the contestations that have become increasingly visible since Rubin's 1992 prediction, focusing her attention on the struggle over masculinity—its meanings, bodies, and both social and sexual productivities—that the "border" between lesbian butch and FTM might be said critically to represent. Halberstam's essay hoped to rework the political future of masculinity, refusing al-

together its critical application to genetic male bodies and producing a theoretical space for what she called the "transgender butch that did not presume transsexuality as its epistemological frame" (Halberstam 1998: 146). In this, she marked the divide between the desire for bodily transformation and "the possibility of the non-operated-upon transgender person" (Halberstam 1998: 146).

21 "Masculinity Without Men" is the subtitle of Halberstam's introduction (1998: 1). The phrase appeared a year earlier in the title of an essay that sought to think about straight femininity and its relation to masculine identifications: see Cox et al. 1997.

22 It is important to stress, as Halberstam does, that the emphasis on alternative masculinities is not, in and of itself, enough to guarantee its political effectiveness. She writes, "Not all models of masculinity are equal, and as butches and transsexuals begin to lay claims to the kinds of masculinities they have produced in the past and are generating in the present, it is crucial that we also pay careful attention to the function of homophobia and sexism in particular within the new masculinities. . . . Gender variance, like sexual variance, cannot be relied on to produce a radical and oppositional politics simply by virtue of representing difference. . . . I suggest we think carefully, butches and FTMs alike, about the kinds of men or masculine begins that we become and lay claim to: alternative masculinities, ultimately, will fail to change existing gender hierarchies to the extent to which they fail to be feminist, antiracist, and queer" (Halberstam 1998: 173).

23 I am echoing Janice Radway (1999) here, whose essay "What's In a Name?" cogently explores the problem of naming for American studies' field formation.

24 If we return to one of the founding texts of Anglo-American feminism, for instance, we encounter the crisis status of "woman" in a text far removed from the theoretical deployments of postmodernism. In *A Vindication of the Rights of Woman*, Mary Wollstonecraft so radically dis-identifies with the symbolic investment and cultural production of the category of woman that her work has been characterized by Susan Gubar as an instance of "feminist misogyny." More recently, Ann Snitow has written about how feminism posed for her a way to dis-identify coherently with woman as an act of political resistance. For the former, see Gubar 1995; for the latter, see Snitow 1990.

25 Intellectual arguments do not exist fully apart from pragmatic ones, though in the remainder of this chapter I will focus on the critical implications of the former. The most recurrent pragmatic arguments for changing the name of Women's Studies concern the proclivities of deans; the politics of student populations for whom, ironically, *gender* may be perceived as more conservative than *women;* faculty expertise and research agendas; and institutional pressures to redefine Women's Studies as a domain friendly to and inclusive of men.

26 Unlike those who view this detachment as the tragic end of feminism, I am inclined to read our shock at the consequences of institutionalization as an effect of our radically undertheorized relationship to the academy and knowledge production, on one hand, and to institutionalization as a form of political intervention, on the other.

27 A number of feminist methodologies have been developed to seek to overcome this traditional subject-object split. The feminist study of epistemology, for instance, espe-

cially as it is performed in the domain of science and technology, has greatly challenged the distance paradigm inherited from traditional disciplines by trying to think about how the production of knowledge is a dialectical effect. Yet it seems to me that feminism's own creation of itself as an interdisciplinary entity cannot escape this distinctive problem of modern knowledge formations, no matter how much we turn to standpoint theories or participant-observer modes of inquiry. For in making women into objects of study and in arguing for the knowledge content of women's experience and everyday practices, feminism has implicitly conceded to certain terms of legibility in and by the institution.

28 Readers familiar with Brown's "The Impossibility of Women's Studies" (1997) will note that, rather than citing women's incoherence as a primary reason for the dissolution of the institutional site of Women's Studies, I advocate a rigorous pursuit of this incoherence as the problematic that animates the field.

29 At my former university, it is interesting to note, the School of Biological Science did not even collect sex data on enrollment, although it did keep close account of the racial and ethnic diversity of its undergraduate population.

The Present and Our Past: Simone de Beauvoir, Descartes, and Presentism in the Historiography of Feminism

We're, like, stuck in Nerdsville.—Jennifer/Mary Sue in *Pleasantville* (1998)

Il y a une infinité de Descartes possibles.—Paul Valéry

In *Pleasantville* (1998), Gary Ross's cinematographically high-tech para-
ble of the notorious "family values" debate of the late-twentieth-century
United States, two California siblings of the '90s are abruptly relocated to
small-town America in 1958, as depicted in a popular television series,
"Pleasantville." Not coincidentally reminiscent of "Leave It to Beaver,"
the show's suburban white fences and father George's "Honey, I'm
home!" greeting to the picture-perfect Betty, his patient, martini-toting
wife, lock *Pleasantville* and the past it represents into frozen scenarios of
routine and oppression. Uncomfortably drained of the color that be-
tokens her postmodern habits, Jennifer, now absorbed as Mary Sue into
the nuclear family of the black-and-white TV show, proceeds to shake
things up by introducing her 1950s high-school cohort to the passions
linked with body culture and sex. She eventually turns to reading, however, as a new form of obsession; director-writer Ross wittily scripts Jennifer's private enlightenment as the result of discovering the texts of
D. H. Lawrence, indirectly suggesting that the gap between the mind and
the body is never as extreme as it seems. Brother David, the 1950s Bud,
although initially content to take up his role as a resident Pleasantville
nerd and soda jerk, soon follows suit by turning from TV-culture freak

into champion of art, literature, and non-routinized labor. In a fantasy of progressivism associated in the film with sexual liberation (and technically enabled by the companion achievements of an ever more sophisticated film science), the color of the single red rose that leaps out of its black-and-white background at the basketball star, Jennifer/Mary Sue's first sexual conquest, soon bleeds out into *Pleasantville*'s entire architectural, emotional, and ideological landscape. The women of *Pleasantville*, of course, appear to be the most liberated by contact with the future. Mother Betty in particular is freed from her housewifely role, literally given color and contour as the subject of "scandalous" large-scale public art. When, in a replay of the trial scene from *To Kill a Mockingbird*, the white male fathers of Pleasantville are finally forced to cede their authority to the liberated "coloreds" seated in the second-floor gallery of the courtroom, the ideological superiority of our present over their past is assured both narratively and cinematographically as color washes over the town and into the minds of Pleasantville's previously black-and-white populace. Belying David/Bud's initial claims, then, that "they are happy this way," the overall message of the film is that ignorance is not bliss. Indeed, the only way that the sins of the past are to be redeemed is by bringing that past up to speed and into line with a present of late-twentieth-century norms.

But the story is (of course) never quite so simple. In crafting a tale about the excitement of taking postmodern progress, openness, and excitement back to a uniformly white, male, and even fascistic past, *Pleasantville* elides—even as it displays—the dubious privileges inherent in that past's acceptance of the future goods of prejudice and violence, for example, from David's and Jennifer's ecologically, epidemiologically, and emotionally scary '90s world. *Pleasantville*'s depiction of life in the '50s also overlooks—or, at least, fails to represent—the fact that such issues were already part of the fabric of life at the time. This is not to say that Ross's clear advocacy of a variety of freedoms in the film is not to be applauded. Yet a number of on-line comments about *Pleasantville* that can be found at http://www.us.imdb.com, and particularly those offered by teenage viewers criticizing the film's several oversimplifications, underscore the problem of telling a story about the liberation of a "nerdy" and despicable past by the present that relies—literally and figuratively— on black-and-white cartoons of "their" always already boring cultural oppression and repression and "our" colorful freedom. Such gestures obscure the complexities of both eras and of their relationship to each other by relying on an implicit narrative of progress, even if it is told in this film in reverse. It is only ironic that the film redeems "Nerdsville" by relying on one of the chronologies that postmodern feminists in particular have associated so intimately with repressive ideologies of Enlightenment humanism by choreographing the relationship between present and past in a disappointingly monodirectional and predictably progressivist way.

That Ross was aware of the dangers—and weaknesses—of creating such a starkly represented hierarchy of oppression and liberation and stretching it over indistinct megaperiods only identifiable as "them then" and "us now" nevertheless emerges out of the gender politics and opposing plot resolutions for David/Bud and Jennifer/Mary Sue. The man-child returns to the future in "feminized" form at the end of the film, a sensitive boy of the 1990s now worldly-wise about the emotional needs of his single-mom parent. Going back to the future represents progress for him. Mary Sue, however, who, as she herself notes, must turn away from the body to regain her color in an act of intellection rather than intercourse, decides to stay put—indeed, to become somewhat of a nerd herself by going to college. A simplistic gender-bending scenario and swap might have had Mary Sue become "manly" as she sets off on her studies, matching Bud's taking on of the nurturing role with a parallel virilization. The film thwarts this expectation by involving Mary Sue in a moment of decidedly heterosexual intellectual courtship in the final scene. All body in the '90s, she can both be "embodied" (albeit in a conventional way) and engage in a life of the mind in the past. Going back thus represents going forward for Jennifer/Mary Sue. Precisely because of this reversal, viewers such as myself may be pardoned for trying to make out the title on the spine of the book from which Jennifer/Mary Sue reads in her last scene, for we would like to know what she will go on to study after she has so paradoxically been introduced to the "pleasures of the text" by the likes of *Sons and Lovers*. Might Jennifer/Mary Sue have in her hands a late '50s edition of *Le discours de la méthode* [Discourse on method, 1637] by that alleged theorist of the mind-body split, René Descartes, on whose work the very conceit of her character is based? Or ought we to imagine her reading Simone de Beauvoir's *Le deuxième sexe* [The second sex, 1949], available in English as of 1953, preparing for '60s feminism by studying the very female philosopher to whom Judith Butler attributes the "putting to rest" of the "Cartesian ghost" (Butler 1998: 29)? Given the logic of her "redemption" at the hands of the past, I would argue that we may want to imagine that Jennifer/Mary Sue is reading Descartes (the farther back in time, the better), and that she has found a means of liberation for herself in his thought.

I begin with a reading of *Pleasantville*'s narrative manipulations of the relationship between the past and the present—and with the question of Jennifer/Mary Sue's college reading—because they give me a way of thinking about the chronology of the stories that get told about the relationship between the "them" and the "us" of the past in recent historiography of both feminism and Women's Studies. I am especially interested in the way that the history of feminism and of its "main issues" is produced as a consequence not only of what we assign to students of feminism to read in our classes (usually not Descartes, and increasingly less often even Simone de Beauvoir), but also how we teach them to construct chronologies of knowledge and theory formation as a result. Here I am referring not to the possibility of students' encountering highly nuanced depictions of the gender politics of ancient Greece, or of the inner and outer lives of medieval female saints, or of the complex sexuality and intellectual and bodily labor of the women of the sixteenth through the twentieth centuries that literary scholars, political theorists, and women's historians have made accessible to us in both their research and their disciplinarily specific classes over the past twenty years. Rather, I am interested in assessing the overall inclination of many programs and courses in interdisciplinary Women's Studies to assume that the key issues of feminism about which students need to know began to emerge only in the 1960s and '70s, if not in the 1990s, and have moved only forward ever since. Accompanying this assumption is the implicit claim that reaching back before these years can represent nothing other than antiquarian—and potentially politically incorrect—knowledge projects.[1]

My point is the following: If we ask students to begin thinking feminism as a matter of complexity only in our postmodern present, or, in a related gesture, if we pass on to them the habit of seeing the "origins of feminism" only from a presentist perspective, one that judges the past interesting only when and if it "reflects back [to us] histories of modernist or postmodernist identities" (Biddick 1998: 83), we neglect to interrogate our own investments in the need to construct that present—our present, in other words—as the culmination of a narrative of the victors. When we fail, that is, to challenge both students and ourselves to theorize alterity as an issue of change over time as well as of geographical distance, ethnic difference, and sexual choice, we repress and refuse to confront not only the "thickness" of historical difference itself, but also the dimensions of what is perhaps the most pressing issue in Women's Studies today—namely, the impact on its fundamental critical task of the gradual institutionalization of the field as an academic discipline, a development fueled, I would argue, by our (self)implication in a narrative of progress whose hero(in)es inhabit only the present. This image of progress tends to legitimate—even as it masks—the absorption of the field's and our energy into the traditional mechanisms of mass instruction, administrative bureaucracy, and, in particular, the trap of a kind of quick and competitive knowledge production that can be measured only in the currency of the late postmodern academic realm: publication. Increasing the speed at which the feminist critique proceeds in this way, so that the most recent is also the best, may be responsible for a specific kind of collateral damage—namely, the creation of a permanently antagonistic relationship among past, present, and future knowledge projects within the discipline as a result of locking feminist theory into the reactive position as the only legitimate stance for feminist scholars vis-à-vis one another as well as toward other fields. Failing to reflect on the progressivist chronologies that organize the historiography of feminism will ultimately slow down rather than secure the interdisciplinarity stabilization that most Women's Studies programs claim they desire by overlooking potential allies in fields such as classics and comparative religious studies, for example, not usually recognized as intrinsically related to the project of feminism in standard accounts of the field.

The gradual paling of the difference between Women's Studies as an academic formation and the other, "traditional disciplines" represents one of the single most challenging issues for academic feminists today. Most of us try desperately every day to navigate the stormy waters where institutional careerism and politically meaningful work (also in the classroom) meet, sometimes by trying to distinguish between the two categorically, and sometimes by collapsing them into compensatory versions of each other. These struggles for self-siting within and outside the academy consume large amounts of energy and time. It may well be that because we have been so consumed with them, we have also too long overlooked, ignored, and repressed the fact that we will remain caught in this paralyzing impasse as long as we historicize the discipline only as a narrative of ever greater understanding, ever greater inclusiveness, and ever greater critique. The majority of introductory courses in our now thirty-something-year-old discipline begin (as mine have), for example, with either selections from or (less often) the entirety of *Le deuxième sexe* and move only forward. In so doing, they attempt to create "disciplinary security" (Biddick 1998: 1–2) by identifying all that is pre-Simone—and thus representative of humanism, the Enlightenment, "the canon," and the past all in one—as the "despised" Other, as different from and even antithetical to "our concerns." The curricular, scholarly, and theoretical chronologies created by the "disavowal" not only of the local historical nature of our current agendas, but also of the possibility that the complex sedimentations of the past might themselves yield potentially useful versions and visions of our future disciplinary Selves, can yield only the kind of presentism that characterizes *Pleasantville* by preventing a critical analysis of the ideology of the progressive narrative that has come to script the institutional, intellectual, and political behavior of our field in black-and-white ways.

In what follows, I outline the coordinates of this presentism as it informs late-twentieth-century Women's Studies by indicating, first, the ways in which its chronologies inhabit some recent feminist work. My examples are the cases of Descartes and "Cartesian thinking," on the one hand, and of Simone de Beauvoir, on the other, as two prominent inhabitants of our collective theoretical and intellectual landscape. Associated with rationalism and identified as the bogeyman of patriarchal tradition personified, Descartes functions rhetorically in many— although not all—accounts of recent feminist theory as the beginning of the end for women because of the (in)famous mind-body split allegedly at the center of his thought, a split in which women are said to be identified with the inferior second term. De Beauvoir's work has been made to serve the founding of modern feminism in a similar, although somewhat more complex, fashion. She is either the much celebrated, originary intellectual woman and author of the history of women's oppression, or the typical Eurocentric who failed to address not only difference, but also differences among women around the world. The final part of this chapter tries to muddy the waters of contemporary approaches to the chronology of feminism and its issues by displacing these (both positively and negatively) idealized renderings of Descartes and de Beauvoir as they crowd the pages of many (but, again, by no means all) recent texts, and by substituting for them a different kind of historical embodiment of both her and his ideas.

I have to admit, finally, that in conceiving this chapter, I was originally attracted to the prospect of finding and inventing (from the Latin *invenio*, to find) a "political Descartes" in the early to mid-seventeenth century, when it was a radical act to declare the mind to be free of the body, especially as that body was implicated in and constrained by all manner of oppressive regimes of power and knowledge rooted in early modern religious and nationalist political orthodoxies and conflicts. This Descartes wrote in the vernacular rather than Latin to reach out to a broad audience that included women, and he served as the philosopher-adviser of a distinguished female head of state, Queen Christina of Sweden, as well as a learned correspondent with other illustrious female intellectuals of the time.[2] No sexist Dead White Male he. Yet indulging in such a reading would have led me down exactly the same path of presentist scholarship that I seek to challenge, because I would only have been defending Descartes by pointing out how much he "really was" on "our" side. It is perhaps not by chance that many of the bitter battles over de Beauvoir's legacy have been and continue to be organized in this same way, only as a matter of its and her significance for "us" and our— rather than her—historical institutional and political concerns. Ultimately, I chose to follow a different kind of historiographic model, one that would acknowledge the possibility of the "infinity of Descartes"— and de Beauvoir—of which Paul Valéry writes (1957 [1937]: 794) by adding another potentially politicized Descartes to the seventeenth-century one described earlier. My specific example is, then, the Descartes whose thought figured prominently in the political landscape of France in the 1920s–40s, during the period just predating de Beauvoir's writing of *Le deuxième sexe*. Investigating the interwar and wartime contexts in which this Descartes moved may make it possible for us to question our investment in telling monolithic stories about his and her place in the history of (Western) feminist theory based on the conceit of how much better— politically and intellectually, ideologically and materially—our present is than a past framed in black-and-white terms. By liberating de Beauvoir and Descartes from univocal narratives about their respective places in feminism and allowing them to circulate within multiple political, social, and moral contexts, we disrupt presentist logic by turning back, even stopping, the clock long enough to allow the other colors of various pasts to emerge.

Founding Moments: Simone de Beauvoir and the Cartesian Ghost

It will not have escaped the attention of those with even a passing interest in the work of Simone de Beauvoir that both she and her texts, particularly *Le deuxième sexe,* have been invested over at least the past twenty years with the status and function of having founded second-wave feminism. Considered "one of the most influential and perceptive feminist books ever written" by Jean Crimshaw in (1986: 45), even if it deserves a critique because it tends to recommend that women seek autonomy by becoming like men (1986: 46), and deemed an "anchoring text" by Margaret Atack (1998: 32), *Le deuxième sexe* has the dubious distinction of being one of the most often invoked, yet recently most seldom read, of the "founding texts" of Western feminism, even though its publication in English was one of the "most influential events in twentieth-century women's history," according to Deborah G. Felder's very respectable volume of the same name (1999: 210–14). This failure to read is not absolute, of course. And yet, the ways in which *Le deuxième sexe* is read, when it is read, are even more revealing of its status in current feminist thinking about itself than might be its complete elision. Stevi Jackson's *Women's Studies: Essential Readings* (1993), for example, begins its section on "Feminist Literary Criticism" with a brief selection from de Beauvoir's famous book; the useful anthology edited by Linda Nicholson and published by Routledge, *The Second Wave: A Reader in Feminist Theory* (1997), ratifies this inaugural gesture by beginning its history-of-"our"-feminism-enacted-as-anthology with a seven-page excerpt from the introduction. Thus, parts of *Le deuxième sexe* can be read in the late twentieth century, even if they are very small parts indeed. Editorial decisions that cannibalize texts and render the pieces foundational as fragments in this way—although of course dictated by press mandates, market requirements, and bottom lines (and typical of anthologies in nearly all disciplines)—nevertheless have the curious effect in this particular case of recommending to students an approach to the history of feminism that trades in fetish objects, whereby an arbitrary moment stands in for "feminism's past." Weighed down with an overload of symbolic baggage, these moments provide an excuse for, and may even function as, potential models of dislocated theoretical behavior and disconnected knowledge production of other kinds, too.

Ironically, the reception of de Beauvoir herself has proceeded in exactly the opposite direction. Her (sexualized) body was and is the focus of most accounts of her work—from François Mauriac's early remark that reading *Le deuxième sexe* made him "entirely familiar with Beauvoir's vagina" (as quoted in Fallaize 1998: 8) to the ongoing obsession with her relationship to Sartre and the recent publication of her passionate correspondence with the American writer, Nelson Algren, presented to its English-language readers in a volume entitled *A Transatlantic Love Affair* (de Beauvoir 1998 [1997]), so designated, perhaps, to suggest that in these letters we will find even more of an embodied Simone.[3] The fragments of *Le deuxième sexe* as they appear in Jackson's and Nicholson's anthologies, as well as in any number of introductory Women's Studies' lectures ("One is not born, but rather becomes, a woman"), nevertheless usually circulate strangely detached from this body (even as it too is available to us in fetishized form), disengaged from the intellectual and political complexities of the situation in which their author wrote. The sanitized bits of text that many students encounter are thus made to stand in for and replace the complex political and philosophical positions, as well as the intertextual practices, of *Le deuxième sexe*, which indicate their very specific placement in a historical narrative that does not begin but, rather, ends with de Beauvoir.

Such presentations of de Beauvoir and her work also mask the dislocation that the original French text of *Le deuxième sexe* experienced at the hands of its American translator, H. M. Parshley, professor emeritus of zoology at Smith College (see de Beauvoir 1989 [1953]). Parshley famously cut the text and mistranslated key existentialist terms (see Simons 1999 [1983]) even as he provided English readers with "explanatory" footnotes that reference primarily the U.S. context. The move is a classic one, based on a replaying of the "translatio studii et imperii" topos, that U.S. post–World War II ideology of "our" legitimate postwar inheritance of European power and ideas; it had the effect of highlighting 1950s U.S. American experience and research as the primary legitimating locations and telos of de Beauvoir's theories and claims (see de Beauvoir 1989 [1953]: 28, 30, 314, and passim). U.S. readers and critics of *Le deuxième sexe* who reminisce about what reading the book meant for them and for feminism in the 1960s inadvertently tell another version of this same story, the temporality of which dictates that there are no "befores," only "afters," of de Beauvoir. Susan Brownmiller's *In Our Time: Memoir of a Revolution* (1999: 13, 20, 257) continues the trend set early on by Betty Friedan in "It Changed My Life" (1976: 387–403) in this respect. By indexing de Beauvoir's significance as a matter only of her impact on the U.S. women's movement and by citing her most famous text in its English translation (and thus failing to gloss that translation's inaccuracies and omissions), cultural historians and anthologizers alike engage in a similarly "imperialistic" story of cultural transmission, in which there is really only one (namely, "our") ending.

Equally accepted is the somewhat more specialized story told about de Beauvoir and *Le deuxième sexe* as another kind of beginning, albeit an *ex negativo* one, of the "New French Feminism" so hugely influential in the U.S. academy in the 1980s and early '90s. The critiques of de Beauvoir as "humanist, existentialist, and egalitarian" by such well-known figures as Hélène Cixous, Julia Kristeva, and Luce Irigaray, who are most often identified with "psychoanalytical, differentialist, deconstructionist, and postmodern" feminism, have been described in detail by several scholars, most recently by Catherine Rodgers (1998), but notably earlier by Toril Moi. Moi claimed in 1994 that the "French feminists" considered de Beauvoir a "theoretical dinosaur" (1994: 182); Moi's earlier *Sexual/Textual Politics: Feminist Literary Theory* (1985), whose enormous impact on North American students of feminism can be measured in terms of the fact that the book went through nine editions in its first six years, briefly insists that it is important to tell a somewhat more nuanced story about the ongoing effect of de Beauvoir's work on French theorists such as Monique Wittig and Christine Delphy (Moi 1985: 98). But what the several generations of U.S. students of feminism cutting their teeth on the alleged differences between Old and New World feminist theory took away from Moi's 1985 book was the lesson taught by its politics of the page and by the stark distinction between two different brands of Anglo-American feminist criticism and French feminist theory made there, a distinction and selection that suggested that it was only after de Beauvoir that "French feminism"—with its greatly reduced personnel—became important. A beginning of sorts.

We must pardon Moi's deployment of de Beauvoir in the inadvertent service of a presentist narrative about feminism in 1985 when we acknowledge her magisterial achievement in *Simone de Beauvoir: The Making of an Intellectual Woman* (1994), as well as in the several lengthy essays examining de Beauvoir's work that appeared in Moi's *What Is a Woman?* (1999), both of which thickened the picture immeasurably. Yet when we look to the only form in which most U.S. students might have had access to the history of French feminism prior to the appearance of Moi's 1985 book, the picture is not such a pretty one. In Elaine Marks and Isabelle de Courtivron's very important collection, *New French Feminisms, an Anthology* (1980), de Beauvoir stands as the sole inhabitant of the section labeled "Beginnings." Even though other excerpts from *Le deuxième sexe* and from interviews with and publications by de Beauvoir appear later in the anthology under such headings as "Warnings," "Manifestoes," and "Utopias," her identity as totem founder is marked by her inscription in this inaugurary, yet lonely, textual position. Along with translations of selections from Kristeva's "Semeiotike," published in *Desire in Language* (Kristeva 1980), and "Women's Time" (1981 [1979]), *New French Feminisms* provided for nearly half a decade nearly the only textual window onto—indeed, the only English-language version of—the feminist theory that was to make such a distinct impression upon much U.S. academic feminism in subsequent years. In *New French Feminisms*, of course, fragments of other works in addition to de Beauvoir's are asked to work overtime to tell the (hi)story of feminism. Yet even after the publication of translations of Irigaray's work by Cornell University Press in 1985 (see Irigaray 1985b, 1985c) and the appearance both in hardcover and in the more affordable paperback of books such as Gayle Greene and Coppélia Kahn's *Making a Difference* (1985) and Elaine Showalter's *The New Feminist Criticism*, both of which contained reliable essays "processing" French feminism for large audiences of U.S. undergraduates, the same story was told. In this story, there is no need to go any further back than de Beauvoir "Englished" in the production of the genealogy of "our" present concerns.

There has been a return recently to de Beauvoir and *Le deuxième sexe* not only by Moi, but also by Mary Evans (1998), Kate and Edward Fullbrook (1993), Eva Gothlin-Lundgren (1996 [1991]), Margaret Simons (1999), and Karen Vintges (1996 [1992]), a return that not only reconnects her work to her intellectual, institutional, and political body in immensely useful ways, but also complicates both a chronology and a geography of feminism that would declare itself able to do without pre-de

Beauvoir and non-U.S. European knowledges. Such monumentalizing nevertheless merely confirms her status in the by-now-familiar narrative of how contemporary U.S. feminism and Women's Studies "began" in the 1960s, when the select number of (primarily white) U.S. feminists, now canonized as its "founders" (see King 1994), read and "translated" de Beauvoir into the local version of feminism. This is the feminism that, since the mid-1980s, has moved ever forward, always in need of being (progressively) challenged, revisioned, and revised from multiple perspectives, to be sure, but, save for the occasional reference to Mary Wollstonecraft and Sojourner Truth, seldom allowed to consider the relevance of pre-1949 or 1953 events.

In an unsettling parallel narrative, Descartes has haunted both the margins and the centers of twentieth-century feminist theory in similar ways. My choice of this ghostly metaphor is deliberate, as there is a curious conflation in much feminist work of the individual person and material oeuvre of the seventeenth-century philosopher himself and the only occasionally nuanced "Cartesian tradition" and "Cartesian mind-body split." That is, even though Judith Butler had cautioned already in 1986 that "Cartesian 'man' is not the same as the man with distinct anatomical traits" (1998: 37), thereby offering a strategy for distinguishing between Descartes and his work, on the one hand, and what has been construed and constructed as "the Cartesian inheritance in the Enlightenment and post-Enlightenment West," on the other, influential volumes such as Alison Jagger and Susan Bordo's *Gender/Body/Knowledge: Feminist Reconstructions of Being and Knowing* (1989) specifically target— with nary a footnote or line of textual analysis—both Descartes individually as the primal bogeyman and his work in general as definitively exemplary of the evils of "Western thinking" writ large (Jagger and Bordo 1989: 2–3). In this volume, some 350 pages strong, the French philosopher is actually discussed only once, by Ruth Berman, and then as the author and progenitor of the "rigid dualism" and separation of body and mind (Berman 1989: 235). In Berman's article, as in Bordo's earlier book, *The Flight to Objectivity: Essays on Cartesianism and Culture* (1987), Descartes and Cartesianism are allowed to collapse easily into each other, obviating the need for student-readers to have recourse to any closer analysis of the philosopher's writings or the historical context in which they were produced (see also Bordo 1987: 116, as quoted in Bordo 1999: 3). Indeed, in light of the role Descartes is asked to play in these sorts of narratives about "the feminist critique," it can only be seen as a critical and disciplinary irony that Berman appears to have relied for her assessment of Descartes on the excerpts from his oeuvre that appear in a volume produced in 1947, *Man and the Universe: The Philosophers of Science,* edited by S. Commins and R. N. Linscott; she thus subtly reproduces in her argument a reliance on the very Cold War canonization and authority of the "great male thinkers" school of the history of philosophy that she seeks to challenge. It is important to note that, like Toril Moi, Bordo subsequently revised her earlier claims about feminism's relationship with the philosopher of the mind-body split in her immensely useful anthology *Feminist Interpretations of René Descartes* (1999). There she allows her contributors to sculpt "thicker" pictures of the multiple historical and philosophical landscapes inhabiting and inhabited by Descartes in his past as well as in our postmodern present in fascinating detail. Bordo specifically includes "antimasculinist" readings of Descartes by Stanley Clarke and James A. Winders, among others, that move beyond "conventional readings" of the philosopher as the beginning of women's end (Bordo 1999: 14).

Yet, Bordo's claim in her introduction that it has been the feminist position "all along," that "it is the dominant cultural and historical renderings of Cartesianism, not Descartes 'himself,' that are the object of [its] criticisms" (Bordo 1999: 2), is belied—or at least made difficult for the feminist layperson to access—by the pervasiveness in feminist theory in the late 1980s and 1990s of precisely these conventional claims, along with more indirect arguments that Descartes and his thought gave rise to some of the "deepest categories" of "Western philosophy," categories that obliterate "differences of gender" by celebrating the Cartesian "male subject of reason." Here Seyla Benhabib, in "Feminism and Postmodernism: An Uneasy Alliance," paraphrases one of the "grandiose metanarrative[s]" (1995: 24) that subtend Jane Flax's oracular claims in *Thinking Fragments: Psychoanalysis, Feminism, and Postmodernism in the Contemporary West* (1990) in order to critique them. Benhabib's objections to Flax are well taken. And yet, Flax, in both *Thinking Fragments* and earlier work, was very influential; citations of her rendering of Cartesianism form a veritable refrain in numerous accounts of feminism's tasks. Indeed, even though Jean Crimshaw, for example, attempted in *Philosophy and Feminist Thinking* to develop her analysis of the several oversimplifications of receptions of Cartesian categories as instrumental in defining the "male-

ness of philosophy" (1986: 53–4) by critiquing Flax's "Political Philosophy and the Patriarchal Unconscious" (1983: 58–60), and specifically
Flax where she invokes Descartes (Flax 1983: 58–60), the top billing
given to Flax in Crimshaw's book allows the alleged Cartesian conspiracy
to survive in occulted form. For when Crimshaw ultimately decides that
while neither universal nor "homogeneous" (1986: 65), many "differing
sorts of philosophical theories" do indeed relegate women "to second
place" (1986: 69), and thus that "there are indeed important senses in
which philosophical theories can be seen as male" (1986: 70), she is
ultimately singing the same song. It is a tune still audible several years
later, in Marilyn Frye's essay on feminism and philosophy in Cheris
Kramarae and Dale Spender's important *The Knowledge Explosion: Generations of Feminist Scholarship* (1992). There Frye generalizes not only
about "almost all of western philosophy," but also about "most feminist
philosophers," who "reject . . . the mind-body dualism" (Frye 1992: 128).
Without naming Descartes, she thus allows his categories to continue to
shape the contours of this very brief, yet also terribly influential historiographic sketch of feminism's philosophical genealogy and present
claims. Part 1 of *The Knowledge Explosion* claimed to map "the disciplines," and part 2 claimed to delineate "the debates" in an attempt
to chart not only the substantial "achievements of Women's Studies"
(Kramarae and Spender 1992: 1) but, more important, also to encourage
feminists to "continue [their] commitment to transformation" of the
academy (Kramarae and Spender 1992: 9) as the millennium neared. In
1992, then, moving into the future still meant forging ahead on the basis
of inherited claims about Descartes' and Cartesianism's role in fixing the
terms of feminism's debates.

It is unfortunate that in spite of the more differentiated picture of
Descartes sketched in Bordo's 1999 anthology, volumes of feminist theory published by influential presses have continued to trade in critical
cartoons about some of the key elements of Enlightenment philosophy
up until the very cusp of and, indeed, into the new century. Some of this
approach is undoubtedly the result of the accelerated economy of citation
necessitated by the apocalyptic 2000 deadline itself and thus by the pressure to produce fin de siècle-type statements. Such pressures nevertheless encourage critical practices that create "coverage" of the Cartesian
tradition only via its mediations in feminist work that have themselves
become canonical. Alison Assiter's appeal to Irigaray's reading of Des-

cartes in *Enlightened Women: Modernist Feminism in a Postmodern Age* (1996: 45, 70–71, 74–75), and Barbara Arneil's rendering of Bacon and Descartes through the lens of Keller and Chodorow in *Politics and Feminism* (1999: 86–87, 131, 132), provide examples here. The practice also subtends and, I would argue, will extend into an indefinite future the now increasingly predictable critique of Eurocentrism, also in Western Women's Studies, that has dominated feminism during much of this same time. Many (although not all) postcolonial feminist theorists now feel the need to do no more than gesture toward the tradition of "European thinkers," never pausing to consider which subset of the many populations of the greater Eurasian continent they are supposing gave birth to these thoughts or, indeed, how, when, and why these parts of Europe came to stand in for "Europe" writ large. (They are certainly not targeting the eastern parts of Europe, for example, so long considered the despised Other of Western Europe that, according to Larry Wolff, provided the West with its first example of "underdevelopment, a concept [now applied] all over the globe" [1994: 9]). In her important book *Reorienting Western Feminism: Women's Diversity in a Postcolonial World* (1998), Chilla Bulbeck tries to be more precise about the "source" of the problematic hesperization of both culture and theory. Yet she (Bulbeck) still uses Moira Gatens's reading of Descartes as one of main textual anchors of her critique (Gatens 1991: 44). It was Gatens, of course, who found Simone de Beauvoir's work itself flawed by her (de Beauvoir's) fundamental acceptance of "a philosophical dualism of the most orthodox kind"—specifically, the "mind-body" distinction (Gatens 1991: 2), which leads her to accept the "clustering" of "femininity, the female body, and woman" (Gatens 1991: 48–59). Although not claiming that Descartes was the originator of such dichotomous thinking, Gatens—and thus Bulbeck in turn—accepts his work as a prominent and influential articulation of it. Anyone, including even the foremother of feminism, raised in the tradition of European philosophy that addresses such issues thus must be included among those whose work reveals "an implicit bias against women" (Gatens 1991: 60) related to his. Such strange citational bedfellows make it difficult for students—and for us—to think of that past, a period both broadly and narrowly understood as anchored by the Cartesian and de Beauvoirian poles, as harboring anything other than repressive ideologies and positions, giving them and us apparently little reason to investigate its complexities in greater detail.

My story of contemporary feminism's and Women's Studies' presentist chronologies as visible in the way de Beauvoir and Descartes function as coordinates in them can be brought to an end with a reference to
Susan Gamble's recent *Routledge Critical Dictionary of Feminism and Postfeminism* (2000). A welcome resource, the volume includes a short but
dense article on Simone de Beauvoir (Gamble 2000: 195). "The Cartesian legacy" is mentioned only once, however, in Pamela Sue Anderson's
essay, "Feminism and Philosophy," as part of a tradition that "serves
to justify the sexual division of labor" (Anderson 2000: 149). No other
entry appears either on Cartesianism or on Descartes that might direct
students to investigate this legacy in greater depth. In 2000, then, feminism's temporal frame had become even narrower, with Descartes drop-
ping out of the picture nearly entirely, replaced and usurped by de Beauvoir, his philosophical next-of-kin, in genealogical pride-of-place. The
move is significant, first, because it foreshortens the timeline of feminism in a moment of considerable intellectual and pedagogical importance. By this I mean that, precisely because it is to such handbooks and
collections (not unlike the one in which this chapter appears) that students will increasingly refer as our postmodern history extends into the
future and they—and we—seek to orient them- and ourselves in the
textual superabundance of end-of-the-century/beginning-of-the-century
historiographies of feminism's critical, political, and personal worlds, we
must monitor the kind of presentist messages sent in them with special
care. Indeed, the very title of Gamble's handbook—with "feminism" and
"postfeminism" competing for the reader's attention—suggests that this
is precisely the kind of temporal schema that will shape our future if we
do not do so, for what the double-whammy appears to want to do is let the
curtain fall on that past by suggesting that in 2000 we are already part of
the "post." An accelerated economy of knowledge, indeed.

In what follows, I seek to interrupt the momentum of such unexamined moves forward by moving backward to a place and time—namely,
the early twentieth century in France, when Descartes' work inhabited a
far more complex world. This world was, of course, also Simone de
Beauvoir's world as a young student of philosophy and a maturing feminist theorist. In this world, there is evidence that Descartes' ideas may
have represented not a demon reification of "the mind-body split," but a
set of terms with which to think about political ethics. Butler has famously remarked on the importance of kidnapping narratives for ends

perhaps in conflict with those narratives' original intents (Butler 1994: 128). Interestingly, Butler comments specifically in this context on the possible "resignification" of the "narrative of modernity associated with European conceptions of emancipation," the narrative that she argues in fact "required and instituted slavery." Butler calls for an "appropriation" of even such suspect narratives as a "pragmatic" gesture of "decontextualization" that allows for their "re-contextualization" for "a political purpose for which [they were] explicitly not devised." I do not find the narrative of a political ethics problematic in this way, but I do know that a claim for a "political reading" of Descartes' oeuvre will seem suspicious to some. It is thus that I deploy Butler's method in an anti-presentist gesture by decontextualizing late-twentieth-century feminism's freezing of Descartes' significance into only the founder of the mind-body split, and recontextualizing his work as part of the politics of early-twentieth-century world of interwar and wartime France. In so doing, I come not to praise Descartes but, rather, to disinter his work from its (mostly) static position in narratives of feminism's origins. Slavoj Žižek has called for an analysis of the "spectre of the 'Cartesian paradigm' [that] roams around, simultaneously proclaimed dead and feared as the ultimate threat to our survival" (6). While I do not seek, as Žižek does, to "reassert the Cartesian subject" writ large (1998: 2), I am persuaded with him that even in its denial, "Cartesian subjectivity continues to be acknowledged by all academic powers as a powerful and still active intellectual tradition" (1998: 1). The robustness of this tradition in the tense and dangerous Europe of the 1920s, '30s, and '40s is one that we would do well to consider before excluding Descartes from our current discussions and concerns.

I am, finally, not the first to yoke Descartes and de Beauvoir together in an examination of issues central to feminism. In 1986, Butler herself commented on de Beauvoir's successful articulation, via Hegel, of the "limits of a Cartesian version of disembodied freedom" (Butler 1998 [1986]: 37–38). In 1998, Sonia Kruks cast the relationship somewhat differently—namely, as one in which de Beauvoir "adopts the Cartesian distinction between freedom [*liberté*] . . . and power [*puissance*]" (1998 [1990]: 50) in order to defend her own position vis-à-vis Sartre on the "situation" of the individual. The very fact that these two Descartes—one advocating a problematically "disembodied freedom"; the other theorizing the relationship between precisely that freedom and the body's ac-

cess to its performance—can coexist in feminist receptions of de Beauvoir nevertheless models for us the very principle of multiplicity of which
Valéry wrote. It is this variety and complexity of reception, and a methodology that will permit the production of theoretical and political significance for the past, to which I draw attention here. N. Katherine Hayles
wrote recently about the need to "keep disembodiment from being re-
written, once again, into prevailing concepts of subjectivity" in what she
calls the "posthuman" age of cybernetics (1999: 5). In what follows, I re-
embody Descartes not as a literal, but as a textual, body and active participant in the complex materiality of early-twentieth-century Europe. This
return to a past may initially appear "nerdish"—indeed, may seem to
concern only the processing of "the important ideas" by "dead white
men" of European high culture. My argument, however, is that going
back to their past may offer a different way to consider our feminist
futures.

"An Infinity of Possible Descartes": The Politics and Ethics
of Philosophy in Simone de Beauvoir's Europe

In 1937, the Bibliothèque Nationale in Paris mounted an extraordinary
exhibit on the life and work of René Descartes. The show stands out in
the history of the institution not only because of the richness represented
by the some 900 texts and artifacts assembled there, all associated with
Descartes as philosopher, scientist, and citizen of the early modern pan-
European *respublica literaria,* but also because of the political semiotics of
the exhibit and its content. The Ninth International Congress of Philosophy held in Paris at the same time as the exhibit opened was designated
the "Congrès Descartes" (Cain 1937: i), and sixty-seven of the 300 lectures held there by an international array of scholars were devoted to his
work. Yet the timing of both the conference and the exhibit made it clear
that, in spite of the apparently hagiographic impulse behind these joint
events, it was not the man but his texts that were of central, symbolic
importance, because 1937 of course marked the three-hundredth anniversary of the publication of his famous *Discourse de la méthode* rather
than any particular date in the philosopher's life. The focus on texts
would have been a familiar strategy to visitors to the French national
library, who would have remembered the 1933 exhibit there devoted to
the work of François Rabelais, timed to coincide with the four-hundredth

anniversary of the publication of his famous *Pantagruel*. More recently—indeed, in that very same year (1937)—the Bibliothèque Nationale had mounted an exhibit devoted to one of the most famous authors of French classical drama, Corneille, recognizing the three-hundredth anniversary of the publication of one of his well-known plays, *The Cid*, in the same year as Descartes' *Méthode*. Again, it was to a textual monument that the exhibit paid its respects.[4]

This foregrounding of the importance of textual afterlives is visible in the 1937 Descartes exhibit. Indeed, one of its most fascinating aspects must have been the sixty-two or so editions of the *Discourse de la méthode* on display, fifty-two of which were editions in the original French published between 1637 and 1931, and ten of which were translations into Dutch, Latin, Spanish, Polish, Portuguese, and even Hebrew. The multiple editions offered proof positive of the continuous fascination with and viability of Cartesian thought in the highly contentious context of National Front-led France. I return later to the significance of this specific moment of actualizing Cartesian thought in post-Cartesian times. First, however, it is interesting to note that in this exhibit, no German translations of Descartes' most famous text were displayed, even though the German reception of the Cartesian system had created a stir in Paris by 1929, when Edmund Husserl had lectured at the Sorbonne. The lectures were later published under the title of the *Cartesianische Untersuchungen* [Cartesian investigations] after his death. There are several ways to read this absence. It points to the fact that there was no love lost between the French and the Germans during these post-Treaty of Versailles years. Acknowledging the important German reception of Descartes would have meant offering a figurative olive branch to the enemy when doing so would surely have been perceived as a nearly traitorous act. An additional moment of the symbolic politics of exclusion can be observed in the absence of German scholarship from the inventory of "important" treatments of Descartes that Cain, director of the Bibliothèque Nationale, cites in the catalogue's foreword. The work of Flemish, Czech, Spanish, and Italian scholars is mentioned, but no Germans are named (Cain 1937: ii). The political tensions that exploded into the second continent-rending military conflict of the century over the next several years can thus be felt in the selectivity principles that organized the texts on display.

However, internal French institutional politics and generational preferences may also have played a role in the choice of how to package the

Cartesian legacy at this particular time and place. After all, one of the most highly profiled receptions of Husserl's Parisian lectures had been by the young Jean-Paul Sartre, who had traveled to Germany in the fatal year of 1933 to study Husserl's thinking in greater detail (Matthews 1996: 60). Sartre was only twenty-four when he heard Husserl, twenty-eight when he went to Germany, and thirty-two when the Descartes exhibit opened at the Bibliothèque Nationale. The primary organizers of the exhibit, however, represented predominantly the intellectual and philosophical older guard, among them Paul Valéry and, more important, the venerable Léon Brunschvicg (1869–1944), "un des maître officiels" [one of the official masters] of the French philosophical scene (Messaut 1938: 9) and Professor of Philosophy at the Sorbonne since 1909. Brunschvicg was the author himself of numerous highly specialized treatments of the Cartesian philosophy in the 1910s and '20s, collected in his *Écrits philosophiques* (1951–58). He was also the author, however, of the more generally accessible *Descartes et Pascal: Lecteurs de Montaigne* [Descartes and Pascal as readers of Montaigne], originally published in 1942 in Neuchatel, Switzerland, after Brunschvicg, a Jew, had fled into exile in the south of France in 1940, when he was no longer permitted to publish in his native land. He was nearly seventy at the time of the Descartes exhibit but had nevertheless been immensely influential in the teaching of the younger generation, including the likes of Sartre, for nearly half a century.

De Beauvoir's memoirs of her student days give a lively account of the intellectual and institutional politics of some of those years. They are littered with references to Brunschvicg and his Descartes. In the late 1920s, for example, it appears to have been something of a badge of courage among the younger generation, still students, to be chosen to present position papers in Brunschvicg's lectures, yet also privately to take a critical stance toward his readings of the philosophical tradition (de Beauvoir 1974: 310–11, 344). Nearly all serious students of philosophy in France had worked with him, either in their preparatory courses at one of the numerous Parisian lycées (high schools) where he taught or at the Sorbonne. Indeed, both de Beauvoir and the pacifist Simone Weil had written lengthy theses under Brunschvicg's direction in the late 1920s. De Beauvoir's was on the seventeenth-century German philosopher Leibniz (see Moi 1994: 52; de Beauvoir 1974: 266), Weil's was on "Science and Perception in Descartes." Brunschvicg apparently thought very little of Weil's penetrating treatment of the cogito (Pétrement 1973: 150–57) and gave it a barely passing grade. De Beauvoir, however, had already written a lengthy study on Descartes, "Descartes and the Ontological Fallacy" (1974: 223), and at the time she wrote her dissertation on Leibniz, she was already associating with the likes of fellow students Sartre and the future existential phenomenologist Maurice Merleau-Ponty. As de Beauvoir was researching and writing the thesis on Leibniz for Brunschvicg, she reports in her memoirs, the group around Sartre developed a rather self-impressed "club," to which only the "best minds," including Socrates and Descartes—as well as themselves—could belong (1974 [1958]: 321). A possible origin of this anchoring of their private caste system in the persons of these two philosophers in particular—why not Aristotle, for example, or Hume?—may in fact be found in Brunschvicg's somewhat later account, articulated in lectures in 1939–40, but published only after his death, of the origins of "l'esprit Européen" [the European soul] in precisely these select philosophers of the European past (see Brunschvicg 1947). Sartre and company were thus obviously familiar enough with Brunschvicg's readings of the philosophical tradition to be able to play with—as well as critique—them when they saw fit. De Beauvoir, a member of this crowd by this point, was thus perhaps better able than Weil to adopt a more orthodox approach to philosophizing and thus find Brunschvicg's favor. In any case, in 1937 and from Brunschvicg's point of view (he appears to have been the prime mover behind the exhibit at the Bibliothèque Nationale), there would thus have been no need to accentuate the German reception of Descartes or, indeed, even to highlight the newfangled—and still emerging—existentialist take on the great philosopher's work, because he (Brunschvicg) had already provided a thorough, if somewhat more traditional, account of the philosopher's system much closer to home.

Yet the question of what constituted a "traditional" approach to Descartes during these and subsequent years is crucial to pose, because Brunschvicg's "critical idealism" (de Beauvoir 1974: 234, see also 344; Messaut 1938: 163), although influential, was neither as simple as it seemed nor the only approach to Descartes that was current during the tense interwar and wartime years in France. The idealist reading of Descartes understood him primarily as a "rationalist" (Brunschvicg, 1944 [1942]: 141). In such a reading—and here I refer to one of Brunschvicg's somewhat later (originally 1942) treatments of Descartes for evidence— the relationship between the human subject and the material world takes place primarily through both perception and mental representation. As Descartes famously explains,

> Je trouve dans mon esprit deux idées du soleil toutes diverses: l'une tire son origine du sense . . . par laquelle il me paraît extrêmement petit; l'autre est prise des raisons de l'astonomie, c'est à dire de certaines notions nées avec moi, ou enfin est formée par moi-même de quelque sorte que ce puisse être, par laquelle il me paraît plusieurs fois plus grand que toute la terre [I find in my spirit/soul two very different ideas of the sun. The one finds its origin in the senses and makes the sun appear extremely small to me. The other is derived from the logic of astronomy, which is to say from certain notions/ ideas to which I gave birth, which were, in other words, ultimately formed by my Self in whatever way this can be said to be possible. This sun appears to me to be many times larger than the entire Earth]. (Descartes, *Troisième méditation*, as cited in Brunschvicg, 1944 [1942]: 140)

In order for the second, "scientific" idea of the sun to be recognized as "true," the first idea of the sun, based on simple perception, which originates in the body, has to be doubted. The origin of this doubt is thus the consciousness and self-consciousness of the perceiving subject, the famous cogitating I. Choosing the second idea as true—and the issue of choice is important—assumes the authority of this I over the senses and establishes the "truth" of the idea of the sun as something that originates in the mind. The idealist reading of Descartes, which is the reading that many recent feminists have targeted as worthy of critique precisely for its "anti-realism," thus claims that it is less the objects themselves than the mind that "constitutes the objects of perception" (Matthews 1996: 28–29).

And yet, the idealist position, even as articulated here by Brunschvicg, who in fact often seems to be ridiculed in accounts of the more "political" happenings of the time, should not be identified as the only possible reading of Descartes, either in general or by Brunschvicg, as if Descartes could be read only as refusing to consider a more linked version of relationship between the self and the material world. Indeed, "accuser Descartes . . . d'avoir sous-estimé l'expérience, c'est une étrange aberration" [accusing Descartes . . . of having underestimated experience is a strange aberration], wrote André Cresson in his "exposé of his [Descartes'] philosophy" in 1942 (1962 [1942]: 28), citing another book by Brunschvicg, *Descartes* (1937), for support. Indeed, in the later *Descartes et Pascal: Lecteurs de Montaigne*, published in 1942 but drawing on nearly half a century of his own scholarship, Brunschvicg used Descartes' *Sixième méditation* to show that there are in fact two ways to understand the I; "mon esprit, c'est à dire moi-même en tant que je suis seulement une chose qui pense," and "moi-même tout entier, en tant que je suis composé du corps et de l'âme" [my spirit, that is, my Self insofar as I am only a thinking being (and) my Self in its entirety, insofar as I consist in a body and a soul] (Brunschvicg 1944 [1942]: 146). The concepts under discussion here are addressed in Descartes' *Passions de l'Âme* (1649)—namely, how the soul, or spirit, interacts with, responds to, and causes corporeal action (Brunschvicg 1944 [1942]: 146–47). The dimensions of such interactions, of course, provide the very building blocks of a system of political ethics. How can we act well, and how can we do so in all of the materiality of our lives? Such questions surely found their origins in the everything other than other- or anti-worldly conditions of many Frenchmen's and Frenchwomen's lives during these years.

For according to Brunschvicg—at least, in 1942—Descartes was just as committed as his illustrious predecessor, Montaigne, to establishing the means by which human beings could attain "l'autonomie spirituelle" [spiritual autonomy] (1944 [1942]: 147), which would permit us to dispose over our own "libre arbitre" [free will], to become "maîtres de nous-mêmes" [masters over ourselves], and thus to open ourselves up to "un univers de connaissance et d'action" [a universe of knowledge and action] (1944 [1942]: 154). Such statements could be read as signs of political resignation, it is true. In adversity and under conditions of incapacitating oppression, one turns to the only domain over which one has control, one's own spirit and mind, as the sole remaining arena of freedom. The Jew Brunschvicg was clearly writing from a victimized position at this point, unable to publish in his native France, as noted earlier, bereft not only of his position and community but also of both the personal library and the manuscripts that signified his life's work. After his flight, these had been seized and destroyed by the Nazis, against the protests of his remaining colleagues at the Sorbonne (Tenger 1944: 14). Yet at the same time, there is also a distinctly activist dimension to Brunschvicg's appeal to a Cartesian free will. He targets, for example, the notions of "spiritual autonomy" and of a sense of the duty to use "les droits" [the rights] given to us by God to defend "l'humanité" [humanity] (Brunschvicg 1944 [1942]: 149) as the most important ones to remember. Indeed, as Descartes wrote in a letter dated 1645 that Brunschvicg quotes at length, "on doit toutfois penser qu'on ne saurait subsister seul . . . et il faut toujours préférer les intérêts du tout, dont on est partie, à ceux de sa personne en particulier" [one must always remember that one would not know how to survive alone . . . one must always give precedence to the interests of the community of which one forms a part over one's own individual interests] (Brunschvicg 1944 [1942]: 149–50). This quote from Descartes had probably also been in the back—or perhaps even the front—of Brunschvicg's mind when, still in Paris and lecturing for the last time at the Sorbonne in 1939–40, he asserted that it was in fact impossible to treat any topic "d'une analyse strictement philosophique" [from the point of view of a strictly philosophical analysis] without considering it as intimately connected to "la tragédie dont nous ne pouvons detacher notre pensée" [the tragedy from which we are unable to detach our thought], specifically "cette nouvelle guerre" [this new/most recent war] (Brunschvicg 1947: 7).

The philosophical analysis of contemporary political events was by no means new to Brunschvicg. A decade earlier, he had weighed in on matters political with a much criticized article on the "harshness" with which the Germans were treated in the Treaty of Versailles in *La revue des vivants* (July 1931), in which he invoked Spinoza's arguments about how to treat nations defeated in war (Sernin 1985: 297). Yet eight years later, when the tides had turned, Brunschvicg recalled in his 1939–40 lectures on "l'esprit européen" a 1924 article on Kant and the League of Nations that related the importance of Kant's work to Woodrow Wilson after World War I, and analyzed a speech by Nicolas Murray Butler, president of Columbia University, in which Kant and Plato were used to condemn the actions of Adolf Hitler (Brunschvicg 1947: 142). Brunschvicg was already an elderly man when he fled Paris, and the extent to which he could participate in defending the "interests of humanity" by resisting the Nazis may thus have been limited to developing philosophical proofs of the necessity for action. Yet these proofs appear, in at least one case, to have led him to welcome Albert Lautman, a French philosopher and a Jew, into his home after Lautman and others had made a daring escape from a German prison camp in Silesia in 1941. Lautman became an important member of the French Resistance in the south of France, but was captured and executed by the Nazis in 1944. Others who survived and were with Lautman in the camp remember him as an active member of "l'université du camp" [the university in the camp], whose lectures on the "problem of time" were followed avidly by his fellow prisoners (Sirinelli 1994: 550–52). Both Lautman and, in his own way, Brunschvicg thus appear to have found philosophy not only a compelling mode of analysis, but perhaps also a tool of spiritual survival, in the midst of the multiple conflagrations of war. Philosophical discussions of free will and of the individual's ability to act on his own behalf and on behalf of others were thus both central to Brunschvicg's reading of Descartes and key elements of the discourses—and realities—of political action at the time.

Even more radical political mediations of Cartesian positions, however, can be found circulating in Paris during precisely the same decades and in the same contexts in which Brunschvicg and his work traveled. These were again also de Beauvoir's contexts, and it is with a brief indication of these perhaps more recognizable—and yet, also different—political receptions of Descartes that I will end my re-embodiment of his work. In spite of its possible political implications, Brunschvicg's idealist version of Descartes seemed irrefutably traditional to some. It and he were thus under fairly constant attack—or, if that is too strong, they were at least constantly being challenged—by the work of Émile-Auguste Chartier (1868–1951), better known as Alain, on both philosophy in general and on Descartes as "le Prince de l'Entendement" [the prince of understanding] (Alain 1939: 110, 154) in particular, during these same years (on Alain, see Sirinelli 1994: 90–95 and Pétrement 1973: passim). Alain, too, was present, if again only in textual form, in the 1937 Bibliothèque Nationale exhibit as the author of an essay on Descartes that was printed with, and preceded the text of, *Discourse de la méthode* in an edition of that work published in 1927 (see Cain 1937: 100). That Alain was not among those who had planned the exhibit—and thus does not appear at the front of the exhibition catalogue in the lengthy list of the membership of "Comité d'Organisation," where Brunschvicg's name occupies a prominent place—is not surprising, however, because he played a very different kind of role in the political and institutional "microclimate" (Sirinelli 1994: 633) of French politics and philosophy in the years between and including the two world wars.

Of the same generation as Brunschvicg and, indeed, his immediate successor in any number of prestigious lycée jobs teaching philosophy to the future elites of French politics and culture, Alain steadfastly refused either to become absorbed in the class struggle of university advancement to a Chair at the Sorbonne, for example, or to systematize his philosophical thought in any traditional way. Rather, he remained in the position of guru-master to the students of his *khâgne*, or advanced study group at the high-school level, at the Lycée Henri IV until 1933, where he prepared them for the entrance exams in philosophy to the École Normale Supérieure, the training ground for the French professoriate. Beginning in 1921, the publishing house of Gallimard began to publish a twenty-page weekly (later, monthly) collection of short essays, entitled *Libres propos (Journal d'Alain)* [Free words, Alain's paper], in which he and his disciples, who included Simone Weil and Jeanne Alexandre—pacifists, feminists, unionists, founders of "les universités populaires" [peoples' universities] (Pétrement 1973: 117), and members of anti-fascist groups of all kinds—would publish reflections and positions on matters political and philosophical. Through 1936, the size and length of the *Libres propos* increased (Sernin 1985: 304) even as Alain's radical pacifism, the result of his experience in the trenches during World War I (Pétrement 1973: 116), where he saw the best of France's youth cut down all around him, became increasingly out of step with new legislation such as mandatory military service passed in France in response to the growing Nazi threat (Sernin 1985: 346). Although at variance with the anti-German, anti-Nazi position transmitted to us as the only viable political one during these years, Alain's pacifism was a highly "political" stance at the time, one perhaps not nearly so marginal in general as Alain himself appears to have been vis-à-vis the official, academic world of the time.

De Beauvoir was introduced to Alain's ideas and lectures on philosophy by one of his former students who persuaded her that "it's possible to be intelligent and take an interest in politics"; she nevertheless admits that she "continued to rate social questions lower than problems of metaphysics and morals" during her student years (1974: 238). De Beauvoir describes her meeting with one of Alain's best-known acolytes, Weil, at the École Normale as one from which she profited very little because of her (de Beauvoir's) "obstinate refusal" to see what all the fuss was about "suffering humanity." Weil, "attended by a group of Alain's old pupils" (de Beauvoir 1974: 239), ultimately accused de Beauvoir of being a "high-minded little bourgeois," which de Beauvoir apparently had to admit struck close to home. The incident is symptomatic of the reputation that

Alain had for foregrounding ethics rather than metaphysics in his lectures, and that his students had for both articulating and performing a "morale civique" [civic morality] in their lives both while students and thereafter (Sirinelli 1994: 95).

Alain's Descartes was thus, as could be expected, somewhat less orthodox than Brunschvicg's, although I would argue not very distant from it. First and foremost, Descartes was for Alain "homme, et chargé de matière comme nous, empeché de passions comme nous, et gouvernant ensemble corps et âme dans la situation humaine" [a mortal human being and laden with matter like the rest of us, hindered by the same passions as we are, governing the body and the soul together in the human situation] (1939: 110). He thus taught Descartes—and all of the great philosophers, for that matter—from what could be called a differently "presentist" perspective—in other words, precisely not as historical artifacts but as thinkers whose systems grappled with the facts of human existence in the world. Those systems could thus be properly understood only when actualized in the world. A former student, André Bridoux, writes that in Alain's lectures, "Nous n'assistions pas à un exposé des idées de Platon et de Descartes; nous étions en présence de Platon et Descartes . . . sans intermédiaires" [We were not (merely) attending a presentation of Plato's or Descartes' ideas; rather, we found ourselves in their very presence . . . in an unmediated fashion] (Sernin 1985: 123). The immediacy of philosophy that Alain taught is described by another contemporary in a similar way:

> Il n'est pas question ici de faire connaître Descartes, Platon et Hegel, mais d'enseigner selon Descartes, selon Platon et selon Hegel. Tout est dans cette espèce de grâce qui enveloppe le mot "selon": par elle seulement ces hautes pensées acquièrent une actualité qui se peut passer d'historicité [It was not a question then of familiarizing (us) with Descartes, Plato, or Hegel, but of teaching according to Descartes, according to Plato, and according to Hegel. Everything was in this kind of charm/aura that surrounded the words "according to" (French: *selon*). It was by virtue of this word that these lofty ideas acquired a presence that was able to do without historicity]. (As quoted in Sernin 1985: 304)

The systematic grounding of this "actualité" finds its clearest articulation, I would argue, in Alain's collection of essays on philosophy, entitled *Idées* (Ideas), and specifically there in the essay entitled "Étude sur Descartes" (1939: 109–99). *Idées* was originally published in 1932 but was based on essays that had appeared in 1927–28 (Sernin 1985: 303). The volume was reissued in 1939, however, in the very same year that Alain also published collections of his most vehemently anti-militarist essays (Sernin 1985: 396). The coincidence is provocative. The book is clearly designed to give an overview of the oeuvres of various philosophers, such that the student reader may get "le goût de philosophie" [a taste of philosophy] (Alain 1939: 7), and to choose whichever one appeals to him or her as a "maître" [master] (Alain 1939: 8). The fostering of this kind of discipleship system is uncanny, given the way Alain was himself adored by his students. The essay on Descartes in particular begins with a biographical section before moving on to a series of six- to seven-page sections on key Cartesian issues and terms, such as doubt, God, method, the will, understanding, and the imagination. We are allowed to feel the pressures of the political and military conflicts with which the period was most concerned in Alain's decision to place great weight on—indeed, to spend the final third of the essay on—examining the very issue that has subsequently caused such trouble for Descartes: the relationship between the body and the soul. It is well known, and often dismissed, that in his treatise *Traité des passions de l'Âme* [Treatise on the passions], Descartes attempted to locate the connective function between the body and the soul in the infamous "pineal gland." To the disparagement of some, Alain attempts in two chapters of the Descartes essay (1939: 150–55, 178–9) to rehabilitate this organ and theory in the interest of supporting his subsequent claims about the necessary interaction of the body and the mind in acts of free will. The first section devoted to this issue is in fact entitled "L'Union de l'âme et du corps" [The union of the soul and the body], announcing the way in which Alain chooses to interpret the so-called Cartesian dualism. Descartes had recognized the "fait" [fact], according to Alain, that the mind and the body are related (Alain 1939: 151). The issue at stake in the *Traité* is how to negotiate this relationship so that the ability of the individual to exercise her or his "libre arbitre" [free will] is clarified as a metaphysical and moral first principle and duty. In a reading of Descartes not unlike Brunschvicg's, Alain finds that it is in having the choice between the "l'apparence" [appearance] and "l'idée" [the idea] (Alain 1939: 160) and in judging in favor of the idea, that "la pensée libre" [free thought] (Alain 1939: 164) demonstrates its power and prominence. The "pouvoir de douter" [power to doubt] appearances in fact constitutes the power to chose—Descartes also calls it "generosité"

(Alain 1939: 189–94); it is thus doubt and the mind that allow free will to become "efficace" [effectual] in each individual (Alain 1939: 194).

The majority of the *Traité des passions* is devoted to providing a theory of self-control and spiritual autonomy under external conditions of adversity. It was dedicated to the young Princess Elizabeth of Bohemia, granddaughter of James I of England and daughter of the deposed king of Bohemia, Frederick V, who had fled his kingdom in the face of his Catholic enemies during the military fiasco conventionally recognized as the beginning of the Thirty Years' War (1618–48). Elizabeth had queried Descartes on how one could "philosophize" properly when the contingencies of the world lay too heavily about one; her own situation provided a perfect example of such a life. Descartes' answers to her in numerous letters and in the *Traité* contain descriptions of philosophical tasks that are not surprising in this context—namely, how to control one's body and mind under conditions of fear (Alain 1939: 196) and not give in to the "apparence de fatalité" [appearance of fatalism] (Alain 1939: 197). Alain underscores that Descartes counseled the princess to favor "passions favorables à la vie" [passions well disposed to life], such as love, rather than those that oppose it, such as hate and "tristesse" [sadness]. In a significant series of explanations, Alain adduces what he terms a Spinozian reading of Descartes: "Il vaut mieux se nourrir par amour de la vie que par crainte de la mort. . . . L'amour de liberté est aussi plus sain que cette haine que l'on entretient si aisément à l'égard du tyran" [It is far more worthwhile to subsist on the love of life than on the fear of death. . . . The love of liberty is also healthier than the hate that one so easily harbors with respect to the tyrant] (Alain 1939: 197–98). Not idle speculations or the tenets of a feel-good philosophy, Alain's readings of Descartes resonate here with applicability not only to the princess's life, but to the politics and ethics of self-conduct in his Europe. It is thus that Alain can read the early modern texts that he unpacked not only here, but also for generations of students, not at all as philosophical fossils or relics of irrelevant concerns, but as authored by a "homme d'action" [man of action] and "maître de pratique pour tout l'avenir humain" [master (and model) of pragmatism/practicality for all of mankind's future] (Alain 1939: 151).

Alain's actual students had heard his message and heeded it in much the way that Alain appears to have wanted the reader of the 1939 *Idées* to do. It was in 1929–30, for example, that Weil wrote her thesis on Descartes; she had been in Alain's khâgne until 1928. Ironically, her thesis supervisor for the Descartes paper was none other than Brunschvicg (Pétrement 1973: 150).[5] In general, Alain's "doctrine" was of more relevance for her, however, especially as it concerned the primacy of free will, the willing of the good, and the necessity to act in the service of freedom. A former student recounts that one of the main tenets of Alain's philosophy was that "there was no profound distinction between the man of thought, the man of action, and the artist" (Pétrement 1973: 32–33). Thus, when Weil transformed Descartes' "cogito, ergo sum" [I think, therefore I am] into "Je puis, donc je suis. . . . Du moment que je fais, je fais que j'existe" [I can, therefore I am. . . . From the moment that I act, I make myself exist] (Pétrement 1973: 154) in her thesis, she was following Alain's creed. To understand the self is, then, to understand free will. To understand the power of free will, one must act. In Weil's case, this call to act required a refusal of the constraints set on the individual by the world (Pétrement 1973: 154–57), the refusal of inequality and injustice and, ultimately, the refusal of collaboration, even for peace (Sernin 1985: 421). For Alain, the constraints of the world existed in most their abhorrent form in militarism, nationalism, and class hierarchy and prejudice, which all had to be refused absolutely in the here and now. His writings throughout the interwar years and through World War II, and during the occupation of France, represent his unconditional radicalism, a radicalism whose underpinning are audible in his writings on Descartes.

The writings of Brunschvicg and Alain, so instrumental in shaping the thinking of the younger generation of philosophers, including de Beauvoir, during the interwar and wartime years in France, reveal the outlines of a possible embodiment of Cartesian philosophy distinguished by its usefulness as a tool for articulating a political ethics. Not all French receptions of Descartes—or, surely, all of those that emerged in the post-war period—were saturated with the kinds of implications that I have tried to read out of selections of Brunschvicg's and Alain's work. The existentialist version of this ethics, for example, developed in the brief but dense essay on Descartes by de Beauvoir's companion, Jean-Paul Sartre (1946), focuses similarly on the concept of "la liberté cartésienne" [Cartesian liberty, the title of Sartre's essay]. Of central concern to Sartre, as to his master, Heidegger, by this point was the relationship of human freedom to existence, which existence must be both affirmed and refused by the human subject in a demonstration of that subject's autonomy. Sartre finds in Descartes' writings the basic elements of this autonomy, or freedom (Sartre 1946: 52, passim), elements that are the building blocks, he argues, of a kind of radical democratization of freedom. Regardless of "situation," all men have the capacity to choose, "de dire non ou de dire oui" [to say no or to say yes] (Sartre 1946: 19). It is thus not surprising that Sartre refers at the beginning of his essay to Alain's reading of Cartesian "choice" as a matter of judgment (Sartre 1946: 10), as his reading of Descartes in many ways tries to synthesize the Alainian with the Heideggerian position.

It was, of course, de Beauvoir's task to develop an argument that took into account the limitations on freedom that any given individual's "situation" imposed. She actualizes the Alainian-Sartrean-Cartesian moment of "choice" in *Le deuxième sexe,* which she similarly describes as derived from "la morale existentialiste" [existentialist ethics] (949: xxxiv), when she writes there that the individual "n'accomplit sa liberté que par son perpétuel dépassement vers d'autres libertés" [achieves liberty only through a continual reaching out toward other liberties] (1949: xxxiv–xxxv). This premise of the necessity of freedom as choice permeates much of *Le deuxième sexe,* from de Beauvoir's discussion of homosexuality as "une attitude choisie en situation, c'est-à-dire à la fois motivée et librement adoptée" [an attitude chosen in a certain situation—that is, at once motivated and freely adopted] (1949: 1:510, 1:424) to the cases of women as creators of "l'art, la littérature, la philosophie" [art, literature, and philosophy], all of whom "d'abord se poser sans équivoque comme une liberté" [must first unequivocally assume the status of a being who has liberty] (1949: 2:555, 2:711). Sonia Kruks was thus correct in 1990 to point out that de Beauvoir was using a Cartesian move to link her thinking to Sartre's—as well as to move beyond it (1998 [1990]: 50)—when she addressed and problematized the issue of women's access to freedom in *Le deuxième sexe.* But Kruks dwells primarily on the Sartrean connection, much to the disadvantage of the "longer history" of the concept of freedom as it is deployed in that text. Understanding this history would thus of necessity include an in-depth treatment of Descartes' reception during the early twentieth century via a more thorough analysis of the multiple Descartes available in readings by Brunschvicg and Alain, among others, than I have been able to give here.

The colors of the past, even without our interventions, are themselves as deep, and the contours of the past are as complex, as those of the present.

Indeed, in the discussion of the interwar and wartime French Descartes of the 1920s–40s, the past was surely more polychromatic than the black-and-white cartoons of the Enlightenment philosopher and his legacy discussed earlier, the very images of the past to which many of our students have access today. By investigating the contours of the U.S. American, the Soviet, or the French colonial Descartes during these same years, for example, we could fill out the picture by adding a more "multicultural" Descartes. In the process, we might enrich the options for our own choices of theories and methods by considering the possibility of a political and ethical reading of the cogito, one that, for example, enables it to function as a starting point for a theory of agency. I am not suggesting that all feminists must reread all of Western philosophy, or that they must delve into the intellectual, institutional, and political genealogies of their subject matter—although I also think that this might be a good thing. I am concerned, however, that if we persist in handing on to students only the most recent of politically correct objects and methods of study, we reduce the range of ways of thinking about issues by refusing to look at historical models of analysis and critique. If it was—and is—possible to find examples of the grounding of a political ethics in specific past receptions of Descartes, might we not also find in the past ways to address some of our other most pressing questions, such as those concerning identity and difference, the equal distribution of resources, and more democratic state formations, not to speak of more flexible definitions of sexuality, the family, and work? Perhaps it is we who should not be "happy this way." Perhaps it is time to move ahead by moving back. Or if that is too strong, perhaps it is time to challenge the way in which recent generations of feminism have become used to keeping time.

Notes

1 Such presentism also lies behind the much discussed gap between humanistic and social science approaches to feminism, because most assessments of the complex institutional relations between them assume the present structural and methodological differences as timeless oppositions. They thus fail to investigate the genealogy of this alleged split as the odd outcome of past similarities between departments of literary studies and departments of sociology, for example, both of which saw it as their disciplinary destiny during the Cold War to inherit the cultural and methodological goods of a Europe clearly incapable of preserving them safely, as the fighting of two

major wars on European turf in the first half of the twentieth century had shown. Discussions of the topic of the perverse distance between the humanities and the social sciences in the late twentieth and early twenty-first centuries seldom go back even this far, however, and are discussed instead in a manner that literary scholars would call formalist—that is, as methodological artifacts rather than as historical disciplinary formations.

2   Eileen O'Neill traces the intricacies of the reception of the philosopher's ideas among the many "cartésiennes" [female Cartesians] writing at the time, indicating that there was nothing so intrinsically anti-female to his philosophy that it prevented Descartes' thought from finding resonance among women both at the time he wrote and since.

3   Elaine Marks, for example, is fascinated with de Beauvoir's body: see Marks 1998 (1973, 1986).

4   The very difference of the timing of these several exhibits from another, relatively recent show at the Bibliothèque Nationale underscores the centrality of texts to the legacy politics that distinguished the French manner of dealing with their past. In 1931, the library had mounted a show on Goethe, the "father of German classicism," in a centennial celebration of the year of his death. The most (in)famous afterlife that Goethe's texts experienced in France was not observed until somewhat later, when multiple editions of his works in translation were published in Nazi-occupied Paris after 1940 by the famous house of Gallimard. The books appear to have been designed to encourage the availability of work by an author who was considered one of the "First National Socialists" (Assouline 1988 [1984]: 233–34, 246), the master poet of France's new masters. There is a distinct possibility that in 1937, four years after the coming to power of the National Socialists in Germany and at the height of political and military antagonisms between the two countries dating back to the Treaty of Versailles (if not before), veering away from the precedent set by the 1931 Goethe exhibit—and, by implication, from the entire German tradition—was a perhaps partly unconscious, but perhaps also partly deliberate, decision on the part of the committee that designed the Descartes exhibit. That Goethe's texts were transformed into French-language supporters of Third Reich expansionism in subsequent years would only have confirmed the wisdom of this earlier attempt to shackle him and his legacy in 1931 to a specific, and specifically past, moment of embodiment incapable of time-travel and infiltration into French. Conversely, celebrating the ability of illustrious French authors such as Descartes to have abundant and specifically textual afterlives may have signaled the way in which the French thought of their literary and philosophical ancestors as just as, if not more, important because of the ways in which they affected the present.

5   Indeed, although they were initially colleagues, even friends, the split between Alain and Brunschvicg after World War I subsequently caused problems for those of Alain's students who landed in the philosophy faculty at the Sorbonne: see Sirinelli 1994: 466–67. Brunschvicg nevertheless generously acknowledged Alain's philosophical importance in a letter to Alain on the latter's seventieth birthday: see Sernin 1985: 378.

II : INSTITUTIONAL PEDAGOGIES (A FORUM)

Contending with Disciplinarity

Women's Studies, as a paradigm of intellectual inquiry and as institutional site in the academy, has a complex and unstable relationship to traditional scholarly disciplines. At various points in its history, and in different academic settings, the teaching and research practices of Women's Studies can be characterized as multidisciplinary, interdisciplinary, nondisciplinary, and antidisciplinary, or as constituting an emerging or established discipline. The institutional location of Women's Studies in colleges and universities also marks and shapes the relationship of Women's Studies to the local organization of disciplines, most notably in the distinction between Women's Studies programs and departments, but also in the various positioning of Women's Studies units in colleges of humanities, colleges of arts and humanities, supra-college units, or other academic locations.

The extent to which Women's Studies' teaching and scholarship transcends the strictures of disciplinary knowledge has been important to its intellectual viability. Yet what is one of Women's Studies' most rewarding, nourishing aspects also can be challenging, frustrating, and, for some, a deterrent to teaching Women's Studies courses or publishing in Women's Studies venues. The benefits of operating outside the boundaries of conventional disciplinary frameworks, most of which historically have been antagonistic—or, at least, blind—to gender analysis, are clear. These have been explored extensively in Women's Studies scholarship and are reflected in the transdisciplinary institutional mission of most

Women's Studies programs and departments. But there also are problems that stem from the complicated relationship of Women's Studies to the academic disciplines.

Without dismissing the obvious advantages for Women's Studies of existing outside of traditional academic disciplines, I use this essay to explore some vexing issues that stem from this location. I focus particularly on dilemmas that can arise when faculty and students are engaged in scholarly dialogue outside the traditional academic disciplines. Although such concerns certainly are mitigated by institutional arrangements in which faculty lines and degree programs are housed fully within Women's Studies departments, even in such units faculty and students confront a larger academic context of employment opportunities and rewards organized largely along disciplinary lines.

Over the past two decades, I have served terms as director of the Women's Studies programs at the University of Kentucky and at the University of Pittsburgh, both of which are nondepartmental units constituted by faculty and students housed in degree-granting departments. Like the situation in many colleges and universities across the country, these Women's Studies programs rely on faculty such as myself who had little preparation for thinking across disciplinary frameworks. Indeed, many of today's Women's Studies program administrators and department chairs, trained in the graduate schools of the 1960s, 1970s, and early 1980s, were taught to value the intellectual genealogies of particular scholarly niches. The "disciplining" nature of graduate schools of this period privileged scholarly conversations within the boundaries of common intellectual frameworks and retreated from efforts to dilute specialized jargon or to engage in serious cross-disciplinary exchange.

In the 1980s and 1990s, Women's Studies developed a secure and widespread institutional base in universities and colleges across the country, creating pedagogical and scholarly challenges to faculty trained in conventional disciplines. This occurred in two ways. First, the explosion of feminist scholarship in a wide variety of academic fields required faculty to read and introduce students to a tremendous range of ideas and approaches to knowledge, some of which were far afield from the intellectual domain in which they had the most background and felt most comfortable. Second, the classrooms and scholarly exchanges of Women's Studies demanded that faculty read and teach in ways that united (or at least acknowledged) multiple disciplinary stances or that lay outside any traditional disciplinary framework. Women's Studies necessitated learning new approaches to knowledge that were interdisciplinary, multidisciplinary—even nondisciplinary or antidisciplinary.

These challenges to disciplinary knowledge, inherent in the intellectual mission of Women's Studies, have had institutional consequences for Women's Studies programs and departments. On the positive side, Women's Studies has been a valuable intellectual haven from increasingly narrow disciplinary concerns. More problematic, however, has been the often cited tension between traditional university and college structures of disciplinary reward and evaluation for faculty and students and participation in Women's Studies interdisciplinary teaching and scholarship. Equally difficult, although less obvious, have been self-imposed barriers to participation such as faculty resistance to teaching and evaluating feminist scholarship seen as "too far outside" one's disciplinary experience and intellectual command.

One way to explore the promises and pitfalls of inter-, multi-, and antidisciplinarity in Women's Studies is to focus on the teaching of feminist theory classes. I use feminist theory courses as a site in which to examine the issue of disciplinarity in Women's Studies for several reasons. First, feminist theory courses are nearly ubiquitous in Women's Studies, found in small and fledgling programs as well as in large and established departments. Although feminist theory courses are not essential to a Women's Studies curriculum, in most programs and departments these are a (or the) core required course in the curriculum, as is the case in the graduate certificate program at the University of Pittsburgh. Thus, feminist theory courses often carry a special pedagogical burden, as courses meant to convey, in as comprehensive a way as possible, the breadth of feminist thinking across a wide range of subjects and paradigms. Second, feminist theory courses pose particularly thorny issues of disciplinary knowledge, often conveying a skepticism toward disciplinary knowledges while simultaneously tracing feminist theoretical assumptions to the intellectual traditions from which these emerged historically. In practical terms, the attention to traditional—and disciplinary—theories that is required to understand the genealogy of contemporary feminist theorizing may bolster students' understandings of disciplinary traditions at least as much as it provides a sense of the intellectual possibilities of operating outside these traditions.

Feminist theory courses are notoriously challenging to teach. In my experience, feminist theory courses carry an intimidating reputation to faculty (perhaps less so to students), making it difficult to persuade faculty to agree to teach these courses unless they are geared to particular, usually broadly disciplinary, issues and concerns. Unlike other difficult-to-staff courses in which faculty resistance can usually be traced to fears that the students will be unprepared, resistant, or hostile, the widespread unwillingness of faculty to teach feminist theory classes often reflects concerns about operating far afield from one's own academic discipline.

Feminist theory classes pose starkly the gulf between feminist scholarship that is increasingly rooted in inter-, multi-, and antidisciplinarity and the disciplinary preparation of most faculty and students. Teaching such courses requires faculty to find ways to move, and to help students learn how to move, within diverse and even competing theories and epistemologies from multiple disciplines. For faculty in the social sciences and natural sciences, it means thinking about theory and theorizing very differently—that is, not as a framework to guide the collection of empirical data. It requires consideration of issues of aesthetics and humanistic values that rarely intrude in conventional scientific theorizing. For scholars in the humanities, it means confronting theoretical formulations that privilege prediction over explanation or precision over comprehensiveness and those that freight theory with methodological and practical concerns. More intimidating still, teaching feminist theory requires faculty to negotiate scholarly understandings and jargons for which they may have little point of entry and little confidence of competence. The very language of contemporary literary theory and cultural studies can seem impenetrable to students and faculty who operate outside that framework, as can the statistical or empiricist language of the sciences to those from the humanities.

Concerns over the role of theory and the interpretability of jargon also reflect a deeper issue that confronts faculty engaged in interdisciplinary teaching in Women's Studies. As an emerging scholarship, feminist theory largely has been positioned within, or against, disciplinary histories and understandings, making it important to direct students to the antecedents of these ideas and debates. Could we understand Nancy Chodorow without an acquaintance with Freud, or Iris Marion Young without Sartre and Foucault, or Patricia Hill Collins without Marx? Yet time constraints in a course rarely permit more than a quick detour into these intellectual genealogies. Thus, it is difficult to position a discussion of theory that will not seem painfully obvious to some students and incomprehensible to others. Students in such courses tend to be over-prepared for theories that are rooted in their own disciplines and under-prepared to confront ideas based outside those disciplines.

Moreover, inter-, multi-, and antidisciplinary feminist theory courses face the dilemma of superficiality in another way: The wide range of in-tellectual roots within and against which feminist theory is constructed— and the impossibility of understanding each—can be an excuse to skim the surface of disciplinary knowledges. It can permit a "mix and match" of conceptual frameworks from vastly different fields of inquiry without sufficient attention to the complexities of understandings and the com-plicated assumptions in which these knowledges are embedded.

Although such concerns can be paralyzing, they also can be liberating. Feminist theory courses, like other classes within Women's Studies, al-low faculty and students to think about what disparate disciplinary ap-proaches have in common as well as about how they differ. They provide an institutional forum for grappling with the shallow and artificial charac-ter of some disciplinary boundaries, as when cross-disciplinary conversa-tions allow us to see when different jargons obscure identical referents. Feminist theory also can be a site to explore the different approaches and ways of thinking that characterize disciplinary knowledges. It creates a space for challenging one's own disciplinary way of being, and one's own (often unexamined) assumptions about epistemology and about meth-odology and approach. And it can generate a sense of the excitement of thinking and engaging in dialogue outside of a disciplinary box.

Perhaps more explicitly than other pedagogical experiences, the teach-ing of feminist theory forces faculty to position ourselves as learners, to acknowledge our disciplinary blinders, and to take risky intellectual moves outside of those frameworks along with our students. It requires us to acknowledge the shaky ground on which we stand and the threaten-ing, but potentially thrilling, experience of being far from one's intellec-tual home. It forces us to confront what we ask our students to consider: what theory is and what feminist theory can be. Do we want feminist theory to be a nourishing well from which we partake to refresh our largely disciplinary thinking and scholarship? Or do we see feminist theory as a template, a framework, or an approach to knowledge on which we can construct our own scholarship and research?

The challenge of inter-, multi-, and antidisciplinarity in Women's

Studies is to find ways to advance and deepen feminist work within existing disciplines as well as outside these disciplinary frames. The ongoing consolidation of Women's Studies as a distinct field of inquiry and as an institutional unit in universities and colleges will surely decrease tensions about multi-, inter-, and antidisciplinarity in the future by increasing the number of faculty who are trained in a feminist scholarship that is not bound to other academic disciplines. However, it is important to maintain intellectual as well as political and social ties between feminist scholars trained and located in Women's Studies programs and departments and those operating within traditional disciplines. Thoughtful conversations about both the promises and the perils of teaching Women's Studies courses across and outside disciplinary bounds can be one useful mechanism toward this end.

The Past in Our Present: Theorizing the
Activist Project of Women's Studies

Women's Studies began on U.S. college campuses in the late 1960s as
one of the "new knowledges" that emerged from the identity movements
of that decade. One of the first courses was offered at Cornell University
in 1967, and by 1970 courses existed at a number of campuses around
the country, including the State University of New York (SUNY) at Buffalo,
where I was a graduate student in the English department. The first
formal program was approved in that year at San Diego State University,
where I have worked for more than two decades not only as a faculty
member in the Women's Studies department but as its chair for eight
years. Having spent my entire academic career in the development and
maintenance of Women's Studies as an institutional academic discipline, and served recently as president of the National Women's Studies
Association (NWSA), I am deeply committed to the ongoing debate over
what this field was, is, should be, and can be. One way to understand the
present, and plan for the future, is to study the past, so for this essay
I have gone back to one of the earliest articles published on the theory
and practice of Women's Studies, "Women's Studies: A Case in Point"
(1972), cowritten by Christine Grahl, Elizabeth Kennedy, Lillian Robinson, and myself.[1] Using that article as a jumping-off point, I will meditate
on one of the questions that continues to be a point of debate within
Women's Studies, highlighted at the 1999 NWSA conference: the relationship between activism and academics. By thinking about how we understood the question of academics and activism, or theory and practice, in

1972, we can better appreciate its long-lasting influence over the past three decades.

The claim that Women's Studies is the academic arm of the women's movement has been attributed to a number of different sources. One of these is "A Case in Point," in which Grahl, Kennedy, Robinson, and I use a related if subtly different phrase: the "theoretical arm of the feminist movement" (Grahl et al. 1972: 112).[2] The latter phrase harbors two assumptions I will discuss here. The first is that Women's Studies is a theoretical enterprise that is dedicated to more than fact-finding, textual interpretation, and, especially, consciousness-raising (c-r). We felt the need to emphasize the last point, because the idea that feminist education should primarily raise consciousness was, and continues to be, a prominent note in discussions of Women's Studies. We argued in contrast:

> Part of our program is involved in outreach and orientation toward the movement and our courses do serve a consciousness-raising function. But consciousness-raising is not radical education. In fact, conducted in a political and intellectual vacuum, consciousness-raising is neither radical nor education. It is the beginning, not the end, of what we do, and the kind of awareness we try to promote, even at that introductory level, is one focused on elaborating concrete strategies. (Grahl et al. 1972: 112–13)

Our point was that Women's Studies must include a political and intellectual agenda if it is to count as radical education. And that intellectual agenda included the production of theory, without which the political practice in which we are engaged becomes meaningless. Although the article does not directly engage the question of what theory is, it implies that theory is the explanatory grounding for political practice, not an intellectual enterprise in and of itself. In that way, our notion of theory in 1972 differs from some contemporary manifestations of critical theory, which can be, or appear to be, overly abstract and detached from social and political realities. At the same time, however, I would emphasize that "A Case in Point" adamantly rejects the notion that theory is a "male" activity and unnecessary to ground political action. The article, and its authors, were thoroughly committed to the production of theoretical discourses and explanations in the absence of which activists may spin their wheels without direction or purpose. To elaborate that point, I will quote once again from "A Case in Point":

Because our intellectual work has its roots in a serious social movement, we must begin to establish a serious intellectual foundation. We are struggling to understand and control our own experience and we have neither the leisure nor the power—much less the time—to pursue the kinds of questions acceptable in a department that lacks our immediate point of reference and commitment to the real world. (Grahl et al. 1972: 113)

Although many of these words—experience, power, point of reference, real world—have been contested over the past decade, I believe that the message continues to resonate with most practitioners of Women's Studies today. The passage speaks to the profound connection we feel between our academic work and social or political activism. It insists on the serious intent of our educational work, and it roots the production of knowledge in real social relations and commitment to social change. In 1972, at the beginning of the project to define the nature of these social relations and dimensions of this social change, a "serious intellectual foundation" was profoundly needed. What I would highlight in this passage is not the reference to activism—for that is to be expected at that time—but the insistence on intellectual and theoretical work. Written as it was by a collective that included two assistant professors (Kennedy and Robinson) and a graduate student (Zimmerman) who would go on to become significant figures in the development of feminist scholarship, the entire article demands that political practice be informed by theoretical work, and it locates Women's Studies as the place where that relationship can be forged. It cannot be done within feminist organizations alone; nor can it be done in academic disciplines and departments that "lack our immediate point of reference and commitment to the real world."

A second assumption was that Women's Studies not only emerged from the women's movement—as any historical study can verify—but remains part of it. In 1972, that might have seemed self-evident. We felt no need to make that argument in 1972, which we certainly would have had to do even five years previously, or might need to do today. In Buffalo, the Women's Studies program was still a project of Buffalo Women's Liberation (BWL), where it had begun. We saw our purpose as producing activists who would move into BWL, as well as other radical organizations. Indeed, the most intense arguments within the collective in that era (as I recall) concerned the kind of political activists we were trying to create: radical feminists or Marxist socialists—a rather different debate from those that have raged more recently between humanists and social scientists or between postmodernists and cultural feminists. Specifically, we identified ourselves, as Women's Studies teachers and scholars, as "part of the theoretical arm of the feminist movement" (Grahl et al. 1972: p. 112). We recognized then, as now, that institutional Women's Studies was not the only source of feminist theory.

"Women's Studies: A Case in Point," then, clearly articulated what has come to be seen as the essence of Women's Studies: the inextricable and mutually rewarding relationship between academics and academia. But in the 1990s, books, articles, and conference speeches of all types have posited a rift between the two, one that may be mourned or celebrated, attributed to either the activists or, much more often, the academics. Where do the problems lie, and how can they be solved? I will suggest that changes in social relations, including the nature of the women's movement and feminist politics, have dramatically affected this relationship between academics and activism. What we took for granted in 1972—that Women's Studies is "an integral part of women's struggle for self-determination" and "the embodiment of our desire and need to create an education that will contribute to our effectiveness in the struggle"—may need rethinking and reformulating as we move into the twenty-first century.

We must first acknowledge that we cannot go back to the model of activism and academia that existed in 1972. Society has changed, the women's movement has changed, the universities have changed, and Women's Studies has changed. In 1972, feminism, or women's liberation, was a radical, oppositional political movement and discourse. It was brash, new, outrageous, and totally dedicated to the overthrow of patriarchal institutions and ideologies. It was also part of much larger political upheavals tied to the wars of national liberation that were dismantling twentieth-century colonialism. As Elizabeth Lapofsky Kennedy argues in her retrospective on the Buffalo Women's Studies program, we saw no contradiction between our work and that of the Vietnamese National Liberation Front, the Black Panthers, and myriad other organizations dedicated to anticapitalist, antiracist, and anti-imperialist struggles.[3]

Anti-sexist agitation was intricately connected to these struggles, despite the deep sexism of those organizations that had precipitated some of the new women's groups in the first place. Hence, it is not surprising that the uprisings that occurred in the wake of the U.S. invasion of Cambodia in 1970 led our women's liberation group both to participate in organizing an anti-imperialist educational campaign and to "liberate" a women's restroom in order to establish the first child-care center at SUNY, Buffalo.

Like our political work—and this point has been made often before—our intellectual work was iconoclastic, innovative, and interdisciplinary. We were naively ignorant in our belief that no feminist scholarship had existed before us, but most of what we were learning and teaching was indeed the product of our C-R groups and study groups. We were writing the texts as we went along. And the universities in which we found ourselves were reeling from the onslaught of student activism, and responded with a combination of indulgence and repression that was probably unique to the late 1960s and early 1970s.

We don't live in that world anymore. Not that the evils of sexism, racism, capitalism, and imperialism have been vanquished, but the social, political, and intellectual tactics and strategies available to us have changed over the past thirty years. We will need to analyze the relationship between academics and activism, between Women's Studies and women's movements, in light of the social realities of the early twenty-first century, not our nostalgic memories of the 1960s. My own nostalgia for the " '60s" (a period that actually spanned roughly the years 1967 to 1975) revolves around feelings of youthful certainty, optimism, and romanticism. I "remember" (more probably, construct) a period when the nature and causes of women's oppression were clear and self-evident; thus, necessarily, the strategy for ending oppression allowed for no postmodern problematizing. Although I struggled within myself to decide whether the enemy was men as a class or monopoly capitalism, I had no doubt that collective action aimed at the center of the power structure would bring the enemy down. Glory and heroism lay in that struggle; right was right and wrong was wrong; my identity as a woman was whole, unconflicted, and thoroughly rooted in political struggle. These personal memories of the Heroic Age of feminism, multiplied a thousand times over, have helped to construct a public nostalgia that I note, and probably foster, in my Women's Studies students. Whether or not it is a true memory, the conditions that led to and permitted such arrogant and jubilant certainty no longer exist, and new ideas about the relationship among theory, activism, and the academy must be developed.

Toward that end, we might begin by considering what, at the beginning of this new century, we mean by activism. Feminists in 1972 may have differed greatly over the underlying theory and practice of the movement—whether socialism was necessary for women's liberation; whether men as a class or the capitalist state was the enemy; whether we should work within existing institutions or create entirely new ones—but we believed that our goal was to overthrow the centers of power and create an entirely new society. I will venture to guess that the goal of many feminists today is not the total overthrow of existing power structures, but the practical amelioration of women's wounds—or the "empowerment" of women, which may or may not have a radical, transformative analysis behind it. Whether the reason behind this change is our greater skepticism about the workings of power or our greater stake in the system itself, I find myself wondering whether what we mean by activism has become synonymous with community service, or, in current academic jargon, "service-learning." I have observed that the activist goals of Women's Studies to which students are most attracted center on domestic-violence work. Individual women are certainly helped by battered women's shelters and services, and profoundly so, but it is not clear to me that this work necessarily does anything to transform the balance of power or undermine oppressive institutions in the larger society. Indeed, the emphasis within Women's Studies on volunteer activities, whether in the public sector or in the nonprofit agencies that employ so many of our graduates, may actually reinforce current power structures and relations by taking on some of the work that used to be considered the responsibility of the state.

I believe these are important issues to raise and questions to ask for a number of reasons. First, universities are increasingly encouraging, even requiring, service-learning, and thus what we in Women's Studies have always understood to be the essence of our radical activism could become yet another graduation requirement, something that must be done for the accumulation of credits, not because it is integrated into the student's understanding of her or his responsibility for social change.[4] Second, we need to ask whether we are preparing students for a life of activism or of volunteer work and philanthropy. How does our understanding of "community service" differ from that of, say, social work—or even fraternities and sororities? Third, one measure of our success is the institutionalization of feminist (and other radical) projects through non-profit agencies, and, hence, the professionalization of community service, or activism, that may be no different from that of academic Women's Studies. Finally, I believe we should begin to interrogate the primacy we tend to give to activism over academics, because our academic work may be of equal—or even greater—value than activism. I do not speak only of the academic research that is directly and obviously useful to community activists. Not only can we not predict what scholarship may prove valuable in the future, the intellectual realm—research, experimentation, critical reading, theorizing—is valuable for its own sake. For that matter, much as the convents of early medieval Europe preserved literacy during centuries of decline, Women's Studies programs could prove to be the repositories of feminist knowledge in future periods of repression or complacency.

My conclusion is that we imperatively need to forge new relationships between political activism and scholarship that are not dependent on mythology or nostalgia, and that respect the goals of both activism and academia.[5] In 1972, when the relationship between the women's liberation movement and the emerging field of Women's Studies was clear and direct, Grahl, Kennedy, Robinson, and I argued that without a strong intellectual and theoretical base, our political work would be aimless and unproductive. Because we were situated as academics in universities, we saw it as our responsibility to take ourselves seriously as scholars and develop that intellectual base. At the beginning of the twenty-first century, in a very different political and social climate, it seems to me that our responsibilities to be scholars is even stronger than it was in 1972. As universities are increasingly reshaped according to corporate agendas, as social welfare becomes privatized and Women's Studies students find themselves in the position of modern ladies bountiful, as the productive space between theory and practice threatens to grow into an unbridgeable chasm—for all these reasons and more, we need committed Women's Studies scholars to produce the theories, questions, and data that shape and influence meaningful social and political activism.

Notes

1 Grahl et al. 1972.
2 Specifically, we identify ourselves as Women's Studies teachers and scholars, as "part of the theoretical arm of the feminist movement" (Grahl et al. 1972: p. 112). We

recognized then, as now, that institutional Women's Studies was not the only source of feminist theory.

3 See Kennedy 2000.

4 In California, for example, Governor Gray Davis has proposed that community service be a graduation requirement for all students in the California State University and University of California systems.

5 For a related analysis stressing the relationship between activism and institutionalization, see Orr 1999b.

JUDITH KEGAN GARDINER

Rethinking Collectivity: Chicago Feminism, Athenian Democracy, and the Consumer University

In the early 1970s, a male faculty member at my urban public university opposed our nascent Women's Studies Program as dangerously communistic, and one female student wanted the faculty and students in the organizing collective to live together communally with our children and partners and pool our incomes. A generation later, there is less hostility and less utopianism surrounding Women's Studies, more feminist scholarship to master, more acceptance of the process-oriented pedagogy that Women's Studies often fosters, and a firmer institutional base for the program within the university. Those initial fears and hopes about collectivity, however, were not irrelevant responses to our socialist feminist ideology of equality and empowerment.[1]

Rather, they were founded on the challenges that our ideas posed to American individualism and traditional university structures. A founder, sometimes acting director, and continuous participant in our Women's Studies Program for more than twenty-five years, I here reconsider our history and ponder our future as we continue to face the contradictory pressures of consumer individualism, the corporatized public university, and our vision of social transformation. What remains of our earlier socialist feminist goals of equality, consensus, and collaboration? How do they affect our program now, and how should they guide its future?

The Women's Studies program at the University of Illinois at Chicago (UIC), like many others, has its roots in the women's liberation movement. I arrived on campus as an Assistant Professor of English in 1969 and joined groups protesting the American war in Vietnam. I and a few other female faculty in these groups found ourselves defending women's liberation, before we had joined its ranks ourselves, against charges that feminism was trivial, exclusively personal, or divisive to leftist activism. We then formed a student and faculty women's group and affiliated with the Chicago Women's Liberation Union, an umbrella organization for local socialist feminist activists. We sought a "comprehensive interdisciplinary" Women's Studies curriculum, "tutoring and counseling to expand women's vocational opportunities (for instance, in science and math), outreach to women in the community to share resources with them, research on women," more propitious learning conditions, a child-care center, and adequate women's health services on campus.[2]

Trained on the left, we knew to come to meetings prepared and to write persuasive proposals. We expected not to win our goals quickly or completely, but to persevere and sometimes prevail. In our campaign to establish a campus child-care center, for example, in which I was involved as the mother of two small daughters, faculty collaborated with a student group that held a baby-in. When they brought their noisy children to administrators' offices, we faculty members temperately urged the administrators to respond to this student demand, and we sustained our joint efforts until the center was well established.[3]

All of the program's founders were Euro-American, and most were then middle-class heterosexual women in our twenties and young thirties. Because we came from the mixed left, we welcomed men as well as women in our classes, and we sought coalitions with other groups, especially those working for African American, Latin American, and gay and lesbian studies. However, our beliefs and style undoubtedly limited participation by women unlike ourselves, as did the heavy time commitments required for collective work. We believed our Women's Studies program should be noncompetitive, nonhierarchical, collaborative, and empowering to women, as well as antiracist, anticlassist, and antiheterosexist. Together we designed our first interdisciplinary Women's Studies courses, teaching for several years on unpaid overload under an experimental rubric. Subsequent campaigns institutionalized Women's Studies faculty and administrative lines and secured permanent program status within the college of Liberal Arts and Sciences. Among our goals was the fostering of a public university as a place to learn about the world and change it in progressive ways, a goal that implied changing university structures—or, at least, providing alternative models within them.

The organizing group that established our program set up as its governing body a Women's Studies Committee of active faculty, students, and staff—but mostly faculty—a body later ratified by the college administration. The Women's Studies Committee sought to involve all its members in the program's decisions. For many years, roles, tasks, and spokeswomen rotated. At least two committee members at once routinely met with campus administrators. All decisions were made by consensus, even when this led to protracted meetings, and all meetings ended with a round of "criticism and self-criticism" (a practice we believed inspired by Chinese revolutionaries) that encouraged self-consciousness about group process and the group's adherence to feminist goals. All reports and other documents were circulated among the group for comment and revision. We also tried to implement these egalitarian feminist ideals in our teaching collectives, assignments, and relations with students.

Over the years, the Women's Studies program changed as it expanded. We increased faculty lines, acquired paid staff, established courses and concentrations recognized by the university, and developed an internship program. The core faculty helped found our campus's Center for Research on Women and Gender, Chancellor's Committee on the Status of Women, and Office of Women's Affairs. Because in recent years our university claims an urban mission to the state legislature and to the public, our program's commitment to serving the community was sometimes helpful to the administration, which supported our conferences on fair housing, activist research, and other topics, and our workshops on antisexist and antiracist pedagogy. Some of our goals thus converged with the university's policies, partly because core Women's Studies faculty served on some of the university committees that draft documents and shape policy. Meanwhile, the Women's Studies Committee, which still serves as the program's chief policy-making body and still tries to achieve consensus on key decisions, has grown to twenty people. It includes the director, the six other UIC faculty with some percentage of official appointment in Women's Studies—four tenured and two tenure-track—the long-term administrator, each year's teaching and research assistants, and other students, faculty, and staff representing campus programs for women. Although authority to make programmatic decisions still rests with the Women's Studies Committee as a whole, the core faculty members recently have begun to meet separately on occasion, reporting their discussions to the full committee. These separate faculty meetings confined tedious detail about course scheduling to the faculty concerned and complied with university statutes about voting in our program's first tenure case, but they also recalled an earlier dynamic before the Women's Studies Committee included so many representatives from affiliated groups. Clearly, the new meeting structure indicates an effort to restore and consolidate core faculty power.

Many of the open conflicts our program faced in the past involved a clash between egalitarian ideals and hierarchical structures. We first taught our core courses through a teaching collective that included undergraduates, graduate students, and faculty; this group assembled anew each term to teach introductory, interdisciplinary core courses. The practice provided the students with wonderful opportunities to gain planning, organizing, and teaching skills. However, it was enormously labor-intensive, each section requiring new and lengthy preparations and continuous mentoring of the student collective members. After about a decade, it was discontinued.

In another conflict, the program's first paid staff member had an anti-hierarchical conception of her role. An early graduate of our program, she enjoyed membership in the course teaching collectives, developed program relationships with off-campus women's groups, and did not type others' work for them. As the program grew, a new director refused these conditions, while the staff member regarded changes in the distribution of responsibilities and power in the program as attacks not only against her job but also against feminist principles. After several painful months, the Women's Studies Committee agreed to replace her with a secretary (sponsoring her move to another job in the university). Other conflicts involved our tactical disagreements in the course of the defeat of a dean's plan to fold the program into the Sociology Department (though none of us were sociologists); our decision not to defend a radical feminist colleague accused of racial insensitivity in murky circumstances; and our rejection of some faculty's proposals to be designated Women's Studies core faculty because they wanted to teach specialized courses without participating in core program teaching or administration.[4] We made an intense commitment to Women's Studies teaching and service a prerequisite for joining the core. This stabilized the program's coherence and ideology but reduced the participation of faculty women of color and others whose primary commitments were elsewhere.

All these struggles can be seen as involving power within collectivity.

After ending the teaching collectives, faculty still shared some tasks with teaching assistants and included activist projects as assignments for students enrolled in courses, but they no longer involved undergraduates in course planning. This allowed faculty to retain control over course content and reduced planning and mentoring time, although one faculty member associated with the teaching collective recently said, "In my view, discontinuing collective teaching tore the radical heart out of the program." Hiring a secretary rather than sharing all tasks meant that office work was more efficient and the director's time freed, at the price of a more conventional division of labor, although the secretary did become a member of the policy-making Women's Studies Committee. Faculty meeting separately in the past month have held more extensive discussions about candidates for the director's position, even when discussion continues in the full committee. In each case, the core materialist feminist faculty preserved our own fairly egalitarian, hard-working, and participatory collegiality, but by reducing the power and participation of others. Within the group, we held ourselves accountable to one another. We held open discussions of salary raises in the Women's Studies Committee and strategized to maximize the group's pool by justifying special merit raises for individual faculty in staggered years. We kept our procedures for tenure as open as possible within university guidelines, and junior faculty have told us how useful they found this shared information. Probably facilitating our good working relationships was the fact that, although we were allies, the faculty were not one another's lovers or rivals, personally or professionally. Thus, the core faculty followed democratic processes within the group and worked in coalition with others but on terms we sought to control, a tendency that is accelerating now that the core faculty has begun to hold some discussions separately.

As a materialist feminist, I ask who benefits from any practice. Our students benefit from opportunities to develop leadership and critical knowledge in the program, and some of our graduates attain good academic jobs and influential community positions. The university benefits from our labor and gains credit for our community service. Despite the hazards of burnout and forgone research time, we core faculty perhaps benefit most from our program in being able to teach within a structure that we shape in congruence with our beliefs. We have developed an ethos of cooperation and mutual support within which we demystify university procedures, mentor junior faculty, and construct win-win solutions when faced with attempts to pit us against one another or other units. Trying to theorize feminist agency not as an individual attribute but as an ongoing and interactive process, I have come to believe that acting in concert with others can create a collective identity that mobilizes action for change, and, further, that our belief in our own efficacy spurs such actions.[5]

Thus, much of our program's effectiveness comes from structuring opportunities in which its constituents can act according to feminist principles and so effect personal changes, while simultaneously reinforcing our commitments to institutional and social transformation.

All successes, of course, rest on exclusions, forgone opportunities, and challenges still unmet. I have already suggested that our program's apparently democratic and participatory structure rests on maintaining core faculty dominance. The conflicts we faced in the past often pitted that core against the interests of some students, staff, other faculty, and administrators. Now, as the program has become more institutionalized, there are more perquisites to be sought. For example, there are now more faculty trained in feminist theory or scholarship who might enjoy teaching our courses without sharing our ideology and commitment to service. Personally, I feel that we core faculty need to be open to sharing power and decision-making, especially with our students, but I also think that democratic faculty power is even more important and more imperiled now than it was a generation ago. Without diminishing the role of students, support staff, or untenured instructors, such faculty power must still be articulated and fought for in the face of recent faculty downsizing, powerful administrative agendas, and the realignment of the public university with corporate interests.

These current conditions pose two related dangers to our program's materialist feminist ideals that I want to highlight: the dangers of Athenian democracy and of consumer individualism. By Athenian democracy I mean the participatory equality of an elite that rests on the unacknowledged labor of others whom it disfranchises or ignores. Many of the struggles of the Women's Studies program I have detailed might be construed in this light. At present, I would defend the core faculty's power as well as seek to improve our accountability to other constituencies within Women's Studies. Both the power and the accountability are necessary, I think, in sustaining a commitment to work for gender justice and a more democratic university rather than simply adapting to the university's usual structures and rewards. That is, I believe that we core faculty should continue thinking of ourselves as working for collective goals, even as we reassess the nature and membership of such collectivity.

In addition to the internal struggles within our program, we also face graver though less immediate dangers. Universities in general have come to rely less on tenured faculty, and more on part-time and temporary staff. Decisions at public universities are increasingly made by administrators who are accountable to legislators and businessmen, not to the community at large. Recent mission statements for our university tell us to train proper employees for the state's enterprises. At the same time, a pervasive corporate ideology depletes public resources in favor of an all-embracing market economy that claims it alone comprehends and fulfills all individual needs. These forces are also not very enthusiastic about supporting the humanities and social sciences, especially those deemed critical of the status quo. Because of campaigns to erode public support for higher education and to redirect university funds from faculty to administration and technology, fewer apprentice scholars are achieving full faculty-guild status than did a generation ago, despite the nation's need for university teachers. Although our Women's Studies program has only a few teaching and research assistants, and several of them are involved in campus unionization campaigns, we still need to join efforts that enlarge the narrowing sphere in which democracy can be practiced, in universities as in society at large. This includes struggles to retain faculty privileges, such as secure employment and academic freedom. I think these struggles are most principled in conjunction with efforts to extend such privileges, to expand and democratize access to other university resources, and to try to persuade the public as well as the university of the case for Women's Studies programs and feminist scholarship.

If bureaucratic and corporate ideologies position students as employees-in-training, they also interpellate them as education consumers to be enticed, pleased, and placated, but not to be involved in decisions about university governance or the construction of knowledge. Although images proliferate in our culture, media monopolies constrict the number of viewpoints and ideas discussed. The tendency toward corporate oligopolies hyping dominant viewpoints and deauthorizing unconventional views is likely to be intensified with the current marketing of commercially programmed course packages and educational assessments as cheaper, more uniform, and more reliable than human teachers steadily employed by universities. Public responses to feminism, too, are frequently poured through the same ideological funnels. Among such ideas, I see the ideological correlative to the Athenian democracy mentioned earlier, which keeps egalitarian catchwords and ideals in circulation but narrows their application and empties them of transformative meaning. One such thought funnel posits that groups or ideological movements such as feminism are always and intrinsically the enemies of individuals, and specifically that feminism, therefore, must be totalitarian, unneeded, outmoded, coercive, and gender-divisive, in opposition to, rather than congruent with, individuals' efforts to achieve a just and fulfilling life.

Let me illustrate these attitudes regarding feminism with a few student comments from a freshman honors course I taught recently on "Family Facts and Gender Theories."[6] None of the students in the course had prior familiarity with Women's Studies, and all of them expressed devotion to general principles of fairness and equality. What those principles meant in practice, of course, was at issue. For some of these students, feminism is unnecessary because its aims have already succeeded. "I don't really consider myself to be a feminist because I have never really experienced any gender inequality in my life," wrote one young woman. "I was raised totally equal to my brother. I never felt threatened in my work or school experiences either. I suppose that since I don't see any real inequality in my life I don't see a real need to be fighting for it. . . . Hopefully I will never feel discriminated against." This attitude may hold up a monitory mirror to the limits of Athenian democracy, even in Women's Studies, which may fight for its own freedoms without considering larger contexts.

Perhaps the bedrock of many students' responses to feminism, however, is their belief in individualism, expressed as the right to choose opinions from the current marketplace of ideas, which they imagine as containing all possible ideas, properly packaged for speedy ingestion. At the same time, they see all political groups as rigid and totalitarian by definition, and they believe that all attempts to persuade other people of one's views are both coercive and doomed to fail. Thus, a second female student wrote, "I would love for men and women to be equal, but I don't plan on standing on the street corner, cursing every man that walks by, or getting on stage and trying to persuade women to leave their husbands and join the feminist movement. Some of this has to do with the nega-tivity put on feminists by society. I think a lot of it, though, has to do with my feelings towards interfering in other peoples' lives. . . . I personally hate it when other people give me advice. . . . If I don't like others' advice, who's to say that others will like mine. So, instead of being a hypocrite, I give them the freedom to choose what they want to do." This liberal "freedom to choose" may also imply a comfortable abrogation of respon-sibility for one's group privilege and an inoculation against differing views about gender, sexuality, or society.

These are familiar views, to be sure, and my point is not to take my students to task but to let their comments help me suggest some crucial directions for academic Women's Studies now: to theorize, imagine, narrate, and, to the best of our ability, actively demonstrate noncoercive collectivity, to show the limits of consumer freedom, and to envision models of feminist equality in addition to shared housework or expanded job opportunities for women. Another of my female students, for exam-ple, wrote the class, "Sorry, I am not a feminist, but I think we should be seeing more women and men as being equal household heads. . . . Women should have any kind of career they choose; it is a violation of human rights to not let them." Students now have images of egalitarian couples, if not a clear sense of the constraints on achieving that equality, and they have a liberal vocabulary of "human rights." However, we may have been less successful in putting before them models of egalitarian groups that work for change and in theorizing noncoercive, minimally exclusionary collective subjects. Feminist pedagogy aspires to the sense of an enhancing group, though within the paradoxical inequality shared by teachers and students. Part of the tenacity of the family as metaphor is that it, too, provides a known model for such interactions. I suggest that it will continue to be useful to tell stories about group interactions among feminists, including their satisfactions, differences, and resolutions, in order to help break down simplistic oppositions between totalized groups and free individuals. Such stories might also help break down the common attitudes of all-or-nothing or winner-take-all, in which finding any imperfection or inconsistency in a group or ideology excuses discard-ing it altogether rather than working to improve it. It is in this spirit that I discuss some of the complicities and complications of my role as a core faculty member within an evolving Women's Studies program.

The desire for radical democracy faces different fields of power now from those it faced thirty years ago. In a globally privileged American society in which women's wage labor is taken for granted without equality in social opportunities as a whole, socialist or materialist feminist vision is necessary to counter the false and limited choices of consumer individualism, in the university and outside it, with models of the productive, active, imperfect participation of people working together for common ideals of equity and progress. Even our language in countering consumer individualism is currently impoverished. Despite a useful literature on feminist organizations, there is still relatively little discussion of the synergies of feminist groups that enhance each member's development as well as expand the possibilities for human social life.[7]

Analyses of Women's Studies' role in various hierarchies, and its commitments to democracy, power-sharing, cooperation, and public service, continue to be necessary, both as we consider our power as professors and as we analyze the contradictory positions of public universities. Among the models I think useful, then, are those of feminist collectivity, one of which I have described in our Women's Studies program. Such a model does not pretend to be a static ideal; rather, it is an example that needs to be critiqued, theorized, revised, and lived.[8]

Notes

1   In 1982 I wrote, "Socialist feminism sees sexism as culturally pervasive, but it defines American women's immediate enemy specifically as capitalist patriarchy, and it is committed to collective action for change" (Gardiner 1982: 631). Because of the fall of communism and reaction against the self-styled socialist countries, some theorists now prefer the title "materialist feminism," a term my students usually interpret to mean "greedy." See, e.g. Hennessy and Ingraham 1997. In her textbook on feminist theories, to cite a current taxonomy, Rosemarie Putnam Tong describes the older form as "socialist feminism" and more recent materialist feminisms under such rubrics as "global feminism": Tong 1998: 118–29, 226–36.

2   Quoted from the UIC student newspaper *Illini*, November 27, 1972, summarizing Circle Women's Liberation Union leaflets in circulation at that time.

3   The Circle Children's Center recently celebrated its twenty-fifth anniversary.

4   Part of my point is that this summary comes from my perspective as a core Women's Studies faculty member. Other participants in these struggles would probably characterize them differently.

5   I edited a book on this topic that includes essays by my colleagues Sandra Bartky, Stephanie Riger, and Margaret Strobel. Riger writes specifically on efficacy beliefs, while Strobel writes on the activism and feminism of Chicago Women's Liberation

Union members: see Greene and Kahn 1995: esp. 1–20 (my introduction), 52–68 (Margaret Strobel's "Consciousness and Action: Historical Agency in the Chicago Women's Liberation Union"), and 169–77 (Julie Nelson-Kuna and Stephanie Riger's "Women's Agency in Psychological Contexts").

6 All quotations are taken from student comments on the course listserv for Honors 102/English 170, "Family Facts and Gender Theories: The Shakespeares, the Freuds, and the Simpsons," University of Illinois at Chicago (fall 1998), with the students' permission. Although the class was ethnically diverse, the three students quoted were all young Euro-American women of working- or middle-class backgrounds.

7 See, for example, Riger 1994 and its citations.

8 In addition to UIC's Women's Studies program, I have been a member of the editorial collective for the interdisciplinary journal *Feminist Studies* since 1989. My colleague Clark Hulse used the term "Athenian democracy" in another context. For comments, suggestions, and quotations, I thank Noel Barker, Sandra Bartky, Jessica Purdy, Jaclyn Sea, Margaret Strobel, Stephanie Riger, and Laura Wilson. The viewpoints expressed, however, are my own.

JEAN C. ROBINSON

From Politics to Professionalism: Cultural Change in Women's Studies

It's hard to avoid the maternal metaphor for those of us who were there at the beginning of Women's Studies. And the maternal looms even more apparent as we recognize the generational differences between the early Women's Studies programs of the late 1970s and the more developed programs of the late 1990s. Thus, it is no surprise that early Women's Studies faculty feel a measure of discomfort when faced with the urge toward professionalization and departmentalization that is a hallmark of the 1990s. In this essay, I muse on these generational differences and focus in particular on what I perceive as significant cultural changes between the early and the contemporary period. As one who was involved in early Women's Studies, and as one who matured professionally through administering a Women's Studies program, my own views have been shaped by my experiences of being a "foremother" of Women's Studies at Indiana University.

When Women's Studies was born in the mid-1970s, politics was its midwife. During the early years, to be active in Women's Studies programs was also to declare publicly an ideology and a political stance in the academy. Women's Studies seemed to demand a revolutionary attitude toward institutional change. By the mid-1990s, Women's Studies had ceased to be a site for publicly declaring that politics was personal; the rhetoric of the early period has been replaced by demands for professionalism and academic integrity. Women's Studies is still engaged in struggle, but the struggle is from within, involving a questioning of both the conservative nature of disciplinary knowledge and of the founding everyday practices of Women's Studies in the academy. To "do" Women's Studies remains a political act, but the politics and the institutional culture surrounding Women's Studies have indeed changed dramatically. Is Women's Studies less "revolutionary" now than it was at its inception?

Certainly, there are many of us who were involved in the early Women's Studies programs who mourn what appears to be a loss of community and a loss of spirit within Women's Studies. One could claim that Women's Studies appears to have dropped any pretense at all of making revolution within the academy, as I did in my first draft of this chapter. Initially, I thought of the current state of Women's Studies as antirevolutionary. I was, and am, concerned that the increasing focus on professionalism and departmentalization has encouraged Women's Studies to move closer to accepting the norms of current academic life. And superficially, it is this normalization that appears to have created a different culture from that which we envisioned twenty years ago. Yet on reflection, it is also clear to me that, although the culture has changed, Women's Studies remains a revolutionary act. The academy and the university are still resistant to women—both as participants and as subjects. Women's Studies continues to embody the spirit of resistance: It defies the norms of academic disciplinarity and seeks legitimacy for invoking gender and power as suitable subjects for academic enquiry.

I started coordinating a Women's Studies program in the late 1970s. Our program had a coordinator rather than a director because we wanted to embody a style of administration that was open and nonhierarchical and that relied on active participation of faculty and students at the decision-making level. The real practice of running a Women's Studies program involved hours of discussion, argument, and consensus-building. The faculty and students who participated in the Women's Studies program then were concerned that having a director who directed would diminish the participatory principles that we saw as fundamental to the practice of Women's Studies.

Our goal was the uncovering and discovering and propagation of research on women. It was a heady time, for none of the faculty involved had any formal training at all in Women's Studies, and only a mere few had training in interdisciplinary work. Yet all of us were committed professionally and politically to the creation of a place in the university that recognized and honored women's lives and contributions. We were also committed to creating an interdisciplinary endeavor that drew on the insights of humanities and social-science scholars, with an episodic nod to the natural sciences and mathematics. We used the discourse of the time—we were openly feminist and claimed that we were engaged in the task of transforming learning and knowledge. We also self-consciously thought of ourselves as revolutionary, in that we were seeking to transform a male-dominant institution into one that valued women and women's contributions. We thought that we were inclusive and believed that we had developed ties to the larger surrounding community. Indeed, we believed that Women's Studies was an evolving model of how academic life and thought could be a bridge to the world outside. It seems to me in retrospect that this first generation of Women's Studies faculty and administrators were convinced of the significant contribution we were making to change the academy, but that we were rather naive about how forms of knowledge are created and sustained. We had not yet interrogated fully the ways in which power can be structured in the academy, and thus we presumed that our brand of revolutionary fervor could truly transform the academy, the experience of students, and the understandings we had of gender, sexuality, and power.

During my interviews for the coordinator's position, I was asked questions that elicited conversations about Women's Studies' mission and feminist ideology in the academy. Could men be in Women's Studies? Did one have to be a feminist to teach in Women's Studies? Is our purpose in the classroom to create feminists? How would I ensure that everyone—faculty, staff, community women, students—felt welcome and involved in our project? How could we reach beyond the white feminist core of Women's Studies faculty and students? I was also asked the more conventional academic questions: What characterizes and distinguishes feminist research? How does interdisciplinarity differ from, or move beyond, disciplinary study and learning? How would I pursue my research agenda while coordinating a program? Clearly, some of these questions sought to differentiate Women's Studies from more conventional disciplines; I can assure you that the questions political scientists asked me exhibited little if any concern with the teaching mission, with bridging to the community, or with race, gender, or class issues. But to note this should not elide the point that even early on, Women's Studies was possessed of the same tensions that pervade the rest of the academy. There was, and is, a simultaneous desire to establish something new while accruing legitimacy and support from within the conventional academy.

The Women's Studies culture that we consciously tried to create, though, was one that eschewed conventional notions about success in the academy. In its place, we glorified participation, relevance, and social change. We thought that the project we were establishing was one that would change not only what we taught and researched, but also how we made decisions about personnel, quality, and legitimacy.

Although Women's Studies sought to be political, the academy inhibited us. We knew we couldn't get approval for a program in feminist studies at a conservative Midwestern university. We knew we couldn't exclude men from classes, as Mary Daly has sought. As coordinator, I certainly came to realize quickly that the practices of the academy, and of the particular academic institution, meant that we had to appear—in some ways, at least—to fit in.

At the beginning, I think, the faculty, many of whom were young and perhaps naive, believed that we could chart a new course for scholarship and for scholars. But the reality of the academic research institution was that tenure was important for the Women's Studies faculty, most of whom were untenured and potentially at risk just for doing Women's Studies. Doing Women's Studies in committee meetings or in the classroom or in research had to be complemented with doing the regular work of our disciplines. (There were always conversations about one's "acceptable" research, which seldom, except among the lit scholars, was on women.) Women and the few men involved in early Women's Studies work did Women's Studies mostly on the side, on their own time, as an adjunct to that which they had been hired to be and do.

The impact of this was profound. When choices had to be made about teaching or research, untenured faculty took enormous risks if they insisted on doing work "only" on Women's Studies issues. Most faculty ended up choosing, if choice it was, to put Women's Studies second. "I will do more teaching for the program after tenure," they would say, or "Once I get tenure, I can then begin to do the interesting research on women and power." Inevitably, we had to search harder and farther for faculty who would be given released time to teach Women's Studies courses on the "margins." Eventually, Women's Studies programs became convinced that we could not continue with the model of bringing faculty together from a variety of disciplines and departments. As we began to ask for faculty of our own, Women's Studies started on the road to professionalization and departmentalization.

These kinds of hard decisions ultimately led as well to different kinds of leadership patterns and organizational structures for Women's Studies. As faculty from outside the program had to opt out of committee meetings, coordinating over a relatively short period of time really did become more like directing. The director, as at my university, was one of the few faculty with a budgeted line in the program. Engaged in the day-to-day work of teaching, research, and administration, it was perhaps inevitable that the director more and more took on the traditional roles of departmental chair, and intensive participation on the part of faculty and students diminished considerably. Inexorably, we moved farther from the Women's Studies organizational culture—a culture that worshiped inclusiveness, participation, and discussion, so consciously created in the late 1970s and early 1980s.

It was almost a mantra that Women's Studies would, and should, disappear, once the disciplines took on their morally mandated task of integrating women into the broader arts and sciences curriculum and into research. When my program received a National Endowment for the Humanities grant to integrate Women's Studies into the curriculum, we argued that once introductory and upper-level courses included significant material on women and perspectives from Women's Studies, then perhaps there would be less need for a separate undergraduate Women's Studies curriculum. Simultaneously, and perhaps problematically, we also claimed that the interdisciplinary study of sex and gender required a level of expertise that could not be found within individual departments or solely from disciplinary training.

Many of us recognized the tension of what we argued. At one and the same time, we argued for disbanding Women's Studies (at the proper time, of course) and we argued for our necessity for the university and for the broader community of knowledge. As we sought to incorporate Women's Studies research into the regular offerings of the campus, the faculty became even more enmeshed in the tensions. In order to persuade departments and deans and other "serious" faculty that we were engaged in a legitimate academic project, we increasingly took on the discourse and practices of particular disciplines. At the same time, we argued loudly and consistently for the particular methodologies and standpoints embedded in the burgeoning research in Women's Studies.

But rather than changing the other fields, we became more like them. And in doing so, we not only adapted ourselves to different disciplinary models, but we also moved closer to the mainstream organizational model of academic life.

It is not that the goals of integration, or the desire for budgeted faculty, were necessarily misguided. Rather, it is that the university has extraordinarily powerful everyday practices that proved stronger than the new modes we were trying to establish. Perhaps in the process of institutionalizing Women's Studies with directors, faculties, and core curriculum, we were not creative enough to avoid the hegemonic influences of the academy and the university as institution. Certainly, in attempting to transform (or in light of real practices, influence) the canon in disciplines, we believed that we had to become more like "them" in order to be heard.

My issue here, though, is not with the question of integration or with the effort to legitimize Women's Studies as an acceptable academic pursuit. Rather, the question was whether Women's Studies could remain politically engaged and defiant of traditional academic disciplines. Could Women's Studies adherents resist the incessant calls to become like one of the boys? The pressure to become yet another (legitimate) department pursuing knowledge in the standardized methods of late-twentieth-century North American academe have proved ever more powerful. Women's Studies programs sometimes seem torn between retaining the old (yes, even twenty-five years can seem old in this revised context) social and cultural construction, or going back to the even older one (although even here we are talking about less than a hundred years) prevalent in most of our universities.

The discourse has certainly shifted. The world has shifted. Revolution takes different forms in different times, and if at first glance Women's Studies programs no longer are heralded as sites of revolutionary change, they nevertheless are engaged in action that seeks to reframe knowledge and power. But alongside the continuing resistance expressed in Women's Studies classrooms and in the research and writings of Women's Studies scholars, there is also a new refrain. It is this refrain—one that talks of departmentalization, institutionalization, and professionalization—that seems discordant to the foremothers of Women's Studies but may be necessary to the next generation.

I remind myself occasionally that it is important to remember that

Women's Studies programs and faculty have been training Women's Studies scholars for twenty years. There is now a core of rigorously trained interdisciplinary scholars at most research universities who focus on questions relating to gender, sexuality, and power. Compared with the scene twenty years ago, the scholars are remarkably sophisticated and confident. They are certainly more knowledgeable about methodology, theory, and discourse than were the early founders of Women's Studies. But like their foremothers, the younger generation came to, and continue to find, Women's Studies because they are searching for different ways to answer the gender-sex paradox in our cultures. I believe that the younger generation of Women's Studies scholars is certainly political in its choice to be part of even a less politicized version of Women's Studies, because Women's Studies still elicits questions of legitimacy and place from most other disciplines, as well as from the broader intellectual community. (How else can one explain, for instance, the *New York Times Book Review*'s insistence on always having antifeminists review feminist scholarship and literature?)

Yet for the younger generation, more than for my generation, being in Women's Studies is a professional choice, as well. For us, it could not be and was not an available option, except for the lucky few. To see Women's Studies as a professional option is also to recognize that Women's Studies is, in innumerable ways, like any other department or discipline.

Regardless of the initial political motivation to become involved in Women's Studies, the professionalization of Women's Studies has continued the erosion of the cultural themes of participation and community that were the foundations of early Women's Studies. Perhaps this is a proverbial chicken-and-egg story: Did the move to professionalization lead to a lessening of community, or did the community weaken and create a void for professionalization to fill? I am not sure, although I suspect that the Women's Studies culture we thought we created was in fact at risk: We sometimes deluded ourselves about the extent of involvement and participation, about the lack of hierarchy, about our ability to bridge to the community. And as we have recognized in the past decade, what we thought was stable and secure can never be. For whatever reasons—and perhaps time is the best explanation—Women's Studies has become a legitimate and institutionalized presence in the university.

In becoming so, it has adapted to the forms with which we are all familiar: powerful chairs, junior faculty anxious about tenure, research questions chosen because they can get published. In some Women's Studies programs, student participation takes the form of attending class, and faculty participation consists of trying to protect the program from outsiders. What was once an institutional attempt to create an inclusive site for discussing the lives and study of women has, at some universities, become an exclusive and guarded place for those who are professional scholars in the field. It appears that the fledgling cultures we tried to establish two decades ago have been subsumed by the quest for mature, recognized academic forms. The culture that remains—at least, in terms of structure, participation, and decision-making—often seems little different from the culture in the larger university.

And yet Women's Studies is still a place where resistant ideas are voiced, where opposition to cultural and social norms is accepted, and where the very subjects of study still have to be justified to a doubting, highly critical academic community. The scholars and students who choose to work in Women's Studies remain at risk, just as they were twenty years ago. Legitimacy has yet to be conferred on the Women's Studies project. Budgets and faculty lines are not secure; majors and postgraduate programs are still questioned; scholars of sex and gender continue to struggle over whether to be affiliated with such a risky endeavor before tenure. Politics, in other words, is still at the heart of Women's Studies, because the institutions in which we exist have not fully accepted that we are an integral part of the knowledge process. In many ways, we are still fighting to be included.

Inclusion is not only an issue that Women's Studies faces toward the larger academic community and the university. It is also an issue from within. Women's Studies politics is perhaps even more conflictual now than it was twenty years ago, however, because of the generational struggles over what Women's Studies should be, who it should include, and how it should be governed. The trend toward professionalizing and departmentalizing means that faculty who have long considered themselves as "doing" Women's Studies—voluntarily, if on the side—are slowly being excluded from Women's Studies units that are operating as departments. Now more than ever, there appear to be several classes of Women's Studies scholars: those who have faculty lines and whose tenure and promotion, teaching and research, are judged solely within the Women's Studies unit, and those who may do Women's Studies research and teaching in their disciplinary homes but who do not have formal appointments in Women's Studies. Not surprisingly, this also turns out to be a generational divide.

What Women's Studies programs and departments are struggling with now is how to respect and incorporate the different interests and needs of these different classes within one unit. That may be difficult, if not impossible. Clearly, what is important personally and professionally for those faculty whose livelihood and future is determined by Women's Studies programs will be quite different from the concerns of tenured faculty in other departmental homes. I don't believe that the solution is to focus only on those on the "inside." This seems to me to be a fundamental break with the Women's Studies culture established twenty-odd years ago. And it neglects the many contributions that have been, and will be, made by scholars outside the formal Women's Studies unit. We must recognize, though, that Women's Studies scholars on the "outside," while having a serious stake in the Women's Studies project, nevertheless have less direct commitment and risk than their "inside" counterparts. Scholars formally and publicly affiliated with Women's Studies need autonomy to make decisions about their careers, the curriculum they offer, and the bases on which personnel decisions are made. I believe that what was good and useful in the old Women's Studies culture should be revived so that Women's Studies encourages and facilitates a broader community of Women's Studies scholars and students. If Women's Studies is to be true to its founding principles, even as it necessarily changes and develops, then there has to be a serious commitment to discussing these generational and institutional differences openly among Women's Studies scholars. Out of these conversations, we might be able to construct new cultures that will ensure the longevity of the Women's Studies project. Such cultures must take into account the dominant hegemony of departments and traditional academic forms while establishing creative, if not revolutionary, processes of inclusion.

Battle-Weary Feminists and Supercharged Grrls:
Generational Differences and Outsider Status
in Women's Studies Administration

Administrative posts are not generally held by academic tyros, but in Women's Studies, assistant professors and lecturers serve as directors or chairs.[1] Placing untenured or non-tenure-track faculty in Women's Studies leadership positions should provoke disciplinary, institutional, and professional-development concerns, as well as internal political ones. Junior administrative positions may demonstrate an institution's lack of financial commitment to Women's Studies. Non-tenured administrators may also perpetuate the idea that Women's Studies is "less professional" than other units. On the level of the individual, tenure-track administrators are at risk when lip service alone is given to the importance of service and administrative contributions. All of these factors place Women's Studies and its administrators in institutionally insecure positions, undermining our ability to function effectively, to compete for resources, and even to govern ourselves. I consider these possibilities—particularly the last—in this chapter. I identify obstacles that may be faced when outsiders assume Women's Studies leadership positions and describe how these obstacles are exacerbated when the administrators are chronologically young and institutionally junior.

The condition of being untenured in a Women's Studies directorship is one I have experienced and witnessed. I became an acting director in a program that had a history of selecting young feminists as leaders. The previous permanent director believed she might have been the youngest one in the country. After a successful tenuring, she became an associate dean. Recently, the program hired its first outside senior-level director. I sat on the search committee and read files from applicants who were already Women's Studies administrators at the level of lecturer or visiting assistant professor and who were seeking more secure positions. I now teach in a Department of Women's Studies, under a chair who was hired as an assistant professor when no internal candidates stepped forward. Three years after she became chair, she received tenure and promotion. She had been an assistant professor on the campus twenty years earlier and had left academia. She was in the highly unusual position of being a new hire and a liminal insider. For most new directors, however, outsider status is unavoidable, and its consequences are unmistakable.

As a relatively new academic unit, Women's Studies differs from more established counterparts in that its founders may remain on campus. Women's Studies was established on most campuses through agitation by a handful of committed faculty members, who proposed courses, taught them, and fought for institutional recognition. Next, they selected one among them to lead. When all of the founders had the opportunity to serve as administrator (or repeatedly to turn down the post), the institution's first generation of Women's Studies leadership ended. A national search was likely authorized. The fruits of these searches constituted a "next generation" of Women's Studies administrators, hired into existing programs or departments. New administrators were outsiders, overseeing or sharing governance with founding faculty. In some cases, the new administrators were senior-level hires and contemporaries of the program's originators, who therefore shared (or were perceived as sharing) feminist political or academic experiences. For junior administrators, tenure-track or instructor faculty status may also indicate relative youth. Differences in age and experience between a Women's Studies administrator and faculty members are likely to lay the foundation for additional internal struggles. I confine my remaining remarks to two situations that I believe new administrators should be prepared to face and all Women's Studies faculty to recognize and address. I label these scenarios "battle-weariness" and "supercharged grrls."

Administrators in every discipline manage "battle-weary" faculty who obsessively replay old conflicts and whose belligerent focus pervades their dealings on campus. Working with these faculty members, a new administrator must determine the relevance of felt problems to current situations. She must establish relationships with faculty, as well as with oft-hated deans, provosts, and presidents. Managing and supporting the battle-weary can take a tremendous amount of time. Women's Studies administrators tend to face greater demands than those in other disciplines because the battles of yesteryear were often collective, long-standing, and especially painful for the faculty. Many founding faculty invested tremendous personal and professional energy in Women's Studies, whether out of political commitment or out of frustration with traditional units. Faculty conflicts are likely to have involved members of the administration or selected department chairs. Women's Studies may have provided a safe haven in an otherwise hostile environment, with the coordinator, director, or chair positioned as the sustainer of this haven. Women's Studies is likely to have devolved from those halcyon days (whether nostalgically or actually remembered) in which faculty worked together against a common nemesis. Today's battles are probably less colorful and more insidious, and internal divisions may even have taken precedence over them.

Learning, evaluating, and negotiating the institutional and individual histories surrounding the unit are necessary tasks for any new administrator, but in Women's Studies, peculiar challenges arise. New administrators were not there during the university's Women's Studies battle royal. As a result, founding faculty may not view outside administrators as allies or as effective assuagers of the battle-weary, creating mutual disappointments and resentments about the status of their feminist community. When the administrator is chronologically young, the chasm widens. Not only are the institutional battles unfamiliar to her, but she may encounter an additional level of mistrust based on generational differences. A junior administrator cannot know the nuances of her senior colleagues' institutional pain, and she cannot "appreciate" their historical struggles, either. To be sure, some junior faculty may contribute to these imbalances by being "ungrateful"—a generational phenomenon that Diane Elam has described as the "nonpayment of debt" (1997: 62). Conversely, established feminists may interpret as a betrayal any changes proposed by their juniors, replaying the "dutiful daughter complex" (Elam 1997: 62). Such perceptions and understandings could, at their worst, bring the functioning of Women's Studies to a halt.

Change of any kind is rendered more suspect when a Women's Studies outsider is proposing it. "We tried that five years ago, and it didn't work" or "The provost would never approve that" might prove popular refrains at faculty meetings. An outside administrator may be subjected to endless institutional-history lessons inscrutably supposed to translate into present policy ("When X was dean, he promised us a budget increase every year but never gave us a dime"). Or, almost as difficult, a new administrator may be "protected" from internecine struggles that affect her ability to do her job ("I can't tell you the whole story—just know that you can't ask Chair X to cross-list a course"). If there have been difficulties between Women's Studies and the higher administration, a new administrator may be in a quandary. Her colleagues may believe that the best relationship with the dean or the provost is no relationship, promoting self-marginalization as a badge of pride. A new director or chair risks alienating her colleagues by colluding with the administrative enemy, and she risks jeopardizing the future growth of Women's Studies with continued separatism. These are not necessarily dilemmas peculiar to Women's Studies, but among a faculty with high expectations for consensus and a commitment to progressive political principle (along with, perhaps, a distrust of those in power and a highly personalized investment in the unit), the conflicts must be more painfully felt. When the conflicts are experienced by a junior administrator, the stakes are high indeed: continuing a friendly relationship with senior colleagues, who are likely to oversee her renewal or tenuring, versus doing what she believes is best for Women's Studies. Her decision-making abilities may be paralyzed.

What is most dangerous about the manifestations of faculty battle scars is that they keep the focus on the past rather than on the future of Women's Studies. If faculty members set an agenda for a new administrator that repeatedly educates her about the past, then they may inadvertently short-circuit what could be accomplished next. Rather than seeking important avenues for development, battle-weary Women's Studies faculty prefer to stay in their hard-won foxholes. At a meeting of the faculty, staff, and students of one Women's Studies program with which I was involved, senior faculty members spent much of the scheduled time expressing fears that the university would abolish Women's Studies. Naturally alarmed, I asked questions that met with murky, paranoid answers, until I, too, felt half-certain that we were doomed. Later I set up a meeting with the administrator. "Why," I asked her, "do they think that the program is going to be abolished?" She replied, after much reflection, "There's nothing specific, really. It's just that Women's Studies is always under fire."

I do not want entirely to belittle her sentiment that Women's Studies is always under fire. Recent fracases at the State University of New York at New Paltz and in Arizona's public universities come to mind (Ingalls 1988; "State" 1999). The popular media remains fond of publishing exposes of our supposedly lightweight classrooms. In the case of the program of which I was a part, however, our budget was minuscule. Ours was one of the more than half of existing Women's Studies units described as "poverty level" by the National Women's Studies Association. The number of students enrolled in Women's Studies courses appeared to be large and sustainable. Women's Studies was one of the most cost-effective units of that university. We enrolled our fair share of students, offered campus programming at a level unheard of elsewhere, and made the university feel good about its commitment to gender equity—all on a shoestring. Short of a sea change among the trustees or the state legislature, it was difficult to imagine Women's Studies being abolished there. But the issue of Women's Studies' survival surfaced often, and it took up a good deal of our time. Worrying about our survival (which I came to believe was never in question) prevented us from discussing what we wanted or needed—putting us in an entirely reactive rather than a proactive mode.

If the professional baggage—again, whether real or imagined—of the Women's Studies faculty creates hurdles for the administrator interested in focusing on the future, so does the model of what I will call the "supercharged grrl." Faculty in Women's Studies are spread notoriously thin in their teaching, advising, co-curricular programming, and committee responsibilities. Senior faculty earn their burnout. But these conditions create enormous difficulties for a new administrator who is hired not only because she is less expensive, but also precisely because she is "young" and "energetic." As Darlene Hantzis and I wrote in our essay on feminist generational differences, " 'Older' feminist colleagues would make us understand that we are their successors around the tables; we make them proud (of themselves and of us); they have enabled us to fight on, and we enable them to take a well-earned rest. One of the difficulties of this logic . . . is that more bodies are needed around the tables" (Looser and Hantzis 1995: 242). Some in Women's Studies may look to a junior administrative hire as a "supercharged grrl" who will take over where they left off, allowing them to breathe easily after their years of service. Other junior Women's Studies faculty usually are not in a professional position that allows them to take up the slack.

There is no surer way to create a similarly burned-out and embittered next generation in Women's Studies than to give a new administrator all of the work, none of the assistance, and a heap of expectations. In a program or department in which there are significant generational divides, there may be a perception that the new blood should do the work while the seasoned faculty serve largely as supporters, having paid their dues. Ostensibly ceding control, the senior faculty may at the same time desire continuity. A junior administrator who accepts the agenda of the senior faculty may find herself doing all of their work alone, albeit with their support. Or she may refuse their agenda and do all of her work alone, in the midst of their disappointment or resentment and at her own professional risk. (When the senior faculty do not agree on an agenda— as is often the case—her job is no easier.) Hiring a junior administrator is an effective, albeit unintentional, way for founders to retain de facto power over the unit without exerting much effort. Senior faculty do not look to hire a junior administrator for this nefarious reason; the hiring of junior administrators certainly has much more to do with financial exigencies. But nefarious effects are possible, regardless of beneficent intentions.

Some of the problems facing the "supercharged grrl" arise from Women's Studies' inherited (if resisted) structures of academic hierarchization. Senior faculty can neither unequivocally mentor a junior administrator—who is, in some sense, their supervisor—nor conceive of her as a peer. A junior administrator is responsible for promoting and managing the careers of her faculty, the very same people who are likely to be overseeing her own. Making these conditions worse is the refusal of some senior faculty to acknowledge power imbalances within Women's Studies (as if wishing them away will make them go away), denying in the process their own institutional power. The ability to sit back and rely on others to do the work is largely the purview of the powerful. Colleagues who perceive their contributions to Women's Studies as significant in the past rather than as necessary in the present put their own hard-won gains in peril.

There may be good reasons for a junior administrator to take the helm, but the hazards can outweigh the benefits. Senior and junior faculty must work together to ensure that Women's Studies' administrators achieve the same professional security, pay, and support that accrue to those leading other units. Until that is achieved, we must more openly

acknowledge and address our generational differences and take ownership of and responsibility for the kinds of institutional power that each of
us wields. Generational conflicts may be more acutely felt in Women's
Studies, a smaller academic community in which collective action and
collaborative governance have been the norm and in which volunteerism, non-compensation, and a lack of financial autonomy persist. The
problems I have outlined in these anecdotes and scenarios, though not
the most pressing obstacles that we face, may prevent us from working
together effectively.

There are, of course, senior Women's Studies faculty who actively
support a junior administrator's initiatives and leadership.[2] And there
may be junior administrators whose lack of interpersonal savvy provokes
rifts. Until more of us are willing to speak of and to our differences, our
expectations, and our disappointments, however, such conflicts will remain underground and perhaps intractable. I welcome feedback from
senior faculty who feel themselves mischaracterized or misunderstood
by my descriptions, as well as from junior administrators who have—or
have not—noticed generational obstacles in their Women's Studies work.
As Marilyn Boxer puts it, "If the time has come to assess 'where have we
been, where are we going?' in women's studies . . . the enterprise must be
shared" (1998: xviii).

Notes

I thank Robyn Wiegman for her thoughtful e-mail conversations and superb editorial
suggestions. Some of the language in this chapter comes directly out of her pointed
questions.

1 My claim is grounded in anecdotal evidence and in an unscientific perusal of ads in
the *Chronicle of Higher Education,* necessarily speculative information. It is difficult to
know, for instance, who was hired in searches for assistant or associate professors.
Less mistakable are ads such as one that appeared in March 1999 seeking an ABD ("all
but dissertation" Ph.D. candidate) for a renewable-term appointment as Women's
Studies director at a large state university.

2 I have been fortunate to work with senior Women's Studies faculty who have been
actively supportive, including Jane Bakerman, Myrna Handley, Becky Hogan, and
Star Olderman.

Taking Account of Women's Studies

Women's Studies has made it—into course catalogues, timetables, committees, conferences, journals, books. It has also made it into the university budget, that ultimate arbitrator of intellectual legitimation. Sort of. Women's Studies is all too often caught in fiscal limbo for reasons that are becoming increasingly clear. Consider for a moment that one of the intellectual and political strengths of Women's Studies is that it is widely interdisciplinary and from its inception has drawn on resources from disciplines across the university. Humanities, arts, social sciences, natural and medical sciences have all contributed to the running of Women's Studies.

This may seem on the surface like one big intellectual and political party, a daily celebration of the far-reaching influences of Women's Studies. But the institutional-party permit has a big price. The result is that Women's Studies is often viewed by the fiscal powers that be as a "borrowed-time" discipline, where specialists are constantly trying to find time to teach, study, and do research in Women's Studies in addition to the responsibilities they have to a primary field of research. Nice work if you can get it.

To some extent, this disciplinary double-entry bookkeeping has been reduced by the introduction of dedicated lines of faculty that devote all or the majority of their time to Women's Studies. However, growing numbers of students routinely outstrip the addition of faculty, sending Women's Studies directors back to the trenches to find yet more willing recruits. It's a good thing that Women's Studies is so very interdisciplinary, or pressed directors would have run out of new troops a long time ago. Yet it takes little foresight to see that the recruitment market is not infinitely expandable or the labor of the university infinitely exploitable. Goodwill and good humor go only so far; there are only so many teachers in any one university, and only some of them are going to have an interest in Women's Studies, no matter how interdisciplinary it is. So for Women's Studies to prosper and expand as it should, its budget cannot continue to remain flat or heavily dependent on soft funding opportunities generated by exploiting available staff.

To argue for the desirability, for the necessity, of the autonomy of Women's Studies, especially in such blatantly fiscal and administrative terms, has not always been—and maybe for some still is not—an acceptable line to pursue. Once upon a time, it was thought that Women's Studies should not have its own budget, its own lines, its own resources, its own institutionally sanctioned administrative engine. In short, the argument was that Women's Studies should not really be a full-fledged academic department at all. Although this would hardly be a surprising position to maintain if one were against Women's Studies, it has less predictably also been the stance taken by its own supporters. "With friends like that . . . ," the university administrator might mumble. The story was supposed to be that Women's Studies should stand outside the structure of the institution and, at the same time, be firmly placed as an intellectual offering within the university. To succumb to being part of the structure of the institution would be tantamount to Women's Studies' selling out its political principles. Women's Studies could not be a critic of the university's knowledge practices if it became a traditional part of the university curriculum, administered in the same old ways.

I will say straight away that to take such a position now, in the age of the corporate university whose motivating principles are increased profitability in the face of shrinking market shares, is the closest thing an academic discipline can get to institutional suicide.[1] The idealism of Women's Studies can quickly be replaced by the profits of Golf Course Studies. Now, in putting it this way, I am not suggesting that Women's Studies sell its political soul to the highest bidder, regardless of the compromises it has to make. Rather, I am trying to underline the fact that is university accountancy—that accountability within the university is to a certain extent measured by the accounting department, whether we like it or not. For Women's Studies to remain on the margins—without adequate resources and without attracting the number of students that it could—neither forces the political hand of the university nor funds the very projects that Women's Studies is so invested in carrying out.

Women's Studies stands to become more of a force to be reckoned with if it is institutionally recognized as a department with hard funding that is as financially accountable to the institution as are more traditional subjects. However, the important move that Women's Studies can make is that it can indeed become a department without simultaneously taking on the rigidity of a discipline. In doing this it can begin to challenge the terms and conditions under which the university is used to operating. Part of the negotiation that Women's Studies as a department will have to make is preserving, even intensifying, all of its various interdisciplinary connections while arguing for its fiscal, administrative, and disciplinary autonomy. In order to survive and grow, Women's Studies needs to be viewed by the institution as a financially and intellectually autonomous discipline that continues to explore its interdisciplinary commitments. Budgets need to allow for multiple staffing possibilities and research opportunities; they need to be structured to include both lines for dedicated faculty and lines shared with other disciplines and departments.

The bottom line—in fiscal, epistemological, and political terms—is that Women's Studies is an "interdisciplinary discipline." Its very strength is that it draws on multiple disciplines without being simply reducible to any one of them. And precisely because Women's Studies is so interdisciplinary, it needs to have a departmental "center," a common ground where its work takes place—a material and mental space in which Women's Studies scholars can meet, converse, think. This is as crucial for research development as it is for teaching, for if Women's Studies is to retain the force of its interdisciplinary inquiries, there must be an institutional site where these connections can be formulated and refined. Budgets must address this fact sooner rather than later, because Women's Studies cannot forever exist on borrowed time.

It can be easier, though, to explain why Women's Studies is an interdisciplinary department and needs an appropriate budget than it is to carry out the practical administration that actually draws resources into Women's Studies on an ongoing basis. It's not enough to say, "Let there be Women's Studies," and henceforth a new budget is approved. One of the main challenges facing the shoring up of hard funds for Women's

Studies is establishing and maintaining the criteria by which work in Women's Studies will be judged worthy of funding: accountability in the face of accountancy. Although sheer student numbers alone answer some budgetary questions, they certainly do not satisfy others, and it is important to scrutinize what other types of criteria are being imposed.

It seems obvious that the criteria for judgment should not be plucked from any one discipline that contributes to Women's Studies. However, to say that there is no Ur-discipline to which Women's Studies should appeal does not rule out the fact that such disciplinary high courts do get installed as the ultimate arbitrators of work in Women's Studies. To take one example that is close to my current academic home, for the purposes of research funding in Britain, Women's Studies is subject to evaluation by the sociology panel. The temptation, of course, is for Women's Studies submissions to increase their holdings in sociology stocks as the quickest route to a legitimate intellectual portfolio under the terms of assessment. If it is not fiscally feasible simply to hire more sociologists who do Women's Studies, then those already engaged in Women's Studies at any one institution could do worse than pursue research that could be judged favorably by the disciplinary criteria of sociology. The invitation is certainly there for a wholesale shift within Women's Studies to sociological approaches to women's literature, women's history, women's art, women's work, women's music, women's whatever, as long as the approach is sociological in some way.

In saying that, I do not mean to belittle sociological research. It is definitely useful; it is obviously necessary. However, it is also not the only type of research that needs to be pursued in the name of Women's Studies. Although sociologists have made important contributions to Women's Studies, that is not the same thing as saying that Women's Studies *is* sociology. In submitting itself to sociology, Women's Studies is left in the precarious position that, each time it is reviewed, it must negotiate the fact that it is *not* simply an intellectual subset of sociology.

My example here is limited to some extent; it is a local one for me, a specifically national one for others. Yet the problems to which the situation in the United Kingdom calls attention are equally applicable to tenure reviews, research-funding decisions, hiring committees, and editorial boards in the United States whose task it is to arbitrate work in Women's Studies. Part of the solution here goes back to why it is important to establish Women's Studies as an autonomous department that is granted the usual institutional control over its own academic practices and is not seen as a station on the way to some other "real" discipline that can be pointed to as the fiscally and intellectually responsible department. It is close to impossible to orchestrate the practical administration of judgment without some kind of departmental center—and again I am referring to a physical as well as intellectual space—in which those involved in Women's Studies can discuss how they will indeed make their judgments without appeal to another party. Judging the interdisciplinary work of Women's Studies requires bringing not only different disciplinary criteria, but also the specifically interdisciplinary criteria of Women's Studies, into play. Multiple sets of criteria are applied. This is not a one-size-fits-all discipline.

So although it is certainly necessary to establish criteria for what constitutes good work in Women's Studies that is deserving of funding and promotion within the university, one of those criteria might well be the extent to which the work does indeed meet some of the criteria of the other discipline or disciplines with which it engages. Research that focuses on Women's Studies topics within the medical sciences might not, for instance, look like or be judged by precisely the same criteria applied to Women's Studies investigations that center primarily on literary studies. Of course, this is more complicated than the more straightforward evaluations that most departments produce, and matters become increasingly complex in the case of Women's Studies work that ranges across multiple disciplines. Disciplinary methodologies conflict, and Women's Studies will have to negotiate this problem. There will be times when specific disciplinary methodologies are challenged, perhaps even flaunted, and some way is needed to make a distinction between incompetent and critically challenging work. An appeal to a single subject review board, as is the case of Women's Studies and sociology in the United Kingdom, is a poor way indeed to resolve such matters on intellectual or financial grounds. Women's Studies must retain a commitment to challenging the sort of disciplinary rigidity that often manifests itself as some inflexible notion of the "departmental standard" that frequently fails to take account of important intellectual and political challenges to what constitutes knowledge production. At the same time, the only way for Women's Studies to have the necessary degree of flexibility and autonomy over hiring, promotion, and tenure decisions (as well as more day-to-day control over the allocation of its internal resources) is to become a department.

Taking account of the accounting that lies behind the administration of Women's Studies, then, does not have to be an argument for simply giving in to market forces. Women's Studies can continue to be a resistant force within the university, insisting that accountability exceeds accounting and making strategic interventions into the managerialism that universities are increasingly promoting. But Women's Studies will not be heard if its voice is only a tiny squeak from the margins that always begins by insisting that it should be taken seriously. Women's Studies cannot negotiate from a position of strength without a solid financial commitment on the part of the university. That is, Women's Studies will have the resources with which to be critical of centers of power only if it is not relegated to the financial margins of the university's budget. And this means taking on the structure of funding that goes along with the serious financial allocations that are given only to departments. Departmental status ensures that Women's Studies is not just another soft-funded studies program that can be wiped off the budget on a mere fiscal whim. To be a department is to be ensured, in these volatile fiscal times, that the university is committed to the acquisition of knowledges about women.

Women's Studies would not be anywhere without its interdisciplinary strengths, and although becoming a department should not determine entirely what its future holds, it does guarantee that it will have an institutional future at all. Women have been marginal for long enough within the academy. Isn't it time that we take account of Women's Studies?

Notes

1   When I say "corporate university" I am not limiting my analysis to the handful of newly formed, blatantly "for profit" universities, many of which enjoy a virtual existence by exploiting the degree-granting potential of the Internet. Rather, I want to emphasize the market-driven tendencies of all universities today as they increasingly adopt the structures and principles of corporate capitalism. For a perceptive analysis of this trend, see Readings 1996. Biddy Martin explores the significance of Readings's remarks for Women's Studies in Martin 1997.

Nice Work, If You Can Get It—and If You Can't? Building Women's Studies Without Tenure Lines

Women's Studies practitioners are justifiably excited these days about the development of our field as an "interdiscipline." As other contributors to this volume explain, the growing number of free-standing departments of Women's Studies with tenure lines of their own has "made a space" in academic institutions for the new methodologies and new subject matter peculiar to the interdisciplinary feminist study of women and gender. When job candidates with Ph.D.s in Women's Studies enter tenure-track jobs in Women's Studies departments, they are more than free to produce new forms of knowledge by pursuing modes of scholarship that might not be deemed "tenureable" in traditional disciplinary departments. Indeed, they find themselves in situations that foster and encourage unconventional, boundary-breaking thought. What Ph.D. in Women's Studies with academic ambitions wouldn't like to land a tenure-track job in a Women's Studies program or department?

Nice work, if you can get it! But for anyone to get it, it has to be there in the first place. A look at the 1997–98 "Job Tracks" register in *Lingua Franca* shows there were only thirty-four full-time junior hirings that year in "Afro-Am/Ethnic/Women's Studies" in the entire United States ("Job Tracks" 1998). *Lingua Franca*'s numbers are never perfect, but they provide a general estimate. The National Women's Studies Association is promising to produce statistics about how many of those jobs are actually devoted to Women's Studies, and how many Ph.D.s in Women's Studies and in other fields are competing for those jobs each year. Say, for the sake of argument, that maybe a third of those thirty-four were not Afro-Am or Ethnic but, rather, Women's Studies jobs. That would mean there were maybe ten or a dozen opportunities last year for junior faculty to enter tenure-track jobs devoted to our interdiscipline. Even without recourse to statistics, we know there are certainly hundreds, probably thousands, more Women's Studies practitioners seeking academic jobs each year than these few positions can accommodate. Where are they going? Doubtless, those who find jobs are finding them in the so-called traditional disciplinary departments. I want to complicate the opposition that is being set up in the national Women's Studies community between programs that hire faculty into Women's Studies tenure lines and these "traditional departments." I will argue that departments in all the disciplines are gradually becoming less traditional as their tenure-track personnel are becoming more interdisciplinary, and that the long-term radical transformation of "traditional departments" is as worthy a goal as the more obviously exciting project of developing Women's Studies tenure lines in those institutions where it is possible to do so.

Indeed, not every institution of higher education has tenure lines to give to Women's Studies programs—or to any other programs, for that matter. A closer look at "Job Tracks" shows that the institutions who are hiring junior faculty into tenure-track lines in Women's Studies and ethnic studies fall into a comparatively small subset of colleges and universities. In 1997–98, they were flagship schools in large state systems (Rutgers University; University of Arizona; University of Iowa; University of Minnesota; University of North Carolina, Chapel Hill; University of Washington; University of Wisconsin, Madison), "elite" private schools (Dartmouth; Columbia; Simon's Rock of Bard; Wellesley), or large campuses within state systems in Arizona (Arizona State University hired four junior faculty in these subjects last year) or California (with three hires each at Cal State's Northridge and Long Beach universities, and one each at Fresno and San Francisco). Some institutions are falling outside this general pattern. (It would be interesting to know why the University of Louisville had three such hires last year, and what kinds of circumstances enabled such schools as the City University of New York, Lehman; Dakota-Wesleyan; Indiana State University; Massachusetts-Boston; and Minnesota-Duluth to devote tenure lines to ethnic studies or Women's Studies.) But the message of the list is clear: Although the number of tenure lines in Women's Studies and ethnic studies has grown exponentially in the past two decades, it is still tiny, given the pool of untenured practitioners of Women's Studies—trained by Women's Studies graduate programs or by disciplinarily defined departments—who are seeking academic jobs.

I may be the only director of Women's Studies I know who is not looking to add tenure lines to the program I administer. Dedicated faculty lines? I don't want them; I don't need them—I won't ask for them. I realize that as a programmatic policy, this sounds counterintuitive, maybe even perverse. It is, however, a pragmatic position for an interdisciplinary program to adopt in the current era of university budget-crunches, and—as we have learned in the nine-year history of the Women's Studies program at the University of Vermont, where multimillion-dollar budget crises are almost as common as blizzards—it can be powerfully effective as a strategy for making Women's Studies programs grow in climates where everything else seems to be wilting under conditions of budgetary drought. It is also, it seems to me, a crucial strategic position for Women's Studies programs to adopt in those hundreds and thousands of institutions of higher education—ranging from impoverished state schools to under-endowed private colleges and community colleges and everything in between—whose resources are so strapped as to make the dedication of tenure lines to Women's Studies unlikely or impossible. In what follows, I am speaking to those Women's Studies practitioners who are responsible for fostering feminist teaching and scholarship in this vast majority of colleges and universities. I am advocating a long-term strategy for radical transformation of the "traditional disciplinary departments" themselves, with a goal of eventually dissolving the departmental structure of higher education in favor of a fully interdisciplinary organization for the production of knowledge. This seems to me our best hope for ensuring the future of Women's Studies in times of retrenchment.

Clearly, the situation is different in some places, but evidently universities like mine have reached the limits of our resources—of money and of time. No longer will budgets increase to accommodate innovation; nor can faculty possibly do more teaching, service, and research than is already required. Anything that any one program requests and wins from a central administration is something that another program will lose. Any tenure line my program might gain after hard-fought negotiations with a dean is a tenure-line taken from another department of my college, left battered and resentful after its own hard-fought battle. Such piecemeal reallocation is already in full swing at a school such as the University of Vermont (UVM), where every retirement, resignation, or death in a tenured position results in the line's being "frozen" while the administration considers whether that line could be put to better (read, more "cost-efficient") use in another program. By the time tenure-track hires are authorized, years after the vacancies occurred, no one can remember who exactly it is that's being replaced. No one really knows where the new "line" has come from, but everyone can see that no line is ever really "new," because nearly all programs and departments are operating with fewer lines than they had ten years ago.

Everybody who has been a chair or a director knows that these conditions contribute to a defensive sense of embattlement within departments and programs. I would be tempted to call it paranoia, except that there's nothing delusional about it. The threat of losing tenure lines is constant and real; the challenge of reconfiguring programs to function with fewer tenure-track faculty is a pressing question everywhere, in classics and English, chemistry and art, as well as in Women's Studies, where there are few if any tenure lines to take away in the first place. In a zero-sum game, it seems, Women's Studies would stand only to gain from any transaction; our victory, though, would inevitably be someone else's grimly grudging loss.

If some economic miracle were to befall UVM, resulting in all deserving programs' receiving as many tenure lines as would be necessary to support their ideal curriculum, our program would of course joyfully accept the windfall. Now, mind you, I'm not sure that would necessarily be in the best interest of the evolving intellectual goals of the Women's Studies program. Indeed, it would mean we could hire permanent faculty into lines configured to fit the current notion of what the field of Women's Studies ought to be. That dream department would contain faculty conversant in all the branches of feminist theory as it exists in the new century: There would be postcolonial feminists and womanists; liberal, radical, and third-wave feminists; poststructuralist feminist literary and cultural critics; positivist feminist social scientists; feminist performance artists; and someone who could teach the sort of courses one assumes Donna Haraway might teach. There would be a glorious spread of races, ethnicities, nationalities, abilities and disabilities, ages, and especially sexualities. There would be transsexuals, gay and straight women and men, people who are ambisexual, and people who are "questioning."

How many people would be in this dream department? The variety I have sketched out is an only slightly hyperbolic representation of the current Women's Studies-affiliated faculty at UVM (well, except that we don't really have anybody like Donna Haraway), a list that includes about ninety permanent and adjunct faculty (out of an Arts and Sciences faculty of around four hundred). Perhaps if we could control the representation of various scholarly approaches and forms of experience by doing all our own hiring instead of being at the mercy of other departments' hiring decisions, we could achieve something like the same diversity with a tenure-track faculty of, say thirty—about the size of the UVM English Department, for example.

To be sure, the existence of such a dream department would make a significant space for the development of Women's Studies as an interdiscipline. (And I do take seriously the distinction we Women's Studies practitioners are currently making between merely "multidisciplinary" and truly "interdisciplinary" research and teaching.) I wonder, though, whether we are not placing too much emphasis on the idea that such space must literally be a place on a specific college campus, to the disadvantage of the work that gets produced in the virtual spaces academic life offers us. Are the intellectual communities we can find through the Internet, national and regional conferences, and publications incapable of fostering genuinely interdisciplinary thought? The idea of a "safe space" for feminist work includes an assumption that truly new modes of interdisciplinary thinking will meet resistance from tenure committees in traditionally conceived departments, as many Women's Studies scholars with "joint appointments" have found. This may be true at the more prestigious institutions that have managed to develop tenure lines in Women's Studies. But is it equally true at the many less-well-endowed schools where there is always less at stake in tenure decisions? Might not scholars in disciplinarily defined departments encounter less resistance from colleagues willing to defer to their Women's Studies expertise than could arise among members of a Women's Studies department deeply divided along theoretical and political lines? How can we be certain that tenure lines in Women's Studies are the best way to go?

In the absence of an economic miracle, of course, these questions are hardly worth debating, as they are moot. Things being what they are at institutions such as mine, no tenure lines can be added to the Women's Studies program without first being denied to the other departments of the college, and as no one really knows what the origins of a given line might have been, everyone looks with suspicion on any recently established program that seems to be getting what they themselves might have been forced to give up. If I could hire a full-time faculty member specializing in postcolonialist perspectives on international feminisms, the English Department would see her as replacing the Romanticist whose line has been "frozen" for four years, the Sociology Department would think she was there in place of the theorist who retired, the History Department would consider her to be occupying the position properly belonging to its departed Asia specialist, and so forth. As "frozen" positions are always rapidly "defrosted" and reallocated (or, even more often, sublimated, the way ice-cube trays eventually become empty in a frost-free freezer), no more than one department would be right about the origins of the new Women's Studies line, but all the departments would be resentful. In subsequent years, if I were to contact those chairs to ask whether they would offer their regular sections of "Feminist Literary Theory and Criticism," "Sociology of Reproduction," "Women in U.S. History," and other mainstays of the Women's Studies program, their willingness to cooperate with our curricular needs would be seriously curtailed.

When I became director of Women's Studies, my predecessor, the sociologist Joan Smith, advised me that a Women's Studies program's only hope in the zero-sum game of university budgeting is to cultivate relationships with established departments and programs in order—to put it bluntly—to infiltrate them until they are so transformed they hardly resemble their former selves. The idea is to do everything possible to make sure that tenure lines in other departments are being filled with feminist scholars, and that those professors, once hired, cross-list their courses with Women's Studies, and, in the long run, stay at UVM. That might sound like an even more unrealistic goal than adding tenure lines to Women's Studies programs would be, but I think it is as manageable as it is inspired. As she put it to me, "You go to the chairs of all the departments and make them believe that Women's Studies is not here to take anything away from them; on the contrary, Women's Studies is here to help them, to supply programming and events that will enhance their offerings, to make their programs better and their lives easier." By thus seeming to position ourselves as helpmeets to the traditional departments, Women's Studies may appear to be slipping demurely into that all-too-familiar position of the academic distaff. The key, though, is that this is a matter of appearances, of making the departments believe our goal is simply to facilitate their work. More important than the short-term facilitation is the long-term infiltration. The degree of cooperation a Women's Studies program can elicit from departments in this way is very high, and the results of that cooperation can be a significant increase in Women's Studies course listings and feminist tenure-track hirings in all departments of the college.

What does a dedicated tenure line (especially the "partial" tenure lines Women's Studies often gets) buy you, anyway—or even three of them, or five? Our program "owns" one-half of one feminist economist, and that translates for us into her teaching one course for us, free of cost to the Women's Studies instructional budget, every fourth semester. How a 50 percent increment of a full-time salary got translated into so insignificant a proportion of her five-course-per-year teaching load is another story, but I think it's not atypical in situations in which interdisciplinary pro-grams "share" faculty with departments. Departments will always have the upper hand in working out the "deals" (as they will inevitably have more clout in the tenure decisions made about "shared" faculty). To be sure, if our program had three full-time faculty members in dedicated lines, that would mean we could offer fifteen courses a year that were scheduled independently by Women's Studies, with no help or coopera-tion from other departments. As it is, we have the budget to offer only four such courses a year, by buying out faculty time from home depart-ments. But what would it cost us to get those three faculty lines, if it meant antagonizing the other departments of the college? How many of the forty-five cross-listed courses now offered each semester would we still have to our credit? We would have the advantage of holding more control over the coherence of our curriculum, but we would have the disadvantage of having the feminist perspectives being taught in our program limited to what those three faculty could convey. The cost to the program in terms of interdisciplinary breadth of course offerings and diversity of feminisms would be heavy.

More important, it seems to me, than filling Women's Studies lines and thus sacrificing the goodwill of other departments, is to foster rela-tions with those departments that make it possible for Women's Studies to participate actively in recruiting and retaining new tenure-track faculty across the college. What if the Romanticist, the social theorist, and the historian of Asia—once authorized to be hired—could all also be feminists, maybe even postcolonialist feminists? Given the pre-eminence of feminist scholarly approaches across the humanities, fine arts, and social sciences, almost every search for an assistant professor at UVM results in a pool of finalists that includes at least one candidate with a commitment to feminist teaching and scholarship, and more often than not that candidate becomes the home department's first choice. We have found that a friendly call to department chairs from the Women's Studies Personnel Committee, offering to entertain any visiting job candidates who have interests in gender or Women's Studies at an informal breakfast or lunch, goes a long way toward attracting the best feminist candidates to accept the jobs, once offered. Sometimes the departments seek our feedback on the candidates we have taken to breakfast with colleagues from other departments whose gender-centered interests intersect with theirs; sometimes they do not. Over the long run, though, the part we can play in recruiting the strongest feminist candidates pays off in the contributions those candidates make to their own departments' curricula and scholarly agendas, once they are hired, promoted, and tenured.

And once feminist scholars join the tenure-track faculty, the Women's Studies program—with its brown-bag lunches and feminist theory discussion groups, its sponsorship of visiting lectures and its modest augmentation of travel allowances, its potluck dinners and its weekly teas, its influence on the Faculty Senate and its mentoring of student activists—plays a significant role in maintaining an intellectual and social climate that will retain feminist scholars. The kind of money it takes to maintain these aspects of a program is trivial compared with the financial commitment required by tenure lines. Even in the toughest budgetary situations, Women's Studies programs can make a compelling case for such comparatively minor financial support. At UVM, at least, the returns on this strategy are calculable: In the past five years, the number of tenured and tenure-track faculty affiliated with the Women's Studies program has grown from forty-one to seventy-eight, with no special help from the Dean's Office in defining new hires to suit our purposes. Not all of the affiliated faculty—new hires or old-timers—define "feminism" as I do. Their teaching and research represents a genuine diversity of approaches to what it means to use gender and sexuality as primary categories of analysis across the disciplines. This, for now, achieves my goal for the program—but only for now.

I want to stress that I am outlining strategies that seem to me practical for the way we now live, in colleges and universities whose very limited resources are divided up along traditionally understood departmental lines. For what it's worth, I believe that the future of colleges such as mine is not in departments at all, but in interdisciplinary programs. Inevitably, the traditional disciplinary boundaries dividing up institutional resources will dissolve, as they have already begun to dissolve in our scholarly and pedagogical practices across the disciplines. Anyone who has recently sat on a hiring committee in the humanities, fine arts, or social sciences knows that the most exciting feminist candidates for tenure-track positions are doing genuinely interdisciplinary work, whatever discipline their Ph.D.s might represent. As these scholars are hired and tenured into disciplinarily defined departments, the departments themselves are being transformed. It is my hope and my belief that before I retire, departments as we know them will no longer exist. That time may come, but not before those traditional departments contain enough tenured faculty who can recognize the wisdom and the necessity of reorganizing the institutional structure of higher education on the model that Women's Studies, as an interdiscipline, has been developing for twenty-five years.

As I think about institutional transformation, I take the very long view, mainly to keep from being discouraged. For now, I think Women's Studies programs that cannot count on getting tenure lines should not squander that most precious of resources, energy, in struggling to get them at any cost. Our best hope for radical institutional change is to keep modeling interdisciplinary teaching and scholarship across the university as we continue to infiltrate from within.

The Politics of "Excellence"

> The question becomes how to link diverse feminisms without requiring either equivalence or a master theory. How to make these links without replicating cultural and economic hegemony?—Inderpal Grewal and Caren Kaplan (1994: 19)

Those of us who work in U.S. state university systems are increasingly compelled by system administrators to define our programs or departments in the instrumentalist discourse of "mission review," "public accountability," and "student outcomes assessment." In other words, we are compelled to define our place within a contemporary university-becoming-transnational corporation. That becoming signifies a temporal and functional transformation of the public university that is uneven and apparently contradictory; it means a shift from a university mission that served the nation primarily by inculcating a "useful common culture" in the interests of statist consumerism to one that serves primarily transnational corporations by inculcating "efficiency and productivity" in the interests of the "globalization" of capital. Women's Studies' emergence 20-plus years ago challenged, from an increasingly critical transdisciplinary perspective, the production of knowledges that reproduced the patriarchal, racist, consumerist logic of the nation-state. The most pointed attacks on Women's Studies have derived primarily from this nationalist agenda, which has increasingly sought to maintain itself, especially through "reform" initiatives such as those carried out historically in general education curricula across the country, against the erosion of the nation-state. Such attacks continue even today, overlapping with the much more recent pressures on Women's Studies directors to define their programs' "mission" in the corporate logic of "accountability" and "efficiency."

Both of the logical economies inherent in the transformation of the university rely on the "idea of America," though they each construct this ideology differently: One invokes it overtly as a moral imperative and ground for the reproduction of a "shared democratic culture"; the other relies on it implicitly as a technological ground and imperative for "democratic and economic efficiency" that can be exported and reproduced globally. These logical economies increasingly utilize the rhetoric of "excellence" to describe their separate—though ultimately indissolubly related—aims. Both, I would claim, are antagonized by the potentialities of transdisciplinary programs such as Women's Studies, which are engaged in thinking the resistance to "scattered hegemonies," as suggested by (among many others) Grewal and Kaplan's discussion of "transnational feminist practices" quoted earlier. The pervasiveness of the rhetoric of "excellence" in both these initiatives is symptomatic of the becoming with which Women's Studies must now reckon. Transdisciplinary Women's Studies programs of the future will need to develop "new analyses of how gender works in the dynamic of globalization and the countermeasures of new nationalisms, and ethnic and racial fundamentalisms" (Grewal and Kaplan 1994: 19) if they are to be relevant, critical, and oppositional practices within the transnational corporate university.

General education, through which many U.S. Women's Studies courses and programs are introduced to undergraduates, is one of the most visible battlegrounds for this transformation of the university. A fundamental imperative of the increasingly corporatized university and its overdetermination of "accountability" is the standardization of general education curricula. State University of New York (SUNY) Provost Peter D. Salins, in a recent report on general education for the SUNY system, wrote, for example, that "there is increasing evidence that employers value the personal and intellectual qualities provided by a strong general education as much as technically focused experience. . . . A rigorous general education can prepare students to know how to learn, and to adapt readily to rapid changes in workplace expectations" (Salins 1998: 5). (Salins is referring to a U.S. Department of Education statement that "today's college graduates will pursue between 6 and 12 different vocations during a working lifetime".) This standardized core, which reduces the differential dynamics of lived experience to a quantifiable category, allows the university to be "accountable" to the taxpayers and its "customers" and, especially, to the transnational corporations that increasingly demand workers with transferable technological skills and a "common core experience." Defining that "common core" is also the goal of conservative administrators and educators who seek to reinscribe the centrality of an American heritage and Western civilization perceived to have been "shattered" in the aftermath of the 1960s student protests.[1] Both initiatives rely on a conception of general education that celebrates the triumphalist idea of an America (understood not only as liberal democracy but also capitalism) and the West that "won" the Cold War. Salins's report makes this clear. Hailing a general education that "enriches our political system, our society and our culture," he claims that "the modern American university can be one of the most effective institutions available to support the nation's ideals of free inquiry and democratic access to prosperity and power" (Salins 1998: 6)—especially in an age of fractious ethnic conflict and uneasy development of democratic and free-market principles.[2] In other words, although the way in which each initiative celebrates that "idea" points to an apparent contradiction in the current general-education debates, it seems increasingly clear that they both rely on and universalize this idea of America—and use the rhetoric of "excellence" to promote their agendas. I'd like to sketch out some practical implications of this "politics of excellence" for U.S. public higher education, using SUNY, the largest state-university system, synecdochically, then join with others to call for a new thinking of transdisciplinary programs such as Women's Studies in the twenty-first-century corporate university.

This transformation of the university has profound ramifications both for the education of students in U.S. universities as well as the exportation of U.S. knowledge production globally, as Bill Readings details in his provocative book *The University in Ruins* (1996). His pointed exposure of how "excellence" informs this shift is crucial for my own thinking about these issues. "Excellence" in his analysis "has become the unifying principle of the contemporary University. . . . As an integrating principle, excellence has the singular advantage of being entirely meaningless, or to put it more precisely, non-referential" (Readings 1996: 22). He argues that this new quantitative rhetoric has accompanied the transformation of the traditional role of the university as a consequence of the decline of the nation-state and the subsequent disappearance of a "national culture." For Readings, this transformation is basically complete, so that a nationalistic ideology no longer operates in the university. I would suggest, based on general-education reform initiatives across the United States in the mid- to late 1990s, that his conclusions were premature, though I believe he was right about the direction of the transformation. That both aspects of this becoming can be subsumed under the banner of "excellence" only reinforces his insight regarding the term's inherent meaninglessness.

Evidence of the corporatization of knowledge is everywhere manifest in general education "reform" today. Duke University's new "matrix" model of general education, which one of its faculty members favorably called "a 'total quality management' approach to curriculum change" is one example.[3] But this momentum is most dramatically and ominously manifest in the struggle over general education that has been taking place within SUNY since the early to mid-1990s. Under Governor George Pataki, the SUNY system has been transformed (with accompanying "downsizing") from being a "state-supported" to a "state-assisted" university system.[4] Yet as state funding has decreased, political micromanaging has increased, pursued by both public and private bodies that are driven by a special "interest" in determining issues of access to the university as well as what students "should" learn once they enter. These "special interests" represent their micromanaging as delivering greater fiscal "accountability" to state taxpayers, greater "value" for the consumers (that is, students and their families), and greater educational "preparation" of workers for the corporate sector. Yet their "interest" also reveals a reactionary agenda for "restoring" a narrow, nationalistic American and Western heritage. As I believe the SUNY example makes clear, traditional faculty control over curriculum is being undermined in favor of non-academic technocrats and the special corporate interests they represent, under the guise of a reactionary nationalist agenda that is intended to insure that the transnational agenda will be guided and determined by a very particular "idea of America." All these initiatives are subsumed under the rhetoric of "excellence."

Working with such "special-interest" groups in New York State such as Change-NY (which calls itself an "anti-tax group") and the Empire Foundation for Policy Research, several self-proclaimed "activist" members of the SUNY Board of Trustees (with the support of conservative faculty groups such as the state branch of the National Association of Scholars) have, over the past several years, increasingly attempted to dictate models of general education that would standardize the curriculum for the sixty-four campus SUNY system. "Standardization" here means undermining the potential of transdisciplinarity and pluralism represented by programs such as Women's Studies, as well as making the curriculum serviceable to the corporate sector by increasing the technologization of learning. In December 1995, the board presented a report to the governor and legislature titled "Rethinking SUNY," a multiyear approach to achieving greater fiscal accountability and greater student and faculty "productivity." In July 1996, a report titled "SUNY's Core Curricula: The Failure to Set Consistent and High Academic Standards" appeared.[5] Published by the "special interests" mentioned earlier, it purports to be an analysis of each SUNY campus's general-education curriculum (but not of their course syllabi). Quoting conservative "reformers" such as Matthew Arnold and Arthur Schlesinger Jr., this report found what it called "incoherence"—an "almost a complete lack of structure"—and, tellingly, an excess of "narrow and esoteric" courses accepted as suitable for general education requirements throughout the system.

The report erroneously claims that the majority of SUNY campuses have succumbed to "multiculturalism," meaning that students are "force[d] to take courses that often have an ideological or political bent. . . . Instead of a balanced treatment of different cultures, these campuses offer politicized courses that focus on grievances of different groups, whether based on sex, race, or class" (SUNY's Core Curricula 1996: 22). Among those deemed "not appropriate as core courses" were "Feminism: Literature and Cultural Contexts" and "Sexuality in Literature" (for the "Interpreting Texts in the Humanities" requirement at one campus); "Myths and Folktales of American Indians" (for the "Non-Western Traditions" requirement at a second campus); "Puerto Rico: People, History and Culture" (for the "Cultural and Historical Perspectives" requirement at a third campus); "Introduction to African-American History," "Anthropology of Gender," and "Environmental Economics" (to fulfill a Writing-Intensive requirement at a fourth campus); and "World Food Crisis" (for a "Natural Science" requirement at a fifth campus) (SUNY's Core Curricula 1996: 28–29). One can detect the ideological subtext that this list of prohibitions (and the report includes others) has in common: aspects of

American or Western life that the "idea" of America has been historically silent about because their study would constitute obstacles in the progress of transnational capital.

The report begins with testimonials under the heading "Praise from the Business and Academic Communities," which link this nationalistic version of general-education "reform" together with the corporate logic that the university increasingly serves. For example, William E. Simon, former U.S. Secretary of Treasury (1974–77), states: "The study on SUNY's core curriculum . . . should serve as a wake-up call for SUNY's leaders. As in every other area of the marketplace, consumers will catch on that a product is worthless. SUNY's leaders should recognize that parents and students can vote with their checkbooks for the education that prepares young people for lives as productive and educated citizens." Kay S. Hymowitz, senior fellow at the conservative Manhattan Institute, states: "[The report's] thorough depiction of SUNY's fragmented and incoherent curriculums not only reveals the extent to which SUNY is failing to provide employers a needed assurance that its diploma has real heft. It also demonstrates how SUNY is letting down the thousands of students for whom a public university is the only hope for both upward mobility and for a meaningful introduction to a common, democratic culture" (SUNY's Core Curricula 1996). The report concludes with an ominous threat in the section "Next Steps": "SUNY need not accept low academic standards. SUNY campuses already have the authority to independently reform their core curricula. And, *if the campuses fail to act or fail to act properly,* the SUNY Board of Trustees has the legal authority to set academic standards for the campuses" (SUNY's Core Curricula 1996: 30; emphasis added).

Two subsequent events reveal overlapping implications of this dual-edged agenda, which introduce a "common democratic culture" in the name of corporate accountability. One was the attack on SUNY-New Paltz's annual Women's Studies conference in 1997; the other was the December 1998 mandate by the trustees of a core curriculum for the SUNY system without consultation with the faculty. As symptomatic of the university-becoming-transnational corporation, they provide especially telling examples of what is at stake for Women's Studies programs nationally.

Together with their allies in the public sector, certain trustees—as well as John Ryan, then SUNY's chancellor, attacked the New Paltz Women's

Studies conference ("Revolting Behavior: The Challenges of Women's Sexual Freedom"), attempting not only to undermine the long-standing Women's Studies transdisciplinary program there *but to remove the college president* for his support of the program and the conference. The controversy generated national media attention, including coverage in the *Chronicle of Higher Education*, the *New York Times,* and CBS News's "60 Minutes," which incorporated the New Paltz conference as the lead-in to a story ("Sexuality 101") that lamented the rise of queer studies in U.S. universities and quoted the SUNY trustee Candace DeRussy and members of the "special-interest" groups mentioned earlier, as well as SUNY-New Paltz's embattled president, Roger Bowen.[6]

Teresa L. Ebert, Associate Professor of English at SUNY-Albany (one of the four research universities in the system), responded to the New Paltz controversy in an op-ed piece for the *Schenectady Daily Gazette,* in which she rightly observed that "what is really scandalous in SUNY" was not the Women's Studies conference but the "dumbing down of SUNY: the concerted effort to reduce the education of citizens to what is basically nothing more than job training" (Ebert 1997). She noted that Albany "is closing down its German Department and marginalizing English, French and other humanities programs, [while] it is creating a number of new administrative positions and supporting such projects as CETL (Center for Excellence in Teaching and Learning), which is a loosely disguised form of skills training" (Ebert 1997). Ebert's conclusion is that the mostly working- and middle-class students that SUNY serves "are expected to settle for a cultural education based on popular culture manufactured by corporations. They are thus left out of any serious debates on, for example, gender and sexuality that do not fit the formulas of mainstream cliches given to them by their bottom-line education" (Ebert 1997). Her assessment, as the report earlier clearly suggests, is right on target in critiquing the university's transnational interests; it does not, however, address the simultaneous reactionary nationalism that marked much of the outcry over the New Paltz conference. This version of general education lends itself to the transnational "excellence" agenda by reducing the traditional American general-education program to "skills" and the idea of America as the epitome of technological knowledge and practice.

In December 1998, the SUNY Board of Trustees voted 10-3 to adopt a new standardized general-education curriculum for the system's

370,000 students; the curriculum was distributed to campus academic officers only a week before the board meeting and formulated without consultation with faculty, following the letter and spirit of the 1996 "SUNY's Core Curricula" report. The trustees' model dictates American history and Western civilization, as well as distribution requirements in basic skills and disciplinary knowledges, but it also justifies itself in the name of increased efficiency, accountability, and productivity. Interdisciplinary programs are given no visible place in the new core curriculum. Following systemwide faculty outrage over the trustees' action, which resulted in a vote of "no confidence" in the Board of Trustees, the plan was debated by a General Education Task Force appointed by the provost in the summer of 1999; the task force generated ten "learning outcomes" as opposed to a narrow set of ten specific courses.[7] The mandate was to take effect in the fall of 2000; at this writing, campuses were still uncertain about how the system planned to assess the learning outcomes. No new funds had been allocated to ease the burden on campuses scrambling to comply.[8]

As the SUNY example reveals, Women's Studies as transdisciplinary practice must resist the leveling imperative of the "politics of excellence" that mark the transformation of a university rooted in the idea of America, albeit one that serves competing and sometimes contradictory interests. In seeking to define itself as an "interdiscipline," positioning itself in the shifting spaces of power as disciplines attempt to reregulate what counts as "legitimate" knowledge production and how these create "global subjects" serving transnational interests, Women's Studies should heed Susan Stanford Friedman's recent reminder that "interdisciplinarity is as much a cultural formation subject to change and politics as disciplinarity" (1998b: 310). Women's Studies should continue to interrogate the logic of reactionary nationalisms as well as the instrumentalist logic of transnational corporatism; it must adopt pedagogical strategies aimed at transforming the construction of both knowledge and subjects, thereby generating new modes of inquiry in the "borders" or "interstices" of such constructions. The transdisciplinary thinking inaugurated by Women's Studies in conjunction with studies in ethnicity, postcoloniality, and queer studies "articulate[s] the relationship of gender to scattered hegemonies such as global economic structures, patriarchal nationalisms, 'authentic' forms of tradition, local structures of domination, and legal-juridical oppression on multiple levels" (Grewal and Kaplan 1994: 17). It thus enables students to recognize the relay from the

240   Jeanette McVicker

local to the global while maintaining historically, geographically, and culturally specific and concrete perspectives. Women's Studies can open up spaces of resistance even within the corporate "University of Excellence," maintain vital links to the activist practices of building affiliated communities, and foster the development of "critical citizens." In other words, one initiative of Women's Studies should be to think the contradictions inherent in these agendas.[9]

Notes

My deep thanks to William V. Spanos for his invaluable advice and for reading early drafts.

1   For a compelling genealogy of the American university and the role of general education, particularly during the Cold War and the Vietnam war, see Spanos 1993.

2   In *The University in Ruins*, Bill Readings suggests that the transformation in North American universities is "part of the process of Americanization [that] cannot be understood as simply the expansion of U.S. cultural hegemony ... 'Americanization' in its current form is a synonym for globalization ... that recognizes that globalization is not a neutral process" (1996: 2). I agree with Readings that it is not neutral. See Salins 1997, in which he argues that in order for America to overcome its growing move toward "ethnic federalism" and achieve its pre-1960s status as a "civic nation," it must reclaim the idea of assimilation.

3   See Schneider 1999.

4   According to United University Professions (UUP), the faculty and professional staff union for SUNY, the university has gone from 90 percent state-tax-dollar support in 1986–87 to 46 percent in 1996–97. This information, based on SUNY's Office of Institutional Research, was presented in a memo dated November 16, 1996, by Fredonia UUP President Richard Reddy to members of the UUP Temporary Task Force on Variable Campus-Based Tuition. I thank him for the information.

5   "SUNY's Core Curricula" was a joint project of the New York Association of Scholars and the Empire Foundation for Policy Research.

6   For more details about SUNY-New Paltz's 1997 Women's Studies conference and the aftermath, see the program's Web site at http://www.newpaltz.edu/wmnstudies. The 1998 conference took up the controversy and dedicated itself to a thoughtful exploration of censorship, academic freedom, and Women's Studies with the theme "Silencing Women/Voices of Resistance."

7   The "no confidence" vote was cosponsored by the faculty union, the UUP, and the University Senate, the primary systemwide faculty-governance body. The vote was unanimous among the four-year colleges and universities in the system, though the actual impact of the vote was of course negligible. It did, however, inspire the provost to appoint a task force to "review the mandate" and make recommendations for implementation.

8   Campuses have had to submit their revised general-education plans to the provost's implementation task force (composed primarily of administrators and a few faculty)

in order to be certified as compliant with the trustees' mandate. Although some flexibility has been allowed, campuses have received very mixed signals depending on whom they have dealt with on the task force. In addition, the immense impact on history and language departments has been completely unaddressed, as have system-wide assessment procedures. The significance of the SUNY situation is revealed in a *New York Times* story that covered the entrance of the American Association of University Professors (AAUP) in the summer of 2000 into the SUNY fray. In that story, AAUP General-Secretary Mary Burgan was quoted as saying, "We are determined to find ways to counter such dire encroachments on the integrity of a great institution like SUNY": see Arenson 2000.

9 For a more in-depth and general version of this essay, see McVicker 1999.

Academic Housework: Women's Studies and Second Shifting

I started teaching introductory Women's Studies courses in 1986, but it was only after I read Arlie Hochschild's *The Second Shift* in 1989 that I realized how the three universities at which I have taught—College of the Holy Cross, Miami University, and University of Wisconsin-Madison (a fair ground for generalizing, I hope)—set up the expectations for labor in Women's Studies programs. As I will show, Hochschild's thesis of dual-career heterosexual couples and the second shift has its parallel in the division of labor in the university. Hochschild's major point is that there is a "cultural cover-up" of the disjunctive inequality between men's and women's labor: Men control time at home, especially in terms of choosing which chores to do and the regularity of getting them done. Women do more at home than their partners do. Unconsciously or not, academic administrations, I contend, expect women—and particularly Women's Studies professors—to follow out those models in ways that they generally don't for male faculty members. The very language ascribed to Women's Studies is a language of academic "service." The result is that Women's Studies teachers do the second shift of academe, which amounts to a whole range of expectations of female faculty and "feminized" labor.[1] This essay will explain the effects of this second shift in the context of university calls for accountability and debates over academic values. The "real work" of the academy goes on, business as usual in traditional departments, and most female faculty working within those departments must then do two sorts of labor: the first, that for which they are hired, promoted, and rewarded; the second—they are told—that which they do out of their commitment or interest. And so they perform the domestic work of academe—the nurturing, sustaining, fostering of students, a labor made "natural" because of their interest in furthering a Women's Studies agenda. Their committee work and administrative appointments cover the business of the academic world, and their ostensibly naturalized care-giving is their pleasure to do, or, they tell themselves, it is their duty—as feminists—to uphold. The second shift then winds up hurting Women's Studies faculty's "home" careers insofar as what Hochschild terms the "smooth choicelessness" of many male faculty and administrators allows them to neglect anything but what they see as "their own work," most often research.

Perhaps it is not at all surprising that the same expectation often holds true in Women's Studies programs or departments, particularly for those who are joint-appointed (working within a traditional department in addition to an interdisciplinary one). That means a double share of committee appointments, often a double load of meetings and assignments in Women's Studies that takes place after the "regular" hours of one's home department. The two kinds of institutional discrimination operate together, reinforcing each other. The first just expects female faculty to do more than male colleagues; the second subordinates the interdisciplinary program to the "home" department. So goes the logic of enforced volunteerism, a result of split appointments as a compromise between no support and full support.

Hochschild's study determines psychological and cultural attitudes toward domestic duties among dual-career heterosexual couples, documenting those attitudes in ten case studies across class and race lines. While Hochschild envied the "smooth choicelessness" of her male colleagues who did not have to worry about their children or bring them into the office, she also remarked on how their power lives on in stratified relations at home, regardless of whatever equality women might have gained at work. Her research revealed that women were "far more deeply torn between the demands of work and family life than were their husbands" (1989: 6). Their ambivalence played itself out in spoken resentment against their spouses or, if that remained unarticulated, in often passive-aggressive resistance to their spouses' politics of time control and their extra leisure. Hochschild's study concludes that women, more than men, are forced to accept the alienated life of the public work-domestic labor split, along with being held to higher standards due to social expectations for working mothers. But Hochschild does not conclude that women should refuse to do domestic labor. She instead argues that the psychological cost of their labor is an ambivalence about their relationship to the institution (in this case, marriage).

Women's Studies work is not only constructed around a similar model of domestic labor; it is also perceived along domestic lines—taking care of the "family" or one's academic "sisters," addressing the extra-systemic needs of women and men. Twenty years or so into the institutionalization of these programs across the country, those associated with Women's Studies are still trying to justify Women's Studies as a discipline and as a legitimate—and necessary—response to ideological pressures and the intellectual demands of our students. These now familiar accusations come as new attacks, as if departments of anthropology and sociology weren't also responses to ideological pressures in the 1920s and 1930s; as if liberal education itself weren't a response to ideological pressures in nineteenth-century education. These departments, too, were once "new" to the academy as social pressures created academic disciplines. The academy changes by virtue of what it considers central and marginal to its evolving missions. That Women's Studies is still trying to define itself as central reveals not only the politics of such normalizing, but also the politics of funding.[2]

Thus, the analogy of Women's Studies Program to the conventional heterosexual marriage assures that whatever we do in "private"—that is, in programs—is our own business, as long as Women's Studies professors do the "home" work in departments (which often turns out to be the department's housekeeping, such as formal and informal mentoring, work with students rather than in research, social events). In Zora Neale Hurston's terms, the "oldest human longing" is not for speech but for space, one of the most contested arenas in academic life (1978 [1973]: 18) The physical distance of the home department and program— separated on campus—also leads to particular confusion about institutional allegiance, because the "home department" generally signifies the previously all-male place "where even the feminist scholar has a chance to escape the domestic by participating in and having a relation to a knowledge formation that is deemed legitimate" (Wiegman, personal correspondence, 1999). Yet the "home" department is marked by the domestic register, while the "program" (the domain where most Women's Studies work gets done) is—by this logic—extra-familial, a personal-is-political commitment that confounds the traditional home-work division. Or, in the convolutions of many departments, the home-"home department" split makes the academic workplace a version of the domestic, privatized home, where certain scholars do research and don't do what amounts to "windows"—service or introductory teaching. The other or outside status of the "program" suggests something not fully legitimate, not home; it is the uncanny of the university, where the university has relegated its own repressed unconscious. If the university has a Women's Studies program, so this logic goes, then there must be no inequality of women or troubled gendered climate. In light of these pressures, Women's Studies is often split internally, because the originating idea of Women's Studies is based on a liberal claim about human equality, then devoted to understanding differences such as gender, class, and race among women. Arguably, this liminality used to benefit Women's Studies programs, insofar as they could develop outside of the rules of traditional departments. However, that liminality also works against Women's Studies programs now as they jockey to maintain institutional power. As we will see, the foundational ambivalence emerges at the center of Women's Studies program and allegiances to the university.[3]

"Chronic Ambivalence"

In Women's Studies today, we see this conflicted relationship to home departments—fostered by the cavalier attitude with which home departments treat the commitments of their joint-appointed or shared faculty. As one colleague recently remarked, she not only feels double-shifted, but, given the ways in which traditional departments dismiss interdisciplinary programs, she often feels double-shafted. Although the exhaustion of managing the double load may take its toll in the short run and on individual professors, the ambivalence that the institutional relationship fosters may also be the site of new resistance, as I will explain later.

The second shift of Women's Studies, then, can amount to a series of repeated self-justifications, by which intellectual and innovative energies are siphoned off. One way to understand the status of Women's Studies programs is to consider how writing programs—in the 1970s and '80s—came to be considered feminized. Women's Studies is most obviously "feminized" given its female faculty, but writing programs have been rendered so by the equation of composition studies with a second-class—or second-shift—status. As Carol Hartzog has written about writing-program administration, writing programs that serve an interdisciplinary purpose often face the same disrespect and the same academic politics of debate over whether composition is really an academic discipline (1986: ix). As it is in Women's Studies, writing-program administrations find themselves having to justify their authority in the field. Hartzog explains: "The problem of authority has these, among other, manifestations: faculties disagree about whether or not writing courses are somehow as weighty as other university courses, about whether or not writing courses should be taught by apprentice and temporary faculty members, about whether or not writing deserves and can sustain scholarly investigation, and about whether writing programs exist at the center or at the periphery of the academic enterprise" (1986: 69). This center-margin dichotomy is at the heart of the debate in writing programs as it is in Women's Studies: by forcing programs—whether in writing or Women's Studies or ethnic studies—to argue again and again for legitimacy and validity and "intellectual weight," the programs are politicized and dismissed as ideological matters.

Thus, the activity of Women's Studies seems constantly involved in a mission of self-validation with which other established programs need not burden themselves, even in times of recession. The struggle is one not just for survival but also for academic credibility. As Martha Nussbaum has argued in the *New Republic* (1992), the rise of gay and lesbian studies, like the rise of Women's Studies in the 1960s and '70s, has a primary rationale in liberal education: "The completeness of knowledge itself demands their promotion. And the completeness of knowledge, openness to the facts of history and to arguments about history, is an ideal that conservative opponents of these new forms of study cannot consistently repudiate and still claim to be honoring the time-honored norms of the Western philosophical tradition." And yet, the repudiation, or "second shifting," of Women's Studies goes on in a much more subtle and shrewd way than the academy usually works: as a demand for feminists and lesbian and gay scholars to take on these intellectual duties out of care-giving, guilt, duty—all of the traditional emotional responses long dismissed as irrational, somatic, irrelevant.

When it is not invisible, women's labor quickly becomes subordinated to supporting the smooth reproduction of academic life; thus, women's labor is not regarded as part of the larger project of the pursuit of Western philosophical knowledge. If one has a "home" department, what does that make Women's Studies? Is this an analogy to places or to relations, or both? A "home away from home"? A foreign retreat beyond an immediate "family," a stepchild, or an unsanctioned relation? When there is a conflict between the home department and Women's Studies (as there always is in terms of time), what happens to divided allegiances? Much of the strain for those who work in Women's Studies and Les-Bi-Gay studies and ethnic studies is the forced division of allegiance, in which "home" is the place of sanctioned rewards and "family values." I find that one is often more deeply committed to more powerfully constructed allegiances outside of disciplinary constraints. The pressure to do the double shift is externally imposed, and these pressures make us divided within programs.

Women's Studies professors experience their own double-consciousness by internalizing how the managerial class comes to see them. One feminist teacher at a state university in the South had this to say about working in two departments, English and Women's Studies: "The whole network of public-private metaphors, like 'home' department, the 'woman's work' of advising and mentoring, colleagues as 'sisters' or 'mothers' or 'daughters,' has been very confusing for me and other women I know. It's partly the paradoxes. . . . On the other hand, even though most of my intellectual and emotional network is in Women's Studies, . . . the family metaphors at work there are equally damaging in the expectations for endless nurturing and accessibility that they confer on women faculty" (Ellen Rosenman, personal correspondence, 1992). Because it rationalizes existing power relations, these familial metaphor replicate what is at bottom wrong with the institutional set-ups in which most Women's Studies professors work. A chronic state of ambivalence is thus created when the academy regards Women's Studies as the Ladies' Auxiliary, and female professors are unwittingly compelled to perpetuate this understanding. Evidence of this professorial ambivalence and conflict shows up in unusual places. When I became associate chair of Women's Studies at the University of Wisconsin and then director of the Women's Studies Research Center, I found the following internal memo to new administrators: "If you ever did any rat psych you'll do okay. But this time you're the rat and there's no pellet of food at the end." Another feminist scholar I know from the Southwest skips every third English Department meeting, if only to show the effect of her absence, a strategy that Hochschild accounts for as the "willed illness." Others find their strength in opposition to the "home" department rather than in transformation or change. Still others need to uphold the existing power relations within their "home" departments in order to continue seeing Women's Studies—or another marginal status—as a refuge from the "home."[4] That ambivalence sets up the "home" versus "retreat" opposition of the traditional department versus Women's Studies. In fact, many Women's Studies programs have recently had to address what happens when the "retreat" is itself embattled and divisive, as we internalize the demands and responsibilities of greater institutionalization. And when there are conflicts within the program itself, Women's Studies programs are more intensely scrutinized and more harshly judged because of nearly everyone's utopian expectations of female professors and their program itself.

As long as the institution, our colleagues, and often our students think that labor within Women's Studies is done out of "natural" care-giving or gendered affinity, I see a great challenge in the institutionalization of Women's Studies. And as long as Women's Studies professors and students conceive of labor as nurturing, Women's Studies will still be stymied. Nor can Women's Studies follow a Lysistrata-like strategy: refusing to play with the administration until it stops the war between the patriarchal institution and the feminist counterpart in Women's Studies. This ambivalence is not likely to compel instructors to relinquish Women's Studies work any more than recognition of the second shift—in Hochschild's model—will compel women to stop caring for their families. Another alternative is to change Women's Studies' relationship to the institution, as many have done on an individual basis: by forsaking Women's Studies or symbolically leaving the home department. Instead, we must find a way to explore and exploit that ambivalence. And one way to make that ambivalence potent—rather than buried resentment or self-division or, worse, martyrdom to the various demands of the institution—is to use it to change Women's Studies pedagogy and administration, an endeavor to which I will now turn.

To confront this collective ambivalence is to insist that the institution account more to Women's Studies faculty about the unpaid, unwaged labor of Women's Studies work. Although Women's Studies is itself a field of study and a methodology, it is also expected to be a resource for students who come to us for personal as well as academic guidance on abortion, sexual assault and harassment, and the career counseling we do, in addition to the daily work of educational advising that is so often short shrifted in traditional departments, especially for female students. These expectations are already greater than the disciplinary work of most departments. Although this "outreach" may not be our province or our training, students do expect more from Women's Studies faculty, and many women faculty thus expand their mentoring and act altruistically, perhaps giving more than they could get themselves as students. Women's Studies teachers often suffer because they elicit more transferential responses from students, and we are held accountable for their expectations, along with administrators' demands, so that we are not just unrewarded, but also punished. This generally unrecognized and usually unremunerated part of our labor must be logged, made explicit, and counted as part of merit and promotion advancements. So we need to factor in these demands as part of our job responsibilities, not just make do with these implicit expectations. This may be Women's Studies' next great educational step: to broadcast the demands on female faculty and on Women's Studies as a program. In order to change Women's Studies' relationship to the institution, we must repeatedly and strategically account for the now unrewarded advising and mentoring of undergraduate and graduate students in Women's Studies programs even as increased pedagogical attention is becoming part and parcel of the mission of most universities. Note the popularity of distance learning and post-tenure reviews, two important efforts to shore up the public images of universities as community partners.

One such dossier might address feminist pedagogy itself, which involves teaching critical thinking, feminist inquiry, and social theory; above all, we need to demonstrate how this pedagogy as well as scholarship results from seeing feminism as an intellectual movement. Women's Studies instructors need to address the following questions: How do we deal with the extremes of commitment in our students? What do we do about our accessibility, the "invisible labor" of caretaking involved in "processing" issues with our students? How do we discuss the students' anxieties about taking an overtly ideological course (another instance of our being told we are "different" from other academic departments)?

Because Women's Studies instructors are often stretched to the limits of their abilities and plagued by fatigue from their shifts, they might be tempted to let re-educating the academy slide, hoping that students and colleagues will understand the sacrifice involved in doing both jobs (although a more utopian solution would be to jettison the idea that a single faculty member can do two full-time jobs). We need a more explicit account of the use values of Women's Studies work. Most often, students and colleagues don't grasp this dimension; rather than understanding, there is resentment—on both sides. While the piece of the academic pie allotted to Women's Studies becomes smaller and smaller, Women's Studies faculty cannot do more of the second shift for less. As one of the most accomplished Women's Studies scholars, Susan Stanford Friedman, writes, "In trying to cover so much, the Women's Studies teacher or student self-destructs, a super-woman burned to a crisp by impossible demands" (1998b: 318). As Leora Auslander claims about the Center for Gender Studies at the University of Chicago, "our faculty owe primary allegiance and time to their home departments, and we have limited power to influence renewals, tenure decisions, and promotions. Most of the work done for the Center is invisible and, when noticed, sometimes (understandably) resented by departmental colleagues" (1997: 18). Faculty members are stretched, particularly when the reward system of academe is based on "disciplinary achievement." So the resentment is all around: the "volunteerism" of faculty (Auslander 1997: 19) is dwindling, especially as younger scholars can work on gender within the mainstream, and older scholars are running out of energy and time. Ironically, one reason that newer professors can do so is the exhausting efforts of their joint-appointed predecessors.

Whatever metaphor one uses—the shrinking pie or the burn-out in professorial lives—it means no longer silently accepting the double load, but negotiating the insatiable needs of the academy with the most pressing ones of Women's Studies. In the long run, in an academic culture that still clings to its patriarchal origins yet professes to want to create equal citizens of us all, Women's Studies alone cannot fix the dysfunction. It should come as no surprise if the next generation of Women's Studies faculty repeats this ambivalent academic "family" structure as permanently disgruntled labor, unless the academy sees it in its best interest to change the second shift of Women's Studies work.

Feminist Accountability

Despite this litany of abuses of the university, there is something too politically and intellectually valuable in that unalienated, however unwaged, labor; this is an important vestige of Women's Studies utopian hope. While Bill Readings, among others, has remarked that "accountability is a synonym for accounting in the 'academic lexicon' " (1996: 32). I believe we need to use accountability to our own ends.[5] One Women's Studies advocate puts the dilemma this way: "We are suffering some of the inevitable loss of energy that follows the shift from insurgency to institutional legitimation" (Auslander 1997: 4). Yet why must this loss be "inevitable" once Women's Studies becomes ostensibly legitimated by the university? Are insurgency and oppositional politics alone fueling Women's Studies? Is it that Women's Studies programs have lost the sense of direction implied by the "program" and have, instead, become programmatic? And where does this impasse leave us in terms of active resistance within the academy? Do we agitate for merit awards for second-shift work (rewards that, at best, will result from repressive tolerance), or futilely insist that everyone do the same amount of university service?

What I am recommending is a "feminist dossier" along the lines of a teaching dossier or portfolio, a program-generated document that illustrates the many lines of commitment that feminist instructors provide for the university.[6] Although many of us know that the extra workload for feminist and many female professors extends to the personal, we are reluctant to record such extra labor (for fear, I think, of what it means to us in terms of compensation). In addition to evidence of research and teaching, it might serve us well to document not only work hours (I know of no academic feminist who doesn't lament them), but also methods and efforts that are part of our professional lives. Such a dossier might include: 1) the scope of extra-pedagogical topics we need to address for our students; 2) the interdisciplinary range of our syllabi; 3) our most effective nontraditional assignments, along with a description of the range of our students, many of whom are nontraditional students; 4) our emphasis on ability-based curricula, and especially reports of peer and administrator visits to our classes, to attest to the kinds of teaching methods and successes in feminist classrooms; and 5) the administrative burdens of running interdisciplinary programs. Although feminists have often been quite specific in their descriptions of feminist pedagogy, some analyses from other faculty about our "methods" might go a long way in making our cases. What we do in the classroom, community, and scholarship needs to be offered up (but not as sacrificial rite) to legislators who demand accountability. Feminists can make that legislated accountability work to dispel the pernicious myths of our difference and lack of rigorous practice. By analyzing and explaining our own research and teaching results in such a dossier, we also demonstrate the reflective practices that inform feminist academic work. Accountability in this fashion might also help to debunk the myths of the "radicalness" of feminist methods, a reputation that in our oppositional thinking we might cling to but nevertheless must jettison. As Biddy Martin warns, this binary is most dangerous for Women's Studies: "There are also other sources of negativity such as the mistrust we seem at times to think we owe ourselves as oppositional intellectuals of the possibility of even minimally legitimate forms of authority and distinction, a cynical mistrust that can excuse us from acknowledging how, as educators, we inevitably exercise both. Oppositional stances can sometimes become rigid defenses against political participation" (1997: 105). The persistence of this oppositional model obstructs a modified institutional accounting.

What's the use of doing this sort of "volunteer" work? One way to justify it (yet again) is to make Women's Studies programs a model of and for women's labor generally. Such a dossier would highlight—if it became a national project of Women's Studies programs and departments—less anecdotal, more empirical evidence. We need to document how much women's labor is part of the second shift, how the ethics of feminist volunteerism undergirds the bureaucratic, rationalized work of the university. Although such a new accounting adds more work for already overworked Women's Studies faculty, a record is necessary, even as more unwaged labor. Without such an accounting, the university will never be accountable to its Women's Studies faculty.

Use Value Versus Exchange Value of
Women's Studies Programs

Is the recognition of the second shift—through the documentation of the dossier—enough to change the social forces reinforcing it? It may be laudable to recognize the second shift, but not at the cost of sustaining it. The university economy is dependent on the surplus labor of its faculty; the university needs this surplus to continue, but it is deadlocked on how value is determined. The question of multiple values is now one debated in terms of interdisciplinarity in general, and in terms of Women's Studies in particular. As I see it, two kinds of values exist in the university: use value and exchange value, the former being the unwaged labor we do in

Women's Studies and the latter being most often marked as "disciplinary" labor. Although Women's Studies Programs initially developed by suggesting how a plurality of values would benefit the university—or, at least, be tolerated—the new university is insisting on a more singular value, a new emphasis on the production of exchange value (in terms of prestige and power).

In this way, the gendered model based on these values is inscribed in the university structure, as some work such as that done by Women's Studies programs—although essential to the smooth reproduction of university business—has no exchange value. As long as the university treats disciplinary production as "male," teaching and mentoring are still coded as the "female" end of university reproduction. It's not Women's Studies programs that are unhealthy; it is the climate of surplus labor (and its gendered status) that keeps Women's Studies programs from flourishing. With ever-diminishing resources and ever-negligent support, at a time when Women's Studies professors are more and more absorbed into the disciplines, the decades-long subsistence level of support for Women's Studies programs is being shown to be what it always was: a minimal effort to placate feminist scholars in the profession. The professional managerial class compels Women's Studies scholars (a second class within the university) to do the productive work of teaching and nurturing, thereby perpetuating the second shift. Women's Studies unwaged work has use value (in terms of mentoring and advising) but seemingly no exchange value. In many ways, then, the place determines the value, not the work itself. (We should know that the status of value is also an effect of the greater consideration of tenure and the debate about exchange value of faculty in general.) The non-value of Women's Studies work is arbitrarily defined and exists in a vague or obtuse relation to the wage that Women's Studies faculty receive as a knowledge producer within the university.

Joint-appointed faculty are in an especially good place to articulate the barely repressed, unconscious processes at work in the gendered labor of the university. As joint appointments, many Women's Studies faculty experience the double consciousness and double duties of the academic gender divide. In the end, the most utopian move would be to examine what sort of expectations the university has for all faculty members. A Feminist Dossier in this context would make these expectations more explicit. Feminists have theorized these utopian possibilities of revaluing women's labor within the university, but within the structural limitations of the university, some of this revaluation is impractical, sometimes unthinkable. While one resolution is to demand compensation or combat pay (as I think we should), another is to rethink structurally what the job of the university professor is. That is, how do we negotiate the split that demands that we all be of use value to our students while we are also individually compelled in a market economy to ensure our exchange value through research that can be advertised outside of the university (lest we become fungible)? The debate comes down not to family values or educational value, but to market value.

Notes

A shorter version of this essay appeared in the *Women's Review of Books* (February 1998).

1 See Ruth Rosen's laments about the "intellectual second shift," in which feminist scholars must keep up in multiple fields: the "regular" work of the discipline and the feminist scholarship "that includes theory, the humanities, natural sciences, and the social sciences. The subject matter belongs to no era and to no discipline; it constitutes half of the human race." She argues that we should "excavate the secret lives of academic women" in order to account for the multiple demands on them (1999: A48).

2 Judith Allen (1997), in a very persuasive article about Women's Studies, suggests that we go after donor money in less patriarchal ways than foundations use. In a theoretical essay, Biddy Martin argues—following Readings—that the university has no center (1997: 111).

3 Even trickier than this split, however, is the one between female academics and feminist academics, because this division is the one most closely policed from both sides.

4 Hochschild's new book, *The Time Bind* (1997), documents the retreat from home as an emotionally loaded site to work, a refuge from the ambivalence of familial commitments.

5 See also "Women's Studies on the Edge, Introduction," the special issue of *differences* 9:3 (fall 1997): i–v.

6 What I advocate comes from writing program administrators in their emphasis on documenting program assessment and good pedagogy. Theirs is a lesson we ought to learn well.

(In)Different Spaces: Feminist Journeys from the Academy to a Mall

I came to America more than a decade ago, a feminist: Mary Wollstone-craft, Harriet Tubman, Gertrude Stein, Virginia Woolf, George Sand, Kannagi, the Rani of Jhansi—wind under my feminist wings. I was a Hindu, a Tamilian, a Madrasi, a woman. I came to America a feminist.

I became in the intervening years the wrong "Indian"—the one mistaken for Mexican in California; an East Indian; a non-white Caucasian; an Asian American; an Indian American; a Third World citizen; a woman of color; a South Asian. In the Sophoclean wisdom of the Immigration and Naturalization Service's nomenclature, I was a Non-Resident Alien (tax-paying, of course), and am now a Resident Alien (still tax-paying). Now, when I go across spaces to what I persist in calling home, I am not expatriate, not American citizen, not Tamilian. I have become quite simply a lean, compact, Americanized acronym: NRA (Non-Resident Indian). I have grown to be a very brown alien bird.

In these same years, I have become in the wisdom of Modern Language Association (MLA) nomenclature, a "freeway flyer," a "migrant worker," a "beltway bandit," an "adjunct," a "temp prof."[1] I never found a room of my own in the house of U.S. feminism; I have become part of the undistinguished pool of underemployed "second-class," Third World citizenry in the midst of the First World academe; an immigrant non-success story of high-achieving Asians. Thirteen ways of looking at a brown feminist bird.[2]

Being representative is, perhaps, an implied dictate of this book on feminism—as it is of most books and panels on feminism—and my value on it depends on "the edges that blur" (Rich 1986) between identity and professional experience. My current "I-slot" (Fuss 1989: 34) as unemployed, partially employed, and underemployed makes all those other dozen feminist-speaking positions a luxury I cannot inhabit.

The "problem" has been with us for a long time now and is at least two decades old, we are told, and even then it was an old story. However, it has not been until the past five years or so that the problem has received a stunning range of scholarly scrutiny befitting a Milton or a Shakespeare—or, perhaps, even an Emily Dickinson. The journal *Profession* grows thicker and glossier by the year, filled with erudite exegeses, vituperative analyses, pained narratives of the lost holy grail, and more pie charts and tables than most scholars of English know what to do with. True to our training and expertise, the readings are multilayered, multivalent, and dialogic. Not uncoincidentally, I might add, most of the essays are written by full-time, tenured, not-yet-dead white male professors; some white feminists; a few graduate students; fewer part-time faculty; and, perhaps, here and there an African American, Asian, or Chicana feminist (full- or part-time).

Here are some numbers. The report of the Association of Departments of English (ADE) ad hoc Committee on Staffing ("Report" 1999), and the final report of the MLA Committee on Professional Employment (Gilbert et al. 1997) tell us that between 1975 and 1993, the number of part-time faculty members in English increased 97 percent. The U.S. Department of Education tells us, and feminists agree, that it is during those very same years (between 1975 and 1993) that women entered the academy in larger numbers than ever before, and have been part of the success story in its transformation from an institution of anachronistic behemoths to one filled with sexy intellectuals.[3]

According to the *Digest of Educational Statistics*, as of 1992, white men made up 45.2 percent of full-time faculty in English; white women, 45 percent; women of color, 5.2 percent; and men of color, 4.7 percent (U.S. Department of Education 1995: 234).[4] They are careful to add that this statistic does not include non-resident aliens; I do not figure in this statistic. Clearly, not all groups of women entered the academy in proportionate numbers. When, where, and which women entered the academy, and who and how many of us have been able to stay on remains an untold story—or, perhaps, it is not a story to tell.[5]

Speaking at a roundtable on "Doing Feminism in Interdisciplinary Contexts," Susan Stanford Friedman suggested that, despite our large and successful presence in the academy, feminists are never at home in the academy, and it is precisely this sense of unease that has always been an enabling location for our work as feminists.[6] Although her argument is powerfully persuasive in many ways, it is crucial to ask whether it is that we are never at home in the academy or, in fact, whether for some of us the academy is much too much like home in its replication of the familiar inequities of work and reward. Our continued evocation of familial metaphors of analysis, particularly on the issue of adjuncts, is indicative of the ways in which adjunct labor continues to be gendered, feminized, represented in popular conceptions as "women's choice," and serves as both a rationale and a justification for structural inequities.[7]

Historically, the adjunct problem has always been a "women's problem," and the increasing numbers of white men in the pool, I would argue, is what has brought it unprecedented official attention. In a rare feminist analysis of the issue, Robyn Warhol argues "the gay man or lesbian who follows a partner's tenure track job to become a lecturer, as well as that unusual heterosexual husband who does the same for his wife, is in a feminized position carrying all the disadvantages of a job that has long been institutionally derogated as women's work" (1998: 224–25). Having accurately pointed to the feminization of the position, Warhol can observe uncritically that "they [lecturers at Vermont] teach as only those who love to teach can, and many are active in research, advising, and committee work as well, although they are hardly paid to be" (1998: 225). Here it is: the inextricable knot of work, wages, and love. I want to suggest that much like women's work at home, the system has flourished because we feminists have bought into the ideological fantasy that we work for pleasure and for love. Given the white, middle-class antecedents of the second wave of the feminist movement that put many white feminists in the academy, this particular state of affairs does not seem ironic at all.

As black feminists such as Patricia Hill Collins, bell hooks, Deborah L. King, Evelyn Brooks Higginbotham, and Bonnie Thornton Dill have repeatedly pointed out, the notion of work as a liberatory principle was true only for white, middle-class U.S. feminists, for whom work was a way to escape the strictures of home. For all other women, work has always been integral to their economic survival and, in fact, has had little to do with pleasure or love. Culturally and ideologically, academics in general—but particularly those in the humanities—have internalized the belief that we do what we do not for the money but for the love of it. Women, in turn, under U.S. capitalism are used to the ideological legitimization of women's societal roles and of their related secondary position in the division of labor, which allows them to see their work as secondary and supplemental. Work is not primarily for wages but for self-fulfillment, and this is particularly true for middle-class and white women in this country. The logic that women's work is both secondary and temporary is reflected in the wage structure, in general work expectations, in self-expectations of part-time faculty, and in the unspecified emotional rewards that characterize adjunct academic labor.

Those of us who are feminist academics are not good at talking about wages—especially the relationship of wages to work. And yet, it is the unstated dictates of the relationship of wages to work, and the presumption that we labor not for wages but for love, that presumably has us tongue-tied. Let me provide a context for these arguments through some wage numbers. I work in a coffee shop at a retail mall in suburban America. Initially, I needed to supplement my adjunct income, but increasingly I work there out of choice—a choice I want to contextualize in terms of the academy. At the mall, where I work only part time, I make $10 an hour, get a yearly bonus during the busy season, and have health benefits. Although my work as scholar is seen with mixed bemusement and wonder, it nevertheless gets space in terms of time off to go to conferences (even during the busy season). The rule is simple if inflexible: You get paid for every hour spent on the job, and all work is paid for.

At the local university where I work as an adjunct, I am paid $2,500 a course per semester for my work.[8] Translated into the mall language of hours, and based on national averages of hours worked per week by full-time faculty, this works out to about $8 an hour. I have no health benefits, no bonus, no office, no time off even to attend conferences that are presumably part of my professional life, and my scholarship is seen as secondary to my primary work: teaching. I am expected routinely to do "soft work": attend meetings, do power lunches, volunteer on committees, all in the hope that my increased visibility will bring me rewards in terms of a "real job."[9] And all of this compares to a $7.70 an hour minimum wage to keep people above poverty level voted into law by the city of Baltimore for its lowest-skilled contract laborers.[10] The academy has become the site of what the United States in its imperialism likes to describe as "Third World working conditions."

So what keeps us laboring, then, if the working conditions are so untenable? What keeps us laboring, I want to suggest, is that ineluctable myth: that we work not to put "food on the table" but because we love what we do, and we are good at this. Or as the ADE report somewhat blithely argues: "For some of these individuals [part-time faculty] the attraction to part time teaching is personal rather than economic: they are individuals who enjoy the intellectual stimulation of a college class-room and an academic environment and who do not depend on their teaching appointment as the main source of financial support or health and retirement benefits" ("Report" 1999: 19).

To be fair to the ADE report, it does point out that many of these part-time faculty have other jobs that presumably put food on the table. What the ADE does not address are two related issues: 1) What about those of us for whom this is the only job? and 2) Regardless of whether we do this as primary or secondary source of wages, does the fact that some of us do it for pleasure justify the wage structure that pays $8 an hour to a faculty member for the very same qualifications and work for which a full-time member earns $28 an hour? Nor do they account for that slightly annoy-ing minor detail I brought up earlier: Do our skills as teachers of critical thinking and writing command a mere 50 cents more than the contract laborer? Or can we account for all these discrepancies, as Cary Nel-son and others sometimes do, by saying that this is part of the general corporatization of higher education, on par with the corporatization of America?

One feminist way to intervene in the arguments around wages is not necessarily to draw on the model of corporatization alone, but to revisit that old forgotten argument around family wage. In her classic essay, "The Unhappy Marriage of Marxism and Feminism" (1981), Heidi Hart-mann offers a historical analysis of the emergence of family wages in the United States. She points out that men "argued for wages sufficient for their wage labor alone to support their families. This 'family wage' sys-tem gradually came to be the norm for stable working class families . . . and the non wage-working wife [came to be seen] as part of the standard of living of male workers. Family wages then may be understood as a resolution of the conflict over women's labor power which was occur-ring between patriarchal and capitalist interests at that time" (Hartmann 1981: 105).

That the notion of family wages inheres in arguments about wages for adjunct faculty is made clear when the ADE report quotes David Leslie's figures that "few part timers (10%) report household incomes under $25,000, while over half (52.2%) report household incomes greater than $55,000" ("Report" 1999: 20). The report concludes, as a result, that the economic hardship of part-time employment falls only on those "who become trapped in part-time employment beyond the point where this type of position serves their needs" ("Report" 1999: 20). The ADE also concludes that, although "low pay" in and of itself is "clearly a hardship for individuals who choose to accept part-time employment," it is only so for those who have chosen not to be part of a family unit and asks, "In the light of what is known about the diverse situation of people who choose part-time academic employment, for just how large a segment of the entire group is such employment a hardship?" ("Report" 1999: 20).

The notion of a household income serves as rationalization for the lack of economic hardship for individuals trapped in this system, presumably voluntarily, and entirely frees us of our responsibility as a profession to address, ethically or otherwise, the relationship of work to wages. Further, the model clearly implies a heterosexist view of the family, and even in the absence of such, it makes evident the gendered and feminized position of adjunct labor in the academy. Clearly, among other things, the ADE committee seems quite intent on promoting and preserving healthy family values amid the crumbling facades of academe.

Both the ADE committee and the MLA committee agree not simply to see the problem as a failure on the part of the good intentions of professorial rank faculty and institutions; rather, they offer a "systemic" reading of trends and conditions in higher education. The readings, in the end, smack of self-interest and self-aggrandizement for the currently "overworked," "belabored," and "besieged" tenure-track and professorial-rank faculty, who must, we are told in the recommendations, be given "incentives" to teach in "first year writing or introductory literature courses."

Finally, unwittingly or otherwise, both reports do garner the familiar American rhetoric of choice and freedom for themselves when they state, presumably as a fact, that many part-time faculty choose to be where they are. Even if that were true, as a feminist, I am left with the haunting specter of a similarly cloaked choice: my choice to be a wife, a mother, or a homemaker; and even my choice to be an adjunct made into a benign gesture on the part of institutions who "offer alternatives for individuals whose priorities put family obligations and involvements ahead of the intense demands of a traditional tenure-track academic career" ("Report" 1999: 19). Whose tradition?

It was not so long ago that feminists arguing against traditional definitions of what constitutes work within the academy sought a space in it as a way to redefine what counts as academic labor. It seems ironic that academics are now drawing on the very same, presumably discredited, arguments against women's domestic labor—namely, labor of love, free choice, and family wages—to justify the continued exploitation of adjunct faculty. As feminists in the academy, we have done little to intervene in these arguments or processes.

With the highest degree this land can confer on us, and the most in demand skills in this "age of telecommunications" and "critical thinking," women in academe earn marginally more than the lowest-skilled contract laborer and about the same as a semiskilled retail worker. And most disturbingly and tellingly, the reproduction has been highest in those very disciplines that feminism has helped transform and engender: English, Women's Studies, gay and lesbian studies, ethnic studies, etc. Having successfully challenged the model of unpaid labor for love that we feminists performed at home, we have become silent observers of this peculiar institution at work. Given the potential for feminist interventions on this subject, there has been a curious lack of sustained public critique.[11]

I want to end by invoking and reworking the opening lines of a very different text:

> Between me and the other world there is ever an unasked question: unasked by some through feelings of delicacy; by others through the difficulty of rightly framing it. All, nevertheless, flutter round it. They approach me in a half-hesitant sort of way, eye me curiously or compassionately, and then, instead of saying directly, How does it feel to be a problem? They say, I know of a one-year position at an excellent school that would be ideal for you; or, I know the pay there is peanuts but at least you will be teaching and will be intellectually stimulated instead of working in a mall; or I feel so dreadful about what is happening.

I rewrite William Du Bois's now classic opening to *The Souls of Black Folk* (1903), not because I think the adjunct problem compares in range and magnitude to the race problem, but, rather, to suggest that the problem of the color line, and the gender line, seems very much in place at the beginning of the twenty-first century in our academic world.

What seems urgent for us to do at this moment is reassess the relationship of feminism to politics. Politics subtends and underwrites feminist productions; having successfully politicized the academy to gender, race, sexuality, and class, it would be painful indeed if we failed to politicize ourselves about this particular reproduction. If U.S. feminism is not to suffer from the "historical amnesia" (Christian et al. 1990: 61) that seems to assail it particularly in its moments of self-historicizing, it is crucial to heed these materialities that underpin our existence.

Three decades ago, U.S. feminism gave us the dictum that "the personal is the political." Surely, we did not travel so far, so long, and so wide only to arrive at the door ajar. Surely, we did not travel so far only to be told that for some of us the political is merely the personal.

Notes

Portions of this paper were first presented at the Modern Language Association conference, Chicago, December 1999. Much thanks to Lisa Marcus for her perseverance and commitment in including me on the panel "Feminist Futures, Future Feminisms." I am deeply indebted to Usha Venkatesh for her patient restructuring of my incoherent arguments; to Abhijit Dasgupta for material and nonmaterial support too extensive to list; and to Susan Stanford Friedman, who has been a source of support and inspiration. This paper is dedicated to all those innumerable "others of us" who have generously shared their time, work, anger, triumphs, and defeats with me over many years.

1 The proliferation of various terms for adjunct and part-time labor in the academy, as well as its unquestioned ubiquity of use within academic discourse, particularly in the past five years or more, is itself a good instance of how much we excel at verbalizing away what are essentially material realities of the entire academic world.

2 I am here rewriting Wallace Stevens's familiar "Thirteen Ways of Looking at a Blackbird."

3 I am troping here on Lauren Berlant's use of this term, albeit in very different contexts. See Berlant 1997, 1998.

4 Leslie Bow footnotes this statistic in "Erasure and Representation" (1997), but the focus of her essay and critique are very different from mine. I want to thank her for sharing the earlier version of her essay with me, which helped me think through issues of identity, disciplinarity, and hiring practices, particularly within English and Women's Studies.

5 Until these recent studies, finding reliable numbers for part-time faculty use has been consistently difficult. It is still difficult to find racial and gender breakdowns of part-

time faculty, and neither the ADE report nor the MLA report provides either. Part of this is due at least to the ways in which "part-time" faculty are now tracked at various institutions. Because of American Association of University Professors guidelines regarding fair use of part-time faculty, many now have created euphemistic alternative terms, such as "part-time tenure track."

6   Friedman was not directly addressing the issue of part-time labor, but her evocation of the metaphor of "home" in conjunction with Women's Studies and issues of disciplinarity is an instance of our continued reliance and evocation of familial metaphors. The use of such metaphors is commonplace within debates about issues of adjunct labor: see Kolb 1997, which, despite its trenchant arguments, relies on an uncritical use of familial metaphors.

7   It is important to note that the rhetoric about adjunct labor is also racialized and relies on an often unexamined notion of citizenship. See, for example, the constant use of "two nations" to describe the two worlds within academe. This ties in with my arguments about adjunct labor being constantly othered.

8   The hourly wage is calculated counting a basic minimum of one hour of preparation and one hour of grading and record-keeping for each hour taught. Many administrators argue for an hourly wage calculation based simply on "time spent" in the classroom and the mandatory office hour.

9   At the session at which I presented this paper, some objected to my characterization of part-time work, arguing that in many places they are not expected or required to do "soft work." It was also pointed out that many full-time faculty "shoulder" the "extra burden" of having to work with fewer full-time colleagues. Needless to say, many of the conscientious objectors worked full time, and it remains to be said that many part-time faculty have refused to do work that has not brought them the hoped-for rewards. In any case, much of the reward system for part-time faculty is punitive—that is, it is more a system of withholding the usual rewards that accrue for work.

10 I want to thank Barbara Dayton of Oakton Community College in Illinois for bringing this to my attention at a Midwest Modern Language Association conference in 1997. She also pointed out that the living wage in Chicago was $7.60, and welfare funds paid in Illinois in 1995 to single moms with two children equaled $9.33.

11 At a time that books on this subject are being belted out faster than jobs are being created, there have been hardly any feminist anthologies, workshops, or panels. And as far as I know, at the MLA Women's Caucus, the Gay, Lesbian, Bisexual, and Transgender caucus, and the Committee on the Status of Women in the Profession have not been active with what is seen as the exclusive purview of the Graduate Student Caucus, and the Part Time discussion group. Most senior feminist scholars rarely speak out on this issue, or they do so only to put themselves into the same "victim pool." Only at the 1999 MLA convention did the Committee on the Status of Women in the Profession finally organize a panel on the subject, "All Work and No Pay?" Neither the American Studies Association nor the National Women's Studies Association has paid serious organizational attention to the issue, and most times things are run as "business as usual." Although Cary Nelson's call for a moratorium on all panels on any subject other than this seems bizarre and excessive to many, it does merit thought.

Analogy and Complicity: Women's Studies, Lesbian/Gay Studies, and Capitalism

In her brilliant 1975 essay "The Traffic in Women," Gayle Rubin argues that gender and sexuality are linked in a sex-gender system. Her discussion of this system does not posit either gender or sexuality as an origin point for the sex-gender system. Rather, she proposes that sexuality and gender can be understood as a system in the sense that they are a functional part of the structure of social formations, helping to constitute group boundaries, relations between groups, and internal hierarchies within them. She argues that both gender and sexuality are determined (though not caused) by the economic and political relations among groups. Men establish relations among themselves—kinship relations that are, in the "tribal" contexts she references, political formations—through the exchange of women. This exchange, and thus the economic and political relations among and within social formations, is, she argues, dependent on a binary gender division, an incest taboo, and compulsory heterosexuality. Although the structuralism she borrows from Lévi-Strauss overly stabilizes the relations among gender, sexuality, politics, and economics, her central insight remains powerfully valid: gender, sexuality, economic structures, and what we would now call race, ethnicity, and nation are inextricably interconnected, facilitating and reproducing one another.[1]

In the twenty-five years since that essay was written, many feminist scholars have been hard at work describing these inextricable links. But what is peculiar about this scholarship is that much of it has continued to be framed as an argument against a view that would see gender, race, and class as distinct issues, as if that point had not already been made. And, of course, despite the widespread lip service paid to the "intersectionality" of the various forms of oppression,[2] it is the case that, in the United States, our political and institutional practices were in the 1970s and remain now profoundly determined by a liberal discourse that constitutes subjects as analogous subjects of social identities who contend for "equal" representation and participation in "democratic" institutions with the white male bourgeois subjects who are the normative subjects of rights. So despite the complexity of our analyses of social processes, we find in the academy a proliferation of identity-based programs in Women's Studies, Africana studies, Asian American studies, Mexican American studies, American Indian studies, and, most recently, lesbian/gay/bisexual (LGB) studies, as these committees, programs, and departments are called at the University of Arizona, where I teach. In our institutionalizing practices, then, we would seem to be forgetting our own scholarship.

Most crucially, what is "forgotten" in our construction of identity-based academic programs is a critique of capitalism. "Forgetting" is of course one of the central mechanisms of capitalism; commodity fetishism is in a sense a forgetting of labor: "The mysterious character of the commodity-form consists simply in the fact that the commodity reflects the social characteristics of men's own labour as objective characteristics of the products of labour themselves" (Marx 1977: 164–65). According to Marx, the fetishization of commodities, the attribution to commodities an inherent value, is possible because value does not result from individual labor but from labor as part of a larger social process, a social process that it is difficult for individuals to perceive. So, for example, in our institution-building on behalf of women or gays and lesbians or people of color, we tend to forget that these identities do not have inherent autonomous value but are produced by us as we participate through our individual labor in social-production processes. To "remember" the critique of capitalism would be to locate and analyze our academic production within larger economic and political contexts and to see how, in producing identity-based knowledge and subjects, we participate in global capitalist processes.[3] As I argue at length elsewhere, social formations—including gender, sexuality, and race—are constituted through production and consumption and function, like commodities, as bearers of value and means of production.[4] The academy is a site of production and consumption, and, after Althusser and Foucault, one might even see it as a particularly important site for the production and disciplining of economic and political subjects.[5] A crucial part of my task in this essay, then, will be to situate our individual labor not only as scholars, but also as teachers and administrators (or "servants" of our departments and institutions) in those larger social processes, to show how our work is constrained by and contributes to the production of value in the form of identity.

Focusing on the particularly complex case of the relationship between Women's Studies and LGB studies, I will argue that contemporary capitalism is a context that is both enabling and disabling, both facilitating and co-opting our efforts. However, explaining the ways in which our work is facilitated and co-opted is only part of the story: Both Women's Studies and LGB studies are still seen as a threat—more of a threat to national formations than to global capital, but to national formations that are certainly not yet irrelevant to capital. In a recent article in the *Nation*, Meredith Tax suggests that conservative attacks on Women's Studies (she names the attacks on SUNY-New Paltz, Nassau Community College, and the University of Arizona) are symptomatic of resistance to globalization:

> In the past ten years, nationalist, communalist and religious fundamentalist movements have surfaced all over the world, moving into the power vacuum created as local elites have been overwhelmed by the new global financial ruling class. . . . Civilian populations, especially ethnic minorities, women and children, are caught in between. Atavistic social movements attack feminism . . . as part of their war on modernity itself, for . . . feminism is inescapably secular. (Tax 1999: 24)

She criticizes these fundamentalist movements for their anti-feminism, but she does not confront the complicity between feminist movements and modernization and globalization that her own argument indicates. Instead, in fact, she criticizes the view that "women's movements are symptoms of globalization, rather than the result of autonomous movements for female emancipation" (Tax 1999: 26). The intimate ties between feminist movements and labor movements around the globe and in U.S. history, the circulation of ideologies of "modern" femininity on globalized information networks, and the promotion of certain forms of women's liberation by organizations such as the World Bank, which hope to develop borrowers for micro-credit,[6] suggest that women's movements are hardly autonomous and that much is lost by viewing them as such.

While explicating the complicity of feminism with modernization and globalization is a far too ambitious project for this essay, I do hope here to explore the complicity between contemporary capitalist discourse and the institutional formation of Women's Studies and LGB studies. The authorizing discourse for establishing discrete identity-based units suggests that we are attempting to serve particular students or to create legitimacy and attract resources for scholarly projects that are dismissed and neglected in conventional departments. Although it is certainly the case that such programs open a space for interventionist and emancipatory scholarship and activism, I would like to suggest, in addition, that the institutional structures of discrete programs and departments that we adopt are implicated in and determined by transformations in the global formation of capitalism in ways that undermine their emancipatory potential.

In arguing that our practices are complicit with capital, I state only the inevitable and obvious. There is nothing we do that is not deeply enmeshed in capitalism. At a recent National Women's Studies Association meeting, Gudrun Fonfa, speaking from the audience, described herself as a practicing lesbian separatist and said that she found the idea of queer studies (as opposed to lesbian feminism) to be as unthinkable as a Marxist-capitalist coalition. I might say that it is my fondest hope to embody a queer Marxist-capitalist coalition. There is no pure outside, and attempts to produce such purity will almost certainly be oppressive. Rather than damning our practices as capitalist, what I mean to do in describing their location within capital is to make us aware of our own productivity so that we can understand the constraints on and consequences of our actions and make the possible interventions.

One further caveat: Rubin's piece is in significant part an argument against a Marxism that would subsume feminism as a secondary superstructural issue. I do not mean here to invoke a vulgar economic determinism. Rather, as Spivak argues in "Scattered Speculations on the Question of Value" (1987), I understand the discourses of gender, race, sexuality, and nation to supplement a discourse of economic value that is by itself "discontinuous." In other words, capitalism depends on even as it is served by the hierarchical social formations constituted through discourses of gender, race, sexuality, and nation. Rather than seeing race, class, gender, and sexuality as equivalent or analogous categories, Spivak suggests that these discourses of domination support an international division of labor that allows capitalism (a process of exploitation) to function.

Spivak proposes her analysis of the supplementary relations between gender, race, and nation and economic discourses in opposition to Goux's analogy between the idealist predication of the subject (the subject of consciousness) and the materialist predication of the subject (the subject of labor-power).[7] She points out that the use of analogy renders these two modes of determination independent of each other (as "exclusive predications") and complete unto themselves (each is posited as an internal continuity) (Spivak 1987: 154). It thus "excludes the fields of force that make [each of] them heterogeneous, indeed discontinuous," and "it is to exclude those relationships between the[m] that are attributive and supportive and not analogical" (Spivak 1987: 156).

A critique of analogy will be central to my arguments. "Other" studies programs are often established and legitimated through analogy with one other, and analogy is a particularly prominent feature of contemporary capitalist discourse. (It has been important to the liberal pluralist discourse of the nation-state, as well.) Following Spivak, I find supplementarity to be an important tool in this critique. Supplementarity has been a crucial deconstructive lever in dealing with binary oppositions; it is also quite a useful lever in dealing with analogies, which, like binaries, presuppose that the objects under consideration are externally discrete and internally coherent. Reading supplementarity reverses that presupposition, showing that the objects are externally connected and internally incoherent. In thinking about building political movements, the recognition of external connections and internal incoherences is useful not only for revealing complicity, but also for revealing opportunities on which non-identitarian movements and institutions might be built. I hope in my discussion of Women's Studies and LGB studies to push through the analogic comparison between the two toward a constructive appropriation of their incoherencies and interconnections.

The Global: Analogic Discourse, the Nation-State, and Capitalism

The liberal nation-state has operated through the relentless interplay of binary exclusion and analogic inclusion. This interplay is exemplified by an early-twentieth-century shift in the construction of San Francisco's Chinatown, as Nayan Shah (2001) describes it. Although it is at first imagined as the site of otherness, a classed, raced, sexualized, opium-infused culture that embodied the forbidden desires of a consolidating white bourgeoisie, Chinatown was then re-envisioned as a version of that bourgeoisie itself. This sequence of constructions allowed it to be viewed, in its second manifestation, as a lesser, always striving, instance of bourgeois culture that was still unequal to white culture. The controversy over the National Endowment for the Arts (NEA) yields another example. As I describe in my essay on the NEA, "The Perfect Moment" (1986), in arguing against the conservatives who saw the funding of gay art by the NEA as the legitimation of a homosexuality that should be excluded from the nation, Senator Daniel Moynihan made an analogy between those artists now subject to censorship and the white ethnic groups, now included, who were once subject to censorship. In urging the inclusion by analogy of a new set of groups, he also legitimates the hierarchical positioning of those new-comers as available for exploitation; they are cast as offering, through their difference (their difference being their experience of suffering), an enrichment to the lives of the normative white, straight bourgeois subjects who are implicitly addressed in Moynihan's speech.

The interplay of binary logic and analogy has operated in economic discourse, as well. Adam Smith and David Ricardo both describe a world of national economies that are comparable to each other on the basis of their wealth and productive abilities in various industries or soil quality.[8] They articulate a notion of nations in competition with one another that has persisted up to the present, a notion that sets up a binary division between us and other nations. But they also initiate a comparative discourse that suggests that nations can be ranked in relation to one another and that some division of productive tasks will be to the advantage of all.

Although the binary logic that establishes national boundaries was a particularly prominent narrative structure in the era of Fordist nation-based mass production and consumption, in our post-Fordist era of "globalization" and niched production and consumption, analogy has emerged as the dominant narrative structure (though it has by no means fully displaced the discourse of national competitiveness). With regard to production, networks of Italian family firms have been analogized to the Japanese Kanban system of outsourced suppliers to major corporations, which have been analogized to the friendship networks among Silicon

Valley entrepreneurs who all went to Stanford University together (Piore and Sabel 1984). With regard to consumption, gays and lesbians are also just another form of family to whom advertisements for cars, dining-room tables, and other commodities can be addressed.[9] Gays are like African Americans are like conservative Christians are like women in that all of them have been framed as niche markets for long-distance phone service and credit cards. President Bill Clinton justified International Monetary Fund (IMF) intervention in Indonesia by saying that Indonesians are like Mexicans (previous subjects of IMF intervention) in being a potential market for "our" goods, and thus I suppose they are like gays and African Americans and Christians. As it did in the liberal pluralist discourse of the nation-state, the deployment of analogy in the discourse of globalization works to incorporate all sorts of subjects as equivalent but not equal producers and consumers.[10]

Although the comparison implicit in the analogy among various sites of production and consumption presumes equivalence, it actually involves the hierarchical inscription of differentiated identities. Inevitably, the use of analogy elides both internal discontinuities, such as gender hierarchies within kinship-based communities of production, and external connections, such as the dependence of Silicon Valley entrepreneurs on immigrant sweatshop workers who produce the chips they design. As Ricardo naturalized differences of national wealth in differences of soil quality, the deployment of analogy in globalization discourse legitimates differences of wealth and wage rates in cultural differences and elides the global processes by which various sites have been forcibly arranged on the ladder of so-called development or modernization or civilization. The articulation of a new era of "globalization" would seem to discover anew these analogized sites of production and consumption as if they were previously untouched by capital and had emerged as different through some authentic and autonomous cultural process.[11]

Despite or, rather, because of its central place in liberal political and economic discourse, analogy has and can function as a powerful tool in the articulation of progressive social movements. As Janet Jakobsen points out, citing Laclau and Mouffe (1985), the articulation of equivalence among social struggles can make those struggles recognizable on the mainstream political landscape—and potential allies for one another (Jakobsen [forthcoming]). And certainly, this function of analogy has motivated its use in the efforts to add LGB studies to the list of identity-based academic fields (Roof 1995). However, Jakobsen argues, analogy also separates such movements and elides their connections with one another.

It is crucial in thinking about analogy to recognize that it is relationships being compared and not objects themselves, so the SAT analogy test takes the form of: A is to A's domain as X is to X's domain (Robinson 1997). As Foucault says of the use of analogy in the sixteenth century, "Its power is immense, for the similitudes of which it treats are not the visible, substantial ones between things themselves; they need only be the more subtle resemblance of relations. Disencumbered thus, it can extend, from a single given point, to an endless number of relationships" (1970: 21). That it is relations being compared is also crucial in that it is the isolation of the objects in their own domains that renders each object autonomous (internally continuous and externally discrete) and thus rankable in relation to other objects. For instance, with regard to economic development, Mexican underdevelopment is to Mexico's (underdeveloped) culture as the developed United States is to its (superior) culture; and with regard to civil rights, gays are (not) to sexuality (an immutable biological identity or a choice?) as African Americans are to race (taken to be an immutable biological identity), and therefore gays are (not), like African Americans, legitimate subjects for legal protection from discrimination (Halley 1994: 503).

Judith Butler illustrates the use of analogy to elide connection in her essay, "Against Proper Objects" (1994).[12] In that essay, she critiques the use of an analogy between feminist studies and lesbian and gay studies in the introduction to the *Lesbian and Gay Studies Reader* (Abelove et al. 1993), which, she claims, deploys the analogy in order to establish lesbian and gay studies as an autonomous field. According to Butler, the introduction to the *Reader* asserts that the proper object of gay and lesbian studies is sexuality, while the proper object of feminist studies is gender. It thus suggests that sexuality and gender are discrete domains. As Butler points out, this account of feminist scholarship is certainly a slight to the extensive work on sexuality that has been done under the rubric of feminism, even while it would seem to suggest that sexual difference is not a crucial issue for the study of sexuality. Likewise, in "The Ethics of Analogy," Robinson points out that the frequently deployed analogy between race and sexuality "segregates race and sexuality as objects of analytic and political attention" and "presumes the normative whiteness of the gay subject" (1997).

274   Miranda Joseph

Roof, who like Butler is concerned with the elision of sexual difference, argues that the analogy between LGB studies and other "other" studies, such as Women's Studies and the various ethnic and race studies, is inappropriate because, unlike the differences to which it is compared, it is not "a single category, but a somewhat unstable amalgamation [of lesbian with gay] produced by the complex confluence of institutional politics, consumer culture and gender and sexual anxiety" (Roof 1995: 180). Although she is right to point to the problematic production of internal continuity through the use of analogy, I would suggest that the internal discontinuity she notes for LGB studies is not the feature that differentiates it from other "other" studies, which are also "unstable amalgamations" that have been produced through "complex confluences." The analogy between LGB studies and Women's Studies constitutes both as internally continuous, as somehow complete in themselves, which it cannot be, if gender and sexuality operate as a sex-gender system imbricated in political and economic processes, as Rubin and so many others have argued.

Butler suggests that the analogic pairing of feminist studies and gay and lesbian studies, "a binary frame," excludes from consideration other relevant issues, such as race and class. I think she is actually wrong. Although analogy and binary logics do work in complicity, she conflates them too quickly. Binary logic is a discourse of exclusion, a simple determination of us and them, a mode of self-definition by abjection. Analogics work in precisely the opposite fashion; analogics include, making the other known. As Robinson argues, for instance, the analogy between race and sexuality implies that race is the known term by which we come to know and make familiar a second, unfamiliar term. It moves the inchoate subjects (gays and lesbians) to the grounds of the (supposedly) known, choate, object; positions the unseemly in relation to the seemly, "rendering the struggle for racial justice to the past"—race is figured as a "solution (not a problem) in the American landscape" (1997). Although analogy most frequently might be used to compare two objects, it actually generates a potentially open series of known and included objects. The implication of the analogic comparison of Women's Studies and gender and LGB studies and sexuality is not that race or class should not be considered but, rather, that they should be considered separately, under the rubric of "race studies" or "class studies." And this is, of course, precisely how attention to race is constituted institutionally. It is quite telling that there is no analogically constituted study of class.

Jakobsen's essay addresses the common analogy between Jews and Queers. She argues that we need to move beyond an analogic understanding to a recognition of complicity in the construction of the categories. She points out that the co-articulation of Jews and Queers in Cold War rhetoric posited them not merely as analogous but also as acting together to subvert America. This Cold War anti-Semitic and anti-homosexual discourse, she argues, played a crucial part in a postwar racist resurgence, consolidating white supremacy, rendering blacks the visible enemies in contrast to the invisible Jewish-Queer enemy. She proposes that we might appropriate this complicity, this negative articulation of cooperation between Jews and Queers, as a positive site of alliance. The strategy she proposes—a positive appropriation of complicity rather than the elaboration of analogy—might be a useful strategy for thinking about the relationship between Women's Studies and LGB studies.

The Local: Analogic Discourse, Women's Studies, and LGB Studies at the University of Arizona

I will in this section take up a rather different discursive strategy and style to tell a story about the relationship between Women's Studies and LGB studies at the University of Arizona (UA). Although other institutions would provide different stories and, undoubtedly, others at UA would tell the story differently, I tell my own story here because it has shaped and been shaped by the theoretical perspective offered earlier. This story, I hope, reveals the impact and enactment of capitalist and nationalist discourses at the local level and disrupts the analogy between LGB studies and Women's Studies.

As Jakobsen tells the story (I did not arrive on the scene until '95), a group of queer faculty and graduate students found one another in the wake of a lecture on campus given by Donna Haraway in 1992.[13] This group constituted itself as a formal committee, charged by the provost in 1993 to "promote scholarship and education on Lesbian, Gay and Bisexual issues at the University and in the greater Tucson community."[14] The committee received one year's support to hire a coordinator and began writing grant applications to support a curriculum-development project. At the same time, it founded the Lesbian Looks Film and Video series, which, under Beverly Seckinger's direction, has remained one of LGB studies' major programs.

Under Jakobsen's leadership, LGB studies was established in a complex articulation with Women's Studies:[15] It was constituted as distinct in order to prevent sexuality from being conflated with and subsumed by gender as a rubric of analysis.[16] However, as Jakobsen's line was in Women's Studies and the other LGB faculty were affiliated with Women's Studies, she understood Women's Studies to be the primary source of labor and resources for LGB studies. She successfully lobbied for a sexuality line in Women's Studies (which brought me to UA) and developed a course within Women's Studies titled, "Lesbian and Bisexual Women's Theories/Lives/Activisms." Meanwhile, she also taught a course on queer theory through the Comparative Cultural and Literary Studies (CCLS) program, and the curriculum-development project (ultimately done with internal support) resulted in the creation of two additional sexuality studies courses originating in CCLS and cross-listed with Women's Studies. The next few years, however, saw an increasing separation between Women's Studies and LGB studies—due both to Women's Studies' efforts to push and my efforts to pull LGB studies out of Women's Studies. The question is: Why was the initially complex articulation between the two projects unsustainable?

The initial funding for a coordinator came from the provost and was run through Women's Studies, though clearly earmarked for LGB studies. This funding was not continued after the first year, during which year Arizona's governor (Fife Symington) launched an attack on a course about transgenderism taught by an unpaid graduate student at Northern Arizona University. Efforts to regain funding for an LGB coordinator had a peculiar outcome: Women's Studies agreed to use a line to hire in the field of sexuality studies but did not include the coordinatorship of LGB studies in the structure of the line. In other words, the line (which I fill), rather than being complexly articulated between Women's Studies and LGB studies, was fully incorporated within Women's Studies. The search process itself became a battle over candidates who were imagined to be more or less willing to subordinate sexuality to gender, more or less willing to participate in the norms of the Women's Studies community. After a bloody battle, I emerged as the compromise candidate and arrived at a department riven with tension over the relationship between Women's Studies and LGB studies.

Although I was not committed in an a priori way to institutional separation between LGB studies and Women's Studies, my own scholarly identity was transformed when I was processed through the identity-political job market and took up a job within the identitarian structure of academic programs at UA. Rather than finding a job in which I could practice the poststructuralist, post-Marxist approach to culture and society in which I had been trained (in the Modern Thought and Literature Program at Stanford University, a cultural studies program, at least during my time there), I was hired into a Women's Studies department as "the lesbian," was expected to and did become the head of LGB studies,[17] and, to satisfy my own interests, also affiliated with CCLS. Never having previously thought of myself as doing Women's Studies or LGB studies, as being a "Marxist," I now do Women's Studies and LGB studies, I am a Marxist, and I have become one of the Big Dykes on Campus, which is to say a highly visible (and surveilled) representative of lesbianism.

This transformation has not, of course, been seamless, and my own efforts to separate LGB studies from Women's Studies were largely due to my discomfort with my location in Women's Studies. Founded in 1975, my department in 1995 was still "'70s feminist," in the sense that straight white bourgeois women dominated the agenda and the faculty of the department and in the sense that the ethos of the department was very much about communality and familiality. As Myra Dinnerstein describes in her essay on her experience as the founding director of the program, "A Political Education" (2000), a sense of community, of mutual support, understanding, and pleasure, along with a sense of being on a mission on behalf of women, were the central motivations and rewards experienced by the group of women who founded the program. For me, and I think for the large cohort of junior faculty who joined the department in the mid-1990s, this ethos of communality felt like a normative imposition. But, of course, we had not shared in the struggles that had been bonding experiences for the founders.[18] In an unthoughtful recourse to liberalism that can be understood only as a dialectical opposition to this norm, we have articulated a desire for the department to function as a professional workplace, a place in which a distinction between public and private would actually permit space for greater differences among us. Although many are quick to interpret my alienation as "generational," I find the generational narrative too progressive and self-congratulatory. "Generations" are contingent formations, determined by region, race, institutional setting, etc. As Linda Garber rightly argues at every opportunity, feminism in the 1970s was not exclusively or even primarily "'70s feminism" in the sense in which I have used the term here, nor do all those who were feminists in the '70s share the same views and desires now. However, it is the case that the particular history of my department produced a stark division between senior and junior faculty—a division that has happily been disrupted by recent senior hires.

The Pull

In this context, LGB studies appeared as an opportunity, as a space in which I could act independently of my department to elaborate a professional, intellectual, and social subjectivity that was not supported by my department. As for the founders of Women's Studies, the role of desire for a variety of forms of professional and political sociality in the development of LGB studies at UA cannot be underestimated; the birth and dramatic growth of LGB studies at UA has clearly been due to what Spivak would call "affective desire for labor." My constitution as a subject of consciousness facilitated my productivity as a subject of labor. But in large part due to the work done by the Women's Studies founders, our desires were quite different from theirs; rather than looking from the margins of the academy for the comfort of local community, Jakobsen and I have had the privilege of working from tenure-line positions in Women's Studies toward participation in national scholarly networks. Although the notion of representing and serving an identity-based constituency certainly comes into play in our fund-raising activities, we have generally been quite explicit between ourselves that we are creating a space intended to facilitate our own intellectual and professional development. Conveniently misunderstanding the existing relationship between the two units and encouraged by the senior Women's Studies faculty, I have disarticulated LGB studies from Women's Studies and ultimately formally relocated LGB studies within CCLS. It nevertheless continues to be the case that much of the LGB studies labor is provided by faculty whose lines are in Women's Studies.[19] (Ironically, in the very moment of official separation, Women's Studies hired a lesbian scholar, Elizabeth Lapovsky Kennedy, as its new department head and thus opened previously unavailable opportunities for collaboration.)

The fact that this "opportunity" took the form of yet another identity-political unit is no accident: The eagerness of the institution (various deans, departments, the UA Diversity Action Council, etc.) to fund LGB studies has been remarkable. On one hand, this money rewarded sheer productivity, in relation to which the content of our work was irrelevant, and a large portion of the monies "given" to us were seen by the "givers" as venture capital, money that we would use to bring in more money from outside sources through grant-writing.[20] On the other hand, the eagerness also points directly to the contemporary capitalist context, in which identity circulates as value.

In *The University in Ruins* (1996), Bill Readings argues that the project of the universities for much of the twentieth century has been to produce national subjects through the study of, and training of students in, national cultures and histories. He suggests, however, that the university has undergone a significant transformation in conjunction with the shift from Fordist to post-Fordist capitalism, a shift that entails a decentering and disempowering of the nation-state. He argues that the success of the critiques of traditional disciplines, the emergence of interdisciplinary studies across the university (a development that probably finds its legitimating impetus in the sciences), and the proliferation of "other" studies programs show that the role of the universities in subject and object formation has shifted. The university, he says, is now the "university of excellence," where quantity rather than quality of knowledge production is key, and where the subjectivity produced can be fragmentary and particularized as long as it is also homogeneously productive, as long as the subjects produced bear analogous relations to capital, to production and consumption.

Readings's story is too neat in a number of respects. Certainly, the nationalist university was never the idealized Habermasian bourgeois public sphere for which he seems to yearn; nor was the nation ever as bounded and coherent as he seems to imagine it. In "The International Within the National," Lisa Lowe, like Readings, argues that the traditional role of the universities has been to produce citizens of national culture, but she points out that this has been done through the suppression and disavowal of racial and gender difference (1998: 38–39). Meanwhile, we are not quite done with the nation, as the ongoing exclusionary work of cultural conservatives clearly demonstrates. As Lowe points out, contemporary racial conflicts in the United States are the "material legacy of America's imperial past . . . in which a nation intersected over and over again with the international contexts of the Philippines, Puerto Rico, Mexico, Korea, or Vietnam" (1998: 29–30). Lowe argues that immigration policy has been an ongoing attempt to resolve contradictions between the nation-state and the global economy. We might likewise see debates over public educational policy and ideology—struggles over "academic standards" that code discussions of open admissions, affirmative action, canon reform, and the emergence of Women's Studies, ethnic studies, and LGB studies—as attempts to deal with contradictions between nationalism and economic globalization. However, we might read these debates as revealing not a contradiction but a complex strategy in which the binary exclusionary discourse of nationalism supplements the analogic inclusionary discourse of globalization to produce a hierarchy of political and economic subjects.

Although he dispenses with the nation rather too quickly, Readings's analysis of capital is oddly dated in focusing only on capitalism's production of equivalence. Capitalism has always produced and depended on cultural difference to constitute an international division of labor, but the narrative articulating Fordist mass production and consumption economies did emphasize the erasure of difference and the production of equivalence within the nation. The discourse of post-Fordist capitalism is, by contrast, explicit about its need for and production of "diversity." (Evidence for such explicitness takes the form of diversity policies in employment, including diversity "training" and identity-based employee associations, as well as the noted proliferation of niche-marketing efforts.) Readings's argument suggests that both the university and capital are indifferent to the qualities of the subjects and objects being produced and consumed, and although this production of equivalence certainly is one side of the process of capital expansion, the other side is the production of meaningful differences that allow subjects to be slotted into particular roles within the process of exploitation. Contemporary inclusionary educational policy, including the institutionalization of identity political programs and departments, has to be understood as simultaneously homogenizing an increasingly heterogeneous student population for the market economy (Lowe 1998: 39) and directing those different students into different roles within that economy. In our Women's Studies and LGB studies practices, in producing both subjects and objects of knowledge, we simultaneously produce commodities for identity-based consumption and the subjects of identity who will produce in niched industries and consume niche-marketed commodities.

I teach both "Introduction to Women's Studies" and "Introduction to Sexuality Studies." In the "Introduction to Women's Studies" class, I face a peculiar task: Before I can begin to deconstruct gender, I first must construct gender, must persuade the diverse array of general-education students who find their way into my classroom that women are oppressed, a fact (I don't believe in facts) that they find hard to believe. Not so jokingly, my pet name for the course is "bad things that happen to women." I construct a narrative of oppression and resistance into which I invite my students to write themselves. My task in the "Introduction to Sexuality Studies" class is equally peculiar. Faced with non-urban general-education students who have little conception of the contemporary urban gay and lesbian community, culture, and history that organizes my own identity and scholarship—most do not know what Stonewall is—I find myself trying to produce for them this object only in order to try to take it apart as a social construction. Again, I am inviting them to participate in a narrative of identity and community that I actually find deeply problematic.

What is it that they will, at best, do with these narratives of identity? Purchase the long-distance phone services or credit cards addressed to those identities? Sign the petition supporting American Airlines for its gay-friendly policies that has circulated so relentlessly on e-mail listservs? Become Women's Studies majors? Become feminist or gay "activists," which now means working at a nongovernmental organization? The emphasis in Women's Studies in particular on "practice" is often manifested as internship programs that slot our students into exploitative labor in nonprofit organizations. Given the predominance of women in nonprofit administration, I might very well argue, in the narrowest Althusserean sense, that we act as an ideological apparatus generating particularized subjects for the workforce.

The Push

Having failed in the search process to hire someone who would see sexuality as subordinate to gender, the senior faculty in Women's Studies began to articulate LGB studies as costly to Women's Studies. The costs that were named at various times included not only my teaching and service labor, but also my loyalty. So, for instance, I found myself explicitly asked to prove my loyalty to Women's Studies by "choosing" to teach "Introduction to Women's Studies" instead of "Introduction to Sexuality Studies." Student credit hours, staff time, and copying machine use were also counted. While at some level this accounting seems rational, it is based on a set of highly problematic zero-sum presuppositions.[21] (Under Kennedy's headship, this competitive accounting has ceased.)

For instance, in my view, my service to LGB studies has been in addition to, not instead of, service to Women's Studies and thus could be seen (as my dean, I believe, has seen it) as pure institutional gain. My experience was that I was doing a double shift (I might say), much as Women's Studies-affiliated faculty have done in serving both their home department and their Women's Studies program. As many have pointed out, interdisciplinarity becomes the flexibility of the post-Fordist worker. (Now that LGB studies has enough money to allow me to buy out my own labor from Women's Studies—tenure-track labor that is replaced by adjunct labor—I find myself colluding in the proletarianization of academic labor.) I might say Women's Studies treated my participation in LGB studies in much the way that traditional departments have treated their faculty members' participation in Women's Studies. The analogy that I place under erasure here, between the founding of Women's Studies and LGB studies, was articulated explicitly by one senior colleague over a friendly lunch. She said that she could see that we, the LGB faculty, had the kind of passion for starting something new that she had had in founding Women's Studies, but asked me to admit that it "obviously" took me away from Women's Studies. Although I have often heard feminist faculty contend that their contributions to Women's Studies should have been recognized by their departments as legitimate institutional and intellectual labor, my own senior colleagues nevertheless iterated a discourse of LGB studies' "otherness" from Women's Studies that allowed them to see my work for LGB studies as cost rather than contribution. To the extent that I was doing double duty, this was not due to the "obvious" otherness of LGB studies from Women's Studies but, rather, to the fact that I and my Women's Studies colleagues actively produced a separation between the projects.

The "obviousness" of the competitive relationship between LGB studies and Women's Studies depends on a very particular definition of Women's Studies, a definition that centers gender to the exclusion of the other discourses with which it is "inextricably interconnected."[22] To my colleague, articulating the relationship between Women's Studies and LGB studies as an analogy served to make the emergence of LGB studies less threatening by simultaneously making it familiar and separate, rather than unfamiliar and disruptive. Her need to make it less threatening suggests that the discursive and practical production of a separation between the units indexes not so much the discrete coherence of each as the vulnerabilities and interdependencies of both projects.

Despite certain similarities, my experience has not been the same as that of my senior Women's Studies colleagues, nor has it occurred autonomously of their experience and efforts. I never face the hatred in the eyes of administrators that Dinnerstein describes; in my meetings with administrators the content of the LGB studies project is never questioned. They make (I assume, as it is not actually voiced) an analogy with Women's Studies and the other "other" studies programs (all founded in the same moment at UA) that leads them to accept the legitimacy of the LGB studies project, and, crucially, to feel confident that it will not be a threat to the institution. The administrators' analogic thinking, insofar as it benefits LGB studies, is enabled by the groundwork laid by Women's Studies. The dependence of LGB studies on Women's Studies is revealed even in the very moment the analogy between them is made.

The story I might tell about the dependence of Women's Studies on LGB studies is one we have all heard before. As Butler points out, critiques of heterosexuality have been central to the intellectual content of Women's Studies, and lesbians have contributed a tremendous amount of labor to the creation of Women's Studies. However, this dependence has been, and in my department apparently still is, seen as a source of vulnerability rather than strength. In fact, my colleagues' desires to exclude sexuality studies from Women's Studies may be understood as motivated by a well-founded sense that harboring LGB studies (or maybe, more important, harboring lesbians) endangers Women's Studies politically.

The process of getting Women's Studies' departmental status approved (which occurred in the academic year 1996–97) involved answering regents' questions about the marital status of faculty members. Further, in conjunction with the latest hiring of a lesbian in the department, an administrator, who has been quite supportive of LGB studies, asked the new Women's Studies department head: "Does Women's Studies ever discuss whether there are too many lesbians in the department?" Again, this administrator's concern may have been motivated not by personal homophobia but by a recognition that conservative attacks on the academy, and especially on public education, find their entry point through an attack on feminist and sexuality studies. The content of Women's Studies and LGB scholarship is ridiculed as a way to delegitimate the entire project of public education. For instance, a Women's Studies conference at SUNY-New Paltz in October 1997 entitled "Revolting Behavior: The Challenges of Women's Sexual Freedom" became the occasion for a major right-wing campaign to downsize New York's state university system.[23] Just this spring, the chairwoman of the Arizona House Appropriations Committee threatened to withdraw funding for the Women's Studies programs at all three state universities, in perpetuity, because she was told by a constituent, a parent of a UA student, that one of the courses cross-listed with Women's Studies, a course on "Woman and Literature" originating in the English Department, had "lesbian undertones" (one, and only one, text was by and about a lesbian) and had required that the books for the course be purchased at the women's bookstore in town—"a lesbian environment"—rather than at the university bookstore. As in New York, the context for this attack was an attempt in the legislature to make broad cuts in the university budget, such as eliminating all state funding for the law school and cutting the appropriation for faculty salaries by more than 5 percent (through an increase in teaching time per instructor).

Although I would argue that Women's Studies could protect itself better by making positive claims for the legitimacy and centrality of sexuality studies than by disclaiming LGB studies, such attacks make it possible to understand why Women's Studies might want to distance itself from LGB studies. (These attacks are effective only because those launching them believe, usually correctly, that no one has the will or ability to defend the substantive legitimacy of sexuality studies. It is most often the case that university administrators resort to "academic freedom" in defense of sexuality studies; this is as good as saying that they, too, find the content of this scholarship reprehensible.) In fact, such attacks, like the financial support offered to LGB studies, are part of what Foucault would call the capillary system through which nationalist and capitalist discourses operate locally to discipline what we take up as our own agency, our own choices.

The attacks launched by the state on Women's Studies for harboring lesbians and lesbian studies may seem a contradiction with the encouragement offered by other agents of that state, in the form of dollars, for the development of LGB studies. I would suggest that this is not so much a contradiction as a liberal one-two punch. The conservative (nationalist) boundary-making enacted by some works with the inclusive "diversity" rhetoric of others to produce a hierarchy of subjects. So although LGB studies has received funding from UA based on its "contributions" to the university community, we have also been discouraged from trying to move up the academic hierarchy from committee to program or department and from formalizing our curriculum as a minor or major. To move up the hierarchy in these ways would mean that LGB studies would become a line item in a budget that the legislature would see and that it would have to seek approval from the regents. In other words, we would have to have a direct confrontation with conservatives such as our Appropriations Committee chairwoman, something that neither the deans nor the LGB studies faculty is eager to do. Our location at the bottom of the hierarchy is, of course, a disadvantage in terms of resources, though happily it leaves us relatively free of bureaucratic surveillance (the endless paperwork imposed on departments).

The presence of right-wing (religious and nationalist) legislators has, however, an even more pernicious effect than the limitation on resources. It also disciplines the range of political engagements that can be undertaken by Women's Studies and LGB studies. The legislator who proposed cutting funds for Women's Studies specifically said that Women's Studies would be okay with her, as long as its content was limited to a celebration of women's achievements. In hallway conversation, we rejected such a notion of Women's Studies as a joke, as not at all what Women's Studies is about. However, when the university president asked us to nominate Secretary of State Madeline Albright for an honorary degree, we felt we could not refuse, even though there were no grounds for honoring her as a feminist. In fact, many of us articulated a feminist critique of her policies of military intervention in Iraq and Kosovo. Likewise, in the same week that I was asking the university's president to defend Women's Studies and LGB studies against homophobic attacks in the legislature, I had to decide whether LGB studies should participate in a Students Against Sweatshops action against the president. (We did not at that moment, although we did join in later Students Against Sweatshops actions.)[24] Though these were limited incidents, it is important to recognize that the "conservative" threat can effectively enforce a liberal focus on fetishized identity while chilling critiques of the production of identity.

In "The Impossibility of Women's Studies" (1997), Wendy Brown points out some of the costs to Women's Studies itself of the "tacitly conservative" institutional imperative to constitute Women's Studies as the study of a coherent object (women or gender), in defiance of the insights of our own scholarship. We have, she suggests, impoverished Women's Studies by chasing off to other institutional sites the study of race and sexuality through our own guilt-ridden but nevertheless persistent centering of gender. Much of her account rings true to me. My department, like hers, cannot figure out what body of knowledge would constitute an education in Women's Studies, and we have engaged in battles over the appropriate object of study and teaching: Is it gender or women? Is it anything at all if approached from a feminist perspective? Does the study of race or sexuality qualify as the study of women or gender? But the very fact that these battles take place suggests that the institutional imperative toward coherence in Women's Studies has not fully disciplined us. Women's Studies houses (and in fact is a valuable site of employment for) an incredibly diverse array of scholars. Likewise, Butler would seem to come down overly severely on the editors of *The Lesbian and Gay Studies Reader*. Although their introduction may seem to produce an overly bounded object of study, the collection of essays actually included in the book do not so confine their object. Both Women's Studies and lesbian and gay studies actually evidence an incoherence that defies the analogic institutional discourse through which they are constituted.

Roof argues that, although "the link between identity, epistemology, and discipline appears to open the academy, in practice it restricts thought, limits and consolidates authority under the guise of distributing it, and sequesters individuals within manageable consumer groups with discrete market interests" (1995: 182). In her pessimism about identity studies, she is like Brown in certain ways, I think: far too optimistic about the efficacy of both the structural constraints within which we function and our own efforts to discipline. I am well aware that at the end of one semester of "Intro to Women's Studies," I have definitely not produced fifty new feminists. And if Women's Studies' experience provides an example, we can count on our efforts having unintended and unpredictable effects.

Lowe optimistically suggests that institutionalized interdisciplinary sites such as Women's Studies, ethnic studies, and LGB studies might remain "oppositional forums, productively antagonistic to notions of autonomous culture and disciplinary regulation and to the interpellation of students as univocal subjects" (1998: 41). But what would it take to realize this oppositional potential? Although Brown is prepared to abandon Women's Studies altogether, it seems to me that both Butler's and Brown's accounts might be read as suggesting that we can and should contest the analogic discourse—and the larger social processes in which it is imbricated—through a positive appropriation of the incoherence, the incompleteness of the Women's Studies and LGB studies projects. But that is still no answer. What would a positive appropriation of this incoherence look like?

The embracing of incoherence and incompleteness would not mean merely seeking resolution or coherence at some sort of higher level through coalition or collaboration. As Bernice Johnson Reagon warned in her 1981 speech, "Coalition Politics: Turning the Century," a speech that urged those in attendance at the West Coast Women's Music Festival toward coalition work: "Most of the time you feel threatened to the core and if you don't, you're not really doing no coalescing. . . . You don't go into coalition because you just like it. The only reason you would consider trying to team up with somebody who could possibly kill you is because that's the only way you can figure you can stay alive" (Reagon 1983: 356–57). Coalitions, in her view, are not sites of resolution but, rather, sites at which we must risk the comforts of identity—a mask for the instabilities of subjectivity—in order to confront oppressive social processes.[25] The enabling (or, for that matter, disabling) links among the various participants become available only when those larger processes are centrally in view.

In many places in this essay, I displace the analogy between LGB studies and Women's Studies by describing the development of LGB studies at UA as a dialectical production, an oppositional movement directly related to the constraints imposed within Women's Studies, a contradiction that, it would seem, could be resolved through some sort of improved collaborative efforts. But this is not quite right: LGB studies is analogous neither with Women's Studies nor with its dialectical opposite. Instead, it might best be understood as a *différance* of Women's Studies with itself. Our institutional projects are inevitably a *parole soufflé*—inspired even while spirited away by others, those others that are never fully "other": capitalism, nationalism, diverse identity-based movements.[26] In the face of such inevitable *différance,* it seems to me that, rather than futilely pursuing resolution, our best strategy would be to trace the economic and political dynamics that produce us as different, that produce complex and dynamic relationships among us.

I have tried in a small way to illustrate such a strategy in this essay, taking up identitarian disciplinary formation as a case study within the larger project of contextualizing the production of identity and social formations within economic and political processes. To take such a strategy from the level of analysis and critique, as it exists here (and in Lowe's exemplary work), to the level of productive institutional practice is the next and more difficult challenge. It certainly requires taking up our service work not as a tedious site for a deployment of "common sense" but, rather, as an occasion for creativity. More concretely, we might take our complicity with capital, a complicity that connects us by holding us apart, as the basis for collective action; we might deploy the resources made available to us under the rubric of identity to initiate institutional projects—faculty development, conferences, curriculum development— that center production (understood to be a broad and unstable category in itself) and thus inevitably bring together questions about (and faculty and students concerned with) the discourses of gender, sexuality, race, and nation on which production depends. We are making this attempt at UA with two projects: One is entitled "Sex, Race, and Globalization," sponsored by LGB studies; the other is "Sexuality and the State," a collaboration between Women's Studies and LGB studies. While such efforts might turn out to be merely ameliorative, they might also begin to defetishize identity and produce ongoing alliances (depending on who is included in the initial conceptualization of these projects) that reshape institutional dynamics. In this new century, the urgency of such efforts is greater than ever.

Notes

I have written this essay in the context of an ongoing conversation among the members of my department about the mission of Women's Studies. Although I know that some of my colleagues would not want to be associated with the arguments I make here, I am nevertheless grateful for their contributions to my thinking. I particularly appreciate Elizabeth Lapovsky Kennedy's efforts to have us develop a constructive vision for the future of Women's Studies. The arguments I offer, especially on the implications of analogic discourse for progressive movements, have been developed in collaboration with Janet Jakobsen. But Jakobsen's role in the creation of this essay goes far beyond any single intellectual contribution; as the founder of the Committee on Lesbian/Gay/Bisexual Studies at the UA and as my mentor, she has provided extraordinary leadership and guidance to me in my attempts to fill her shoes as the coordinator of the committee and to sort out my life in Women's Studies. I also thank Robyn Wiegman, Molly McGarry, Janet Jakobsen, Liz Kennedy, Sallie Marston. and Beth Freeman for their thoughtful feedback on earlier drafts.

1   The phrase "inextricably interconnected" was offered by my colleague Susan Craddock in the context of a faculty meeting in which we were trying to write a mission statement for the Women's Studies department. That phrase was in fact included in the statement and is regularly invoked in departmental discussions.

2   On "intersectionality," see Crenshaw 1989: 139.

3   Although it is beyond the purview of this essay to do so, it would be interesting to contextualize the emergence of Women's Studies in relation to the Cold War. Second-wave feminism, the wave that led to the formation of many Women's Studies programs, is usually narrated as at least partly a reaction to the sexism of the New Left and the Civil Rights Movement. However, Daniel Horowitz's recent biography of Betty Friedan suggests that Friedan's liberal feminism emerged through a disavowal of her Old Left roots in the context of the crisis of the Old Left brought on by Stalinism (Horowitz 1998). This suggests that it might be the case that the early institutionalization of Women's Studies (the formation of programs in the 1960s and '70s) required not merely the forgetful fetishization of identity in which we now participate but a more active repudiation of a leftist critique of capitalism. See Milkman 1999 for a review of the Horowitz biography. I thank Molly McGarry for this insight and reference.

4   See Joseph 1998.

5   See Wiegman 1997: 5.

6   Gayatri Chakravorty Spivak discussed this form of what she called "Feminism Without Frontiers" in her keynote address at the 1999 National Women's Studies Association convention. A recent academic defense of this form of feminism can be found in Nussbaum 1999.

7   Spivak (1987: 156) refers to Jean-Joseph Goux's "Numismatiques: An Essay in Theoretical Numismatiques," *Symbolic Economies: After Marx and Freud,* trans. Jennifer Curtiss Gage (Ithaca, N.Y.: Cornell University Press).

8   See Adam Smith, *Wealth of Nations* (Amherst: Prometheus Books, 1991 [1776]); David Ricardo, *On the Principles of Political Economy and Taxation,* ed. Pierro Sraffa (Cambridge: Cambridge University Press, 1951).

9   See Freeman 1997; Chasin (2000); and Joseph, *Against the Romance of Community* (2002), especially chapter 5, "Kinship and Culturalization of Capital: The Discourse of Global/Localization."

10 Neil Smith argues that globalization leads not only to equivalence but also to equality in the sense that wage rates in more developed areas are undercut by the more exploitative conditions elsewhere. However, he also points out that identity markers are explicitly used to hail economic subjects: Within developed regions, a reinscription of race has accompanied privatization, while across the globe certain areas are

red-lined, excluded from flows of capital, through the demonization of particular cultural formations (such as Islam): see Neil Smith, "The Satanic Geographies of Globalization," *Public Culture* 10, no. 1: 184.

11 For a much fuller account of the deployment of analogy in contemporary economic discourse, see Joseph (2002).

12 My return to Rubin's "Traffic in Women" was provoked in part by Butler's citation of that essay Butler 1994.

13 Haraway's visit to campus was sponsored by the Southwest Institute for Research on Women, under the rubric of a grant from the Rockefeller Foundation.

14 This group initially included Janet Jakobsen, Robert Kaplan, Meredith Herbert, Beverly Seckinger, Julia Balen, Maureen Fitzgerald, Leisa Meyer, Barbara Cully, Yolanda Leyva, and Nena Trujillo.

15 The naming of LGB studies, including the "B" but excluding the "T" that is now commonly included, has never been adequately explained to me. We have considered changing the name but have deferred a final decision on the ground that we did not know how to enact a technical name change and we did not know what the implications of that change would be vis-à-vis the university administration. The discussion was an interesting one, as it focused on whether in fact transgender issues were the proper object of a sexuality studies program or whether they would more properly fall under the rubric of Women's Studies, as an issue of gender. Obviously, what this means is that were LGB studies to include the "T," we could open a site of collaboration and connection with Women's Studies.

16 Her concern to distinguish sexuality from gender was hardly idiosyncratic. Although the literature on the relationship of gender and race has focused on showing their mutual imbrication, against a presumption of their distinctness, the literature on the relationship between gender and sexuality has tended to argue for the distinctness of sexuality from gender as a rubric for movements and scholarship, against the presumed obviousness of their connection. In her essay "Thinking Sex" (1993), Gayle Rubin, seeming to reverse her earlier analysis, argues for the inadequacy of feminism, as an analysis of gender, to deal with sexuality. She argues that, because oppression based on sexuality is not exclusively organized through gender, a separate movement for sexual minorities is necessary.

17 I succeeded Jakobsen as coordinator of LGB studies in 1996–97. We alternated in that role, aided by the co-coordinators, Beverly Seckinger and Douglas Weiner, until January 2000, when I became sole coordinator (term ending spring 2002).

18 Between 1993–94 and 1997–98, six juniors were hired into a department that had never hired anyone before. (Those already on the faculty had been brought in from other, often part-time or adjunct, positions in the university.)

19 As of spring 2002, the UA Women's Studies department had five members who do queer or LGB studies. Fourteen people are on the LGBT executive committee, six of whom are in Women's Studies. Those not in Women's Studies are in Media Arts, English Education, Sociology, Art, and one librarian.

    I believe that four of us would claim to do queer, lesbian and gay, or lesbian studies, although I am the only one who was hired specifically to do sexuality studies. And of the eight people who serve on the executive committee of the Committee on LGB Studies at UA, five are employed by Women's Studies. (The others are in media arts, sociology, and anthropology.)

20 Women's Studies has also gained its institutional purchase at UA through its ability to bring in outside money. The Southwest Institute for Research on Women, founded in 1980, is an integral part of the department. It has generated well over $10 million in grants over the past twenty years.

21 At the level of simple incorrectness, the competitive accounting of my teaching labor and student credit hours turned out to be a mistake, as student credit hours actually follow the instructor's line at UA.

22 Actually, some of my senior colleagues are resistant to the idea that Women's Studies should center on the study of gender. "Gender studies," in their view, dilutes and undermines the focus on women.

23 The public ridiculing of the conference began with an article by Roger Kimball in the *Wall Street Journal* titled, "A Syllabus for Sickos" (November 5, 1997, sec. A22). Proposed cuts included elimination of some SUNY campuses altogether; the elimination of graduate and professional programs, day-care, and counseling services; and the privatization of health-care services. For a full account of the attacks on the SUNY system linked to the conference, see Alisa Solomon, "Sexual Smokescreen," *Village Voice*, vol. 42, no. 47 (November 25, 1997), 56. As Solomon says, the use of supposed "tax-payer" outrage about the feminist conference to increase general monitoring of the university and promote budget cuts reiterates the strategy used against the National Endowment for the Arts.

24 UA has a major contract with Nike and is a founding member of the Fair Labor Association, an organization dominated by the very corporations it is intended to regulate. After two years of agitation, in April 1999, the students at UA, along with students at many other campuses around the country, staged a sit-in at the president's office. Though I had passed up the opportunity to support their earlier efforts, I decided to forward all sit-in-related messages to the gay listservs on campus. As I expected, this provoked a response suggesting that sweatshops are not a "gay" issue, which gave me and a number of other participants on the lists the opportunity to explain the relationship of gay identity to global capital. In addition, LGB studies became one of only two academic departments on campus to lend official support to the sit-in (the other was the history department). Even the Women's Studies faculty chose to support the sit-in as individuals rather than as a department (although all but one faculty member did sign a letter of support).

25 Since 1981, poststructuralist feminists have critiqued "coalition politics" for presuming (wrongly) prior stable subjects who join together without being transformed by that joining. Although I agree with that critique in general, it seems to me that Reagon's text can be read precisely as an incitement to transformative collectivity.

26 I am inspired by but also spiriting away Jacques Derrida's *parole* here: see "La parole soufflé," in *Writing and Difference*, trans. Alan Bass (Chicago: University of Chicago Press, 1978).

Institutional Success and Political Vulnerability: A Lesson in the Importance of Allies

On April 2, 1998, the Women's Studies program at the University of Colorado at Boulder won final approval for its B.A. degree in Women's studies from the Colorado Commission on Higher Education. Thus ended three and a half years of highly politicized debate that had raged within the university, in government offices, in the state legislature, and in the press. Even at the very end, the outcome of the vote of the governor's appointed commissioners was uncertain, an appropriate conclusion to the highly charged and unpredictable three-year process.

Although no single factor can explain either the political resistance to, or the successful outcome of, the degree-approval process, certain themes emerge from interviews with a wide range of university and community participants.[1] The reports of these participants, whether they were supportive of or opposed to the Women's Studies proposal, suggest a dynamic tension between the expanding influence of the political right, on the one hand, and the institutional success of Women's Studies, on the other. In this essay, I will explore this tension as it forms an interpretive history of the Women's Studies degree-approval process at Boulder.

Program History

Understanding opposition to the degree requires first some familiarity with the program's history.[2] The founding of the Women's Studies program at the University of Colorado at Boulder was, like others at the time, a product of the women's movement. Largely in response to student initiatives, a group of faculty, students, and community members began meeting in the early 1970s to develop a curriculum of course offerings on the new scholarship on women and gender. These early efforts, although not without opposition, were academically and strategically successful. By the fall of 1974, Women's Studies had been approved as an academic program by the chancellor and was rostered in the College of Arts and Sciences with a full-time faculty director. Courses were offered through two mechanisms: cross-listing classes offered by faculty rostered in regular departments, and teaching classes under the "Experimental Studies" rubric, a category devised by college administrators to respond to the demand for new interdisciplinary courses on nontraditional subjects such as women and gender, race and ethnicity, and culture and the environment.

The Women's Studies course offerings expanded quickly. For example, during the first year, the program's schedule increased from five courses in five departments and programs to twenty-one courses in fourteen different departments and programs. By 1979, a wide array of new interdisciplinary courses and programs—that is, Women's Studies, Black studies, etc.—had grown to such an extent that administrators decided to group the programs together with other, more traditional interdisciplinary programs, such as American studies and humanities, into a single Center for Interdisciplinary Studies. Eventually, the eleven-program center proved too unwieldy; the size, quality, and purposes of its constituent programs were too uneven to operate collegially and efficiently. By 1985, the umbrella unit had been abolished, scattering some programs on their own and eliminating others.

Despite the center's administrative difficulties, the Women's Studies program had flourished under its rubric. By 1980, student demand and course enrollments had swelled sufficiently to justify a certificate program in Women's Studies. Many more students, however, were seeking to major in the field, and in 1983 they were able to do so as a concentration within the American studies major.[3] The decision to establish a concentration rather than to apply for a separate, stand-alone degree was pragmatic. American studies, while small, was an established program within the Center for Interdisciplinary Studies. Sliding a new concentration into this degree program was relatively easy, requiring only the approval of the dean. More important, Women's Studies at the time lacked sufficient numbers of faculty rostered exclusively in the program to win approval through the lengthy process, which involved numerous decision levels: college, campus, university-wide administration, University Board of Regents, and the Colorado Commission on Higher Education. In 1983, the only full-time faculty member in Women's Studies was the director, who also taught courses in sociology. All of the other courses were taught by advanced graduate students, honoraria from the community, and faculty who were rostered in other departments and cross-listed their courses with Women's Studies. Without a core of tenure-line faculty rostered within the program, a separate degree proposal would certainly have failed.

However, by 1994 (the year Women's Studies initiated the separate B.A. degree), those conditions had changed. In the intervening eleven years, Women's Studies had graduated 200 majors in its American studies concentration. They had also awarded one hundred certificates and had graduated thirty minors. In 1988, the program also gained five new faculty lines and the possession of the second-oldest building on campus, the original women's residence hall, called "the Cottage." These gains reflected the recommendations of two external reviews and the commitment of the College of Arts and Sciences to developing both ethnic studies and Women's Studies as high-quality interdisciplinary programs. By 1994, the five faculty lines had been filled. The program had become highly visible and respected in the university, with its faculty noted for their publishing records, campus leadership, and excellence in teaching. In 1994, a blue-ribbon panel evaluated all of the sixty-one programs and departments on campus and ranked the Women's Studies program seventh on the campus as a whole and sixth in the College of Arts and Sciences, where it followed only five highly funded science departments.[4] Moreover, the program's highly successful efforts to raise funds to remodel its historic building had captured the attention and support of influential alumnae, the university's president, and community leaders.[5] Clearly, within the context of the campus and the university as a whole, the Women's Studies program was in an advantageous position to request a stand-alone degree.

Political Context

Colorado state politics have always disrupted the illusion of the university as an ivory tower of disinterested inquiry. Despite the fact that state revenues contribute less than 15 percent to the campus's total operating budget,[6] lawmakers regard the university with a mixture of entitlement and suspicion. The history of the university is filled with examples of members of the legislature involved in campus decision-making, from faculty appointments to student curfews. In the late 1960s, the Boulder campus became known throughout the state for its student activism, hippie lifestyle, left-wing politics, and liberal faculty. This designation has continued to divide the campus and city from the more conservative state. Moreover, the university's governing body, the Board of Regents, is an electoral group of nine, reflective of and responsive to statewide political issues and more locally defined constituencies.

During the fifteen years, roughly from 1980 to 1995, that Women's Studies was making significant institutional gains, the politics in the state were moving increasingly to the right. Although these moves reflected national trends, in Colorado the shift took forms that were to have national as well as local consequences.

The focus of these changes within the state was Colorado Springs, a city of 300,000 located about seventy miles south of the Denver metropolitan area. Home to four military installations, including the Air Force Academy, Colorado Springs began to suffer economically in the early 1980s from federal budget cuts and the loss of military contracts. In an effort to infuse new life into the city's failing economy, the Greater Colorado Springs Economic Development Corporation decided to use the city's traditionally conservative image to lure national and international right-wing religious groups to the region. Touting its conservative, family-oriented climate; beautiful setting; and business-friendly politics (including a generous tax code), the city managed to attract forty-two national religious groups by 1990.[7] These groups ranged from the large and wealthy ($78 million budget) Focus on Family to smaller groups such as the Fellowship of Christian Cowboys and Every House for Christ (Cooper 1995). James Dobson, the founder of Focus on the Family, spelled out the organization's purpose, which was echoed in others of its kind: to strengthen the family by fighting abortion, pornography, euthanasia, premarital (hetero) sex, homosexuality, and humanistic teachings in the schools (Gottlieb and Culver 1992: 7). By 1992, the influence of these groups on local and state politics was stunning. In that year, conservative organizations had placed on the state ballot Amendment 2, which barred anti-bias laws to protect gays and lesbians from discrimination (and in effect nullifying those laws where they existed in Denver,

Boulder, and Aspen). Misleading advertising (such as "No special rights for gays") and the support of right-wing spokesmen such as Republican Senator Bill Armstrong and the University of Colorado football coach Bill McCartney (the founder of the evangelical men's organization Promise Keepers), Amendment 2 passed statewide (and by an almost two-to-one margin in the Colorado Springs area). Two years later, five of the seven Christian-right candidates running for the state assembly were elected, and the three open slots on the State Board of Education also went to the Christian right (Cooper 1995: 9).

Although these events spurred new rounds of socially conservative legislation within the state, other events were occurring nationally that directly affected the university. The conservative attack on liberalized higher education had been systematically and comprehensively developed since the mid-1980s (Messer-Davidow 1993). The conservative strategy included attacks by government officials such as Lynne V. Cheney and William Bennett, a spate of mass-market books by conservatives such as Allan Bloom (1987) and Dinesh D 'Souza (1991), an endless barrage of articles demonizing the left and "tenured radicals" in mainstream periodicals, thousands of criticisms by conservatives in the popular mass media, reports on higher education by conservative think tanks, and numerous actions by citizens and government officials to regulate higher education (Messer-Davidow 1993: 40–42). The goal, according to Ellen Messer-Davidow, was to break what conservatives believed was the liberal monopoly on higher education. One means to achieving that goal was to transform higher education into a free-market model, allowing conservatives to compete and eventually to gain control over cultural production and educational goals (Messer-Davidow 1993: 47–50).

Conservatives were especially vehement in attacking academic feminism and Women's Studies on issues such as rape, abortion, and sexual harassment. Distinguishing academic feminism from a more moderate equal-rights feminism, conservatives criticized academic feminists as radical, lesbian, Marxist, and postmodern (Messer-Davidow 1993: 41–42). These attacks served to link academic feminists to the objects demonized by right-wing Christians, as in Pat Robertson's now (in)famous fund-raising letter, "The feminist agenda is not about equal rights for women. It is about a socialist, anti-family political movement that encourages women to leave their husbands, kill their children, practice witchcraft, destroy capitalism and become lesbians."[8]

These national campaigns, of course, had local parallels. The university's Board of Regents, while never an especially progressive group, had moved steadily to the right. By 1994, the elected board consisted of three Democrats and six Republicans, at least three of whom identified as conservatives. The university itself had been under tighter fiscal control by the conservative legislature with the passage of the Tabor Amendment, which put a ceiling on state spending. (The Tabor Amendment passed the same year as the anti-gay Amendment 2.[9]) The out-gay dean of Arts and Sciences (who had supported the Women's Studies program and its proposal) was under pressure to resign (although his sexual preference was not the official reason for his eventual removal).[10] And a new conservative "think tank," the so-called Independence Institute, had begun to scrutinize the university and its programs.[11] This was the context in which the Women's Studies degree-proposal was initiated.

The Degree-Proposal Process

The impetus for establishing a stand-alone Women's Studies degree began innocently enough with a 1994 student campaign in the College of Arts and Sciences to print the title of majors on diplomas. By the time this request was approved by the Board of Regents and implemented in the college, the faculty in Women's Studies had realized that Women's Studies would have to apply for its own degree. Until this time, students who received a B.A. through the Women's Studies track in American studies received diplomas, like those with B.A.'s in history, sociology, or biology, that said simply "B.A., University of Colorado." There was no indication in either their course work or on their diplomas that their degree was a subset of American studies. Even their transcripts had "Women's Studies" printed on the top. But with the diploma change, the days of the bureaucratically convenient track were numbered. Further, the program's curriculum was becoming global in scope; the "American studies" designation was also substantively inappropriate.

The initial degree proposal glided through university hoops with relative ease and in March 1995 was approved by the regents along with a proposal to convert the Black studies degree to a more encompassing B.A. in ethnic studies. Unlike the ethnic studies degree, however, the Women's Studies proposal hit some snags with staff from the Colorado Commission on Higher Education (CCHE).[12] After a frustrating period in which the faculty tried to respond to an endless supply of staff questions and directives for revision, the Women's Studies proposal died on the table, having failed to win CCHE approval within the requisite six-month period. This failure reflected an increasingly hard-line position within the CCHE to curb what it saw as an excess of costly new degrees (especially from the large Boulder campus), opposition to the idea of Women's Studies by staff assigned to the proposal at the commission, and neglect by campus administrators to mediate the negotiations. Consequently, the degree proposal was effectively tabled, requiring resubmission for the regents' approval.

When the proposal was resubmitted in the fall of 1996, Women's Studies, now newly vulnerable and separated from the vote on ethnic studies, was fair game for the more conservative members of the Board of Regents. In their November 1996 meeting, after intense questioning (for example, "Who needs them [Women's Studies graduates]?"), the board voted to table the decision for sixty days.[13] This was a bigger setback than it first seemed, for the tabling delayed any action until after a new set of CCHE guidelines went into effect on January 1, thus requiring the Women's Studies faculty to begin the whole process anew, from the beginning.

In the spring and fall of 1997, the faculty once more revised its proposal, first as a "concept paper" and then as a full proposal, with each version requiring campus and the regents' approval. After the regents' decision to table the decision the previous fall, however, the Women's Studies degree proposal became a widely debated media topic. At each of the subsequent Board of Regents' meetings, where the Women's Studies proposal was on the agenda (two planning meetings and two full board meetings), the room was filled with faculty, students, community supporters and detractors, the media, and the curious. The regents were heavily lobbied both for and against the proposal, with volumes of letters, email, and telephone messages. Women's Studies majors held placards at spring and fall graduations, announcing "No More Blank Degrees," referring to Women's Studies graduates' decision to have no major listed on their diplomas rather than the American Studies designation.[14] Turnover in campus administration required the newly appointed dean to become familiar with the proposal in the midst of the debate. Top-level administrators, now heavily invested in a successful outcome, began their own intense lobbying efforts. And the newspapers from Boulder to

Denver and Colorado Springs were carrying analysis and opinion. Meanwhile, the Women's Studies program celebrated another kind of success. Having raised $1 million for "the Cottage," they hosted a large dedication of the newly remodeled building, inviting campus and community friends, as well as all of the regents (Bowles and Klein 1983).

By the time of the regents' decision in January 1998, the lines were clear, but the outcome of the vote was not. Students dressed in black lined the perimeter of the room, holding placards, and the faculty joined them when the debate began. The debate, filled with non sequiturs, only added to the uncertainty. One regent who defended his position by quoting Shakespeare's "A rose by any other name would smell as sweet" voted against the proposal. Another, who argued that approval of the degree would "sequester" the faculty from colleagues and recalled a *Murphy Brown* rerun in which the TV character cautioned Women's Studies students against whining, voted for it. Several regents stipulated that their support for the degree required faculty and administration not to request departmental status for Women's Studies.[15] In the end, after the confusing posturing, the female chair (who had been an even-handed but outspoken supporter) crisply broke the 4-4 tie by voting for the degree proposal, thus triggering a roar of approving cheers.[16]

The degree now required only one more vote, the majority approval of the CCHE. With the intense lobbying continuing (now, regents—both for and against the proposal—were also involved with lobbying the state appointees), the commission met in early April with barely a quorum and with an apparently close or tied vote. Again, black-clad students and faculty lined the meeting room. To add to the drama, one of the commissioners who had publicly opposed the degree was the uncle of one of the student majors standing silently at the meeting's edge. After a period of commissioners' questioning the marketability of the degree and the effect of separate degrees on American Studies, the recalcitrant uncle moved for approval. The proposal passed 5-2, to the astonished relief, tears, and cheers of students, faculty, and administrators. As one dazed student remarked, "I'm stunned. . . . We all worked so hard for this. This is wonderful."[17]

The Lessons of Struggle

What are the lessons of this struggle that might be useful to other departments and programs? Although details may vary from region to region and campus to campus, Women's Studies programs in the United States share a common contextual history. During the past twenty years, while Women's Studies became institutionalized as a field of inquiry, the political climate in this country shifted to the right. These moves are related, of course, but the relationship is more complex than simply one of backlash. As Women's Studies programs began to emerge, however tenuously, at colleges and universities, they became embedded in bureaucratic structures, which had the potential to hinder their purposes as well as to assist them. Although college-curriculum committees or administrators may have questioned, changed, or even blocked courses on women and gender, for example, bureaucratic structures such as interdisciplinary course rubrics and individually structured majors also facilitated curriculum development. Many Women's Studies directors and faculty learned how to play the contradictions of bureaucracy as an art form, working the system to establish their programs and courses of study. To do this effectively required knowing well the values of the academy, especially the scholarly and educational value of creating and studying "new knowledge." The early compensatory argument—that is, that women had been excluded from the canon and therefore constituted an important new area of study—legitimated not only Women's Studies but also the study of women in the traditional disciplines. Although this dual influence sparked lively debate in the 1980s among Women's Studies scholars—such as, should Women's Studies be integrated into the various traditional disciplines or be established as a separate field?—the result (both approaches have endured) has strengthened the academic legitimacy of studying women and gender.[18] Thus, Women's Studies was able to develop institutionally in part because the academy supports the expansion of knowledge.

Another conflict that ultimately strengthened the field occurred when women of color critiqued academic Women's Studies (and white feminists) for racism. The intellectual and academic consequences of this critique and its vital transformation of the field have been well documented (see Guy Sheftall 1998). Institutionally and programmatically at the University of Colorado, these changes resulted in increasing numbers of women of color hired into faculty lines in the Women's Studies program. Concomitantly, as more women were hired into the race and ethnic studies program, as men and women from diverse racial backgrounds began to teach gay studies, and as gays and lesbians taught ethnic studies and Women's Studies, the programmatic divisions along the lines of gender, race, and sexual identity were transcended by the identities of the faculty. Although this process was not a simple one, the consequence was to decenter programmatically the individual categories of analysis and to emphasize instead their interconnection.

These intellectual and programmatic alliances both challenged and strengthened Women's Studies' degree bid. On the one hand, the sexual identity of the lesbian faculty as well as the program's course offerings in gay and lesbian studies became a point of deep resistance, especially among some of the regents (see more on this resistance in the following section). On the other hand, the racial identity of the Women's Studies faculty drew support from other administrators, regents, and CCHE staff. For several years, the Boulder campus had been under attack from external and internal groups for its lack of racial diversity (a criticism that continues). With four of its seven tenure-line positions held by women of color, the Women's Studies program had the highest percentage of faculty of color outside ethnic studies. Thus, some officials who took offense at the feminist content of the curriculum were nevertheless persuaded to support the proposal because of the racial distribution of the faculty.

Another important change that occurred in the 1980s and '90s at colleges and universities was the increasing numbers of women participating in higher education. Although women at the University of Colorado did not constitute the majority of those receiving B.A.s—unlike national statistics[19]—they had made significant gains among the faculty. In 1988, women constituted 17 percent of all regular full-time faculty. That number had increased to 25 percent by 1994, an increase of 75 percent.[20] Many newly hired faculty—women and men—had graduated from institutions with established Women's Studies programs and expected the same at Colorado. And some of the recently appointed female administrators had taught and continued to do research in Women's Studies.

These changes and related conditions contributed to eventual success in achieving the Women's Studies degree at the University of Colorado: the legitimacy of studying women and gender within many of the traditional disciplines, the high profile of Women's Studies faculty and the institutional success of the program, the hiring of women of color into the program, the dogged persistence of Women's Studies faculty to keep revising and resubmitting the proposal, and the increasing numbers of female faculty, students, and administrators who took the presence of

Women's Studies as necessary and normal. But the key to making these conditions work in the context of a conservative resistance were the individuals who mediated the tensions informing the effort and its resistance. Although numerous individuals found themselves at various times in this position (including the two female regents), it was the mid-level female administrators, the upper-level male administrators, and the students whose participation clarified and transformed these tensions.

Allies as Mediators

Support from two mid-level female administrators, an associate dean and an associate vice-president, was crucial in making the Women's Studies degree proposal a priority within the university. Both women were members of the faculty at Colorado. Both had taught courses on women within their departments and had published feminist scholarship. Both had a commitment to seeing the Women's Studies degree pass. Each took a strong stand at different times to ensure that higher-ranking administrators saw the importance of the eventual approval of the Women's Studies degree. To accomplish this, the women did not rely solely on the tried-and-true compensatory argument or the diversity strategy. In addition, they placed the success of the Women's Studies degree within the context of other, broader administrative goals.

The Women's Studies proposal was a test case for two areas of university priority. After having been tabled by the Board of Regents, it was one of the first two proposals that had to go through the CCHE's new two-stage approval process. The university had a stake in making sure that it was successful in meeting these requirements. To send forward a weak proposal or one that did not receive full administrative support would have set a damaging precedent for future treatment by a board that was more disposed to eliminating programs than to passing new ones. The system-wide administration came to see that it could ill afford not to support Women's Studies.

Similarly, the newly appointed dean of Arts and Sciences arrived in the middle of Women's Studies' three-and-a-half-year effort. With an intellectual agenda to promote interdisciplinary studies as the cutting edge of new knowledge, he, too, came to see that Women's Studies was a test case and that the attacks on its interdisciplinarity constituted a threat to one of his cherished visions for the college. Although in due time these issues might have become clear to the male administrators, the female administrators made sure that their supervisors understood the strategic importance of the Women's Studies proposal in terms of broader university goals. The women's ability to analyze the broader contexts and to place the degree proposal within an agenda to which the higher-ranking male administrators had already committed themselves was extremely important in sustaining, and in some cases resurrecting, support for the degree.

Although the higher-ranking administrators may have been kept on-track by their female staff, several of them had additional reasons to support the proposal. The chancellor of the campus, vice-chancellor, and dean had all been appointed in the middle of the proposal process. The chancellor had formerly served as systemwide vice-president, where he had become familiar with the Women's Studies degree and had supported it. Perhaps more important, he had labored in the vineyard of scholarship about women. He had co-written a book on health care for older women, his interest in the subject having grown out of his experience as a practicing physician and medical scholar (see Byyny and Speroff 1996). "Women were not getting good health care," he said when asked about his commitment to scholarship about women, "and they had been routinely excluded from clinical trials. I realized that unless the scholarship is there, unless we have the data and research available, public policy will not address women's health needs. And as a result, women will continue to receive inadequate care."[21] Indeed, the chancellor's book became the focus of a dramatic moment at a Board of Regents planning meeting. Speaking for the importance of Women's Studies, he held up his newly published second edition and spoke poignantly of what he had learned in the process of writing the book, how it had personally transformed him, and how he had come to value the scholarship in the field of Women's Studies. Both the chancellor's heartfelt, personal remarks and the regents' cool response had a galvanizing effect on those attending, including the dean. It was after that meeting that the dean began to take a more aggressive personal role in supporting the degree proposal and taking ownership of it. Indeed, it seemed to be the chancellor's personal gesture—and especially the vulnerability displayed—that moved other administrators to take a more vigorous stand for the degree.

As the chancellor and academic vice-chancellor became more involved with lobbying the regents, two related issues began to surface: homophobia and lack of fairness. The opposing regents' public comments had from the beginning indicated their strong political opposition to the program's underlying feminist scholarship. (This was also true of the early staff opposition from the CCHE.) Comments suggesting that Women's Studies was not a legitimate academic program but a political ideology echoed the sentiment, if not the precise language, of Pat Robinson's fund-raising letter. What was not stated publicly, however, was the opposition to lesbian and gay content in the curriculum. Although a supportive regent indicated to Women's Studies faculty early in the process that behind-the-scenes conversation portrayed the program as a "boot camp for lesbians," it was not until the chancellor and vice-chancellor directly addressed the issue in private conversation with individual regents that the issue was confronted. The administrative style was effective: These allies reminded individual regents that the proposal had been approved unanimously at every level of the university. They asked them why they continued to oppose it, inviting regents to discuss what was really concerning them.

By taking a "laid-back," non-confrontational approach, the administrators gave the opposing regents an opportunity to express the homophobic subtext; in fact, they invited them to do so. This approach had the effect of diffusing the strength of the opposition. Acknowledging that the curriculum included lesbian and gay material, the administrators emphasized the academic legitimacy of studying all of social life, including "homosexuality." It also gave them the opportunity to dispel regents' concerns with "indoctrination." These private meetings with the campus's highest-ranking academic officers were especially important not only because they legitimated the gay and lesbian material in the curriculum, but also because they lowered the temperature of the debate. As mediating allies for the program, the chancellor and vice-chancellor were able to respond with detachment to comments that the faculty would have found infuriating. Although the administrators lobbied all the regents, checking in with supporters and listening and responding to opponents, they understandably spent most of their time with the two who represented swing votes. (In the end, one voted for the proposal after speaking against it. The other, having been pressured by conservative state Republicans that they would not support his re-election in the fall, voted against it after ambivalently speaking for it.)

Ironically, the fact that the debate on the proposal took place over a three-and-a-half-year period helped the university's lobbying efforts. It gave administrators an opportunity to educate regents privately as well as publicly at the numerous meetings where the proposal was discussed. The long period of public debate also helped to raise the issue of fairness. As Women's Studies faculty continued to write and revise numerous forms of the proposal, and as they continued to present the proposals at public regents' meetings, they conveyed the message of playing by the rules (even as the rules changed). That approach, combined with their not engaging regents' more inflammatory rhetoric (leaving that to their more dispassionate administrative allies), conveyed the impression over time of reasonable and responsible campus citizens. By not backing down but not reacting, the Women's Studies faculty won supporters in the university community and beyond.[22]

The faculty's matter-of-fact and patient insistence served to influence the students. Although not exactly allies in the sense that the female and male administrators were (the students were a part of the program), the Women's Studies track majors nevertheless were supporting a cause that would serve to benefit future majors. They met weekly, and sometimes more often, to develop strategies, which included developing a letter-writing and e-mail campaign to lobby regents and CCHE members, staging protests at graduation ceremonies, creating an information table (complete with flyers) at the student union, writing letters to newspapers, cultivating allies among other (female and male) students, meeting individually with CCHE staff and campus administrators, and staging with their allies a visible presence at Board of Regents and CCHE meetings. Five of the students also co-wrote an article in a locally published journal on the importance of Women's Studies (see Along et al. 1997). Their efforts increasingly exhibited political sophistication. At times they were direct, vocal, and angry (for example, at demonstrations outside graduation and in letters to newspapers).[23] At other times they used silence to create a strong presence (for example, by staying mute, dressing in black, and holding large posters as they lined the room at Board of Regents and CCHE meetings). In all their efforts, the students argued for the substantive importance of the Women's Studies curriculum. At the same time, however, they effectively used the free-market strategy promoted by the conservative critics of higher education. As consumers of a university education, they demanded that their degree adhere to the principle of truth in advertising. They insisted that their degree represent their course work. One of their posters read: "WE CHOSE CU. WE PAID TUITION. WE DID THE WORK. WE GOT THE GRADES. WE LEAVE HERE TODAY WITH BLANK DIPLOMAS."[24] The students' efforts were not lost on the decision-makers. "Your students," confessed one of the regents at the end of the process, "were very impressive." This seemed a fitting conclusion to a successful effort by a program that had been initiated more than twenty-five years earlier by another generation of students.

Although the effort of allies was crucial for the successful outcome of the degree proposal, it was not apparent at the outset to the Women's Studies faculty that this would be the case. We were slow to recognize the significance of allies for at least two reasons. First, when we began the process, all of the top academic administrators on campus and in the system were on the verge of leaving to retire or to take positions at other institutions. These changes and the ensuing political struggles within the university made it difficult for us to find political allies within the administration who had an ongoing commitment to the institution, let alone to Women's Studies. Thus, in the early stages we were left mostly to fend for ourselves with the help of the female academic associate vice-president.

The second reason we were slow to gain allies was our own limited perspectives. Our success within the university had shielded us from the harsh reality of direct political opposition from the right. Although some of us had experienced conservative criticism to our scholarly work on a national level, and although we were all aware of the conservative influence in the state through Amendment 2 and other measures, we were somewhat naive about our programmatic vulnerability as well as about our symbolic significance statewide to the conservative political agenda. The Women's Studies program on the "flagship" campus of the major research university in the state represented all that the conservatives abhorred: the privilege of the academy, liberalized education, and a feminist curriculum that defied the right's anti-abortion, anti-gay agenda. Once the degree proposal became a public matter, we became a lightning rod for opposition statewide among the conservative regents and staff at the CCHE, within the legislature, in the press, and among the numerous religious organizations and political-action groups. The strategies that had worked to create our success within the university—strategies that drew on academic and scholarly values—were neither sufficient nor, in some cases, effective at all.

It became clear to us only after the opposition was in place that we needed the active and vigorous support of individuals who represented the institution at both the highest and grassroots levels. Although students rallied on their own, faculty found it necessary to continue to educate their administrative allies, to support their lobbying efforts, and to initiate and sustain the communication between Women's Studies and the administration. It was clear to us that our degree proposal—while the primary focus of our energy—was one of many issues that the various administrators were addressing. We needed to stay aware of calendars, schedules, meetings, and articles in the press in order to inform our allies of both anticipated problems and to give them support when they asked for it.

The student and administrative allies were well situated to provide public support for Women's Studies in a way that faculty were not. The degree proposal had become a political issue. It required political means to argue for its approval. At the same time, the argument against Women's Studies as a field was that it was political, not scholarly. We needed allies who could address this paradox by using their political position to represent us as apolitical, scholarly, dispassionate. This was accomplished by university administrators who used the power of their office to legitimate the scholarly and pedagogical appropriateness of our curriculum. And it was accomplished by students who exercised their roles as consumers of education to demand a correct designation for their accumulated coursework and to earn what they argued was a marketable degree in their chosen field of study.

In the process of mediating this paradox, of taking a stand on behalf of Women's Studies, members of these two groups of allies appeared to be transformed. This was especially obvious in the students, who gained confidence, knowledge of bureaucratic procedures, and political acumen. They also developed strong ties among themselves that continued to sustain them (naming themselves the Feminist Student Network) as they took action on other campus issues and served as allies to other groups. Although the female administrators seemed to show less transformation (they both had participated in these kinds of struggles on behalf of feminism before), the male administrators did appear to change. They showed an increasing commitment to the program as the struggle dragged on. Partly, this could have been the result of educating themselves in a field, and thus becoming committed to it. But also, perhaps more subtly, the mere fact of taking a public stand on behalf of the program, then experiencing the denigration to which the faculty had long been subjected, gave them a firsthand grasp of what it feels like to be treated as "Other." Indeed, this direct experience of being treated like the Other may have been the longer-lasting psychological consequence of becoming an ally.

Finally, the struggle gave the administrators and supportive regents experience with defending an academic program that was unpopular with the political right—experience that, unfortunately, they would have to draw on shortly after Women's Studies' success. I will close with this incident to exemplify both the ongoing importance of cultivating effective and committed allies and the treacherous political context that progressive education continues to face.

On March 22, 1998, the television news program *Sixty Minutes* aired a segment on gay studies that outraged a Republican member of the Colorado State Legislature, who was also a member of the Joint Education Committee.[25] Believing that the program depicted Women's Studies, the senator subsequently threatened to hold up all funding for the entire University of Colorado system unless Boulder campus officials cut off funding to the Women's Studies program. By the time university officials were able to get to the source of this threat, they realized the senator's error. But they also realized that when the issue was clarified, the fledgling Gay, Lesbian, Bisexual, Transgender (GLBT) program would be threatened. Once again, faculty educated the administrators about their field of study. And once again, administrators, faculty, and two regents argued for the academic legitimacy of a politically explosive area of the curriculum, this time in the State House.[26] Fielding questions about using state revenues to fund gay studies and confronting fears of indoctrination, the university representatives argued that the field was an important and legitimate area of the curriculum. One of the regents drew the analogy that students take courses on many subjects, including Nazi Germany, as well as diverse religious traditions but that they are not expected to convert to any of those subjects. One of the two Democratic regents noted, "If we do indoctrinate, we're not doing a very good job . . . because the generation coming out of the university is more conservative than the previous one."[27] Although not completely convinced, the committee backed down from the threat, and the university officials returned to campus, having once again defended, for the time being, a politically vulnerable area of the curriculum.

For the faculty in Women's Studies, the degree process and its aftermath have awakened us afresh not only to our political vulnerability, but also to the political importance of our task. If, indeed, the conservative right has identified higher education as the major battlefield of the culture wars, then doing our jobs well within the institution is not avoiding the political but engaging it. In this process, it has been instructive to realize the wider implication of cultivating allies and becoming allies to others. At the same time, however, we struggle against allowing our need for influential and powerful allies to undermine our commitment to transforming the curriculum and the institution. Thus, we find ourselves toeing the narrow line between the twin goals of survival and change, a political-institutional dance that is, indeed, an art form.

Notes

1   Although many individuals involved in this process were interviewed, most did not want to be quoted. Therefore, this interpretive essay is based on a synthesis of information from interviews, personal notes, and articles published in the press.

2   This brief history is drawn primarily from materials in the University of Colorado at Boulder's Women's Studies program—for example, reports, memos, brochures, course schedules, and syllabi.

3   "CU to Offer Degree in Women Studies," *Silver and Gold Record*, April 14, 1983, p. 4.

4   University of Colorado at Boulder, "Enhancing Excellence for the 21st Century," report of the Pursuit of Excellence Task Force (May 16, 1994), 90–92.

5   "Historic UCB Cottage to Get Renovations," *Silver and Gold Record*, October 19, 1995, p. 1, 5.

6   University of Colorado at Boulder, "Just the Facts," Office of News Services (1998–99), 19.

7   Alan Gottlieb and Virginia Culver, "A House Divided?" *Denver Post*, November 11, 1992, sec. C1.

8   "The Stealth Crusade," *Washington Spectator* 19, no. 6 (March 15, 1993), 1.

9   "CU's Response to Tabor Amendment Will Define Future Regents Told," *Silver and Gold Record*, June 13, 1996, pp. 1, 12.

10   "Middleton to Step Down as Dean in '96," *Silver and Gold Record*, September 14, 1995, pp. 1, 12.

11   "CU Wants Women's Studies Degree; Think Tank Says Bad Idea," *Boulder Planet*, January 15–21, 1997, pp. 1, 7.

12   "UCB Ethnic Studies Gains Department Status," *Silver and Gold Record*, October 26, 1995, pp. 1, 8.

13   "Women's Studies Degree Delayed," *Boulder Daily Camera*, November 15, 1996, sec. A1.

14   "CU Graduates Cap It All Off," *Boulder Daily Camera*, December 21, 1997, sec. B3.

15   "Cottage Has Room with a World View," *Colorado Daily*, August 29–31, 1997, 3.

16 "UCB Women's Studies Degree Passes Tough Test with 5-4 Regent Vote," *Silver and Gold Record,* January 29, 1998, p. 8.

17 "Women's Studies OK'd," *Boulder Daily Camera,* January 23, 1998, sec. A1, 14.

18 "CU Women's Studies Gets Own Degree," *Colorado Daily,* April 3–5, 1998, p. 7.

19 "Just the Numbers Please," *Women in Higher Education* 3, no. 5 (1994): 4.

20 Lou McClelland, director of Office of Planning, Budget, and Analysis, University of Colorado at Boulder, e-mail to author, March 22, 1999.

21 Richard Byyny, telephone conversation with the author, August 24, 1998.

22 For example, "Give Women's Studies Its Due," Editorial, *Boulder Daily Camera,* December 9, 1996, sec. B2.

23 Alison Hatch, "King Gets It Wrong Across the Board," Letter to the Editor, *Colorado Daily,* February 7–9, 1997, p. 10.

24 "UCB Women Studies Degree," 8.

25 "Sexuality 101," *Sixty Minutes* (March 22, 1998), CBS, New York.

26 "Legislators Question UCB Faculty Politics, Gay/Lesbian Course Offerings," *Silver and Gold Record,* May 7, 1998, pp. 1, 12.

27 Ibid., 12.

MARYANNE DEVER,
DENISE CUTHBERT, AND LINDSEY POLLAK

Life After Women's Studies: Graduates and the Labor Market

Just as university students were sitting for their final examinations in 1998, an article appeared in the *Australian* entitled, "Relevance Pays Off in Job Search." Prominently positioned on page two of a national newspaper, the article quoted an employment consultant on the difficulty of placing a woman who had majored in Women's Studies. "There is just no job," the consultant explained. "They are not taking someone with that sort of esoteric major" (Armitage 1998). A brief follow-up telephone call to the consultant in question elicited the explanation that a Women's Studies major was difficult for her to "market" to employers, unlike, say, a "broad" major in human resources. Notwithstanding the fact that some of the consultant's mooted difficulty may have related to her own rather sketchy understanding of what a major in Women's Studies might involve, most Women's Studies teachers would probably wish to dispute this characterization of the field and its graduates. But when the initial sense of outrage or exasperation subsides, the question we face is how would we go about doing so?

Some Women's Studies practitioners may argue that more could be achieved in the field if the time regularly spent defending our area of specialization against charges such as these were devoted instead to teaching and to conducting our research (Morris 1998). Others might rightly wish to reject the idea that Women's Studies has to satisfy someone else's unspecified notion of what is "relevant" or "useful." Although many areas within the liberal arts are today increasingly subject to this type of scrutiny, you could well ask why it is that Women's Studies is singled out so consistently and so frequently for the "utility test." Why is it, indeed, that people who apparently have no trouble imagining what you might "do" with French, history, or sociology either draw a blank with Women's Studies or point to the assumed narrowness of a field of study pertaining exclusively to that well-known, numerically dominant minority, women? Perhaps as Women's Studies programs become more successful, numerous, and visible, they naturally attract scrutiny of this order, a pattern suggested by a recent cover story in the *Chronicle of Higher Education,* in which supposedly limited job prospects for graduates provided a way to challenge the overall validity of "proliferating" Women's Studies doctoral programs in the United States (Wilson 1998).[1] And yet, for many feminist academics who situate themselves in critical, even oppositional, relationships to the dominant paradigms of economic rationalism that now pressure academics to justify and legitimize their teaching and research programs in terms of these narrowly conceived, market-driven goals, the very idea of responding to such challenges, of entering into the discourse of graduate labor-market outcomes, may be problematic. That is, it may present the political dilemma of requiring us as feminists to engage with the very structures that elsewhere we work to critique and resist. But can Women's Studies practitioners really afford to continue flinching before the question, "What do you do with Women's Studies?" Is it enough any longer simply to shrug and sigh because our usefulness is not dazzlingly self-evident to all, or alternatively to assert that the vocational lies outside our brief? Or is it rather the case that as professionals in this field we have an obligation to understand and engage critically with what is arguably a significant element in the broader social and political impact of our work in Women's Studies?

We would suggest that consideration of our students' post-graduation experiences in general, and their vocational aspirations in particular, is essential if we are to maintain some meaningful fit between our professed teaching and learning objectives; our students' needs, desires, and aspirations; and the wider context in which important educational and vocational decisions are negotiated. It also represents an opportunity to learn more about what brings students to our programs in the first place. We would suggest further that shifts today in educational, fiscal, and political priorities, both within and beyond the immediate campus environment, are likely to make it increasingly difficult for teachers and researchers, especially those in public institutions, to continue fostering Women's Studies programs and their students in the absence of this type of engagement. After all, in an educational environment that is progressively shaped by the discourses of economic rationalism and the marketplace, many of us have learned firsthand how Women's Studies can find itself in the firing line when arguments are made against maintaining "useless" and "non-vocational" programs of study. And as Alice Kessler-Harris and Amy Swerdlow argue, already "the massive cutbacks in money for higher education in the 1990s have disproportionately affected inter-disciplinary programs outside the traditional mainstream—including women's studies" (Kessler-Harris and Swerdlow 1996). It may well be that as Women's Studies practitioners, we resile from this dilemma at our peril. Indeed, if Beverley Skeggs's astute analysis of the status and progress of Women's Studies in the United Kingdom is any indication, the issue may no longer be whether we should engage with the processes of economic rationalism, but how. Skeggs identifies Women's Studies students' own increasing concern for employment outcomes as a significant dimension of both the current reconfiguration of higher education in many Western societies within a broadly consumerist discourse and the growing rates of unemployment and underemployment among university graduates in many of those same societies (Skeggs 1995). This means, in effect, that many of us are now confronted by an increasing overlap between economic rationalist concerns about the vocational relevance of teaching programs—whether voiced from inside or outside our institutions—and our students' own varying concerns in this regards. And we have few adequate responses.

But if Women's Studies practitioners are to engage productively with this increasingly market-driven, outcome-oriented educational environment, it must necessarily be in ways that do more than simply fulfill the requirements of mere institutional legitimation. Rather than aiming to satisfy the corporate masters, we would argue that feminist research on the post-graduation labor-market aspirations and experiences of Women's Studies students should offer ways to challenge and problematize the limiting and delimited objectives of economic rationalist models for understanding the relationships among educational and political goals, economic benefits, and labor-market outcomes and should provide meaningful insights into the wider project of Women's Studies. Just as we may hope that our critically and politically literate graduates will be placed in employment and take this opportunity to challenge and transform their places of work and—at the macro level—the nature of work itself, we argue that it is necessary for feminist academics to intervene in and, one hopes, transform the existing terms in which discussions about graduates and the labor market take place. This essay explores some of the reasons that the vocational dimensions of Women's Studies should feature more prominently in important debates about the nature, impact, and future of Women's Studies and, using the example of our recent pilot study of students' expectations and aspirations, examines some possible directions for more systematic research into these questions in the future.

Why So Little Debate?

Although feminist scholars and educators have generated valuable debate about questions of gender, employment, and the workplace, there has been surprisingly little discussion of, and even less research on, how Women's Studies programs relate to the domain of the vocational and how Women's Studies graduates fare in the labor market. In many instances, when we as teachers or course advisers are called on to answer the question of "what you *do* with a major or minor in Women's Studies," we can usually offer only the most general of responses, frequently a list of occupations or employment sectors that we believe could or should accommodate graduates with a demonstrated competence in feminist and gender issues. Whether or to what extent they actually do often remains a matter of conjecture. The bottom line is that we have seldom gathered the types of information that would enable us to answer the question, "What do you do with Women's Studies?" in a detailed and informed fashion. Even less attention has been paid to the vocational aspirations with which students enter Women's Studies programs and to the question, "What do you want to do with Women's Studies?"

The only comprehensive reviews of Women's Studies vocational and career questions were those carried out two decades ago in the United States. Part of a series of eight studies that endeavored to assess the impact of the first decade of Women's Studies, *The Relationship Between Women's Studies, Career Development and Vocational Choice* (Bose and Priest-Jones 1980) and *Women's Studies Graduates* (Reuben and Boehm 1980) together attempted to find preliminary answers to such questions as "What is the impact of Women's studies on students' career aspirations?" "Why major in Women's Studies?" and "What do Women's Studies graduates do?" Each volume surveyed the available literature and data, offering promising if sketchy accounts of the positive impact of Women's Studies on students' subsequent labor-market experiences, but their findings were far from conclusive.

Indeed, both sets of authors argued with conviction that, without more detailed and coordinated studies at a national level, the picture would inevitably remain partial, and there would be few definitive, measurable outcomes for practitioners to point to. Among the combined recommendations of the two studies were the need for comprehensive national data-gathering and graduate-tracking, longitudinal studies of Women's Studies cohorts, systematic examination of students' changing aspirations across the period of their Women's Studies enrollment, the development of definitions and measures of the professional and personal transferable skills fostered within Women's Studies, and profiling of the different types of Women's Studies programs emerging in the United States.

It is interesting to note how few of their recommendations have been taken up in practice and how few published studies have followed. Although the political, educational, and employment climates have altered considerably since these reports were published, it could be argued that the need to carry out the number and type of studies they outline has only increased over that period of time. Indeed, as we noted earlier, more and more Women's Studies programs, in common with other areas within the liberal arts, are being asked to justify their activities on the basis of precisely this type of information, particularly as the goals of higher-education institutions become more market-oriented.

This paucity of discussion about the vocational dimensions of Women's Studies puzzled us initially, as in other respects Women's Studies programs and their students have been the subject of a great deal of general scrutiny and speculation since their emergence in the academy more than three decades ago. The most cursory survey of Women's Studies journals and anthologies would suggest that Women's Studies students represented one of the most closely monitored groups of humanities or social-science students today, particularly in the United States and in England. But while there is a body of literature focusing on the impact of Women's Studies on students' post-class and post-graduation behavior, this tends to be concerned primarily with the on-going personal and political impact of their studies[2] rather than on the study-to-work transition or on graduate career paths.

One can account for this trend in a number of ways. We recognize, for example, that Women's Studies programs emerged from strategic political and intellectual agitation by women rather than from employer pressure for specific skills or knowledge. Programs have therefore conventionally viewed their primary roles in terms of women's empowerment with their primary links being to the wider women's movement rather than to the employment sector. It is perhaps natural then that the types of change anticipated, looked for, and documented among our students should belong to the arenas of personal and political transformation. The precise institutional location of many Women's Studies programs may well have played a part, too, because the majority of programs historically have been situated within the liberal arts, an academic area that has until relatively recently rarely considered explicit engagement with vocational outcomes among its primary functions;[3] rather, it has couched its benefits in terms of more "intrinsic" rewards, such as individual self-development.

The fact that Women's Studies takes different political, intellectual, and philosophical forms in different institutions has also probably contributed to the lack of broad-based debate about this issue. For example, the diversity of available programs may not always make discussion of common graduate aims and outcomes particularly easy or meaningful. Alternatively, where Women's Studies programs depend for their core units entirely on existing courses located within the individual disciplines, or where programs rely heavily on the offerings of a single discipline (for example, literature or history), questions of vocational outcomes may well be articulated but exclusively or predominantly in terms of those disciplines rather than in terms of any overarching feminist intellectual or political enterprise. It is also possible that the concentration of Women's Studies programs at the more elite end of the educational spectrum, at some distance from the technical- and vocational-educational arena, has contributed to the absence of significant debate about more pragmatic educational outcomes. Added to this, the strenuous efforts required of feminist educators over the past three decades to establish the intellectual and scholarly credibility of Women's Studies within those same institutions, and the concomitant "race for theory"

(Christian 1987) may have proved difficult to reconcile with more than a passing concern for the vocational elements of Women's Studies. But the absence of published deliberations of these questions probably should not be taken to mean that practitioners themselves have not pondered them, exchanging thoughts and speculations among themselves and with their students in more informal ways.

Framing a Research Agenda

In the 1990s, two studies returned these issues to the Women's Studies agenda. In a 1994 essay, Chris Stearns gives a brief account of a comparative survey of Women's Studies graduates from two U.S. universities (Towson State University in Maryland and Wake Forest University in North Carolina) in which questions relating to the vocational impact of Women's Studies featured prominently. She argues that the collective responses to the survey "reveal the transforming effect of a WMST [Women's Studies] education" with graduates generally indicating significant direct and indirect correlation between their Women's Studies enrollment and the "work they do" (Stearns 1994). It is interesting to note that, beyond any specific knowledge they may have acquired in the course of their studies, when questioned on the impact of Women's Studies on their working lives, these graduates pointed strongly to "interaction with co-workers" (Stearns 1994: 67) or to what we might term "feminist process skills" in communication, organization, and teamwork (Schniedewind 1993). Brief as they are, the instances in which her respondents articulate how they understand the connection between their undergraduate studies and their chosen careers or graduate enrollment are certainly thought-provoking.

Considerably more detailed is Barbara Luebke and Mary Ellen Reilly's book-length qualitative study, *Women's Studies Graduates: The First Generation* (1995), which profiles eighty-nine Women's Studies graduates from a range of programs across the United States, again offering accounts in the graduates' own words of how they relate their studies to their subsequent study, career, and life paths. Through the revealing testimonies of its graduate participants, Luebke and Reilly's work admirably demonstrates the flexible nature of a Women's Studies qualification and the extent to which Women's Studies' ethic of empowerment readily translates from classroom or campus to the workplace. Something very telling about the nature of a Women's Studies qualification is demonstrated in the remarkable range of careers these respondents were pursuing, including graduate studies, journalism, public relations and the media, health care, education, social work and social policy, and so on.

Together, these particular studies are valuable in that they appear to confirm several key assumptions with which Women's Studies practitioners have generally been working. In contrast to the articles from the *Australian* and *Chronicle of Higher Education* cited earlier, these studies suggest that Women's Studies is indeed an enabling qualification that opens up rather than closes off opportunities for its graduates. They also demonstrate that Women's Studies graduates are able to articulate a range of direct and indirect benefits of these programs for their careers. And more important, perhaps, Luebke and Reilly's work offers insights into the ways in which different students derive different vocational benefits from their studies, choosing to engage with the ideas and concepts encountered in Women's Studies in ways that are strategically useful to them. The insights graduates gained from their studies, write the authors, "made them better at what they have done since graduation" (Luebke and Reilly 1995: 199). Graduate tracking of this kind, whether qualitative or quantitative, is clearly an important element in understanding the experience of Women's Studies graduates in the labor market, but evidently a great deal more work needs to be done in this area. In addition to limited data from specific national domains, there are, for example, no comparative international studies that would enable practitioners to construct an extremely revealing snapshot of the differing career paths taken by Women's Studies graduates, and thus the differential social and cultural impact of our work, across a variety of national domains.

We would suggest that in addition to the "slice-of-life" studies that tend to focus on graduates' early labor-market experience or on a single point in their post-graduation working lives, longitudinal studies of graduates' career movements over time also need to be considered. As we know, one of the acknowledged limitations of the traditional early career, or "first-destination," graduate survey method is that it tells us little about the longer-term vocational rewards of specific programs of study (Coyte 1985: 1). Likewise, research on the long-term impact of Women's Studies on students' lives suggests that interest and engagement with the politics and concepts encountered in the classroom actually peaks some time after students leave that environment (Stake and Rose 1994: 410). Therefore, if we are to gain a more complex understanding of whether and in what ways studies of feminism and gender issues affect Women's Studies graduates' long-term career choices, directions, and opportunities, systematic tracking of graduates over longer periods of time will be necessary. Such studies may also assist us in learning not only how individuals' careers are shaped by their studies, but also whether Women's Studies graduates as a cohort are making a collective contribution to changing the nature of different workplaces, increasing their receptivity to the ideas and concepts addressed by Women's Studies. As Diaedre, a graduate student cited in Stearns's article, observes of the future labor-market impact of her peers, "We are also opportunistic. We will virtually be in the vanguard of women looking to create employment opportunities for which [Women's Studies] backgrounds would be an asset. . . . Once we're in the door, we can begin the work of educating our employer" (Stearns 1994: 67).

But graduate tracking, no matter how comprehensive, can provide only one part of the picture—namely, where graduates go. One thing such studies cannot tell us about is employers' recruitment principles and their attitudes toward Women's Studies. If the expressed opinions of the consultant quoted earlier are any indication, this information is clearly crucial to the success our graduates will find in seeking employment. Despite the obvious growth and success of Women's Studies within the academy, it is still something of a well-kept secret for many outside that domain, suggesting that much work remains in establishing dialogues with the broader community about the meaning and value of Women's Studies. Personal experience would seem to indicate that comparatively few people outside the immediate university or college environment, including the friends and families of colleagues and students, have a detailed understanding of what Women's Studies is, believing it to lie somewhere between home economics, biology, and consciousness-raising. This scenario was certainly borne out in research carried out recently by a group of our undergraduate students, who conducted a survey of approximately one hundred members of the public in which "women's health" was commonly selected as the most appropriate description of the course. For some people, then, the question, "What do you do with Women's Studies?" is probably just another way of asking, "What *is* Women's Studies?" And a fair degree of humor, incomprehension, or nervous laughter often greets the explanations.

Given what appears to be the low level of awareness of Women's Studies outside the academy, it seems only reasonable to inquire what potential employers make of our students' academic transcripts. Obviously, employers in women-centered organizations, the community, and educational sectors could be expected to respond positively and with some understanding of the field, but what about other areas? If we accept that upward of 40 percent to 50 percent of new graduate opportunities are open to graduates of any discipline (Perkins 1992: 27), it is likely that many of our graduates are presenting themselves before mainstream graduate recruiters—an impression confirmed, as we show later, by the range of anticipated career paths nominated by the students we have surveyed. What image or understanding, if any, do these potential employers have of the field of Women's Studies? What knowledge and skills, if any, do they associate with its graduates? Do they view a knowledge of women, gender, and equity issues as an asset or a liability in a potential employee? Would they hire a Women's Studies graduate?

Both anecdotal evidence and the results of our survey seem to suggest that many students anticipate meeting varying degrees of ignorance, hostility, and ridicule in the recruitment process. If the recent experience of one of our outstanding graduates who was advised by a recruitment firm to "play down the 'women's thing' " is any indication, these fears may not be groundless. But the real point here is that, to date, no major study of employers' attitudes that would answer these anxieties appears to have been carried out, so we have no way to know how accurate this impression may be.[4] We advocate, then, a program of surveying and selectively interviewing graduate recruiters, personnel officers, careers counselors, and human-resource managers to discover what level of awareness they have of Women's Studies as an academic program and what range of feelings or attitudes they may have toward such programs and their graduates. This style of research might offer practitioners a twofold benefit: Not only would we gather substantial new information on how our field is viewed in the wider employment sector, and thus how graduates from our different programs might fare, but in talking to and interviewing recruiters, human-resource managers, careers counselors, and personnel officers, we would also be playing a positive role in raising awareness of the field of Women's Studies and in debunking myths or stereotypes that may be present. Such contact has the further potential to pave the way for the development of new industry placements and internships, practices that have been shown to have a very positive impact on graduates' employment prospects (Australian Association of Graduate Employers 1997: 26).

At the same time, we must also be willing to listen to and learn from employers and from the existing debate on graduate outcomes generally, as these might allay some of our own and our students' fears and doubts. Existing research suggests, for example, that the vast majority of employers recruiting graduates with generalist degrees are more interested in graduates' transferable personal skills (that is, communication skills, ability to work in teams, verbal reasoning, and confidence) than in the specific knowledge gained from their studies. Indeed, it has been argued that "the better the personal skills the less the discipline seems to matter" (Perkins 1992: 28). This suggests that the field of Women's Studies could benefit from encouraging its students to recognize the genuine vocational strengths of the empowerment and personal transformations they experience, together with those feminist process skills that they develop through their studies.

Integrating Expectations

As a way to establish a firm basis for conducting the specific types of research outlined earlier, we began close to home. Recognizing that as teachers and researchers we had probably come to Women's Studies by very different paths and with different motivations from the undergraduate students with whose immediate and longer-term labor-market experiences we were concerned, we decided to commence our research into this area through a pilot survey examining the expectations of students entering Women's Studies programs. We wanted to explore in detail how they understood the relationship between that enrollment decision and their anticipated career paths, thus replacing the question, "What do you do with Women's Studies?" with, "What do you think you can do with Women's Studies?" or "What do you want to do with Women's Studies?" We felt it would be instructive to learn whether, or to what extent, our students actually viewed their enrollment in vocational terms and how directly they perceived the skills and knowledge developed through Women's Studies as relating to and building toward their subsequent career plans. Among the questions we wanted to explore were: Is this why they chose Women's Studies in the first place? Or were they relying on their other majors for these types of outcomes? Did our students perceive

Women's Studies to be vocational in ways we have never considered? What did they think we were offering them? What did they imagine they would be getting?

We believed that this kind of research would help us understand more about what brings students into our programs, assisting us in making sure there was some meaningful correlation between what we were offering students and the students' own needs, desires, and aspirations. After all, it is one thing for us to establish a set of program objectives and outcomes, and quite another to test those against the objectives and outcomes the students have established for themselves. In this respect, we took our lead from Jean Fox O'Barr, who observed that "if connections are going to be made between what I am teaching and what students are learning, I have to learn much more about the students themselves" (1994: 266). For us, this also meant discovering where students wanted to take the skills and knowledge they encountered and built in our classrooms and admitting the goals and experiences for them that lay beyond the campus and beyond graduation. Moreover, we considered that if we could continue surveying students across the entire period of their enrollment in Women's Studies, it would doubtless yield important insights into the ways in which the programs themselves foster, modify, and inspire particular vocational emphases.

In working through this phase of the research and in analyzing our findings, we have been able to refine our research methodologies in several respects and have also determined that, in addition to examining students' expectations, graduate tracking, and employer-based research, we need to add the further strand by gathering information about Women's Studies programs and researching the attitudes of practitioners involved in their design and delivery. It is hoped that by gathering data on the respective aspirations and expectations of all stakeholders, we will emerge with a clearer picture than we have at present of what our students hope to be able to do with their Women's Studies education and, once in the labor market, how they assess the knowledge, skills, and attributes they have acquired through their feminist and gender education; what the labor market expects of graduates and how the skills and attributes of Women's Studies graduates mesh with these expectations; and whether and in what ways Women's Studies programs and their staff address the post-graduation aspirations of their students and the world of work beyond the walls of the university, whether implicitly or explicitly.

We hope that this work will prove valuable in informing Women's Studies programs practice on many levels.

Pilot Survey of Commencing Students: Overview of Findings

In the first semester of 1998, we developed a pilot survey designed to elicit the attitudes and expectations of enrolling Women's Studies students. The response of staff in other institutions to invitations to participate in the research was overwhelmingly positive. The proposed research clearly struck a chord, as those contacted not only agreed to participate but also expressly inquired whether the data for their programs could later be returned to them for their own use. Discussion among staff at the three participating institutions—Monash and Deakin Universities in Melbourne and Otago University in Dunedin, New Zealand—confirmed the general sense that we all had much to learn from the results. As we were concerned in the first instance to discover as much as possible about what considerations led students to enroll in Women's Studies and the students' expectations of these programs, for the pilot phase of this research we surveyed commencing Women's Studies students in the first few weeks of their course.[5]

The information gathered through these surveys has proved valuable in obtaining a "snapshot" of students at the commencement of their Women's Studies programs. Close scrutiny of this snapshot has reassuringly confirmed a number of our expectations about commencing Women's Studies students—for example, their generally high levels of commitment to the subject area. It has also presented us with surprising and unsettling information, suggesting, among other things, that these students do indeed come to these programs in very different ways and with different expectations from ours and from those we imagined for them. These expectations are different in both kind and quality from what we had anticipated and have confirmed for us the importance of this work.

Perhaps the single most significant finding to emerge from the pilot survey is that personal interest and interest in the subject matter were given by the majority of respondents as their major reason for enrolling in Women's Studies. Of the students surveyed, 61 percent indicated interest in the subject matter as the main reason for enrolling in Women's Studies. The next most frequent reason, scoring 21 percent, was that

Table 1. Summary of Reponses: Main Reason for Enrolling in Women's Studies

a) I was interested in the subject matter	61%
b) Friends or acquaintances recommended Women's Studies to me	11%
c) I had studied gender/feminist issues at school	2%
d) It was a compulsory unit for my course of study	0%
e) Family members suggested this area of study to me	3%
f) I thought it would be easy	1%
g) I thought it would complement my other studies	21%
h) I thought it would enhance my career prospects	3%
i) Other (please specify)	3%
No response	—

Women's Studies would complement their other studies. Interestingly, post-graduation career considerations were selected by only 3 percent of respondents (see table 1). Similarly, when asked to rank the factors influencing their Women's Studies enrollment in order of importance, 73 percent of respondents indicated personal interest as the most important factor, with 80 percent rating it among the top three factors (see table 2).

On the question of perceptions about Women's Studies in relation to other courses of study within the degree program, it is significant to note that the majority of the respondents (64 percent) indicated that they perceived Women's Studies as "neither harder nor easier" than other subjects in their degree program. Only 5 percent of respondents indicated that they understood Women's Studies to be harder than other subjects, while 7 percent understood it to be easier. This is an important finding, given the persistence of the view that enrollment in Women's Studies represents an intellectually "soft" option, a perception that has its origins in the history of aspersions cast against the academic rigor and intellectual validity of Women's Studies programs. Although largely dispensed with, this view rears its head from time to time in venues such as tenure, promotion, and research-funding committees.[6] Although Women's Studies is on par with other subjects areas in respondents' degree programs in terms of perceptions of academic rigor, it is marked as particularly different in students' perceptions of expectations of the classroom experience.

In enrolling in Women's Studies programs, then, the majority of students surveyed follow strong personal interest and commitment; they expect a program offering the same intellectual rigor provided in other subject areas but hold expectations of a significantly different educational experience. This finding confirms other research that emphasizes the high value Women's Studies students place on their educational experience as representing a "room of one's own" in the academy. It also complements further findings from our pilot research, discussed later, pointing to the importance Women's Studies students place on the development of confidence as a desired outcome of their feminist education in particular. Sonia, one of the Women's Studies graduates we have interviewed since completing the pilot survey, explicitly links the particular experience of the Women's Studies classroom to the development of confidence that has been, for her, a crucial attribute in the workplace:

> I found, particularly in the Philosophy Department, most of my classes there were unfortunately dominated by guys. The women were very, very quiet in tutorials. Even if [the ratio of male and female students] was 50-50, the guys would just dominate the discussions. Whereas in Women's Studies, where it was practically all women, there were women who were in my other tutorials and didn't say a word, they'd come to a Women's Studies tutorial and they'd become more vocal. . . . Women's Studies provides an environment where women can develop their confidence. It's made me feel like I can get my opinion across, that I can articulate things, that I have a right to articulate things, that I can approach my manager [in my present workplace] about something and discuss it with him; and feel like I've got an opinion and its valid; that I have a right to say if I'm not satisfied with something, or I feel that something should be changed, or if I've got an idea for something. I feel better about conveying it.[7]

Table 2. Summary of Responses: Rankings of Considerations Influencing Decision to Enroll in Women's Studies (1 = most important; 6 = least important)

	1	2	3	4	5	6
a) Personal interest	73%	11%	8%	4%	0%	.7%
b) Likely success in subject	4%	23%	29%	28%	7%	2%
c) Future career prospects	3%	21%	21%	27%	9%	9%
d) Compatibility with other subjects	16%	32%	22%	13%	4%	4%
e) Family's expectations	0%	1%	3%	8%	43%	39%
f) Friends' attitudes	0%	2%	9%	10%	32%	40%
No response	3%	10%		6%	5%	

Table 3. Summary of Responses: Expectations of the Friendliness/Openness of the Women's Studies Classroom Relative to Other Subjects

a) More open and friendly than other classes	57%
b) Same as other classes	16%
c) Less open and friendly than other classes	0%
d) No particular expectations	25%
No response	2%

In the face of such high expectations of Women's Studies on the part of enrolling students, it is pleasing to note that the overwhelming majority of students surveyed were positive about their initial experiences in their Women's Studies program. As we elaborate later, in describing their expectations and initial experiences of that particular program, the respondents employed a rich and politically inflected vocabulary that showed marked differences from the vocabulary used to describe their expectations of the general degree program of which Women's Studies formed a part. By contrast, where their conceptions and vocabulary appeared to falter was in considering their own relationship to the labor market in general, and the particular relationship their feminist and gender studies might have to it. One revealing indicator of this across respondents from all three institutions was that, despite the fact that the survey itself more frequently used the term "career" (five instances) in preference to the word "job" (two instances), when referring to the labor market respondents themselves almost invariably used the more minimal terminology of "work" and "jobs" to describe their aspirations after graduation, with the word "career" being used by only eight respondents out of the total sample of 150. It might be argued that, with little experience of the labor market beyond the casual or summer job market and subject positions bounded by their present status as students, the respondents were not in a position to make the distinction that we might make among "work," "jobs," and "careers"; hence, the word-frequency data may not bear too much interpretation. But it is also worth considering that this choice of vocabulary may have less to do with the particular position of these students as students than with their position as members of a generation that has lived in the shadow of successive periods of economic recession and—in the Australasian and British contexts, at least—persistently high levels of unemployment. In this respect, the language used by the respondents reflects the reductive terminology of economic-rationalist labor-market discourse in which individuals in search of employment become "job seekers," and a job—indeed, any job—is deemed a successful outcome of the "job search."

In the pilot phase of this research, it has been sobering to confront the degree to which our students' expectations of their labor-market destinations are significantly more constrained than our expectations of and for them. The language used by respondents frequently betrayed anxiety and relatively low aspirations for themselves. This was graphically illustrated by one student who responded to a question requiring her to list three things she hoped to gain from Women's Studies that would help her secure a job after graduation with the bald statement: "To actually get a job!" Although this response is starker than others to this question, it is not isolated. About 14 percent of respondents stated that one of their desired employment-related outcomes from both their general course of study and their particular studies of feminist and gender issues was employment itself. Here we confronted a trend commented on in the English context by Skeggs (1995: 476–77) in which many students today increasingly view and value their education in relation to the employment it will enable them to access on graduation. Yet, as we will discuss later, our pilot survey indicates that as high as these anxieties may run, students are still enrolling in Women's Studies on the basis of personal interest and interest in the subject matter, with career considerations playing a comparatively insignificant role for the majority of students.

It is also possible—and we are currently addressing this question in our research—that there is a distinct gender dimension to the discomfort our respondents felt with the word "career" as a descriptor of their working lives beyond the university. Research by colleagues at other universities, anecdotal evidence, and discussions with our own students raise the possibility that for some young women, the idea of a career is not simply something they cannot imagine themselves pursuing due to low expectations but something they actively resist.[8] This is not so surprising when put in the context of the frequently negative portrayal of "career women" in popular culture. Witness the unattractive, career-focused character played by Sigourney Weaver in the 1988 Hollywood film *Working Girl,* to cite just one example. In addition to such anti-feminist backlash discourses that render "career women" as unfeminine and presented with invidious choices between life and love or career, and either no possibility of combining them or the certain prospect of an exhausting juggling act to do so, there are undoubtedly other factors at work. For example, some of the female students surveyed are likely to be the daughters of "career women" doing the grueling double duty of work in professions that have only barely acknowledged the difficulties faced by women and the home shift. Other students may come from cultures that value marriage and children as non-negotiable constituents of acceptable femininity. Thus, it is likely that when some female students use the term "job" or "work" to describe their imagined employment after graduation, they do so because they believe a "job" is the kind of work that can be combined with some quality of life and the possibilities of getting married and having children, whereas they understand "career" to represent a path that closes off these possibilities.

When it came to addressing employment aspirations explicitly, however, a question asking students to indicate the broad areas in which they planned to make their careers revealed just how greatly our expectations of what Women's Studies students might want to do after graduation could differ from theirs. Our questionnaire provided for six fields of employment, with the seventh option left open for respondents to list other fields that we had not nominated. Some 25 percent of the respondents registered career interests in the "other" category, producing a radically different profile from the one we expected. The category of public service and administration, which we provided and viewed as a likely destination for Women's Studies graduates, was chosen by only 4 percent of respondents as a field in which they wanted to work. Likewise, "women's organizations" was selected by only 8 percent of respondents. Of course, there may be a world of difference between the field of work nominated by a commencing student and where that student ultimately goes, but the fact that a quarter of the students surveyed did not fall into any of the categories we provided certainly gave us cause for reflection. Of the fields of employment we nominated in the questionnaire, only the education and social work-welfare areas rated significantly, both registering 32 percent. In the "other" category, the fields of employment nominated by the respondents themselves included, in order of popularity: health, including psychology and nursing; drama and theater; media, including journalism, film, television, and advertising; the environmental movement; sports and leisure industries; and the armed forces. Although a number of fields nominated by the respondents could be said to have a gendered profile—the nursing profession being a case in point—

others in this category would see Women's Studies graduates moving into mainstream and, in some cases, nontraditional areas of employment, highlighting the need for considerably more research on how the skills and knowledge acquired through a Women's Studies major would be viewed by employers in these fields.

Relations Between Women's Studies and the Labor Market

Although respondents overwhelmingly indicated that post-graduation career plans played very little part in their decision to enroll in Women's Studies (see tables 1 and 2), when students were asked how they saw the skills and knowledge acquired in their Women's Studies' subjects relating to their post-graduation employment plans, a different kind of response emerged (see table 4). Respondents were asked to select a response to finish the statement, "I view the knowledge and skills I develop in Women's Studies as. . . ."

In contrast to the 3 percent of respondents who indicated that post-graduation career plans were a significant factor in their decision to enroll in Women's Studies (see Table 1), once enrolled, the majority of respondents (86 percent) posited at least some relationship between the knowledge and skills acquired in Women's Studies and their career plans, with 15 percent agreeing that Women's Studies was "central" to those plans, and 71 percent indicating that it was "of some importance." The challenge lies in interpreting these figures, particularly the very large percentage (71 percent) of students who chose "of some importance" to complete the statement. Clearly, more research is needed to determine the degree to which students responding that they view their pursuit of Women's Studies as having "some importance" to their later career plans make this response in an informed way. Qualitatively and quantitatively, we need to know whether the response "of some importance" expresses the view that Women's Studies is not as important for their long-term career plans as other courses they take (and on what bases students form this view) or whether it reflects a situation where the students themselves are hopeful but not quite sure what the relationship might be between Women's Studies and their post-graduation career plans. At the very least, we must consider the significant possibility that, as teachers, we may have failed to address adequately the manner in which Women's Studies programs are already vocational and the ways in

Table 4. Summary of Responses: Relationship Between Knowledge and
Skills Acquired Through Women's Studies and Later Career Plans

a) Central to my later career plans	15%
b) Of some importance to my later career plans	71%
c) Unrelated to my later career plans	11%
No response	3%

which the skills and knowledge we teach are transferable to a variety of employment contexts.

We moved a little closer to understanding what vocational benefits students feel they are getting from Women's Studies, relative to their studies generally, from responses to two related questions asking them to nominate three things they hoped to gain from their general course of study and from their Women's Studies program, respectively, that they thought would help them get a job after graduation (see table 5).

In response to the question relating to the general course of study, students' most common responses were the acquisition of knowledge (38 percent) and of skills in written and oral communication and the capacity to express ideas clearly and intelligently (36.4 percent). As mentioned earlier, 14.4 percent of respondents named employment itself one of the three desired labor-market-related outcomes, either indicating some misunderstanding of the question or reflecting the kinds of anxiety already discussed. This response was followed in frequency of nomination by the acquisition of confidence and personal development (14.2 percent); a tertiary qualification and good results (14.2 percent); and research skills (14.2 percent).

A similar question directed specifically at the vocationally significant elements of the Women's Studies component of their studies elicited some useful parallels and some very interesting differences, as table 6 shows.

Most notably, the non-response rate to this question was markedly higher, at 18 percent, than the non-response rate to the question about the general course of study (12 percent). As this question directly followed the question about their desired outcomes from the general course of study, it is possible that a proportion of the students who did not respond to the later question may have felt it repetitive and not answered on those grounds. Certainly, a number of respondents to the later question indicated that their desired outcomes from Women's Studies were the same as those for the overall degree program. There is also the possibility, alluded to earlier, that a proportion of students simply were not sure what, if any, employment-related skills and knowledge their Women's Studies program may be giving them.

Taken together, these two questions showed that there were significant differences between the kinds and quality of answers provided by students about their employment-related expectations of Women's Studies and their expectations for their general course of study. One measure of these differences is provided by an analysis of vocabulary and word frequency in responses (see table 7).

Responding to the question about their general course of study, the 132 students used a common vocabulary: The word "skills" appeared 80 times; the word "knowledge" had a frequency of 61; and "understanding" was used 43 times overall. In formulating their responses to the question specifically on Women's Studies, the same sample of students (excluding those who did not respond to the question) employed a somewhat different common vocabulary, and arguably their choice of words indicated a response that is at once more personal and qualitative, with both a gendered and political inflection. For example, students completing this question used the word "understanding" 73 times; "knowledge" had a frequency of 41; and, interestingly, "skills" and "feminist" (not always used in conjunction with each other) had a frequency of 29 each. This provides, we suggest, one useful means of beginning to understand the different ways in which students think about their Women's Studies

Table 5. Summary of Responses: Labor-Market-Related Expectations of General Course of Study

Name three things you hope to have gained from completing an arts degree that will help you get a job after you graduate:

1. Knowledge	38%
2. Communication/expression skills	36.4%
3. Job/career/profession	14.4%
4. Confidence/personal development	14.2%
5. A qualification/good marks	14.2%
6. Research skills	14.2%
No response	12%

Table 6. Summary of Responses: Labor-Market-Related
Expectations of Women's Studies Program

Name three things you hope to have gained through studying Women's Studies
that will help you get a job after you graduate:

1. Awareness/understanding of women/gender issues	48%
2. Confidence/personal development	28.4%
3. Job/career/profession/work	14.2%
4. Communication/expression skills	10.4%
No response	18%

work in relation to their studies as a whole. Of considerable concern is the relatively low nomination rate of perceived employment-related skills acquired in the Women's Studies programs (29 instances) in relation to the general course of study (80 instances). Although students speak enthusiastically and in qualitatively positive terms about the "understanding" and "awareness" they acquire from Women's Studies, they demonstrate a limited sense of these studies providing "skills" that will serve them in their careers beyond the university.

It is also interesting to note further differences in the ways in which students characterized their desired or predicted outcomes from Women's Studies as distinct from their general course of study. The most frequently nominated outcome students sought from Women's Studies specifically was an awareness or understanding of women's and gender issues (48 percent). Although roughly comparable to "knowledge," the most frequently nominated desired outcome of the general course of study (38 percent), the responses in this category are qualitatively different and more numerous, gender-inflected, and personal. As indicated in the word-frequency analysis, in relation to Women's Studies respondents used the word "understanding" (73 instances) far more frequently than the word "knowledge" (41 instances, as compared with 61 instances in response to the general course of study) to express their epistemological expectations of their Women's Studies programs. This may reflect both the different expectations students have of Women's Studies programs in relation to their general course of study and the degree to which the problematization of knowledge per se is an integral part of the Women's Studies project in a range of institutional contexts. Whatever qualitative difference there may be between the "knowledge" acquired in

Table 7. Analysis of Word Frequency in Responses to Questions 13 and 15.
Most Frequently Used Words (in Order of Frequency)

Q.13 (132 responses)		Q.15 (120 responses)	
skills	80	understanding	73
knowledge	61	knowledge	41
understanding	43	skills	29
		feminist	29

the general course of study and the "understanding" acquired through Women's Studies specifically, Women's Studies students appeared to indicate that an important distinction existed for them.

The second most frequent of the three nominated outcomes was confidence and personal development (28.4 percent), and responses in this category were clearly gender-inflected, with students expressing their hopes that their Women's Studies course would provide them with "determination as a woman," "courage," the "ability to stand up for myself," and "more understanding of myself as a woman in society." We considered it significant that this 28.4 percent response in the personal development and confidence category exceeded by more than 12 percent comparable responses to the question about desired outcomes from the general course of study (14.2 percent), where responses were not markedly gender-inflected and typically gestured toward such things as "a sense of achievement and self-identity," "personal fulfillment," "confidence in expressing my views," and "confidence in achieving my goals." This finding certainly complements trends identified in other research that indicates that Women's Studies programs and students place great emphasis on personal transformation as an objective of both curriculum and pedagogy (Griffin 1994: 13–45). In some instances, respondents to our survey saw a relationship between such personal development or transformation and their career goals—expressing this in explicitly feminist terms, such as acquiring "the strength to unite with women in my chosen field." But for many, the exact nature of the relationship between personal transformation and later career plans remained vague. In part, this may simply result from the fact that our respondents were commencing students with, in most cases, limited knowledge of the world of work, unlike those profiled by Luebke and Reilly who were already in the workforce and therefore better able to able to articulate the precise relationship between the kinds of knowledge, skills and attributes fostered through Women's Studies and those required to survive in an increasingly complex and demanding labor market where a strong and confident sense of self could prove invaluable. But it also suggests that one benefit of the type of research we are undertaking here might be the fostering—among teachers, students and potential employers—of a more detailed understanding of the ways in which the personal is also vocational. After all, as Helen Perkins argues "one of the key determinants of early success in a graduate career and indeed, for that matter, throughout a career, is confidence" (p. 29). The strong connection made by Women's Studies graduates, such as those interviewed by Luebke and Reilly or the comments of Sonia quoted earlier, between a Women's Studies education and the development of personal confidence needs to be better communicated to prospective employers, while prospective and current students could arguably be better served by us if the connections between such personal transformation and the study-to-work transition were made explicit.

Asset or Liability? Concluding Thoughts

As useful as our pilot survey has proved in providing us with information that we have not had about commencing Women's Studies students—their expectations and plans—it is necessarily limited in a number of crucial respects and points to additional future research trajectories. It is probably fair to say that our pilot survey suggests that the high expectations of what Women's Studies programs can offer students in personal, political, and intellectual terms are held despite other considerations. This is a refreshing finding, suggesting that our students are aware of the reductive turn of much current labor-market discourse emphasizing vocational relevance at the expense of other considerations, and that they are making enrollment decisions on other and, for them, more important grounds. In this respect, they appear to value their education in holistic terms, not merely in relation to workplace relevance, a view that Perkins suggests is also shared by at least some graduate employers, who themselves argue that "the purpose of undergraduate learning is not simply or solely to produce people for the world of work" (1992: 30). This broader view of the liberal arts education as an education for life and work is also supported by the findings of a survey of several cohorts of arts, humanities, and social-science graduates undertaken by Gaye Baldwin and Avril Kyle in 1997 (see Baldwin and Kyle 1998).

However, we would contend that, as refreshing as our students' rejection of reductive vocational considerations might be, it is also a matter of concern that so many students tended to view Women's Studies either as vocationally neutral or as a potential vocational liability, especially when such evidence as we have to date (for example, the work of Luebke and Reilly) provides a far different picture. Certainly, a small number of students nominating "work" as one of the desired employment-related outcomes in respect to Women's Studies were rather ambivalent about its likelihood, adding comments such as, "I don't think Women's Studies will help me get a job—in some areas it may hinder" and "Women's Studies won't have a great deal of effect on my getting a job." Comments such as these did not feature in the responses relating to the general course of study. It appears, then, that for a significant number of the students we surveyed, the enrollment scenario goes something like this: Women's Studies probably will not help me get a job, but I have my other courses to do that. In order to understand more fully how these perceptions arise, how they take shape, and how widespread they are, we need more contextual information than we have gathered to date. For example, we need to know more about how students perceive the relationship between their Women's Studies programs and the other majors in which they enroll, especially as 45 percent of the students surveyed indicated the computability of Women's Studies with their other courses as one of the three most influential factors determining their enrollment (table 2). This, of course, begs further questions that can be answered only by tracking these commencing students through their degrees: For how many of these students will Women's Studies become their major field of study? On what basis will the decision to major in Women's Studies be made? How many will continue to combine Women's Studies with another field in the belief that Women's Studies alone will not serve their long-term career interests? If students are overwhelmingly enrolling in Women's Studies out of personal interest, which majors in their degree programs are they selecting on the grounds of career plans? And on what basis is such a decision made? To what extent does personal interest figure prominently in all the enrollment decisions of arts or social science students? Are the factors influencing the Women's Studies enrollment typical or atypical of the way students generally plan their degree programs? In order to gather this information, more extensive research with Women's Studies students over the course of their degrees will be required, as will work with students pursuing majors in other fields within the arts and social sciences.

But if the results of our pilot survey indicate one thing clearly, it is a degree of uncertainty on the part of many students as to what vocational rewards their Women's Studies programs may offer them. For example, the 15 percent of respondents who ranked Women's Studies as being "central" to their later career plans (table 3) listed the following areas of work as their desired career destinations: law and law-related fields; psychology; drama and theater; social work and welfare; education; and business and the commercial sector. The 11 percent of respondents who considered Women's Studies to be "unrelated" to their later career plans listed many of the same areas. How is it that Women's Studies can be viewed as "central" to plans to work in, say, education or theater and performance by one group of students and as "unrelated" to these same fields by another? At the very least, this suggests to us that, in relation to their career plans, there is a need to assist students in taking the guesswork out of their Women's Studies enrollment decisions, particularly as it appears more than likely that our students are not able to see how their Women's Studies majors may fit them for the world of work, because it is not being specifically addressed in the courses we teach. In advocating a greater focus on these issues, we are not suggesting that the employment hopes and anxieties of students dictate how we approach those students. But we are suggesting that, by addressing in a serious and informed way their post-graduation aspirations, we may open productive avenues for dialogue between the academy and the world beyond it, something that has been centrally important to the development of Women's Studies programs and their relationships with larger feminist movements and projects.

Notes

1   The cover of the issue included the subtitle, "Some scholars wonder if graduates will find academic jobs," and the article itself carried the subtitle, "But some scholars worry that choosing a 'non-traditional' field will limit students' prospects." It is worth noting that the term "proliferation" was used in relation to the extremely modest tally of six doctoral programs in Women's Studies throughout the United States. Further, it is interesting in the light of the arguments we make in this essay that Women's Studies was construed in both subtitles as a potentially limiting qualification in career

terms, despite cogent arguments to the contrary advanced in the body of the article that followed.

2   See Pence 1992 and Thomsen et al. 1995.

3   See Eggins 1992 and Lewington 1998.

4   In her article, Stearns refers in passing to a telephone survey she and others appear to have conducted with more than one hundred local employers, who were asked how they would view a job applicant with a qualification in Women's Studies (Stearns 1994: 69, n. 2), but unfortunately no results from this potentially important work appear.

5   At Deakin University and the University of Otago, this involved surveying first-year students; at Monash, where Women's Studies courses commence in the second year, the sample comprised students in the second year of their overall degree program. One hundred fifty students were surveyed; they were predominantly enrolled in generalist degrees such as the bachelor of arts or the bachelor of social science, with small numbers taking Women's Studies as a required component of a vocational degree such as police and justice studies. The survey group included six male students.

6   Ironically, the process of bidding for funds for this research within our university revealed the persistence of some of these prejudices (see Morris 1998). In a debriefing with a senior research colleague after an initial and unsuccessful bid for funding, we were counseled that, while the work was of some merit, it was considered by certain members of the committee to be "political" rather than "intellectual" and to lack "rigor" as a research exercise. At work in this assessment are the dual prejudices against feminist inquiry and against academic consideration of students and their experiences within and beyond the classroom. After an appeal, the research was funded.

7   Interview, June 27, 1999. The graduate's name has been changed to ensure anonymity.

8   Katie Hughes from Victoria University in Melbourne presented evidence at a workshop on new research into Women's Studies students held at Monash University in June 1999 that corroborates our findings on young women's uneasiness with the term "career." The interpretations offered here draw on the discussion that day and on subsequent discussions with students in our programs who were particularly vocal on the impact of negative images of "career women" in the media and in popular culture.

Strangers in the Classroom

In the university where I teach, the Women's Studies program is "un-housed"; it is not under the aegis of any particular department. While this fact engenders a minor irritation as regards access to departmental services, it also enables a genuine attempt toward interdisciplinarity.[1] The chairs of the program are chosen alternately from the social sciences and the humanities, and the courses are taught by a team of two instructors, each selected from either the social sciences or the humanities. Because the program only offers a minor in Women's Studies, the courses offered are limited to introductory surveys. I belong to the English department and so far have participated in team-taught courses with my colleagues from the social sciences. The experience has led me to explore and reflect on institutional and epistemological concerns of interdisciplinarity as they are manifested in the space of a Women's Studies classroom.

Given the insistence that instructors from diverse disciplines teach the Women's Studies courses, the program assumes an equality among the disciplines, so that no single one asserts priority over the others. This assumption of parity is supported by my experience and observation: Junior and senior faculty members tend to team up in accordance with their status, thus removing one serious obstacle to equivalence. The premise of equality is further bolstered by our quotidian, common-sense beliefs that despite disparate histories, goals, languages, and methodologies, the various disciplines can still communicate harmoniously in a classroom that focuses on women. The operative term here is, of course, "women," which, despite its centrality to the whole concern, remains largely undefined. This lack of definition, however, does not automatically grant it a limitless amplification. In fact, the term functions as a restraining mechanism. In other words, the anarchic freedom promised by an undefined term paradoxically confines both the students and the instructors to fairly narrow bounds in a Women's Studies classroom.

The reasons for this self-imprisonment are ideological and pragmatic, and, I believe, related to the founding premise of an interdisciplinary Women's Studies. That is, the initial impetus for forming a program that dealt exclusively with women arose out of the recognition that the various disciplines had hitherto ignored or marginalized women. There had been a widespread feeling that the academic structure, the systems and methods of knowledge acquisition and dissemination, and the routines for establishing precedence among various objects of study within a discipline had all been indifferent to the concerns and issues relating specifically to women. So, for instance, the social sciences had habitually dismissed the effects of cultural changes and of social, political, and economic policies on women's lives; had overlooked the strategies developed by women within familial structures to cope with and adjust to the changing circumstances; and had discounted any serious research into the role played by social, economic, political, and cultural institutions to limit and restrict the participation of women.

History, as a discipline, presented an even stronger case for change. Not only did its content for the most part neglect the lives and contributions of women, but even its interpretive and analytical framework functioned to maintain the status quo. The system of periodization, for example, by which different eras were named after rulers or after activities traditionally associated with men, such as wars, served implicitly to devalue the achievements of women. The research into the effects of major events—revolutions, vast changes in economic structures—on the general populace was limited to studying the changes wrought only in the lives of men, because it was assumed that women's conditions and status changed accordingly.[2] Studies in literature followed a similar trajectory. Barring a few token exceptions, notably from the nineteenth century, female authors had been systematically undervalued and understudied. It was not until after the first half of this century that any serious attention was directed to writings by and about women. The systems of evaluation, which pronounced on the excellence or otherwise of a given piece of literature, were maintained and administered by men who elevated their personal likes and dislikes to the status of the universal, consigning those writings that failed to conform to their expectations to the ranks of the frivolous or the tedious.

Feminist recognition of the enormous lacunae concerning women within all the disciplines was compounded by our dissatisfaction at disciplinary divisions. These boundaries that set history and sociology, or literature and anthropology, apart from each other frustrated any attempts to gain an integrated understanding of the condition of women. In fact, interdisciplinarity became our watchword precisely because it was felt that a redressing of intradisciplinary problems would not lead to any appreciable change in academic structures. That is, even if attention were paid to women within each discipline, this would take the form of merely adding another item to the other topics—a token gesture aimed at short-term conciliation. The borderlines that functioned to demarcate fiefdoms of knowledge seemed as arbitrarily conceived as those that had delimited public and private spheres, academic and activist work. The first radical flush of feminism was impelled by a passionate commitment toward an undermining of such divisions that had contributed to exclusion and disfranchisement of women.

I beg your indulgence for going over well-trodden ground here, but I want to ensure that my critique of the Women's Studies project is not understood as a cavalier dismissal of the problems that Women's Studies sought to address. The situations that I have briefly alluded to certainly warranted the need for interdisciplinary courses in Women's Studies that would then presumably attempt to redress these imbalances and would articulate a more holistic approach—one that would correspond to our lived realities. For instance, one could envisage a scenario in which students are taught about women in the past from a historical perspective, presented with the anthropological research on women in other cultures, and asked to analyze literary texts by and about women. But even this simple formulation is, as I am sure you have recognized, fraught with problems. The formulation itself, calmly and unhesitatingly, acknowledges its dependence on an unexamined and unquestioned object of study—that is, "women." But before I discuss the problems arising from the conundrum posed by "woman," I want to explore another site—tangential to the one occupied by disciplinary edifices—that has also contributed to an ersatz sense of security about our conception of "woman." This is the nondisciplinary academic locus—the space where we enact our daily rituals of social pleasantries and inquiries into one another's work and research interests, and where we attend those committee meetings that are not necessarily connected to our disciplines.[3]

Within these spaces, those of us who are involved with the project of Women's Studies or with research on women participate in creating an implicit conviction that we are all bound by a sense of solidarity. Given our history of acrimonious engagements at times with various institutional structures—academic and political—this feeling of alliance seems almost like a reflexive response. Most of us, either as graduate students or as junior faculty members, participated in the various movements that had challenged the existing disciplinary and academic structures to demarginalize Women's Studies. And all of us, I am sure, have numerous anecdotes and personal experiences that can attest to the myriad problems and obstacles in establishing or being involved in Women's Studies programs and departments—engaging with an indifferent and occasionally hostile institutional administration, as well as having to counter the mildly amused or furtively contemptuous attitude of our peers and faculty members who were not convinced of the worth of such an enterprise and viewed it as a frivolous exercise that drained much needed resources from other areas.

Thus, from a certain point of view, the strictly academic sphere, as well as the social and institutional spheres, can be seen as complicit in maintaining an environment that has devalued any work by and on women. This is assuredly not to suggest that there was some massive, well-coordinated conspiratorial strategy that was impelled by a firm commitment to refusing women proper recognition and space. Rather, it is to suggest that the cultural and political practices current at the time,[4] combined with our personal experiences, led to an insistent perception that it was merely on account of our identity as women that our contributions were being dismissed or ignored. Certainly, some of the objections to the establishment of Women's Studies programs may have been motivated by deeply held altruistic principles of humanism or Marxism, but our ability to make these fine distinctions was clouded by the overwhelming sense of discrimination that we faced. Given this atmosphere, it is no wonder that "woman" became a talisman that drew us to a unified identity—one that would repress all differences that could weaken this solidarity.

In other words, the term "woman" that actuates our courses in the various Women's Studies departments is a cultural construct born out of our sense of social and textual disaffiliation. The nodal point around which our research and teaching has been organized is given part of its authority, in a paradoxical move, by precisely that structuring gaze of power that we were challenging. Let me be clear: I am not attempting to deny our struggles and achievements, or even our agency in bringing about much needed change. I am merely suggesting that the specific configuration of identity we adopted to carry on these struggles to re-fashion the academy was formulated through a process that was responding partly to the exigencies of the moment. In some ways, the point I am trying to make is extremely simple: We felt discriminated against as women; therefore, we came together as women to overcome this discrimination. It is this "therefore," however—this invocation of a causal relationship—that underwrites the facticity of the particular form of our identity. And we extended this identity to all the women in history, who, we felt, had been cavalierly dismissed by the various disciplines. That is, we engaged in a peculiarly contorted move by first extending the identity of the contemporary moment to the past, then using that past to grant authority to the contemporary identity. Thus, the strategic negotiations we had to make in order to insert ourselves into the various fields of discourse fostered an identity whose authority was based on an assumed pre-given origin.

This assumption of an identity representing "woman" thus provided the initiative to constitute a new program—Women's Studies—whose focus and object of knowledge became this quasi-identity that emerged at a particular ideological moment.[5] However, this object of knowledge owes its ascent precisely to that history which had oppressed it. In some ways, this was a re-enactment of the birth of Athena from the head of Zeusian patriarchy. That is, the division between men and women, a division that had enabled us to unify and agitate under the mantle of womanhood, was itself a result of the masculinist ethos.[6] The sexual divide and the gender divide became significant only in the context of discrimination. Given this trajectory of birth and development, it should come as no surprise that Women's Studies has been constantly under attack from within and without.

Adopting this division as our raison d'etre and imbued with the fervor of rescuing this chimerical identity—woman—from centuries of neglect and oppression, a number of women proceeded to set up Women's

Studies as a viable option within the academy. But significant differences, allied to the vaguely defined notions of the "political" and the "intellectual," were emerging within this group. There were those who were firmly committed to the political import of the project. They saw Women's Studies as fulfilling the mission of the university, a mission that had hitherto remained incomplete due to the massive lacuna in its structure. In other words, Women's Studies would fill a void that had existed ever since the other disciplines had been formalized within the university system in the mid-nineteenth century. The existence of this lack for nearly a hundred years indicated the masculinist character of the university and its prevalent sexism, and Women's Studies would now presumably redress this imbalance.

Subscribing to the structure of other disciplines, but firmly opposed to their contents, this group envisaged Women's Studies as encouraging the types of research and teaching that had so far been overlooked and dismissed. The object of knowledge, the founding principle that would orient an enormous range of research and teaching projects, was this "newly found woman." This object provided the impetus for some unquestionably critical work—unearthing writings by women in the fields of literature and philosophy; viewing the social and economic impact of state policies on the lives on women; bringing women's perspectives to the study of history, anthropology, sociology, and so on; uncovering gender-correct role models for female students; emphasizing the importance of what had been dismissed as women's work; and analyzing the influence of gender stereotypes on impressionable minds. The significance of this work provided an important argument for its support, and during the late 1970s and early '80s, when the universities were enlarging their student base, its rhetoric of responding to the needs of a particular constituency—the female students—assured a favorable response from the administration.

Not everything was coming up roses, however. The narrowness of the "object-woman" that had provided the primary impulse to knowledge was being questioned from a number of directions—most notably by lesbians, women of color, and working-class women, who felt excluded by what was then the primary focus. Although responding to these challenges has been an ongoing process marked frequently by dissension and defensiveness, there have also been positive and significant changes in the original blueprint. Not that any of these changes are easy or particularly peaceful, but the commitment to the political magnitude of this work overcomes—or, at least, suppresses for a while—the expressions of disquietude. It is in this atmosphere of uneasy compromises that the demands for solidarity, for presenting a unified front, become especially compelling. Any project based on an identity that, though nebulous, nevertheless exerts enormous authority runs precisely these risks.

It was precisely this reliance on identity that gave rise to another series of remonstrances pertaining to the direction of Women's Studies. These objections emerged from women who felt that an overemphasis on the political had come at the expense of the intellectual rigor of the projects of Women's Studies. Enamored more by the content than by the structure of other disciplines, and excited by the recent work in fields such as psychoanalysis, literary theory, historiography, post-structuralism, and so on, a number of feminists felt radically dissatisfied with the form of identity politics as practiced by Women's Studies.[7] The fear that such politics would reinscribe an essential identity provided another cause for unease. The problem with voicing these objections, however, was that they could be co-opted, and in some cases they seemed indistinguishable from reactionary criticism coming from academic quarters that were uncomfortable with the larger politics of Women's Studies. The danger in expressing one's discontent with the current trend of Women's Studies—its apparent aspiration to be just another discipline in the university and its creed of identity (albeit one that now tried to take race, class, national origin, and sexual orientation into account)—was that these criticisms could be, and were, deployed to undermine the whole purpose of Women's Studies. That is, the criticisms of those who preferred to dismantle the existing Women's Studies programs in favor of a massive reorganization were motivated by orientations that were radically dissimilar to those who preferred to do away with Women's Studies altogether. The initial purpose, as you recall, was to attack the implicit equation of universal humanism with maleness that had been maintained and disseminated admirably by the university systems. The reactionary attacks on the micro-politics of Women's Studies—its demands for resources, departmental recognition, extra faculty lines for scholarship on women—arose from a misplaced belief that other disciplines were somehow apolitical. Women's studies was thus seen as corrupting the purity of the mission of the university, because practitioners in Women's Studies insisted that politics not only had an integral causal relationship to scholarship, but it also provided an ongoing rationale for further research. The idea that academic work exists in an ivory tower has always been a product of a bowdlerized myth, clung to by those whose self-satisfaction is guaranteed only by a radical ignorance about the intertwining of politics and academe.[8]

Allied with the objections to the focus on identity in a separate Women's Studies discipline were the criticisms of those who felt that such separation would merely marginalize the work, providing an easy escape for those who did not wish to engage with the concerns of and about women in their own teaching and research. Ominous predictions of ghettoization impelled some of us to bring such concerns into the mainstream academic disciplines. This perspective viewed the separate Women's Studies departments and programs as inconsequential, at worst, or as stepping stones in the service of better disciplinary knowledge, at best. The revolutionary fervor of transforming the traditional academic disciplinary structure was forgone in favor of incremental additions to the existing knowledge bases.

To date, there has been no acceptable resolution to the dilemma of all these competing visions for bringing gender equality to the university system. Any resolution that could incorporate all of these perspectives, some of which contradict one another directly, is not quite possible. But these oppositions and disagreements have led to a dissatisfaction with Women's Studies from within Women's Studies itself. An open rupture has been avoided in most instances, but I believe that is merely due to the efforts of some of the non-Women's Studies members of the faculty and administration. In fact, our solidarity is to some extent underwritten by the endless horror stories of amazing sexist behavior and attitudes that still prevail on almost all campuses. Thus, the disagreements and the conflicts among the individuals engaged in Women's Studies are swept under the rug while we stubbornly adhere to a superficial belief in our unity. This illusion of solidarity functions, through the years, almost as a prescriptive requirement, and the collaborative instance of an interdisciplinary Women's Studies classroom becomes the exemplar for this fantasy.

In fact, this particular space seems to present the preferred solution to most of the concerns, because interdisciplinarity by definition contains multiple, and even contradictory, perspectives. But how exactly is this space of an interdisciplinary Women's Studies classroom to be understood? What precisely is supposed to take place here? How will this particular instance of pedagogy engage and negotiate with the various stated and unstated educational purposes of the university? How will the bi- or multidisciplinary character of the classroom be cultivated? These are some of the obdurate questions that refuse to be mollified by our collective conjurations of bonding in sisterhood.

Let us begin with some of these issues: How is an interdisciplinary classroom to be defined so that its aims can be communicated easily to all the constituencies it hopes to attract or mollify? The "University Bulletin" describes the course that I have taught, "Introduction to Women's Studies," as follows:

> An interdisciplinary course which introduces the major ideas and concepts of Women's Studies and a variety of gender-related issues. The course provides theoretical tools by which to understand these issues and creates an interdisciplinary foundation of basic concepts and perspectives in Women's Studies. Drawing upon material from a wide range of disciplines: literature, the arts, sociology, language, linguistics, philosophy, psychology, and history, the course prepares the student for more discipline specific courses on women and gender related issues in these and other fields.

The generalized vagueness and lack of specificity in this description may be due partly to the generic conventions of university-bulletin writing, but it is also the result of an attempt to be as inclusive as possible, to cover all the disciplinary bases without specifying how a particular aim—teaching about women and gender-related issues—is to be attained through a particular approach. The indeterminacy regarding the aims of an interdisciplinary Women's Studies classroom exacerbates the issue. The ideological and methodological aspects blend together in a manner that reminds one of nothing so much as the old dictum, "add woman and stir." But what, one may reasonably wonder, is the desirable outcome from taking a course such as this one? Is our goal to introduce students to the various disciplines? The fact that, according to this description, we are supposed to prepare students for higher-level, discipline-specific courses automatically hierarchizes inter- and mono-disciplinarity—a consequence that nullifies the initial definition.

Similar vagueness—or rather, perplexity—about purposes and methods prevails in many of the descriptions at other universities.[9] The problem lies not so much in specific descriptions as in the very organization of most Women's Studies programs. Most such programs are constituted through a scattershot approach, given the initial paucity of fiscal resources. There are very few full-time faculty in the Women's Studies programs; instead, most of the teaching is done either by professors who have joint appointments (in their home disciplines and Women's Studies) or through the cross-listing of various courses in other disciplines.[10] While this approach may lead to multi- or pluri-disciplinarity, it cannot, by any stretch of imagination, be considered interdisciplinary.

In fact, the model most often adopted in Women's Studies courses is one that Jonathan Arac likens to a shop window—"a place for a collection to be displayed" (Arac 1997: 117)—where knowledge is assembled, exhibited, and consumed rather than advanced. This model ensures the convenience of the consumer, without enabling any consideration of inter-relationships that may exist among the objects arrayed in the different windows, other than the fact that they are located under one roof— that is, a format like the one I alluded to earlier, in which the students are introduced to historical, sociological, anthropological, or literary research on women by instructors who are primarily based in these diverse disciplines.[11] This pluralistic, eclectic proposition—"You deal with work; I'll deal with myth and legend; she can talk about the *!Kung* women"—may seem to showcase an impressive variety of approaches, but how specifically is this course to be distinguished from any of the others that we teach individually in our various disciplines?

While teaching *The Mill on the Floss* in my Victorian literature course, for instance, I focus on the text: on its economic and historical context, its use of language, and the literary traditions on which it draws, and I suggest comparisons with the work of other Victorian writers. This is very similar, methodologically, to the Women's Studies course. Both presume an object of knowledge—women in one, and Eliot's novel in another— and proceed to dispense various ways of understanding this object. But this exercise in analogy reveals the impossibility at the core of Women's Studies if it patterns its methodology on traditional disciplines. Although Eliot's text may legitimately be considered an object that requires comprehension and assessment and, in the best of all possible outcomes, leads to a reevaluation of the self that is engaged in this interpretive exercise, extending a similarly enclosed status on "woman," while no doubt expedient, seems nevertheless to be at odds with one's academic and personal integrity. In other words, the term "The Mill on the Floss" is an easily recognizable allusion; it refers directly to a text that, although resistant to any simple categorizations, nevertheless manifests a singular, unique identity, even if we consider that identity to lie only in its physical materiality—the printing, the pages, the title, and so on. The term "woman," however, signifies nothing so much as the elusive incomprehensibility of its referent. Every attempt to impose a rubric of identity comes at the cost of massive exclusions that, in fact, betray the project itself.

This sense of betrayal, I feel, permeates our courses with a constant low-level disquietude, a disquietude that reflects quite unmistakably the unresolved foundational premise of our project. In "The Impossibility of Women's Studies," Wendy Brown suggests that "Women's Studies as a contemporary institution . . . may be politically and theoretically incoherent, as well as tacitly conservative—incoherent because by definition it circumscribes uncircumscribable 'women' as an object of study, and conservative because it must resist all objections to such circumscription if it is to sustain that object of study as its raison d'etre" (1997: 83).

Of course, as Brown acknowledges, this charge of incoherence and conservatism can be laid against all the knowledge projects—Women's Studies, African American studies, and gay and lesbian studies—that emerged from the political movements of the 1960s and expressed a trenchant impatience with the existing academic structures. What began as a deeply radical move—drawing attention to hitherto ignored modalities of being—developed, unfortunately, in the direction of essentializing formulations. In fact, the crystallization of these courses as uncertain and muddled about their purpose while adhering stubbornly to a cautious and circumspect functionality is, ironically, a consequence of their initial radical potential. That is, the very organizations of identity and discipline that were the premier objects of attack became incorporated in precisely those courses that were introduced to rectify the problem.[12]

One of the main problems for Women's Studies and its deflection of radical possibilities lies, I believe, in the impression that the traditional disciplines have an unquestionably secure status, and that it is in our best interests to emulate them. By security of status I am not referring to the benefits of departmentalization (though the loss of such benefits certainly adds a shade of resentment) but, rather, to the perception that research and teaching in the traditional disciplines requires no external justification. This perception relies on selective and self-promoting histories of the disciplines that assert, mendaciously, that the benefits of studying, say, Plato or Adam Smith or quantum physics are paradoxically both self-evident and self-enclosed. That is, research and study in any of these areas adds to the sum of human knowledge—or, at least, to the cognitive capacity of the individual engaged in this study. Hence, their self-evident benefits need no special pleading. And the wisdom gleaned from these areas of study is timeless and universal; there exists no cause to doubt their significance by allying them with specific and local political concerns. In other words, any contingent political advantage that may be derived from these fields of study is merely incidental to their true worth. Just an extra layer of frosting, so to speak.

These assertions suggest that the establishment and growth in the traditional disciplines occurred as a result of teleological progression: As the world became more complex, the human mind naturally gravitated toward sustained study in these fields. It is a nice fable to tell ourselves, especially in these days of dwindling resources and prestige for the academy.[13] However, an overwhelming reliance on the provisional politics of nationalism, statecraft, and the corporate world for the development and direction of research in the traditional disciplines can be gainsaid only by those who have been seduced by visions of stark intellectuality residing chastely in academe's ivory towers.[14] Our virginity, I regret to announce, was always already lost.

Clearly, Women's Studies is too close to its nascence to have developed fully such comforting narratives or to have them widely accepted within the academic mainstream. But perhaps what is even more significant is that the desire to have a narrative of one's own, one that would naturalize a political-cultural moment, is continually frustrated by the commitment to the stated purposes of Women's Studies. It is precisely this philosophical turn, which naturalized exclusion and discrimination within the traditional disciplines, that provided one of the main impetuses for the creation of Women's Studies. And indeed, one of the primary causes for the emergence of the interdisciplinary character of Women's Studies was the necessity to interrupt and suspend these justifying narratives by bringing them into a dialogue with one another. Thus, it is not merely the staffing requirements that mandate interdisciplinarity in Women's Studies. Rather, interdisciplinarity constitutes a principle that is integral to the whole project. The fact that the desire to be consistent to one's intellectual commitments is perpetually at odds with the desire for a secure space where the significance of one's work is taken for granted suggests one of the reasons that the interdisciplinary format in Women's Studies may not have been an unqualified success.[15]

But there are other, more obvious reasons that effective interdisciplinarity has not been an easily attainable goal for Women's Studies. The dissension generated by the move toward particularity and heterogeneity, as opposed to a universal identity for women, has led to a loss of faith in any overarching explanation dealing with women and the purpose of Women's Studies. This absence of a comprehensive meta-outline that might have comfortably supported the slotting of various traditional disciplines at numerous junctures has compounded the problems for interdisciplinarity. In such a situation, the incommensurability between disparate disciplinary objects and methodologies may, in fact, lead to a situation in which the various disciplines barely engage in any conversation with one another. This incompatibility exists not merely among, but also within, many disciplines. Contemporary academe seems to be characterized by nothing so much as internal conflicts within each discipline concerning the preferred modes and rationales to strengthen and increase the influence of said discipline. Acrimonious debates concerning epistemological assumptions and paradigms of knowledge formations within each discipline erupt with increasing frequency during departmental meetings, which are purportedly called to discuss curricular additions or new hires. These multilayered intra- and interdisciplinary polarizations magnify the obstacles in maintaining a fluent and equable conversation among the disciplines.

The social-scientific aspect of Women's Studies, for instance, focuses on the macro-structures, such as society, politics, or economy, that have contributed to the unfavorable condition of women. There is an implicit assumption that a recognition and comprehension of how these structures have functioned can direct us to an evaluation of the changes needed to rectify the oppression and victimization experienced by women. The theoretical readings and qualitative analyses in the social sciences are concretized by the statistical and quantitative data, which help to anchor the academic concepts of gender discrimination to material specificities. Many scholars in these fields are concerned with empirical research, in field studies that help in the gathering of data and evidence regarding the condition of women.

The emphasis on and exploration of these "objects"—that is, the societal and political structures—lends an outward dimension to the social sciences; the histories of these disciplines demonstrate the academic profession's desire to influence policymaking, if not radically to reconfigure the state. However, the significance of the impact of these sciences on the sociopolitical sphere depends on the belief that social science research is conducted in an objective manner based on positive, verifiable, and empirical data. The political establishment that the social scientists seek to influence seems more easily impressed by research that pretends to the status of "objective hard science" and its concomitant claim to "truth" than by qualitative research that foregrounds its subjective biases at the outset. (This suspicion of interpretation apparently does not extend to quantitative work, which is then presumably granted an interpretation-free zone of existence.) The political considerations, such as which type of research is liable to be heard favorably and bring about speedier results in the legislative arena, play a not inconsiderable role in determining the relative value of quantitative and qualitative research.

Indeed, as Jeanne Marceck reports, the social sciences have a highly elaborated scientific method of procedure that enables their practitioners to insist upon the factual veracity of their conclusions. "Many psychologists," she says, for instance, "are deeply distrustful of interpretive ways of working, especially because these ways of working lack procedures for verification equivalent to those claimed by psychology" (1995: 118). For the feminists working in this field, the choices seem rather limited. They can either call into question the methods for data collection and the arrangements and content of some of the questionnaires used for eliciting responses, and suggest procedures for improving statistical analyses and making them more responsive to gender concerns, or they can dispense with quantification completely and join with many humanities-based scholars in a generalized suspicion toward all claims of positivistic truth and objectivity. The latter move, however, marginalizes them within their own disciplinary specialization. The material conditions that structure the academic social sciences, the systems of reward and promotion, publication in top-tier journals, the ability to attract grants, and more are conceived so that empirical, positivist research based on mathematical and scientific models is encouraged and promoted. As Joe Feagin claims in "Soul-Searching in Sociology: Is the Discipline in Crisis?": "Survey and other research projects using advanced statistical methods . . . rarely raised fundamental questions about major institutions, [hence] they were favored by the large underwriters of social research" (1999). Because prestige and influence are both intimately linked to these material conditions, scholars working against the grain may be sacrificing one of the few benefits of working in academe. Thus, philosophical material, and political considerations all seem to work in concert to elevate particular modes of research within the social sciences—modes that attempt to exclude the ambiguities of interpretation—over others.[16]

The humanities seem to present an image that is almost a mirror-reversal of the social sciences. Although similar fractures—between archival researchers and empirical histories, on the one hand, and theories of interpretation and modes of historiography, on the other—threaten a radical split within the various disciplines constituting the humanities, these fractures nevertheless carry a valence that stands in marked opposition to the social sciences. In the fields of literature and art history, for instance, institutional and professional rewards in the form of high salaries, "star" status, publications in top-tier journals, and so on, accrue to those engaged in theoretical, interpretive work; all of this serves implicitly to devalue the others. But the difference between humanities and social sciences does not lie merely in the manner in which the academic-prestige sweepstakes are conducted. From the perspective of social sciences, the humanities, with their relentless concentration on alternative textual interpretations in literature, philosophy, and art history, and their concurrent reliance on personal and subjective responses, tend to be rather narcissistic. Indeed, the focus is more on self-enhancement than on the improvement of society. Virginia Sapiro's distinction between text- and non-text-centered disciplines becomes particularly crucial here in our considerations of interdisciplinarity.[17] Speaking from the perspective of a political scientist, she explains, "the written text [for some of us] is only a medium for holding a conversation about how to solve problems that must be understood in their material dimensions" (Sapiro 1995: 303); she then proceeds to identify a pivotal distinction between those who devote themselves to "understanding what Rousseau or Plato or Marx 'really meant'" and those who try to "figure out the potential for political community by reading smart and thoughtful writers like Rousseau, Plato, or Marx" (Sapiro 1995: 308, n. 25). At this point, I might well be tempted to retort that you cannot use these texts for their recommendations unless you know what they "really meant," but the smug impudence of this rejoinder does nothing substantial to deflect the accusations of political ineffectiveness.

It is, after all, true that we do not read philosophical or literary texts only to intervene in political or economic structures. Every encounter with a work of art is an encounter with the particular; what makes the artwork individual and distinctive is precisely that which resists being subsumed within a generalizable theory with an explicit social or political agenda. I am not denying the effect of political considerations in the election of a specific work, its status within the field, or in what one chooses to emphasize while interpreting it, or even the political import of certain works. I am merely pointing out that the task of studying these works does not authorize any direct intervention in the larger political-socioeconomic arena. This version of politics within humanities constitutes a secondary effect. One can assume, in fact, that social progress or reform will follow, but only in the wake of a more complete and deeply engaged exploration of the subject who is involved in humanistic endeavors.

Further, research in humanities relies less on empirical evidence than on conceptual formations, and the focus splits almost equally among form, style, and language, on the one hand, and the content of the texts, on the other. So, for instance, poetry and fiction by and about women may attest to the specific problems faced by women, but they are also available for a completely different interpretation. We can all remember various texts that deplore violence against women but represent the violence itself in language that is alluring and seductive. The way in which metaphoric expressions might undercut any overt messages of gender oppression, or the manner in which conflicting points of view regarding the proper role of women are represented, elevating one of these perspectives through the deployment of evocative poetic or narrative structures, are all significant areas of inquiry within the humanities. At some level, the purpose of the humanities is a commitment to a constant struggle to hone the interlocution between the text (howsoever defined) and the subject engaged in reading and interpreting it.

Given these irreducible differences of aims, a team-taught, interdisciplinary classroom can easily turn into a site for disciplinary rivalries, indicated either by a studied silence or constant interruptions of one instructor by the other. The situation further deteriorates when a literary critic, as Gayatri Chakravorty Spivak says, "makes like a political economist or a psychoanalyst . . . speaking as an insider of her discipline in terms of her fantasy about what kinds of social value those other disciplines carry" (1989: 221). The sin does not lie in the trespass, per se; it lies rather in an arrogant reliance on a facile and superficial understanding of the aims and orientations of disciplines other than one's own. Although this repeats a common complaint of harrumphing mono-disciplinarians, Spivak seems to be suggesting a more generous proposition: to read and understand empirical, quantitative analysis without prejudging it as epistemologically suspect. Although Spivak mentions literary critics by name—no doubt because English departments have traditionally been more receptive to attempts at interdisciplinarity under the aegis of cultural studies, and hence there are greater numbers of literary critics "making like" knowledgeable assessors of other disciplines—this offense of bad and under-rehearsed performances may in fact be enacted by scholars in all fields.[18] Interruptions such as, "What does this political scientist's use of the metaphoric structure reveal about her subjective biases?" or "If everything is language, then how can we make any political gains?" may turn into intensely rewarding discussions, but more often they have a tendency to backfire disastrously, especially in an introductory-course setting.

One possible remedy would be to divide the semester into two separate halves—each devoted to either the social sciences or the humanities. This division would not only be pragmatic; it would have the added advantage of serving the cause of disciplinary collegiality. It would also, however, almost totally undermine the basic premise of interdisciplinarity. But before we throw up our hands in despair, let us explore an alternative solution. The aims of interdisciplinarity, we must remember, cannot be reconciled with the traditional purposes of the participating disciplines. Therefore, the attempt to maintain the same structures and aims that are current in mono-disciplinary classrooms defeats, at the outset, the cause of interdisciplinarity. After all, interdisciplinarity presumes that the traditional ways of forming each autonomous discipline should be subverted, and that we should be given access to new and excitingly novel methods of producing knowledge. And in an interdisciplinary classroom, it is imperative, I believe, that we attempt accommodation among the concerned disciplines.

This harmony can only be achieved, however, by severely curtailing the contexts and histories of the various disciplines, so that each becomes curiously truncated. The delimitation of the disciplines so they can converse may, in fact, lead to an unfortunate emphasis on the more conservative aspects of each discipline. Each instructor could rely on the most easily understood, clearly bounded, and widely prevalent concepts within the discipline in order to facilitate interdisciplinary dialogue. That is, using only the most familiar approaches within the discipline may prevent a fragmentation of focus and ensure that instructors from other disciplines are able to contribute to the class discussions. So, for instance, literary texts might be read exclusively in relation to women's social and historical realities at the time in which they were written or as a reflection on the lives of their authors. This approach dovetails nicely with the social sciences and possesses an additional advantage of constraining the humanities so that they clearly indicate their use value. In other words, the literary text is used merely as a hook to explore historical and or contemporary sociology, political science, economics, and psychology—not, say, in terms of its relationship to the various literary traditions—to give just one example of what is occluded in such a classroom. However, this amputation situates the materials from humanities merely as other, perhaps more fancifully written, examples of the various social issues that are under discussion. So literature from different temporal or spatial periods is used to illustrate the socioeconomic situations of women in the past or in different areas of the world.

In a classroom where the subjectivities of the humanities hold sway, the social sciences might be reduced to the status of handmaidens to literature and philosophy. They might become a mere addendum to the central conceptualizing theories of humanities, present in the classroom only to be mined for their quantitative analyses and raw data. Such a classroom would adopt an imperially appropriative gesture, regarding the social sciences merely as tools of quick reference. Facts, such as average income or job opportunities for women in a particular period, might be demanded merely to round out the discussion of a literary text set in that particular period. The relationships among the various socioeconomic theories, the causes of their emergence, the inferences they draw, and the assumptions and premises that underlie their methodologies and conclusions might all be completely ignored. These scenarios of disciplinary dominance are hard to avoid; even the most rigorous balancing of syllabi might not lead to a perfect equivalence. Despite our wishes for success in interdisciplinary pursuits, we have, for the most part, been trained in our own disciplinary fields—having initially chosen those academic areas for their power to explain and interpret the world for us. I find it incredibly arduous to forgo my beliefs in the causal power of my discipline, humanities, and in particular, literary and cultural studies, to explain historiography or social-scientific writings. Awareness that a selfish particularity undermines any interdisciplinary project is not often enough to resist the seductions of justifying our academic choices to our colleagues and students. I find myself irresistibly drawn to formulations such as Derek Attridge's "literature is a term . . . capable of destabilizing the discourses and institutions within which it has its being" (1988: 17). Thus, literature, by definition, from this supremely chauvinistic and blinkered perspective, apparently transcends the particularities of other disciplines that have as their objects the various social institutions.

However, my colleagues trust as firmly the ability of their disciplines to resolve and illuminate the concerns that arise in other areas of inquiry. In *The Sociological Imagination*, C. Wright Mills presents perhaps the strongest version of the significance of his discipline as compared to the others: "What fiction, what journalism, what artistic endeavor can compete with the historical reality and political facts of our times? . . . It is the social and historical reality that men want to know, and often they do not find contemporary literature an adequate means of knowing it. They yearn for facts, they search for their meanings, they want a 'big picture' in which they can believe and within which they can come to understand themselves" (1959: 17). Mills's touching confidence in the ability of sociology to respond to all the deeper yearnings of humanity, his partisan advocacy of social science as the discipline par excellence, is countered by similarly parochial assertions about the universality of other disciplines.

This optimism regarding our own particular disciplines pervades an interdisciplinary classroom. Even as we engage with particular units of study—trying to disengage ourselves from disciplinary chauvinism—the biases are almost impossible to eliminate. Every mini-explanation we proffer, or any path of inquiry that we suggest to our students, is based on larger paradigms, on underlying assumptions that are implicit in our discourses. To participate in the classroom by presenting units of study to the students in a piecemeal fashion in order to avoid making these biases explicit may in fact be a disservice both to interdisciplinarity and to our students. However, to reveal all our disciplinary inclinations may suggest to the students that they need to make a choice between the disciplines and their advocate-instructors—an outcome that is equally unwelcome.

Where do our loyalties lie? Is part of our unstated mission, especially in an introductory course at a university that does not offer a major in Women's Studies, to attract students to our own particular specialties? Do we conceive of ourselves as professors of philosophy or anthropology teaching Women's Studies? Or as women teaching this course? Which department provides us with our primary professional identity? Disciplinary politics seem to merge almost imperceptibly into departmental politics. How do we determine the degree of commitment we have to Women's Studies and to our home department? Is teaching in Women's Studies programs just a way to make us more tenurable? More valuable to our home departments and the administration?[19] Or does it in fact make us more vulnerable to those who resent our release time from teaching in the home department? Some of these concerns relate immediately to the material structures of the university and the institutional systems of reward and punishment; others take on a much vaster significance. Although it is true that we are partly interpellated by these material structures, our subjectivities—our own conceptions of self and identity—also bear enormously on the disposition of the Women's Studies classroom. I don't pretend to have the answers to all these questions, but I would like to point out that the spurious unity assumed by the course is fragmented by the conditions of its function.

Even if we hypothesize that most of these doubts are somehow miraculously left at the door and do not play a vital part in the interaction among the instructors, the responses of the students add another crucially significant factor to our consideration of an interdisciplinary Women's Studies classroom. Their reactions to the instructors based perhaps on earlier contacts, or on their history with one of the disciplines, tend to inflect classroom dynamics substantially.

The contradictory expectations of students and faculty do indeed lend a constant undercurrent of anxiety to most classrooms; however, in courses within Women's Studies or gay and lesbian studies, whose justification lies presumably in identitarian formulations, these contradictory expectations assume a formidable import. Courses that are based on corporeal or sexual identity evoke a corresponding desire on the part of the students for validation of that identity. Whereas the faculty attempts to impart discipline-based knowledge, the students may oppose the academic instruction in favor of experiential explorations. This demand by students can also lead to an imbalance within an interdisciplinary context. The humanities, with their emphasis on the exploration of the subject, at times respond more easily to the students' desires than do the social sciences. It is harder to insert oneself into economic or political macro-systems than into novels or poetry that have been chosen in part to corroborate and confirm the experiences of young women.

Students' expectations in Women's Studies place another, less tangible burden on the faculty. Students' need for validation is coupled with implicit solicitations for affection, nurturing, a sense of solidarity, and maybe even some informal therapy. Just as we initially conceived of Women's Studies as promising a radical departure from traditional institutional structures, so do some of the students. They aspire toward an intimate pedagogical scene that would counter the impersonal, distant, and detached academic instruction in which they have hitherto been engaged. Although both the students and the teachers participate in this desire for a learning that is personally supportive, this desire places enormous burdens on faculty who have not necessarily been trained or may not have the requisite resources to fulfill these functions.

The considerable methodological differences between the humanities and the social sciences pose a significant hurdle to any effort to mesh them with each other. For the most part, the emphasis in humanities is on interpretation, whereas within the social sciences a much weightier burden falls on information. Although, as all of us recognize, neither of these labels can necessarily be applied as sole distinctive characteristics to all work within the disciplines—a lot of research in humanities is information-based, just as social-scientific work may be interpretive— these divergent modes become more sharply defined in a classroom setting. The methodological differences evoke varying responses from the students, as well. A number of them feel reassured by the presentation of data and information about the condition of women in society. Despite the depressing statistics and reports, the factual basis of this knowledge grants them an illusion of mastery. The essays they read propose a conceptual thesis, provide various examples to which these conceptualizations can be applied, and then support the conclusions of the authors with fieldwork, data, or statistics. The scientific organization makes knowledge appear solid and tangible, something that can be grasped with intelligent effort and memory and later reproduced for the examinations. This mode of teaching also comforts them because of its resemblance to their learning experiences in the other courses that they take in natural and social sciences, in business, and in engineering, among others.

It is a smaller number of students who respond positively to a mode of learning that places part of the burden of interpretation on them. Struggling with a text that confounds one with multiple interpretations, whose silences and ruptures refuse any singular explanation, and whose obscurity is not immediately dispelled by one presumed to know can be an extremely frustrating experience. The instructor's insistence on engaging with the rhetorical complexities may often provoke the plaintive query: "But what does this have to do with Women's Studies?" Well, nothing really, unless you want to make the feeble argument that attention to all aspects of a woman's craft is part of the syllabus. It is not the case, of course, that rhetorical or linguistic complexities do not provide an entry into the labyrinthine meanings of a text—a text chosen for its relevance to women—but that case is harder to make in the face of students' expectations of an immediate and direct link.

Our approaches to estimating grades for students' written work are also influenced by these methodological differences. A well-organized essay that refers to all the relevant issues covered in class and in reading assignments on a particular topic and is able to articulate precisely the difference between, say, hermaphroditism and transsexualism, may be graded higher by one instructor than an essay that misses some of these points, is fuzzy on certain specific definitions, but engages with one particular reading assignment in greater depth and uncovers complexities not touched on in class discussions. Evaluating the comparative merit of such essays is a constant concern in all teaching situations; however, in the courses that one teaches singly, one is able to impart to the students the valuation that one places on these differing modes of essay writing. This easy communicative clarity is rendered considerably more complex and obscure in an interdisciplinary, team-taught environment. I am not suggesting for a moment that compromises cannot be made, or that negotiations among the instructors do not lead to a satisfactory outcome. I am merely indicating the various hurdles and pitfalls that await all—the students and the teachers—involved in this project.

Most of the practical and tangible classroom issues can be, and for the most part are, amenable to pragmatic resolutions through conversations and compromises by all the involved parties. But these resolutions function rather as impromptu maneuvers to avoid any straining of collegial relationships. All of us involved in such collaborative ventures learn to read when and where it is necessary to defer to the other so as to circumvent open ruptures. But ensuring a relatively harmonious classroom for a semester does not resolve the fundamental tensions and contradictions that are built into the project of an interdisciplinary Women's Studies course. Perhaps some of these anxieties might be allayed if we ensured that the faculty had more than a passing familiarity with the other discipline present in the classroom—that is, study the aims, philosophies, and methodologies, as well as the major current conflicts and debates, of the other discipline or disciplines. At least then we could ensure that we would not pass as experts on the strength of mere acquaintance. That, however, will be possible only if we are given release time in the semester preceding the one in which we teach the course, an outcome whose desirability is exceeded only by the impossibility of its ever coming to fruition.

Even if this option were to be implemented, however, it would not function as a panacea for all the problems. Perhaps we need to rethink the whole project and move firmly away from "woman as object of knowledge." We could return to our founding impulses and attempt an understanding of the sexist biases and assumptions built into the various disciplines. In fact, as best as I recall, the most engaged and exciting class sessions during our team-taught introductory Women's Studies course were those that did not focus directly on women as the object of study. Instead, the object was an author, a theory, or a particular approach within the larger field of Women's Studies, which the two of us analyzed variously in accordance with our disciplinary expertise. These exercises enabled us to enact our disciplinary differences in a contained structure and facilitated the students' access to the complexity of the learning process.

Although my experience and the positive responses of the students endorse this approach, it also unfortunately perpetuates the predicament of Women's Studies if it attempts to gain the stature of a full-fledged discipline. My suggestion foregrounds the mainstream disciplines as the objects of study, though focusing meticulously and explicitly on their aporetic structures. It would mean that we would ruefully have to relinquish our dreams of a comforting narrative that sanctions us as the authority on women—as if such a beast were possible. But perhaps this loss of status as experts within a specialized field might be countered by the expansion of the purview that Women's Studies would henceforth command. The Women's Studies program would be in academe, but not of it—at a slant, as it were, to the mainstream disciplinary formations. Our syllabi would include discussions of the histories and the current structures of various disciplines, their rationales and philosophies, disassembling and exposing their presumptions as and when needed. This would lead not so much to interdisciplinary as to anti-disciplinarity engagements. What is common to all the disciplines are the aporias, the gaps in their structures, the organizing principles that have been forgotten or ignored in the name of professionalism. Women's Studies, along with other similarly oriented knowledge projects, such as African American studies, postcolonial studies, and gay and lesbian studies, would initiate a displacement in the conception and organization of knowledge in contemporary academe. Maybe that is the direction we need to pursue.

Notes

I thank Jessie Daniels, Sharryn Kasmir, Simona Sawhney, and Robyn Wiegman for their extremely helpful comments, not only on the drafts of the essay, but also during the numerous conversations I held with them on this topic. This essay has been particularly difficult to write, mainly because I have had to negotiate between extrapolating from my own involvement in Women's Studies courses and speculating about classroom settings that may not have corresponded to my impressions. It is precisely the felicity of my experience that has granted me the space and freedom to explore and investigate the concerns and the complications associated with teaching an interdisciplinary Women's Studies course. Had it been otherwise, I believe I would have been silenced at the outset by the fear of coming across as reproachful and aggrieved.

1   I do not mean to deny the troubling issues of status or privilege that this homelessness entails. For the moment, however, I am focusing on a different concern.

2   A number of excellent works dealing with women's perspectives on historiography are now available. For more on this topic, see, for instance Scott 1988; Gadol-Kelly 1976.

3   I fully realize the enormity of this site, to which my meager references have not done justice.

4   This refers to the appalling lack of representation in the governing bodies, the restrictive law-and-order situations that implicitly encouraged domestic violence, the cul-

tural mandates such as the unspoken and sometimes explicit commands to be more like men if we wanted to be taken seriously, and so on.

5 I use the term "quasi-identity" because it submerges other aspects—race, sexual orientation, class, national origin—in favor of an identity based solely on sexual characteristics.

6 See also Lyotard 1989.

7 Some of this dissatisfaction may have also arisen from the condescension with which some of the highly respected members of the academy viewed the overtly political nature of Women's Studies. A more-intellectual-than-thou response, so to speak.

8 In an otherwise excellent essay detailing the ills besetting the Women's Studies programs, Wendy Brown seems at times to be criticizing Women's Studies for not being more like the other disciplines. According to Brown, the problem with a political argument justifying the Women's Studies programs is that "it renders dispensable a deep and serious intellectual basis for Women's Studies . . . these arguments affirm the status of Women's Studies as something distinct from the rest of the university's intellectual mission for research and teaching. In effect, by admitting its thoroughly politicized rationale, these defenses replicate the low value that hostile outsiders often accuse Women's Studies of attaching to the caliber of arguments and to intellectual life as a whole" (1997: 91). Not only do these statements assume an opposition between intellectual and political work, accepting unquestioningly the self-definition of mainstream disciplines, but they also expose a strangely naive conception of the mission of the university in society. Brown's valorization of disciplinary knowledge rests on rather shaky foundations. For an early articulation of the intermingling of politics and academe see *The Conflict of the Faculties* (1992), in which Immanuel Kant argues that philosophy should be removed from the political constraints placed on all the other disciplines.

9 The description of the Women's Studies major at the University of Louisville moves uneasily between the methodological and the ideological. The curriculum emphasizes "developing interdisciplinary methods of analysis" without specifying exactly how that is to be achieved, and in a statement regarding the criteria for inclusion as a Women's Studies course suggests that "the course must promote a critical approach to learning [and] the content and method of the course must fall within the general questions, concerns, and methodologies of Women's Studies as a field" (www.louisville.edu/a-s/requirements.html). The ambiguity surrounding these statements— What exactly is the methodology of Women's Studies?—is repeated in a number of other such course descriptions. See the descriptions of the State University of New York at Albany and Stanford University for similar instances.

10 See Boxer 1998 for more data on the state of Women's Studies programs in the U.S. academy.

11 To a certain extent, of course, the "shop-window" is not necessarily limited to interdisciplinary classrooms. As we all know, many large undergraduate classes are organized around a similar model—the instructor feeding her students with the fruits of her research and training, which are then regurgitated by the students in their papers and examinations.

12 This mainstreaming of Women's Studies was not achieved without serious problems and protests along the way. As Boxer relates: "The nation's first Women's Studies program, at San Diego State, split even in its first year, 1970–71," over conflicts relating to program control. The faculty who saw themselves primarily as community activists resigned en masse because they believed that their "collective decision-making and teaching practices would be replaced . . . by professionalism and career interest would overcome political commitment" (1998: 164).

13 We seem to be hard-wired for such selective remembering. Witness the persistence of the Horatio Alger story in the cultural imaginary. Any narrative that enables us to explain our success, or the success of the field to which we have chosen to devote ourselves, in terms of inherent worthiness seems bound to win over one that suggests that luck, being in a particular cultural moment, larger political considerations, media manipulations, or other factors have contributed to our achievements.

14 The formation of scientific societies in the seventeenth and eighteenth centuries in Western Europe to distinguish their culture from what was viewed as backward, superstitious cultures prevailing in the rest of the world; the dependence on Arnold-ian and later Leavisian visions of national culture as exemplified through literature in the nineteenth and early twentieth centuries in England; the funding and research grants available to anthropologists in the twentieth century in Europe and United States to abet state-sponsored foreign policies and domination of other nations; and the current trend toward emphasis on technical competence in the service of trans-national corporations all attest to the immense influence of governments, national politics, and capital on university systems.

15 It should be clear that, for the most part, I have been referring to conditions within the academy. All of us who are affiliated with liberal arts and sciences have to defend and justify our work constantly to the wider public. The practitioners in the newly emerg-ing disciplines in the university, however, have to do this within the scholarly commu-nity as well. For the significance of our work to be taken for granted means that it does not exist on sufferance, with our supporters from other disciplines forever patting themselves on the back for their liberal, egalitarian outlooks. A similar attitude of self-satisfaction at one's open-mindedness, held by, for instance, left-leaning academics toward a scholar of the rise and influence of capitalism would merely reveal the interlocutors as being profoundly lacking in rudimentary knowledge.

16 This tilt, however, is certainly not uniformly apparent for social sciences across the board. Anthropology, for instance, underwent its internal upheaval years ago, and there appears to exist a more equitable system of resource-sharing between the em-pirical and the interpretive branches of scholarship.

17 See Sapiro 1995. Sapiro's essay, along with some of the others in this volume, ex-presses serious dissatisfaction with the pervasive distrust with which humanities' scholars in Women's Studies view the quantitative and empirical research of social scientists.

18 In this connection, Sapiro's assessment of the work of literary critics is particularly instructive. Defending the work of political scientists against attacks by critical theo-rists, she states: "The political theorist who has spent a career focusing on the nature

of the political, the governmental, in all its tangible aspects must have trouble forgetting how the denial of voice and intention can become part of the 'banality of evil,' as Arendt described the character of the Holocaust. Thus, if the empirical urges of political and other social scientists appear banal to those more enveloped in poststructuralism, it is preferable to the more deadly and profoundly painful banalities of life" (Sapiro 1995: 304). Her distempered attack, which maintains an equivalence between poststructuralism and Nazism by attributing to poststructuralism a "denial of voice and intention," betrays a rather lamentable ignorance about the object of her attack.

19 The importance of interdisciplinary studies as economically beneficial for administrations must not be discounted. Although it is certainly true that Women's Studies courses, available as a minor or even as a major, are at present being supported and funded by various university administrations—a result no doubt of the long political battle waged by academic feminists—it is also true that "interdisciplinarity" has become a favorite buzzword of administrations. In fact, interdisciplinarity becomes particularly useful to trim the size of faculties. Interdisciplinarity is also a way of attracting and retaining students—a sort of "two for the price of one" sale in the competitive marketplace of admissions.

"Women of Color in the U.S.":
Pedagogical Reflections on the Politics of "the Name"

All values must remain vulnerable, and those that do not are dead.—Gaston Bachelard (1994 [1958]: 59)

It is easier to retreat to the safety of difference behind racial, cultural and class borders. Because our awareness of the Other as object often swamps our awareness of ourselves as subjects.—Gloria Anzaldúa (1990: 145)

To give a name, is that still to give? One can have doubts about it from the moment when the name not only is nothing, in any case is not the "thing" that it names, not the "nameable" or the renowned, but also risks to bind, to enslave or to engage the other, to link the called, to call him [or] her to respond even before any decision or any deliberation, even before any freedom.—Jacques Derrida (1995: 84)

Turning the experience of teaching in a classroom in Women's Studies into a textual site of critical and analytical investigation is a crucial task. It is important not only for an examination of institutional regimes of power and knowledge, but also for tracing the covert operations of governmentality within the academy. Such operations of power are often viewed as belonging "outside" the political economy of post-Fordism, yet they mesh with the maintenance of interests tied to property, capital, race, and gender privilege. These interests are not confined within the borders of the United States, but they link the United States to global regimes of production, circulation, and consumption of goods and ideas.

The academic modes of production and consumption thus converge with the movement of capital and labor within and outside the borders of nation-states and in conjunction with new forms of globalization. Such new forms of global interconnection rely on the expansion of communication technology, on massive forms of emplacement and displacement of labor and capital, and on the tension and conflicts arising from the imposed temporality of progress and development on the spatial constructions of memory and identity. In this context, representational practices influenced by historical, cultural, and political concerns become essential for the maintenance, and interruption, of those normative regimes of power and knowledge that tend to eliminate all uncertainty by simultaneously containing otherness and transcending differentiated moral subjects. Such representational regimes are historical byproducts of the formation of the centers of accumulation of knowledge defined by forces of colonialism and imperialism in modern global orders.[1]

By treating the institutional framing of knowledge formation as a form of political intervention, my intention is to challenge the process of curricular remembering and forgetting as it tries to constitute a docile body that does and says what the institution permits or dictates (Foucault 1977). The official knowledges of both colonial and post- or neocolonial education continue to rely on the notion of "standards," itself based on normative notions of subjectivity as defined by national, racial, sexual, and class hierarchies. In this case, my purpose is to problematize the institution of knowledge production within which I am located as a participant in the formation of a political will.[2]

Pedagogy and the Politics of Naming

In an attempt to make connections among my experience of teaching "Women of Color in the U.S.," the institutional framing of the course, its textual coding, and the current historical and social conjuncture, I will elaborate on the politics of the name as it relates to pedagogical reflection. My reflection is based on three postulates: first, the vested interest of modern educational institutions in the process of forming naturalized and docile bodies; second, the practice of naming as a mode of both normalization and resistance; and third, the failure of the institution to regulate ambivalence and, through performativity and repetition, to "emplace the dismembering." This last phrase, "the emplacement of dismembering," is meant to describe two related processes. One concerns what becomes "canonical" in modern educational institutions and is normalized as a legitimate form of memory, and the other is a process of forgetting the social and historical conditions that lead to this form of memorizing. In this context, I am interested in both the politics of representation and the possibilities of what Gianni Vattimo (1998: 91) calls "the event-likeness or contingent character of Being."[3]

There are a number of reasons that this course has become for me a site of pedagogically self-reflexive and critical thinking. First, I have been able to teach it on several different campuses both in the United States and in Canada (although in Canada, it was called "Women of Color Cross-Culturally") and to vastly different student audiences (from a majority of White students to a majority of students of color). The course was institutionalized at a different historical moment in each institution but it served in all cases as the representational point of interruption of gender-based curriculum with race. Each classroom context demanded particular performative teaching strategies that required a constant trafficking back and forth between a designed syllabus and the momentum created in the context of the classroom.

Another reason this course became a site of pedagogical reflection for me is the pressure I felt in the class to "repeat and forget," both in terms of the limits of what could, should, or was supposed to be discussed and what silenced our discussion. There is at work here a dynamic yet regulatory process that codifies remembering by the regulation of forgetting and by resistance to decoding. Such dynamism is specifically significant for curricular purposes, because legitimization of any particular form of knowledge is a site of power and of resistance to it. For example, the requirement to celebrate women of color aborted any critical engagement with the politics of knowledge formation. The hyphenated coding of women of color in the United States creates abject spaces and bodies beyond the pale of legitimated classroom discussion. This aspect of teaching is a real challenge to what I view as a critical pedagogy aimed at enhancing and transforming the social imagination; it makes me think of what I call the unbearable pedagogy of limits, which would include the politics of the classroom as socially constructed, historically determined, and mediated through institutionalized relations of race, class, gender, and power.[4]

The tension-provoking aspect of this class, its "making space" for the recognition or dismissal of contradictory and antagonistic forces constructing ontological and epistemological aspects of belonging to multiple categories, especially in the very draining experience of creating a language of possibility that goes beyond the act of "naming," has created in me a need to write about the "event-likeness" of the classroom. In this regard, the classroom experience provides an occasion for the convergence of three sets of expectations: institutional coding, students' identities, and my own desire for coalition-building. This is why my performance in the classroom has become an object of curiosity and fascination, forcing me to reposition myself always in an unsatisfactory relation to these three axes. This fascination is not about autobiographical writing (no such luxury) but a reflexive request to understand those unsettling aspects of the course that provoke tension and conflict while being incorporated in an additive way into Women's Studies curricula.

Finally, I come to the central feature of this particular classroom—that is, as a space to be negotiated by the power of both verbal and non-verbal discursive and material approximation of bodies. The identitarian claims of bodies in the classroom and the importance of pedagogy as a matter of here and now—not to mention those other silent forces—are important components of the discursive production and reception of knowledge in the academic setting of Women's Studies.

Many authors have pointed out how modern educational systems, even in their oppositional forms vis-à-vis traditional disciplines, are located not outside relations of power and privilege but at their center.[5] Without attempting to detail the complexity of the convergence between the economic and the academic modes of production, I will address the conditions of possibility of such complicity in light of teaching "Women of Color in the U.S." I am fully aware of the risk involved in a critique of Women's Studies curricula at a time that academic marginalization (including budget cuts and poverty of resources) is still pressing on Women's Studies programs and departments nationwide. Further, I should also state that I am very conscious of the fact that "Women of Color in the U.S." courses are sometimes the only sites where issues of race are legitimately addressed. Nevertheless, I strongly believe that a critical and reflexive project is even more important for disciplines and interdisciplines that are overtly taking responsibility to make political intervention, precisely because of the importance of considering their disciplinary space as ideological (Grewal and Kaplan 1999). I agree with Gayatri Chakravorty

Spivak that "if academic and 'revolutionary practices' do not bring each other to productive crisis, the power of the script has clearly passed elsewhere" (1993: 53). Further, the pedagogical experiences of internal Third World voices and of the "guest workers" of academe, as well as diasporic scholars who are not assigned to cover either general courses or specialized area studies, create tensions and contradictions.[6]

One should not underestimate the modern institution of knowledge based on the abstraction of mind and the exclusion of bodies. In this case, the presence of difference is by definition a form of displacement of the normative in educational institutions and is measured constantly against what is acceptable and normal. This is to say that such displacement marks a cultural and epistemological *coupure* or distantiation from central features of the classrooms of modernity. These features have legitimized rationalist and masculinist knowledge claims detached from bodies. This tendency has certainly been challenged by the presence of Women's Studies, ethnic studies, and gay and lesbian studies, as well as by other programs and departments based on identity politics. However, certain oppositional modalities that emerged in the context of the institutionalization of departments such as Women's Studies have become complicit with, and even complementary to, masculinist, Eurocentric, and nationalist framings of knowledge production. Such modalities sometimes have turned Women's Studies classrooms into therapeutic, ritualistic, or oppositional spaces that lack scholarly rigor and critical challenges.

Repetition and Forgetting, or the Unbearable Pedagogy of Limits

The history of these courses is connected to women of color's denunciation of the racism and classism inherent in the "unified Women's Movement" between 1972 and 1980 in the United States (Sandoval 1990). "Women of Color in the U.S." courses appear almost exclusively under the auspices of Women's Studies departments and programs.[7] The fundamental premise of the original denunciation was based on the statement that indeed all women are oppressed, but "beyond sisterhood, there is still racism" (Lorde 1981 [1979]: 79). This critique not only provoked tension and division between white women and women of color at professional meetings and conferences, it also brought on a crisis in definitions of "liberation" and "feminism."[8] The safe haven of a unified sisterhood was radically challenged by scholars, teachers, and students identifying with their racialized location. This put pressure on Women's Studies as an institutional site to respond to racism. Such a response took different forms: from hiring faculty of color to adding courses on the topic and publishing a number of "race, gender, class" textbooks. This in turn led to the addition of race to the canon of Women's Studies, which indeed created space for courses based on identity politics in some Women's Studies departments.

However, in the 1990s new tensions emerged from a second, related set of pressures for the internationalization of the Women's Studies curriculum and the expansion of the category of "women of color" to include a speaking position for women from Third World countries. Although for many scholars the collapse of the two categories "women of color in the U.S." and "Third World women" was related to a cartography of resistance and coalition-building vis-à-vis white feminist movements in the West (Mohanty 1991a), this position still entailed contradictions in its inclusion of diasporic Third World women.[9] This tension and contradiction cannot be separated from the hegemonic position of the United States in the world economy and the power of Western cultural imperialism and global feminism to export ideas emerging in the particular context of the United States.[10]

The experience of teaching women of color is bound up with this historical context, and, of course, many critical voices have challenged such politics of recuperation, representation, and inclusion.[11] Even as the term "women of color" has emerged institutionally to critique women within the United States, the stretching of the term to include a global oppositional category of women of color became problematic in the context of the 1990s and the elaboration of postcolonial theory and transnational feminist theories. A fissure appeared, quite predictably, between the U.S. category of "women of color" and the category "Third World," which constitutes in geopolitical terms subjects who are at the same time placed and displaced, resulting in serious contradictions and tensions. Within the context of the United States, I would argue that such contradictions and tensions have found new comfort zones in "multicultural nationalism" (Moallem and Boal 1999) as well as in various expressions of cultural nationalism. The relationship of the category "women of color" to a complex historical past and present frames my experience of teaching this course and is an important component of my understanding of feminism as a site of productive tension and contradiction.

"Women of Color in the U.S.," like a number of classes based in identity politics that were institutionalized in the early 1980s, has been essential in explicitly acknowledging the exclusion of women of color from feminist theories. By creating dialogue about the theoretical subjects that are the objects of a massive assault by dominant culture and multiple indoctrinations of varied discourses, Women's Studies departments have been able to create space for new objects of study, thereby enabling new modes of political intervention. The linguistic and oppositional potential of articulating women of color as a racialized category has been essential not only in challenging white feminist victimization and the pursuit of a "politics of unity" through the exclusion of race, class, sexuality, and power, but also in articulating difference as it is constituted linguistically and culturally. The potential of this course as a site of resistance has been very important in my own pedagogical reflection, which investigates multiple discursive themes that affect subjectivity and voice.

I should explain that, although educational institutions are not located outside the late capitalist formation of global power relations, programs and departments such as Women's Studies have a particular history that can be traced to the new social movements rather than to nineteenth-century disciplinary practices. The peculiar history and location of such departments often puts Women Studies in a defensive mode, delaying critical engagement with its own problematic status as a discipline because it is always "under attack." I agree with Elspeth Probyn (1996) that we need to revitalize and reformulate the point and direction of academic political interventions at the present juncture. Falling into the defensive mode of "let's resolve the contradiction after the fall of the main enemy" is the byproduct of an oppositional logic that ignores complexity and multiplicity.[12] In discussing the limits of the model of "giving voice" to multiple discourses and locations, Norma Alarcón makes the point that "to privilege the subject, even if multiple-voiced, is not enough" (1990: 366). Although the recognition of the knowledge of a situation is itself a site of privilege, as Alarcón noted, it should also be remembered that the category "women of color," exists in an intertextual relation with the field of Women's Studies that has not been willing to think its relation to the rubric of "color," which it nevertheless institutionally owns. It is important to recognize, with Teresa Cordova (1998: 18), that the university and the educational system emerged out of slavery and colonialism dedicated to a system of privilege and Eurocentric regimes of knowledge and power. Thus, racial politics cannot be separated from the expansion of corporate and multicultural capitalism and its cultural formations in naming and constructing academic subjectivities and voices. The projection of U.S. racial politics onto the global situation disguises cultural imperialism as a major component of postcolonial societies. In this sense, cultural politics in the context of academe cannot be separated from the importance of making social, cultural, political, and economic issues the primary categories for understanding the curriculum.

The Disjunction of the Curriculum and the Classroom

Here is an entry from my diary:

> I am excited about the possibility of getting together in a class like this. This class permits—under this name, under this title—certain discussions; and certain reflexive practices become possible. I am excited not only about the possibilities of rethinking coalition building and the political formations related to the very subject of this class, but also the potential for challenging and changing the positions both of myself and my students. However, I am anxious about the outcomes of surnaming, the original lack of meaning in the very concepts of "women," "color" and the "U.S." and the pedagogical consequences of my addressing students, students addressing me and students addressing each other. (Berkeley, Calif., January 1994)

The "positioned" in me as well as in the students has always been an important aspect of teaching the course. I am referring to "the positioned" as a component of one's subjectivity and identity either imposed from outside or assumed from the inside. It is also about the politics of location, enabling or disabling moves in and out of identity frames, holding or withholding belief in their foundation. The politics of positionality in a classroom such as this one, where knowledge about the "other" or the "self" is sought within the epistemological borders of those bodies marked by their "color," "ethnicity," or "culture," as opposed to those without it or privileged enough to be camouflaged under the sign of normativity, is especially complex and multidimensional. At times, white students resisted the fact that the course had something to do with "whiteness" rather than knowledge about women of color; in this case, race mattered only for "the others."[13] At times, the very presence of students belonging to "border zones" (and their claims and disclaimers of belonging) leads to both productive confusion and intolerance of ambiguity in a society where recognition of the "self" is increasingly complicitous with the consumerist moment of capitalism. Such disjunctures challenge and question the comforting aspects of an identity politics that remains secure in the homogenizing notions of cultural nationalism of various forms. It also challenges my positioning as a "woman of color" in the United States for recognition of what positions me not only in relation to the racial constructions of modernity and the machinery of the state, but also in the national imagining of my colleagues or students in so far as there is a match or mismatch with naturalized notions of women of color and the U.S. location. Although the connection of the category "woman of color" to "Third World" facilitates a "speaking" position for me where I can talk about my experience of racialization not only in the United States but also as it relates to the experience of colonialism and postcolonial subject formation, the framing of the course "in the U.S." raises a whole series of questions in terms of what should or should not be discussed, and who may or may not legitimately teach it.

In this case, what is not evident is the embodied experience of being in a classroom, because an immigrant body does not fit the territorialist and nationalist requirement of "the U.S." Thus, one could claim that negotiating power and authority in the classroom is neither a matter of institutional location (because such courses respond to the particular need of an imagined audience and student satisfaction is a must for the institution) nor an easy task in relation to students' expectation of who may legitimately speak. In this case, as A. Henry Giroux (1993: 3) notes, an uncritical appeal to a discourse of authenticity in identity politics suppresses differences within their own "liberatory" narratives. For example, in the context of my course at the University of California, Berkeley, my "foreign-ness" became a source of my "illegitimate intervention" not only in the choice of materials that were discussed in the classroom but also in terms of the transnational connections that the class encouraged between global and local forms of racialization.[14] This was manifested both in the classroom discussions and in some of the student evaluations. For example, one student commented in her evaluation:[15]

> Depicting the Korean shop owners during Los Angeles riots was the
> worst piece of trash I have ever seen. To trash the entire African

American race and portray Koreans as it did was an insult to everyone. [She refers to a film screening and lecture by Elaine Kim on *L.A. Riots*.] To pick a film such as this to illustrate a point was not in the interest of the class. There was no focus on women born and raised in America or at least comparison to shed light on her foreign examples.

Yes, indeed, my perception of teaching such a course is influenced by the idea of the "name" as a lure or an occasion for attentiveness, a relation of non-relation, where the normal and normative explanations of the world are interrupted, and where the very possibility of thinking as departure is created. However, my diasporic body, my accent, and my connection to a location beyond the borders of the United States fail to create the classroom as an occasion for creating a place where cultural politics are practiced.[16] This gap, this state of being, surprised and inspired me in subsequent versions of the course to reexamine the limits of naming and to open a dialogue on the name and its deconstruction. On another campus, when I invited a colleague of color to give a talk in my class, she refused to do what she promised and instead started to interrogate my students about what they had learned about race, implicitly addressing both me as an outsider and my students as vulnerable to the ideological mystification at the heart of U.S. politics of race. On this occasion, I was reminded of the importance of teaching the historical and social postcolonial context in the racialization of women globally and in the United States.

From these experiences, it seems to me that indeed naming is the way both to make a certain reality "proper" and, at the same time, to make it disappear. So although it is very important to pay attention to the historical importance of naming in the context of the institutionalization of Women's Studies, it is also essential to pay attention to the normalization of the proper name in what is concealed and disappeared. What I precisely mean by normalization is the mission accompli of race in the universalization of the category of women of color and its epistemological distancing from its genealogy and intertextuality with the category of women within the real and imaginary borders of the United States. The classroom is haunted by the apparition of dissimulated reality—that is, bodies marked by their deviance from hegemonic and hegemonizing notions of normative bodies. Here the overexploited body of Third World women in the very construct of the proper name throws into crisis the category "women of color in the U.S." at the expense of concealment and reconstitution of Third World women.[17]

This process is certainly marked by the disjunctive meaning of teaching a subject of importance, on the one hand, and being in the classroom, on the other hand. It is specifically influenced by what becomes constitutive of the classroom as a theater of cruelty, in what Himani Bannerji calls "the social relations of teaching and learning as relations of violence" (1992: 6), where some students, instead of asserting creative control over knowledge production, assert control over the instructor's body. In this case, pedagogy has to be transformed into the decolonization of one's self and body in the face of domination and in the name of learning.

The Body Politics of the Classroom Encounter

The pedagogical encounters in this class have made me aware of a multiplicity of positionalities along the axes of gender, race, class, sexuality, and power. In my view, "corporeal manifestations of hegemony" (to use the phrase of Peter McLaren and Henry A. Giroux [1995: 48]) are not structured in a hierarchical mode. They are rather negotiated with regard to multiple forms of exchange in a classroom. Such pedagogical encounters cannot be abstracted from the embodied experience of the classroom, where students not only unwittingly consent to domination but also sometimes find pleasure in the form and content through which such domination is manifested. The need to totalize, systematize, and control creates a train of the unspeakable and works against a deconstructionist approach of praising latency, formlessness, and plurality in the classroom. The need for pedagogical mediation means the spontaneous decoding and interpreting of the sign systems of those bodies that become a principal site of theatrical and political intervention, establishing a body politics rooted in the individual presence of the postcolonial subject in educational institutions. So being in a classroom goes beyond the text that privileges the performance of mind over body in relation to the bodies in the classroom. As noted by Judith Butler, "the speech act is performed bodily, and though it does not instate the absolute or immediate presence of the body, the simultaneity of the production and delivery of the expression communicates not merely what is said, but the bearing of the body as the rhetorical instrument of expression" (1997: 152). What makes the instructor distinguishable from the instructions (a presupposed set of readings exchanged in a classroom) is the representation of this embodiment. If we define performance as action that occurs on a given occasion, both the course materials and what the institution expects from the instructor in terms of those frames of meaning that transcend the classroom and authorize and contain their variety in the institutional space become radically distinguishable from the performance as an event in which we would always be experiencing something else each time. In this sense, the classroom is not the enactment but the act itself. This brings me to the second point I would like to make in relation to the classroom as it is caught up in the social and political exigencies of the moment: Because the performance is, above all, a historical process, it may even be the element against which one is performing.

The third point to consider is the question of complicity with the very mechanisms of authority that one seeks to subvert white men's rules of the classroom. The classroom is like a field in which one confronts her audience and within which the work's relative worth is determined. The question of complicity is important in relation to what is being re-created in a spirit of dialogue, a community of discourse between students and instructor. This spirit of dialogue is an important transformative aspect of the classroom, where both my students and I have been able to create new roles and new identities, to define, and often redefine, our roles in the community proper. To transform an audience of students in a classroom into a community is a difficult and rather romantic task. It is a task that can be tackled under the banner of the proper name, requiring generalization, formalization, and homogenization, in contrast to the ambiguous spirit of a classroom in its potential contingency.[18] If the coming together of the students and myself as a community is what one would aim for, my failure to achieve this, and my students' failure to carry it through, would be a point of concern over my performance and a cause of self-reflection about my own pedagogical complicity with the God of the institution. The classroom is a space where the instructor's body is expected not to express emotion or feelings—that is, to (appear to) lack all interiority; hence, the postcolonial rejection of a Eurocentric and logocentric emphasis on absence creates a discrepancy between the linguistic and the performative. To expose the postcolonial educator's body to the activity of seeing (the gaze) creates a constant need for and against forgetting and repetition. It also becomes an occasion for an awareness of the body as an object and a subject within a larger discursive economy of voice and movement that stresses the theatrical and the performative as predicated on the idea of an exchange in which those engaged are physically present to one another. In this sense, pedagogy is what we think, do, and discuss here and now. It may be that pedagogy can be defined only as interruption, as a revolution that requires "making no appeal to the permanence of any institutionality."[19]

Notes

I thank Robyn Wiegman, Caren Kaplan, Inderpal Grewal, and Iain Boal, who gave me excellent feedback and support on various versions of this paper. I am also grateful to my teaching assistants Rinate Abastido and Sonia Rogenby, who encouraged me to write about my teaching experiences. An earlier version of this paper was presented at a panel at the annual Modern Language Association Meeting, San Francisco, December 1998. I thank Rachel Lee for inviting me to be on that panel.

1 The term "centers of calculation" is adopted from Latour (1987), a highly original study of science and technology that maps out the cumulative character of modern science that connects and transforms scattered resources into a network that achieves domination at a distance.

2 I agree with Foucault that "the role of the intellectual is not to tell others what they have to do. The work of an intellectual is not to shape others' political will; it is through that analysis that he carries out in his field, to question over and over again what is postulated as self-evident" (1988 [1984]: 265).

3 The Italian philosopher Gianni Vattimo's critique of metaphysical essentialism and foundationalism is useful for a rethinking of any nostalgic search for an ultimate and unshaken foundation.

4 I am with David Haver when he refers to Deborah P. Britzman's notion of queer pedagogy as "a relation to limit, a relation to that which cannot bear to think, of what is for a certain enlightenment unbearable" (1997: 290).

5 Bourdieu (1984) pointed out that economic and cultural capital are both the objects and the weapons of a competitive struggle between classes.

6 In my academic life both in Canada and in the United States, I have been reminded covertly and overtly of my "immigrant" status in terms of what it permitted or prohibited for me in academe. For example, when I won a competitive doctoral fellowship as a Ph.D. student in Canada, some of my classmates let me hear that they resented the disbursing of Canadian resources to foreigners like me. On another occasion, a colleague of color overtly reminded me that only a "U.S.-born" woman of color was able properly to understand race relations in the United States and be trusted as a true advocate for the causes of women of color in the United States. I find a very similar logic at work between this discourse in academe and the anti-immigrant and xeno-

phobic discourses outside academe—for example, "immigrants steal our jobs," and so on. The "guest-worker" logic denies full citizenship even when one is legally and institutionally a citizen.

7   It may be taught as "Race, Gender, Class" or "Ethnic Women in the U.S." in some Women's Studies departments.

8   This tension was reflected in professional organizations, as well as in a number of extremely important texts, such as *This Bridge Called My Back* (Moraga and Anzaldúa 1981). Women of color questioned the silencing mechanisms in the women's movements. Audre Lorde, one of the pioneers, made connections among racism, classism, and homophobia and called for the "recognition of differences among women" (Lorde 1981 [1979]). This moment of crisis led to an outing of women of color at the 1981 National Women's Studies Association Conference, where an organizing committee exclusively for "Third World" women provoked a storm of controversy (Sandoval 1990).

9   This tension has generated both "essentialist" and "anti-essentialist" identity claims and a place for the investigation of "who is included" and "who is excluded" in the women of color category or other identity-based categories. See, among others, Roof and Wiegman 1996; Women of South Asian Descent Collective 1993; and Kadi 1994.

10 For an illuminating discussion of Western cultural imperialism and global feminism, see Grewal and Kaplan 1994, 1996, 1999.

11 Bannerji (1993: xiii–xiv) problematizes the token presence of nonwhite women in academe. She argues that, although this presence moves from the margin to the center, it is nevertheless contained within a descriptive boundary through the gestures of inclusion and multiculturalism. Ella Shohat (1998: 7) problematizes both reductionist and single-hyphen boxes as not allowing for the polysemy in the politics of color.

12 I learned this lesson during the revolution of 1979 in Iran, where everyone was postponing women's issues and minority issues until the post-revolutionary era, without understanding that the first groups subjected to discrimination by the post-revolutionary state would again be women and minorities.

13 A response to this position has led to important feminist scholarship on whiteness. See, for example, Frankenberg (1993, 1997).

14 The rejection of the inclusion of any subject that had to do with the so-called foreign-born women became on a number of occasions a site of consensus-making between some of my white students and my students of color. In this case, territorial nationalism was a hegemonizing force and worked against cultural nationalism. For example, in a class session focusing on the representation of South Asian diasporas, some students challenged the readings as irrelevant to the experience of U.S. women of color.

15 Student evaluations have been a very interesting spur to reflection for me. Although on many occasions I have learned from the students' comments, on others I have observed the most blatant expressions of xenophobia and racism.

16 I agree with bell hooks that "only the person who is most powerful has the privilege of denying their body" (1994: 137).

17 I am with Derrida (1995) in thinking that what constitutes the name, the proper name, is originally renaming.

18 As hooks remarks, "The classroom remains the most radical space of possibility in the academy" (1994:12).

19 I refer to William Haver's (1997: 290) interpretation of Deborah P. Britzman's intervention in "Is There a Queer Pedagogy?" (1995).

Negotiating the Politics of Experiential Learning in Women's Studies: Lessons from the Community Action Project

Drawing on lessons from the Community Action Project (CAP), an experiential class project I developed for use in a large introductory Women's Studies course, this chapter explores the continued significance of experiential learning for Women's Studies. My goals with the CAP are twofold: first, to teach lessons in politics, collective action, and feminist analyses; and second, to help students develop investigatory and political skills that can complement a developing critical consciousness. From a feminist pedagogical perspective, the development of critical consciousness provides students with the ability to call into question taken-for-granted understandings of their social, political, economic, and academic life (see, for example, Luke and Gore 1992; Mayberry and Rose 1999; Weiler 1998). In this chapter, I demonstrate how community action as a pedagogical strategy permits us to move beyond the early consciousness-raising approaches in Women's Studies classrooms while retaining some of the valuable lessons derived from experiential learning.

The CAP serves as a semi-structured exercise in identifying sites of intervention and strategies for social change that can be implemented within the time frame of a ten-week course. The CAP provides students, who rarely come to the course with experience as self-initiated political actors, the opportunity to move from individual-level personal concerns to collective action while simultaneously developing a sense of how patterns of inequality circumscribe their everyday lives in ways that are often invisible to them.

The CAP project forms part of the requirements for the second in a three-quarter-year-long introductory Women's Studies series. The first quarter focuses on "Gender and Feminism in Everyday Life" and the third on "Gender and Popular Culture." The second course, entitled "Reproducing and Resisting Inequalities," demonstrates how inequalities of gender, race, class, sexuality, and colonialism are embedded in institutions generally thought to be "value-free." In the first part of the course, we examine the institutional formations of science, medicine, agriculture, the capitalist economy, citizenship, and the state through a historical and international lens. In the second half of the course, we emphasize how women's community-based and international organizing challenge local, national, and global processes of inequality. The CAP gives students the experiential base from which to understand how to link local community actions with broader struggles for social change and feminist theorizing about these processes.

I draw on my own research and experiential learning about community activism as well as on the rich body of feminist literature that explores the construction and reproduction of inequalities and resistance strategies to help guide the class project. For almost twenty years, I have been exploring the processes by which diverse women develop their commitment to community-based activism and how this relates to a process of politicization (see Naples 1998a, 1998b). My research affirms the important relationship among positionality, constructions of community, the development of oppositional consciousness, and willingness to engage in political action that has been implicit in many feminist theoretical perspectives, especially materialist feminist frameworks. These lessons led me to consider the ways in which I might give my Women's Studies students the opportunity to learn how to "do politics" and, in the course of this activity, discover firsthand how inequality is reproduced in institutions that shape our daily lives as well as how they can effectively challenge these patterns of inequality.

Feminist Activism, Consciousness-Raising, and Women's Studies

In the context of the women's movement of the late 1960s and early 1970s, feminist faculty across the United States developed innovative pedagogical strategies designed to draw on female students' personal experiences and incorporate processes of dialogue and reflexivity into classroom interaction and course assignments (see, for example, Maher and Tetreault 1994). Early Women's Studies classes used journal writing, autobiographical essays, and oral histories of family and community members, among other techniques, to provide students with the opportunity to explore how their personal lives were shaped by processes of oppression often hidden from view (see, for example, Bunch and Pollack 1983). The notion of the "personal is political," the central tenet of consciousness-raising (CR) groups of this period, provided the pedagogical framing for many of these classroom exercises. However, these techniques could be adopted without incorporating the group process and collective action that had been central aspects of CR during the women's movement of the late 1960s and 1970s (see, for example, Kenway and Mondra 1992: 156).

The CR group process enabled women to share their experiences, define and analyze the social and political mechanisms by which women are oppressed, and develop strategies for social change. Many radical feminists of this era viewed CR as "a starting point for feminism, a place from which to begin doing more public, activist organizing, rather than an end in itself or an investigative model" (Hogeland 1998: 25; see also Gearhart 1983; MacKinnon 1989; Quest Staff 1981). Lisa Hogeland (1998) reports that, although personal experiences served as the beginning for feminist analysis, CR groups were to switch their energies to political projects such as abortion rights, expansion of child-care services, employment and educational equity, and fighting violence against women. Therefore, radical feminist explications of CR included linking personal issues to political analyses for the purposes of political action (also see Bunch and Pollack 1983; Stanley and Wise 1983; Weiler 1998). In fact, many second-wave women's movement activists viewed CR as the method through which feminist political analysis and action proceeded.

The newly defined curricular area of Women's Studies was initially viewed by many feminist faculty as the academic arm of the women's movement (for example, see Boxer 1982; Bunch and Pollack 1983). As Sandra Krajewski, chair of the Department of Women's Studies at the University of Wisconsin-La Crosse, notes, initially "activists taught Women's Studies at a time when connecting theory and practice meant connecting academic theories and community activism. Theory was informed by the realities of specific struggles in a given community, and was tested by the clarity of the analysis and insight it offered" (1999:5).

However, with the institutionalization of Women's Studies, links to women's movement goals and feminist organizations began to weaken.

In some cases, academic administrators required Women's Studies faculty to distance themselves from activist organizations and controversial issues. Krajewski reports that when the battered women's shelter opened in her community in 1978, an administrator at the university warned the Women's Studies director to avoid associating with the new shelter and addressing the issue of battering.

With the institutionalization of Women's Studies, and in the context of the ongoing backlash against feminist and multicultural challenges to androcentric educational models, experiential approaches to feminist pedagogy have come under attack from critics both within and outside Women's Studies (see Minnich 1998; Patai and Koertge 1995). Embedded within these diverse critiques is a fear that by valorizing women's experiences over other ways of knowing, Women's Studies classrooms do not measure up to academic standards of "excellence" (see, for example, Hogeland 1998). Feminist faculty also worried that such gynocentric strategies might reinscribe a feminized notion of women, one grounded in essentialist constructions of "womanhood." Although most of these concerns circulate around the use of CR, emotionality, and autobiography, all approaches to experiential learning have come under scrutiny.

Institutional factors and conservative political forces only partially explain the resistance to experiential learning by some Women's Studies faculty (see Patai and Koertge 1995).[1] Developments within feminist scholarship contributed to the increasing ambivalence toward experiential strategies in Women's Studies. Poststructuralist analyses, which call into question what "counts as experience" (Scott 1992: 37), as well as critiques of certain essentializing interpretations of standpoint epistemologies form powerful cautions against valorizing women's experience in the Women's Studies classroom. Furthermore, as materialist feminist standpoint epistemologists such as Nancy Hartsock (1983) and Dorothy Smith (1987) point out, oppositional consciousness is not an inevitable outcome of experience; nor, I would add, is it an inevitable outcome of CR strategies (Naples 1999; also see Kirsch 1999; Mohanty 1995).

Because CR groups typically grew out of localized interpersonal networks, the political analyses developed in these groups are typically limited by the homogeneity of the group. The lack of diversity within specific CR groups circumscribes their potential as sites through which to develop an intersectional critique of hegemonic relations of power. Deborah Gerson (1995: 30), in an analysis of the limits of 1970s CR groups for developing effective political strategies to fight institutional forms of oppression, points out that even when these groups did attempt to negotiate diversity, CR "as a tool to overcome divisions among women" often failed to move beyond the local "culture of reflexivity" to explore the relations of ruling organizing structurally different experiences among women. In Gerson's words, "The problem: difference; the solution: change consciousness" (1995: 33). Furthermore, as hooks (1984a) points out, CR strategies do not necessarily provide the context through which we can recognize how social structural dynamics such as capitalism, colonialism, or racism shape our experiences.

Recognizing the limits of CR as a pedagogical strategy, Women's Studies faculty have experimented with approaches that might produce a "more intellectually sound, more politically and theoretically sophisticated" approach to CR in the Women's Studies classroom (Hogeland 1998: 166; see also Anderson et al. 1997; Benmayor 1991; Mayberry and Rose 1999; McDaniel 1999). For example, Hogeland highlights Estelle Freedman's "Small Group Pedagogy: Consciousness Raising in Conservative Times" (1990) as an illustration of one successful strategy. Freedman includes CR in her course as a separate component, one that takes place outside the classroom through small group processes and journal writing. However, the institutionalization of Women's Studies in the academy constrains the development of collective political action that characterized the CR groups of the 1970s. With power differentials between teachers and students, and among students, and the surveillance of Women's Studies curriculum by bureaucratic bodies within the academy, feminist faculty often find it difficult to incorporate the "commitment to praxis" in their classrooms (Weiler 1998). Given the contradictions of institutionalization, what strategies can Women's Studies faculty employ to retain a pedagogical commitment to feminist praxis? In the remainder of this chapter, I demonstrate the possibilities of teaching feminist praxis through an experiential approach.[2] This goal seems especially important given the so-called post-feminist political context of the 1990s.

Experiential Learning, Politicization, and Community Action

Ironically, although activist strategies in the Women's Studies classroom are often viewed with suspicion, problem-solving learning and internship programs have received renewed legitimacy within the academy (see Bojar 2000; Dickinson 1999; "Special Issue" 1999).[3] Responding to a 1999 discussion that occurred on the Teach Sociology listserv, Elizabeth Strugatz argued that problem-solving learning can be used to "teach lifelong skills such as learning how to find information, how to think critically about that information and come to one's own conclusions about the problem, [and] how to work in groups and overcome conflict." Working with Kansas State University's Women's Resource Center and Kansas Center for Rural Initiatives, Torry Dickinson (1999: 56) initiated a targeted internship program that would prepare traditional and non-matriculated community students to support women who want to start micro-enterprises and cooperatives."[4] Students learn to help women start micro-businesses and give them the skills to start their own businesses. Women's Studies programs have also used internships to familiarize students with the work of feminist organizations such as battered women's shelters, the National Organization for Women, National Abortion and Reproductive Rights League, and welfare-rights organizations (see Bojar 2000).

Women's Studies students are often disappointed when they observe firsthand how professionalization and bureaucratization interferes with feminist practice within these organizations. Furthermore, as a consequence of the success of feminist activism, some women's shelters and related organizations have now been established by professional groups or through government initiatives without a feminist analysis of the issues they address. In addition, with demands for service often outstripping resources, even staff who retain a feminist vision have less time for political activism.

Not surprisingly, as I reviewed the CAPs completed for my course, I found that students encountered similar dilemmas. Many want to jump quickly into a service mode in response to specific needs they have identified. Through a process of politicization, which sometimes requires a painful recalculation of their taken-for-granted beliefs about gender, race, class, and sexuality, students began to recognize the broader conditions and institutional practices that contribute to the specific problems they target. The process of politicization parallels CR in some ways. However, it explicitly directs attention to the political actions that are necessary to challenge inequality. The CAP provides a context through which students explore how dominant ideologies and organizational practices obscure systemic patterns of oppression. It also incorporates the goal of political action directly into the learning process.

CAPs can be conceptualized as class-initiated problem-solving strategies (see, for example, Short 1999) or linked with targeted internship programs (see, for example, McDaniel 1999; Romanoff et al. 1999). In either form, CAPs can facilitate teaching the investigatory and political skills that can complement students' growing critical consciousness. The CAP begins from the students' personal concerns but quickly moves them outward to the larger context of their social, political, economic, and cultural lives. The CAP provides a site in which students can experience a process of politicization through group interaction and political analysis of the problem or issue they choose (although there is no guarantee that this will occur). Although "working the steps" and completing weekly reports on their group's progress does not leave much time and space for discussion of personal experiences related to the projects, as is more typical in a CR group context, personal experiences did provide the foundation for a number of CAPs.

For example, Bahareh Myers helped initiate the group named How to Make the Most of Your Research Experience, which developed guidelines for students and faculty in biological sciences field research independent studies (BIO199).[5]

> This community action project caught my interest as a result of the negative experiences I have had, in the past, with BIO199 research. When I started doing the research, I had just assumed that the professor had the authority to make you do whatever he [or] she wanted. This incorrect assumption has caused me much grief. For instance, on my first days at research, the professor took me to a small, dark isolated stock room and placed me in front of a paper shredding machine. He then told me that my job for the next few hours would be to shred stacks of paper. . . . On my second week at research, I was placed in front of a photocopying machine and then told to copy a stack full of death certificates. Being trapped in a small photocopy room for four hours copying people's death certificates overwhelmed me with anxiety and depression. I will always remember the tears of anger and frustration each day as I left the research facilities. (Myers 1995: 1–2)

Myers subsequently quit her research job and did not pursue another assignment because she thought that other jobs would be just as tedious.

The next year, Myers's roommate returned home to complain about her research assignment. She told Myers that "her professor constantly yells at her and calls her useless. In addition, when time came for her to leave for the day, he would complain about her to the other students in the laboratory" (Myers 1995: 3). After hearing about her roommate's experiences, Myers understood that she "was not the only person to go through this deeply degrading and dehumanizing experience doing research. I realized that, in this situation, the personal is political. What I first thought was only my problem turned out to also be a problem for countless others" (Myers 1995: 3).

She brought up the issue in her discussion group and found that several other students had similar experiences. Myers and her CAP group found that, rather than gain research experiences, many students complained that they are primarily asked to do clerical or other non-academic work. Some students also complained of sexual harassment. This CAP group developed an information sheet explaining what students should expect from their research experience and how to protect their rights. It was specifically addressed to female students, although both male and female students find this form useful. This two-page form detailing the rights and responsibilities of students and teachers is now included with the BIO199 application form.

Students who were drawn to address violence against women sometimes explained their motivation to create a CAP on this topic as a consequence of personal experiences of abuse. In the final reports from individual members of these groups, a number of students described their personal experiences of acquaintance rape or growing up in a household where their father abused their mother. Although few of these individual stories are shared in the large lecture course, they are often brought up in the small discussion groups or with other CAP members. Because we have developed a close working relationship with the Center for Women and Gender Education, which sponsors groups for survivors of sexual assault, those dealing with eating disorders, and adult children of alcoholic parents, among others, we encourage students to seek out these avenues of support, if needed.

As in many Women's Studies classrooms, the topics we discuss often trigger memories or emotional responses that cannot be dealt with effectively in the classroom. However, the CAP offered these students an activist strategy for dealing with these issues. As Myers explained in her final report, when she recognized that her personal problem was collectively experienced, she understood that it could become the focus for political action. This process was empowering for her, as she was able to help improve the situation for other students. Because the experiential project was embedded in a larger pedagogical context in which we read and discussed feminist activism and the reproduction of inequality from a social-structural perspective, the "personal" and "political" were analytically linked in both theory and practice. In this way, the CAP as implemented in a group context retains some of the features of CR. The CAP used as a requirement for the introductory course propels the students to action, even if their only motivation initially is a grade. In addition, many students emphasize the importance of finding their "voice" through their participation in the project. As one student explained in her final report, "This class experience made me aware of my potential to voice my opinion and make a difference if I am willing to put forth the effort" (Au 1994: 8).

Implementing the Community Action Project

Despite the contradictions of the CAP as an assignment in a required course for which a grade is given, reviewing the projects from 1994 to 1999, I recognized that they continually re-inspired my own sense of political possibilities for a new generation of Women's Studies students. The first course I taught in Women's Studies at the University of California, Irvine (UCI), was titled "Social Perspectives on Gender." It was the second of the three-quarter introductory series in a new interdisciplinary Women's Studies major established in the fall of the 1992–93 academic year. My job was to teach feminist perspectives in the social sciences. The first course was intended as an interdisciplinary overview, and the third highlighted humanities perspectives on gender. My initial goal in introducing Women's Studies students to community action through the CAP was to teach them the skills of political and institutional analysis in order to enhance their effectiveness as agents of change in their everyday lives. Furthermore, because most of the students had little understanding of what "doing politics" entailed, I offered the CAP as an experiential means by which they could begin to learn what constitutes political action and from there see how gendered, racialized, and class-differentiated processes were often hidden from view in the institutions that pervade our everyday lives.

The students are asked to conceptualize a project that will leave a legacy beyond the ten-week quarter. From the start, they must consider how to ensure the continuity of their work and what political strategy would help them accomplish this goal. The CAP is implemented through a series of specific steps. Although the CAP is a group project, each student submits a short weekly report on the progress made by the group for each step as indicated in this outline.[6] The final report on the CAP is a comprehensive narrative of the history of the project including: 1) evaluation of group process and the project itself; 2) incorporation of assigned readings as appropriate; and 3) integration of the comments provided by the teaching assistant or instructor on the progress reports.

The students encounter difficulties at four junctures: 1) defining the problem that will be the focus of their CAP; 2) constructing a project that can be implemented in the course of ten weeks; 3) identifying the relevant actors in different institutional sites who have power to make the changes they envision and getting these actors to respond; and 4) working in groups. In the next section, I will describe how the students, teaching assistants, and I deal with these problems. I will also discuss how we negotiate relationships with other units on campus, especially the Center for Women and Gender Education, that are implicated in the students projects. I will then outline the diversity of themes that have emerged from the projects over the past six years and illustrate how these were linked to class content. Then I will discuss the legacy of certain projects on campus and in the wider community and conclude by exploring the limits of community action for teaching intersectional, cross-cultural, and transnational feminist praxis.

Defining and Coordinating Community Action Projects

At the first meeting of each discussion group, students are asked to identify issues of concern to them that affect women on campus, in the communities in which they live, or in the broader social environment. Themes for projects are listed on the board. Between the first and second meetings of the discussion group, students write a short statement that describes why they believe it would be important to address a particular issue. These statements are used to facilitate the formation of small groups. Students read their statements in an attempt to encourage other students to join with them. When all students feel that their issues have been raised and considered, and a defined number of projects has been outlined, small groups of five to eight are formed in which the specified issues chosen are further clarified and the specific action steps are developed. Before reaching consensus on a particular action plan, group members gather information about the feasibility for each plan proposed.

In some cases, a number of students quickly see that they have overlapping interests and agree to join together. Sometimes, however, only one or two students are interested in a particular topic. When this occurs, we usually work with these students to see how they might refocus their interests to choose a group that has a sufficient number of members to proceed. Because many tasks are involved in producing a CAP in such a short time frame, groups of four or fewer are typically unable to implement the project effectively. If the concern expressed is a broad one, such as racism in the community or sexual harassment on campus, the group may decide to construct a series of actions that could be implemented over an extended period, but one specific aspect of the plan must be implemented within the ten-week quarter.

The teaching assistants assigned to the course are charged with the responsibility for ensuring effective coordination among CAP projects, campus programs and administrative staff, and community groups. With the current class size of 210, each teaching assistant supervises three sections, with approximately twenty-six students and at least five CAP groups in each section. In some cases, students in different sections come up with the same topic for their CAP. The teaching assistants must then work together to make sure that these separate groups coordinate with each other to develop somewhat different focuses for their interventions. During my weekly meetings with the teaching assistants, we identify which groups are working on similar projects and attempt to put the groups together in order to encourage them to differentiate their CAPs or to coordinate their community actions. Although it is possible, broadly speaking, to identify and prevent duplication among groups in different sections, it is not possible to avoid contrasting views of similar issues.

By way of example, during the winter quarter of 1998, groups in two different sections defined their CAP in terms of campus safety. One group focused on testing the effectiveness of the Safety Escort Service and determined that the long response time posed a problem for women who needed to use the service. They investigated further and found that one explanation for the delay was the lack of available escorts. Further, due to lack of escorts, the service stopped in the early evening. Working with the student government and Department of Campus Parking and Transportation, they developed strategies to increase the number of escorts and to extend the hours of service. The second group decided to explore the availability and effectiveness of pepper spray to counter sexual assault and to increase awareness and access for UCI students. This group's final presentation prompted a heated discussion among class members about this strategy, because the first group had also investigated its effectiveness and came to the conclusion that pepper spray was relatively ineffective because it had to be sprayed directly into the eyes and could be easily avoided by the attacker.

Providing students with the space to identify and specify their community actions does require giving up some control. In a private discussion with a member of one group who was working on establishing a support group for incest survivors, and as a consequence of what she was sharing with me, I decided to inform her that I was also an incest survivor. I had, in fact, written about it (albeit without much detail about the abuse) in a chapter that appears in *Feminism and Social Change*, edited by Heidi Gottfried (Naples with Clark 1996). During the last week of classes, I have each group briefly describe its project and what it accomplished or learned from it. This student presented for her group and in the course of her presentation enthusiastically told the class that I, too, was a survivor of incest. Now, to be fair, she had asked me just before class if that would be okay. If I had had more time, I would have explored with her why she thought this was necessary for her presentation, but after coming out to her about it, and in an effort to support her decision to come out to the class about herself as an incest survivor, I felt I could not withhold my consent.

In another instance, a group working on breast cancer seized the opportunity to educate men on campus about their risk for the disease. Misreading the statistics on the extent of the problem, the group created a flyer and distributed it throughout campus with the following statement: "It is estimated that out of 1,400 men, 200 will be diagnosed with breast cancer." The report from which the group took this statistic actually said that in a study of 1,400 men diagnosed with breast cancer, 200 died from the disease. When I attended the group to hear its CAP presentations, I read the flyer and noticed the error. After a brief lesson in reading statistical information, I asked group members to retrace their steps, go through each flyer, and cross out the sentence with the erroneous statistic.

The most difficult challenge faced by the teaching assistants was negotiating conflict and uneven division of labor within groups. In some cases, teaching assistants were unaware of such problems until the end of the quarter. As one member of the 1999 class wrote in her final report, "Our group lacked cohesiveness and direction from the very beginning. I came to dread each group meeting. . . . I was frankly disappointed at the lack of maturity and communication skills of my fellow group members, I also take blame on myself for not handling the situation more effectively" (Tarbell 1999: 6).

She went on to detail the problems as follows: "lack of focus" (that is, "We never clearly defined and limited our project—its title, goals, or the activities necessary to accomplish it"), "lack of commitment" ("The entire group was present at a meeting only two times"); "lack of leadership" ("When no one stepped up to the task, I should have provided more direction"); and "lack of communication" ("People in the group did not clearly express their opinions and goals and did not clearly understand the concerns of other members").

In addition to the challenges of coordination across the projects and within each group, we have found even more difficulties managing the relationships that are forged by students with other units across campus. When I first began using the CAP at UCI, Paula Goldsmid, Director of the Center for Women and Gender Education,[7] called to tell me that the Women's Studies students were descending on the center and asking the staff to help with their CAPs. Campus Assault Prevention Program Coordinator Donna-Jean Louden was especially swamped with requests for assistance.

After discussing possible solutions, we determined that the students needed guidelines to help negotiate how and when to approach the center for help. First, center's staff would meet with groups only as a whole. Initially, students from the same group would approach them individually, unaware that another member of their group had already done so. Second, the students needed to explore a number of other options before going to the center. There were Web sites, community groups, and other sources of information the students need to identify before making an appointment with the center's staff. Third, groups needed to be clear about what they wanted to do for a CAP before their meeting with a staff member. The center's staff were then invited to speak to the class at the beginning of the quarter to discuss the procedures that would protect their time while retaining their role as consultants for relevant CAPS.

Although the Center for Women and Gender Education is the most important site on campus to which the students can turn for assistance with their projects, each year I receive calls from one or more other units who have been targets of CAPS. These include the Campus Police, Student Health Services, Campus Housing, the *New U* (the UCI student newspaper), and other academic schools and departments. As the size of the class grew from 70 in 1994 to 210 in 1999, it became increasingly difficult to coordinate the frequency with which individual groups contacted these and other programs on campus. However, because the CAP has been implemented for six years, most relevant units now understand the purpose of the project and have typically been supportive, even when they are the target of the proposed actions.

Working the Steps

I recall the resistance the first time I used the CAP in the Women's Studies class from students who felt that "it took too much time," "they didn't know where to begin," and that "it was too hard working in groups outside of discussion period," which is scheduled for one hour per week. When I explored their resistance with them, it became clear that they had in fact spent little time outside class on the project. In fact, the main problem was that they felt burdened because the CAP made them uncomfortable. It required skills that they had yet to develop, including working in groups, finding information outside of the library, and researching through interviewing and other interpersonal strategies. Once I realized the source of their resistance, I began to provide more specific guidelines. For example, I included the following in the CAP outline for the first step:

> Tasks for this step include identification of relevant community groups established to address the issue, phone calls to these groups to clarify the current status of work on this issue, interviews with key individuals who are employed by these groups. The groups and individuals may be identified through phone books, resource guides,

networking with resource people who are knowledgeable about the area. The broader the search, the better. All this information is needed for you to move effectively to the next step.

Providing more specific direction for CAP members also helped the teaching assistants, because many of them had never engaged in community action.

For those students who begin the CAP with a lot of enthusiasm, the process of defining a specific project usually takes them through a period of disillusionment. As Lisa Ross, a member of a group concerned with women and AIDS, wisely reflected:

> In the beginning everyone talked as though we were going to save the world, but I had my doubts. I think a lot of community action fails because they set unreachable goals for themselves. Workers all have a dream that they want to see come true. That is what promotes community action. But these dreams are huge; if it were not a huge dream, then it would not require social reform to make it into reality. If social action groups would set smaller goals for themselves instead of trying to change the world all at once, then there would be more positive social reform because movements would have more of a foundation. (Ross 1994: 3)

Ross described the first meeting of the group as follows: "We wasted a lot of time discussing the impossible. Our first meeting consisted of everyone sitting around and discussing our TV broadcasts and our celebrity endorsers while I sat quietly and tried not to destroy their fantasies" (Ross 1994: 5). After a series of discussions about forming a "doable" project, Ross reported that the group realized "that we are four students" and "AIDS is a worldwide epidemic. We could not make a difference on a big level, but by making our community the University, then we as students managed to get something done" (Ross 1994: 6).

At the next step (designed for implementation during weeks three and four of the quarter), students are asked to analyze the community and institutional context for the problem they are addressing. This step usually poses the most difficulty for the students in that they are asked to move from a general definition of the problem to a more focused framework through which to determine the institutional and political forces that contribute to the problem they have defined. To provide some guidance for the group-work process necessary to complete this step in the action plan, I instructed the students to "brainstorm alternative strategies to reach the desired outcome and indicate top strategies. Remember this is a group project, and all group members' points of view must be evaluated before moving ahead with a specific strategy."

Step three (which ideally should occur during weeks four and five) takes the students into a more detailed analysis of the institutional and political context for their action plan. Here they must consider who occupies positions of power (both formal and informal decision-makers) in the institutional arenas that are the targets for their interventions. The group then decides how it will contact each person and what strategies to adopt in order to influence them. A parallel goal for this step is to identify likely obstacles and opponents, as well as to discuss how to negotiate the resistance. Another aspect of this step in the action plan is to determine who might be likely allies in the political-change effort. After identifying which individuals or organizations will most likely benefit from the action, group members determine how they will be contacted (for example, by letter, phone, or in person) and which member or members of the group will make each contact.

Once the group has assessed the institutional and political context and considered potential allies and potential hindrances, the group must develop its specific strategy. During this step, group members develop a timeframe for implementing the specific action and consider the resources they will need.[8] This step is often linked with the next one, which involves broadening the constituency for the action plan. Students are expected to complete this step by week five. The targeted date for implementation of the CAP (step seven) is week six or seven of the quarter.

If the CAP group is successful in keeping to the timeframe (and many are not for one reason or another), the next two week weeks can be devoted to evaluating the project (step seven) and group process (step eight). For step seven, the group members assess what they have achieved, what they would do differently if they were to implement a similar project in the future, and what new community actions might follow the one they have just completed. Step eight involves a critical assessment of the group process. In addition, although the students have been asked to consider their work in light of the class readings, lectures, and discussions through the quarter, this step formalizes this exercise. They are asked to analyze their project in terms of the themes and concepts discussed in class—for example, understanding how "relations of ruling" (D. Smith 1987, 1990) are embedded in different organizations (for example, science, medicine, agriculture, land policy, politics); how colonialism, sexism, racism, poverty, and homophobia can be challenged in everyday life; and the difficulties of coalition-building.

The separate reports generated for each of the steps are then used by the students to construct their final report. They are also asked to identify ways to publicize the results of their CAPS. Depending on the focus of the CAP, students can consider sending announcements to the local newspapers and radio stations. Copies of selected reports are kept on file in the Women's Studies program office for other students to learn about these efforts. In this way, the students in future classes will benefit from the work done by the students who came before them. In a few cases, students have used these reports as jumping-off points for their projects, thus extending or following up on the work that has already been accomplished. In some cases, strategies chosen by previous groups were used by students in the next cohort. The overall list of topics and issues addressed is also shared with each new cohort.

Themes Emerging from the Community Action Programs

Because the students are required to identify topics of interest to them rather than assigned by me or the teaching assistants, the CAPS illuminate which issues or concerns are the most salient for them and, as important, how the students understand what counts as politics. Here the lessons of politics and feminism are given meaning in the context of where the students are in their learning process. There is a great deal of continuity from year to year in the topics that students identify for the CAPS (which may be partly a factor of their knowledge about the topics and issues addressed by previous cohorts). The most prevalent area of concern is violence against women. This includes preventing sexual harassment and acquaintance rape, increasing safety on campus, multicultural sensitivity in battered women's shelters, self-defense, and anti-stalking measures. For example, after researching the problem of stalking and identifying how to reach students with this information, one CAP group developed a brief description of stalking and the steps students could take to protect themselves; they gained approval to insert the description in the annual *Student Survival Guide* given to all incoming students.

The next set of concerns relate to health. CAPS focused on college women and eating disorders, increasing the awareness of breast health among younger women and women of different minorities, stress management for university women, raising awareness about the risk of dioxins in high-absorbency tampons, prevention of cervical cancer, teenage sexuality, women and AIDS/HIV prevention, HIV testing, and HIV prevention in a local high school. One group was interested in promoting anonymous HIV testing for women on campus. The group felt that many women resisted getting tested because they felt a stigma was attached and were afraid that their parents or others would find out that they had been tested. As one student explained in her final report, "It was not until I enrolled in a Women's Studies class at UCI that I became aware of the differences between confidential testing and anonymous testing for HIV." Along with four other students, she decided that the group wanted "to identify and address the barriers that may exist [that] could prevent women from taking advantage of anonymous on-campus testing." As a consequence of their investigation, they developed a series of recommendations for the Health Education Office on campus and a flyer titled, "What You Should Know About Anonymous HIV Testing at UCI."

The third theme is contraception. For example, several CAPS worked to increase education about, and awareness and accessibility of, both men's and women's condoms on campus. Many of these groups produced flyers for distribution through the Health Services and Center for Women and Gender Education that continue to be used by staff and peer educators.

Education was the next most popular topic for student projects. I define this category broadly to include projects that encouraged female students to enter the sciences as well as a campaign to place the Equal Educational Opportunity Initiative (EEOI) on the November 1998 ballot. The initiative was designed in response to the passage of Proposition 209, which ended affirmation action in admissions to the University of California. The EEOI read: "In order to provide equal opportunity, promote diversity, and combat discrimination in public education, the state may consider the economic background, race, sex, ethnicity, and national origin of qualified individuals." In addition to educational forums and a petition drive, the students contacted UCI's assistant vice-chancellor for enrollment services, assistant vice-chancellor of counseling and health services, and director of the Counseling Center to explore the strategies

UCI was adopting in order to ensure racial and ethnic diversity within the student body.

The next set of issues concerns parenting, child care, and gender socialization. CAPs were organized to address a variety of concerns, including the lack of high-quality day care for UCI students who are parents. One of my favorite projects in this category involved working with the managers of South Coast Plaza, a large and popular shopping center in Orange County, to challenge the distribution of gender-stereotyped toys at the carousel, an amusement ride in the mall. This group investigated who managed the carousel and who made the decisions about which toys would be given out. After a series of meetings with relevant managers and submitting a petition that outlined why they thought that this practice was ill-conceived, the students persuaded store managers to change their toy-distribution strategy. Now if you take your child to the carousel at South Coast Plaza, your child can choose the toy she likes rather than automatically receive a gender-stereotyped toy.

The next topic that drew the students' attention was the negative images of women in various media. Several groups challenged sexist images in advertising. For example, one group focused on a local health club that used a very sexist depiction of a woman in its advertising campaign. As part of their CAP, these students investigated previous campaigns against sexist advertising, noting that in 1971 the National Organization for Women had protested National Airlines for using an ad campaign that featured an attractive woman saying, "Fly Me." They discovered that the company mandated that flight attendants wear buttons with the slogans "Fly me" and "We make you feel good all over." As one student reported, on the picket line outside "the ticket offices of National Airlines, they carried signs like, 'Haven't you heard, I'm not a bird'" (Tran 1993: 2). As in this example, the students were regularly teaching one another about different feminist issues, historical events, and political strategies they uncovered through their CAP-related research. Consequently, the students' research enriched the educational content presented in the course and contributed to building a learning community that engaged them in the educational process.

There are always two or three groups each year who choose a topic related to promoting Women's Studies. For example, one group targeted a local high school and worked with teachers to help develop a feminist studies curriculum; another group designed and implemented strategies to recruit male students to Women's Studies; and a third group worked to counter negative stereotypes of feminism among students at UCI. The last group developed a flyer titled, "Who Are Feminists?" which is used by staff and peer educators at the Center for Women and Gender Education. Less frequent topics include equal promotion and representation of women's sports on campus. These projects are often initiated by female athletes enrolled in the class who emphasize how little support and visibility women's sports are given in the student newspaper and by Cheers, the group that promotes attendance at sports events.

A number of groups have focused on discrimination in employment and housing. One group that called itself Live and Let Live targeted the UCI apartment complex Verano Place for its discrimination against lesbian and gay couples. The strategy to persuade Verano Place housing authorities to reconsider their rental policy (which precluded gay and lesbian couples from living together unless both were enrolled as students) included a position paper, a petition drive, and a staged homosexual wedding on campus.

As this brief overview of selected projects reveals, students initiated research on a variety of topics that could not be covered in a ten-week syllabus. Because they identified the topics of most interest to them, they frequently brought a lot of enthusiasm to their research and analysis of the problems and institutions that were the focus of their projects. Of course, because the course attracts a large number of students who are more interested in fulfilling a campus-wide breadth requirement than in the topic of "Resisting and Reproducing Inequalities," it would be misleading to claim that every student approaches the CAP with tremendous energy and enthusiasm. However, I have found that, after a short period of frustration and resistance at the very beginning of the course, the majority of the students do come to appreciate the value of the CAP for their learning process and political development.

Legacy of the Community Action Programs

Beyond the pedagogical value of the CAPS, there have been a number of projects that have made a lasting impact on the campus and in the community. One of the main topics of concern for the students over the years has been rape awareness and safety on campus. During the first year of the CAP, 1994, a group came together with a concern about sexual harassment. As part of the process through which the group was attempting to define a specific action, it discovered that the annual orientation manual, called the *Survival Guide*, did not include any information on sexual harassment. Although the guide did tell students not to walk dogs on campus and where to get discount tickets for shows at the university theater, it failed to provide students with information on sexual harassment. The group investigated who was responsible for producing the *Survival Guide*, met with the relevant people, and proposed including in the *Guide* a paragraph on sexual harassment. Following a review of university publications on sexual harassment and in consultation with Paula Goldsmid of the Center for Women and Gender Education, the group drafted a paragraph that was subsequently inserted into the *Survival Guide*. One of the students expressed her enthusiasm for their success in her final report as follows: "It was really exciting that as students we could influence and motivate faculty members into action!" (Mitchell 1993).

In 1995, another CAP group, inspired by the success of the first year's group, developed a paragraph on acquaintance rape that was inserted into *The UCI Residents' Guidebook*. Another group concerned about rape prevention and calling itself Dare to Be Heard worked in collaboration with Joan Ariel, then Academic Coordinator (and Women's Studies Librarian) of the Women's Studies Program, and Donna-Jean Louden, Campus Assault Prevention Program Coordinator, to develop a proposal for a feminist self-defense course. This course is now regularly taught at the Center for Women and Gender Education. A 1999 CAP successfully changed the telephone number for the Safety Escort Service from one that was difficult to memorize to 824-SAFE.

The following year, a CAP group reviewed the processes by which students were informed about rape prevention and determined that first-year students needed more information earlier in their careers at UCI. The group titled its project, "Could You Be Next?" and developed a proposal that it submitted to two housing complexes where first-year students were assigned and called for annual rape awareness and prevention workshops for dorm residents. Working closely with Louden, the group obtained approval for its proposal.

Obviously, not all efforts to work on campus or with community groups have been successful, although, regardless of the outcome, students come away with a great deal of knowledge about the intersection of race, class, and gender and institutional politics. Because UCI's population is more than 50 percent Asian American, a number of projects have focused on advocating for the rights of Asian American women in a variety of settings. One CAP group discovered that Interval House, a shelter located in a predominantly Vietnamese community in Westminster, served a predominantly white European American population. This group worked with shelter staff to identify obstacles preventing Vietnamese American women from using the shelter. Drawing on readings from the course, the students developed a proposal for establishing a bilingual and multicultural community board that they presented to the staff. Their proposal was met with "mixed responses." The shelter director explained that the shelter could not initiate such a program without approval of funding agencies, including the California Department of Social Services. In her final report, a group member, Hanh Nguyen, acknowledged that the group might have achieved more success if it had had the time "to garner more support from the Vietnamese community itself by going to Vietnamese-owned businesses, especially run by women, speaking on the Vietnamese channel" (1995: 7), among other strategies.

Groups have increasingly turned to the Internet as a site for their political actions. I have been somewhat cautious in my support of this strategy, because Web pages must be updated regularly and need to be linked to other relevant sites. Other concerns I have include the risk of duplication; the difficulty, in some cases, of constructing this intervention as political action; the extensive time needed to gather the data and source materials; and the technical expertise that often prohibits many members of the group from participating. One group created a Web page to promote women's sports on campus. It reported that in the first week and a half that the page was available, it had received 300 hits, and almost a dozen people had signed up for the e-mail listserv connected to it. This group optimistically said that it would keep the page going after the course. Given time constraints, the diversity of projects, and the problems tracking students after they leave the course, it is difficult to access how many CAPS outlast the term and to determine, for those who do continue, how they continue. My general sense is that few CAPS do continue, even when students express an interest in doing so, given that they encounter other demands on their time or lose track of group members as they graduate or move on to other classes.

However, some students individually continue to demonstrate a commitment to community action or other forms of community-based work while at UCI, although it would be difficult to determine how long that involvement continues after graduation. Ranu Mukherjee, whose project concerned addressing the problem of eating disorders among UCI students, wrote: "Even though my project is over, I really want to continue doing something about this problem that affects so many young women. . . . I am really interested in this subject and I want to make sure that I am constantly involved in something that I feel so strongly about" (1999: 6). Hanh Nguyen explained why she expected to continue her work on behalf of battered women in the Vietnamese American community. She wrote in her final CAP report: "I have a personal stake in continuing this effort because this is my community. Domestic violence is never talked about in the Vietnamese community because it is sanctioned for men and shamed for women. However, my social location as a middle class student provides me with opportunities to tap into resources such as [English] language [proficiency] that will aid abused women" (1995: 10).

Unlike many who bemoan the loss of a commitment to political activism among the younger generation of feminists, I have witnessed firsthand their energy and enthusiasm for challenging patterns of inequality in diverse of institutions and social practices.

Through the investigatory process and activist interventions they choose for their CAPs, students learn about the "extralocal organization of everyday experiences" (DeVault 1999: 49) or "how things work" to reproduce inequality (D. Smith 1990: 34). These lessons also illustrate the feminist critiques of "objectified and authoritative knowledge" as embodied in "professional, scientific, and other academic discourses" (Smith 1999: 31). As they uncover how corporations test and market certain products, or as they examine the practices of certain professions, they empirically test some of the premises of the feminist analyses presented in class. Therefore, the experiential approach reinforces the instructional content of the introductory course, "Reproducing and Resisting Inequalities," which explores the social organization of knowledge and the processes of inequalities that are woven in and through institutions.

Teaching Feminisms Experientially

Over the years, students have expressed a variety of positive and negative feelings about working in groups to accomplish the project. Among the problems they report are difficulty in scheduling meetings outside of class time, determining an effective division of labor, negotiating the different degrees of participation that contributes to some group members' performing a disproportionate amount of work, and achieving consensus. UCI and, consequently, the Women's Studies introductory sequence draw a diverse student body. In some cases, this diversity posed challenges for the process of group consensus-building. In other cases, it served as a resource. Nayomi Munaweera, who worked on a project concerned with increasing Vietnamese American women's access to services for battered women, wrote that "the fact that we were of diverse racial backgrounds was really more of an advantage than not. We really represented a multicultural slice of America since we were a Vietnamese, an African American, a Caucasian, a Latina, and a Sri Lankan" (1995: 8). And students who did not achieve the level of consensus or cooperation that Munaweera reports often agreed that, despite their difficulties, working in groups is a necessary part of fostering change.

Experience working in the CAP groups highlighted many themes of class discussion, sometimes providing painful lessons. Shadi Aryabod, who worked on the EEOI campaign discussed earlier, remarked on the gender division of labor that occurred within her group:

> With one exception, the division of labor in the group was delineated according to invisible rules about gender appropriate tasks. For instance, men were reluctant in helping with poster making since they believed that our "pretty, female hand-writing" were more appropriate than their "manly hand-writing"! In addition, they practically monopolized our "public relations" activities by not sharing the information with the others. If any contacts were given out, they tended to be the less influential ones. Finally, all the letters and flyers that went out in the first part of our project contained the signatures of the two male co-organizers, in spite of the fact that one of the three founding co-organizers was a female. (1998: 5)

Once she recognized the pattern of gender inequality, she developed an alternative strategy to ensure her active participation in outreach and group decision-making:

> Hence, after a short period of disillusionment, I realized that I could not afford to sit back and hope that they would consider my opinions. Therefore, I took it upon myself to change my approach. I

began to make plans and to seek the assistance of other women in the group. Moreover, I started to make contacts with predominant members of the University and the community. . . . These contacts proved to be, not only of great importance to our efforts, but helped me learn more about myself and activism. (Aryabod 1998: 5)

In her final report, Aryabod reflected on this experience and recognized her own process of politicization. Referring to an article we discussed in class by Celene Krauss (1998), Aryabod (1998: 6) wrote: "I came to experience first hand how the valuable knowledge women have is commonly subjugated and not taken into consideration."

By researching their chosen topics and discovering certain information on their own, the students developed a deeper understanding of the issue than if they only heard it discussed in class or in assigned reading. For example, Tenisha Powers, whose group focused on date rape, reported in her final paper:

This was a total learning experience in so many different ways. First of all was the knowledge I received just studying date rape. I knew date rape happened but I was unaware of how frequently it occurred. I myself held some of the misconceptions about date rape, for example, believing that most rapists were strangers to the victim. It is amazing how many women are raped by someone they knew. . . . Once people know what date rape is more women would be more willing to come forward with their stories and more men would think twice before pressuring a woman into sex. (1999: 5)

Many students expressed frustration in their final reports about the limited timeframe for the project. In considering why her other two group members were less enthusiastic about the CAP, Anna Vasquez wrote: "I feel that many students felt rushed and arranged to have workshops for the sake of getting the project done and over with. I feel that these people could be capable of so much more given ample time" (1994: 7). However, despite their frustrations regarding the limited time they had to implement the CAP, many other students came to view it as a valuable experience.

Most students were able to draw connections between the CAP and feminist theorizing. In my first introductory Women's Studies class at UCI, in the winter of 1993, I introduced students to the different "feminisms":

liberal or reform feminism; socialist and Marxist feminisms; radical feminism; lesbian feminism; Third World feminisms. Various other categories of feminisms appear in Women's Studies texts, including historical categorizations such as "first-wave" (up to 1950) and "second-wave" (1950–early 1980s) feminisms (Humm 1992); labels that refer more to specific theoretical frameworks, such as psychoanalytic feminism (Humm 1992; Tong 1989); and designations connected to the racial-ethnic identities or social locations of the authors or that center race, postcolonial analyses, or gendered processes of global capitalism such as black feminism, multicultural feminism and global feminism (Collins 1990; Jaggar and Rothenberg 1993; Lorber 1994). Terry Haywoode (1991) analyzes dimensions of "working-class feminism." Maxine Baca Zinn and Bonnie Thornton Dill (1996: 323–24) describe "multiracial feminism" that locates both men and women "in multiple systems of domination." African American women and Latinas have created terminology that self-consciously rejects the feminist label such as "xicanista" and "womanist" (Castillo 1995; Walker 1983; also see Johnson-Odim 1992; Mohanty 1991b). In a recent effort "to contribute to the creation of multi-centered, women-affirming, and transformative politics," Angela Miles (1996: x–xi) demonstrates how "types of feminism usually perceived as absolutely different, even opposing, share important integrative principles." Her articulation of "integrative feminisms" further challenges rigid distinctions between liberal, radical, and socialist feminisms (see also Sandoval 1991).

For students in an introductory course in Women's Studies, such a complexity of feminisms is often confusing, to say the least. Although presenting the variety of feminisms does contest the very limited constructions of feminism that circulate in the media and popular discourse, teaching multiple feminisms as typologies could also undercut the students' ability to appreciate the complex political traditions, theoretical debates, and historical factors that contributed to the articulation of the diverse feminist approaches. Given the short timeframe for the class, it is also difficult to give the students a more textured historical, comparative, and international introduction to diverse women's movements' relationship to different feminisms. However, in the context of the CAP, political interventions that the students identify for their change project become resources for more grounded discussions of different feminist strategies.

For example, one recent CAP group was interested in finding a way to address the educational needs of students in other parts of the world. The group discussed the factors that contribute to illiteracy and determined that lack of resources was a key factor. From this recognition, it decided that it would mount a campaign to raise funds from local businesses to send school supplies to a rural community in Kenya with which one of the students was familiar through her neighbor, who had founded the Center for Indigenous Knowledge. When I discussed the proposal with the group, I asked the students to consider how this intervention would challenge the system of inequality that underlay the problem of illiteracy and how the action they proposed would address gender inequality. The group then continued their discussion without me to revise their CAP in response to the issues I raised. They returned a week later to tell me that they would revise their project to target the sororities on campus to see whether they would be willing to sponsor an annual drive to raise funds for school supplies for schoolchildren in Kenya.

This left me with another dilemma. When do I use my authority to veto a project if it does not reflect a more complex understanding of politics? I have learned that, although I can provide some structure and guidance, I cannot tell a group that it needs to find another type of community action. I do use the process of topic selection and discussion of possible interventions to teach about the theoretical differences in political actions. However, in the course of ten weeks it is not always possible for students to redirect their efforts. Fortunately, the action steps they do take can always be understood within different feminist frameworks. School supplies to Kenya as a strategy to fight illiteracy reflects a liberal response to inequality that continues to inform social-welfare policy. A project such as this one gives me the opportunity to discuss liberal, postcolonialist, and Third World feminisms in the context of a very particular action devised by members of the class. Rather than highlight the limits of their intervention, I can acknowledge the contribution that these students make to class discussion.

Limits and Possibilities of Community Action

Community-based activism as a political strategy is limited in a number of significant ways. These limitations apply regardless of whether the collective actions emerge in a particular neighborhood or university context. Some critics argue that community activism by definition rarely transcends the local; nor, in many cases, is it likely to continue after the particular issue and targeted problem is resolved. Even when particular actors or community organizations attempt to build coalitions with others beyond their local community, limited time and resources often prevent effective coalition-building. Furthermore, issue-based community activism often contributes to a narrow focus that renders invisible the larger political and economic factors in which the particular concern is embedded. Therefore, group members often had difficulty extending their political and economic analysis beyond the immediate context. Furthermore, it is not surprising that few CAPS focused on international issues. This is of particular concern because the course is designed to reveal the intersection of the local, international, and global in the production of knowledge, the reproduction of inequalities, the organization of women's everyday lives, and resistance strategies.

Since 1994, only three groups have focused on international issues. Of course, this is not surprising given the strong recommendation that groups target an identifiable community that they can contact directly and attempt to influence in the ten-week timeframe. However, one group became interested in promoting awareness of indigenous Mexican women's struggles in Chiapas. This group was formed after a student in the class discussed her summer trip to Chiapas and emphasized that there was a need to raise awareness about the political and economic situation there. She suggested establishing a Web page with information about the circumstances surrounding the struggle and what interested people might do to support the indigenous people. In addressing my concerns about using the Web for its project, the Chiapas group was able to demonstrate how it would maximize the Internet for raising awareness about this issue and create a page accessible to UCI students that would predominantly serve as a link to relevant sites that already had an institutional sponsorship to ensure that the information on linked Web pages is updated regularly.

In an effort to promote a more international and intersectional framework for the CAPS, I have explored how materialist feminist analyses and Dorothy Smith's institutional ethnography can provide epistemological tools to help students link the so-called micro-social world with the macro processes that shape our world.[9] Smith describes her institutional ethnographic approach as a "method of inquiry, always ongoing, opening things up, discovering" (1992: 88). Institutional ethnography is a sociological method that can be "accountable to people's lived experience" and "as a means of making visible the social relations that organize and shape our lives" (Smith 1992: 190). In fact, in the introduction to their edited collection of case studies inspired by Dorothy Smith's institutional ethnography approach to standpoint analysis, Marie Campbell and Ann Manicom (1995: 12) argue that institutional ethnography permits researchers and activists "to discover how people's lives are ordered, managed, ruled—to support interests that are not their own." The method of institutional ethnography highlights the extra-local processes that organize everyday life. Students are asked to examine relevant texts, organizational practices, and institutional relationships to explore how things are put together in order to reproduce inequalities in specific settings (also see DeVault 1999). Due to the influence of phenomenology, Marxism, and poststructuralism, institutional ethnography has an inherently interdisciplinary reach. Although Smith's particular project is to help construct a sociology that starts from and can speak to the everyday actualities of people's lives, her methodology for social critique and textual and institutional analyses has much to offer interdisciplinary feminist pedagogical practice. The institutional and political knowledge that students derive from their investigation of how things are put together in order to make the changes they propose illustrates the link between institutional ethnography and activism.

As a feminist pedagogical tool, the CAP challenges some of the basic tenets of contemporary academic production. At the close of the 1990s, we find increasing pressure on colleges and universities to maximize faculty labor while raising the bottom line through large course sizes, distance learning, and computer technology. Those of us in joint positions are further engaged in this process as our service commitments and curriculum offerings are expanded to serve the needs of two diverse units. On the one hand, like other problem-solving exercises and internships, the CAP serves this goal well by encouraging the students to become "self-taught" in a variety of topics that we cannot cover in a ten-week quarter. On the other hand, the CAP as an experiential group project challenges the privatization of academic knowledge production. Students begin to recognize how the individualized approach to higher education inhibits the development of certain kinds of knowledge, privileging self-interest and competition among students rather than cooperation and group learning. The project also provides a context through which students can critique the academy as a site of social control as well as discover how it is linked to other institutions to reproduce patterns of inequality. Finally, students come to recognize their own position within these institutions as well as their ability to challenge oppressive institutional practices. In some instances, they succeed in making small changes within the university or their community. In many instances, these changes are fleeting. Regardless of the specific outcome, the CAP group process offers one strategy for incorporating social-change-oriented pedagogy into the Women's Studies curriculum. In other words, the institutionalization of Women's Studies does not mean the inevitable loss of feminist praxis in the feminist classroom. It demonstrates how we might reinvent ourselves as feminist educators as well as help our students resist the privatized and apolitical discourse and practice that accompanies life in the academy and beyond.

With the development of university-based Centers for Women, among other organizations for support and grassroots political engagement, Women's Studies classrooms are no longer the only formal sites in colleges and universities where consciousness-raising and empowerment occur. We now occupy the institutional location from which to develop further strategies that link the personal to the political to the theoretical in new and creative ways. Moreover, given the growth in size of our Women's Studies classrooms (especially at the introductory level), we need to find epistemological and pedagogical approaches that lend themselves to feminist education without marginalizing the important insights of early CR strategies.

Yet I also have to acknowledge my ambivalence about the use of such a challenging project in the large introductory Women's Studies class. When I began the project, the class was limited to seventy students. Working with one teaching assistant, I was able to intervene more directly in the implementation of CAPS as well as more quickly link the specific action steps in which the students engaged with the course material. However, as the class size grew to the current enrollment of 210, with four teaching assistants, I felt increasing unease about the feasibility of effectively implementing this experiential project. Many of the teaching assistants are themselves new to community action and are consequently unsure in their role as CAP facilitators. Ideally, I would like to see the CAP offered within the context of an upper-division course that is limited to no more than forty students. I would also like to create a related course for teaching assistants interested in linking theory and feminist practice. Although we have discussed these options in our Women's Studies program, we currently do not have the faculty time and resources to offer these courses.

Different academic settings provide different contexts for the use of experiential projects such as the CAP. Marjorie DeVault ends her discussion of institutional ethnography with the following coda: "The dynamic of borrowing and extending—picking up tools and reshaping them, testing their malleability and observing their performance, noting their problems and making corrections—is the essential dynamic of research as resistance" (1999: 53). I offer the CAP and the lessons I have learned from it in the same spirit, for I believe that experiential learning is a dynamic process that can invigorate our teaching and our feminist praxis in the classroom and beyond.

Notes

I thank all the students in ws50B for their work on the CAPs. I owe a great deal of gratitude to Robin Goldberg, who taught the course in the winter quarters of 1996 and 1997; to Paula Goldsmid and Donna-Jean Louden for graciously sharing their valuable time and wisdom with the students; and to the following graduate teaching assistants for their essential role in guiding the CAPs to completion: Jennifer Boyle, Cindy Cheng, Michelle Grisat, Clara McLean, Chrisy Moutsatsos, Julie Park, Beth Quinn, Beth Rayfield, Charlene Tung, and Clare Weber. I express special appreciation to the Women's Studies student Rosalia Vassalla, who helped me systematize the CAP reports. My thanks to Karen Bojar, Jennifer Boyle, Marjorie DeVault, Michelle Grisat, Adina Mack, Chrisy Moutsatsos, Karen Tice, Charlene Tung, and Robyn Wiegman for helpful feedback on an earlier draft of this chapter.

1 Lisa Hogeland (1998: 166) points out that most critiques of Women's Studies "simply replay the critiques of CR itself (as bourgeois, as therapeutic, or as self-indulgent) among late 1960s radicals." Hogeland also notes how attacks on Women's Studies are financed by conservative research institutes "in conjunction with other attacks on higher education, which does differentiate them from New Leftist sniping at Women's Liberation" (1998: 176).

2 See Coates et al. 1998 for a discussion of the challenges graduate students face in negotiating feminism research and activism.

3 See also Elizabeth Strugatz, e-mail on teachsoc@vance.irss.unc.edu, May 22, 1999. In many cases, internships are developed in response to employers' interests in training an educated workforce with employment-relevant skills. Some students, especially those from middle- and upper-class backgrounds who have not found it necessary to seek employment while going to college, can gain many advantages from internships in the community. For working-class students, internships are a mixed bag. On the one hand, they can provide experience that contributes to their upward mobility better than do the minimum-wage jobs they often hold while attending college. These experiences, coupled with the letters of recommendations from professionals in not-for-profit community organizations, could enhance their employability following graduation. On the other hand, internships are typically unpaid and require working-class students to engage in volunteer work while juggling paid jobs and college. Students who are parents find internship requirements even more unmanageable.

4 By "targeted," Dickinson means that "all community placements would, in some way, relate to increasing women's self-sufficiency through the development of microenterprises, cooperatives, or flexible business networks (where people from related businesses cooperate together)" (1999: 56).

5 Since the introductory Women's Studies series can be used by students for the college-wide Diversity and Humanities sequence, we attract a large number of science—especially, biology—majors (approximately one-third of the class). All biology majors are given the opportunity to pursue independent experimental laboratory or field research under the supervision of a professor in the School of Biological Sciences or College of Medicine.

6 Anna Ascencio (1999: 6) emphasized that the weekly reports provided a way to ensure that each member of the group participated regularly in group activities. She explained in her final report: "We had to learn to compromise and be democratic in order to keep the peace and be fair. The workload was relatively fair among us, and I think that was due to the weekly reports that we had to turn in. The reports served as a way of self-monitoring what we did and didn't do."

7 The Center for Women and Gender Education, previously called the UCI Women's Resource Center, was established in 1975 to provide a site on campus for women to gain support, learn, and discuss gender-related issues, and to celebrate women's achievements. The center sponsors a peer educators' program in which students develop and implement their own programs related to women's issues and gender education.

8 If funds are required, the group must find a way to raise money through contributions (for example, from the local copy center or stationery store) or other creative means. This has been a challenge for the students, as it adds another labor-intensive activity to the process. Some groups decide to forgo fund-raising and actually chip in collectively to fund their projects. Although in most cases the expense is minimal, the class

implications of this decision provides an opportunity to discuss how differential access to financial and other resources advantages some groups over others.

9 Feminist materialist approaches to standpoint epistemology argue for the continued significance of the social analyst who starts from the "standpoint" of women's everyday lives and, in Dorothy Smith's approach, does not end analysis at the level of individual women as "knowers" but explores and explicates "what [they do] not know—the social relations and organization pervading [their] world but invisible in it" (1992: 91).

What Should Every Women's Studies Major Know? Reflections on the Capstone Seminar

A major in Women's Studies should be more than a loose amalgamation of courses on women, the gender system, and the relationship of gender to other systems of stratification in transnational context. Whatever the constraints imposed by their funding problems, staff shortages, and general vulnerability, Women's Studies programs typically aim for some level of curricular coherence and cumulative progression from the introductory, through the intermediate, and on to the advanced level of courses for undergraduate degree programs. In general, where the pragmatics of a particular institution have allowed it, programs have instituted a sequence for majors, minors, or certificate students that begins with an interdisciplinary course or courses at the introductory level, moves through intermediate or advanced courses with either a disciplinary or interdisciplinary focus, and concludes with a capstone seminar. Although numerous textbooks have been published for introductions to Women's Studies, and although there has been considerable dialogue on what should be covered in the evolving introductions to Women's Studies, much less has been available on the capstone seminar.

Just what should every undergraduate major know about Women's Studies before graduation? Designing the capstone seminar for Women's Studies majors lands feminist faculty smack-dab in the middle of the key issues of our new area of inquiry. For some, Women's Studies is an interdisciplinary field in which feminist questions and knowledge from a variety of disciplines are brought to bear on work in one of the traditional disciplines. For others, Women's Studies is a new discipline, with its own body of knowledge and methodology, the basis for newly proliferating Ph.D. degrees. Little consensus exists, however, about what constitutes the core body of knowledge and methodology of Women's Studies that should be passed on at the graduate or undergraduate level. Moreover, the desire for intellectual breadth and the need for scholarly depth require constant negotiation as we recognize the rapid pace of change in higher education and as the conventional borders among disciplines are increasingly porous and frequently transgressed. These questions shape our everyday lives as feminist teachers and scholars and frame the curricular design of degree programs. Thinking about them is crucial, as well, in the development of the capstone seminar.

Should the seminar provide an opportunity for a specialized research project that gives a student hands-on experience with in-depth research design, critical thinking, evidence collecting, and argumentation? Or, conversely, should the capstone experience in Women's Studies emphasize breadth and an integrative interdisciplinarity that pulls together the disparate pieces of the major? Do we want majors to tunnel deep or get a bird's-eye view of the field as they prepare to leave the cocoon of classroom learning? Should the seminar reflect the faculty member's own areas of expertise or specialized field of research? And how should the seminar relate to what many regard as the intellectual "glue" that holds the major together—namely, feminist theory—especially given that a number of programs use their main feminist theory course as a capstone seminar? I do not want to propose a single answer for these questions; nor have I systematically surveyed the variety of seminars that are actually being offered in the United States, let alone in what is increasingly becoming a worldwide movement in higher education. Instead, my intent is to encourage a dialogue about the capstone seminar by reflecting on what I have been doing in my annual efforts since 1992 to design and refine a course that effectively concludes the undergraduate curriculum for majors.

The type of seminar I have developed rests on the foundation of what the students have already taken for their Women's Studies major at the University of Wisconsin-Madison, which has a large, relatively well-funded program with some sixteen budgeted faculty with joint appointments and forty more faculty with non-budgeted appointments in the program. Students choose from a combination of interdisciplinary courses budgeted and taught in the program and discipline-based courses budgeted either through the program or a variety of departments throughout the campus. Majors are required to take at least two of the three introductory-level interdisciplinary courses—the science course and either the humanities or the social science introduction. Majors must also take one Women's Studies course in each of five areas: theory, U.S. women of color or women in non-Western societies, biology and health, humanities, and social sciences. And finally, they must either complete another major or take an additional nine to twelve credits in an area of concentration with some methodological or substantive coherence (such as a department or an interdepartmental cluster).[1] Students in the honors program are required to write a senior thesis, but the program does not have enough faculty to make this a requirement, or even an option, for all majors. An internship course—long desired—is currently being implemented as an option.

With this demanding set of requirements as a foundation, the Women's Studies majors have been exposed to a range of courses, some interdisciplinary and some discipline-based. Most—perhaps as many as 80 percent—of the students are double majors. Roughly half the students have either a concentration or another major in the social sciences (e.g., sociology, social welfare, law and society, psychology, political science); approximately a third are humanities-based (e.g., English, French, communications, comparative literature, philosophy); a tiny number (usually one to three students) are science majors; and the remainder have a major with another interdisciplinary unit, such as Afro-American studies or law and society. With an occasional exception, all the majors are women. The capstone seminar was designed to enroll about fifteen students in their final semester as undergraduates, ensuring a small-class experience as the endpoint of the major. But the runaway success of the major—we have about 200 majors, with numbers still increasing—has meant that the course has had to accommodate enrollments of 25–38, hardly conducive to seminar-like pedagogy and work assignments, a fact that has affected the course I have designed.

On the whole, these Women's Studies majors are eager to leave school but anxious, if not downright terrified, about graduating. Even those who have well-formulated career objectives often want to take time off before undertaking arduous postgraduate degrees or finding the "perfect" job in their field. Many lack confidence about being able to get into the graduate and professional schools they select; others are uncertain about how to look and be competitive for an interesting job that would allow them to use what they have learned in school. Like many public universities, career advising is at a minimum at UW-Madison, and the Women's Studies majors often experience impending graduation as being set adrift on a sea of uncertainty. Quite a number of Women's Studies majors are impatient with classroom learning in their final semester of school and are eager to get out into the community to put into practice their feminist idealism and desire for social justice.

Designing a stimulating and effective capstone seminar for the kinds of students I teach requires a delicate balancing of what they will be responsive to, given where they're "at," and what I think they need to learn as both of these factors are mediated by what I am capable of teaching at an advanced undergraduate level. After one unfortunate experience, I discovered that most students were very unhappy with a seminar aimed at deepening their knowledge of feminist theory, particularly because most had just completed the feminist theory course required for majors. Having watched a colleague face wholesale revolt against her attempt to teach an aspect of her research specialization, I didn't even attempt to focus the capstone on a narrow topic that I happened to know a great deal about. Although this is the model of many capstone seminars in the traditional disciplines, I could see how majors in an interdisciplinary field such as Women's Studies would find this too limiting. In addition to feminist theory, my areas of special expertise are located in the humanities, especially literary studies, cultural studies, and the arts. Where would any topics or methodologies I chose leave the students whose feminist interests and skills were based more in the social sciences or sciences, especially quantitative ones? A vast chasm separates feminist hermeneutics for reading *l'écriture féminine*—how women (or men) "write the feminine body"—for example, and feminist statistical analysis of patterns in women's sexual behavior, even though the issue of gender and sexuality underlies both topics.

For related reasons, I also hesitated to attempt a seminar in which the goal was to get each student to design a research topic related to her (or his) special interest and expertise. This model is the other major format of capstone seminars at UW-Madison, with history majors, for example, working with primary sources and related historiography on a specific topic in the discipline of history. But how could I—with thirty-some students ranging over the humanities, social sciences, and sciences— effectively direct all those projects, particularly when a large number of them would inevitably require knowledge of scholarly literatures and methodologies with which I was not familiar? Through trial and error, characterized by continuing refinement, I have designed a seminar that is ambitiously interdisciplinary but rooted in fields and methods I can handle; it is extensively theoretical without being directly devoted to feminist theory; and it is analytically rather than research-oriented.

The fundamental objective of my capstone seminar as it has evolved begins with the acknowledgement of the students' position as graduating seniors. They are on the cusp—the threshold between the need for a retrospective look back at what they have learned as Women's Studies majors and a prospective look forward at what they might be facing after graduation. Thresholds are liminal spaces, in between one thing and another, as theorized in many fields (from the anthropology of Victor Turner to the postcolonial theory of Homi Bhabha to the border consciousness of Gloria Anzaldúa). They are borderlands between the past and the future. In the case of Women's Studies majors, the seminar is the liminal site between being undergraduate students and being postgraduates—either out in the "big wide world" or moving on into some form of professional training.[2] The capstone seminar is an ideal place for students to shuttle between looking backward and looking forward, between gaining a perspective on what they have learned and fortifying themselves for what they will face after graduation. I want, in short, for the seminar to fulfill two needs simultaneously: to pull together what they have learned in their Women's Studies classes and to help prepare them for a future life (vocational and personal) in which their Women's Studies majors can play a significant and positive role. Because I firmly believe that what they will need in the future will increasingly involve the ability to negotiate transcultural contacts and effects inside and outside the United States in an increasingly globalized world, I place the retrospective and prospective dimensions of the seminar within a broadly comparative and transnational frame. To meet this double objective, I organize the seminar around three main focuses: 1) the History and Theory of Women's Studies (three weeks); 2) Feminist Epistemologies: Theory and Practice in Reading and Writing Women's Lives (ten weeks); and 3) the Third Wave: The New Generation of Feminists and Your Future. Any one of these is sufficient for a whole term, but each has its distinctive contribution to overall course objectives, and the mix prevents the seminar from dragging or becoming repetitive.[3] I will address the theoretical underpinnings and aims for each section in turn, then offer critical reflections on the limitations of this approach to the capstone seminar.

The objective of the first section of the seminar is to provide a brief overview of the diachronic evolution of Women's Studies as a field in higher education and to enhance the students' ability to articulate a synchronic definition of Women's Studies that is flexible enough to incorporate diverse forms but precise enough to demonstrate a conceptual understanding of underlying issues. Immersed in many specific areas of Women's Studies, our students have by their senior year a strong, phenomenological sense of the field but little systematic knowledge of its history or theoretically precise mappings of its boundaries. One could argue that majors in all fields should be introduced to the shape and history of their discipline as such, although such meta-analysis is more typically reserved for graduate education, with its greater emphasis on professionalization. But because Women's Studies is a new field, a political field, and often under attack, I think graduating majors need for their own survival to be able to explain and justify their Women's Studies major in concrete and persuasive terms. It is important, as well, for the field of Women's Studies to turn out majors who are effective ambassadors for their major after graduation.

Given the complexity of the topic, the three weeks I devote to the theory and history of Women's Studies is woefully condensed and incomplete. Nevertheless, it often hits the students with the force of the famous feminist "click"—the lightbulb epiphany of revelation that puts things in place and makes them much clearer about how to explain to others what their major is all about. I remind them that after they graduate, they will face many questions from prospective employers, professional schools, graduate programs, friends, lovers, family, and so forth about what Women's Studies is and why they majored in it. These questions will range, I warn them, from the knowledgeable and supportive, to the ignorant and mildly curious, to the suspicious and downright hostile. They are quick to tell me that they have already faced these questions a lot—and out pour, with relief, a lot of the stereotypes about Women's Studies and feminists they have been confronting for years: It's not a serious academic major; it's full of man-hating lesbians; it's "politically correct" (PC); it won't prepare you for life; you can't get a job with a Women's Studies major; and so forth. They express considerable frustration with these accusations and how they have attempted to answer them, especially when the challenges come from people they care about, such as family members, friends, and partners. This frustration is useful, providing considerable motivation to engage them in definitional and historical analysis.

Rather than provide students with a ready-made definition of Women's Studies, I use a brainstorming pedagogy to elicit their own definitions. What emerges is often heartfelt, thus getting them to reflect on their direct experience in the classroom for the purposes of metacritical analysis. It is also often fragmentary, unsystematic, and even contradictory. As one might expect, it shows little awareness of historical struggles that undergird the field—the conflict within Women's Studies and the conflict Women's Studies has faced within the academy and from society at large. Nor does it show much comparative knowledge of Women's Studies in different locations—in different kinds of academic settings, in K–12 educational institutions, in community advocacy organizations such as rape crisis centers, or in different parts of the globe.

In getting the students to develop a synchronic definition of Women's Studies, I encourage them to work toward an umbrella definition, one that encompasses considerable diversity of opinion on what constitutes feminism, as well as what kinds of locations the "educational arm of the women's movement" comes into being. Definitions tend to police borders, drawing lines between what is included and what is excluded from a category. Theory itself, by its very emphasis on structure and system, often fixes. It is important in Women's Studies, however, to resist sectarian borders that narrow the field or establish insiders and outsiders based on the particular political values or positionality of definers. Narrow orthodoxies not only isolate Women's Studies; they also cover up differences among people in Women's Studies. I therefore encourage porous definitional boundaries, inclusive and flexible. But I do devote considerable attention to getting students to articulate what the many constitutive components of Women's Studies are and why Women's Studies fits under the general rubric of feminism (itself broadly defined) in its advocacy of social justice and in its transformative impact on traditional disciplines.[4]

Supplementing their synchronic analysis, the focus on the diachronic development of Women's Studies in the past thirty years develops the students' understanding of the political processes and practices that have made the diverse forms of Women's Studies possible and that continue to subject Women's Studies to change and growth. Because of time constraints, I turn the spotlight onto Women's Studies in higher education in the United States, with only supplementary reference to the global spread of Women's Studies, where different kinds of feminist movements have combined with very different academic institutions to produce geographically distinct forms of Women's Studies around the world.[5] (The notion of what I call "locationally" or "geographically" specific analysis is as important as understanding the temporally or historically specific analysis.) Students find that their individual menu of Women's Studies courses begins to fall into a coherent pattern, particularly as they learn about the theoretical, institutional, and political factors that have shaped the stiff requirements for the major. On the whole, they are fascinated to hear about the professional and political issues that underlie their coursework, information that would have been of little interest to them in introductory courses in Women's Studies—the evolving debates about differences among women in the curriculum, feminist pedagogy, governance issues, institutional homes for Women's Studies, degree programs, faculty and staffing issues, disciplinarity versus interdisciplinarity, program versus department structures, "autonomy" versus "integration," academics versus activism, and the like.[6]

Even more important, they discover that aspects of their collaborative definition of Women's Studies have a history—even a politically charged and fraught history—and did not just "happen" without conflict. For example, students included without prompting in their definition of Women's Studies attention to differences among women based on race, class, sexuality, religion, and so forth. They were often unaware, however, of the historical process that produced this now consensual insight of multipositionality. I assign introductions to such Women's Studies texts as *All the Women Are White, All the Men Are Black, But Some of Us Are Brave* (Hull, Scott, and Smith 1982), *Lesbian Studies: Present and Future* (Cruikshank 1982), and *Third World Women and the Politics of Feminism* (Mohanty et al. 1991) from the 1980s to show them the pioneering and difficult role played by such feminists as Barbara Smith, Margaret Cruikshank, Gloria T. Hull, Alice Chai, and Chandra Mohanty. Learning the history of the developing discourse of differences among women in

Women's Studies in the United States helps students to see how the divisions that run like an undercurrent in Women's Studies classrooms are still with us today and still need hard work to negotiate. Understanding Women's Studies as the result of an ongoing historical process that takes place in specific locations also gives the majors a sense of participating in the future shaping of Women's Studies.

For the final topic in the section on the Theory and History of Women's Studies, I turn to the PC debate and the attacks on Women's Studies made across the spectrum of political views. My objective here is twofold: to develop an understanding of the place of Women's Studies in the contemporary "culture wars" and to provide students with strategies for forming and defending their own positions on these issues effectively. I also want to legitimate critique from within Women's Studies—that is, the formation of critique aimed at strengthening Women's Studies. After asking students to brainstorm on the meanings of the term "political correctness" (or "PC" as they hear it used in the media and in their everyday lives), I have them read Ruth Perry (1992) on the history of the term—from its origins in the left, particularly as a form of mocking self-critique, to its appropriation by the right and the National Association of Scholars as an all-out assault on Women's Studies, ethnic studies, gay/lesbian/queer studies, and postmodern or poststructuralist studies. A range of articles attacking PC-ness and Women's Studies by John Taylor (1991), Christina Hoff Sommers (1992), Karen Lerhman (1993), Daphne Patai and Noretta Koertge (1995), and Barbara Epstein (1992) acquaint students with different kinds of attack, including the anti-feminist, the unsympathetic feminist, and the Women's Studies-identified feminist. These sample articles taken from various venues in the popular, highbrow, and academic media offer good opportunities to explain such issues as rhetoric, visuals, audience, promotion, funding, and publication industries. They also allow me to make the crucial distinction between the pernicious use of the category "political correctness" to dismiss the entire project of Women's Studies and the necessity for the category within Women's Studies as a mechanism to challenge tendencies toward feminist orthodoxy or fundamentalism. Many students experience impatience with feminist PC-ism in their classes and among friends; they need permission to be critical of feminism as a way of maintaining its openness to change.[7]

For the substantial middle section of the seminar, I foster interdisciplinarity by focusing on a topic that is central to Women's Studies across the humanities, social sciences, and sciences so that students who have emphasized different divisions can experience it as significant for their past and future work. I suspect this kind of thematic focus is quite common in Women's Studies capstone seminars, and I can envision any number of topical or controversial focuses that could make for lively interdisciplinary examination. I focus on the epistemological issue of feminist interpretation itself. How do feminists read and thus create meaning in examining women's lives?[8] What are the contexts of interpretation? What are the modes or genres in which interpretations take shape, and what impact do those forms have on the content? Who is the audience for these interpretations? What are their effects? How do the structures of power affect interpretative acts? Where are agency and authority located? How are they negotiated?

My intent in shaping ten weeks around the theory and practice of interpretation is to problematize feminist acts of meaning-making. I want to break down the unexamined assumption that students might have acquired in their Women's Studies major that if an interpretation is "feminist," it is "good." To some extent, the very success of Women's Studies classes in teaching students to critique sexist, racist, heterosexist, classist, ageist (and so forth) cultural formations and institutions implicitly fosters the notion that a feminist perspective inoculates one against the problematics of interpretation. Moreover, the creative tension between objectivist and constructivist epistemologies in Women's Studies sometimes leaves students confused. On the one hand, they learn that all knowledge comes from a given perspective and is not value-free; but on the other hand, they often assume that feminist knowledge is "true," or at least more "true" than non-feminist knowledge.[9] In subjecting feminist epistemology to sustained interrogation in the seminar, I address both the retrospective and prospective objectives of the course. Students rethink past courses, and they are very quick to see the implications of these questions for their future vocations and personal lives. Meaning-making is a human activity across the globe and throughout the course of one's life, in all its aspects. Feminist meaning-making needs to be open to rigorous self-examination, challenging any tendency toward orthodoxy, cliché, or closure.

Among a number of other readings, Sherna Berger Gluck and Daphne Patai's collection *Women's Words: The Feminist Practice of Oral History*

(1991) is a superb text to use to raise these issues.[10] The essays variously demand rigorous self-reflexivity about feminist research. Katherine Borland's " 'That's Not What I Said': Interpretive Conflict in Oral Narrative Research" (1991) for example, narrates how her feminist interpretation of her grandmother's story angered her grandmother, who did not accept the "spin" Borland as feminist folklorist gave to the tale. Facing the competing agencies and narrative authority of research subject and researcher led her to question the power relations between them and ultimately propose a collaborative model for a negotiated text that represents both views of the meaning of the story. A number of essays raise questions about the politics and ethics of feminist research, particularly when the research subject is of a different, especially less-privileged, class, race, religion, or nationality from the researcher. The ways in which contradictory subject positions mediate a research situation is interestingly evident in Sondra Hale's account of her unsuccessful interview with a prominent Sudanese feminist who came from a more privileged class than Hale but from a "Third World country" and who had her own plans for how to use Hale in her factional disputes in Sudanese politics.[11]

I follow up these and other theoretical writings on the problematics and politics of feminist interpretation with eight weeks of a case-study approach, taking up selected texts that reveal particularly complex instances of mediation. Influenced by my training in literary and cultural studies, I use a text-centered approach to feminist epistemology, one that stresses the relationship between "how" a feminist text means and "what" it means—that is, the interplay between form and content within a large context.[12] The "text" can be written, oral, or visual; it can be produced as research, art, literature, popular culture, and so forth; it usually has multiple agendas, meanings, audiences, agencies, and effects; it can be mainstream, avant-garde, or produced for a single community; it can be "local," "global," or "transnational" in its reach. The point I want to get across to the students is that feminist "texts" are the result of interpretive acts; they come in all forms and are produced in different sites for different purposes and with different effects.

Adapting principles of semiotics, I insist that texts be understood not in isolation but as part of a communication system that includes a producer, a text, and a receiver. (The "producer" can be plural; the text has "intertexts"—that is, texts to which it alludes, echoes, revises, etc.—and the "receiver" is often multiple, changing over time.) This system exists within multiple historical and geographical contexts that influence every aspect of production, textuality, and reception. I introduce the concepts of mediation and teleology (or "agenda," a word the students are more comfortable with) to show how institutions, ideology, and culture in general enter into the semiotic system. At first, mediation is a difficult concept for many students, particularly for those who think of communication in positivist terms as an unmediated transfer of information, ideas, feelings, or opinions. A schematic chart using stick figures helps materialize and personalize these philosophical concepts. It is a chart I use repeatedly in teaching the texts, adding to it visually to represent the constitutive parts of a specific interpretive text. And it is a chart that some venturesome students reproduce on the board in the class sessions where they do the teaching (more on this later).

In a difficult and politically charged juggling act, I select eight feminist texts for sustained analysis over an eight-week period. My goal is to put together a diverse package that exhibits difference, "border" crossing, and commonality—within the United States, transnationally, and generically. Thus, I use texts that represent different racial, ethnic, religious, class, sexual, and geopolitical identities, juxtaposing, for example, texts such as Janet Campbell Hale's Coeur d'Alene autobiography *Bloodlines*, Julie Dash's mythopoetic-historical film about a Gullah family *Daughters of the Dust*, Kim Chernin's biography-autobiography *In My Mother's House*, Barbara Meyerhoff's video ethnography *In Her Own Time*, the playwright and actor Anna Deavere Smith's *Fires in the Mirror or Twilight*, Gish Jen's novel on American multiculturalism *Mona in the Promised Land*, and Lindsy Van Gelder and Pamela Brandt's journalistic romp through U.S. lesbian cultures in *The Girls Next Door*.

Texts produced outside the United States about women in different parts of the globe serve a key function, jolting students into an awareness of their own American context and introducing through often radical conjunctures alternate gender systems and activisms. Texts such as Medea Benjamin/Elvia Alvarado's *Don't Be Afraid, Gringo! A Honduran Woman Speaks from the Heart*, Fatima Mernissi's *Dreams of Trespass: Tales of a Harem Girlhood*, Sharan-Jeet Shan's *In My Own Name*, Mariama B.'s *So Long a Letter*, and Nawal el Saadawi's *Memoirs from the Women's Prison* help students to "travel," getting them to see different cultural formations of familiar feminist issues such as family, sexuality, religion, and resistance. This particular stir-fry of differences is intended to break up stereotyped notions of "difference" based on simple binaries of victim and victimizer; make visible the agencies embedded in all differences; show the multicultural grid of race and ethnicity inside and outside the United States; emphasize the interactive nature of multipositionality in all cultures; examine what Inderpal Grewal and Caren Kaplan call "transnational" interconnections between the global and the local; explore how feminist ideas travel globally and take root in particular local formations; and identify sites for coalition. Comparative analysis based on identification of similarities and differences complements a conjuncturalist method that I borrow from anthropology. Blending ethnography and literary studies, I call the latter cultural parataxis, emphasizing ways in which the radical juxtaposition of different cultures illuminates each and brings into focus connections that might not otherwise be evident.[13]

Generic or modal difference is another concept I represent in the selection of texts. A range of methods of production and textual forms is consistent with the interdisciplinary aims of the seminar and very important in developing a sophisticated understanding of mediation.[14] (In their initial emphasis on the content of a text, a number of students regularly fail to distinguish among a novel, an oral history, an autobiography, a biography, and an ethnography and thus miss the methodological and generic differences that shape the production and reception of that content.) Explaining that all modes of interpretation attempt to represent a "truth" as the producer or producers see it, I suggest that different modes or genres can be placed on a spectrum between the imagined opposites of "fact" and "fiction," each of which represents a different pathway to "truth" or meaning. These include such types as history (oral and written), sociological survey (using qualitative methods), ethnography, journalism, biography, documentary film, autobiography, feature film, performance, and novel. Introducing genre or modal distinctions that affect the methodology or the forms of the texts, I try to get the students to see how what literary scholars often call the generic "horizon of expectations" affects both the text's creator and reader or viewer. We expect, for example, that a novel is based on fictional events while an autobiography is about actual events; we assume that an ethnography describes a "real" community; we know that a performer is impersonating, inhabiting, or symbolically representing an other; and so forth. Getting students to see the "borders" among these modes, I then introduce the concept of generic hybridity, the mixing of types that gets its special effects through transgressing the horizon of generic expectations. This notion of the clashing and blending of different modes facilitates the deconstruction of the binary of "fact" and "fiction," helping students to see how various fictions are implicit in any account of facts and conversely how the realm of "fact" or the "real" exists as referent for fictions.

Running through all the modal forms of interpretation is narrative as a fundamental, meaning-making activity of human interpretation, present to a lesser or greater extent across the humanities, social sciences, and sciences. Narrative exists in some form in all eight case-study texts, depending on the conventions of storytelling such as setting, characters, narrators, sequencing of events, and often even such particularly literary elements as imagery, figural language, complex plotting, and suspense. Arlie Hochschild's *The Second Shift* (1989), for example, textualizes her sociological ethnography of contemporary housework by borrowing from the conventions of magazine writing about couples, who come to life for the students as their troubled marriages unfold. The students remember the vivid "characters" in her study in part because she is an effective storyteller. Conversely, the students on the whole found some other ethnographies based on in-depth interviewing "boring," at least in part because the authors did not handle narrative as well—books such as Greta Foff Paules's *Power and Resistance Among Waitresses in a New Jersey Restaurant* (1991) and Elizabeth Kennedy and M. Davis's *Boots of Leather, Slippers of Gold* (1993). However valuable their research findings, these books use few direct quotations; where they appear, they are short, undercontextualized, or overedited, with the result that the individual women on whose lives the research is based do not come fully into focus and tend to blur one with another. Even in sociological or ethnographic research, where the intent is to characterize representative trends, not tell good stories about individuals, the use of effective narrative strategies can have a great impact on the reception of the text. Getting students to see this process at work helps teach them how they themselves use narrative in making meaning about their own lives, in creating their own and others' identities in acts of memory.

The danger of heightening students' awareness of how a text means and the communication system within which it operates is that the content of the texts gets lost. My intent to heighten students' reflexivity about the processes of representation and reception reflects what is known in anthropology as the "postmodern turn" as much as it does my background in literary studies. In pursuit of this awareness, I nevertheless believe it is important not to go too far. Exclusive focus on epistemological and representational issues runs the risk of erasing what knowledge is about—in the case of our seminar, the lives of women in the context of gender and other systems of stratification. In bringing to visibility the role of multiple mediations, I do not want to suggest that the content of those lives is irretrievably unknowable and therefore not worth attempting to learn about or articulate. What is needed, I tell the students, is attention to the interplay in a given text of the politics and process of meaning-making with the meaning that is being made about women's lives. To ignore the content of a text is to subject the women represented in it to double erasure—first, by conventional knowledge that ignores them, and second, by excessive reflexivity. Hence, I advocate and model for them a negotiated or dialogic relationship between objectivist and subjectivist feminist epistemologies.

I also use these eight weeks of textual analysis to hand the reins of the class over to the students, on the grounds that as graduating seniors, they have learned enough from their Women's Studies majors to teach themselves. I schedule the seminar so that we are in class twice a week, breaking the tradition of seminars meeting in single once-a-week blocks. I run the first class on a given text, providing through a mixed lecture and discussion format the necessary context—conceptual, historical, biographical, formal, etc. Well in advance, students are assigned to groups responsible for leading the discussion on each text for the second class period of the week. They are required to meet on their own, hand out in advance a set of discussion questions for the other students, and then lead a discussion about these questions. I stress that these are not to be presentations, an assignment that I often find deadly in both undergraduate and graduate classes. Rather, they are responsible for setting the agenda for discussion and leading the students through a series of topics for all but the last five to ten minutes of the class period. This assignment stresses collaborative teamwork and oral self-presentation in a group, skills that I explain are necessary in many job situations. I sit silent, for the most part, during their discussions, intervening only to provide factual information. What I want is for students to set their own agendas for discussion, learn to talk effectively with one another over an hour without help from me, and experience what it means to work one's way as a group out of controversy, muddles, and even boredom. I use the last minutes of the class to reflect back to them what I have seen them accomplish as a group or to clarify factual, conceptual, or textual matters. Often, I am able to use my response to their discussions as a springboard for introducing the next text in the following week, thus weaving together what they have done on their own with my objectives for the seminar. The downside of this pedagogy is that it is often hard for me to sit silent when I see them having problems or ignoring significant issues or parts of a text. The upside, however, is that this pedagogy fosters their independence, developing their sense that they leave school fortified not only with specific knowledge but also with the ability to keep learning, forming analyses, and articulating ideas in collaborative settings.

The final two weeks of the seminar, The Third Wave: The New Generation of Feminists and Your Future, encourage students to think about the future—their own as well as the future of Women's Studies and feminism.[15] Reflecting my age and number of years teaching Women's Studies, I think of this section as the time in which I emphasize my need to "pass the torch," to persuade the students that they are the budding leaders of a movement that is emphatically not dead (media reports to the contrary) but alive and evolving in transnational and global directions we cannot fully imagine today. The common rhetoric of feminist "waves"— first wave (Enlightenment–1920), second wave (1965–1990), and third wave (1990–)—misleads in many ways. It is insufficiently global, in the first place, using the feminist movements in the West, especially in Britain and the United States, as the defining periodization for all. It tends to obscure the significance of how the second and third waves, unlike the first and second waves, overlap historically. This in turn can produce definitions of each wave that are inaccurately monolithic. Moreover, it can be very misleading to explain differences in feminist theory and praxis primarily in generational terms, using the family model (especially of fraught relationships between mothers and daughters) to characterize differences that need to be understood in more broadly historical, political, or theoretical terms. In spite of these problems with the wave rhetoric, however, there is an important generational issue at stake at the millennium. Emerging in the North American academy in the late 1960s, Women's Studies has been around long enough to produce multiple generations. We are engaged in the growing pains of learning how to reproduce ourselves—something "first-wave" feminism did not do very successfully—and how to make affiliations and coalitions worldwide. It is critical, I believe, to instill in Women's Studies majors a sense that as they progress in their vocational and personal lives, they need to seize the reins of leadership and self-definition for the future.[16]

As much as I generally like this formula for a capstone seminar that has evolved over time, with constant adjustment of the syllabus, readings, and writing assignments, I will conclude with a few critical remarks. First, the analytic, comparative, and text-centered approach I use does not give majors an opportunity for an in-depth research project designed to reflect each student's particular area of interest and expertise. For the few majors who opt to write a senior thesis, this is not a problem. But a strong argument can be made for requiring majors to develop an individualized project that is more complex than the conventional term paper, but less sustained than a full thesis.

Second, the seminar's focus on getting students to rethink their own experience in Women's Studies and to project its continuing influence on their lives has the positive effect of validating the personal and enhancing self-reflexivity about their experience—both familiar projects of U.S. feminism, particularly for women whose degrees help guarantee a societal status that is at the very least middle class. However, although "the personal is political," not everyone's "personal" is the same worldwide. Nor does validating the personal and individual ensure the understanding of the need for systemic transformation or a recognition of how the success of some women often depends on the continuing struggles and inequality of others—particularly for U.S. women in a transnational context. My attempt to stress differences among women worldwide and the interlocking ("glocational") nature of global effects and indigenized feminist formations aims to interrupt the over-personalization of the students' understanding of Women's Studies. Nevertheless, I am continually aware of the difficult and delicate balance to be sought between fostering the students' future agency and insisting that they look beyond their own relatively privileged situations as future college graduates in the United States.

Third, the objective of full interdisciplinarity around the epistemological issues of interpretation is not as achievable as I have hoped. Although I am familiar with the general principles and problematics of the "scientific method" and integrate discussion of them into the theoretical and case-study sections of the course, the seminar does not give equal weight to methods and processes of interpretation that are heavily quantified or experimental, as in survey research or the lab sciences, which involve complex research designs, sophisticated modeling, and advanced statistical analysis. I don't attempt to incorporate case studies of such research in the eight-week portion of the course because I do not have the expertise to cross the considerable chasm between qualitative work in the humanities and social sciences and quantitative methodologies. I deal regularly with the empirical—with concepts of data and how it is produced. But data that is collected through such methods as in-depth interviewing, participant observation, or open-ended questionnaires is far more obviously mediated by the interpretive eye of the researcher than data produced through some version of scientific method. Teaching students how to locate the often subtle, disguised, or mathematically embedded subjectivities of quantified research is beyond my skill level. Moreover, for faculty such as myself based in the humanities, "data" is first and foremost "texts"—that is, representations themselves are the object of study. As I have written elsewhere (Friedman 1998b), I believe that the methodological divide between the quantitative and the qualitative at the advanced level is so substantial that full interdisciplinarity in Women's Studies is not feasible at this point. Although I do my best to validate quantitative interpretation in the seminar, I recognize that my particular background privileges the qualitative and thus helps to reinforce the gender division of research and higher education that preserves the "hard" sciences and the quantitative social sciences primarily for men.

In addition, my particular disciplinary background in narrative studies accounts in part for the heavy emphasis I place on issues of narrative in meaning-making acts of interpretation across the divisions of knowledge. Yet to mute the interdisciplinary and disciplinary emphases of the seminar that come out of my background in the humanities and narrative studies in the interest of equity would at the same time reduce the intellectual level of the seminar. To work at an advanced level in one way seems to necessitate working at a less advanced level in another. In compensation, I make this (inter)disciplinary problematic itself a subject of discussion in the course, pointing out to students that this negotiation between interdisciplinarity and disciplinarity is endemic to Women's Studies at all levels, from the institutional and intellectual to the political.[17]

A final concern about the capstone seminar I have developed is its strong focus on women as students and women as both the subjects and objects of interpretation. In doing so, I have followed what has become the conventional emphasis on women in Women's Studies to compensate for the continuing androcentrism of most courses in the academy. I stress that this has not meant "women" in isolation from a broader understanding of the gender system, which, I would argue, has been a concern of Women's Studies right from the beginning. But as feminist studies has become mainstreamed into both traditional disciplines and the new interdisciplinary fields such as cultural studies, race and ethnic studies, postcolonial studies, and gay/lesbian/bisexual/transsexual studies, there has been a concomitant rise in "gender studies," a term whose meanings vary depending on its institutional location. Sometimes feminists have used the name "gender studies" for strategic purposes, with its more neutral resonance as camouflage. However, sometimes the term "gender studies" signals a shift in emphasis from women and the gender system to the gender system as it relates to both men and women. The growth of gender studies in general has important implications for the future of Women's Studies, ones that are well worth more open dialogue. There are oppositional, subterranean currents in the U.S. academy about whether, on the one hand, "gender studies" represents a retreat from an openly political stance and feminist advocacy, and on the other hand, whether "Women's Studies" is passé, old-fashioned, mired in "identity politics" and essentialism, isolated or too nationally focused, not sufficiently "hip" with the newer fields of queer studies, poststructuralist theory, and transnational studies. I am not in sympathy with either type of dismissal. I see as great a need as ever for Women's Studies to exist as a distinct intellectual enterprise and organizational structure. However, I also think it is vital for Women's Studies to keep changing along with the shifting tides and landscapes of higher education in a global context. Just where the still untheorized distinctions between "Women's Studies" and "gender studies" will lead, I am not sure. To date, I have not found an effective way to integrate this issue into the capstone seminar.

I will conclude briefly by reasserting that my intent in reporting on the kind of capstone seminar I have developed has not been to advocate for a single model of "what every Women's Studies major should know." Rather, I am interested in starting a dialogue in the field about what kinds of seminars work effectively as a final course in a cumulative Women's

Studies curriculum in different academic settings and with different kinds of students. We need more discussion about the variety of ways in which Women's Studies faculty design capstone seminars around the fact that they often come at a very special moment in the lives of undergraduates, a moment very much caught in the borderlands between the past and the future.

Notes

1   We encourage the double major primarily to maximize students' ability to do post-graduate work in a discipline if they so choose and to protect them against the still considerable ignorance of or hostility to the Women's Studies major as a rigorous and legitimate academic enterprise. For specifics on the UW-Madison Women's Studies program, see the Web site at http://polyglot.lss.wisc.edu/wsp/.

2   I repeatedly use this phrase with the students instead of the more common "the real world" to emphasize that higher education is very much part of the "real world," with power structures and conflict within the academy and a powerful role as a major societal institution in relation to the "outside" world. The cliché of the academy as an "ivory tower" is one that I often critique in class to deconstruct the misleading binaries of academics and activism, theory and practice.

3   One of the major complaints I hear from Women's Studies majors about their Women's Studies courses is that the courses are repetitive: Either the same course hammers in its major themes with too much repetition, or the Women's Studies courses tend to repeat one another, sometimes using the same readings or making the same points. Some of this results, I believe, from faculty trained in different disciplines relying on a core set of readings outside their disciplines, with the result that students get the same readings from different teachers. More curricular coordination is needed to ensure greater diversity of readings and topics across the curriculum, but this is difficult to actualize, particularly in universities with strong traditions of academic freedom.

4   For sample theoretical formations, I assign Howe 1984; Friedman 1997; and Kesselman et al. 1995, which is particularly useful for its inclusion of students' voices.

5   Howe 1997 usefully introduces the students to Women's Studies outside the U.S. context. Marilyn Boxer's classic survey, "For and About Women: The Theory and Practice of Women's Studies in the United States" (1982), serves as an excellent introduction to the early political and institutional debates; see also Boxer 1998.

6   Particularly useful readings on these debates include Allen and Kitch 1998; Bowles and Klein 1983; Chai 1985; Cruikshank 1982; Florence 1984; Friedman 1998b; hooks 1989; Hull and Smith 1982; Jordan 1985; McIntosh and Minnich 1984; and Mohanty et al. 1991.

7   Instead of asking students to do feminist critiques of this material (a well-honed skill for seniors), I use two writing assignments that emphasize persuasive argumentation and use of evidence for a stated position: first, a concise "letter to the editor"; second, a

short "position paper" in which they must fairly represent one of the charges made against Women's Studies in the readings, explain the significance of the charge for Women's Studies, and then agree or disagree with the charge, defending their position with specific examples from their own experience or reading. Many students find this kind of writing very difficult. Some defend Women's Studies vociferously but without sufficient evidence, asking readers to accept their word on authority. Others write as if preaching to the converted, not taking into account the need to persuade the unpersuaded or the hostile. I stress the importance of evidentiary use of their own experience in Women's Studies classes as well as the rhetorical skills needed in many future job or advocacy situations requiring verbal or written analysis of a problem and proposal for what should be done about it.

8 Although we examine women's lives in the context of the gender system and other axes of difference, I select texts that focus centrally on women; the same approach could be used more broadly for gender formations affecting men as much as women.

9 I have written about these competing epistemologies as important for Women's Studies in "Making History" (1995), an essay that is included in Friedman (1998c: 199–227).

10 The use of Gluck and Patai's rigorous, scholarly collection *Women's Words* (1991) in the context of Patai's later coauthorship with Noretta Koertge of *Professing Feminism* (1995), with its shoddy methodology and mass-media appeal, is itself an effective political lesson for students.

11 See Hale 1991. For other theoretical readings I have found useful, see Heilbrun 1988; hooks 1989; Jordan 1985; Shostak 1989; and Swindells 1989.

12 Epistemology is a traditional branch of the discipline of philosophy. Although I have some knowledge of the field, literary and cultural studies have been more influential in shaping how I work with these questions. A feminist philosopher would no doubt design the course on this topic quite differently, as would a scientist or a quantitative social scientist.

13 For anthropological conjuncturalism, see, for example, Alarcón 1990; Clifford 1988; Frankenberg and Mani 1993; and Visweswaran 1994.

14 See Marjorie Pyrse's theoretical formulation of the linkage between what she calls "critical interdisciplinarity" and "cross-cultural insight" in advocating for the disciplinarity hybridity of a transnational and multicultural Women's Studies (Pyrse 1998).

15 I added this section of the course in response to some dissatisfaction expressed in anonymous student evaluations for syllabi in which the case-study texts concluded the seminar. Many expressed a lack of closure along with anxiety about their futures. I use Rebecca Walker's collection, *To Be Real* (1995), containing personal essays by young feminists writing against what they perceive as the orthodoxies of second-wave feminism and about the impact of third-wave feminism on their lives, and Barbara Luebke and Mary Ellen Reilly's *Women's Studies Graduates: The First Generation* (1995), a report on an open-ended survey questionnaire sent to selected former Women's Studies majors about the relationship of their degrees to their vocational and personal experience. They are both pioneering and flawed, and thus pedagogically useful.

16 The options for the final project build on this need by asking students to do on their own what the authors did in the case-study texts. They choose among doing autobiographies, biographies, or oral histories of an event; an essay appropriate for Walker's *To Be Real;* or a journal on their volunteer or paid work as feminists. All options require a second, reflexive paper about the mediating processes and forms of their efforts. This assignment tends to temper students' eagerness for critique with a measure of empathy born of experiencing the actual difficulty of producing effective texts. In short, feminist theory about interpretation becomes feminist praxis.

17 One solution for a program is to involve different faculty in the teaching of the capstone seminar, if faculty in the sciences or quantitative social sciences are available and willing to teach it.

**LAURA E. DONALDSON,
ANNE DONADEY, AND JAEL SILLIMAN**

Subversive Couplings: On Antiracism and Postcolonialism in Graduate Women's Studies

We are three women of varying sexual, racial, and national backgrounds who are core faculty members of the University of Iowa's Women's Studies program, which welcomed its first class of Ph.D. students in the 1998–99 academic year. In the context of our graduate program, we are exploring ways of making postcolonial and antiracist critiques central to its curriculum, and we share some of our concerns and strategies in this chapter.

The recent emergence of Ph.D. programs in Women's Studies represents a culminating moment for Women's Studies in the academy. After twenty-five years of often marginal institutional existence and reliance on the intellectual labor of other disciplines, Women's Studies has finally gained independence through the creation of its own graduate programs. Given the larger public context of backlash against affirmative action (and now ethnic studies programs) and the conservatism of the past decade, such an achievement stands out as all the more remarkable. The nascent emergence of doctoral-level Women's Studies provides many benefits, including more highly trained students as well as more control over the feminist curriculum. But perhaps the greatest gain is the ability to influence the production of knowledge at every level. This era of unprecedented possibility in Women's Studies also constitutes a time of unprecedented danger, however. Indeed, the rite of passage into graduate education brings its own set of problems and temptations. One of the most pressing dangers comes from the very nature of university-based graduate programs: the creation of experts whose mastery of certain fields grants them a sometimes disproportionate legitimacy in disseminating their views. When one combines this factor with the overwhelming whiteness of the faculty and students in Women's Studies (and other) doctoral programs, a troubling vision emerges of the potential for polarization between credentialed and noncredentialed feminist scholars and the creation of even more tension between Euroamerican women and women of color. The central positioning of postcolonial and antiracist views within Women's Studies curricula will intervene in such polarizations because these perspectives attend to the conditions under which knowledge is produced, as well as the continued troubling split between intellectuals and activists in feminist movements. These angles of vision deconstruct and demystify the white solipsism and imperialist epistemologies that predominately white faculties and student bodies often (but not always) engender. It is for this reason and many more that the dissemination of these critical perspectives within Women's Studies assumes a new urgency.

Conservative attacks on Women's Studies programs such as the ones listed by Inderpal Grewal and Caren Kaplan in their chapter in this volume are part of what they call "the backlash narrative." These must be strongly countered. The fact that Women's Studies as a field of knowledge production continues to come under attack by regressive forces, however, should not cause its practitioners to retreat into a defensive posture that will prevent us from perceiving and incorporating progressive critiques into our scholarship and teaching. We offer this call for the subversive couplings of antiracism and postcolonialism in feminist inquiry because we are deeply committed to the field of Women's Studies and because we believe, for the reasons stated in this chapter, that this paradigm shift will help Women's Studies respond to the backlash by increasing the relevance, centrality, and sophistication of its intellectual frameworks.

In this chapter, we will address the following issues: the often sharp divide between faculty who privilege gender, or gender and sexuality, as analytical frameworks and those who also incorporate race, colonialism, and class; the pedagogical strategies that will foster multiaxial analysis in the next generation of feminist scholars; and the curricular content that will facilitate this kind of learning. In the fraught contexts surrounding discussions of antiracism and postcolonialism, their integration at the curricular and critical center of graduate Women's Studies is a subversive coupling. Although many discussions of postcolonialism refer to the way in which discourses of race support or perpetuate colonialism, few have attended to the development of antiracist movements and how they have changed the contours of the previously colonized world. (For example, in *Key Concepts in Post-Colonial Studies* [Ashcroft, Griffiths, and Tiffin 1998], the authors define "anti-colonialism" but have no category for "antiracism.") Likewise, the inclusion of postcolonial views in antiracist theories is often lacking.

Unlike many authors in this volume whose critical practice embodies the subversive coupling we advocate, these perspectives have not always been integrated into Women's Studies curricula. Many scholars and activists also perceive postcolonialism and antiracism as very different realities: Postcolonialism signifies entanglement with a system of domination (colonialism) that may or may not be a struggle for decolonization, while antiracism implies a struggle against oppressive systems (here, white supremacy). Both white women and women of color in the United States have tended to construe the intellectual and political practice of postcolonialism and antiracism as a divisive wedge rather than as an occasion for solidarity. For example, bell hooks complains that many "Third World nationals" bring to this country the same kind of contempt and disrespect for blackness that is most frequently associated with white Western imperialism. She argues that this group has often failed to interrogate the ways in which they enter a racialist hierarchy "where in the eyes of whites they automatically have greater status and privilege than individuals of African descent" (hooks 1990: 94). As a model of how this process works, hooks cites a Women's Studies program whose predominately white faculty hold negative views of certain black women. Members of the faculty ask a "Third World national" to explain why the black women are "angry" and "hostile." By assuming the role of mediator or go-between, the postcolonial intellectual reinscribes the well-known role of the colonial interpreter who translates "the Natives"—her African American colleagues—to those in power, here representatives of a predominately white, mainstream academic feminism.

The reverse is true, as well, as many people of color in the United States have been taught and may have internalized colonialist ideas regarding people in the "Third World." This exists as the flip side to the danger hooks perceives in the relatively privileged position "Third World" scholars may be granted over U.S. scholars of color. Moreover, global patterns of dominance (an extension of the colonial encounter) have resulted in many "Third World" students gaining doctoral training in the United States. When this training does not include an examination of colonial and neocolonialist practices, colonial misrepresentations are reinforced and exported back to the countries from which the students came, thus perpetuating intellectual colonization. Further, U.S. domination, and the inequities between the academies of the "First World" and "Third World" often amplify the voices of such Western-trained scholars. Their credentials might, in some instances, give them undue influence abroad as authentic voices and at home as "experts." Because of all these conundrums (and more), we view postcolonialism and antiracism as crucial components of any Women's Studies curriculum. Postcolonial critiques are essential for understanding both gender issues within the United States and the neocolonialist relationships of the United States to the rest of the world, while experiences of race and class are profoundly inflected by the colonial forces that produce and maintain them. Patriarchal and racist ideologies were reformulated through colonial discourses and structured both the systemic and personal relationships between colonizer and colonized. To understand, for example, the experiences of Puerto Rican, Mexican, or Caribbean women who now live in the United States, it is essential to understand how colonial forces shaped their position in their own countries and continue to shape their experiences in the United States today. For these women, the ongoing economic and political relationships of their countries to the "First World" lead to very distinct experiences in the United States. The nexus of feminism, postcolonialism, and antiracism consequently holds great promise for graduate Women's Studies, especially in the creation of curricula and modes of analysis that could function as liberating models of scholarship for the academy. Before this can take place, however, one needs to address the issue of knowledge production and, more particularly, how postcolonialism and antiracism might transform the knowledge production of graduate Women's Studies.

Field Formation and the Production of Knowledge

The task of defining postcolonialism and antiracism is a daunting one and has taxed the abilities of many a contemporary critic. For the purposes of this essay, we are adopting the following definitions: Postcolonialism refers to "a process of disengagement from the whole colonial syndrome, which takes many forms" (see Loomba 1998: 19), while antiracism implies a struggle against white supremacy and other oppressive deployments of "race."[1] Both terms facilitate what Leela Gandhi has called the epistemological and pedagogic reterritorialization of the non-Western—or we would add, non-white—world (Guy-Sheftall 1998: 45). According to Gandhi, this reterritorialization involves exposing the humanist pretense of political disinterestedness and provincializing the knowledge claims of the "West" that the collaboration of modern imperialism and nationalism have made universal (Gandhi 1998). Gayatri Chakravorty Spivak has described the latter task more specifically as "anthropologizing" the West—that is, studying the various cultural systems of Africa, Asia, Asia Pacific, and the Americas as if peopled by historical agents. Only then, she argues, "can we put together the story of a cosmopolitanism that is global, gendered, and dynamic" (Spivak 1993: 278)—and only then will feminist scholars put together the story of a graduate Women's Studies that is transnational and antiracist as well as gendered.

An essential part of this story is recognizing that issues of difference are fundamental to the viability to Women's Studies programs (Guy-Sheftall 1998: 329). The University of Iowa Ph.D. program has addressed this concern by incorporating these issues into the core "feminist foundations" course and by requiring that all students take a series of courses foregrounding the experiences and concerns of women of color or "Third World" women. If the latter were to stand on its own, however, it would embody what one might call a band-aid approach to issues of difference. Guy-Sheftall, who completed a study of racial and global perspectives in graduate Women's Studies education for the Ford Foundation, worries about how this model might perpetuate the expectation that diversity will be handled in elective rather than core courses.[2] A related concern is that many "diversity" courses are located outside the direct offerings of Women's Studies programs, and their content is consequently difficult to monitor. Although our diversity requirement does make an explicit commitment to teaching and learning non-white knowledges, the reterritorialization of the non-Western world in Women's Studies also requires a systemic recognition that colonialism and racism exist as far more than just economic and political systems. It entails, for example, incorporating at every level—including core and feminist theory courses—the knowledge that, in its drive for economic domination, colonialism created new class structures and restructured gender relations.

It is for these reasons that, in planning our "Foundations of Feminist Inquiry" graduate course, the entire faculty met several times to collaborate in devising a multidisciplinary syllabus that included postcolonial and antiracist materials throughout the semester rather than congregating them in one or two weekly sessions. Through this integration, we hoped to convey the idea that gender cannot be examined without close attention to the way in which colonialism transformed power structures, including gendered power relations. To understand women's roles, positions, and aspirations, colonial history cannot be elided since it constitutes a profoundly important base on which current understandings must be built.[3] This should not and cannot be only a "Third World" feminist agenda—just as the issue of diversity should not be construed only as an elective—but must also be a central project for Women's Studies if it is genuinely committed to creating alternative politics and epistemologies. Without this understanding, Euroamerican feminists risk extending an asymmetric ignorance about most of the world's women and exacerbating the tensions among Women's Studies scholars in different locations. Without this understanding, they also risk perpetuating colonial representations that prevent the formation of "communities of resistance" across boundaries of race, class, ethnicity, and national background. Provincializing the production of "First World" knowledge also transforms the practice of the everyday classroom.

One example of this process comes from something as mundane as the form that our Women's Studies program uses for its undergraduate and graduate course evaluations. At Iowa, departments may design their own forms; that this is a difficult enterprise is shown by the fact that our program has revised the questions on its form several times in the recent past. The current document begins by asking students whether an instructor taught the class from "a feminist perspective." This question is problematic for a number of reasons—not the least of which is its implication that "a" feminist orientation can travel across cultural, racial, and national boundaries. When one of us mentioned this in a faculty meeting, however, it was dismissed by a few colleagues as not relevant, and even counter-productive. Yet the concern remains: In courses on American Indian or postcolonial women, whose viewpoints challenge many presuppositions of the Euroamerican women's movement, questions about "a" (presumably univocal) feminist perspective become unanswerable and perpetuate the colonialist assumptions that we have tried, through our teaching and research, to disable. Because the three questions that follow that one on the form ask whether the instructor adequately addressed issues of race, class, and sexuality (but not gender), the first query clearly implies that "feminist" means "gender" (and conversely, that race, class, and sexuality have little to do with gender), thus perpetuating a monist way of thinking challenged by the subversive coupling of postcolonialism and antiracism. And what of those who use different signifiers for their political advocacy on behalf of women? "Womanism" and "critical race feminism" are two alternatives that come to mind. Both of these descriptions emerge from the experiences and struggles of U.S. women of color—the first emerging from the imagination of Alice Walker and its appropriation by African American feminists, and the second from women of color doing critical legal theory— and both necessitate that one filter gender, race, class, and sexuality through one another. Yet this point of view is occluded by the terminology of a single course evaluation form that privileges certain conceptions of feminism and gender over others. In discussions about how best to revise our form, suggestions have included beginning with the question: "Did the feminist perspective in this class address the intersection of race, class, gender, and sexuality?" The question, "Did the instructor teach the class from a feminist perspective?" could then be rephrased more accurately as "Were feminist interpretations and analyses of gender presented in this class?"

Another illustration of what course evaluations tell us about the production of knowledge in Women's Studies originates in another question on our form, this one asking whether the instructor incorporated course material on sexual orientation. In a recent set of evaluations from Laura Donaldson's (undergraduate) "Race, Class and Gender in the U.S." course, many students responded affirmatively to this particular inquiry: "Yes, something other classes of mine have not" and "Yes, there was always an understanding that sexual orientation is a part of the interlocking oppressions of our society." However, there were also a significant number who expressed ambivalence or uncertainty. Their responses included "occasionally, but not really" and even one that answered with a resounding "No!" What interests us about these particular responses is that, in this course, at least two of the seven books on the syllabus directly confronted issues of sexuality and sexual orientation. One of the first books read in the course, Mab Segrest's *Memoir of a Race Traitor* (1994), is the narrative of a white lesbian woman who insists on, and painfully excavates, the connections among her own raced and gendered identity, white supremacy, anti-Semitism, and homophobia. Another, Zillah Eisenstein's *Hatreds* (1996), discusses issues of sexuality in a transnational frame. Despite this, some students in the class clearly failed to understand how the texts engaged issues of sexuality, albeit multivocally. Donaldson's interpretation of their negative responses is that many students are so used to gender- and sexuality-only paradigms that they do not and cannot recognize the problematic of sexuality when it is integrated into race, class, and colonial analysis. The issue of the evaluation form is one that the Women's Studies faculty will revisit as we strive to design questions that best reflect the learning process that we wish to model to our students.

Ironically, even though Women's Studies is an interdisciplinary field that has continued to stretch the parameters of other disciplines, its own boundaries can constrain its production of feminist knowledge. Because it began as a way to bring women's issues into a male-centered world of research and teaching, the main emphasis of Women's Studies courses understandably foregrounds women writers and women's lives. This emphasis can make it difficult to teach courses foregrounding postcolonial and antiracist perspectives. Jael Silliman observed, for instance, that when she first began teaching the "Introduction to Women's Studies" course, she inherited a syllabus that inconsistently included women of color perspectives. The students in the course also wanted to focus mainly on issues important for the white women's movement. Some bluntly let her know that they did not think it was necessary to spend time on women of color perspectives because at the University of Iowa, which is a predominantly white campus, those issues were not relevant to them. Silliman sensed that they responded in this way because they must have sensed subconsciously that women of color perspectives were only added on, and thus not integral to the course. In other words, women of color perspectives were not crucial for informing their perspectives and understandings of the world. The way in which a syllabus is structured and presented—the politics of its presentation—is a crucial factor in whether these perspectives will be incorporated and embraced. When postcolonial perspectives are included as an essential feature of the course, as in the earlier example, it does not seem like one more dimension or layer with which students must struggle. She subsequently incorporated race and class perspectives along with postcolonial critiques, and the students now find them immensely satisfying. Now, for instance, when this course examines issues of reproductive rights, it looks at mainstream struggles for expanding reproductive choice, critiques by women of color who articulate how their reproductive rights have been systematically undermined, and "Third World" women's responses to population-control agendas. This enables students to see the struggle for reproductive rights in all its complexity and to appreciate the different priorities various groups of women have regarding this issue. Silliman observes that, since this multilayered set of perspectives has been integrated throughout the course, she has met with little student resistance.

Silliman's experience teaching "Introduction to Women's Studies" has been echoed by courses at the graduate level. Anne Donadey notes that her graduate course in feminist criticism, which she structures around antiracist and postcolonial viewpoints, has taught her a great deal about the "politics of presentation." Although these perspectives were an integral part of the course, the title "Feminist Criticism" and the fact that students' earlier encounters with the topic had mostly followed monist lines, meant that most of them assumed it would be taught mainly through the lens of gender. She further relates that several outspoken white students specifically resented the course's focus on the linkages between race and gender. Donadey notes that she still gets some of these responses, but they do not erupt with as much force as they did the first time she taught the class. This is due, in great part, to the way she now sets up the first three weeks of classes with readings that encourage students to reflect on the following issues: their own racial-identity development,[4] the impact of racism and white privilege on their lives,[5] ethical issues in feminist scholarship and teaching,[6] classroom dynamics,[7] student counter-resistance to liberatory pedagogy,[8] and the role of emotions in the learning process.[9] The essay by Beverly Tatum (1992), which presents theories of racial-identity development as they apply to classroom experience, is particularly helpful (although it deals only with models of blackness and whiteness). Providing ways of thinking about racial-identity development allows students to put their feelings and those of others in a larger psychosocial context and to realize that they are going through a general process, which may in turn reduce anxiety and counter-resistance. Tatum notes that at one stage of the model, students are often tempted to withdraw from class through absenteeism or by not turning in assignments. Alerting students to this possibility seems to reduce its incidence (Tatum 1992: 6–7).

It is also helpful to students and faculty to keep in mind that white people who become aware of institutional racism and white privilege may react to the discomforting nature of this newfound awareness either by assuming an antiracist position or by refusing this new knowledge and "reshaping [their] belief system to be more congruent with an acceptance of racism" (Tatum 1992: 15), thereby transforming their guilt feelings into anger directed against people of color. This "reintegration stage" is expressed in the Women's Studies classroom when students consistently refuse to let go of their monist parameters even after being shown many times that they are oppressive to women of color. Speaking about Women's Studies education, Paula Rothenberg (1988) makes the point that when the curriculum is integrated from the start, there is less student counter-resistance—a fact that has been confirmed by Donadey's experience in teaching an undergraduate version of "Feminist Criticism." Because the prerequisite for this class is completion of the "Introduction to Women's Studies" course, she has found that students are much more likely to consider the integrated study of gender, race, colonialism, class, and sexuality as part and parcel of feminist inquiry. There has consequently been no need to assign a set of preparatory readings for this group of students.

All of the preceding scenarios for the production of knowledge in Women's Studies beg the question of their institutional contexts—in our case, a major research university—and it is to the constraints and challenges offered by this context that we now devote our attention.

Constraints and Challenges

It is somewhat of a paradox that Ph.D. programs in Women's Studies are emerging at a time of mounting conservatism: Institutions of higher education are becoming increasingly controlled by boards of regents and state legislatures, and radical feminist concerns are often being domesticated through their absorption into some of the more diffuse rhetorics of gender studies. This paradox may unfortunately reduce the margin for maneuvering and give Women's Studies programs incentives to align with mainstream ideas about scholarship, curricula, and "professionalism." Our program's negotiation of a fifteen-hour "disciplinary" requirement provides an illustrative microcosm of this vexed issue. In addition to core courses in Women's Studies, our program mandates that all graduate students take fifteen hours of coursework in a discipline of their choice. From the beginning, however, we had significant conflicts over how to interpret this requirement. Some members of the faculty insisted that grounding in a determinate scholarly mode was necessary for students and that the requirement only meant working in traditional disciplines such as anthropology, history, or English. In her essay "(Inter)disciplinarity and the Question of the Women's Studies Ph.D.," Susan Stanford Friedman notes the potentially positive effects of those knowledge boundaries known as "disciplines," writing: "The word's resonance with systematic, sustained, and highly skilled labor, even craftsmanship, is as significant for me as its association with punishment. Academic disciplines not only regulate and certify but also enable expertise and depth of knowledge" (1998b: 309). At best, then, advocating a strict interpretation of our requirement emphasized these undoubtedly positive outcomes of working within traditional disciplinary boundaries. At worst, this attitude proved a stumbling block to faculty officially appointed or professionally engaged with other multidisciplinary programs (American Indian/Native studies, Latin American studies, South Asian studies) as well as those engaged in interdisciplinary work (postcolonial studies) or who held interdisciplinary Ph.D.s (religion and literature). It also acutely concerned doctoral students who wanted to work in such multidisciplinary fields. In addition to the beneficial associations evoked by Friedman, however, an academic discipline is also "an accumulative, cooperative project for the production of knowledge, the exercise of power, and the creation of careers."[10] Consequently, a strict interpretation of our disciplinary requirement aligned our multidisciplinary, and sometimes interdisciplinary, program with cautious, mainstream notions of "proper" scholarship.[11] Fortunately, we were able to negotiate an agreement that students could petition to substitute work in any duly constituted field of scholarship, subject to faculty approval—although some remained uneasy about this compromise. Although we settled this particular issue, it nevertheless stands in for a plethora of similarly problematic questions.

One such question is the area of hiring. Although Women's Studies is in the process of defining itself as an interdisciplinary field, it largely relies on traditional disciplinary boundaries or identity rubrics (such as women of color or lesbian studies) in hiring faculty. Yet to create a new intellectual field, it must carve out areas of expertise that cut across disciplines. Women's Studies needs to create the space for this kind of field formation to occur within hiring processes that are usually shaped by budgetary limits and administrative interests. For example, the University of California, Irvine, framed a new position in the International Political Economy of Gender. The university wanted to find someone working outside nationalist parameters to think about the economy from a gender perspective, and it wanted to make these gender and economy concerns central to the curriculum. Several years ago, our own program conducted a search under a Gender, Culture, and Politics rubric designed to attract those with interdisciplinary research and teaching interests in social science or history. These two creative, substantive frames of a subfield demonstrate the importance of thinking beyond the intellectual rubrics of departments to identify areas of core knowledge within Women's Studies. If Women's Studies is truly to be a new field, not an amalgamation of the separate study of women from various disciplines, then it will need the flexibility and creativity to forge such appointments and foster such intellectual lines of inquiry. It is precisely this flexibility that leads Friedman, a long-time member of the University of Wisconsin-Madison's Women's Studies program, to argue against Women's Studies Ph.D.s, and at this point we would engage her objections—particularly those that turn on issues of interdisciplinarity and hiring.

Friedman articulates several "pragmatic" factors that have triggered her opposition to the Women's Studies Ph.D., including budgetary and pedagogical considerations. Her first worry, however, is about "newly graduated students eagerly grasping their interdisciplinary Ph.D. degrees in hand and even more eagerly entering the job market" (1998b: 304). In Friedman's scenario, most academic doors will be closed to them because most hiring processes follow traditional categories for specialization. Further, given the shrinking job market for virtually all the disciplines, the interdisciplinarity of these new Ph.D.s will harm their hopes and dreams to join the professorate. She pessimistically concludes: "The hiring and promotion patterns for feminists in the American Academy today are such that it would be very difficult for people with interdisciplinary Ph.D.s in Women's Studies to succeed on the academic market" (1998b: 305). At the end of her essay, Friedman admits that her opposition to doctoral programs in Women's Studies seems based on an acquiescence with current structures of knowledge in the Euroamerican academy, and she frets about her possible "failure of imagination" (1998b: 319). We also wonder why feminist scholars not only fail to imagine the possibilities of a Women's Studies Ph.D., but also distort the trajectory of interdisciplinary Ph.D.s in higher education.

One might, for example, look at the hiring rates for the history of consciousness Ph.D. at the University of California, Santa Cruz, or at Emory University's Institute of Liberal Arts (or the ILA, where Laura Donaldson received her Ph.D.). The ILA grants only interdisciplinary Ph.D.s and constitutes a separate department with its own budget, faculty positions, and economic support for students in the form of research and teaching assistantships; the history of consciousness program has propelled some of America's most gifted academics into positions ranging from feminist studies to psychology, literature, and anthropology.[12] Friedman's argument that the shrinking job market necessitates a disciplinary Ph.D. falls short when one notices that Ph.D.s from these interdisciplinary programs match and sometimes even exceed the hiring capabilities of their disciplinary peers because they can apply for positions in multiple fields. For every student whose career becomes stalled betwixt and between disciplines, there are least as many whose interdisciplinary qualifications make them more attractive to college and university departments. This is especially true in a shrinking academic job market in which departments are seeking to hire those who can teach a wide variety of courses. Further, established programs such as American studies, African American studies, and Women's Studies have a need for scholars trained in these interdisciplines. We agree that graduate programs, including Women's Studies, have an ethical obligation to prepare their potential graduates for careers in academe and elsewhere. Falling back on the rhetoric of scarcity and the stereotype of interdisciplinarity as inherently superficial, however, does not advance the cause of feminist scholarship. If institutional hiring processes work against creating the kind of intellectual subject that Women's Studies needs to establish, then we must work to transform these institutional structures rather than allow them to define our goals and vision for the future.

Indeed, it was precisely so that cross-disciplinary exchange could lead to new insights and areas of study that Women's Studies programs were established outside of disciplines. Such mobile traversal and permeation of previously impenetrable epistemological boundaries frequently induce a crisis of identity within many disciplines, as well as within the larger institution itself. One need only contemplate how issues of representation and writing have transformed anthropology, or how issues of culture have transformed the study of English, to realize this. It is this boundary-busting capacity of feminism, postcolonialism, and antiracism that will occupy the remainder of this chapter.

Mutual Suspicion or Productive Crisis?

If academic and "revolutionary" practices do not bring each other to productive crisis, the power of the script has clearly passed elsewhere.—Gayatri Chakravorty Spivak, *Outside in the Teaching Machine* (1993)

Kwame Anthony Appiah once described postcolonialism as a space-clearing gesture that creates room for non-European knowledges.[13] Spivak more pointedly asserts that "there can be no doubt that the apparently crystalline disciplinary mainstream runs muddy if these [postcolonial] studies do not provide a persistent dredging operation" (1999: 1). These analogies conjure somewhat irreverent fantasies of faculty operating bulldozers/dredging machines and demolishing/digging out the epistemological edifice/conceptual silt of the master's house/river. These images also evoke the capacity of postcolonialism and antiracism to transform and bring to crisis the frameworks on which they are brought to bear. They also bring each other to productive crisis. To paraphrase Spivak's epigraph in this section, we affirm that if postcolonial or antiracist and feminist practices do not bring each other to productive crisis, the power of the script has clearly passed elsewhere.

In *Woman, Native, Other,* Trinh Minh-ha offers a salient example of this productive crisis by reminding readers of both the historical contexts and the universalizing dangers (defining different contexts as similar with regard to the "West" as norm) of the term "Third World" (1989: 97–98). It is important to keep in mind both the differences and the similarities among women living in the "Third World"; "Third World" nationals in the United States; and U.S. women of color, as well as the differences and similarities within each group (along class lines, obviously, but also along such axes as religion, marital status, sexual orientation, age, caste, language, and nationality). As Ania Loomba has noted, combining feminism and postcolonialism would alert us to ways in which the category "black woman," for example, does not account for the tremendous cultural, racial, and locational differences internal to this term—all of which, according to Loomba, would complicate the relationship between black women and colonial or racist ideologies (1998: 166).

In the United States, issues of colonization often tend to be racialized, making invisible the connections among class, race, and colonial practices. This leads to the danger of collapsing difference into sameness. For example, concerns of women in the "Third" and "Fourth" worlds were reconfigured according to racial parameters by feminists residing in the United States in the 1980s in order to highlight a "common context of struggle" among women of color worldwide (Mohanty 1991a: 7). The danger here is not only that "Third World women" as a category can become subsumed under the concerns of U.S. women of color, but also that colonization becomes subsumed under the category of racism. Similarly, the differences among the historical situations of internally diverse minoritized peoples in the United States are usually erased by the overarching rubric of race. This is a problem that Native activists in the United States have long recognized: Defining American Indians as an ethnic or "minority group" transforms their demands for state and federal fulfillment of treaty rights and sovereignty into a less threatening struggle over civil rights and racialized identity. With few exceptions, Native nations are conspicuously absent from most postcolonial theory and studies of contemporary colonial discourse. Works by Native scholars are rarely included in anthologies and syllabi, and when they are, it is often in a way that undermines the very issues they discuss. An example is the recent (and otherwise excellent) anthology *Dangerous Liaisons* (McClintock, Mufti, and Shohat 1997), in which the sole essay on

Native issues is placed under the subheading "Gender and the Politics of Race" rather than under "Contesting Nations." Outside the U.S. context, in former white-settler colonies such as Australia and Canada, the lack of race analysis in postcolonial studies has contributed to a very problematic emphasis on the (white) settler as the emblematic postcolonial subject. Although postcolonial critics who hold this view insist that former white-settler colonies should be included in the category "postcolonial," this argument ignores both the neocolonial position that some of these countries occupy and their continued colonial exploitation of aboriginal peoples. We consequently resist teaching or theorizing the United States, or other predominately white former colonies, as "postcolonial" because to do so covers over the power asymmetries whose demystification are at the heart of postcolonial analysis.

The question of the production of knowledges that do not erase histories of non-dominant groups is for us at the heart of postcolonial, anti-racist, and Women's Studies. Just as white settlers can use postcolonial analysis to escape complicity in historical and discursive colonialism, Euroamerican students (and faculty) often use knowledge about "others" as a way of avoiding issues about their own complicity with the structures and ideologies of oppression. The presupposition that oppression is only about "others" (meaning those who are not white) is exactly why, when we teach about race and colonialism, we include classroom materials that not only raise questions about students' immediate contexts, but also construct a complex grid of cultural and social exchange. In Donaldson's undergraduate "Race, Class, and Gender in the U.S." course, for example, she provides such a multidirectional framework by studying how immigrant populations were victimized by American white supremacy, but also how their resistance to this oppression changed American history; how the realities of U.S. racism affected the relationships of immigrants with their home countries as well as the interethnic solidarity that emerged among various groups (for example, the Japanese-Mexican labor associations created in California during the 1920s and '30s). The class also studies the social and psychological processes that link seemingly disparate phenomena. Their status as symbolic and physical crimes of control link the very diverse contexts of anti-gay hate crimes in the United States and the use of rape as a war tactic in Bosnia—not to mention the way in which the latter repeats the same genocidal tactics used in the Angloeuropean conquest of American Indians. Another example of such linking is how the socio-psychological process of projection—that is, resolving internal contradictions by "projecting" them onto other entities—informs the circulation of stereotypes in the arenas of U.S. racism and international colonialism. These are only some of the ways in which Donaldson's pedagogy incorporates a postcolonial and transnational perspective on the processes of U.S. racism, sexism, and classism.

Feminism, postcolonialism, and antiracism also bring one another to productive crisis—and not mutual suspicion—in Donaldson's graduate "American Indian Women's Literature" course. In this course, the subversive equation is that the sexual division of labor in most American Indian societies equals balance and reciprocity rather than hierarchy and dominance. This equation, combined with an emphasis on sovereignty, challenges many of the most deeply held beliefs and paradigms of the Euroamerican women's movement. Donaldson recounts, for instance, that she once assigned Wilma Mankiller's autobiography, *Mankiller: A Chief and Her People* (1993), as a text in this course and especially directed students' attention to those sections discussing a Cherokee woman's conflicts with the principle of affirmative action—not because she opposed it, but because it infringed on the ability of the Cherokee Nation to make its own decisions about governance. The majority of students, who were predominately Euroamerican, expressed puzzlement about, or hostility to, this view. It was very difficult for most to conceptualize a feminist movement (a label that Mankiller accepts) not defined by the Euroamerican foundation of individualist autonomy. However, a course thematizing the lives, concerns, and literary texts of American Indian women confronts the silence in contemporary Native North American scholarship on the traditional and contemporary gender roles of Native women—not to mention misogyny, domestic abuse, and a whole host of other ills connected to the colonial history of Indians and whites.

In conclusion, unless and until graduate (and undergraduate) Women's Studies incorporates the multiaxial perspectives of postcolonialism and antiracism into its knowledge base, it is at best consigned to parochialism, and at worst to destructive patterns of neocolonialist racism. If, as Uma Narayan suggests, multicultural education cannot be seen as a simple task of replacing "ignorance about Other cultures" with "knowledge" but, rather, necessitates that we understand how different contexts affect various issues (1997: 104), then postcolonial and antiracist scholarship nurtures this aspiration. Training our graduate students to be attentive to the workings of power and disempowerment in diverse contexts helps them to become researchers, teachers, and advocates whose vision will be inclusive and synthetic. They (and we) will be encouraged constantly to seek to expand our vision, to uncover our blind spots, and to place our individual or local concerns in a broader, transnational framework. They will also learn that striving toward inclusiveness is a life-long goal, not something one learns once and for all in the first year of graduate school. Postcolonial and antiracist perspectives will also help Women's Studies programs build strong alliances with our counterparts in ethnic studies programs as well as with other movements for social change—alliances that, at present, seem to be sorely missing. Although these perspectives are certainly not panaceas for all the challenges facing women in the academy, they do offer some tools and viewpoints that are essential for realizing the considerable potential of feminist analysis. Their subversive coupling moves us beyond a mere correction of the past toward the possibility of transformation. On such critical encounters hang the intellectual—not to mention the ethical—credibility of graduate Women's Studies.

Notes

1 Our notions of postcolonialism and antiracism are related to the ways in which Grewal and Kaplan use the term "transnational" to indicate a feminism that knows it is not "free of asymmetrical power relations" yet involves "forms of alliance, subversion, and complicity within which asymmetries and inequalities can be critiqued" (see the chapter by Kaplan and Grewal in this volume). Their definition of "transnational" has changed since the publication of *Scattered Hegemonies* (1994), in which they defined it more as a deconstructive movement between the local and the global.

2 Guy-Sheftall completed this study for the years 1969 to 1992.

3 See Sangari and Vaid 1993: 17.

4 See Tatum 1992. See also Hardiman and Jackson 1992.

5 See Bohmer and Briggs 1991. See also McIntosh 1998.

6 See hooks 1989. See also Patai 1991; Mohanty 1991a, 1991b.

7 See Rakow 1991.

8 See hooks 1994. See also Rothenberg 1988.

9 See Narayan 1988.

10 See Bove, as cited in Spanos 1986: 52.

11 The terms "multidisciplinary" and "interdisciplinary" are not interchangeable. We define "multidisciplinary" as scholarship that enriches its subject by drawing on several different disciplines (for example, literature and history); interdisciplinary

work goes beyond this in that the rigorous combining of several different disciplines actually transforms the way one practices all of them. Needless to say, the latter happens far less frequently than the former, and what is often called "interdisciplinary" is actually "multidisciplinary."

12 Including Deborah Gordon, Caren Kaplan, Katie King, and Chela Sandoval, among others.

13 See Kwane Anthony Appiah, *In My Father's House: Africa in the Philosophy of Culture* (London: Methuen, 1992), 240.

Afterword: Continuity and Change in Women's Studies

Locating Feminism offers a survey of Women's Studies at the dawn of the twenty-first century. We have been in constant confrontation with our institutions, which often question the validity of our new field. This volume, written by several generations of scholars, shows that, despite opposition, every kind of Women's Studies is going on in this world.

Since I left teaching in the mid-1980s, Women's Studies has gone deeper with its questions. We thought the study of women would be a temporary phase; eventually we would all go back to our disciplines. I remember the day in 1977 when I said in lecture, "Women, we" and asked myself in a flash, "Women, we: Who am I talking about?" Early on we recognized the narrowness of our original conceptions. I looked for articles on Black, Native American, and Chinese women in the United States and found few; I asked the three untenured women in those fields at Berkeley to lecture in my classes. Together we came upon strains of similarity but also large differences in the lives of women. This is work still to be done, as Rachel Lee's splendid essay shows.

When I joined the editorial board of *Women's Studies International Forum* in 1980, another level of discovery commenced. "Feminism" was not a shared word or idea; women around the world, no matter their lot, were strategizing to improve life for themselves and their families. Here was a more nuanced view of woman's resistance. "Women in development" was getting a bad name; the U.S. government and the international agencies it dominated often contributed, knowingly or not, to the subordination of women. Feminist scholars entered the debates, pointing out what these women accomplished each day and asking them what kind of help would help. Quickly, our subject matter was expanding, and with it the questions about how to conduct our studies. *Theories of Women's Studies* (1983), which I edited with Renate Klein, included a number of germinal essays on feminist methods. Among other questions, scholars took up the subject-object split of traditional research.[1] Since then, there has been a veritable flood of books on research practices.

From the beginnings of our field, feminist scholars wanted our academic work to have an impact on lives of women outside the academy. In the 1970s and '80s, we agonized about whether university work had any meaning in the "real" world. When asked during our fifth-year review what they got out of Women's Studies, our students replied: "Confidence." After graduation, they often returned to tell us how their education had helped them. Our small seminars, using the new feminist pedagogy, had taught them to speak up; they recognized discrimination and had some sense of how to address it.

Though the faculty soon saw that our graduates were using Women's Studies in the world, we seldom recognized that we, in fact, were doing political work within the university. We spent hours strategizing, cultivating allies, finding out about our detractors. We learned to work the system. Despite all the talk of theory in the past decade, women have been eminently practical and politically savvy, as the essays by Robyn Warhol and Marcia Westkott point out. At the University of Illinois, Chicago, the program tries to give students a living example of collectivity through program governance. With institutionalization comes hierarchy. Judith Gardiner and her colleagues show an unusual commitment to ideas that animated us early on, but that many have abandoned because it is so time-consuming and unwieldy to make group decisions.

Women's Studies advocates understand that all politics is local—thus, the different forms of Women's Studies we see in the United States and around the world. Yet we have tried to gather together nationally and internationally. Our national association has had some of the same internal problems as individual programs. But we desperately need an effective advocacy group. For example, one would hope that our National Women's Studies Association (NWSA) would address the appalling exploitation of part-time teachers and lecturers, the majority of them women, an exploitation that Sivagami Subbaraman addresses in this volume, as

458   Gloria Bowles

well as the use by Women's Studies programs of untenured "junior administrators," which Devoney Looser describes. Getting the word out about the kind of research of graduates and their careers undertaken by Maryanne Dever, Denise Cuthbert, and Lindsay Pollak is also the job of a national organization. Faculty know that students benefit from our labors, but we still have to make this argument to skeptical colleagues. In 1979, I got an outside grant to teach "Women's Studies and Careers." Students wrote résumés and interviewed women who had careers like those they thought of pursuing. Graduates returned to tell us about their experiences in the workplace. Two students surveyed our graduates and wrote a paper addressing the question, "What do you do with a major in Women's Studies?" The same question is alive in this volume. There are some signs that the NWSA is taking on these challenges.[2]

Above all, Women's Studies practitioners today are overwhelmed by the too-muchness of their lives as teachers and administrators and scholars. In the 1970s, we could read everyone's work, because there was so little of it. Now feminist scholars must pick and choose. This leaves us frustrated, because we really want to know everything. The scope of our field has led some to assert that ours is necessarily an inter- (or trans-) disciplinary discipline. That same capaciousness is the very reason others argue that feminist scholarship is too big to be a coherent study and thus is best pursued within the existing disciplines, whose brick and mortar ensures that our scholarship will be responsible and rigorous. The traditional disciplines are changing, too, this argument maintains. Sabina Sawhney's honest essay is interesting in this regard. A professor of English, she feels intellectually comfortable in her discipline and found unsatisfying an experience of interdisciplinary team-teaching.

Successful collaboration, whether in teaching or writing, is rare. And academe still does not for the most part reward the collaborations of teachers or writers. For a few years at Berkeley in the mid-1970s, we were lucky to have an experimental interdisciplinary college funded by outside money. Strawberry Creek College was expensive because two faculty members taught each small seminar. Faculty and graduate students who already had interdisciplinary bents were selected to teach at Strawberry. Out of this group some of us were able to find fruitful collaborations. When in 1976 I taught a class on the "private-public split" with a colleague in political science, we brought different knowledge to the table. But we shared feminist perspectives, and we "clicked" intellectually. My two years in this community was the most satisfying pedagogical experience I ever had.[3]

Theories of Women's Studies (1983) envisioned an interdisciplinary discipline with its own department. At a conference organized by the Spencer Foundation in 1999 to discuss the study of women in the new century, a group of prominent feminist scholars readily admitted that they did not know how to do interdisciplinary work. They agreed that this task will be left to another generation, those women pursuing Ph.D.s in Women's Studies.[4] But will the structures of academe be ready for them?

In the mid- to late 1980s, five women were hired at Berkeley as full professors with joint appointments in Women's Studies. All of them were known as excellent scholars in their fields, but few had experience in Women's Studies. Some said openly that they did not know whether they believed in it. Of the five, one has retired, one has returned to the East Coast, and three have left Women's Studies for the Berkeley departments of their original disciplines, where prestige and power lie. In 2000, a sixth faculty member decamped to a department, showing once again how deadly joint appointments can be for our field. It is extremely wearing constantly to have to defend one's field of study; it is not surprising that women choose a more secure home in an established discipline. As long as interdisciplinary work is little respected and unrewarded, Women's Studies will not be able to test its potential as an inter- or transdisciplinary discipline or, as Robyn Wiegman puts it, "a knowledge formation."

We might be better prepared if we taught Women's Studies theory along with feminist theory and poststructuralism. With a seminar on "Theories of Women's Studies," Berkeley students had a chance to join the ongoing conversation about the history and ideas of our field. Should not such a class be a regular part of our core curriculum? Since the book that came out of the seminar, there have been many more volumes on feminist methods than on the interdisciplinary project. Our call in "Theories of Women's Studies" for "autonomous" Women's Studies, a discipline in its own right housed in its own department, is a promise that has gone largely unfulfilled.

Some argue that Women's Studies is too big and complex to be "disciplined." I am probably less troubled by these arguments than some because of my background in comparative literature. I never quite knew what "comp lit" was but chose it because I lacked belief in the validity of studying a single language and literature. So I feel comfortable with the capacious, even as I read those who dig down into the systems of older disciplines to produce feminist scholarship. I admire this work as long as it does not retreat to the tiny speck. Imagination can save us from such drudgery.

Of course, the most obvious change in feminist scholarship from the mid-1980s and through the 1990s was the entry of critical theory in its various guises. As Rosi Braidotti of the department of Women's Studies at Utrecht has pointed out, "In European academia, the movement of thought known as poststructuralism, far from being the prestigious site of high theory—as it seems to be in the United States—has retained a marginal and radical 'wing,' with barely any institutional pull."[5] In the United States, "theory" came to denote only the theorizing based in modern European philosophy. Too often other legitimate ways of thinking were seen as less important. For example, U.S. feminist scholarship has suffered a split between the poststructuralists and the empiricists. Having lived abroad to study European languages, I always felt that Americans were too easily seduced by continental philosophy. In the 1970s, feminists wrote convincingly about the social construction of knowledge; this idea ribbons its way through Dale Spender's prodigious oeuvre. But Foucault's dissection of the power to produce knowledge immediately had more cachet. In the 1980s, we needed an analysis like the one finally offered in 1998 by Clare Moses, who in her essay "Made in America: 'French Feminism' in Academia" shows how a few thinkers of "Psych et po" and others became "the French feminists," while numerous, more overtly political groups were ignored.[6] This is a prime example of how Americans tend to adopt foreign ideas without a sense of the context from which they spring.

Interestingly, Women's Studies has never taken hold in Europe the way it has here, in part because of the greater rigidity of Europe's educational systems. But one must point out that American pragmatism is also a form of theory. The ability of women to figure out how to do Women's Studies in their particular locality is a testament to our practicality and our political skills.

Of course, one can use theory as a tool for explication or be used by it. Like all else, it is a question of degree. We have suffered the excesses of poststructuralism and deconstruction. Some French thinkers writing in the 1960s adopted ambiguity as a weapon against famed French (read, bourgeois) *clarté*. Initiated into this dense, often playful language through translation, some scholars have tried to imitate it, with damaging consequences for our scholarship. The clarity of prose, the common language to which feminists once aspired, has too often been replaced by jargon, with its predictable lexicon. Not all of us are philosophers. Above all, it is disturbing to hear such inaccessible language taken up by graduate students and young faculty who should be on the lookout for their own voices. It is possible to explicate difficult ideas in lucid prose; such writing should be our model.[7]

I hope that we are entering a period of correction, when we have a perspective on both the contributions and the pitfalls of modern European philosophies, as we now have some critical distance on existentialism and Marxism. I am certain that this correction will be accelerated if we listen to the ideas of women who live and work in the big world outside the United States and Europe.

Our debates about whether a flood of European ideas derailed feminist thought have been so heated precisely because, since its inception, our field has been interested in theory that has practical consequences. Ideas have power in the real world. In reading this volume, I found it amazing and heartening that, even after years of the powerful impact of postmodernism, one still hears the echoing refrain of our pioneer days: Are we doing anything useful?

Women's Studies remains a particularly self-critical discipline. We didn't want to be like the other disciplines. We wanted to change the "multiversity," making it less impersonal and more democratic. Our analysis in the 1960s of the university as servant of the military-industrial complex is akin to the "corporatization of knowledge" analyzed by Jeanette McVicker in this volume. Women's Studies remains exceedingly ambitious. Although the title of Robyn Wiegman's chapter emphasizes feminist research into masculinity ("The Progress of Gender: Whither 'Women'?"), her essay is a veritable summation of the major theoretical moves of the past decade. Our pedagogy is no less ambitious. Nancy Naples teaches a class in experiential learning that combines work in the field and a sophisticated reading list. Jane Newman wants to go back centuries with students for whom World War II is ancient history. The young students of Caren Kaplan and Inderpal Grewal probably have little experience outside their milieu, but these professors want to enlarge their worlds with global feminist analysis. And to do this, the professors first need vast and detailed knowledge themselves. Susan Stanford Friedman teaches a final "capstone" class which includes theories of Women's Studies, feminist interpretive strategies and, finally, Women's Studies and careers.

Despite our prodigious efforts, the university often does not appreciate what we do. (This is the "housework" theme eloquently argued by Dale Bauer.) Women's Studies, ethnic studies, nonprofit studies in a business school—all are swimming against the academic mainstream. Certainly, we should know our limits and learn to say no. At the same time, we may be disappointed if we expect large rewards from the very institutions we challenge. In this sense, too, our work is political. We do it because we believe in it. At a conference on Women's Studies at the University of California, Irvine, in 1984, I said I constantly had to "hold up my values against the values of the institution, which are not all bad, but which can dominate us." Few academic books written today will influence their moment, and fewer still will stand any test of time. Some faculty enjoy writing and publishing, but many do it to survive. Yet we know that good teaching can change a student's life. Many of us heard, and hear, that famous line in Women's Studies: "This course changed my life."

Women's Studies still requires generosity, courage, and vision. That has not changed.

Notes

1 See Bowles and Klein 1983. In *Strategies for Women's Studies in the Eighties* (1984), I extended the arguments of *Theories*, with essays by integrationists, advocates of "autonomous" Women's Studies, and multicultural scholars.

2 The NWSA newsletter that came out after the Albuquerque conference addressed the need to help administrators and to document the successes of Women's Studies graduates: see *NWSAction*, vol. 10, no. 2 (1999).

3 The Collegiate Seminar Program, or Strawberry Creek College—so named for the stream running through campus—was founded by Charles Muscatine and funded by the Fund for Innovative Post-Secondary Education. Undergraduates received ten credits (two-thirds of their course load) for seminars in which they actively participated and wrote substantial research papers.

4 Marilyn Boxer, personal communication, October 5, 1999. Professor Boxer attended the meeting in Chicago in late fall, called by the Spencer Foundation and Catharine Stimpson, titled, "Women's Studies and the Study of Women: What Should We Know About Them and Their Influence?" The charge of the conference was to outline the major research questions of the future.

5 See Braidotti 1997.
6 See Moses 1998. See also Brodribb 1992.
7 For example, an unusually lucid explication of ideology can be found in Belsey 1991. In this essay, one feels the writer has completely understood the difficult texts she has read and reinterpreted them for her reader.

Abelove, Henry, Michele A. Barale, and David Halperin, eds. 1993. *The Lesbian and Gay Studies Reader*. New York: Routledge.

Abusharaf, Rogaia. 1998. "Unmasking Tradition." *The Sciences* (March–April): 23–27.

Alain. 1939. *Idées*. Paris: Paul Hartmann.

Alarcón, Norma. 1990. "The Theoretical Subject(s) of This Bridge Called My Back and Anglo-American Feminism." In *Making Face, Making Soul/Haciendo Caras: Creative and Critical Perspectives by Feminists of Color*, ed. Gloria Anzaldúa. San Francisco: Aunt Lute Books.

Albrecht, Lisa, and Rose M. Brewer, eds. *Bridges of Power: Women's Multicultural Alliances*. Philadelphia: New Society Publishers, 1990.

Alexander, M. Jacqui, and Chandra Talpade Mohanty, eds. 1997. *Feminist Genealogies, Colonial Legacies, Democratic Futures*. New York: Routledge.

Allen, Judith A. 1997. "Strengthening Women's Studies in Hard Times: Feminism and Challenges of Institutional Adaptation." *Women's Studies Quarterly* 25, no. 1–2 (spring–summer): 358–87.

Allen, Judith A., and Sally L. Kitch. 1998. "Disciplined by Disciplines? The Need for an Interdisciplinary Research Mission in Women's Studies." *Feminist Studies* 24, no. 2 (summer): 275–300.

Alongi, Ingrid, Amy Kane, Sani Keskimake, Karen Lozano, and Beth Ross. 1997. "Is Women's Studies Endangered?" *Circles* 1, no. 4: 38–40.

Anderson, Mary, Lisa Fine, Kathleen Geissler, and Joyce R. Ladenson, eds. 1997. *Doing Feminism: Teaching and Research in the Academy*. East Lansing: Michigan State University.

Anderson, Pamela Sue. 2000. "Feminism and Philosophy." In *The Routledge Critical Dictionary of Feminism and Postfeminism*, ed. Susan Gamble. New York: Routledge.

Anzaldúa, Gloria. 1987. *Borderlands/La Frontera*. San Francisco: Aunt Lute Books.

——, ed. 1990. "La conciencia de la mestiza: Towards a New Consciousness." In *Making*

Face, Making Soul/Haciendo Caras: Creative and Critical Perspectives by Feminists of Color. San Francisco: Aunt Lute Books.

Arac, Jonathan. 1997. "Shop Window or Laboratory: Collection, Collaboration, and the Humanities." In *The Politics of Research,* ed. E. Ann Kaplan and George Levine. New Brunswick, N.J.: Rutgers University Press.

Arenson, Karen W. 2000. "SUNY Fight over Curriculum Mirrors Larger Debate." *New York Times,* June 6, sec. B1–B2.

Armitage, Catherine. 1998. "Relevance Pays Off in Job Search." *The Australian,* November 23, p. 2.

Arneil, Barbara. 1999. *Politics and Feminism.* Oxford: Blackwell.

Aryabod, Shadi. 1998. "Community Action Project Report." Unpublished paper, University of California, Irvine.

Ascencio, Anna. 1999. "Community Action Project: Final Report." Unpublished paper, University of California, Irvine.

Ashcroft, Bill, Gareth Griffiths, and Helen Tiffin, eds. 1998. *Key Concepts in Post-Colonial Studies.* London: Routledge.

Assiter, Alison. 1996. *Enlightened Women: Modernist Feminism in a Postmodern Age.* New York: Routledge.

Assouline, Pierre. 1988 (1984). *Gaston Gallimard: A Half-Century of French Publishing,* trans. Harold J. Salemson. San Diego: Harcourt Brace Jovanovich.

Atack, Margaret. 1998. "Writing from the Centre: Ironies of Otherness and Marginality." In *Simone de Beauvoir's* The Second Sex. *New Interdisciplinary Essays,* ed. Ruth Evans. Manchester, Engl.: Manchester University Press.

Attridge, Derek. 1988. *Peculiar Language: Literature as Difference from the Renaissance to James Joyce.* London: Methuen.

Au, Ami Danice. 1994. "Group Action Project Final Report." Unpublished paper, Women's Studies Program, University of California, Irvine.

Auslander, Leora. 1997. "Do Women's + Feminist + Men's + Lesbian and Gay + Queer Studies = Gender Studies?" *differences* 9, no. 3: 1–30.

Australian Association of Graduate Employers. 1997. "A National Survey of Graduate Employers: Report." Melbourne: Australian Association of Graduate Employers.

Bachelard, Gaston. 1994 (1958). *The Poetics of Space.* Boston: Beacon Press.

Baldwin, Gaye, and Avril Kyle. 1998. "Survey of Arts, Humanities and Social Science Graduates—1986 and 1991 Cohorts." Final report, Monash University, Faculty of Arts, Melbourne.

Bannerji, Himani. 1996. "On the Dark Side of the Nation: Politics of Multiculturalism and the State of 'Canada.' " *Journal of Canadian Studies* 31, no. 3 (fall): 103–28.

—, ed. 1993. *Returning the Gaze: Essays on Racism, Feminism and Politics.* Toronto: Sister Vision Press.

Bannerji, Himani, Linda Carty, Kari Dehli, Susan Heald, and Kate McKenna. 1991. *Unsettling Relations. The University as a Site of Feminist Struggles.* Toronto: Women's Press.

Barlow, Tani. 1993. "Colonialism's Career in Postwar China Studies." *positions* 1 (spring): 224–67.

Bassnett, Susan, and Harish Trivedi. 1999. "Introduction: Of Colonies, Cannibals and

Vernaculars." In *Post-Colonial Translation: Theory and Practice*, ed. Susan Bassnett and Harish Trivedi. New York: Routledge.

Bellei, Sérgio Luiz Prado. 1998. "Brazilian Anthropology Revisited." In *Cannibalism and the Colonial World*, ed. Francis Barker, Peter Hulme, and Margaret Iverson. Cambridge: Cambridge University Press.

Belsey, Catherine. 1991. "Constructing the Subject: Deconstructing the Text." In *Feminisms: An Anthology of Literary Theory and Criticism*, ed. Robyn R. Warhol and Diane Price Herndl. New Brunswick, N.J.: Rutgers University Press.

Benhabib, Seyla. 1995. "Feminism and Postmodernism: An Uneasy Alliance." In *Feminist Contentions: A Philosophical Exchange*. New York: Routledge.

Benmayor, Rina. 1991. "Testimony, Action Research, and Empowerment: Puerto Rican Women and Popular Education." In *Women's Words: The Feminist Practice of Oral History*, ed. Sherna B. Gluck and Daphne Patai. New York: Routledge.

Berlant, Lauren. 1997. *The Queen of America Goes to Washington City: Essays on Sex and Citizenship*. Durham, N.C.: Duke University Press.

——. 1998. "Collegiality, Crisis, and Cultural Studies." *Profession* 98: Bowles, G105–16.

Berman, Ruth. 1989. "From Aristotle's Dualism to Materialist Dialectics: Feminist Transformation of Science and Society." In *Gender/Body/Knowledge: Feminist Reconstructions of Being and Knowing*, ed. Alison Jagger and Susan Bordo. New Brunswick, N.J.: Rutgers University Press.

Bernheimer, Charles, ed. 1995. *Comparative Literature in the Age of Multiculturalism*. Baltimore, Md.: Johns Hopkins University Press.

Bhabha, Homi. 1994. *The Location of Culture*. London: Routledge.

Biddick, Kathleen. 1998. *The Shock of Medievalism*. Durham, N.C.: Duke University Press.

Bloom, Allan. 1987. *The Closing of the American Mind*. New York: Simon and Schuster.

Bohmer, Suzanne, and Joyce L. Briggs. 1991. "Teaching Privileged Students About Gender, Race, and Class Oppression." *Teaching Sociology* 19, no. 2 (April): 154–63.

Bojar, Karen. 1998. "Volunteerism and Women's Lives: A Lens for Exploring Conflicts in Contemporary Feminist Thought, Historical Importance, and Socioeconomic Value of Women's Contributions as Volunteers." In *Women's Studies in Transition: The Pursuit of Interdisciplinarity*, ed. Kate Conway-Turner. Newark, N.J.: University of Delaware Press.

——. 2000. "Service Learning and Women's Studies: A Community College Perspective." In *The Practice of Change: Concepts and Models for Service Learning in Women's Studies*, ed. Barbra Balliet and Kerissa Hefferman. Merrifield, Va.: American Association of Higher Education.

Boone, Joseph A., and Michael Cadden, eds. 1990. *Engendering Men: The Question of Male Feminist Criticism*. New York: Routledge.

Bordo, Susan. 1987. *The Flight to Objectivity: Essays on Cartesianism and Culture*. Albany: State University of New York Press.

——. 1993. *Unbearable Weight: Feminism, Western Culture, and the Body*. Berkeley: University of California Press.

——, ed. 1999. *Feminist Interpretations of René Descartes*. University Park: Pennsylvania State University Press.

Borges, Jorge Luis. 1971. "Pierre Menard, Author of the *Quixote*." In *Labyrinths*. Harmondsworth, Engl.: Penguin.

Borland, Katherine. 1991. " 'That's Not What I Said': Interpretive Conflict in Oral Narrative Research." In *Women's Words: The Practice of Oral History*, ed. Sherna Berger Gluck and Daphne Patai. London: Routledge.

Bose, Christine E., and Janet Priest-Jones. 1980. *The Relationship Between Women's Studies, Career Development, and Vocational Choice*. Washington, D.C.: National Institute of Education.

Bourdieu, Pierre. 1984. *Distinction: A Social Critique of the Judgment of Taste*. London: Routledge and Kegan Paul.

Bow, Leslie. 1997. "Erasure and Representation: Asian American Women in the Academy." *Profession* 97: 215–21.

Bowles, Gloria, and Renate Duelli Klein. 1983. *Theories of Women's Studies*. London: Routledge and Kegan Paul.

Bowles, Gloria, ed. 1984. *Strategies for Women's Studies in the Eighties*. Oxford: Pergamon.

Boxer, Marilyn. 1982. "For and About Women: The Theory and Practice of Women's Studies in the United States." *Signs* 7, no. 3 (spring): 661–95.

——. 1998. *When Women Ask the Questions: Creating Women's Studies in America*. Baltimore, Md.: Johns Hopkins University Press.

Braidotti, Rosi. 1997. "Comment on Felski's 'The Doxa of Difference': Working Through Sexual Difference," *Signs* 23, no. 1 (fall): 24.

——. 1997. "Uneasy Transitions: Women's Studies in the European Union." In *Transitions, Environments: Feminisms in International Politics*, ed. Joan Scott, Cora Kaplan, and Debra Keates. New York: Routledge.

Britzman, Deborah P. 1995. "Is There a Queer Pedagogy? or, Stop Reading Straight." *Educational Theory* (www.ed.uiuc.edu/EPS/Educational-Theory/Contents/1995__2.asp).

Brodribb, Somer. 1992. *Nothing Mat(t)ers: A Feminist Critique of Postmodernism*. New York: New York University Press.

Brown, Wendy. 1997. "The Impossibility of Women's Studies." *differences* 9, no. 3 (fall): 79–101.

Brownmiller, Susan. 1999. *In Our Time: Memoir of a Revolution*. New York: Dial Press.

Brunschvicg, Léon. 1937. *Descartes*. Paris: Les Éditions Rieder.

——. 1944 (1942). *Descartes et Pascal: Lecteurs de Montaigne*. New York: Brentano's.

——. 1947. *L'Esprit Européen*. Neuchatel: Éditions de la Baconnière.

——. 1951–58. *Écrits philosophiques*. 3 vols. Paris: Presses Universitaires de France.

Bulbeck, Chilla. 1998. *Re-orienting Western Feminism: Women's Diversity in a Postcolonial World*. New York: Cambridge University Press.

Bunch, Charlotte, and Sandra Pollack, eds. 1983. *Learning Our Way: Essays in Feminist Education*. Trumansburg, N.Y.: Crossing Press.

Butler, Judith. 1990. *Gender Trouble: Feminism and the Subversion of Identity*. New York: Routledge.

——. 1994. "Against Proper Objects." *differences* 6, no. 2–3: 1–26.

——. 1997. *Excitable Speech. A Politics of the Performative*. New York: Routledge.

——. 1998 (1986). "Sex and Gender in Simone de Beauvoir's *Second Sex*." In *Simone de Beauvoir. A Critical Reader*, ed. Elizabeth Fallaize. New York: Routledge.

Byyny, Richard, and Leon Speroff. 1996. *A Clinical Guide for the Care of Older Women: Primary and Preventative Care.* 2d ed. Baltimore, Md.: Williams and Williams.

Cain, Julien. 1937. *Descartes. Exposition organisée pour le IIIe Centenaire du Discours de la Méthode.* Paris: Bibliothèque Nationale.

Campbell, Marie, and Ann Manicom. 1995. Introduction to *Knowledge, Experience, and Ruling Relations*, ed. Marie Campbell and Ann Manicom. Toronto: University of Toronto Press.

Castillo, Ana. 1995. *Massacre of the Dreamers: Essays on Xicanisma.* New York: Plume.

Chai, Alice. 1985. "Toward a Holistic Paradigm for Asian American Women's Studies: A Synthesis of Feminist Scholarship and Women of Color's Feminist Politics." *Women's Studies International Forum* 8, no. 1: 59–66.

Chapman, Kathleen, and Michael Du Plessis. 1997. " 'Don't Call Me Girl': Lesbian Theory, Feminist Theory, and Transsexual Identities." In *Cross-Purposes: Lesbians, Feminists, and the Limits of Alliance*, ed. Dana Heller. Bloomington: Indiana University Press.

Chase, Cheryl. 1998. "Hermaphrodites with Attitude: Mapping the Emergence of Intersex Political Activism." In "The Transgender Issue," *GLQ: A Journal of Gay and Lesbian Studies* 4, no. 2: 189–211.

Chasin, Alexandra. 2000. *Selling Out: The Gay and Lesbian Movement Goes to Market.* New York: St. Martin's Press.

Cheah, Pheng, and Bruce Robbins, eds. 1998. *Cosmopolitics: Thinking and Feeling Beyond the Nation.* Minneapolis: University of Minnesota Press.

Chen, Kuan-Hsing. 1992. "Voices from the Outside: Towards a New Internationalist Localism." *Cultural Studies* 6, no. 3 (October): 476–84.

——. 1994. "Positioning Positions: A New Internationalist Localism of Cultural Studies." *positions* 2, no. 3 (winter): 680–710.

Chilly Collective, ed. 1995. *Breaking Anonymity: The Chilly Climate for Women Faculty.* Waterloo, Ont.: Wilfred Laurier Press.

Chow, Rey. 1993. *Writing Diaspora: Tactics of Intervention in Contemporary Cultural Studies.* Bloomington: Indiana University Press.

Christian, Barbara. 1987. "The Race for Theory." *Cultural Critique* 6: 335–45.

Christian, Barbara, Ann duCille, Sharon Marcus, Elaine Marks, Nancy K. Miller, Sylvia Schafer, and Joan W. Scott. 1990. "Conference Call." *differences* 2 (fall): 52–108.

Clark, Vèvè, Shirley Nelson Garner, Margaret Higonnet, and Ketu H. Katrak, eds. 1996. *Antifeminism in the Academy.* New York: Routledge.

Clarke, Stanley. 1999. "Descartes's Gender." In *Feminist Interpretations of René Descartes*, ed. Susan Bordo. University Park: Pennsylvania State University Press.

Clifford, James. 1988. *The Predicament of Culture: Twentieth-Century Ethnography, Literature, and Art.* Cambridge, Mass.: Harvard University Press.

Coates, Jacky, Michelle Doods, and Jodi Jensen. 1998. " 'Isn't Just Being Here Political Enough?' Feminist Action-Oriented Research as a Challenge to Graduate Women's Studies." *Feminist Studies* 24, no. 2: 333–46.

Cochran, Jo Whitehorse, Donna Langston, and Carolyn Woodward, eds. 1991. *Changing Our Power.* Dubuque, Iowa: Kendall/Hunt.

Collins, Patricia Hill. 1990. *Black Feminist Thought: Knowledge, Consciousness, and the Politics of Empowerment.* New York: Routledge.

Combahee River Collective. 1982. "A Black Feminist Statement." In *All the Women Are White, All the Men Are Black, But Some of Us Are Brave*, ed. Gloria T. Hull, Patricia Bell Scott and Barbara Smith. Old Westbury, N.Y.: Feminist Press.

Cook, Kathryn, Renea Henry, and Joan Scott. 1997. "The Edge Interview." *differences* 9, no. 3 (fall): 132–55.

Cooper, Marc. 1995. "God and Man in Colorado Springs." *Nation* 260, no. 1 (January 2): 9–12.

Cordova, Teresa. 1998. "Power and Knowledge: Colonialism in the Academy." In *Living Chicana Theory*, ed. Carla Trujillo. Berkeley, Calif.: Third Woman Press.

Cox, Ana Marie, Freya Johnson, Annalee Newitz, and Jillian Sandell. 1997. "Masculinity Without Men: Women Reconciling Feminism and Male-Identification." In *Third Wave Agenda: Being Feminist, Doing Feminism*, ed. Leslie Haywood and Jennifer Drake. Minneapolis: University of Minnesota Press.

Coyte, Philip. 1985. *Graduates in the Labour Market.* Sydney: University of Sydney Careers and Appointments Service.

Cresson, André. 1962 (1942). *Descartes, Sa Vie, Son Oeuvre, avec un Exposé de sa Philosophie.* Paris: Presses Universitaires de France.

Crenshaw, Kimberlé. 1989. "Demarginalizing the Intersection of Race and Sex: A Black Feminist Critique of Antidiscrimination Doctrine, Feminist Theory, and Antiracist Politics." *University of Chicago Legal Forum:* 139–67.

——. 1995. "Mapping the Margins: Intersectionality, Identity Politics, and the Violence Against Women of Color." In *After Identity: A Reader in Law and Culture*, ed. Dan Danielsen and Karen Engle. New York: Routledge.

Crimshaw, Jean. 1986. *Philosophy and Feminist Thinking.* Minneapolis: University of Minnesota Press.

Cruikshank, Margaret, ed. 1982. *Lesbian Studies: Present and Future.* Old Westbury, N.Y.: Feminist Press.

Daly, Mary. 1978. *Gyn/Ecology: The Metaethics of Radical Feminism.* Boston: Beacon.

Davis, Angela. 1983 (1981). *Women, Race, and Class.* New York: Vintage Books.

Davis, Angela, and Elizabeth Martinez. 1994. "Coalition Building Among People of Color." In "Enunciating Our Terms: Women of Color in Collaboration and Conflict," special issue of *Inscriptions* 7: 42–53.

Dean, Jodi. 1996. *Solidarity of Strangers: Feminism After Identity Politics.* Berkeley: University of California Press.

de Beauvoir, Simone. 1949. *Le deuxième Sexe.*, 2 vols. Paris: Gallimard.

——. 1959 (1958). *Memoirs of a Dutiful Daughter*, trans. James Kirkup. New York: Harper and Row.

——. 1989 (1953). *The Second Sex*, trans. H. M. Parshley. New York: Vintage.

——. 1998 (1997). *A Transatlantic Love Affair. Letters to Nelson Algren.* New York: New Press.

——. 1999 (1954). *America Day by Day*, trans. Carol Cosman. Berkeley: University of California Press.

Derrida, Jacques. 1995. *On the Name*, ed. Thomas Dutoit. Stanford, Calif.: Stanford University Press.

DeVault, Marjorie L. 1999. *Liberating Method: Feminism and Social Research.* Philadelphia, Pa.: Temple University Press.

Dickinson, Torry D. 1999. "Reunifying Community and Transforming Society: Community Development, Education, and the University." In *Research in Community Sociology* 9, ed. Dan Chekki. Greenwich, Conn.: JAI Press.

Dinnerstein, Myra. 2000. "A Political Education." In *The Politics of Women's Studies: Testimony from Thirty Founding Mothers.* New York: Feminist Press.

Drakulic, Slavenka. 1996. *The Taste of a Man.* Trans. Christina Pribichevich Zoric. London: Abacus.

D'Souza, Dinesh. 1991. *Illiberal Education: The Politics of Race and Sex on Campus.* New York: Free Press.

Du Bois, W. E. B. 1903. *The Souls of Black Folk.* New York: Penguin.

Ebert, Teresa L. 1997. "Sensationalists Miss Out on Real Scandal at SUNY." *Schenectady Daily Gazette,* November 23, sec. F1.

Edelman, Lee. 1990. "Redeeming the Phallus: Wallace Stevens, Frank Lentricchia, and the Politics of (Hetero)Sexuality." In *Engendering Men: The Question of Male Feminist Criticism,* ed. Joseph A. Boone and Michael Cadden. New York: Routledge.

Eggins, Heather, ed. 1992. *Arts Graduates, Their Skills and Their Employment: Perspectives for Change.* London: Falmer Press.

Eichler, Margaret. 1990. "What's in a Name? Women's Studies or Feminist Studies?" *Atlantis* 16, no. 1 (fall): 40–56.

Eisenstein, Zillah R. 1996. *Hatreds: Racialized and Sexualized Conflicts in the 21st Century.* New York: Routledge.

Elam, Diane. 1997. "Sisters Are Doing It to Themselves." In *Generations: Academic Feminists in Dialogue,* ed. Devoney Looser and E. Ann Kaplan. Minneapolis: University of Minnesota Press.

Ellmann, Maud. 1993. *The Hunger Artists: Starving, Writing, and Imprisonment.* Cambridge, Mass.: Harvard University Press.

Emberley, Peter C. 1996. *Zero Tolerance: Hot Button Politics in Canada's Universities.* Toronto: Penguin.

Enloe, Cynthia. 1990. *Bananas, Beaches, and Bases: Making Feminist Sense out of International Politics.* Berkeley: University of California Press.

Epstein, Barbara. 1992. "Political Correctness and Identity Politics." In *Beyond P.C.: Toward a Politics of Understanding,* ed. Patricia Aufderheide. St. Paul, Minn.: Greywolf Press.

Evans, Mary. 1997. "Negotiating the Frontier: Women and Resistance in the Contemporary Academy." In *Knowing Feminisms: On Academic Borders, Territories and Tribes,* ed. Liz Stanley. London: Sage.

Evans, Ruth, ed. 1998. *Simone de Beauvoir's "The Second Sex": New Interdisciplinary Essays.* Manchester, Engl.: Manchester University Press.

Fallaize, Elizabeth. 1998. Introduction to *Simone de Beauvoir. A Critical Reader,* ed. Elizabeth Fallaize. New York: Routledge.

Feagin, Joe. 1999. "Soul-Searching in Sociology: Is the Discipline in Crisis?" *Chronicle of Higher Education,* October 15, sec. B4–B6.

Fekete, John. 1994. *Moral Panic: Biopolitics Rising.* Montreal: Robert Davies.

Felder, Deborah G. 1999. *A Century of Women. The Most Influential Events in Twentieth-Century Women's History.* Secaucus, N.J.: Carol Publishing Group.

Flax, Jane. 1983. "Political Philosophy and the Patriarchal Unconscious: A Psychoanalytic Perspective on Epistemology and Metaphysics." In *Discovering Reality: Feminist Perspectives on Epistemology, Metaphysics, Methodology, and the Philosophy of Science*, ed. Sandra Harding and Merrill B. Hintikka. Boston: D. Reidel.

——. 1990. *Thinking Fragments: Psychoanalysis, Feminism, and Postmodernism in the Contemporary West*. Berkeley: University of California Press.

Foucault, Michel. 1970. *The Order of Things: An Archeology of the Human Sciences*. New York: Random House.

——. 1977. *Discipline and Punish: The Birth of the Prison*, trans. Alan Sheridan. London: Allen Lane.

——. 1998. "The Concern for Truth." In *Politics, Philosophy, Culture: Interviews and Other Writings, 1977–1984*, ed. L. D. Kritzman. New York: Routledge.

——, ed. 1980. *Herculine Barbin: Being the Recently Discovered Memoirs of a Nineteenth-Century Hermaphrodite*, trans. Richard McDongall. New York: Colophon.

Frankenberg, Ruth. 1993. *White Women, Race Matters: The Social Construction of Whiteness*. Minneapolis: University of Minnesota Press.

Frankenberg, Ruth, ed. 1997. *Displacing Whiteness*. Durham, N.C.: Duke University Press.

Frankenberg, Ruth, and Lata Mani. 1993. "Crosscurrents, Crosstalk: Race, 'Postcoloniality' and the Politics of Location." *Cultural Studies* 7, no. 1 (May): 292–310.

Fraser, Nancy. 1989. *Unruly Practices: Power, Discourse, and Gender in Contemporary Social Theory*. Minneapolis: University of Minnesota Press.

Freedman, Estelle B. 1990. "Small Group Pedagogy: Consciousness Raising in Conservative Times." *National Women's Studies Association Journal* 2, no. 4 (fall): 603–23.

Freeman, Elizabeth. 1997. "Property, Promiscuity and the Gay and Lesbian Marriage Rights Movement." Paper presented at the Sixth Annual Cultural Studies Symposium, Kansas State University, Manhattan, Kansas, March 6–8.

Freeman, Jo, ed. 1995. *Women: A Feminist Perspective*. Dubuque, Iowa: Mayfield.

Friedan, Betty. 1975. "It Changed My Life." In *Writings on the Women's Movement*. New York: Random House.

Friedman, Susan Stanford. 1997. "Women's Studies." In *Dictionary of Multicultural Education*, ed. Carl A. Grant and Gloria Ladson-Billings. Phoenix: Orynx Press.

——. 1998a. "Doing Feminism in Interdisciplinary Contexts." Paper presented at the Modern Language Association meeting, San Francisco, December 29.

——. 1998b. "(Inter)Disciplinarity and the Question of the Women's Studies Ph.D." *Feminist Studies*, 24, no. 2 (summer): 301–25.

——. 1998c. *Mappings: Feminism and the Cultural Geographies of Encounter*. Princeton, N.J.: Princeton University Press.

Frye, Marilyn. 1978. "Lesbian Feminism and the Gay Rights Movement: Another View of Male Supremacy, Another Separation." In *The Politics of Reality: Essays in Feminist Theory*. Trumansburg, N.Y.: Crossing Press.

——. 1992. "The Body Philosophical." In *The Knowledge Explosion: Generations of Feminist Scholarship*, ed. Cheris Kramarae and Dale Spender. New York: Teacher's College Press.

Fullbrook, Kate, and Edward Fullbrook. 1993. *Simone de Beauvoir and Jean-Paul Sartre: The Remaking of a Twentieth-Century Legend.* New York: Harvester Wheatsheaf.

Fuss, Diana. 1989. *Essentially Speaking: Feminism, Nature, and Difference.* New York: Routledge.

Gadol-Kelly, Joan. 1976. "The Social Relation of the Sexes: Methodological Implications of Women's History." *Signs* 1, no. 4 (summer): 809–24.

Gallop, Jane. 1997. *Feminist Accused of Sexual Harassment.* Durham, N.C.: Duke University Press.

——. 1999. "Resisting Reasonableness." *Critical Inquiry* 25, no. 3 (spring): 599–609.

——, ed. 1995. *Pedagogy: The Question of Impersonation.* Bloomington: Indiana University Press.

Gallop, Jane, and Elizabeth Francis. 1997. "Talking Across." In *Generations: Academic Feminists in Dialogue,* ed. Devoney Looser and E. Ann Kaplan. Minneapolis: University of Minnesota Press.

Gamble, Susan, ed. 2000. *The Routledge Critical Dictionary of Feminism and Postfeminism.* New York: Routledge.

Gandhi, Leela. 1998. *Postcolonial Theory: A Critical Introduction.* New York: Columbia University Press.

Gardiner, Judith Kegan. 1982. "An Interchange on Feminist Criticism: On 'Dancing Through the Minefield.'" *Feminist Studies* 8, no. 3 (fall): 629–35.

Gatens, Moira. 1991. *Feminism and Philosophy: Perspectives on Difference and Equality.* Bloomington: Indiana University Press.

Gates, Henry Louis, Jr. 1986. *Race, Writing, and Difference.* Chicago: University of Chicago Press.

Gearhart, Sally Miller. 1983. "If the Mortarboard Fits . . . Radical Feminism in Academia." In *Learning Our Way: Essays in Feminist Education,* ed. Charlotte Bunch and Sandra Pollack. Trumansburg, N.Y.: Crossing Press.

Gerson, Deborah A. 1995. "Practice from Pain: The Ambivalent Legacy of Consciousness Raising." Unpublished paper, University of California, Berkeley.

Gilbert, Sandra M. 1999. Letter to the Editor. *Critical Inquiry* 25, no. 2 (winter): 399–400.

Gilbert, Sandra M., et al. 1997. "Final Report of the MLA Committee on Professional Employment." Modern Language Association, New York.

Giroux, Henry A. 1993. "Living Dangerously: Identity Politics and the New Cultural Racism: Toward a Critical Pedagogy of Representation." *Cultural Studies* 7, no. 1: 1–27.

Gluck, Sherna Berger, and Daphne Patai, eds. 1991. *Women's Words: The Feminist Practice of Oral History.* New York: Routledge.

Gordon, Avery, and Christopher Newfield, eds. 1996. *Mapping Multiculturalism.* Minneapolis: University of Minnesota Press.

Goto, Hiromi. 1994. *A Chorus of Mushrooms.* Edmonton: NeWest Press.

Gottlieb, Alan, and Virginia Culver. 1992. "A House Divided?" *Denver Post,* November 1, sec. C1.

Grahl, Christine, Elizabeth Kennedy, Lillian Robinson, and Bonnie Zimmerman. 1972. "Women's Studies: A Case in Point." *Feminist Studies* 1, no. 2 (fall): 109–20.

Greene, Gayle and Coppélia Kahn, eds. 1985. *Making a Difference: Feminist Literary Criticism*. London: Methuen.

—. 1995. *Provoking Agents: Gender and Agency in Theory and Action*. Urbana: University of Illinois Press.

Grewal, Inderpal. 1996. *Home and Harem: Imperialism, Nationalism, and the Culture of Travel*. Durham, N.C.: Duke University Press.

—. 1999. "Women's Rights as Human Rights: Feminist Practices, Global Feminism, and Human Rights Regimes in Transnationality." *Citizenship Studies* 3, no. 3 (November): 337–54.

Grewal, Inderpal, and Caren Kaplan. 1994. *Scattered Hegemonies: Postmodernity and Transnational Feminist Practices*. Minnesota: University of Minnesota Press.

—. 1996. "Warrior Marks: Global Womanism's Neo-Colonial Discourse in a Multicultural Context." *Camera Obscura* 39 (September): 5–33.

—. 1999. "Transnational Practices and Interdisciplinary Feminist Scholarship: Refiguring Women and Gender Studies." Paper presented at the Boundaries in Question Conference, University of California, Berkeley, March 5.

Griffin, Gabrielle. 1994. *Changing Our Lives: Doing Women's Studies*. London: Pluto Press.

Gubar, Susan. 1995. "Feminist Misogyny: Mary Wollstonecraft and the Paradox of 'It Takes One to Know One.'" In *Feminism Beside Itself*, ed. Diane Elam and Robyn Wiegman. New York: Routledge.

—. 1998. "What Ails Feminist Criticism?" *Critical Inquiry* 24, no. 4 (summer): 878–902.

—. 1999. "Critical Response: Notations in Medias Res." *Critical Inquiry* 25, no. 2 (winter): 380–96.

Guerrero, Marie Anna Jaimes. 1997. "Civil Rights and Sovereignty." In *Feminist Genealogies, Colonial Legacies, Democratic Futures*, ed. M. Jacqui Alexander and Chandra Talpade Mohanty. New York: Routledge.

Gunew, Sneja. 1994. *Framing Marginality: Multicultural Literary Studies*. Melbourne: Melbourne University Press.

—. 2000. "Operatic Karaoke and the Pitfalls of Identity Politics: A Translated Performance." In *Thinking Through Feminism*, ed. Sara Ahmed, Jane Kilby, Celia Lury, Maureen McNeil, and Beverley Skeggs. London: Routledge.

—, ed. 1990. *Feminist Knowledge as Critique and Construct*. London: Routledge.

—. 1991. *A Reader in Feminist Knowledge*. London: Routledge.

Gunning, Isabelle. 1992. "Arrogant Perception, World-Travelling, and Multicultural Feminism: The Case of Female Genital Surgeries." *Columbia Human Rights Law Review* 23, no. 189: 189–248.

Gupta, Akhil. 1998. *Postcolonial Developments: Agriculture in the Making of Modern India*. Durham, N.C.: Duke University Press.

Guy-Sheftall, Beverly. 1998. "Engaging Difference: Racial and Global Perspectives in Graduate Women's Studies Education." *Feminist Studies* 24, no. 2 (summer): 327–32.

—. 1995. *Women's Studies: A Retrospective*. New York: Ford Foundation.

Halberstam, Judith. 1998. *Female Masculinity*. Durham, N.C.: Duke University Press.

Hale, Sondra. 1991. "Feminist Method, Process, and Self-Criticism: Interviewing Sudanese Women." In *Women's Words: The Practice of Oral History*, ed. Sherna Berger Gluck and Daphne Patai. London: Routledge.

Hall, Jacquelyn Dowd. 1983. " 'The Mind That Burns in Each Body': Women, Rape, and Racial Violence." In *Powers of Desire: The Politics of Sexuality*, ed. Ann Snitow, Christine Stansell, and Sharon Thompson. New York: Monthly Review Press.

Hall, Stuart. 1986. "Gramsci's Relevance for the Study of Race and Ethnicity." *Journal of Communication Inquiry* 10, no. 2 (summer): 5–27.

Halley, Janet. 1994. "Sexual Orientation and the Politics of Biology: A Critique of the Argument from Immutability." *Stanford Law Review* 46, no. 3 (February): 503–68.

Haraway, Donna. 1988. "Situated Knowledges: The Science Question in Feminism and the Privilege of Partial Perspective." *Feminist Studies* 14, no. 3 (fall): 575–99.

—. 1990. "A Manifesto for Cyborgs: Science, Technology, and Socialist Feminism in the 1980s." In *Feminism/Postmodernism*, ed. Linda Nicholson. New York: Routledge.

Hardiman, Rita, and Bailey W. Jackson. 1992. "Racial Identity Development: Understanding Racial Dynamics in College Classrooms and on Campus." *New Directions for Teaching and Learning* 52 (winter): 21–37.

Harris, Trudier. 1984. *Exorcising Blackness: Historical and Literary Lynching and Burning Rituals*. Bloomington: Indiana University Press.

Hartmann, Heidi. 1981. "The Unhappy Marriage of Marxism and Feminism." In *The Second Wave: A Reader in Feminist Theory*, ed. Linda Nicholson. New York, Routledge.

Hartsock, Nancy. 1983. *Money, Sex, and Power: Toward a Feminist Historical Materialism*. New York: Longman.

Hartzog, Carol. 1986. *Composition and the Academy*. New York: Modern Language Association.

Haver, David. 1997. "Queer Research; or, How to Practice Invention to the Brink of Intelligibility." In *The Eight Technologies of Otherness*, ed. Sue Golding. London: Routledge.

Hayles, N. Katherine. 1991. "Constrained Constructivism: Locating Scientific Inquiry in the Theater of Representation." *New Orleans Review* 18, no. 1 (spring): 76–85.

—. 1999. *How We Became Posthuman: Virtual Bodies in Cybernetics, Literature, and Informatics*. Chicago: University of Chicago Press.

Haywoode, Terry. 1991. "Working Class Feminism: Creating a Politics of Community, Connection, and Concern." Ph.D. diss., The City University of New York.

Heilbrun, Carolyn. 1998. *Writing a Woman's Life*. New York: Ballantine.

—. 1999. Letter to the Editor. *Critical Inquiry* 25, no. 2 (winter): 397–400.

Hennessy, Rosemary, and Chrys Ingraham, eds. 1997. *Materialist Feminism: A Reader in Class, Difference, and Women's Lives*. New York: Routledge.

Hine, Darlene Clark, and Earnestine Jenkins, eds. 1999. *A Question of Manhood: A Reader in Black Masculinity in the United States*. Bloomington: Indiana University Press.

Hochschild, Arlie. 1989. *The Second Shift*. New York: Avon Books.

—. 1997. *The Time Bind*. New York: Metropolitan Books.

Hogeland, Lisa Maria. 1998. *Feminism and Its Fictions: The Consciousness-Raising Novel and the Women's Liberation Movement*. Philadelphia: University of Pennsylvania Press.

hooks, bell. 1981. *Ain't I a Woman? Black Women and Feminism*. Boston: South End Press.

—. 1984a. *Feminist Theory: From Margin to Center*. Boston: South End Press.

—. 1984b. "Men: Comrades in Struggle." In *Feminist Theory: From Margin to Center*. Boston: South End Press.

——. 1989. "Feminist Scholarship: Ethical Issues." Pp. 42–49 in *Talking Back: Thinking Feminist/Thinking Black*. Boston: South End Press.

——. 1990. *Yearning: Race, Gender, and Cultural Politics*. Boston: South End Press.

——. 1994. *Teaching to Transgress: Education as the Practice of Freedom*. New York: Routledge.

Horowitz, Daniel. 1998. *Betty Friedan and the Making of the Feminist Mystique*. Amherst: University of Massachusetts Press.

Howe, Florence. 1984. "Myths of Coeducation." In *Myths of Coeducation*. Bloomington: Indiana University Press.

——. 1997. " 'Promises to Keep': Trends in Women's Studies Worldwide." *Women's Studies Quarterly* 25, no. 1–2 (spring–summer): 404–21.

Hull, Gloria T., and Barbara Smith, eds. 1982. *All the Women Are White, All the Men Are Black, But Some of Us Are Brave*. Old Westbury, N.Y.: Feminist Press.

Hulme, Peter. 1998. "Introduction: The Cannibal Scene." In *Cannibalism and the Colonial World*, ed. Francis Barker, Peter Hulme, and Margaret Iverson. Cambridge: Cambridge University Press.

Humm, Maggie, ed. 1992. *Modern Feminism: Political, Literary, Cultural*. New York: Columbia University Press.

Hurston, Zora Neale. 1978 (1937). *Their Eyes Were Watching God*. Urbana: University of Illinois Press.

Hurtado, Aida. 1989. "Relating to Privilege: Seduction and Rejection in the Subordination of White Women and Women of Color." *Signs* 14, no. 4 (summer): 833–55.

——. 1996. *The Color of Privilege: Three Blasphemies on Race and Feminism*. Ann Arbor: University of Michigan Press.

Ingalls, Zoe. 1988. "Organizer of Controversial Women's Studies Event at New Paltz Experienced 'the Eye of the Storm.' " *Chronicle of Higher Education*, May 8, sec. A10.

Irigaray, Luce. 1985a. "Commodities Among Themselves." In *This Sex Which Is Not One*, trans. Catherine Porter. Ithaca, N.Y.: Cornell University Press.

——. 1985b. *Speculum of the Other Woman*, trans. G. C. Gill. Ithaca, N.Y.: Cornell University Press.

——. 1985c. *This Sex Which Is Not One*, trans. C. Porter and C. Burke. Ithaca, N.Y.: Cornell University Press.

Jackson, Stevi, et al. 1993. *Women's Studies: Essential Readings*. New York: New York University Press.

Jagger, Alison, and Susan Bordo, eds. 1989. *Gender/Body/Knowledge: Feminist Reconstructions of Being and Knowing*. New Brunswick, N.J.: Rutgers University Press.

Jagger, Alison, and Paula Rothenberg, eds. 1993. *Feminist Frameworks: Alternative Theoretical Accounts of the Relations Between Men and Women*. New York: McGraw-Hill.

Jagose, Annamarie. 1997. " 'Feminism Without Women': A Lesbian Reassurance." In *Cross-Purposes: Lesbians, Feminists, and the Limits of Alliance*, ed. Dana Heller. Bloomington: Indiana University Press.

Jakobsen, Janet. Forthcoming. "Queers Are Like Jews, Aren't They? Analogy and Alliance in Theory and Politics." In *Queers and the Jewish Question*, ed. Daniel Boyarin, Daniel Itzkovitz, and Ann Pellegrini. New York: Columbia University Press.

Jeffords, Susan. 1989. *The Remasculinization of America: Gender and the Vietnam War.* Bloomington: Indiana University Press.

"Job Tracks: Who Got Hired Where, 1997–98." 1998. *Lingua Franca* 8 (February): 69.

Johnson-Odim, Cheryl. 1992. "Common Themes, Different Contexts: Third World Women and Feminism." In *Third World Women and the Politics of Feminism,* ed. Chandra Talpade Mohanty, Ann Russo, and Lourdes Torres. Bloomington: Indiana University Press.

Jordan, June. 1985. "Report from the Bahamas." In *On Call: Political Essays.* Boston: South End Press.

Joseph, Miranda. 1996. "The Perfect Moment: Christians, Gays and the NEA." *Socialist Review* 26, no. 3–4: 111–44.

——. 2002. *Against the Romance of Community.* Minneapolis: University of Minnesota Press.

——. 2002. "Family Affairs: The Discourse of Global/Localization." In *Queer Globalization: Citizenship and the Afterlife of Colonialism,* ed. Arnaldo Cruz-Malav and Martin Manalansan. New York: New York University Press.

Joseph, Suad, ed. Forthcoming. *Women and Human Rights in Muslim Communities.* Berkeley: University of California Press.

Kadi, Joanna. 1994. *Food for Our Grandmothers: Writings by Arab American and Arab Canadian Feminists.* Boston: South End Press.

Kaplan, Caren. 1996. *Questions of Travel: Postmodern Discourses of Displacement.* Durham, N.C.: Duke University Press.

Keating, Analouise. 1998. "(De)Centering the Margins? Identity Politics and Tactical (Re)Naming." In *Other Sisterhoods: Literary Theory and U.S. Women of Color,* ed. Sandra Kumamoto Stanley. Urbana: University of Illinois Press.

Kennedy, Elizabeth Lapovsky. 2000. "Dreams of Social Justice." In *The Politics of Women's Studies: Testimony from Thirty Founding Mothers,* ed. Florence Howe. New York: Feminist Press.

Kennedy, Elizabeth Lapovsky, and Madelaine D. Davis. 1993. *Boots of Leather, Slippers of Gold: The History of a Lesbian Community.* New York: Routledge.

Kenway, Jane, and Helen Mondra. 1992. "Feminist Pedagogy and Emancipatory Possibilities." In *Feminisms and Critical Pedagogy,* ed. Carmen Luke and Jennifer Gore. New York: Routledge.

Kesselman, Amy, Lily C. McNair, and Nancy Schniedewind, eds. 1995. *Women's Images and Realities, a Multicultural Reader.* London: Mayfield.

Kessler-Harris, Alice, and Amy Swerdlow. 1996. "Pride and Paradox: Despite Success, Women's Studies Faces an Uncertain Future." *Chronicle of Higher Education,* April 26, sec. A64.

Kim, Elaine H. 1998. "Dangerous Women: Korean Immigrant Women in the United States." Paper presented at the annual meeting of the American Studies Association, Seattle, Washington, November 19.

King, Katie. 1994. "What Counts as Theory? Travels Through Several Histories of U.S. Feminism." In *Theory in Its Feminist Travels: Conversations in U.S. Women's Movements.* Bloomington: Indiana University Press.

Kirby, Vicki. 1987. "On the Cutting Edge: Feminism and Clitoridectomy." *Australian Feminist Studies* 5 (summer): 35–55.

Kirsch, Gesa E. 1999. *Ethical Dilemmas in Feminist Research: The Politics of Location, Interpretation, and Publication.* Albany: State University of New York Press.

Kolb, Katherine. 1997. "Adjuncts in Academe: No Place Called Home." *Profession* 97: 93–103.

Koshy, Susan. 1999. "From Cold War to Trade War: Neocolonialism and Human Rights." *Social Text* 58 16, no. 3 (spring): 1–32.

Krajewski, Sandra. 1999. "Women's Studies: Returning to Our Activist Roots and Achieving Tenure Along the Way." *Feminist Collections: A Quarterly of Women's Studies Resources* 20, no. 3 (spring): 4–7.

Kramarae, Cheris, and Dale Spender, eds. 1992. *The Knowledge Explosion. Generations of Feminist Scholarship.* New York: Teacher's College Press.

Krauss, Celene. 1998. "Challenging Power: Toxic Waste Protests and the Politicization of Working Class Women." In *Community Activism and Feminist Politics: Organizing Across Race, Class and Gender,* ed. Nancy A. Naples. New York: Routledge.

Kristeva, Julia. 1980. *Desire in Language: A Semiotic Approach to Literature and Art,* ed. Leon S. Roudiez; trans. Thomas Gora, Alice Jardine, and Leon S. Roudiez. New York: Columbia University Press.

——. 1981 (1979). "Women's Time." In *Feminist Theory: A Critique of Ideology,* ed. Nannerl O. Keohane, Michelle Z. Rosaldo, and Barbara C. Gelpi; trans. Alice Jardine and Harry Blake. Chicago: University of Chicago Press.

——. 1982. *Powers of Horror: An Essay on Abjection.* Trans. Leon S. Roudiez. New York: Columbia University Press.

Kruks, Sonia. 1998 (1990). "Beauvoir: The Weight of Situation." In *Simone de Beauvoir: A Critical Reader,* ed. Elizabeth Fallaize. New York: Routledge.

Laclau, Ernesto, and Chantal Mouffe. 1985. *Hegemony and Socialist Strategy: Towards a Radical Democratic Politics.* London: Verso.

Lang, Sabine. 1997. "The NGOization of Feminism." In *Transitions, Environments, Translations: Feminisms in International Politics,* ed. Joan W. Scott, Cora Kaplan, and Debra Keates. New York: Routledge.

Latour, Bruno. 1987. *Science in Action.* Cambridge, Mass.: Harvard University Press.

Lee, Benjamin. 1995. "Critical Internationalism." *Public Culture* 7, no. 3 (spring): 559–92.

Lehrman, Karen. 1993. "Off Course." *Mother Jones* (September–October): 45–51, 66–68.

Lenton, Rhonda. 1990 "Academic Feminists and the Women's Movement in Canada: Continuity or Discontinuity." *Atlantis* 16, no. 1 (fall): 57–68.

Levernz, David. 1986. "The Politics of Emerson's Man-Making Words." *PMLA* 101, no. 1: 38–56.

Lewington, Jennifer. 1998. "Professors in Canada Adopt New Tactics to Demonstrate Why Their Work Matters." *Chronicle of Higher Education,* June 19, sec. A47, A49.

Lionnet, Françoise. 1995. *Postcolonial Representations.* Ithaca, N.Y.: Cornell University Press.

Loomba, Ania. 1998. *Colonialism/Postcolonialism.* London: Routledge.

Looser, Devoney. 1997. "Gen X Feminists? Youthism, Careerism, and the Third Wave." In

Generations: Academic Feminists in Dialogue, ed. Devoney Looser and E. Ann Kaplan. Minneapolis: University of Minnesota Press.

Looser, Devoney, and Darlene Hantzis. 1995. "Of Safe(r) Spaces and 'Right' Speech: Feminist Histories, Loyalties, Theories, and the Dangers of Critique." In *PC Wars: Politics and Theory in the Academy,* ed. Jeffrey Williams. New York: Routledge.

Looser, Devoney, and E. Ann Kaplan, eds. 1997. *Generations: Academic Feminists in Dialogue.* Minneapolis: University of Minnesota Press.

Lorber, Judith. 1994. *Paradoxes of Gender.* New Haven, Conn.: Yale University Press.

Lorde, Audre. 1981 (1979). "An Open Letter to Mary Daly." In *This Bridge Called My Back: Writings by Radical Women of Color,* ed. Cherrie Moraga and Gloria Anzaldúa. New York: Women of Color Press.

——. 1987. "Man Child: A Black Lesbian Feminist's Response." In *Sister Outsider.* Trumansburg, N.Y.: Crossing Press.

Lowe, Lisa. 1996. *Immigrant Acts: On Asian American Cultural Politics.* Durham, N.C.: Duke University Press.

——. 1998. "The International Within the National." *Cultural Critique* 40 (fall–winter): 29–47.

Luebke, Barbara F., and Mary Ellen Reilly. 1995. *Women's Studies Graduates: The First Generation.* New York: Teacher's College Press.

Lundgren-Gothlin, Eva. 1996 (1991). *Sex and Existence: Simone de Beauvoir's The Second Sex,* trans. Linda Schenck. London: Athlone.

Luke, Carmen, and Jennifer Gore, eds. 1992. *Feminisms and Critical Pedagogy.* New York: Routledge.

Lyotard, Jean-Francois. 1989. "One of the Things at Stake in Women's Struggles." In *The Lyotard Reader,* ed. Andrew Benjamin. Oxford: Basil Blackwell.

MacKinnon, Catherine A. 1989. *Toward a Feminist Theory of the State.* Cambridge, Mass.: Harvard University Press.

Maher, Frances A., and Mary Kay Thompson Tetreault. 1994. *The Feminist Classroom.* New York: Basic Books.

Malkki, Liisa. 1994. "Citizens of Humanity: Internationalism and the Imagined Community of Nations." *Diaspora* 3, no. 1 (spring): 41–68.

Mankiller, Wilma P. 1993. *Mankiller: A Chief and Her People.* New York: St. Martin's Press.

Marceck, Jeanne. 1995. "Psychology and Feminism: Can This Relationship Be Saved?" In *Feminisms in the Academy,* ed. Domna C. Stanton and Abigail J. Stewart. Ann Arbor: University of Michigan Press.

Marchak, M. Patricia. 1996. *Racism, Sexism, and the University: The Political Science Affair at the University of British Columbia.* Montreal: McGill University Press.

Marks, Elaine. 1998 (1973, 1986). "Encounters with Death in *A Very Easy Death* and The Body in Decline in *Adieux: A Farewell to Sartre.*" In *Simone de Beauvoir: A Critical Reader,* ed. Elizabeth Fallaize. New York: Routledge.

Marks, Elaine, and Isabelle de Courtivron, eds. 1980. *New French Feminisms: An Anthology.* Amherst: University of Massachusetts Press.

Martin, Biddy. 1996. "Sexualities Without Genders and Other Queer Utopias." In *Femininity Played Straight: The Significance of Being a Lesbian.* New York: Routledge.

—. 1997. "Success and Its Failures." *differences* 9, no. 3: 102–31.

Martin, Biddy, and Chandra Talpade Mohanty. 1986. "Feminist Politics: What's Home Got to Do with It?" In *Feminist Studies/Critical Studies,* ed. Teresa de Lauretis. Bloomington: Indiana University Press.

Marx, Karl. 1977. *Capital,* vol. 1, trans. Ben Fowkes. New York: Random House.

Matthews, Eric. 1996. *Twentieth-Century French Philosophy.* Oxford: Oxford University Press.

Mayberry, Maralee, and Ellen Cronan Rose, eds. 1999. *Meeting the Challenge: Innovative Feminist Pedagogies in Action.* New York: Routledge.

McClintock, Anne, Aamir Mufti, and Ella Shohat, eds. 1997. *Dangerous Liaisons: Gender, Nation, and Postcolonial Perspective.* Minneapolis: University of Minnesota Press.

McDaniel, Judith. 1999. "When the Community Is the Curriculum: Teaching Women's Studies Activism and Organizations." *Feminist Collections: A Quarterly of Women's Studies Resources* 20, no. 3 (spring): 35–37.

McDermott, Patrice. 1998. "Internationalizing the Core Curriculum." *Women's Studies Quarterly* 26, no. 3–4 (fall–winter): 88–98.

McIntosh, Peggy. 1998. "White Privilege and Male Privilege: A Personal Account of Coming to See Correspondences Through Work in Women's Studies." In *Race, Class, and Gender: An Anthology,* ed. Margaret Andersen and Patricia Hill Collins. Belmont, Calif.: Wadsworth Publishing.

McIntosh, Peggy, and Elizabeth Minnich. 1984. "Varieties of Women's Studies." *Women's Studies International Forum* 7, no. 3: 139–48.

McLaren, Peter, with Henry A. Giroux. 1995. "Radical Pedagogy as Cultural Politics Beyond the Discourse of Critique and Anti-Utopianism." In *Critical Pedagogy and Predatory Culture: Oppositional Politics in a Postmodern Era,* ed. Peter McLaren. London: Routledge.

McVicker, Jeanette. 1999. "General Education for the Transnationalized Masses." *Crossings,* no. 3: 41–55.

Messaut, J. 1938. *La philosophie de Léon Brunschvicg.* Paris: Librairie Philosophique J. Vrin.

Messer-Davidow, Ellen. 1993. "Manufacturing the Attack on Liberalized Higher Education." *Social Text* 36 (fall): 40–48.

Miki, Roy. 1998. *Broken Entries: Race, Subjectivity, Writing: Essays.* Toronto: Mercury Press.

Miles, Angela. 1996. *Integrative Feminisms: Building Global Visions, 1960s–1990s.* New York: Routledge.

Milkman, Ruth. 1999. "Before the Mystique." *Women's Review of Books* 16, no. 9 (June): 1.

Mills, C. Wright. 1959. *The Sociological Imagination.* Oxford: Oxford University Press.

Minnich, Elizabeth Kamarck. 1998. "Review Essay: Feminist Attacks on Feminisms: Patriarchy's Prodigal Daughters." *Feminist Studies* 24, no. 1 (spring): 159–75.

Minow, Martha. 1997. *Not Only for Myself: Identity, Politics, and the Law.* New York: New Press.

Moallem, Minoo, and Iain Boal. 1999. "Multicultural Nationalism and the Poetics of Inauguration." In *Between Woman and Nation: Nationalisms, Transnational Feminisms, and the State,* ed. Caren Kaplan, Norma Alarcón, and Minoo Moallem. Durham, N.C.: Duke University Press.

Modleski, Tania. 1991. *Feminism Without Women: Culture and Criticism in a "Postfeminist" Age*. New York: Routledge.

Mohanty, Chandra Talpade. 1991a. "Cartographies of Struggle." In *Third World Women and the Politics of Feminism*. ed. Chandra Talpade Mohanty, Anne Russo, and Lourdes Torres. Bloomington: Indiana University Press.

———. 1991b. "Under Western Eyes: Feminist Scholarship and Colonial Discourses." In *Third World Women and the Politics of Feminism*, ed. Chandra Talpade Mohanty, Anne Russo, and Lourdes Torres. Bloomington: Indiana University Press.

———. 1995. "Feminist Encounters: Locating the Politics of Experience." In *Social Postmodernism: Beyond Identity Politics*, ed. Linda Nicholson and Steven Seidman. Cambridge: Cambridge University Press.

Moi, Toril. 1985. *Sexual/Textual Politics: Feminist Literary Theory*. London: Methuen.

———. 1994. *Simone de Beauvoir: The Making of an Intellectual Woman*. Oxford: Blackwell.

———. 1999. *What Is a Woman? And Other Essays*. Oxford: Oxford University Press.

Moraga, Cherrie, and Gloria Anzaldúa, eds. 1981. *This Bridge Called My Back: Writings by Radical Women of Color*. New York: Women of Color Press.

Morgan, Robin, ed. 1984. *Sisterhood Is Global: The International Women's Movement Anthology*. New York: Anchor Press.

Morris, Bonnie J. 1998. "Women's Studies: Prejudice and Vilification Persist." *Chronicle of Higher Education*, June 19, sec. A56.

Morris, Rosalind C. 1994. "Three Sexes and Four Sexualities: Redressing the Discourses on Gender and Sexuality in Contemporary Thailand." *positions* 2, no. 1 (spring): 15–43.

Moses, Clare. 1998. "Made in America: 'French Feminism' in Academia." *Feminist Studies* 24, no. 2 (summer): 241–73.

Naples, Nancy A. 1998a. *Community Activism and Feminist Politics: Organization Across Race, Class, and Gender*. New York: Routledge.

———. 1998b. *Grassroots Warriors: Activist Mothering, Community Work, and the War on Poverty*. New York: Routledge.

———. 1999. "Toward a Comparative Analysis of Women's Political Practice: Explicating Multiple Dimensions of Standpoint Epistemology for Feminist Ethnography." *Women and Politics* 20, no. 1: 29–57.

Naples, Nancy A., with Emily Clark. 1996. "Feminist Participatory Research and Empowerment: Going Public as Survivors of Childhood Sexual Abuse." In *Feminism and Social Change: Bridging Theory and Practice*, ed. Heidi Gottfried. Urbana: Illinois University Press.

Narain, Mona. 1997. "Shifting Locations: Third World Feminists and Institutional Aporias." In *Generations: Academic Feminists in Dialogue*, ed. Devoney Looser and E. Ann Kaplan. Minneapolis: University of Minnesota Press.

Narayan, Uma. 1988. "Working Together Across Difference: Some Considerations on Emotions and Political Practice." *Hypatia* 3, no. 2 (summer): 31–47.

———. 1997. *Dislocating Cultures: Identities, Traditions, and Third World Feminism*. New York: Routledge.

Newfield, Christopher. 1989. "The Politics of Male Suffering: Masochism and Hegemony in the American Renaissance." *differences* 1, no. 3: 55–87.

Nichols, Mike, dir. 1988. *Working Girl*. Trimark.

Nicholson, Linda. 1994. "Interpreting Gender." *Signs* 20, no. 1 (fall): 79–105.

Nicholson, Linda, ed. 1997. *The Second Wave. A Reader in Feminist Theory*. New York: Routledge.

Nussbaum, Martha C. 1992. "The Softness of Reason: A Classical Case for Gay Studies." *New Republic* 207, no. 3–4 (July 19): 26–27, 30, 32, 34–35.

——. 1997. *Cultivating Humanity: A Classical Defense of Reform in Liberal Education*. Cambridge, Mass.: Harvard University Press.

——. 1999. *Sex and Social Justice*. New York: Oxford University Press.

O'Barr, Jean Fox. 1994. *Feminism in Action: Building Institutions and Community Through Women's Studies*. Chapel Hill: University of North Carolina Press.

O'Neill, Eileen. 1999. "Women Cartesians, 'Feminine Philosophy,' and Historical Exclusion." In *Feminist Interpretations of René Descartes*, ed. Susan Bordo. University Park: Pennsylvania State University Press.

Orr, Catherine M. 1999a. "Negotiating Class Interests and Academy-Community Divides: The Case of Women's Studies' Emergence at the University of Minnesota." *Feminist Collections: A Quarterly of Women's Studies Resources* 20, no. 3 (spring): 2–4.

——. 1999b. "Tellings of Our Activist Pasts: Tracing the Emergence of Women's Studies at San Diego State College." *Women's Studies Quarterly* 27, no. 3–4 (fall–winter): 212–29.

Patai, Daphne. 1991. "U.S. Academics and Third World Women: Is Ethical Research Possible?" In *Women's Words: The Feminist Practice of Oral History*, ed. Sherna Berger Gluck and Daphne Patai. New York: Routledge.

Patai, Daphne, and Noretta Koertge. 1994. *Professing Feminism: Cautionary Tales from the Strange World of Women's Studies*. New York: Basic Books.

Paules, Greta Foff. 1991. *Dishing It Out: Power and Resistance among Waitresses in a New Jersey Restaurant*. Philadelphia, Pa.: Temple University Press.

Pence, Dan. 1992. "A Women's Studies Course: Its Impact on Women's Attitudes Toward Men and Masculinity." *National Women's Studies Association Journal* 4, no. 3 (fall): 321–35.

Perkins, Helen. 1992. "Association of Graduate Recruiters." In *Arts Graduates, Their Skills and Their Employment: Perspectives for Change*, ed. Heather Eggins. London: Falmer Press.

Perry, Ruth. 1992. "A Short History of the Term Politically Correct." In *Beyond P.C.: Toward a Politics of Understanding*, ed. Patricia Aufderheide. St. Paul, Minn.: Greywolf Press.

Pétrement, Simone. 1973. *La vie de Simone Weil*. 2 vols. Paris: Fayard.

Philip, Marlene Nourbese. 1992. *Frontiers: Selected Essays and Writing on Racism and Culture, 1984–1992*. Stratford, Ont.: Mercury Press.

——. 1995. "Signifying: Why the Media Have Fawned over Bissoondaths Selling Illusions." *Border/Lines Magazine* 36: 4–11.

Piore, Michael, and Charles F. Sabel. 1984. *The Second Industrial Divide: Possibilities for Prosperity*. New York: Basic Books.

Probyn, Elspeth. 1996. *Outside Belongings*. New York: Routledge.

Prosser, Jay. 1998. *Second Skins: The Body Narratives of Transsexuality*. New York: Columbia University Press.

Pryse, Marjorie. 1998. "Critical Interdisciplinarity, Women's Studies, and Cross-Cultural Insight." *National Women's Studies Association Journal* 10, no. 1 (spring): 1–22.

Quest Staff, eds. 1981. *Building Feminist Theory: Essays from Quest*. New York: Longman.

Radway, Janice. 1999. " 'What's In a Name?' Presidential Address to the American Studies Association, 20 November, 1998." *American Quarterly* 51, no. 1 (March): 1–32.

Rakow, Lana F. 1991. "Gender and Race in the Classroom: Teaching Way Out of Line." *Feminist Teacher* 6, no. 1 (summer): 10–13.

Readings, Bill. 1996. *The University in Ruins*. Cambridge, Mass.: Harvard University Press.

Reagon, Bernice Johnson. 1983. "Coalition Politics." In *Home Girls: A Black Feminist Anthology*, ed. Barbara Smith. Latham, N.Y.: Kitchen Table Press.

—. 1992 (1981). "Coalition Politics: Turning the Century." In *Race, Class, and Gender: An Anthology*, ed. Margaret L. Andersen and Patricia Hill Collins. Belmont, Calif.: Wadsworth.

"Report of the ADE Ad Hoc Committee on Staffing." 1999. *ADE Bulletin* 122: 1–26.

Reuben, Elaine, and Mary Jo Boehm Strauss. 1980. *Women's Studies Graduates*. Washington, D.C.: National Institute of Education.

"Rethinking SUNY." 1995. Report from SUNY Board of Trustees to Governor George Pataki and Leaders of the New York State Legislature, December 1.

Rich, Adrienne. 1979. *On Lies, Secrets, and Silence: Selected Prose, 1966–1978*. New York: Norton.

—. 1986. "You Who Think I Find Words for Everything." In *Your Native Land, Your Life*. New York: Norton.

Riger, Stephanie. 1994. "Challenges of Success: Stages of Growth in Feminist Organizations." *Feminist Studies* 20, no. 2 (summer): 275–300.

Riley, Denise. 1988. *"Am I That Name?" Feminism and the Category of 'Women' in History*. Minneapolis: University of Minnesota Press.

Robinson, Amy. 1997. "The Ethics of Analogy: Critical Discourse on Race and Sexuality." Lecture given at the Stanford Humanities Center, Stanford, Calif., March 20.

Rodgers, Catherine. 1998. "The Influence of *The Second Sex* on the French Feminist Scene." In *Simone de Beauvoir's The Second Sex: New Interdisciplinary Essays*, ed. Ruth Evans. Manchester, Engl.: Manchester University Press.

Romanoff, Bronna, Chrys Ingraham, Pat Dinkelaker, and Jennifer MacLaughlin. 1999. "Women Changing the World: A Course in Community Collaboration." *Feminist Collections: A Quarterly of Women's Studies Resources* 20, no. 3 (spring): 42–44.

Rony, Fatima Tobing. 1995. *On Cannibalism*, 6 min., film.

—. 1996. *The Third Eye: Race, Cinema, and Ethnographic Spectacle*. Durham, N.C.: Duke University Press.

Roof, Judith. 1995. "Buckling Down or Knuckling Under: Discipline or Punish in Lesbian and Gay Studies." In *Who Can Speak: Authority and Critical Identity*, ed. Judith Roof and Robyn Wiegman. Urbana: University of Illinois Press.

Rosen, Ruth. 1999. "Secrets of the Second Shift in Scholarly Life." *Chronicle of Higher Education*, July 30, sec. A48.

Ross, Gary, dir. 1998. *Pleasantville*. New Line Cinema.

Ross, Lisa. 1994. "Women with AIDS: Community Action Report." Unpublished paper, Women's Studies Program, University of California, Irvine.

Rothenberg, Paula. 1988. "Integrating the Study of Race, Gender, and Class: Some Preliminary Observations." *Feminist Teacher* 3, no. 3 (fall–winter): 37–42.

Rouse, Roger. 1995. "Thinking Through Transnationalism: Notes on the Cultural Politics of Class Relations in the Contemporary United States." *Public Culture* 7, no. 2 (winter): 353–402.

Rubin, Gayle. 1975. "The Traffic in Women: Notes on the 'Political Economy' of Sex." In *Toward an Anthropology of Women,* ed. Rayna R. Reiter. New York: Monthly Review.

——. 1984. "Thinking Sex: Notes for a Radical Theory of the Politics of Sexuality." In *Pleasure and Danger: Exploring Female Sexuality,* ed. Carole S. Vance. New York: Routledge.

——. 1992. "Of Catamites and Kings: Reflections on Butch, Gender, and Boundaries." In *The Persistent Desire: A Femme-Butch Reader,* ed. Joan Nestle. Boston: Alyson Publications.

——. 1993. "Thinking Sex: Notes for a Radical Theory of the Politics of Sexuality." In *The Lesbian and Gay Studies Reader,* ed. Henry Abelove, Michele A. Barale, and David Halperin. New York: Routledge.

——. 1994. "Sexual Traffic." Interview in *differences* 6, no. 2–3 (summer–fall): 62–99.

Salecl, Renata. 1994. *The Spoils of Freedom: Psychoanalysis and Feminism After the Fall of Socialism.* New York: Routledge.

Salins, Peter D. 1997. *Assimilation, American Style.* New York: Basic Books.

——. 1998. "General Education: Overview and Recommendations. Office of the Provost and Vice Chancellor for Academic Affairs." Report. State University of New York Central, Albany, New York.

Sandoval, Chela. 1990. "Feminism and Racism: A Report on the 1981 National Women's Studies Association Conference." In *Making Face, Making Soul. Haciendo Caras. Creative and Critical Perspectives by Women of Color,* ed. Gloria Anzaldúa. San Francisco: Aunt Lute.

——. 1991. "U.S. Third World Feminism: The Theory and Method of Oppositional Consciousness in the Postmodern World." *Genders* 10 (spring): 1–24.

Sangari, Kumkum, and Sudesh Vaid. 1993. "Recasting Women: An Introduction." In *Recasting Women,* ed. Kumkum Sangari and Sudesh Vaid. New Delhi: Kali for Women.

Sapiro, Virginia. 1995. "Feminist Studies and Political Science—and Vice Versa." In *Feminisms in the Academy,* ed. Domna C. Stanton and Abigail J. Stewart. Ann Arbor: University of Michigan Press.

Sartre, Jean-Paul. 1946. "La liberté Cartésienne." In *Descartes,* ed. Jean-Paul Sartre. Paris: Trois Collines.

Schneider, Alison. 1999. "When Revising a Curriculum, Strategy May Trump Pedagogy." *Chronicle of Higher Education* (February 19): A14.

Schniedwind, Nancy. 1993. "Teaching Feminist Process Skills in the 1990s." *Women's Studies Quarterly* 21, no. 3–4 (fall–winter): 17–30.

Schor, Naomi. 1992. "Feminist and Gender Studies." In *Introduction to Scholarship in Modern Languages and Literatures,* ed. Joseph Gibaldi. 2d ed. New York: Modern Language Association of America.

Scott, Joan W. 1988. *Gender and the Politics of History*. New York: Columbia University Press.

——. 1992. "Experience." In *Feminists Theorize the Political*, ed. Judith Butler and Joan Scott. New York: Routledge.

——, ed. 1997. "Women's Studies on the Edge." Special issue of *differences* 9, no. 3 (fall).

Sedgwick, Eve Kosofsky. 1985. *Between Men: English Literature and Male Homosocial Desire*. New York: Columbia University Press.

——. 1992. "Gender Studies." In *Redrawing the Boundaries: The Transformation of English and American Literary Studies*, ed. Stephen Greenblatt and Giles Gunn. New York: Modern Language Association of America.

Segal, Lynne. 1990. *Slow Motion: Changing Masculinities, Changing Men*. New Brunswick, N.J.: Rutgers University Press.

Segrest, Mab. 1994. *Memoir of a Race Traitor*. Boston: South End Press.

Sernin, André. 1985. *Alain: Un sage dans la cité, 1868–1951*. Paris: Éditions Robert Laffont.

Shah, Nayan. 2001. *Contagious Divides: Epidemics and Race in San Francisco's Chinatown*. Berkeley: University of California Press.

Shohat, Ella. 1992–93. "Staging the Quincentenary: The Middle East and the Americas." *Third Text* 21 (winter): 95–106.

Shohat, Ella, ed. 1998. *Talking Visions. Multicultural Feminism in a Transnational Age*. Cambridge, Mass.: MIT Press.

Short, Kayann. 1999. " 'Why Shop?' Week': Shopping, Service-Learning, and Student Activism." *Feminist Collections: A Quarterly of Women's Studies Resources* 20, no. 3 (spring): 32–33.

Shostak, Marjorie. 1989. " 'What the Wind Won't Take Away': The Genesis of Nisa—The Life and Words of a !Kung Woman." In *Interpreting Women's Lives: Feminist Theory and Personal Narratives*, ed. Personal Narrative Group. Bloomington: Indiana University Press.

Showalter, Elaine. 1985. *The New Feminist Criticism: Essays on Women, Literature, and Theory*. New York: Pantheon.

Simons, Margaret A., ed. 1999. *Beauvoir and "The Second Sex": Feminism, Race, and the Origins of Existentialism*. Lanham, Md.: Rowman and Littlefield.

——. 1999 (1983). "The Silencing of Simone de Beauvoir: Guess What's Missing from *The Second Sex?*" In *Beauvoir and The Second Sex: Feminism, Race, and the Origins of Existentialism*, ed. Margaret Simons. Lanham, Md.: Rowman and Littlefield.

Sirinelli, Jean-François. 1994. *Génération intellectuelle: khâgneux et normaliens dans 1'entre-deux-guerres*. Paris: Presses Universitaires de France.

Skeggs, Beverley. 1995. "Women's Studies in Britain in the 1990s: Entitlement Cultures and Institutional Constraints." *Women's Studies International Forum* 18, no. 4: 475–85.

Smith, Dorothy. 1987. *The Everyday World as Problematic: A Feminist Sociology*. Toronto: University of Toronto Press.

——. 1990. *Conceptual Practices of Power*. Boston: Northeastern University Press.

——. 1992. "Sociology from Women's Experience: A Reaffirmation." *Sociological Theory* 10, no. 1 (spring): 88–98.

———. 1999. *Writing the Social: Critique, Theory, and Investigations.* Toronto: University of Toronto Press.

Smith, Joan, ed. 1996. *Hungry for You: From Cannibalism to Seduction: A Book on Food.* London: Chatto and Windus.

Smith, Valerie. 1990. "Split Affinities: The Case of Interracial Rape." In *Conflicts in Feminism,* ed. Marianne Hirsch and Evelyn Fox Keller. New York: Routledge.

Snitow, Ann. 1990. "A Gender Diary." In *Conflicts in Feminism,* ed. Marianne Hirsch and Evelyn Fox Keller. New York: Routledge.

Sommers, Christina Hoff. 1992. "Sister Soldiers." *New Republic* (October 5): 29–33.

Spanos, William V. 1986. "The Appolonian Investment of Modern Humanist Education: The Examples of Matthew Arnold, Irving Babbit, and I. A. Richards." *Cultural Critique* 1: 7–72.

———. 1993. *The End of Education.* Minneapolis: University of Minnesota Press.

"Special Issue: Academy/Community Connections." 1999. *Feminist Collections* 20, no. 3.

Spivak, Gayatri Chakravorty. 1987. "Scattered Speculations on the Question of Value." In *In Other Worlds.* New York: Methuen.

———. 1989. "The Political Economy of Women as Seen by a Literary Critic." In *Coming to Terms: Feminism, Theory, Politics,* ed. Elizabeth Weed. London: Routledge.

———. 1993. *Outside in the Teaching Machine.* New York: Routledge.

———. 1999. *A Critique of Postcolonial Reason.* Cambridge, Mass.: Harvard University Press.

Stake, Jayne E., and Suzanna Rose. 1994. "The Long-Term Impact of Women's Studies on Students' Personal Lives and Political Activism." *Psychology of Women Quarterly* 18, no. 3: 403–12.

Stanley, Liz, ed. 1997. *Knowing Feminisms: On Academic Borders, Territories and Tribes.* London: Sage.

Stanley, Liz, and Sue Wise. 1983. *Breaking Out.* London: Routledge and Kegan Paul.

"State Lawmakers Question Women's Studies at Arizona Public Universities." 1999. *Chronicle of Higher Education,* February 26, sec. A28.

Stearns, Chris. 1994. "Is There Life After Women's Studies: An Update to the Original Inquiry." In *Women's Studies im internationalen Vergleich,* ed. H. Flessner, M. Kriszio, R. Kurth, and L. Potts. Pfaffenweiler, Ger.: Centaurus-Verlagsgesellschaft.

Stein, Arlene. 1997. "Sex, Kids, and Therapy: The Decentering of Lesbian Feminism." In *Sex and Sensibility: Stories of a Lesbian Generation.* Berkeley: University of California Press.

Stoller, Nancy E. 1995. "Lesbian Involvement in the AIDS Epidemic: Changing Roles and Generational Differences." In *Women Resisting AIDS: Feminist Strategies of Empowerment,* ed. Beth E. Schneider and Nancy E. Stoller. Philadelphia, Pa.: Temple University Press.

Stone, Sandy. 1991. "The *Empire* Strikes Back: A Posttranssexual Manifesto." In *Body Guards: The Cultural Politics of Gender Ambiguity,* ed. Julia Epstein and Kristina Straub. New York: Routledge.

Stryker, Susan. 1998. "The Transgender Issue: An Introduction." *GLQ: A Journal of Lesbian and Gay Studies* 4, no. 2: 145–58.

"SUNY's Core Curricula: The Failure to Set Consistent and High Academic Standards."

1996. Report. New York Association of Scholars and Empire Foundation for Policy Research. July.

Swindells, Julia. 1989. "Liberating the Subject? Autobiography and 'Women's History'—A Reading of the Diaries of Hannah Cullwick." In *Interpreting Women's Lives: Feminist Theory and Personal Narratives,* ed. Personal Narrative Group. Bloomington: Indiana University Press.

Tadiar, Neferti Xina M. 1995. "Manila's New Metropolitan Form." In *Discrepant Histories: Translocal Essays on Filipino Cultures,* ed. Vicente L. Rafael. Philadelphia, Pa.: Temple University Press.

Tarbell, Kathryn. 1999. "Community Action Project Final Report." Unpublished paper, University of California, Irvine.

Tatum, Beverly Daniel. 1992. "Talking About Race, Learning About Racism: The Application of Racial Identity Development Theory in the Classroom." *Harvard Educational Review* 62, no. 1 (spring): 1–24.

Tax, Meredith. 1999. "World Culture War." *Nation* 268, no. 18 (May 17): 24–28.

Taylor, John. 1991. "Are You Politically Correct?" *New York Magazine* (January 21): 32–40.

Tenger, Robert. 1944. Note de 1'Editeur in *Descartes et Pascal: Lecteurs de Montaigne* ed. Robert Tenger. New York: Brentano's.

Thomsen, Cynthia J., Andra M. Basu, and Mark Tippens Reinitz. 1995. "Effects of Women's Studies Courses on Gender-Related Attitudes of Women and Men." *Psychology of Women Quarterly* 19, no. 3: 419–26.

Threadgold, Terry. 1998. "Gender Studies and Women's Studies." In K*nowing Ourselves and Others: The Humanities in Australia into the 21st Century,* ed. Reference Group for the Australian Academy of the Humanities. Canberra: Commonwealth of Australia.

Tong, Rosemarie Putnam. 1998 (1989). *Feminist Thought: A More Comprehensive Introduction,* 2d ed. Boulder, Colo.: Westview Press.

Tran, Lisa. 1993. "Women's Studies 50B Community Action Project: Final Report." Unpublished paper, Women's Studies program, University of California, Irvine.

Trask, Haunani-Kay. 1993. *From a Native Daughter: Colonialism and Sovereignty in Hawai'i.* Monroe, Maine: Common Courage Press.

Trinh, T. Minh-ha. 1989. *Woman, Native, Other: Writing Postcoloniality and Feminism.* Bloomington: Indiana University Press.

Tsing, Anna Loewenhaupt. 1997. "Transitions as Translations." In *Transitions, Environments: Feminisms in International Politics,* ed. Joan Scott, Cora Kaplan, and Debra Keates. New York: Routledge.

U.S. Department of Education. 1995. *Digest of Education Statistics.* National Center for Education Statistics, NCES 95-029. Washington, D.C.: Government Publications Office.

Valéry, Paul. 1957 (1937). "Descartes." In *Valéry, Oeuvres,* vol. 1, ed. Jean Hytier. Paris: Gallimard.

Vasquez, Anna. 1994. "Community Action Project Report." Unpublished paper, University of California, Irvine.

Vattimo, Gianni. 1998. "The Trace of the Trace." In *Religion. Cultural Memory in the Present,* ed. Jacques Derrida and Gianni Vattimo. Stanford, Calif.: Stanford University Press.

Vickers, Jill. 1996. "Difficult Choices: The Knowledge Strategies of Feminist Social Science and the Knowledge Needs of Women's Movements." In *Quilting a New Canon: Stitching Women's Words,* ed. Uma Parameswaran. Toronto: Sister Vision Press.

Vieira, Else Ribeiro Pires. 1999. "Liberating Calibans: Readings of Antropofagia and Haroldo de Campos' Poetics of Transcreation." In *Post-Colonial Translation: Theory and Practice,* ed. Susan Bassnett and Harish Trivedi. London: Routledge.

Vintges, Karen. 1996 (1992). *Philosophy as Passion: The Thinking of Simone de Beauvoir,* trans. Anne Lavelle. Bloomington: Indiana University Press.

Visweswaran, Kamala. 1994. *Fictions of Feminist Ethnography.* Minneapolis: University of Minnesota Press.

Walker, Alice. 1983. *In Search of Our Mothers' Gardens: Womanist Prose.* New York: Harcourt Brace Jovanovich.

Walker, Rebecca, ed. 1995. *To Be Real: Telling the Truth and Changing the Face of Feminism.* New York: Anchor Books.

Wallace, Michele. 1990 (1979). *Black Macho and the Myth of Super Woman.* London: Verso.

Ware, Vron. 1992. *Beyond the Pale: White Women, Racism, and History.* London: Verso.

Warhol, Robyn. 1998. "How We Got Contracts for Lecturers at the University of Vermont: A Tale of (Qualified) Success." *Profession* 98: 223–28.

Warner, Marina. 1998a. "Fee Fi Fo Fum: The Child in the Jaws of the Story." In *Cannibalism and the Colonial World,* ed. Francis Barker, Peter Hulme, and Margaret Iverson. Cambridge: Cambridge University Press.

——. 1998b. *No Go the Bogeyman: Scaring, Lulling and Making Mock.* New York: Farrar, Straus, and Giroux.

Weiler, Kathleen. 1998. "Freire and a Feminist Pedagogy of Difference." In *Minding Women: Reshaping the Educational Realm,* ed. Christine A. Woyshner and Holly S. Gelford. Cambridge, Mass.: Harvard Educational Review.

Wells, Ida B. 1970. *Crusade for Justice: The Autobiography of Ida B. Wells.* Chicago: University of Chicago Press.

Wiegman, Robyn. 1997. "Queering the Academy." *Genders* 26: 3–22.

——. 1999. "What Ails Feminist Criticism? A Second Opinion." *Critical Inquiry* 25, no. 1 (winter): 362–79.

Wilson, Robin. 1998. "Ph.D. Programs in Women's Studies Proliferate on the Campuses." *Chronicle of Higher Education,* November 27, sec. A10–12.

Winders, James A. 1999. "Writing Like a Man (?): Descartes, Science, and Madness." In *Feminist Interpretations of René Descartes,* ed. Susan Bordo. University Park: Pennsylvania State University Press.

Wolff, Larry. 1994. *Inventing Eastern Europe: The Map of Civilization on the Mind of the Enlightenment.* Stanford, Calif.: Stanford University Press.

Women of South Asian Descent Collective. 1993. *Our Feet Walk the Sky: Women of the South Asian Diaspora.* San Francisco: Aunt Lute Books.

Wong, Nellie. 1991. "Socialist Feminism: Our Bridge to Freedom." In *Third World Women and the Politics of Feminism,* ed. Chandra Talpade Mohanty, Anne Russo, and Lourdes Torres. Bloomington: Indiana University Press.

Yeatman, Anna. 1990. *Bureaucrats, Femocrats, Technocrats: Essays on the Contemporary Australian State.* Sydney: Allen and Unwin.

——, ed. 1998. Activism and the Policy Process. Sydney: Allen and Unwin.

Yee, Shirley. 1997. "The 'Women' in Women's Studies." *differences* 9, no. 3 (fall): 46–64.

Zinn, Maxine Baca, and Bonnie Thornton Dill. 1996. "Theorizing Difference from Multi-racial Feminism." *Feminist Studies* 22, no. 2 (summer): 321–31.

Zinn, Maxine Baca, and Bonnie Thornton Dill, eds. 1994. *Women of Color in U.S. Society*. Philadelphia: Temple University Press.

Žižek, Slavoj. 1989. *The Sublime Object of Ideology*. London: Verso.

——. 1994. *The Metastasis of Enjoyment: Six Essays on Women and Causality*. New York: Verso.

——. 1998. "Cogito as a Shibboleth." In *Cogito and the Unconscious*, ed. Slavoj Žižek. Durham, N.C.: Duke University Press.

DALE M. BAUER is Professor of English and Women's Studies at the University of Kentucky. She is the author of *Feminist Dialogics* (1988) and *Edith Wharton's Brave New Politics* (1994) and has edited the books *Bahktin and Feminism* (1991) and *"The Yellow Wallpaper"* (1998). Her current work is on sex-expression and style in American women's writing from 1860 through 1950. She is the coeditor (with Phil Gould) of the *Cambridge Companion to Nineteenth-Century American Women's Writing* (2001).

KATHLEEN M. BLEE is Professor of Sociology at the University of Pittsburgh and has served as Director of Women's Studies at the University of Pittsburgh and the University of Kentucky. Her books include *Women of the Klan: Racism and Gender in the 1920s* (1991); *No Middle Ground: Women and Radical Protest* (1998); *The Road to Poverty: The Making of Wealth and Inequality in an American Region* (1998); *Feminism and Antiracism: International Struggles for Justice* (2001); and *Inside Organized Racism: Women in the Hate Movement* (2002).

GLORIA BOWLES was the founding coordinator of Women's Studies at the University of California at Berkeley, where she received her Ph.D. in Comparative Literature and taught from 1976–85. She is the author of *Louise Bogan's Aesthetic of Limitation* (1987). With Renate Klein, she edited *Theories of Women's Studies* (1983), a classic text on Women's Studies as a discipline in its own right. She edited *Strategies for Women's Studies in the Eighties* (1984), which extended the arguments of *Theories,* in essays by integrationists, advocates of "autonomous" Women's Studies, and multiculturalists. She is now completing "Living Ideas: A Personal/Political History of Berkeley Women's Studies, 1973–85," and her next book will be about the joys of language learning and travel in Spanish-speaking countries.

DENISE CUTHBERT holds degrees from the University of Queensland and the University of Sydney and is currently Associate Dean of Graduate Research at Monash University in Melbourne. Her research interests include gender and cultural difference, indigenous issues, postcolonialism, and feminism. She has published recently in such journals as *Cultural Studies, Hecate, Year's Work in Critical and Cultural Theory,* and *Journal of Australian Studies.* She and Maryanne Dever are the coauthors of *Feminist Perspectives on Postcolonialism* (1999).

MARYANNE DEVER is Director of the Centre for Women's Studies and Gender Research at Monash University, Melbourne. She has taught at the University of Hong Kong, where she helped to found the Women's Studies Research Centre. Her articles have appeared in *Feminist Teacher, Tulsa Studies in Women's Literature,* and the *Asian Journal of Women's Studies.* She edited *Australia and Asia: Cultural Transactions* (1997). Her research interests include feminist pedagogy, feminist research methodology, women's writing, postcolonialism, and cross-cultural feminism.

ANNE DONADEY is Associate Professor of French and Women's Studies at San Diego State University. She has recently published a book on women writers from Algeria, *Recasting Postcolonialism: Women Writing Between Worlds* (2001). She has published articles in journals such as *NWSA Journal, World Literature Today, Studies in Twentieth-Century Literature, French Cultural Studies,* and *The French Review.* She is currently at work on a book-length study of postcolonial feminist writers from the Middle East, Africa, the Caribbean, and the United States.

LAURA DONALDSON is of Scotch-Irish and Cherokee descent and teaches postcolonial women's writing as well as American Indian studies (with an emphasis on American Indian-First Nations women). She is the author of *Decolonizing Feminisms: Race, Gender and Empire-Building* (1992) and is working on two book-length projects: "The Skin of God: American Indian Writing as Colonial Technology" and

"Postcolonial Appropriations and Signs of Orpah: Biblical Reading in the Contact Zone." Her essays have been published in such journals as *Diacritics, Cultural Critique, Signs,* and *American Indian Quarterly.*

DIANE ELAM teaches at the University of Wales, Cardiff, where she is Professor of English Literature and Critical and Cultural Theory. She is the author of *Romancing the Postmodern* (1992) and *Feminism and Deconstruction: Ms. en abyme* (1994), as well as coeditor with Robyn Wiegman of *Feminism Beside Itself* (1995).

SUSAN STANFORD FRIEDMAN is the Virginia Woolf Professor of English and Women's Studies at the University of Wisconsin-Madison, where she has had a joint appointment with the Women's Studies Program since 1975. She served as Associate Chair of the program in charge of curriculum development from the program's founding in 1975 until 1981; she has designed and taught four interdisciplinary courses for the program, including the humanities introduction and the capstone seminar for majors. She is the author of *A Woman's Guide to Theory* (1979); *Psyche Reborn: The Emergence of H.D.* (1981); *Penelope's Web: Gender, Modernity, H.D.'s Fiction* (1990); and *Mappings: Feminism and the Cultural Geographies of Encounter* (1998); the editor of *Joyce: The Return of the Repressed* (1994); and coeditor of *Signets—Reading H.D.* (1991). Her most recent articles on Women's Studies appeared in the special issue on the Ph.D. in Women's Studies (summer 1998) and in the forum on feminism and interdisciplinarity (summer 2001), both in *Feminist Studies.*

JUDITH KEGAN GARDINER is Professor of English and of Gender and Women's Studies at the University of Illinois at Chicago. She is the author of *Rhys, Stead, Lessing, and the Politics of Empathy* (1989); *Masculinity Studies and Feminist Theory: New Directions* (2001); and the editor of *Provoking Agents: Gender and Agency in Theory and Practice* (1995). She is a member of the editorial collective of the journal *Feminist Studies,* and her essays on feminist and psychoanalytic theory and on women writers have been published in such journals as *Critical Inquiry, Feminist Studies, Signs,* and *Tulsa Studies in Women's Literature.*

INDERPAL GREWAL is Professor and Director of the program in Women's Studies at the University of California, Irvine. She is the author of *Home and Harem: Nation, Gender, Empire, and the Cultures of Travel*

(Duke, 1996); coauthor (with Caren Kaplan) of *Introduction to Women's Studies: Gender in a Transnational World* (2002); and the coeditor of *Scattered Hegemonies: Postmodernity and Transnational Feminist Practices* (1994). She is one of the founders of Narika, a Berkeley-based nonprofit agency working on South Asian women's issues.

SNEJA GUNEW has taught for more than twenty-five years at various universities in England, Australia, and Canada. She has published widely on multicultural, postcolonial, and feminist critical theory and is currently Professor of English and Women's Studies at the University of British Columbia. She is the author of *Framing Marginality: Multicultural Literary Studies* (1994) and *Postcolonial Multiculturalisms: Bodies, Communities, Nations* (forthcoming. She has edited and coedited four anthologies of Australian women's and multicultural writings and is the editor of *Feminist Knowledge: Critique and Construct* (1990) and *A Reader in Feminist Knowledge* (1991). She also coedited, with Anna Yeatman, *Feminism and the Politics of Difference* (1983). Her current work is in comparative multiculturalism and in diasporic literatures and their intersections with national and global cultural formations, using theoretical frameworks deriving from postcolonialism and critical multicultural theory.

MIRANDA JOSEPH is Associate Professor of Women's Studies at the University of Arizona, where she is also Coordinator of the Committee on Lesbian/Gay/Bisexual Studies. She is the author of *Against the Romance of Community* (2002) and "The Performance of Production and Consumption," *Social Text* 54 (spring 1998). She has been a Rockefeller Fellow at the Center for Lesbian and Gay Studies, CUNY Graduate Center (1997–98) and a Bunting Fellow at Radcliffe College (1999–2000).

CAREN KAPLAN is Associate Professor of Women's Studies and Chair of Women's Studies at the University of California, Berkeley. She is the author of *Questions of Travel: Postmodern Discourses of Displacement* (Duke, 1996) and the coeditor of *Scattered Hegemonies: Postmodernity and Transnational Feminist Practices* (1994); *Between Women and Nation: Nationalisms, Transnational Feminisms, and the State* (Duke, 1999); and *Introduction to Women's Studies: Gender in a Transnational World* (2002).

RACHEL LEE is Associate Professor of English and Women's Studies at the University of California, Los Angeles. She is the author of *The Americas of Asian American Literature: Gendered Fictions of Nation and Transnation* (1999), which addresses current debates on the relationship between Asian American ethnic identity, national belonging, globalization, and gender. Her essays on location, territory, and critical regionalism in the context of Asian American cultural criticism have appeared in *Cultural Critique, boundary 2,* and various anthologies.

DEVONEY LOOSER is former Acting Director of Women's Studies at Indiana State University and currently Assistant Professor of Women's Studies and Anthropology at the University of Wisconsin-Whitewater. She is the author of *British Women Writers and the Writing of History, 1670–1820* (2000); the editor of *Jane Austen and Discourses of Feminism* (1995); and coeditor, with E. Ann Kaplan, of *Generations: Academic Feminists in Dialogue* (1997).

JEANETTE MCVICKER is Associate Professor of English at State University of New York College at Fredonia. She completed a four-year term as Director of Women's Studies, in which the program was reactivated after nearly ten years of dormancy. She has also completed a three-year term on Fredonia's general-education committee. She coedited the *Selected Papers* from the 7th and 8th Annual Conferences on Virginia Woolf (1998–99). She is working on a long-term project on the modernisms of Woolf, Katherine Anne Porter, and Zora Neale Hurston.

MINOO MOALLEM is Associate Professor and Chair of Women's Studies at San Francisco State University. She is the coeditor, with Caren Kaplan and Norma Alarcón, of *Between Woman and Nation: Nationalisms, Transnational Feminisms and the State* (Duke, 1999). She is currently working on a book manuscript, "Between Warrior Brother and Veiled Sister: Islamic Fundamentalism and the Cultural Politics of Patriarchy." Trained as a sociologist, she writes on feminist theory, gender and fundamentalism, globalization, and Iranian cultural politics and diasporas.

NANCY A. NAPLES is Associate Professor of Women's Studies and Sociology at the University of Connecticut, having also served on the faculty of the University of California, Irvine, and Iowa State University. Her work has appeared in *Gender and Society, Feminist Economics,* and *Signs,* among other journals and books. She is the author of *Grassroots Warriors: Activist Mothering, Community Work, and the War on Poverty* (1998) and editor of *Community Activism and Feminist Politics: Organizing Across Race, Class, and Gender* (1998). With Manisha Desai, she coedited *Women's Activism and Globalization: Linking Local Struggles and Transnational Politics* (2002); and with Karen Bojar, she coedited *Teaching Feminist Activism: Strategies from the Field* (2002).

JANE O. NEWMAN is Professor of Comparative Literature and a member of the core faculty in Women's Studies at the University of California, Irvine. The author of *Pastoral Conventions: Poetry, Language and Thought in Seventeenth-Century Nuremberg* (1990) and *The Intervention of Philology: Gender, Learning, and Power in Lohenstein's Roman Plays* (2000) and of articles on feminist theory and historiography, political theory, and literary and material culture in the sixteenth and seventeenth centuries. She directed the Women's Studies Program at the University of California, Irvine from 1998 to 1999 and in 2002 was appointed as the Pay Equity/Advancement for Women Faculty Advisor in the School of Humanities at UC-Irvine.

LINDSEY POLLAK is a graduate of Yale University. She completed a Master of Arts in Women's Studies at Monash University and now works in New York. She is the coauthor of *Women for Hire: The Ultimate Guide to Getting a Job* (2002).

JEAN C. ROBINSON is Dean of the Office of Women's Affairs and Professor of Political Science at Indiana University. Her academic career began with a half-time position coordinating the Women's Studies program at Indiana University in 1977, which became a tenure-track position in 1980. She served as Director until 1982, then returned as Acting Director for two years in 1991. She does cross-national research on women, family policy, and state feminist agencies, and teaches political science, East Asian languages and cultures, Russian and East European studies, and honors courses as well as Women's Studies.

SABINA SAWHNEY teaches in the English Department and the Women's Studies program at Hofstra University. Her research and teaching interests include critical and feminist theory, postcolonial literature and theory, and Victorian studies. She has published articles in such anthologies as *Feminism Beside Itself* (1995); *Who Can Speak? Authority and Critical Identity* (1995); *Sexy Bodies* (1996); and *Narratives*

of Nostalgia, Gender and Nationalism (1997). She is currently working on a book-length project, "Scrambled Histories: The Unpunc-
tual Postcolonial."

JAEL SILLIMAN is Assistant Professor in Women's Studies at the University of Iowa. She is the author of *Jewish Portraits, Indian Frames:
Women's Narratives from a Diaspora of Hope* (2001) and the coeditor
of two anthologies: *Dangerous Intersections: Feminist Perspectives on
Population, Environment, and Development* (1999) and *Policing the
National Body: Race, Gender, and Criminalization* (2002). She is the
author of several articles on social movements, transnational feminist politics, environmental justice, and reproductive rights and
health issues.

SIVAGAMI SUBBARAMAN lives in Maryland, working mostly at a coffee
shop in a suburban mall, and "adjuncting." She taught most recently for the Women's Studies program at Macalester College and
has taught at the University of Maryland, College Park. Her publications include "Catalog-ing Ethnicity: Clothing as Cultural Citizenship," *Interventions* 1 (1999), and "Of Job Trails and Holy Grails for
Feminists Out There: A Postmodernist Cautionary Tale," in the anthology *On the Market: Surviving the Academic Job Search* (1997). She
presents papers regularly at a variety of conferences and refuses the
title "independent scholar" as a protest against academe's indifference to material realities. She is now back in the "academic world"
but in a nonfaculty position, doing Web development and diversity
work out of the Office of Human Relations Programs at the University of Maryland.

ROBYN WARHOL is Professor and Chair of English and former Director of
Women's Studies at the University of Vermont, where roughly 25
percent of the Arts and Sciences faculty self-identify as "Women's
Studies-affiliated." She is the author of *Gendered Interventions: Nar-
rative Discourse in the Victorian Novel* (1989) and coeditor, with Diane
Price Herndl, of *Feminisms* (1991, 1997). Her latest book is *Having a
Good Cry: Feelings and Popular-Culture Forms* (forthcoming).

MARCIA WESTKOTT is Professor Emeritus, University of Colorado at
Boulder, where she directed the Women's Studies Program from
1988 to 1994. She has a Ph.D. in sociology from the University
of Pennsylvania. She has published numerous works on the psychology of women, including *The Feminist Legacy of Karen Horney*

(1986), and on Women's Studies as a field, including "Feminist Criticism of the Social Sciences," *Harvard Educational Review* (1979) and "Personalized Learning," with Gay Victoria, in *The Courage to Question* (1992). Her current interests include East-West concepts of the (gendered) self.

ROBYN WIEGMAN is the Margaret Taylor Smith Director of and Associate Professor of Women's Studies at Duke University. She has published *American Anatomies: Theorizing Race and Gender* (Duke, 1995) and four edited collections: *Feminism Beside Itself* (1995), *Who Can Speak? Authority and Critical Identity* (1995), *AIDS and the National Body: Writings by Thomas Yingling* (Duke, 1997), and *The Futures of American Studies* (Duke, 2002). She is currently completing a manuscript, "Object Lessons: Feminism and the Knowledge Politics of Identity."

BONNIE ZIMMERMAN is Professor of Women's Studies at San Diego State University, where she also chaired the department from 1986–92 and 1995–97. She has been a Women's Studies practitioner since 1970, when she participated in founding another of the country's oldest programs, at the State University of New York at Buffalo. In 1998–99, she served as President of the National Women's Studies Association. She is also known for her work in the field of lesbian studies.

Female genital surgery, 80

Feminism: academic, 3–4, 130, 133; black, 260, 301; cultural, 77–78; definition of, 89, 113, 120, 128; French, 150, 461; history of, 144–52, 156, 187; institutionalization of, 130, 139 n.26; as knowledge formation, 51, 55, 70, 79, 107, 128–29, 133, 140 n.27, 144–45, 240–41, 275; second wave, 53, 134–35 n.4; third wave, 53, 431; Third World, 87; transnational, 76, 79

Feminist knowledge: across the disciplines, 50, 177–79, 182, 228, 230–231, 264, 434; commodification of, 113, 156; genealogies of, 180; instrumentalization of, 53; and social change, 55, 185, 187–88, 192, 232, 306, 310, 383–415

Feminist theory, 64, 134 n.3, 147, 151–54, 179, 184, 186; and poststructuralism, 112, 135 n.9, 347, 386, 411, 461; and practice, 183, 186, 188, 435 n.2; socialist/materialist, 191, 200 n.1, 384; standpoint theory, 77, 99, 386

Flax, Jane, 153–54

Foucault, Michel, 274

Friedman, Susan Stanford, 448–50

Frye, Marilyn, 135 n.6, 154

Gamble, Susan, 156

Gatens, Moira, 155

Gender studies, 66, 106, 128, 130, 131, 134 n.1, 434

Generational differences, 2, 202, 208–11, 213, 215, 217, 432, 457

Globalization, 6, 131, 273, 281, 368–69

Grahl, Christine, 183–86, 189 n.2

Grewal, Inderpal, 233–34, 240, 371, 439

Gubar, Susan, 92

Guy-Sheftall, Beverly, 442–43, 455 n.2

Halberstam, Judith, 138–39 n.20, 139 nn.21, 22

Hartmann, Heidi, 262

Hartzog, Carol, 249

Heterosexuality, 115, 245–46

Hochschild, Arlie, 245–46, 257 n.4, 429

Homophobia, 115, 305, 309

Homosexuality, 297

Homosociality, 114–15, 117

Humanities, 172 n.1, 181, 341, 355–56, 361

Human rights, 72

Identity: as object of study, 109, 129–31, 268, 286, 345, 347–48; politics, 54, 64, 372, 374

Individualism, 198, 200

Internationalization, 56, 73–74, 78

Intersectionality, 54, 64, 77, 111, 131, 133, 136, 268

Intersexuality, 122–23

Irigaray, Luce, 115–16

Jaggar, Alison, 152

Jeffords, Susan, 116–18, 137 n.14

Kaplan, Caren, 233–34, 240, 371, 439

Kennedy, Elizabeth, 183–86

Kramarae, Cheris, 154

Kruks, Sonia, 171

Lee, Benjamin, 74

Lesbian, 124; butch, 124–25, 138; feminism, 124, 138; identity, 124

Lowe, Lisa, 280–81

Luebke Barbara, 318–19, 334–35, 436 n.15

Malkki, Liisa, 73

Marginality: commitment to, 49, 88, 249, 364, 371; fetishization of, 84, 104 n.17

Marks, Elaine, 151

Martin, Biddy, 131, 255

Masculinity: alternative, 139 n.22; differences among, 110–11, 116, 118–19, 136 n.14; female, 125–26, 138; male, 109–11, 113, 115, 117, 137 n.14; as object of study, 108, 119, 126, 134 n.3

McDermott, Patrice, 101 n.6

Mills, C. Wright, 359

Modeleski, Tania, 135 n.7, 135 n.8, 135 n.9, 136 nn.10, 11

Modernity, 372

Mohanty, Chandra, 82, 100 n.1, 373, 452

Moi, Toril, 151

Multiculturalism, 55, 74, 134 n.2, 237

Women's Studies programs (*cont.*)
226, 228, 230–31, 246, 249, 260, 302,
435, 439; and funding, 285; governance,
193–96, 203, 206, 209, 295, 350, 423;
history of; 50, 70, 88, 92, 133, 135, 185,
192, 202, 204, 212, 301, 317, 342–44,
372, 384–85, 421, 457–58, 462; institutionalization of, 4, 44, 49, 178, 183, 196,
205, 207, 218–23, 224–32, 250–51,
293–94, 301, 313, 344, 351, 372, 385, 387;
internationalization of, 57, 423; and the
job market, 224–25, 418; labor, 102 n.8,
197, 245–57, 258–66, 259, 285, 312–38;
the major, 94–95, 298–99, 303, 416–

37; nationalism in, 70–71, 78, 234;
Ph.D. in, 224, 417, 438, 448, 450, 460;
professionalization, 202–3, 206–9, 388;
progress, narrative of, 88, 90, 94, 135,
145; relation to ethnic studies, 69, 275,
455; relation to LGBT studies, 269, 271,
275–79, 277, 282–89; and state legislatures, 285–86, 293, 296–97, 307; and
tenure, 102 n.8, 195, 222, 228, 230–32,
253, 263, 283, 295, 459; and women's
community, 52

Zinn, Maxine Baca, 100 n.1, 104 n.18, 408
Žižek, Slavoj, 157

Library of Congress Cataloging-in-Publication Data
Women's studies on its own : a next wave reader in
institutional change / edited by Robyn Wiegman.
p. cm. — (Next wave)
Includes bibliographical references and index.
ISBN 0-8223-2950-6 (cloth : alk. paper)
ISBN 0-8223-2986-7 (pbk. : alk. paper)
1. Women's studies. 2. Women's studies—United States.
I. Wiegman, Robyn. II. Series.
HQ1180 .w6876 2002   305.4'071—dc21   2002004596

remedy, that can we tackle its narrowness, its embeddedness in a particular location. Forgoing the critical surplus of oppositional mobility, Crenshaw constructs a remedial agenda for black women that seeks redress vis-à-vis the U.S. political economy in the late twentieth century rather than celebrating "women of color's" marginality to the state. In this respect, Crenshaw's essay spurs a critical reassessment of Sandoval's "oppositional" mobility. While Sandoval highlights multiplicitous mobility as graceful, Crenshaw in contrast emphasizes the collision of several routes as traumatic rather than as enlarging:

> If an accident happens in an intersection, it can be caused by cars traveling from any number of directions and, sometimes, from all of them. Similarly, if a Black woman is harmed because she is in the intersection, her injury could result from sex discrimination or race discrimination. . . . Providing legal relief only when Black women show that their claims are based on race or on sex is analogous to calling an ambulance for the victim only after the driver responsible for the injuries is identified. But it is not always easy to reconstruct an accident: Sometimes the skid marks and the injuries simply indicate that they occurred simultaneously. . . . In these cases . . . no driver is held responsible. (Crenshaw 1989: 149)

Where Sandoval heralds the guerrilla ability of a woman of color to "transform [her] identity according to [one's] readings of power's formation" (Sandoval 1991: 15), Crenshaw characterizes shape-shifting (or fitting one's shape into those forms already recognized by power formations, such as the court or current antidiscrimination statutes) as a deficit, because too often women of color—black women, in particular—cannot fit their shape into the one size that is offered. Her enunciation of the trauma rather than of the open-ended possibilities of "women of color's" flexible identities might mark the emergence of a woman-of-color *transformative* political subjectivity. I mean transformative precisely in the sense of seeing what we possess (guerrilla abilities, flexibility and grace, a mobile disposition) not merely as heroic, though such qualities certainly are, but also as something we can change. Portraying black women as underserved by national protections—as "countryless women," to use Ana Castillo's phrase (Castillo 1994: 24)—Crenshaw characterizes justice as a more complete coverture of black women by the interventionist state.

In claiming a terrain on which black women would be not merely the oppositional mode but the centered subject, Crenshaw stakes a claim that, in emphasis of the earlier point, has its own limited vision. For the Hawai'ian activist Haunani-Kay Trask, such appeals to the U.S. courts would be a misguided appropriation of territory already seized from indigenous peoples. Defining her feminist project in terms of indigenous land rights and woman's "*mana*" (power, authority), Trask refuses to romanticize her exquisite dispossession and argues for a political terrain, a sovereignty, and a transformative political subjectivity, albeit aimed at a different territorial object from that defined by Crenshaw. Can these two programs for action coalesce? The answer is, probably not. However, the contradictions internal to the different domains to which various women of color speak constitute the challenge represented by the bodies of knowledge produced by women of color in distinction to the ease of noting women of color's convergence in opposition to the center. Thus, the challenge for Women's Studies in developing a slate of classes on "women of color" will be to collaborate, paradoxically, on points of disagreement and catalysts of disidentification, controverting over-investments in "women of color" as a "new model for unity" (Zinn and Dill 1994: xv).[18] Although it is certainly admirable, this emphasis on "unity" tends to obscure the legitimacy of other modes of conceptualizing and narrating "women of color" as also a site of difference and struggle—as itself a discourse in need of critique and deconstruction.

In short, the struggle for women of color is not—as perhaps implicitly envisioned—to be answered in (white) feminism's self-ameliorating actions on race, not in some other agent's ability to read or see women of color's mobile practices, and not in our inhabiting the space of promised teleological guarantee on behalf of feminism, but in our scrutiny of our own articulations of women of color as community, methodological consistency, temporary coalition, or that which is secured by a teleological guarantee. (For instance, Sandoval seems not to want such a guarantee, whereas Crenshaw and Trask do.) Essentially, I suggest that women of color and Third World feminism seek out the places that are haunted by ghostly presences not yet articulated.[19]

The Yearning to Travel

To envision "women of color," and Women's Studies on the whole, as somehow a better mode of consciousness, as materially disposed to